Lecture Notes in Computer Science 4450

Commenced Publication in 1973
Founding and Former Series Editors:
Gerhard Goos, Juris Hartmanis, and Jan van Leeuwen

Tatsuaki Okamoto   Xiaoyun Wang (Eds.)

Public Key Cryptography – PKC 2007

10th International Conference
on Practice and Theory in Public-Key Cryptography
Beijing, China, April 16-20, 2007
Proceedings

 Springer

Volume Editors

Tatsuaki Okamoto
NTT Laboratories, Nippon Telegraph and Telephone Corporation
Japan
E-mail: okamoto.tatsuaki@lab.ntt.co.jp

Xiaoyun Wang
Shandong University and Tsinghua University
China
E-mail: xywang@sdu.edu.cn

Library of Congress Control Number: 2007923868

CR Subject Classification (1998): E.3, F.2.1-2, C.2.0, K.4.4, K.6.5

LNCS Sublibrary: SL 4 – Security and Cryptology

ISSN   0302-9743
ISBN-10   3-540-71676-9 Springer Berlin Heidelberg New York
ISBN-13   978-3-540-71676-1 Springer Berlin Heidelberg New York

Springer is a part of Springer Science+Business Media

springer.com

©International Association for Cryptologic Research 2007
Printed in Germany

Typesetting: Camera-ready by author, data conversion by Scientific Publishing Services, Chennai, India
Printed on acid-free paper   SPIN: 12042999   06/3180   5 4 3 2 1 0

Preface

The 10th International Conference on Theory and Practice of Public-Key Cryptography (PKC 2007) was held at Tsinghua University in Beijing, China, April 16–20, 2007. PKC is the premier international conference dedicated to cryptology focusing on all aspects of public-key cryptography. The event is sponsored by the International Association of Cryptologic Research (IACR), and this year it was also sponsored by the National Natural Science Foundation of China (NSFC) and Tsinghua University.

The conference received 118 submissions, and the Program Committee selected 29 of these for presentation. The Program Committee worked very hard to evaluate the papers with respect to quality, originality, and relevance to public-key cryptography. Each paper was anonymously reviewed by at least three Program Committee members.

Extended abstracts of the revised versions of the accepted papers are in these proceedings. The program also included three invited lectures by Rafail Ostrovsky with UCLA, USA, Shige Peng with Shandong University, China and Adi Shamir with the Weizmann Institute of Science, Israel. Two papers regarding the invited lectures are included in these proceedings. The PKC 2007 Program Committee had the pleasure of awarding this year's PKC best paper award to Xavier Boyen and Brent Waters for their paper, entitled "Full-Domain Subgroup Hiding and Constant-Size Group Signatures."

We are extremely grateful to the Program Committee members for their enormous investment of time and effort in the difficult and delicate process of review and selection. We gratefully acknowledge the help of a large number of external reviewers who reviewed submissions in their area of expertise. We also thank the PKC Steering Committee for their support.

Electronic submissions were made possible by the Web Review system, iChair, developed by Thomas Baignéres and Matthieu Finiasz at EPFL, LASEC. We would like to thank Thomas Baignéres and Matthieu Finiasz for their great support.

We deeply thank Andrew C. Yao, the General Chair, for his effort in organizing and making this conference possible. The great scientist was the source of the success of PKC 2007.

We are grateful to all the Organizing Committee members for their volunteer work. In addition, we would like to thank Wei Yu for his enormous support in installing and operating the iChair system in the review process and editing of these proceedings.

We wish to thank all the authors, for submitting papers, and the authors of accepted papers for their cooperation.

February 2007   Tatsuaki Okamoto
                                                              Xiaoyun Wang

PKC 2007

The 10th International Conference on Theory and Practice of Public-Key Cryptography

Tsinghua University, Beijing, China, April 16–20, 2007

Sponsored by the *International Association of Cryptologic Research (IACR)*, *National Natural Science Foundation of China* and *Tsinghua University*.

General Chair

Andrew C. Yao, Tsinghua University, China

Program Co-chairs

Tatsuaki Okamoto, NTT, Japan
Xiaoyun Wang, Tsinghua University, China

Organizing Committee

Andrew C. Yao .... Tsinghua University, China
Xiaoyun Wang .... Tsinghua University, China
Yuexuan Wang .... Tsinghua University, China
Xiaoming Sun .... Tsinghua University, China
Hongbo Yu .... Tsinghua University, China
Qi Feng .... Tsinghua University, China
Meiqin Wang .... Shandong University,China

Program Committee

Feng Bao .... I2R, Singapore
Jung Hee Cheon .... Seoul National University, Korea
Alfredo De Santis .... University of Salerno, Italy
Yvo Desmedt ....UCL, UK
Giovanni Di Crescenzo .... Telcordia Tech., USA
Steven Galbraith .... Royal Holloway University of London, UK
Juan Garay .... Bell labs, USA
Jonathan Katz .... University of Maryland, USA
Kwangjo Kim .... ICU, Korea
Hugo Krawczyk .... IBM, USA
Arjen Lenstra .... Lucent, USA
Anna Lysyanskaya .... Brown University, USA
Alfred Menezes .... University of Waterloo, Canada
Kazuo Ohta .... University of Electro-Communications, Japan

Rafail Ostrovsky .... UCLA, USA
Dingyi Pei .... Guangzhou University, China
David Pointcheval .... ENS, France
C. Pandu Rangan .... IIT Madras, India
Hovav Shacham .... Weizmann Institute, Israel
Igor Shparlinski .... Macquarie University, Australia
Serge Vaudenay .... EPFL, Switzerland
Frances Yao .... City University of Hong Kong, Hong Kong, China
Moti Yung .... Columbia University, USA
Yuliang Zheng .... University of North Carolina at Charlotte, USA

Steering Committee

Ronald Cramer .... CWI and Leiden University, The Netherlands
Yvo Desmedt .... University College London, UK
Hideki Imai (Chair) .... AIST and Chuo University, Japan
Kwangjo Kim .... Information and Communications University, Korea
David Naccache .... ENS, France
Tatsuaki Okamoto .... NTT, Japan
Jacques Stern .... ENS, France
Moti Yung .... RSA Laboratories and Columbia University, USA
Yuliang Zheng (Secretary) .... University of North Carolina at Charlotte, USA

External Reviewers

Michel Abdalla	Yuichiro Esaki	Yutaka Kawai
Patrick Amon	Serge Fehr	Aggelos Kiayias
Paolo D Arco	Anna Lisa Ferrara	Eike Kilt
Joonsang Baek	Matthieu Finiasz	Woo-Hwan Kim
Thomas Baigneres	Pierre-Alain Fouque	Thorsten Kleinjung
Caroline Belrose	Rosario Gennaro	Yuichi Kokubun
Olivier Billet	Nick Howgrave Graham	Vlad Kolesnikov
Colin Boyd	Jens Groth	Yuichi Komano
Dan Brown	Shai Halevi	Takahiro Kondo
Qingjun Cai	Safuat Hamdy	Chiu-Yuen Koo
Sebastien Canard	Yoshikazu Hanatani	Noboru Kunihiro
Melissa Chase	Darrel Hankerson	Kaoru Kurosawa
Carlos Cid	Jason Hinek	Taekyoung Kwon
Scott Contini	Qiong Huang	Rob Lambert
Cecile Delerablee	James Hughes	Kristin Lauter
Alex Dent	Sebastien Kunz Jacques	Munkyu Lee
Konidala M. Divyan	Ellen Jochemsz	Jin Li
Junwu Dong	Pascal Junod	Yong Li
Dang Nguyen Duc	Marcelo Kaihara	Vo Duc Liem
Ratna Dutta	Alexandre Karlov	Seongan Lim

Perret Ludovic
Daegun Ma
Benoit Chevallier Mames
Barbara Masucci
Alex May
Alexander May
Maria Meyerovich
Anton Mityagin
Satoshi Miyagawa
Payman Mohassel
David Molnar
Jean Monnerat
Siguna Mueller
Phong Nguyen
Phong Q. Nguyen
Takashi Nishide
Haruki Ota
Duong Hieu PHAN

Sylvain Pasini
Kenny Paterson
Manas Patra
Ludovic Perret
Benny Pinkas
Tal Rabin
Leonid Rayzin
Pankaj Rohatgi
Bagus Santoso
Benjamin Smith
Martijn Stam
Ron Steinfeld
Rene Struik
Willy Susilo
Chunming Tang
Emmanuel Thome
Xiaojian Tian
Jacques Traore

Berkant Ustaoglu
Jose Villegas
Ivan Visconti
Martin Vuagnoux
Shabsi Walfish
Brent Waters
Christopher Wolf
Duncan S. Wong
David Woodruff
Yongdong Wu
Guomin Yang
Jeong Hyun Yi
Kazuki Yoneyama
Hyojin Yoon
Xiaolai Zhang

Table of Contents

Signatures II

Multivariate Cryptosystems

Encryption

Protocols II

Invited Talk II

Number Theoretic Techniques

Public-Key Infrastructure

Full-Domain Subgroup Hiding and Constant-Size Group Signatures

Xavier Boyen[1] and Brent Waters[2,*]

[1] Voltage Inc., Palo Alto
xb@boyen.org
[2] SRI International
bwaters@csl.sri.com

Abstract. We give a short constant-size group signature scheme, which we prove fully secure under reasonable assumptions in bilinear groups, in the standard model. We achieve this result by using a new NIZK proof technique, related to the BGN cryptosystem and the GOS proof system, but that allows us to hide integers from the full domain rather than individual bits.

1 Introduction

Group signatures, introduced by Chaum and van Heyst [19], allow any member of a certain group to sign a message on behalf of the group, but the signer remains anonymous within the group. However, in certain extenuating circumstances an authority will have the ability to revoke the anonymity of a signer and trace the signature. One of the primary motivating use scenarios of group signatures is in anonymous attestation, which has practical applications such as in building Trusted Platform Modules (TPMs). Group signatures have also attracted much attention in the research community where several constructions have been proposed [1,2,3,5,6,9,12,13,14,15,16,25,27,29].

The most efficient group signature constructions given only have a proof of security in the random oracles model and either are based on the Strong-RSA assumption in Z_n [2,3,16] or use bilinear groups [9,11,17]. Solutions in the standard model can be derived from general assumptions as first shown by Bellare et. al. [5].

Recently, two efficient group signature schemes were respectively proposed both by Boyen and Waters [13] and Ateniese et al. [1] that did not use random oracles. The two solutions took different approaches and have different features.

The Boyen-Waters construction used a two-level hierarchical signature, where the first level corresponds to the signer's identity and the second level is the message to be signed. The scheme hides the actual identity in the first level by using bilinear groups of composite order and applying a mechanism from the recent Non-Interactive Zero-Knowledge (NIZK) result of Groth, Ostrovsky, and

---

* Supported by NSF CNS-0524252 and the US Army Research Office under the CyberTA Grant No. W911NF-06-1-0316.

T. Okamoto and X. Wang (Eds.): PKC 2007, LNCS 4450, pp. 1–15, 2007.

Sahai [23]. The two drawbacks of the Boyen-Waters result are that the number of group elements in the signature are logarithmic in the number of signers in the group and that the anonymity property is only secure against chosen-plaintext attacks, as opposed to chosen-ciphertext attacks. The need for a logarithmic number of group elements results from the fact that a signer must prove that the blinded first level identity was computed correctly. The authors needed to use the model for CPA attacks because the tracing authority used the knowledge of the factorization of the order to trace members.

The Ateniese et. al. scheme works in asymmetric bilinear groups. Their scheme has signatures with a constant number of group elements and has chosen-ciphertext security. However, its proofs of security rely on interactive assumptions where the adversary has access to an oracle; therefore, these assumptions are inherently non-falsifiable [28]. In addition, the scheme has the drawback that if a user's private key is compromised then it can be used to revoke the anonymity of that user's past signatures. Although, it should be pointed out that some schemes have used this property as an advantage in Verifier-Local Group signatures [11].

Groth [21] also gave a recent group signature scheme that was proven CCA-secure in the standard model under the decisional Linear assumption [9]. Signatures in his scheme technically consist of a constant number of group elements, however, as noted by the author the constant is too large for real systems and in practice his constant will be much more than $\lg(n)$ for any reasonable number of n signers. The result does though, give a feasibility result under a relatively mild assumption.

In this paper we give a new construction of a group signature scheme that addresses some of the drawbacks of the Boyen-Waters [13] solution. Following their scheme we use a two-level hierarchical signature as the basis for our signatures, where the first level specifies the identity. However, we use a new signature on the first level based off an assumption related to Strong Diffie-Hellman (SDH) [8] that we call the Hidden Strong Diffie-Hellman, which like SDH and Strong-RSA has the property that the adversary has flexibility in what he is allowed to return to the challenger. The signature has the property that if the signer gives a signature on an arbitrary group element this can be used to break our assumption. We provide efficient proofs of well-formmess that use techniques beyond those given in [23], including proofs of encrypted Diffie-Hellman tuples. One disadvantage of this approach is that it uses a stronger assumption for unforgeability than CDH, which was used in the Boyen-Waters [13] scheme. However, we emphasize that this assumption is falsifiable.

2   Preliminaries

We review a number of useful notions from the recent literature on pairing-based cryptography, which we shall need in later sections. First, we briefly review the properties that constitute a group signature scheme and define its security.

We take this opportunity to clarify once and for all that, in this paper, the word "group" by default assumes its algebraic meaning, except in contexts such as "group signature" and "group manager" where it designates a collection of users. There should be no ambiguity from context.

2.1   Group Signatures

A group signature scheme consists of a pentuple of PPT algorithms:

- A group setup algorithm, *Setup*, that takes as input a security parameter 1^λ (in unary) and the size of the group, 2^k, and outputs a public key PK for verifying signatures, a master key MK for enrolling group members, and a tracing key TK for identifying signers.
- An enrollment algorithm, *Enroll*, that takes the master key MK and an identity ID, and outputs a unique identifier s_{ID} and a private signing key K_{ID} which is to be given to the user.
- A signing algorithm, *Sign*, that takes a group member's private signing key K_{ID} and a message M, and outputs a signature σ.
- A (usually deterministic) verification algorithm, *Verify*, that takes a message M, a signature σ, and a group verification key PK, and outputs either `valid` or `invalid`.
- A (usually deterministic) tracing algorithm, *Trace*, that takes a valid signature σ and a tracing key TK, and outputs an identifier s_{ID} or the failure symbol $\perp$.

There are four types of entities one must consider:

- The group master, which sets up the group and issues private keys to the users. Often, the group master is an ephemeral entity, and the master key MK is destroyed once the group is set up. Alternatively, techniques from distributed cryptography can be used to realize the group master functionality without any real party becoming in possession of the master key.
- The group manager, which is given the ability to identify signers using the tracing key TK, but not to enroll users or create new signing keys.
- Regular member users, or signers, which are each given a distinct private signing key K_{ID}.
- Outsiders, or verifiers, who can only verify signatures using the public key PK.

We require the following correctness and security properties.

Consistency. The consistency requirements are such that, whenever, (for a group of 2^k users)

$$(\mathsf{PK}, \mathsf{MK}, \mathsf{TK}) \leftarrow Setup(1^\lambda, 2^k),$$

$$(s_{ID}, K_{ID}) \leftarrow Enroll(\mathsf{MK}, \mathsf{ID}), \qquad \sigma \leftarrow Sign(K_{ID}, M),$$

we have, (except with negligible probability over the random bits used in *Verify* and *Trace*)

$$Verify(M, \sigma, \mathsf{PK}) = \mathtt{valid}, \qquad \text{and} \qquad Trace(\sigma, \mathsf{TK}) = s_{ID}.$$

The unique identifier s_{ID} can be used to assist in determining the user ID from the transcript of the *Enroll* algorithm; s_{ID} may but need not be disclosed to the user; it may be the same as ID.

Security. Bellare, Micciancio, and Warinschi [5] characterize the fundamental properties of group signatures in terms of two crucial security properties from which a number of other properties follow. The two important properties are:

Full Anonymity which requires that no PPT adversary be able to decide (with non-negligible probability over one half) whether a challenge signature σ on a message M emanates from user ID_1 or ID_2, where ID_1, ID_2, and M are chosen by the adversary. In the original definition of [5], the adversary is given access to a tracing oracle, which it may query before and after being given the challenge σ, much in the fashion of IND-CCA2 security for encryption.

Boneh, Boyen, and Shacham [9] relax this definition by withholding access to the tracing oracle, thus mirroring the notion of IND-CPA security for encryption. We follow [9] and speak of *CCA2-full anonymity* and *CPA-full anonymity* for the respective notions.

Full Traceability which requires that no coalition of users be able to generate, in polynomial time, a signature that passes the *Verify* algorithm but fails to trace to a member of the coalition under the *Trace* algorithm. According to this notion, the adversary is allowed to ask for the private keys of any user of its choice, adaptively, and is also given the secret key TK to be used for tracing—but of course not the enrollment master key MK.

It is noted in [5] that this property implies that of *exculpability* [4], which is the requirement that no party should be able to frame a honest group member as the signer of a signature he did not make, not even the group manager. However, the model of [5] does not consider the possibility of a (long-lived) group master, which leaves it as a potential framer. To address this problem and achieve the notion of *strong exculpability*, introduced in [2] and formalized in [26,6], one would need an interactive enrollment protocol, call *Join*, at the end of which only the user himself knows his full private key; the same mechanism may also enable concurrent dynamic group enrollment [6,27].

We refer the reader mainly to [5] for more precise definitions of these and related notions.

2.2   Bilinear Groups of Composite Order

We review some general notions about bilinear maps and groups, with an emphasis on groups of *composite order* which will be used in most of our constructions. We follow [10] in which composite order bilinear groups were first introduced in cryptography.

Consider two finite cyclic groups G and G_T having the same order n, in which the respective group operation is efficiently computable and denoted multiplicatively. Assume that there exists an efficiently computable function $e : G \times G \to G_T$, called a bilinear map or pairing, with the following properties:

– (Bilinearity) $\forall u, v \in G$, $\forall a, b \in \mathbb{Z}$, $e(u^a, v^b) = e(u, v)^{ab}$, where the product in the exponent is defined modulo n;

- (Non-degeneracy) $\exists g \in G$ such that $e(g, g)$ has order n in G_T. In other words, $e(g, g)$ is a generator of G_T, whereas g generates G.

If such a bilinear map can be computed efficiently, the group G is called a bilinear group. We remark that the vast majority of cryptosystems based on pairings assume for simplicity that bilinear groups have prime order. In our case, it is important that the pairing be defined over a group G containing $|G| = n$ elements, where $n = pq$ has a (ostensibly hidden) factorization in two large primes, $p \neq q$.

2.3 Complexity Assumptions

We make use of a few complexity assumptions: computational Diffie-Hellman (CDH) in the prime-order bilinear subgroup G_p, Subgroup Decision in the group G of composite order $n = pq$, and a new assumption in G_p related to Strong Diffie-Hellman (SDH) that we call HSDH.

CDH in Bilinear Groups. The CDH assumption states that there is no probabilistic polynomial time (PPT) algorithm that, given a triple $(g, g^a, g^b) \in G_p^3$ for random exponents $a, b \in \mathbb{Z}_p$, computes $g^{ab} \in G_p$ with non-negligible probability. Because of the pairing, CDH in G_p implies a "Gap DH" assumption [24] and should not be confused with the vanilla CDH assumption in usual non-pairing groups. It is also subsumed by the HSDH assumption we describe later.

The Subgroup Decision Assumption. Our second tool is the Subgroup Decision assumption introduced in [10]. It combines features of bilinear pairings with the hardness of factoring, which is the reason for working with bilinear groups of composite order.

Informally, the Subgroup Decision assumption posits that for a bilinear group G of composite order $n = pq$, the uniform distribution on G is computationally indistinguishable from the uniform distribution on a subgroup of G (say, G_q, the subgroup of order q). The precise definition is based on the subgroup decision problem, which we now define.

Consider an "instance generator" algorithm $\mathcal{GG}$ that, on input a security parameter 1^λ, outputs a tuple (p, q, G, G_T, e), in which p and q are independent uniform random λ-bit primes, G and G_T are cyclic groups of order $n = pq$ with efficiently computable group operations (over their respective elements, which must have a polynomial size representation in λ), and $e : G \times G \rightarrow G_T$ is a bilinear map. Let $G_q \subset G$ denote the subgroup of G of order q. The subgroup decision problem is:

> On input a tuple $(n = pq, G, G_T, e)$ derived from a random execution of $\mathcal{GG}(1^\lambda)$, and an element w selected at random either from G or from G_q, decide whether $w \in G_q$.

The advantage of an algorithm $\mathcal{A}$ solving the subgroup decision problem is defined as $\mathcal{A}$'s excess probability, beyond $\frac{1}{2}$, of outputting the correct solution. The probability is defined over the random choice of instance and the random bits used by $\mathcal{A}$.

The HSDH Assumption. Last, we need to introduce a new assumption we call Hidden SDH by analogy to the SDH assumption [8] from which it descends. We present it in the next section.

3   The Hidden Strong Diffie-Hellman Assumption

We introduce a new assumption in the prime-order bilinear group G_p. It is a variant of the Strong Diffie-Hellman (SDH) assumption proposed in [8]. It is slightly stronger, but retains the attributes of the original assumption of being non-interactive, falsifiable, and provably true in the generic bilinear group model.

The Strong Diffie-Hellman assumption in bilinear groups states that there is no probabilistic polynomial time (PPT) adversary that, given a $(\ell + 1)$-tuple $(g, g^\omega, g^{\omega^2}, \dots, g^{\omega^\ell}) \in G_p^{\ell+1}$ for a random exponent $\omega \in \mathbb{Z}_p^*$, outputs a pair $(c, g^{1/(\omega+c)}) \in \mathbb{Z}_p^* \times G_p$ with non-negligible probability. (The parameter ℓ is defined externally.) What makes the SDH assumption useful is that it implies the hardness of the following problem:

> On input two generators $g, g^\omega \in G_p$, and $\ell-1$ distinct pairs $(c_i, g^{1/(\omega+c_i)})$ $\in \mathbb{Z}_p^* \times G_p$, output an additional pair $(c, g^{1/(\omega+c)}) \in \mathbb{Z}_p^* \times G_p$ such that $c \neq c_i$ for all $i = 1, \dots, \ell - 1$.

This argument was used by Boneh and Boyen [8] as the basis of their secure signature constructions. In particular, Boneh and Boyen's primordial "weakly secure signature" on a message c is nothing more than the group element $g^{1/(\omega+c)}$. Much of their paper is concerned with securing these signatures against *adaptive* chosen message attacks, but for our purposes this is unnecessary.

However, an inherent trait of the general notion of signature is that verification requires knowledge of the message. Since in our group signature the first-level "message" is the identity of the user, we would like to keep it as hidden as possible, since at the end of the day we need to blind it. To facilitate this task, we build a modified version of the Boneh-Boyen "weak signature" above that does not require knowledge of c in order to verify. It is based on the Hidden SDH assumption, a straightforward extension to the SDH assumption where the "message" c is not given in the clear.

The Hidden Strong Diffie-Hellman Problem. We first define the ℓ-HSDH problem as follows:

> On input three generators $g, h, g^\omega \in G_p$, and $\ell - 1$ distinct triples $(g^{1/(\omega+c_i)}, g^{c_i}, h^{c_i}) \in G_p^3$ where $c_i \in \mathbb{Z}_p$, output another such triple $(g^{1/(\omega+c)}, g^c, h^c) \in G_p^3$ distinct of all the others.

Observe that the well-formedness of a triple $(A, B, C) = (g^{1/(\omega+c)}, g^c, h^c)$ can be ascertained without knowing c by verifying that $e(A, g^\omega B) = e(g, g)$ and that $e(B, h) = e(C, g)$. In these verifications, the Diffie-Hellman relationship

(g, h, g^c, h^c) serves as a discrete-log NIZK proof of knowledge of c. Notice that contrary to the SDH problem statement [8], here we allow c or some c_i to be zero.

We define the advantage of an HSDH adversary $\mathcal{A}$ as its probability of outputting a valid triple. The probability is taken over the random choice of instance and the random bits used by $\mathcal{A}$.

Definition 1. *We say that the ℓ-HSDH assumption holds in a family of prime order bilinear groups generated by $\mathcal{GG}$, if there is no PPT algorithm that, for sufficiently large $\lambda \in \mathbb{N}$, solves the HSDH problem in the bilinear group $(p, G_p, e) \leftarrow \mathcal{GG}(1^\lambda)$ with non-negligible probability. Here, ℓ may be either an explicit parameter to the assumption, or some polynomially bounded function of the security parameter λ.*

It is easy to see that for any $\ell \geq 1$, hardness of the ℓ-HSDH problem implies hardness of the ℓ-SDH problem in the same group, which itself requires the CDH problem to be hard in that group. To bolster our confidence in the new complexity assumption, we can prove an $\Omega(\sqrt{p/\ell})$ lower bound on the complexity of solving the HSDH problem in generic bilinear groups, provided that $\ell < \sqrt[3]{p}$. Notice that HSDH does not rely on the composite order n, so the generic group model can apply. The proof will appear in the full paper.

4   Anonymous Hierarchical Signatures

As our first step toward short group signatures, we build a hierarchical signature with the signer identity at the first level and the message being signed at the second level, such that the whole signature can be verified without revealing the identity.

In a hierarchical signature, a message is a tuple comprising several atomic message components. The crucial property is that a signature on a message $(m_1, \ldots, m_i)$, also acts as a restricted private key that enables the signing of any message extension $(m_1, \ldots, m_i, \ldots, m_j)$ of which the original message is a prefix. In some schemes, the hierarchy has a maximum depth d, in which case we must have $i \leq j \leq d$. Here, we shall only consider 2-level hierarchical signatures, in which the first level is concerned with user identities, and the second level with messages proper. Notice that 2-level hierarchical signatures and identity-based signatures are equivalent notions: the identity-based key is just a fancy name for a signature on a first-level atomic component.

We use the HSDH assumption to construct a short two-level hierarchical signature that can be verified without knowing the user identity at the first level. Our construction makes a hybrid of two schemes, one at each level.

First Level. At the first level, we devise a variant of the "primary" deterministic Boneh-Boyen signatures from [8, §3.2]. Recall that Boneh-Boyen signatures are constructed in two stages, beginning with a primary "weak" deterministic signature, which is subsequently hardened with a sprinkle of randomness. The primary signature is weaker for the reason that in the forgery game, the opponent must submit all the signing queries up front, rather than adaptively as in the full Boneh-Boyen signature.

In the context of group signatures, this up-front attack model is perfectly adequate for signatures on user identities, since, in group signatures, user identities are not subject to adaptive attacks. Indeed, since there are only polynomially users in a group, their identities can be assigned from a polynomially sized set of integers. Furthermore, these unique identifiers can all be selected in advance by the group manager, and assigned to the users as they enroll in the system.

We shall make one modification to the primary Boneh-Boyen signatures. The modification will allow them to be verifiable without knowledge of the user identity. This is where our new HSDH assumption will come into play.

Second Level. At the second level, where the actual messages are signed, we can work with any secure signature scheme that can be meshed into an upward hierarchy. Hierarchical identity-based encryption schemes with "adaptive-identity security" make good candidates, since we can turn them into signatures schemes that are existentially unforgeable against adaptive chosen message attacks. We shall use a signature based on Waters' IBE scheme [30] for this purpose.

4.1   Hybrid Scheme

Let thus λ be the security parameter. User identities will be modeled as integers taken from a (non-public) polynomially sized random set $\{s_1, \ldots, s_{2^k}\} \subset \mathbb{Z}_p$ where $k = O(\log(\lambda))$. For convenience, we use sequential identifiers $\mathsf{ID} = 1, \ldots, 2^k$ to index the hidden identities s_{ID}, which are kept secret. Messages will be taken as binary strings of fixed length $m = O(\lambda)$. In the description that follows, g is a generator of the prime order subgroup G_p; therefore all group elements in the basic hierarchical signature scheme will have prime order p in G and G_T.

Setup(1^λ): To setup the system, first, secret integers $\alpha, \omega \in \mathbb{Z}_p$ are chosen at random, from which the values $\Omega = g^\omega$ and $A = e(g, g)^\alpha$ are calculated. Next, two integers $y, z' \in \mathbb{Z}_p$ and a vector $\boldsymbol{z} = (z_1, \ldots, z_m) \in \mathbb{Z}_p^m$ are selected at random. The public parameters and master key are

$$\mathsf{PP} = \left(g, \ \Omega = g^\omega, \ u = g^y, \ v' = g^{z'}, \ v_1 = g^{z_1}, \ \ldots, \ v_m = g^{z_m}, \ A = e(g, g)^\alpha \right)$$
$$\in G^{m+5} \times G_T$$

$$\mathsf{MK} = \left(\omega, \ g^\alpha, \ s_1, \ldots, s_{2^k} \right) \ \in \mathbb{Z}_p \times G \times \mathbb{Z}_p^{2^k}$$

The public parameters, PP, also implicitly include k, m, and a description of (p, G, G_T, e). The master key, MK, is assumed to contain the secret list of user identities, $\{s_1, \ldots, s_{2^k}\} \subset \mathbb{Z}_p$.

Extract(PP, MK, ID): To create a private key for the identity s_{ID} associated with the user of index $1 \leq \mathsf{ID} \leq 2^k$, return

$$K_{\mathsf{ID}} = \left((g^\alpha)^{\frac{1}{\omega + s_{\mathsf{ID}}}}, \ g^{s_{\mathsf{ID}}}, \ u^{s_{\mathsf{ID}}} \right) \ \in G^3$$

Sign(PP, K_{ID}, M): To sign a message represented as a bit string $M = (\mu_1 \ldots \mu_m)$ $\in \{0,1\}^m$, using a private key $K_{\text{ID}} = (K_1, K_2, K_3) \in G^3$, select a random $s \in \mathbb{Z}_p$, and output

$$S = \left(\ K_1, \ \ K_2, \ \ K_3 \cdot \left(v' \prod_{j=1}^{m} v_j^{\mu_j}\right)^s, \ \ g^{-s} \ \right) \in G^4$$

Verify(PP, M, σ): To verify that a signature $S = (S_1, S_2, S_3, S_4) \in G^4$ is valid for a message $M = (\mu_1 \ldots \mu_m) \in \{0,1\}^m$, check whether

$$e(S_1, \ S_2 \varOmega) \overset{?}{=} A \qquad \text{and} \qquad e(S_2, \ u) \overset{?}{=} e(S_3, \ g) \cdot e(S_4, \ v' \prod_{j=1}^{m} v_j^{\mu_j})$$

It the equality holds, output `valid`; otherwise, output `invalid`.

Notice that in this case we did not verify the signer's identity, ID, only the message, M. However, signatures remain linkable because S_2 and S_3 are invariant for the same user.

4.2   Existential Unforgeability

The hybrid scheme is existentially unforgeable against adaptive chosen message attacks, and is anonymous at the first level. We shall now state and prove the unforgeability property, which will be needed later on when building group signatures.

Theorem 1. *Consider an adversary $\mathcal{A}$ that existentially forges the hybrid two-level signature scheme in an adaptive chosen message attack. Assume that $\mathcal{A}$ makes no more that $\ell - 1 \ll p$ signature queries and produces a successful forgery with probability ϵ in time t. Then there exists an algorithm $\mathcal{B}$ that solves the ℓ-HSDH problem with probability $\tilde{\epsilon} \approx \epsilon/(4m\ell^2)$ in time $\tilde{t} \approx t$.*

The proof of this theorem uses a two-prong strategy, one for each level. At the first level, we give a reduction based on the ℓ-HSDH assumption, where $\ell = 2^k$ is the number of secret user identities in the master key list (or the number that we have actually used). At the second level, we construct a reduction from the CDH assumption in the bilinear group G_p, but since CDH is implied by HSDH, we get a single reduction from HSDH for both levels at once. All reductions are in the standard model.

Proof. The proof may be found in the full paper.

5   Constant-Size Group Signatures

We now describe the actual group signature scheme, based on the hierarchical signature scheme above. It is obtained from by obfuscating the user identity, and replacing it by a NIZK proof of it being well formed. We also need to incorporate a tracing mechanism, which is achieved by using a trapdoor into the NIZK proof.

5.1   Related Schemes

The group signature we describe invites comparison with two earlier schemes that also feature compact signatures and provable security without random oracles. One of the earlier schemes is due to Boyen and Waters [12,13], the other to Ateniese et al. [1].

The key difference with the earlier Boyen-Waters group signature scheme [12,13], is that the earlier scheme relied on an all-purpose bit hiding technique due to Groth, Ostrovsky, and Sahai [23] to conceal the user identity. Unfortunately, each bit had to supply its own NIZK proof in the final signature, which resulted in a logarithmic-size group signature. The present scheme manages to give a single short proof for the entire identity at once. This makes the resulting signature much shorter, comprising only a small, constant number of group elements.

One of the main differences with the Ateniese et al. [1] scheme, is that the latter relied on very strong, interactive complexity assumptions in order to implement the corresponding NIZK proofs. The present scheme is simpler, and arguably rests on firmer ground.

5.2   Core Construction

The group signature scheme is described by the following algorithms.

Setup(1^λ): The input is a security parameter in unary, 1^λ. Suppose we wish to support up to 2^k signers in the group, and sign messages in $\{0,1\}^m$, where $k = O(\lambda)$ and $m = O(\lambda)$.

The setup algorithm first chooses $n = pq$ where p and q are random primes of bit size $\lceil \log_2 p \rceil, \lceil \log_2 q \rceil = \Theta(\lambda) > k$. From this, it builds a cyclic bilinear group G of order n. Denote by G_p and G_q the cyclic subgroups of G of respective order p and q. The algorithm also selects a generator g of G and a generator h of G_q. Next, the algorithm picks two random exponents $\alpha, \omega \in \mathbb{Z}_n$, and defines $A = e(g,g)^\alpha \in G_T$ and $\Omega = g^\omega \in G$. Finally, it draws $m + 2$ random generators, $u, v', v_1, \ldots, v_m \in G$.

The public information consists of the bilinear group, (n, G, G_T, e), and the public values,

$$\mathsf{PP} = \left(\ g,\ h,\ u,\ v',\ v_1,\ \ldots,\ v_m,\ \Omega = g^\omega,\ A = e(g,g)^\alpha\ \right)$$
$$\in G \times G_q \times G^{m+3} \times G_T$$

The master enrollment key, MK, and the group manager's tracing key, TK, are, respectively,

$$\mathsf{MK} = \left(\ g^\alpha,\ \omega\ \right) \in G \times \mathbb{Z}_n \qquad\qquad \mathsf{TK} = q \in \mathbb{Z}$$

Enroll$(\mathsf{PP}, \mathsf{MK}, \mathsf{ID})$: Suppose we wish to create a signing key for user ID, where $0 \le \mathsf{ID} < 2^k < p$. Upon enrollment in the group, the user is assigned a secret unique value $s_\mathsf{ID} \in \mathbb{Z}_n$, to be later used for tracing purposes. This value must be chosen so that $\omega + s_\mathsf{ID}$ lies in $\mathbb{Z}_n^\times$, the multiplicative group modulo

n. Based on the hidden identity s_{ID}, the signing key to be given to the user is constructed as,

$$K_{\text{ID}} = (K_1, K_2, K_3) = \left(\ (g^\alpha)^{\frac{1}{\omega + s_{\text{ID}}}}, \ g^{s_{\text{ID}}}, \ u^{s_{\text{ID}}} \ \right) \in G^3$$

Here, K_1 is essentially a deterministic Boneh-Boyen signature on s_{ID}, which is not disclosed. Rather, K_2 and K_3 provide a NIZK proof of knowledge of s_{ID} by the issuing authority. There is also a supplemental constant exponent α that will matter at the second level. The newly enrolled user may verify that the key is well formed by checking that (cfr. Section 4),

$$e(K_1, K_2 \, \Omega) \overset{?}{=} A \qquad \text{and} \qquad e(K_2, u) \overset{?}{=} e(K_3, g).$$

Sign(PP, ID, K_{ID}, M): To sign a message $M = (\mu_1 \ldots \mu_m) \in \{0, 1\}^m$, a user with a signing key K_{ID} proceeds as follows.

First, K_{ID} is used to create a two-level hybrid signature with the message M at the second level. To do so, the user chooses a random $s \in \mathbb{Z}_n$ and computes the (randomized but unblinded) hybrid signature,

$$\theta = (\theta_1, \theta_2, \theta_3, \theta_4) = \left(K_1, \ \ K_2, \ \ K_3 \cdot \left(v' \prod_{i=1}^{m} v_i^{\mu_i} \right)^s, \ \ g^{-s} \right)$$

Notice that this initial signature satisfies the regular verification equations: $e(\theta_1, \theta_2 \, \Omega) = A$, and $e(\theta_2, u) = e(\theta_3, g) \cdot e(\theta_4, v' \prod_{i=1}^{m} v_i^{\mu_i})$.

Next, θ must be turned into a blinded signature that is both verifiable and traceable, but remains unlinkable and anonymous to anyone who lacks the tracing key. To proceed, the signer picks four random exponents $t_1, t_2, t_3, t_4 \in \mathbb{Z}_n$ and sets,

$$\sigma_1 = \theta_1 \cdot h^{t_1}, \qquad \sigma_2 = \theta_2 \cdot h^{t_2}, \qquad \sigma_3 = \theta_3 \cdot h^{t_3}, \qquad \sigma_4 = \theta_4 \cdot h^{t_4}.$$

Additionally, it computes the two group elements,

$$\pi_1 = h^{t_1 t_2} \cdot (\theta_1)^{t_2} \cdot (\theta_2 \, \Omega)^{t_1}, \qquad \pi_2 = u^{t_2} \cdot g^{-t_3} \cdot \left(v' \prod_{i=1}^{m} v_i^{\mu_i} \right)^{t_4}.$$

The final signature is output as:

$$\sigma = \left(\sigma_1, \sigma_2, \sigma_3, \sigma_4, \pi_1, \pi_2 \right) \in G^6.$$

Verify(PP, M, σ): To validate a group signature σ on a message M, the verifier first calculates,

$$T_1 = A^{-1} \cdot e(\sigma_1, \sigma_2 \, \Omega), \qquad T_2 = e(\sigma_2, u) \cdot e(\sigma_3, g)^{-1} \cdot e(\sigma_4, v' \prod_{i=1}^{m} v_i^{\mu_i})^{-1}.$$

Then it checks whether,

$$T_1 \overset{?}{=} e(h, \pi_1), \qquad T_2 \overset{?}{=} e(h, \pi_2).$$

If both equalities hold, the verifier outputs `valid`; otherwise, it outputs `invalid`.

These tests show that $(\sigma_1, \sigma_2, \sigma_3, \sigma_4)$ is a valid 2-level hybrid signature once the random blinding factors are removed; the extra elements (π_1, π_2) serve to convince the verifier that the blinding factors were affixed correctly.

Trace(PP, TK, σ): Let $\sigma = (\ldots, \sigma_2, \ldots)$ be a signature assumed to pass the verification test for some message M, which will not be needed here. To recover the identity of the signer, the tracing authority first calculates $(\sigma_2)^q$ using the tracing key TK. Then, for each auspicious identity ID_i, it tests whether,

$$(\sigma_2)^q \overset{?}{=} (g^{s\mathsf{ID}_i})^q.$$

The tracer outputs the recovered identity, $\mathsf{ID} = \mathsf{ID}_i$, upon satisfaction of the above equation.

Remark that tracing can be done in constant time — the time to compute $(\sigma_2)^q$ — with the help of a lookup table of associations $(g^{s\mathsf{ID}_i})^q \mapsto \mathsf{ID}_i$ for all users in the group. Since the value $(g^{s\mathsf{ID}_i})^q$ can be calculated once and for all for each user ID_i, for instance upon a user's initial enrollment, the amortized cost of tracing is indeed essentially constant.

Next we state the security properties of our constant-size group signature scheme.

5.3 Full Anonymity (Under CPA Attack)

We prove the security of our group signature scheme in the anonymity game against chosen plaintext attacks. First, we show that an adversary cannot tell whether h is a random generator of G_q or G. Next, we show that if h is chosen from G then the identity of a signer is perfectly hidden, in the information theoretic sense.

Theorem 2. *Suppose no t-time adversary can solve the subgroup decision problem with advantage at least ϵ_{sd}. Then for every t'-time adversary $\mathcal{A}$ where $t' \approx t$ we have that $\mathrm{Adv}_{\mathcal{A}} < 2\,\epsilon_{\mathrm{sd}}$.*

Proof. We use a game switching argument where Γ_0 is the real group signature anonymity game, and Γ_1 is a game in which the public parameters are the same as in the original game except that h is chosen randomly from G instead of G_q. We denote the adversary's advantage in the original game by $\mathrm{Adv}_{\mathcal{A}}$, and in the modified game by $\mathrm{Adv}_{\mathcal{A}, \Gamma_1}$.

First, in Lemma 1, we show that the two games are essentially indistinguishable, unless the Decision Subgroup assumption is easy. Second, in lemma 2, we use an information-theoretic argument to prove that in the game Γ_1 the adversary's advantage must be zero. The theorem follows from these results.

Lemma 1. *For all t'-time adversaries as above, $\mathrm{Adv}_{\mathcal{A}} - \mathrm{Adv}_{\mathcal{A}, \Gamma_1} < 2\,\epsilon_{\mathrm{sd}}$.*

Lemma 2. *For any algorithm $\mathcal{A}$, we have that $\mathrm{Adv}_{\mathcal{A}, \Gamma_1} = 0$.*

Proof. The proofs of these two lemmas are given in the full paper.

5.4   Full Traceability

We reduce the full traceability of the group signature scheme to the existential unforgeability of the underlying hybrid signature construction of Section 4.

Theorem 3. *If there is a (t, ϵ) adversary for the full traceability game against the group signature scheme, then there exists a $(\tilde{t}, \epsilon)$ adaptive chosen message existential unforgeability adversary against the two-level hybrid signature scheme, where $t \approx \tilde{t}$.*

Proof. We prove this theorem in the full paper.

6   CCA-Security

In the introduction we stated that the two primary drawbacks of the scheme of Boyen and Waters [12,13] are that the signature grew logarithmically with the number of signers and that the scheme was not CCA secure. In this work we addressed the first limitation (furthermore in a practical way), but left the second one open. Here we explain some of the challenges in achieving CCA security while using the subgroup paradigm for proofs.

In both this paper and the Boneh-Waters scheme the authority uses knowledge of the factorization of the group order in order to trace. In order to achieve CCA security we will clearly need to take a different approach since all known CCA proof techniques depend upon a simulation knowing partial decryption information (e.g. consider the two key paradigm of Dolev, Dwork and Naor [20]).

One tempting direction is to provably encrypt (in a simulation sound manner) the identity of the signer in a CCA-secure cryptosystems derived from one of the recent bilinear map-based IBE systems of Boneh and Boyen [7] combined with the techniques of Canetti, Halevi, and Katz [18]. Then we could allow the tracer to have the decryption key for this system, but not know the group's factorization. However, there is one large problem with this technique. The subgroup-based NIZK techniques only prove soundness in one subgroup. It is easy to see that a corrupt signer can provably encrypt his identity and then randomize the encryption in the other subgroup. Since the decryption authority will not know the factorization, his view of the identity will be indistinguishable from random. Therefore, it seems more complex techniques are necessary to achieve CCA-security will using subgroup based proofs. This might also be an argument for basing future group signature schemes on proof systems [22] derived from the decisional Linear assumption [9].

References

1. Giuseppe Ateniese, Jan Camenisch, Susan Hohenberger, and Breno de Medeiros. Practical group signatures without random oracles. Cryptology ePrint Archive, Report 2005/385, 2005. http://eprint.iacr.org/.
2. Giuseppe Ateniese, Jan Camenisch, Marc Joye, and Gene Tsudik. A practical and provably secure coalition-resistant group signature scheme. In *Proceedings of Crypto 2000*, volume 1880 of *Lecture Notes in Computer Science*, pages 255–70. Springer-Verlag, 2000.
3. Giuseppe Ateniese, Dawn Song, and Gene Tsudik. Quasi-efficient revocation of group signatures. In *Proceedings of Financial Cryptography 2002*, 2002.
4. Giuseppe Ateniese and Gene Tsudik. Some open issues and directions in group signatures. In *Proceedings of Financial Cryptography 1999*, volume 1648 of *Lecture Notes in Computer Science*, pages 196–211. Springer-Verlag, 1999.
5. Mihir Bellare, Daniele Micciancio, and Bogdan Warinschi. Foundations of group signatures: Formal definitions, simplified requirements, and a construction based on general assumptions. In *Advances in Cryptology—EUROCRYPT 2003*, volume 2656 of *Lecture Notes in Computer Science*, pages 614–29. Springer-Verlag, 2003.
6. Mihir Bellare, Haixia Shi, and Chong Zhang. Foundations of group signatures: The case of dynamic groups. In *Proceedings of CT-RSA 2005*, Lecture Notes in Computer Science, pages 136–153. Springer-Verlag, 2005.
7. Dan Boneh and Xavier Boyen. Efficient selective-ID secure identity based encryption without random oracles. In *Advances in Cryptology—EUROCRYPT 2004*, volume 3027 of *Lecture Notes in Computer Science*, pages 223–38. Springer-Verlag, 2004.
8. Dan Boneh and Xavier Boyen. Short signatures without random oracles. In *Advances in Cryptology—EUROCRYPT 2004*, volume 3027 of *Lecture Notes in Computer Science*, pages 56–73. Springer-Verlag, 2004.
9. Dan Boneh, Xavier Boyen, and Hovav Shacham. Short group signatures. In *Advances in Cryptology—CRYPTO 2004*, volume 3152 of *Lecture Notes in Computer Science*, pages 41–55. Springer-Verlag, 2004.
10. Dan Boneh, Eu-Jin Goh, and Kobbi Nissim. Evaluating 2-DNF formulas on ciphertexts. In *Proceedings of TCC 2005*, Lecture Notes in Computer Science. Springer-Verlag, 2005.
11. Dan Boneh and Hovav Shacham. Group signatures with verifier-local revocation. In *Proceedings of ACM CCS 2004*, pages 168–77. ACM Press, 2004.
12. Xavier Boyen and Brent Waters. Compact group signatures without random oracles. Cryptology ePrint Archive, Report 2005/381, 2005. http://eprint.iacr.org/.
13. Xavier Boyen and Brent Waters. Compact group signatures without random oracles. In *Advances in Cryptology—EUROCRYPT 2006*, volume 4004 of *Lecture Notes in Computer Science*, pages 427–444. Springer-Verlag, 2006.
14. Jan Camenisch. Efficient and generalized group signatures. In *Advances in Cryptology—EUROCRYPT 1997*, Lecture Notes in Computer Science, pages 465–479. Springer-Verlag, 1997.
15. Jan Camenisch and Jens Groth. Group signatures: Better efficiency and new theoretical aspects. In *Proceedings of SCN 2004*, pages 120–133, 2004.
16. Jan Camenisch and Anna Lysyanskaya. Dynamic accumulators and application to efficient revocation of anonymous credentials. In *Advances in Cryptology—CRYPTO 2002*, volume 2442 of *Lecture Notes in Computer Science*, pages 61–76. Springer-Verlag, 2002.

17. Jan Camenisch and Anna Lysyanskaya. Signature schemes and anonymous credentials from bilinear maps. In *Advances in Cryptology—CRYPTO 2004*, volume 3152 of *Lecture Notes in Computer Science*. Springer-Verlag, 2004.
18. Ran Canetti, Shai Halevi, and Jonathan Katz. Chosen-ciphertext security from identity-based encryption. In *Advances in Cryptology—EUROCRYPT 2004*. Springer-Verlag, 2004.
19. David Chaum and Eugène van Heyst. Group signatures. In *Advances in Cryptology—EUROCRYPT 1991*, volume 547 of *Lecture Notes in Computer Science*, pages 257–65. Springer-Verlag, 1991.
20. Danny Dolev, Cynthia Dwork, and Moni Naor. Non-malleable cryptography (extended abstract). In *Proceedings of STOC 1991*, pages 542–552, 1991.
21. Jens Groth. Simulation-sound NIZK proofs for a practical language and constant size group signatures. In *Proceedings of ASIACRYPT 2006*, Lecture Notes in Computer Science, pages 444–459. Springer-Verlag, 2006.
22. Jens Groth, Rafail Ostrovsky, and Amit Sahai. Non-interactive Zaps and new techniques for NIZK. In *Advances in Cryptology—CRYPTO 2006*, Lecture Notes in Computer Science. Springer-Verlag, 2006.
23. Jens Groth, Rafail Ostrovsky, and Amit Sahai. Perfect non-interactive zero knowledge for NP. In *Advances in Cryptology—EUROCRYPT 2006*, Lecture Notes in Computer Science. Springer-Verlag, 2006.
24. Antoine Joux and Kim Nguyen. Separating decision Diffie-Hellman from computational Diffie-Hellman in cryptographic groups. *Journal of Cryptology*, 16(4), 2003.
25. Aggelos Kiayias and Moti Yung. Extracting group signatures from traitor tracing schemes. In *Advances in Cryptology—EUROCRYPT 2003*, Lecture Notes in Computer Science, pages 630–48. Springer-Verlag, 2003.
26. Aggelos Kiayias and Moti Yung. Group signatures: Provable security, efficient constructions and anonymity from trapdoor-holders. Cryptology ePrint Archive, Report 2004/076, 2004. http://eprint.iacr.org/.
27. Aggelos Kiayias and Moti Yung. Group signatures with efficient concurrent join. In *Advances in Cryptology—EUROCRYPT 2005*, Lecture Notes in Computer Science, pages 198–214. Springer-Verlag, 2005.
28. Moni Naor. On cryptographic assumptions and challenges. In *Advances in Cryptology—CRYPTO 2003*, Lecture Notes in Computer Science, pages 96–109. Springer-Verlag, 2003.
29. Dawn Xiaodong Song. Practical forward secure group signature schemes. In *ACM Conference on Computer and Communications Security—CCS 2001*, pages 225–234, 2001.
30. Brent Waters. Efficient identity-based encryption without random oracles. In *Advances in Cryptology—EUROCRYPT 2005*, volume 3494 of *Lecture Notes in Computer Science*. Springer-Verlag, 2005.

A Direct Anonymous Attestation Scheme for Embedded Devices

He Ge[1,*] and Stephen R. Tate[2]

[1] Microsoft Corporation, One Microsoft Way, Redmond 98005
hege@microsoft.com
[2] Department of Computer Science and Engineering
University of North Texas, Denton, TX 76203
srt@cse.unt.edu

Abstract. Direct anonymous attestation (DAA) is an anonymous authentication scheme adopted by the Trusted Computing Group in its specifications for trusted computing platforms. This paper presents an efficient construction that implements all anonymous authentication features specified in DAA, including authentication with total anonymity, authentication with variable anonymity, and rogue TPM tagging. The current DAA construction is mainly targeted for powerful devices such as personal computers, and their corresponding application areas, but is not entirely suitable for embedded devices with limited computing capabilities (e.g., cell phones or hand-held PDAs). We propose a new construction with more efficient sign and verify protocols, making it more attractive for embedded devices. We prove that the new construction is secure under the strong RSA assumption and the decisional Diffie-Hellman assumption.

Keywords: Direct Anonymous Attestation, Group signature, Privacy, Authentication, Trusted Computing Platform, Cryptographic Protocol.

1 Introduction

In this paper, we present an efficient direct anonymous attestation scheme for embedded devices. DAA is a group signature variant designed to protect the privacy of the owner of a trust computing platform, and has been adopted by the Trusted Computing Group, an industry consortium developing standards for "trusted computing platforms." A group signature is a privacy-preserving signature scheme introduced by Chaum and Heyst [12]. In such a scheme, there are two basic types of entities: a group manager and certain number of group members. The group manager issues a group membership certificate/credential for each group member. Later, based on its own group membership certificate, a group member can sign a message on behalf of the group without revealing its identity. That is, a third party can only verify that the signature was produced by a legitimate group member without being able to find which particular one. Only the group manager is able to open a signature and reveal its originator (in some cases this ability is held by a separate party known as an "open authority"). In addition, signatures signed

---

* Work done while at the Department of Computer Science and Engineering, University of North Texas.

T. Okamoto and X. Wang (Eds.): PKC 2007, LNCS 4450, pp. 16–30, 2007.

by the same group member cannot be identified as from the same source, i.e., "linked." Recently, the study of group signature schemes has attracted considerable attention, and many solutions have been proposed in the literature (e.g., [1,4,5,7,8,9]).

1.1 Background

The Trusted Computing Group [21] (TCG) is an industry consortium formed to develop standards for Trusted Computing Platforms. A trusted computing platform is a computing device integrated with a cryptographic chip called a trusted platform module (TPM), which is designed and manufactured in a way such that all parties can trust cryptographic computing results from this TPM. Based on the TPM, a trusted computing platform can implement many security related features, such as secure boot, sealed storage, and software integrity attestation. More information about TPMs and trusted computing platforms can be found at the TCG website [21].

TPMs are tamper-resistant cryptographic chips. When a TPM is manufactured, a unique RSA keypair, called the Endorsement Key (EK), is created and stored in the protected area of the TPM. The EK might be generated inside a TPM, or imported from an outside key generator. The public part of the EK is authenticated by the manufacturer, while the private part of the EK will never be revealed to the outside. A TPM independently performs cryptographic computations inside itself, and even its manufacturer cannot obtain knowledge of these computations. TPMs are embedded into computing devices by a device manufacturer, and these devices are called trusted computing platforms when coupled with appropriate software. At the heart of trusted computing platform is the assumption that TPMs should independently work as expected, and be "trusted" by remote parties. Essentially, trusted computing platforms are based on trust of TPMs.

The deployment and use of TPMs introduces privacy concerns. If the authentication of a TPM is directly based on its EK, all transactions by the same TPM can be linked through the public part of the EK. Furthermore, if the TPM is associated with a user's identity, the user may suffer a loss of privacy. To protect the privacy of a TPM owner, two solutions have been proposed in the TPM specifications.

Privacy in the TPM v1.1 specification is based on a trusted third party, called a Privacy CA. A TPM generates a second RSA keypair called an Attestation Identity Key (AIK). The TPM sends an AIK to the Privacy CA, applying for a certificate on the AIK. After the TPM proves its ownership using a valid EK, the Privacy CA issues a certificate for this AIK. Later, the TPM sends the certificate for this AIK to a verifier, and proves it owns this AIK. This way, the TPM hides its identity during the transaction. Obviously, this is not a completely satisfactory solution, since each AIK creation needs the involvement of the Privacy CA, and compromise of the Privacy CA (or a dishonest Privacy CA) can destroy all privacy guarantees.

An alternate solution added in TPM v1.2 is called Direct Anonymous Attestation (DAA), adopting techniques from group signatures: A TPM applies for a credential from an issuer, and later the TPM generates a special signature using this credential. A remote verifier can verify the signature has been constructed from a valid credential without the ability to recover the underlying credential. Different signatures based on the same credential might be linkable or unlinkable depending on a verifier's requirements. If the method implements unlinkable authentication, it is called total anonymity. It should be noted that the open operation defined in standard group signature schemes, which allows the group manager to learn the creator of a signature, is not included in DAA for privacy protection.

Variable anonymity [22] is a conditionally linkable anonymous authentication, in which the signatures signed by the same TPM in a certain time interval are linkable. However, when the signing parameters change, the signatures across the different periods cannot be linked. When the time interval becomes short, the method works like perfectly unlinkable authentication. When the period never expires, this leads to pseudo-anonymity. A verifier can adjust the time interval to detect suspicious attestation. If too many attestation requests come from the same TPM in a period of time, it is likely this TPM has been compromised.

Rogue TPM tagging is about the revocation of the key of a corrupted TPM. When a broken TPM is discovered and identified by its EK, its secrets will be published on the revocation list. A verifier can identify and exclude any rogue TPM on the list, and an issuer can refuse to issue new credentials to a TPM with a revoked EK.

The current solution for DAA is due to Brickell, Camenisch, and Chen [6], which we refer to as the BCC scheme in this paper. The BCC scheme is designed mainly for devices with powerful computing capabilities such as personal computers. The scheme is quite complex with high computing overhead. To expedite the authentication process, the computation has been distributed between a TPM and the host into which the TPM is embedded. The TPM finishes the computation related to the signature generation, while the host finishes the computation related to anonymity. The BCC scheme works fine with personal computers. However, it would be an expensive solution for devices with low computing capabilities, such as cell phones, hand-held PDA, etc.

1.2 Our Results

In this paper, we propose a new construction that can carry out all required features in DAA (total anonymity, variable anonymity, and rouge TPM tagging), and has much more efficient sign and verify protocols.

Our construction is built up from the group signature scheme due to Camenisch and Michels [8], which we will refer to as the CM scheme. We directly adopt their join protocol. However, our sign and verify protocols are totally different. We have devised an efficient way to carry out anonymous authentication with much less computation. So far we are not aware of any similar method being adopted in other cryptographic constructions for anonymous authentication. Due to the simplicity and efficiency of our method, the new construction is more appealing for embedded devices with low computing capability. We will demonstrate this point in Section 4.6 when we present a performance analysis.

However, we also need to point out that the join protocol, which we directly adopt from the CM scheme, is not an efficient one. Furthermore, the security argument for the join protocol assumes a static adversary, while the counterpart in the BCC scheme can be proved secure under an adaptive adversary. However, we consider this to be a minor issue in real applications. The join protocol is the way a TPM obtains its anonymous certificate/credential. In practice, the join protocol normally is conducted in the system setup stage, and is run infrequently in later phases. Meanwhile, the join protocol generally should be completed in more strict environments with rigorous security requirements, so security under static attack should be reasonable and acceptable. Furthermore, the join protocol may not be the only option for certificate generation. In some applications, certificates could be produced at manufacturing time, just as the endorsement key (EK) is. In such a situation, the join protocol might not even be necessary.

The rest of this paper is organized as follows. The next section introduces the model for our construction. Section 3 reviews some definitions, cryptographic assumptions, and building blocks of our proposed scheme. Section 4 presents the proposed scheme. Security properties are considered in Section 5. Finally, we summarize and give conclusions in Section 6.

2   The Model

This section introduces the model for direct anonymous attestation, which is a variant of the group signature model [1]. Both these two models support procedures Setup, Join, Sign, and Verify, while DAA further supports mechanism such as variable linkability and rogue group member identification, i.e., rogue TPM tagging.

Definition 1. *Direct anonymous attestation is a digital signature scheme with two types of participants: the certificate issuer, and TPMs. It consists of the following procedures:*

- **Setup:** *For a given security parameter σ, the issuer produces system-wide public parameters and a group master key for group membership certificate generation.*
- **Join:** *An interactive protocol between a TPM and the issuer. The TPM obtains a group membership certificate to become a group member. The public certificate and the TPM's identity information are stored by the issuer in a database for future use.*
- **Sign:** *Using its group membership certificate and private key, the TPM creates an anonymous group signature for a message.*
- **Verify:** *A signature is verified to make sure it originates from a legitimate TPM without knowledge of which particular one.*
- **Rogue tagging:** *A rogue TPM can be identified and excluded for the group.*

Similar to a group signature, DAA should satisfy the following properties:

- **Correctness:** Any valid signature can be correctly verified by the Verify protocol.
- **Forgery-Resistance:** A valid group membership certificate can only be created by a TPM and the issuer through the Join protocol.
- **Anonymity:** It is infeasible to identify the real TPM of a signature unless this TPM is on the revocation list.
- **Unlinkability:** It is infeasible to link two different signatures of the same TPM.
- **Non-framing:** No one (including the issuer) can sign a message in such a way that it appears to come from another TPM.

3   Definitions and Preliminaries

This section reviews some definitions, widely accepted complexity assumptions, and building blocks that we will use in this paper.

3.1   Number-Theoretic Assumption

Definition 2 (Special RSA Modulus). *An RSA modulus $n = pq$ is called special if $p = 2p' + 1$ and $q = 2q' + 1$ where p' and q' also are prime numbers.*

Definition 3 (Quadratic Residue Group QR_n). *Let Z_n^* be the multiplicative group modulo n, which contains all positive integers less than n and relatively prime to n. An element $x \in Z_n^*$ is called a* quadratic residue *if there exists an $a \in Z_n^*$ such that $a^2 \equiv x \pmod{n}$. The set of all quadratic residues of Z_n^* forms a cyclic subgroup of Z_n^*, which we denote by QR_n. If n is the product of two distinct primes, then $|QR_n| = \frac{1}{4}|Z_n^*|$.*

We list two properties about QR_n which will be be used in the later security proof.

Property 1. *If n is a special RSA modulus, with p, q, p', and q' as in Definition 2 above, then $|QR_n| = p'q'$ and $(p' - 1)(q' - 1)$ elements of QR_n are generators of QR_n.*

Property 2. *If g is a generator of QR_n, then $g^a \bmod n$ is a generator of QR_n if and only if $GCD(a, |QR_n|) = 1$.*

The security of our techniques relies on the following security assumptions which are widely accepted in the cryptography literature. (see, for example, [1,2,9,10,15]).

Assumption 1 (Strong RSA Assumption). *Let n be an RSA modulus. The* Flexible RSA Problem *is the problem of taking a random element $u \in Z_n^*$ and finding a pair (v, e) such that $e > 1$ and $v^e = u \pmod{n}$. The* Strong RSA Assumption *says that no probabilistic polynomial time algorithm can solve the flexible RSA problem with non-negligible probability.*

Assumption 2 (Decisional Diffie-Hellman Assumption for QR_n). *Let n be a special RSA modulus, and let g be a generator of QR_n. For two distributions (g, g^x, g^y, g^{xy}), (g, g^x, g^y, g^z), $x, y, x \in_R Z_n$, there is no probabilistic polynomial-time algorithm that distinguishes them with non-negligible probability.*

Kiayias et al. have investigated the Decisional Diffie-Hellman Assumption over a subset of QR_n in [17], i.e., x, y, z are randomly chosen from some subsets, truncation of QR_n. They showed that the Decisional Diffie-Hellman Assumption is still attainable over subsets of QR_n with the size down to at least $|QR_n|^{1/4}$.

3.2   Building Blocks

Our main building blocks are *statistical honest-verifier zero knowledge proofs of knowledge* related to discrete logarithms over QR_n [10,11,16]. They include protocols for things such as knowledge of a discrete logarithm, knowledge of the equality of two discrete logarithms, and knowledge of a discrete logarithm that lies in certain interval, etc. We introduce one of them here. Readers may refer to the original papers for more details.

Definition 4 (Protocol 1). *Let n be a special RSA modulus, QR_n be the quadratic residue group modulo n, and g be a generator of QR_n. Let α, l, and l_c be security parameters that are all greater than 1, and let X be a constant number. In the following protocol, Alice knows x, the discrete logarithm of T_1 (so $g^x \equiv T_1 \pmod{n}$), where $x \in [X - 2^l, X + 2^l]$. After the protocol is executed, Bob is convinced that Alice knows the discrete log x of T_1 such that $x \in [X - 2^{\alpha(l+l_c)+1}, X + 2^{\alpha(l+l_c)+1}]$.*

1. *Alice picks a random $t \in \pm\{0,1\}^{\alpha(l+l_c)}$ and computes $T_2 = g^t \pmod{n}$. Alice sends (T_1, T_2) to a verifier Bob.*
2. *Bob picks a random $c \in \{0,1\}^{l_c}$ and sends it to Alice.*
3. *Alice computes*
$$w = t - c(x - X),$$
   which she sends to Bob. Notice that an honest Alice knows a value of $x \in [X - 2^l, X + 2^l]$, so given the range in which t and c were selected, an honest Alice will produce a w that satisfies $w \in [-2^{\alpha(l+l_c)+1}, 2^{\alpha(l+l_c)+1}]$ (actually in a slightly smaller interval than this, but this is a sufficiently tight bound for our purposes).
4. *Bob checks that $w \in [-2^{\alpha(l+l_c)+1}, 2^{\alpha(l+l_c)+1}]$ and*
$$g^{w-cX} T_1^c \equiv T_2 \pmod{n}.$$

   If both tests pass, then Bob is convinced that Alice knows the discrete logarithm of T_1 and that it lies in the range $[X - 2^{\alpha(l+l_c)+1}, X + 2^{\alpha(l+l_c)+1}]$.

Remark 1. The parameter $\alpha > 1$ is used since we do not know the size of the group QR_n, and determines the statistical closeness of our actual distribution to the ideal one. In other words, α determines the statistical zero-knowledge property of this protocol. For a more in-depth discussion and analysis, we refer the reader to [8].

Remark 2. Using the Fiat-Shamir heuristic [14], the protocol can be turned into a non-interactive "signature of knowledge," which is secure in the random oracle model [3]. We will introduce our new signature scheme in the manner of a "signature of knowledge" in the next section.

4   The Direct Anonymous Attestation Scheme

In this section, we describe our method for implementing direct anonymous attestation. As mentioned earlier, our construction is based on the same group certificate as the CM scheme [8]. However, the sign and verify protocols are re-designed.

4.1   System Parameter Setting

The certificate issuer picks a security parameter σ, and generates the system parameters as follows:

- n, g: n is a special RSA modulus such that $n = pq$, where p and q are each at least σ bits long (so $p, q > 2^\sigma$), and $p = 2p' + 1$, and $q = 2q' + 1$, with p' and q' both being prime. g is a random generator of the cyclic group QR_n. n, g are public values while p and q are kept secret by the group manager.

- α, l_c, l_s, l_b: Security parameters that are greater than 1.
- X, Y: constant integers. $Y > 2^{\alpha(l_c+l_b)+1}$, and $X > 2Y + 2^{\alpha(l_s+l_c)+2}$.
- Two strong collision-resistant hash functions: $\mathcal{H}_1 : \{0,1\}^* \to Z_n^*$, and $\mathcal{H}_2 : \{0,1\}^* \to \{0,1\}^{l_c}$.

An illustration of the system parameters is the setting of $\sigma = 1024$ (so n is 2048 bits), $\alpha = 9/8$, $X = 2^{792}$ (99 bytes), $Y = 2^{520}$ (65 bytes), $l_s = 540$, $l_b = 300$, and $l_c = 160$.

4.2 Join Protocol

We adopt the same join protocol as in the CM group signature. A TPM obtains its group membership certificate as a keypair (E, s), such that s is prime, $s \in (X, X + 2^{l_s})$, and

$$E^s \equiv g \,(\text{mod } n).$$

s is the TPM's private key and is kept secret by the TPM. For further details on how the join protocol works, see [8].

4.3 Authentication with Total Anonymity

The idea of our method for implementing authentication with total anonymity is as follows: the TPM picks a random blinding integer $b < s$, computes $T_1 = E^b = g^{s^{-1}b} \,(\text{mod } n)$, $T_2 = g^b \,(\text{mod } n)$. Then the TPM sends (T_1, T_2) to a verifier along with a proof that (T_1, T_2) is constructed from a legitimate keypair. Thus, a TPM's keypair is covered by this blinding integer b. The requirement for $b < s$ is important, which will be seen more clearly in the later security proof.

This method is very different from the one used in many group signature schemes (e.g., [1,6,8]). In those schemes, a group member basically adopts the ElGamal encryption to hide its identity [13]. For instance, in the CM group signature, a group member hide itself by computing

$$T_1 = Ey^b \,(\text{mod } n), \quad T_2 = g^b \,(\text{mod } n),$$

where y is the group manager's public key. Afterwards, the task for the group member is to prove that (T_1, T_2) was constructed from a legitimate keypair, which is much less efficient than our method.

Now, we introduce our sign protocol. For a message m, the TPM executes the following steps to complete the sign protocol:

1. Generate a random $b \in_R [Y - 2^{l_b}, Y + 2^{l_b}]$, $t_1 \in_R \pm\{0,1\}^{\alpha(l_s+l_c)}$, $t_2 \in_R \pm\{0,1\}^{\alpha(l_b+l_c)}$, and compute

$$T_1 = E^b \,(\text{mod } n), \quad T_2 = g^b \,(\text{mod } n); \quad d_1 = T_1^{t_1} \,(\text{mod } n), \quad d_2 = g^{t_2} \,(\text{mod } n); .$$

2. Compute:
$$c = \mathcal{H}_2(g||T_1||T_2||d_1||d_2||m);$$
$$w_1 = t_1 - c(s - X), \quad w_2 = t_2 - c(b - Y).$$

3. Output (c, w_1, w_2, T_1, T_2).

To verify a signature, the verifier computes

$$c' = \mathcal{H}_2(g||T_1||T_2||T_1^{w_1-cX}T_2^c||g^{w_2-cY}T_2^c||m),$$

and accepts the signature if and only if $c = c'$, $w_1 \in \pm\{0,1\}^{\alpha(l_s+l_c)+1}$, and $w_2 \in \pm\{0,1\}^{\alpha(l_b+l_c)+1}$.

4.4 Authentication with Variable Anonymity

To achieve variable anonymity, each signature will belong to a "linkability class" that is identified using a "linkability class identifier," or LCID. All signatures made by the same TPM with the same LCID are linkable, and in an interactive authentication protocol the LCID can be negotiated and determined by the TPM and verifier. For example, to link authentications to a single server over a single day, the LCID could simply be the server name concatenated with the date. If the same LCID is always used with a particular server (e.g., the server name), then the result is a pseudo-anonymity system. If complete anonymity is desired, the signer can simply pick a random LCID (which is possible if the server is not concerned with linkability and allows arbitrary LCIDs).

The TPM derives a generator j of QR_n by hashing the LCID of this signature.

$$j = (\mathcal{H}_1(LCID))^2 \pmod{n}.$$

To implement variable anonymity, we add the following computations to the Sign protocol:

$$T_3 = j^s \pmod{n}, \quad d_3 = j^{t_1} \pmod{n},$$
$$c = \mathcal{H}_2(g||j||T_1||T_2||T_3||d_1||d_2||d_3||m);$$

and outputs $(c, w_1, w_2, T_1, T_2, T_3, m)$. The verifier then computes

$$c' = \mathcal{H}_2(g||j||T_1||T_2||T_3||T_1^{w_1-cX}T_2^c||g^{w_2-cY}T_2^c||j^{w_1-cX}T_3^c||m).$$

Since j will remain unchanged for a certain time interval, the same TPM will always produce the same T_3 during this interval. The frequency of T_3 will be used by the verifier to identify suspicious authentication, and may refuse to provide further services. Since j changes in different periods of time, this ensures the unlinkability of the same TPM between periods.

4.5 Rogue TPM Tagging

As described earlier, TPMs are manufactured to provide tamper-resistance. Otherwise, the basic benefits of trusted computing platforms would become meaningless. However, in extreme circumstances, a TPM may be compromised and its keypair exposed, so a verifier should be able to identify the attestation request from rogue TPMs. To do so, the secrets of a corrupted TPM (e.g., EK, E, and s) should be published on the revocation list. For a keypair (E, s) on the revocation list, a verifier checks

$$T_1^s =? T_2 \pmod{n}.$$

If the equation holds, the request comes from a revoked TPM.

4.6 Performance Analysis

We present a performance analysis of our scheme in the section. It can be observed that the computation complexity in our scheme is dominated by the modular squaring and multiplication operations. To estimate the computation cost, it is sufficient to count total modular squarings and multiplications in the protocol. For simplicity, we estimate the computation cost based on techniques for general exponentiation [19]. For a particular exponentiation operation, let m_1 be the bit length of the exponent, and m_2 be the number of 1's in the binary representation. Then the total computation cost can be estimated as m_1 squarings and m_2 multiplications. For example, if $y = g^x \pmod{n}$, and $x \in_R \{0,1\}^{160}$, then the expected number of 1's in x is 80, so the total expected computation includes 160 squarings and 80 multiplications.

Suppose we set $\sigma = 1024$, so n is 2048 bits (p, q are 1024 bits). We further choose $\alpha = 9/8, l_c = 160, l_s = 540, l_b = 300$. We also set $X = 2^{792}$ (99 bytes), $Y = 2^{520}$ (65 bytes). This parameter setting conforms to the requirements of the decisional Diffie-Hellman assumption over the subset of QR_n. We can observe that most bits of s, b are 0's. The computation with exponent b has 520 squarings and 151 expected multiplications. For authentication with total anonymity, a TPM needs 2352 ($520 \times 3 + 792$) squarings, and 958 ($151 \times 2 + 520/2 + 792/2$) multiplications.

We have counted the total exponent bit-length in the BCC scheme, which is 25844 for authentication with total anonymity. However, due to the computation distribution between the TPM and its host, efficient algorithm for mult-based exponentiation can be used on the host part (Algorithm 15.2 in [18]). According to our counting result, in the BCC scheme, the total exponent bit-length for the TPM is around 4088, and 12098 for the host. So the total exponent bit-length is 16186 ($4088 + 12098$), which includes 16186 squarings and 8093 expected multiplications. If we assume the cost of squaring is equal to that of multiplication (squaring can be at most two times faster than multiplication), our scheme is about 7 ($24279/3310$) times faster than the BCC scheme. Even if we only consider the computation inside the TPM, our scheme is almost 2 ($6132/3310$) times faster than the BCC scheme. For variable anonymity, our scheme needs 5561 modular multiplications, which still can be carried out by the TPM alone.

It should be noticed that the computation can also be distributed in our scheme. T_1, T_2, d_2, w_2 can be calculated by the host, and T_3, d_1, d_3, w_1 must be computed inside the TPM. Generally speaking, this should be unnecessary since all the computation can be done by the TPM alone.

Without the distribution of computation, the system design can be greatly simplified. Thus, our method is more appropriate for mobile devices with low computing capabilities.

5 Security Properties

We first propose a lemma that deals with the valid range of system parameters.

Lemma 1. *If* $X > 2^{\alpha(l_s+l_c)+2}$, $\alpha, l_s, l_c > 1$, *then* $(X - 2^{\alpha(l_s+l_c)+1})^2 > X + 2^{\alpha(l_s+l_c)+1}$.

Proof.

$$(X - 2^{\alpha(l_s+l_c)+1})^2 - (X + 2^{\alpha(l_s+l_c)+1})$$

$$= X^2 - X2^{\alpha(l_s+l_c)+2} + 2^{2\alpha(l_s+l_c)+2} - X - 2^{\alpha(l_s+l_c)+1}$$

$$= X(X - 2^{\alpha(l_s+l_c)+2} - 1) + 2^{2\alpha(l_s+l_c)+2} - 2^{\alpha(l_s+l_c)+1}$$

Since $\alpha, l_s, l_c > 1$, and $X > 2^{\alpha(l_s+l_c)+2}$, the equation is greater than 0.   □

Next we introduce an extension version of the lemma due to Shamir [20].

Lemma 2. *Let n be a special RSA number. Given values $u, v \in QR_n$ and $x, y \in Z$ such that $GCD(x, y) = r < x$, and $v^x \equiv u^y \pmod{n}$, there is an efficient way to compute a value z such that $z^k \equiv u \pmod{n}$, where $k = x/r$.*

Proof. Since $GCD(x, y) = r, r < x$, using the extended Euclidean GCD algorithm, we can obtain values α and β such that $\alpha x/r + \beta y/r = 1$. Then we have

$$u \equiv u^{\alpha x/r+\beta y/r} \equiv u^{\alpha x/r}u^{y\beta/r} \equiv u^{\alpha x/r}v^{\beta x/r} \equiv (u^\alpha v^\beta)^{x/r} \pmod{n}.$$

Therefore, setting $k = x/r$ and $z = u^\alpha v^\beta$, we have $z^k \equiv u \pmod{n}$.   □

Based on this lemma, we can immediately obtain a corollary for later proof.

Corollary 1. *Let n be a special RSA number. For given values $u, v \in QR_n$ and $x, y \in Z$ such that $x > y$ and $v^x \equiv u^y \pmod{n}$, there is an efficient way to compute values (x, k) such that $x^k \equiv u \pmod{n}$.*

Proof. Since $x > y$, we have $GCD(x, y) = r, 1 \leq r \leq y < x$. Due to Lemma 2, we can find a pair (x, k) such that

$$x^k \equiv u \pmod{n},$$

where $k = x/r$. Therefore $y \leq k \leq e$.   □

Now, we start addressing the security of our scheme. We need to address the issue of keypair forgery in case an attacker can obtain a set of legitimate keypairs. A successful attack is one in which a new keypair is generated that is valid and different from current keypairs. The following theorem shows that, assuming the strong RSA assumption, it is intractable for an attacker to forge such a keypair. This analysis assumes a static adversary, not an adaptive adversary who can adaptively obtain polynomial amount of keypars at his own choice.

Theorem 1 (Forgery-resistance). *If there exists a probabilistic polynomial time algorithm which takes a list of valid keypairs, $(E_1, s_1), (E_2, s_2), \ldots, (E_k, s_k)$ and with non-negligible probability produces a new valid keypair (E, s) such that $E^s \equiv g \pmod{n}$ and $s \neq s_i$ for $1 \leq i \leq k$, then we can solve the flexible RSA problem with non-negligible probability.*

Proof. Suppose there exists a probabilistic polynomial-time algorithm which computes a new legitimate keypair based on the available keypairs, and succeeds with some non-negligible probability $p(\sigma)$. Then we construct an algorithm for solving the flexible RSA problem, given a random input (u, n), as follows (the following makes sense as long as u is a generator of QR_n, which is true with non-negligible probability for random instances — we consider this more carefully below when analyzing the success probability of our constructed algorithm):

1. First, we check if $GCD(u, n) = 1$. If it's not, then we have one of the factors of n, and can easily calculate a solution to the flexible RSA problem. Therefore, in the following we assume that $GCD(u, n) = 1$, so $u \in Z_n^*$.
2. We pick random prime numbers $s_1, s_2, \ldots, s_k$ in the required range $s \in [X - 2^{\alpha(l_s+l_c)+1}, X + 2^{\alpha(l_s+l_c)+1}]$, and compute

$$r = s_1 s_2 \ldots s_k,$$

$$g = u^r = u^{s_1 s_2 \cdots s_k} \pmod{n}.$$

Note that since the s_i values are primes strictly less than either p' or q', it must be the case that $GCD(r, |QR_n|) = 1$, so Property 2 says that g is a generator of QR_n if and only u is a generator of QR_n.

3. Next, we create k group keypairs, using the s_i values and E_i values calculated as follows:

$$E_1 = u^{s_2 \cdots s_k} \pmod{n}$$
$$E_2 = u^{s_1 s_3 \cdots s_k} \pmod{n}$$
$$\vdots$$
$$E_k = u^{s_1 s_2 \cdots s_{k-1}} \pmod{n}$$

Note that for all $i = 1, \ldots, k$, raising E_i to the power s_i "completes the exponent" in a sense, giving $E_i^{s_i} = u^{s_1 s_2 \cdots s_k} = u^r = g \pmod{n}$.

4. We use the assumed forgery algorithm for creating a new valid keypair (E, s), where $s \in [X - 2^{\alpha(l_s+l_c)+1}, X + 2^{\alpha(l_s+l_c)+1}]$, and $E^s = g = u^r \pmod{n}$.
5. If the forgery algorithm succeeds, then s will be different from all the s_i's. By Lemma 1, s cannot be the product of s_i, s_j, $1 \leq i, j \leq k$. Therefore, either $GCD(s, s_1 s_2 \cdots s_k) = 1$, or $GCD(s, s_1 s_2 \cdots s_k) = s_i$, $1 \leq i \leq k$. In the first case, due to Lemma 2, we can find a pair (y, s) such that

$$y^s = u \pmod{n}$$

so the pair (y, s) is a solution to our flexible RSA problem instance. In the second case, assume $s = v \times s_i$, then $v < X - 2^{\alpha(l_s+l_c)+1}$, and $GCD(v, s_1 s_2 \cdots s_k) = 1$ (or $GCD(v, r) = 1$). We then have

$$E^s \equiv E^{v s_i} \equiv u^r \pmod{n}.$$

Again by Lemma 2, we can find a pair (y, v) such that

$$y^v = u \pmod{n},$$

so the pair (y, v) is a solution to our flexible RSA problem instance.

We now analyze the probability that the above algorithm for solving the flexible RSA problem succeeds. The algorithm succeeds in Step 1 if $GCD(u, n) \neq 1$, so let P_1 represent the probability of this event, which is negligible. When $GCD(u, n) = 1$, the algorithm succeeds when the following three conditions are satisfied: (1) $u \in QR_n$, which happens with probability $\frac{1}{4}$, (2) u is a generator of QR_n, which fails for only a negligible fraction of elements of QR_n, due to Property 1, and (3) the key forgery algorithm succeeds, which happens with probability $p(\sigma)$. Putting this together, the probability that the constructed algorithm succeeds is $P_1 + (1 - P_1)\frac{1}{4}(1 - \text{negl}(\sigma)) p(\sigma)$, which is non-negligible.   □

In step 5 of the proof about forgery resistance (Theorem 1), we can obtain a corollary as follows.

Corollary 2. *Under the strong RSA assumption, it is intractable to forge a keypair* (E, s) *such that s lies in the interval* $(0, X - 2^{\alpha(l_s+l_c)+1})$ *or* $(X + 2^{\alpha(l_s+l_c)+1}, (X - 2^{\alpha(l_s+l_c)+1})^2)$*, and* $E^s = g \pmod{n}$*.*

Proof. In step 5 of the proof for Theorem 1, if $s \in (0, X - 2^{\alpha(l_s+l_c)+1})$, since all $s_i \in [X - 2^{\alpha(l_s+l_c)+1}, X + 2^{\alpha(l_s+l_c)+1}]$ are prime, then $GCD(s, s_1 s_2 \cdots s_k) = 1$, and we can solve a flexible RSA problem.

If $s \in (X + 2^{\alpha(l_s+l_c)+1}, (X - 2^{\alpha(l_s+l_c)+1})^2)$, due to Lemma 1, s can not be the product of any $s_i s_j$, $i, j < k$. Thus the proof is as before to solve a flexible RSA problem. Therefore, under the strong RSA assumption, we have the corollary as given above.   □

Now we address the security of the sign and verify protocol.

Theorem 2. *Under the strong RSA assumption, the interactive protocol underlying the Sign and Verify protocol is a statistical zero-knowledge proof in honest-verifier mode that the TPM holds a keypair* (E, s) *such that* $E^s \equiv g \pmod{n}$ *and s lies in the correct interval.*

Proof. The proofs of completeness and statistical zero-knowledge property (simulator) follow the standard method. Here we only outline the existence of the knowledge extractor.

In the sign protocol, the TPM proves $T_2 \equiv g^b \pmod{n}$, and $b \in [Y - 2^{\alpha(l_c+l_b)+1}, Y + 2^{\alpha(l_c+l_b)+1}]$. This is a statistical honest-verifier zero-knowledge protocol that is secure under the strong RSA assumption. b can be recovered by a knowledge extractor following the standard method.

We need to show a knowledge extractor is able to recover the legitimate keypair once it has found two accepting tuples. Let (T_1, T_2, d_1, c, w_1), $(T_1, T_2, d_1, c', w_1')$ be two accepting tuples. Without loss of generality, we assume $c > c'$. Then we have

$$T_1^{w_1-cX} T_2^c \equiv T_1^{w_1'-c'X} T_2^{c'} \equiv d_1 \pmod{n}.$$

It follows that

$$T_1^{(w_1'-w_1)+(c-c')X} \equiv T_2^{c-c'} \equiv g^{b(c-c')} \pmod{n}. \tag{1}$$

By the system parameter settings, we require $X > 2Y + 2^{\alpha(l_s+l_c)+2}$, and $Y > 2^{\alpha(l_c+l_b)+1}$. Then we can have

$$(c - c')X > (c - c')(Y + 2^{\alpha(l_c+l_b)+1} + 2^{\alpha(l_s+l_c)+2}).$$

Since we already have $b < Y + 2^{\alpha(l_c+l_b)+1}$, we further obtain

$$(c - c')X > (c - c')(b + 2^{\alpha(l_s+l_c)+2}).$$

Since $w_1, w_1' \in \pm\{0,1\}^{\alpha(l_s+l_c)+1}$, $w_1' - w_1$ is at least $-2^{\alpha(l_s+l_c)+2}$. Since $c - c'$ is at least 1, we finally have

$$(w_1' - w_1) + (c - c')X > b(c - c').$$

Due to Corollary 1, we can solve Equation 1 to obtain a pair (E, s) such $E^s \equiv g \pmod{n}$, $s \le (w_1' - w_1) + (c - c')X$.

In our parameter settings, $(w_1' - w_1) + (c - c')X < (X - 2^{\alpha(l_s+l_c)+1})^2$. Due to Corollary 2, s must be a legitimate keypair in the correct interval. Therefore, (E, s) is a valid keypair, which completes the proof. □

For variable anonymity, $(j, T_3, d_3; T_1, T_2, d_1)$ are used to prove equality of the discrete logarithms of T_3 with base j, and T_2 with base T_1. This is also a statistical honest-verifier zero-knowledge protocol which has been proved secure under the strong RSA assumption.

Finally, we present a theorem for the unlinkability of a TPM's signatures.

Theorem 3 (Unlinkability). *Under the decisional Diffie-Hellman assumption over subset of QR_n, the protocol implements anonymous authentication such that it is infeasible to link the transactions by a TPM with different LCID.*

Proof. To decide whether two transactions are linked to a TPM, one needs to decide whether two equations are produced from the same E.

$$T_1, T_2 \equiv g^b \equiv T_1^s \pmod{n}$$
$$T_1', T_2' \equiv g^{b'} \equiv (T_1')^s \pmod{n}$$

Since T_1, T_1' are random generators of QR_n, under the DDH assumption it is infeasible to decide whether or not there exist an s such that $T_1^s \equiv T_2$, and $(T_1')^s \equiv T_2'$. The same argument can be applied to variable anonymity, in which case

$$T_3 \equiv j^s \pmod{n}, \ T_3' \equiv j'^s \pmod{n}$$

where j, j' are two random generators of QR_n in different periods of time. □

6   Conclusion

In this paper, we have presented an efficient direct anonymous attestation scheme for Trusted Computing Platform. We adopt the same group certificate as the CM group signature scheme with new sign and verify protocols. Our construction supports authentication with total anonymity, variable anonymity, and rogue TPM tagging.

Compared to the current construction for DAA (the BCC scheme), our scheme has more efficient sign and verify protocols, thus all computation can be completed in the TPM alone, making the computation distribution in the BCC scheme unnecessary. Therefore, our scheme is more attractive for embedded devices, such as cell phone, PDA, etc.

Finally, we proved our construction is secure under the strong RSA assumption and the decisional Diffie-Hellman assumption.

References

1. G. Ateniese, J. Camenisch, M. Joye, and G. Tsudik.   A practical and provably secure coalition-resistant group signature scheme.   In *Advances in Cryptology — Crypto*, pages 255–270, 2000.
2. N. Baric and B. Pfitzmann.   Collision-free accumulators and fail-stop signature schemes without trees. In *Advances in Cryptology — Eurocrypto*, pages 480–494, 1997.
3. M. Bellare and P. Rogaway. Random oracles are practical: A paradigm for designing efficient procotols.   In *First ACM Conference On computer and Communication Security*, pages 62–73. ACM Press, 1993.
4. D. Boneh, X. Boyen, and H.Shacham. Short group signatures. In *Advances in Cryptology — Crypto'04, LNCS 3152*, pages 41–55, 2004.
5. D. Boneh and H. Shacham.   Group signatures with verifier-local revocation.   In *Proc. of the 11th ACM Conference on Computer and Communications Security (CCS 2004)*, pages 168–177, 2004.
6. E. Brickell, J. Camenisch, and L. Chen. Direct anonymous attestation. In *ACM Conference on Computer and Communications Security*, pages 132–145, 2004.
7. J. Camenisch and J. Groth. Group signatures: Better efficiency and new theoretical aspects. In *Security in Communication Networks (SCN 2004), LNCS 3352*, pages 120–133, 2005.
8. J. Camenisch and M. Michels. A group signature scheme based on an RSA-variants. Technical Report RS-98-27, BRICS, University of Aarhus, Nov. 1998.
9. J. Camenisch and M. Stadler.   Efficient group signature schemems for large groups.   In *Advances in Cryptology — Crypto'97, LNCS 1294*, pages 410–424, 1997.
10. J. Camenisch and M. Stadler. A group signature scheme with improved efficiency. In *Advances in Cryptology — ASIACRYPT'98, LNCS 1514*, pages 160–174, 1998.
11. A. Chan, Y. Frankel, and Y. Tsiounis. Easy come - easy go divisible cash. In *K. Yyberg, editor, Advances in Cryptology – Eurocrypt'98, LNCS 1403*, pages 561 – 574. Sringer-Verlag, 1998.
12. D. Chaum and E. van Heyst. Group signature. In *Advances in Cryptology — Eurocrypt*, pages 390–407, 1992.
13. T. ElGamal. A public key cryptosystem and a signature scheme based on discrete logarithms. In *Advances in Cryptology — Crypto*, pages 10–18, 1984.
14. A. Fiat and A. Shamir. How to prove yourself: practical solutions to identification and signature problems. In *Advances in Cryptology — CRYPTO'86, LNCS 263*, pages 186–194. Springer-Verlag, 1987.
15. E. Fujisaki and T. Okamoto. Statistical zero knowledge protocols to prove modular polynomial relations. In *Advances in Cryptology — Crypto*, pages 16–30, 1997.
16. E. Fujisaki and T. Okamoto. A practical and provably secure scheme for publicly verifable secret sharing and its applications. In *Advances in Cryptology – EUROCRYPTO'98*, pages 32–46, 1998.

17. A. Kiayias, Y. Tsiounis, and M. Yung. Traceable signatures. In *Advances in Cryptology—Eurocypt, LNCS 3027*, pages 571–589. Springer-Verlag, 2004.
18. W. Mao. *Modern Cryptography: Theory & Practice*. Prentice Hall PTR, 2004.
19. A. J. Menezes, P. C. Oorschot, and S. A. Vanstone. *Handbook of Applied Cryptography*, pages 613–619. CRC Press, Inc, 1997.
20. A. Shamir. On the generation of cryptograpically strong psedorandom sequences. *ACM Transaction on computer systems*, 1, 1983.
21. TCG. http://www.trustedcomputinggroup.org.
22. TCG. TPM V1.2 Specification Changes: A summary of changes with respect to the v1.1b TPM specification, 2003.

Anonymous Signatures Made Easy

Marc Fischlin[*]

Darmstadt University of Technology, Germany
marc.fischlin@gmail.com
www.fischlin.de

Abstract. At PKC 2006, Yang, Wong, Deng and Wang proposed the
notion of anonymous signature schemes where signatures do not reveal
the signer's identity, as long as some parts of the message are unknown.
They also show how to modify the RSA scheme and the Schnorr scheme
to derive anonymous signatures in the random oracle model. Here we
present a general and yet very efficient approach to build such anonymous schemes from ordinary signature schemes. When instantiated in
the random oracle model, our solution is essentially as efficient as the
original scheme, whereas our construction also supports an almost as efficient instantiation in the standard model.

Keywords: Anonymity, perfectly one-way hash function, randomness
extractor, signature scheme.

1 Introduction

In an anonymous signature scheme, introduced by Yang et al. [9], a signature σ
to a message m should hide the identity of a signer. That is, one should not be
able to tell whether σ has been produced by the user with public key pk_0 or by
the user with public key pk_1. This holds as long there is some hidden residual
randomness in the signed message m, otherwise one can easily check the validity
of m and σ with respect to the public keys.

Yang et al. discuss several applications of anonymous signature schemes such
as authenticated key-transportation with client anonymity and anonymous paper
reviewing. Another example are anonymous auctions where bidders can publish
their bid and sign the bid prepended by some hidden random string, such that
the bidder's identity remains secret and is only revealed if winning the auction.
Yang et al. also show that well-known signatures schemes like RSA and Schnorr
do not have the anonymity property, yet can be turned into anonymous ones (in
the random oracle model).

OUR RESULTS. Here we give a very simple and yet general construction method
for anonymous signatures from arbitrary signature schemes. Depending on the
instantiation of the underlying tools in our transformation we either get an

---

[*] This work was supported by the Emmy Noether Program Fi 940/2-1 of the German
Research Foundation (DFG).

T. Okamoto and X. Wang (Eds.): PKC 2007, LNCS 4450, pp. 31–42, 2007.

anonymous scheme in the random oracle model, which is essentially as efficient as the original signature scheme, or we get a solution in the standard model with a marginal loss in efficiency only (assuming the existence of regular collision-intractable hash functions[1]).

For the underlying idea suppose for the moment that we have an unforgeable but identity-revealing signature scheme producing signatures σ of length ℓ. Assume further that the unknown message m is distributed uniformly over ℓ-bit strings. If we now define a modified signature scheme where we let $\sigma' = \sigma \oplus m$, then the new scheme would clearly retain unforgeability. At the same time, signatures should still look random to an attacker who is oblivious about m and should thus provide anonymity. The fallacy in this argument —in addition to the overly optimistic assumption about completely random and unknown messages— is that the original signature value σ itself depends on m and thus σ' may not be uniformly distributed anymore.

The solution for the problem with arbitrary message distributions is to use randomness extractors [6,5,8]. Such extractors gather a sufficient amount of "smooth" randomness $\mathsf{Ext}(m)$ from an input m, as long as the input distribution has some intrinsic entropy. That is, if sufficiently large parts of the message are unknown to an attacker, the extracted value $\mathsf{Ext}(m)$ still looks like a uniformly distributed variable.[2] Hence, instead of using the message m to mask the signature we now add the value $\mathsf{Ext}(m)$.

For the second problem, dependencies between the signature of the message and the extracted randomness, we will introduce special randomness extractors whose output $\mathsf{Ext}(m)$ looks random, even if one sees an additional (possibly randomized) hash value $\mathsf{H}(m)$ of the message m. Given such a "good" hash function and extractor combination we can compute the signature σ for the hash value $\mathsf{H}(m)$, and then mask this signature with the extracted value $\mathsf{Ext}(m)$ of the original message:

$$\mathsf{Sig}'(sk, m) = \mathsf{Sig}(sk, \mathsf{H}(m)) \oplus \mathsf{Ext}(m).$$

We note that, if the hash function or the extractor are randomized, then the signature will also include the (public) randomness used to evaluate the functions. It is also worth noticing that signatures constructed as above actually achieve the stronger notion of being pseudorandom, and that this even holds if an attacker knows the secret signing key.

INSTANTIATIONS. It remains to specify how to build a "good" hash function and randomness extractor pair. In the random oracle model this is very easy. Namely, for a random function H simply define the hash function to be $H(0, \cdot)$ and the randomness extractor to be $H(1, \cdot)$, such that both functions essentially yield

---

[1] A function is regular if any image has the same number of pre-images.

[2] In the literature randomness extractors are typically defined to produce an output that is statistically close to the uniform distribution. Here we merely need the relaxation to computational indistinguishability where the output *appears* to be random *for efficient observers*. We will use this algorithmic relaxation throughout the paper.

independent outputs $\mathsf{H}(m) = H(0, m)$ and $\mathsf{Ext}(m) = H(1, m)$ for non-trivially distributed messages m. Note that with this instantiation the derived signature scheme is basically as efficient as the original scheme.

To get a solution in the standard model we deploy so-called perfectly one-way hash functions [2,3] where it is infeasible to distinguish between randomized hash values $(\mathsf{H}(x; r), \mathsf{H}(x; r'))$ of the same pre-image x, and hashes $(\mathsf{H}(x; r), \mathsf{H}(x'; r'))$ of independent values x, x'. Take the first part of such a pair $(\mathsf{H}(m; r), \mathsf{H}(m; r'))$ for our message m as the hash input to the signature scheme, and the second part of the pair to be the output of our extractor (appropriately modified to yield pseudorandom outputs). Then the values appear to come from independent inputs m and m' and we get the desired computational independence of the two parts.

Very efficient instantiations of perfectly one-way hash function can de derived, for example, from regular collision-intractable hash functions, together with universal hash functions [3]. Namely, the randomized hash evaluation $\mathsf{H}(m)$ is described by picking an almost universal hash permutation π as public randomness and outputting $h(\pi(m))$ for a regular collision-intractable hash function h. According to our approach this hash function also defines the basic steps of our extractor, except that we have to produce a pseudorandom output. This additional property can be accomplished, for instance, by applying another almost universal hash function ρ to the $h(\pi(m))$ portion and by stretching the outcome with a pseudorandom generator G, i.e., the extractor's output for public randomness π, ρ equals $\mathsf{Ext}(m) = G(\rho(h(\pi(m))))$.

We remark that the informal discussion above hides some technical nuisances. For instance, if we use the suggested instantiation through the perfectly one-way hash functions, then the fact that we apply universal hash functions twice and stretch the final output with a pseudorandom generator, only yields a provably secure solution if we start with enough hidden entropy in the message. This entropy bound exceeds the one for the random-oracle based solution, but still appears to be within reasonable bounds for most applications.

RELATIONSHIP TO RING SIGNATURES. Ring signatures [7] allow each user from an "ad-hoc" group, the ring, to sign a message such that the signer's identity remains secret, yet everyone can verify that the message has been signed by someone in the ring. In this sense, anonymous signatures are an attenuation of ring signatures, because for anonymous schemes the signer's identity only remains undisclosed as long as the parts of the message are unknown. In fact, this weaker requirement allows us to give a simple and yet general construction of anonymous signatures, whereas ring signatures typically depend on specific assumptions (e.g. [7,4]) or are rather feasibility constructions as in [1]. One advantage of anonymous signatures over ring signature schemes is that anonymity is not bound to a certain group.

Our approach shows that there are anonymous signature schemes which are not ring signatures. Given the complete message m one can easily "peel off" the mask $\mathsf{Ext}(m)$ in our construction and figure out the signer's identity by checking the validity with respect to the keys. It remains an interesting open problem if there is a general and efficient transformation from anonymous signatures to ring signatures (by that we refer to a transformation which does not involve general non-interactive zero-knowledge proofs as in [1]).

ORGANIZATION. In Section 2 we introduce the notions of unforgeability and anonymity of signature schemes. In Section 3 we present the construction of the hash function and extractor pairs. In Section 4 we prove our derived anonymous signature scheme to be secure.

2   Preliminaries

For an algorithm A we write $x \leftarrow A(y)$ for a (possibly random) output x of A for input y. Likewise, $x \leftarrow X$ for a set X denotes a uniformly chosen element x from X, and with $x \leftarrow \mathcal{X}(y)$ we refer to x sampled according to distribution $\mathcal{X}$ (parameterized by input y). To make the random coins in probabilistic processes more specific we sometimes write $x \leftarrow A(y; \omega)$ for the output of algorithm A on input y for random coins ω. We say that an algorithm or a distribution is efficient if it runs in polynomial time in its input length (and, unless stated differently, we assume that efficient algorithms are probabilistic).

SIGNATURE SCHEMES. A signature scheme $\mathcal{S} = (\mathsf{SKGen}, \mathsf{Sig}, \mathsf{SVf})$ consists of efficient algorithms such that SKGen on input 1^n generates a key pair $(sk, pk) \leftarrow \mathsf{SKGen}(1^n)$, algorithm Sig for input sk and a message $m \in \{0,1\}^*$ outputs a signature $\sigma \leftarrow \mathsf{Sig}(sk, m)$, and algorithm SVf for input pk, m and σ returns a decision bit $d \leftarrow \mathsf{SVf}(pk, m, \sigma)$. Furthermore, for all security parameters $n \in \mathbb{N}$, all keys $(sk, pk) \leftarrow \mathsf{SKGen}(1^n)$, all messages $m \in \{0,1\}^*$ and all signatures $\sigma \leftarrow \mathsf{Sig}(sk, m)$ it holds $\mathsf{SVf}(pk, m, \sigma) = 1$.

A signature scheme $\mathcal{S}$ is *existentially unforgeable under adaptively chosen-message attacks* (or, for short, *unforgeable*) if for any efficient algorithm $\mathcal{A}$ the probability for $(sk, pk) \leftarrow \mathsf{SKGen}(1^n)$ and $(m^*, \sigma^*) \leftarrow \mathcal{A}^{\mathsf{Sig}(sk, \cdot)}(pk)$ such that $\mathsf{SVf}(pk, m^*, \sigma^*) = 1$ and m^* is not among the queries to oracle $\mathsf{Sig}(sk, \cdot)$, is negligible (as a function of n). We say that $\mathcal{S}$ is *strongly unforgeable* if we relax the requirement on the adversarial output (m^*, σ^*), such that $\mathsf{SVf}(pk, m^*, \sigma^*) = 1$ and m^* has never been answered with σ^* by oracle $\mathsf{Sig}(sk, \cdot)$, i.e., the message m^* may have been signed by $\mathsf{Sig}(sk, \cdot)$ previously but then the adversarial signature σ^* must be new.

ANONYMOUS SIGNATURES. For anonymity we adopt the strongest notion given by Yang et al. [9], called anonymity under chosen-message attacks. This notion basically says that no efficient algorithm $\mathcal{D}$ should be able to distinguish whether a message m (generated secretly according to a distribution $\mathcal{M}$) has been signed with secret key sk_0 or sk_1. This should even hold if $\mathcal{D}$ gets to learn other signatures for chosen messages. See [9] for a discussion of this notion.

In comparison to the original definition we consider here the most simple case of two users and public keys, respectively, among which $\mathcal{D}$ must distinguish (instead of polynomially many users). Security for the case of two users implies anonymity for polynomially many users, because the two "target keys" can always be guessed among the polynomially many keys (with sufficiently large probability).

In addition, as for ring signatures [1] we also consider the notion of anonymity with respect to *full key exposure* where the signer's identity cannot be determined even if one knows the signing keys of the two users. This guarantees anonymity even if the adversary corrupts the users and gets to know the secret key.

Definition 1. *A signature scheme S is called* signer anonymous under adaptive chosen-message attacks *(or simply* anonymous*) with respect to distribution M if for any efficient algorithm D the random variables $Exp_{S,M,D}^{anon,b}(n)$ for $b = 0, 1$ are computationally indistinguishable:*

> *Experiment $Exp_{S,M,D}^{anon,b}(n)$:*
> *let $(sk_0, pk_0) \leftarrow \mathsf{SKGen}(1^n)$ and $(sk_1, pk_1) \leftarrow \mathsf{SKGen}(1^n)$*
> *sample $m \leftarrow M(pk_b)$ and compute $\sigma \leftarrow \mathsf{Sig}(sk_b, m)$*
> *let $d \leftarrow D^{\mathsf{Sig}(sk_0, \cdot), \mathsf{Sig}(sk_1, \cdot)}(pk_0, pk_1, \sigma)$*
> *output d*

The scheme is called anonymous with respect to full key exposure *if the random variables are still computationally indistinguishable, even if D gets the secret keys sk_0, sk_1 as additional input.*

The definition above considers anonymity with respect to designated distributions M, i.e., the signature scheme itself may depend on the distribution in question. Such schemes may be sufficient in some settings, but it often seems be desirable to have schemes which are anonymous with respect to any distributions from a larger class C_M, e.g., including all efficient distributions with non-trivial entropy. The definition extends straightforwardly to this case by demanding anonymity with respect to any distribution M from C_M. For the constructions we mostly focus on the case of designated distributions and briefly discuss how our solutions extend to classes of distributions.

3   Constructing Hash-and-Extractor Combinations

Recall from the introduction that our goal is to design a (probabilistic) randomness extractor whose output still looks random, even if one sees an additional hash value of the extractor's input. We first recall the two required primitives, hash functions and randomness extractors. Both algorithms will be randomized in the sense that they get an auxiliary random input and compute the output from the input and this random string, and the random string becomes part of the output (public randomness).

HASH FUNCTIONS AND EXTRACTORS. A (probabilistic) hash function $H = (\mathsf{HKGen}, \mathsf{H})$ consists of efficient algorithms such that HKGen on input 1^n returns a key K and H on input a key K and a string $x \in \{0,1\}^{i(n)}$ picks a random string $r \leftarrow \{0,1\}^{t(n)}$ and outputs an image $y \leftarrow \mathsf{H}(K, x; r)$ (to which one appends the randomness r). The hash function H is called *collision-intractable* if for any efficient algorithm $\mathcal{C}$ the probability that for $K \leftarrow \mathsf{HKGen}(1^n)$ and $(r, x, x') \leftarrow \mathcal{C}(K)$ it holds $x \neq x'$ but $\mathsf{H}(K, x; r) = \mathsf{H}(K, x'; r)$, is negligible (as a function of n). Note that we define such collisions x, x' with respect to the same random string r, as required for our applications.

We next define randomness extractors [6,5,8]. Recall that we want to combine a hash function and an extractor and we therefore extend the basic definition of extractors and allow the key generation algorithm of the extractor to depend on hash function keys. Namely, a (strong[3]) extractor $\mathcal{E} = (\mathsf{EKGen}, \mathsf{Ext})$ *associated to hash function* $\mathcal{H}$ consists of two probabilistic algorithms such that EKGen for input $K \leftarrow \mathsf{HKGen}(1^n)$ returns a random key $E \leftarrow \mathsf{EKGen}(K)$, and algorithm Ext for input E and $x \in \{0,1\}^{i(n)}$ picks a random string $u \leftarrow \{0,1\}^{d(n)}$ and outputs an $\ell(n)$-bit string $e \leftarrow \mathsf{Ext}(E, x; u)$ (to which one appends again the randomness u).

The extractor $\mathcal{E}$ (associated to $\mathcal{H}$) is called *pseudorandom* for distribution $\mathcal{X}$ if the following two random variables (one describing a hash value and the related extractor output, and the other one a hash value and an independent random output) are computationally indistinguishable:

- Let $K \leftarrow \mathsf{HKGen}(1^n)$, $x \leftarrow \mathcal{X}(1^n)$, $y \leftarrow \mathsf{H}(K, x; r)$, and $E \leftarrow \mathsf{EKGen}(K)$, $u \leftarrow \{0,1\}^{d(n)}$ and $e \leftarrow \mathsf{Ext}(E, x; u)$. Output the tuple $(K, r||y, E, u||e)$.
- Let $K \leftarrow \mathsf{HKGen}(1^n)$, $x \leftarrow \mathcal{X}(1^n)$, $y \leftarrow \mathsf{H}(K, x; r)$, and $E \leftarrow \mathsf{EKGen}(K)$, $u \leftarrow \{0,1\}^{d(n)}$ and $v \leftarrow \{0,1\}^{\ell(n)}$. Output the tuple $(K, r||y, E, u||v)$.

In the literature it is usually assumed that the extractor's output is statistically close to uniform. For our purpose it suffices that the output cannot be efficiently distinguished from random. This also requires a form of nontriviality of the distribution $\mathcal{X}$, usually demanding that the min-entropy $H_\infty(\mathcal{X}) = \min_x -(\log \mathrm{Prob}[\mathcal{X}(1^n) = x])$ of $\mathcal{X}$ is super-logarithmic (so called *well-spread* distributions). We also note that we get the regular definition of extractors by setting $K = 1^n$ and letting $\mathsf{H}(K, x; r)$ and r be the empty strings. In this case we drop the addendum "associated to $\mathcal{H}$" and simply speak of regular extractors.

INSTANTIATIONS. As for the existence of such extractors we give two examples. Assume that we work in the random oracle model, for random function $H : \{0,1\}^* \to \{0,1\}^{\ell(n)}$. Define $H(0, \cdot)$ as the collision-intractable hash function. Then it is easy to see that $\mathsf{Ext}(\cdot) = H(1, \cdot)$ is a (deterministic) extractor (associated to $H(0, \cdot)$) which is pseudorandom for any fixed well-spread distribution $\mathcal{X}$. This is so because the super-logarithmic min-entropy of $\mathcal{X}$ prevents a distinguisher to query $H(0, \cdot)$ or $H(1, \cdot)$ about a randomly sampled and secret pre-image x, except with negligible probability, making the hash values independent and uniformly distributed.

To get a solution in the standard model, which is only slightly less efficient, assume that we have a 2-value perfectly one-way hash function (with public randomness) [2,3], i.e., where hash value pairs $(\mathsf{H}(K, x; r), \mathsf{H}(K, x; r'))$ of the same

---

[3] The term "strong" typically refers to extractors that give the auxiliary random input as part of the output. Since this is always the case here we usually do not mention this explicitly.

pre-image x are indistinguishable from hash value pairs $(\mathsf{H}(K,x;r),\mathsf{H}(K,x';r'))$ of independent pre-images x,x'. Formally, a *perfectly one-way hash function* (with respect to distribution $\mathcal{X}$) is a probabilistic collision-resistant hash function $\mathcal{H}$ such that the following random variables are computationally indistinguishable:

- Let $K \leftarrow \mathsf{HKGen}(1^n)$, $x \leftarrow \mathcal{X}(1^n)$ and $r,r' \leftarrow \{0,1\}^{t(n)}$. Compute $y \leftarrow \mathsf{H}(K,x;r)$ and $y' \leftarrow \mathsf{H}(K,x;r')$. Output the tuple (K,r,r',y,y').
- Let $K \leftarrow \mathsf{HKGen}(1^n)$, $x,x' \leftarrow \mathcal{X}(1^n)$ and $r,r' \leftarrow \{0,1\}^{t(n)}$. Compute $y \leftarrow \mathsf{H}(K,x;r)$ and $y' \leftarrow \mathsf{H}(K,x';r')$. Output the tuple (K,r,r',y,y').

Very efficient perfectly one-way hash functions (for any fixed well-spread distribution $\mathcal{X}$) can be derived from any regular collision-resistant hash function [3].

The perfectly one-way hash function basically allows us to compute two hashes of the same input but such the hash values appear to originate from independent inputs. Hence, if we now take the first hash value for the signing process and apply a regular extractor $\mathcal{E}_{\mathsf{reg}}$ to the second hash value, the result will almost look as if we have run both algorithms on independent inputs.

On a technical side, we note that the regular extractor $\mathcal{E}_{\mathsf{reg}}$ (not associated to a hash function) gets as input a hash value sampled according to the distribution which picks $x \leftarrow \mathcal{X}(1^n)$, $K \leftarrow \mathsf{HKGen}(1^n)$ and $r \leftarrow \{0,1\}^{t(n)}$ and which returns $\mathsf{H}(K,x;r)$. We denote this distribution by $\mathcal{H}(\mathcal{X})$, and we say that such an extractor is pseudorandom with respect to $\mathcal{H}(\mathcal{X})$ if the extractor's output is indistinguishable from random, even when given K and r in clear.

We remark that the distribution $\mathcal{H}(\mathcal{X})$ "essentially preserves" the entropy of the input distribution $\mathcal{X}$. That is, if $\mathcal{X}$ is well-spread and efficient, then with overwhelming probability over the choice $K \leftarrow \mathsf{HKGen}(1^n)$ and $r \leftarrow \{0,1\}^{t(n)}$, the min-entropy of $\mathsf{H}(K,\mathcal{X}(1^n);r)$ remains super-logarithmically. Else, for a random input key K, sampling $r \leftarrow \{0,1\}^{t(n)}$ and $x,x' \leftarrow \mathcal{X}(1^n)$ would yield a non-trivial collision with noticeable probability (i.e., because of the min-entropy of $\mathcal{X}$ the values x,x' will be different with overwhelming probability, whereas the hash values collide with noticeable probability by presumption about the entropy loss of H). The entropy of $\mathcal{H}(\mathcal{X})$ can be determined explicitly in terms of the entropy of $\mathcal{X}$ and the "entropy loss" of $\mathcal{H}$. In particular, if we use the construction of $\mathcal{H}$ via regular collision-resistant hash functions [3] then a (fixed) min-entropy $\lambda(n)$ of $\mathcal{X}$ yields a distribution $\mathcal{H}(\mathcal{X})$ with min-entropy at least $\lambda(n)/6 + 3$.

Recall that we usually consider an extractor $\mathcal{E}_{\mathsf{reg}}$ as the composition of a statistical randomness extractors, producing output which is statistically close to the uniform distribution, and a cryptographically-secure pseudorandom generator G. Note that the pseudorandom generator G needs to be able to stretch the short random input of, say, super-logarithmically many bits, into a pseudorandom output of polynomially many bits. Whether G achieves such an expansion factor or not depends on the concrete implementation. But we can safely assume for any pseudorandom generator that, if G takes n^c inputs bits (for some constant $c > 0$), it can stretch this input to any output of polynomial size. Thus, using the [3] perfectly one-way hash function, we get a secure construction if the starting distribution has min-entropy $\Omega(n^c)$. Below, however, we still state our result in its general form, assuming that we have a good extractor with respect to the distribution $\mathcal{H}(\mathcal{X})$.

Construction 1. *Let $\mathcal{H}$ be a hash function and $\mathcal{E}_{reg}$ be a regular extractor (for distribution $\mathcal{H}(\mathcal{X})$). Define extractor $\mathcal{E} = (\mathsf{EKGen}, \mathsf{Ext})$ associated to $\mathcal{H}$ as follows:*

- *The key generator EKGen on input K generates $E_{reg} \leftarrow \mathsf{EKGen}_{reg}(1^n)$ and outputs $E \leftarrow (E_{reg}, K)$.*
- *The extraction procedure Ext on input E, $x \in \{0,1\}^{i(n)}$ and $u = r\|u_{reg} \in \{0,1\}^{t(n)+d(n)}$ computes $e \leftarrow \mathsf{Ext}_{reg}(E_{reg}, \mathsf{H}(K, x; r); u_{reg})$ and outputs e.*

We next prove that the derived extractor is pseudorandom:

Proposition 1. *Let $\mathcal{H}$ be a perfectly one-way hash function (for distribution $\mathcal{X}$) and $\mathcal{E}_{reg}$ be a pseudorandom extractor (for distribution $\mathcal{H}(\mathcal{X})$). Then $\mathcal{E}$ in Construction 1 is an extractor associated to $\mathcal{H}$ which is pseudorandom (with respect to distribution $\mathcal{X}$).*

Proof. Consider the random variable

Let $K \leftarrow \mathsf{HKGen}(1^n)$, $x \leftarrow \mathcal{X}(1^n)$ and $r, r' \leftarrow \{0,1\}^{t(n)}$. Let $E_{reg} \leftarrow \mathsf{EKGen}_{reg}(1^n)$ and $u_{reg} \leftarrow \{0,1\}^{d(n)}$. Compute $y \leftarrow \mathsf{H}(K, x; r)$ and $e_{reg} \leftarrow \mathsf{Ext}_{reg}(E_{reg}, \mathsf{H}(K, x; r'); u_{reg})$. Output $(K, r\|y, (K, E_{reg}), r'\|u_{reg}\|e_{reg})$.

which describes the output of our extractor $\mathcal{E}$ for a random sample x (together with the additional hash value). By the computational indistinguishability of the perfectly one-way hash function this variable is indistinguishable from the following random variable, where we pick an independent input x' for the "extractor's hash value":

Let $K \leftarrow \mathsf{HKGen}(1^n)$, $x, x' \leftarrow \mathcal{X}(1^n)$ and $r, r' \leftarrow \{0,1\}^{t(n)}$. Let $E_{reg} \leftarrow \mathsf{EKGen}_{reg}(1^n)$ and $u_{reg} \leftarrow \{0,1\}^{d(n)}$. Compute $y \leftarrow \mathsf{H}(K, x; r)$ as well as $e_{reg} \leftarrow \mathsf{Ext}_{reg}(E_{reg}, \mathsf{H}(K, x'; r'); u_{reg})$. Output $(K, r\|y, (K, E_{reg}), r'\|u_{reg}\|e_{reg})$.

It next follows from the pseudorandomness of the extractor $\mathcal{E}_{reg}$ that the previous random variable with independent inputs x, x' is indistinguishable from the following random variable, where we replace the extractor's output by a random value:

Let $K \leftarrow \mathsf{HKGen}(1^n)$, $x \leftarrow \mathcal{X}(1^n)$, $r, r' \leftarrow \{0,1\}^{t(n)}$ and $E_{reg} \leftarrow \mathsf{EKGen}_{reg}(1^n)$. Pick $u_{reg} \leftarrow \{0,1\}^{d(n)}$ as well as $v_{reg} \leftarrow \{0,1\}^{\ell(n)}$. Compute $y \leftarrow \mathsf{H}(K, x; r)$. Output $(K, r\|y, (K, E_{reg}), r'\|u_{reg}\|v_{reg})$.

The indistinguishability of this final variable from the starting case proves the claim. $\qquad\square$

Our extractors so far work for specific distributions $\mathcal{H}(\mathcal{X})$. In particular, they depend (only) on the knowledge of the min-entropy of distribution $\mathcal{H}(\mathcal{X})$. Hence, such extractors also work with classes $\mathcal{C}_{\mathcal{H}(\mathcal{X})}$ of distributions, as long as any such distribution $\mathcal{H}(\mathcal{X}) \in \mathcal{C}_{\mathcal{H}(\mathcal{X})}$ obeys a fixed lower bound $\lambda(n)$ on the min-entropy (e.g., $\lambda(n) = \omega(\log n)$ if one assumes a strong pseudorandom generator G, or $\lambda(n) = n^c$ for some constant $c > 0$ if we assume standard pseudorandom generators).

4   Constructing Anonymous Signatures

With the primitives of the previous section we can now give the formal description of our transformation from any regular signature scheme to an anonymous one. We assume without loss of generality that the signature size is bounded by some publicly known polynomial $\ell(n)$ (such a bound exists by the limited running time of the signature algorithms), and that the extractor $\mathsf{Ext}(E, m; u)$ produces $\ell(n)$-bit outputs e. Below, if we mask the signature σ with e it is understood that the signature is padded with zeros if necessary, i.e., $\sigma \oplus e = (\sigma || 0^{\ell - |\sigma|}) \oplus e$.

Note that our construction of the extractor (associated to a hash function) requires that the message has some fixed input length $i(n)$ (which nonetheless can depend on the security parameter). We therefore assume that messages to be signed have exactly $i(n)$ bits, and that the distribution $\mathcal{M}$ itself is defined over such bit strings. This requirement can be implemented by hashing longer messages first with some collision-intractable hash function. Accordingly, we have to consider the distribution of hashed messages then (which, by the collision-intractability, is also well-spread if the original message distribution is).

Construction 2. *Let $\mathcal{S}$ be a signature scheme, let $\mathcal{H}$ be a hash function and $\mathcal{E}$ be an extractor (associated to $\mathcal{H}$). Define the following signature scheme $\mathcal{S}' = (\mathsf{SKGen}', \mathsf{Sig}', \mathsf{SVf}')$:*

- *The key generation algorithm $\mathsf{SKGen}'(1^n)$ runs $\mathsf{SKGen}(1^n)$ to get a key pair (sk, pk). It also runs $\mathsf{HKGen}(1^n)$ to generate a key K for the hash function, as well as a key $E \leftarrow \mathsf{EKGen}(K)$ for the extractor. It outputs $sk' \leftarrow (sk, K, E)$ and $pk' \leftarrow (pk, K, E)$.*
- *The signing algorithm $\mathsf{Sig}'(sk, m)$ samples $r \leftarrow \{0,1\}^{t(n)}$ and $u \leftarrow \{0,1\}^{d(n)}$, computes a signature $\sigma \leftarrow \mathsf{Sig}(sk, \mathsf{H}(K, m; r))$ as well as $\tau \leftarrow \sigma \oplus \mathsf{Ext}(E, m; u)$ and finally outputs $\sigma' \leftarrow \tau || r || u$.*
- *The verification algorithm $\mathsf{SVf}'(pk', m, \sigma')$ for $\sigma' = \tau || r || u$ first computes $\sigma \leftarrow \tau \oplus \mathsf{Ext}(E, m; u)$ and then outputs $\mathsf{SVf}(pk, \mathsf{H}(K, m; r), \sigma)$.*

Proposition 2. *Let $\mathcal{S}$ be an unforgeable signature scheme, let $\mathcal{H}$ be a collision-intractable hash function and $\mathcal{E}$ be an extractor (associated to $\mathcal{H}$). Then $\mathcal{S}'$ in Construction 2 is an unforgeable signature scheme.*

Note that we do not need to assume that $\mathcal{E}$ is a good extractor for proving unforgeability. This property will only be required for the anonymity proof.

Proof. We show that we can transform any forger $\mathcal{A}'$ on the derived scheme $\mathcal{S}'$ into one on the original scheme, essentially preserving the running time and success probability of $\mathcal{A}'$. We assume without loss of generality that $\mathcal{A}'$ always outputs a new message m^* in the forgery attempt (i.e., such that m^* has never been signed by the signing oracle before).

For transforming the attacker $\mathcal{A}'$ into one for the underlying signature scheme we let $\mathcal{A}^{\mathsf{Sig}(sk,\cdot)}(pk)$ run a black-box simulation of $\mathcal{A}'$ for input $pk' = (pk, K, E)$ where keys K and E are generated by $\mathcal{A}$ by running $\mathsf{HKGen}(1^n)$ and $\mathsf{EKGen}(K)$. Then, $\mathcal{A}$ simulates the signing oracle Sig' for $\mathcal{A}'$ as follows:

> Each time $\mathcal{A}'$ submits a message $m \in \{0,1\}^{i(n)}$ to its (putative) sign-ing oracle attacker $\mathcal{A}$ first picks $r \leftarrow \{0,1\}^{t(n)}$ and $u \leftarrow \{0,1\}^{d(n)}$ and forwards $H(K, m; r)$ to its oracle Sig to get a signature σ. Algorithm $\mathcal{A}$ next computes $\tau \leftarrow \sigma \oplus \mathsf{Ext}(E, m; u)$ and $\sigma' \leftarrow \tau || r || u$ and returns σ' on behalf of Sig' to attacker $\mathcal{A}'$.

When $\mathcal{A}'$ eventually outputs a forgery attempt $(m^*, \tau^* || r^* || u^*)$ we let $\mathcal{A}$ compute $\sigma^* \leftarrow \tau^* \oplus \mathsf{Ext}(E, m^*; u^*)$ and let it return $(H(K, m^*; r^*), \sigma^*)$.

It is easy to see that the simulation above perfectly mimics an actual attack. Hence, in the simulation above $\mathcal{A}'$ outputs a successful forgery with the same probability as in an attack on the derived scheme. By the collision-intractability of $\mathcal{H}$ we can also conclude that, with overwhelming probability, $H(K, m^*; r^*)$ is different from all hash values that $\mathcal{A}$ has passed to its oracle Sig previously (else, since m^* is different from all previously signed messages, it would be straightfor-ward to derive a successful collision-finder against the hash function). It follows that, if $\mathcal{A}'$ produces a successful forgery against the derived scheme with no-ticeable probability, then so does $\mathcal{A}$ in the attack on the underlying signature scheme. $\qquad\square$

Theorem 3. *Let $\mathcal{S}$ be a signature scheme, let $\mathcal{H}$ be a hash function and $\mathcal{E}$ be an extractor (associated to $\mathcal{H}$) which is pseudorandom with respect to distribution $\mathcal{M}$. Then $\mathcal{S}'$ in Construction 2 is an anonymous signature scheme (with respect to $\mathcal{M}$). It is even anonymous with respect to full key exposure.*

Here we merely require that the extractor is pseudorandom; the original signa-ture scheme and the hash function only need to be efficient. This fact also shows anonymity against full key exposure.

Proof. Fix an arbitrary attacker $\mathcal{D}$ against the (basic) anonymity property and some distribution $\mathcal{M}$. We need to show that the outputs of the random variables $\mathbf{Exp}_{\mathcal{S}',\mathcal{M},\mathcal{D}}^{\mathrm{anon},b}(n)$ for $b = 0, 1$ are indistinguishable. In the sequel we also fix the bit b.

In experiment $\mathbf{Exp}_{\mathcal{S}',\mathcal{M},\mathcal{D}}^{\mathrm{anon},b}(n)$ we now change the way the challenge signature for $m \leftarrow \mathcal{M}(pk_b)$ is computed as follows. As before we sample $r \leftarrow \{0,1\}^{t(n)}$ and $u \leftarrow \{0,1\}^{d(n)}$ and compute a signature $\sigma \leftarrow \mathsf{Sig}(sk, H(K, m; r))$. But now we let $\tau \leftarrow \sigma \oplus v$ for an independent random value v, instead of computing $\tau \leftarrow \sigma \oplus \mathsf{Ext}(E, m; u)$ as before. We output $\sigma' \leftarrow \tau || r || u$ for the modified value τ. We denote this experiment by $\mathbf{Exp}_{\mathcal{S}',\mathcal{M},\mathcal{D}}^{\mathrm{mod\text{-}anon},b}(n)$.

It follows from the pseudorandomness of the extractor (associated to $\mathcal{H}$) that the way we compute the signature in the modified experiment cannot change the output behavior of experiment $\mathbf{Exp}_{\mathcal{S}',\mathcal{M},\mathcal{D}}^{\mathrm{anon},b}(n)$ noticeably. Else it would be easy to construct an algorithm $\mathcal{B}_b$ (with b hardwired into its description) which gets

$(K, r||y, E, u||v)$ for $v = \mathsf{Ext}(E, m; u)$ or random v as input, and which success-fully distinguishes these two cases (by simulating $\mathcal{D}$ in experiment $\mathbf{Exp}^{\mathrm{anon},b}_{\mathcal{S}',\mathcal{M},\mathcal{D}}(n)$ for fixed bit b and using the given values to prepare the challenge signature). Hence, $\mathbf{Exp}^{\mathrm{anon},b}_{\mathcal{S}',\mathcal{M},\mathcal{D}}(n)$ and $\mathbf{Exp}^{\mathrm{mod\text{-}anon},b}_{\mathcal{S}',\mathcal{M},\mathcal{D}}(n)$ are computationally indistinguish-able for both $b = 0, 1$.

But in experiment $\mathbf{Exp}^{\mathrm{mod\text{-}anon},b}_{\mathcal{S}',\mathcal{M},\mathcal{D}}(n)$ the signature $\tau||r||u$ for $\tau \leftarrow \sigma \oplus v$ is now independently distributed of σ and it follows that the output $\mathbf{Exp}^{\mathrm{mod\text{-}anon},b}_{\mathcal{S}',\mathcal{M},\mathcal{D}}(n)$ for both $b = 0, 1$ is identical. In conclusion, the random variables $\mathbf{Exp}^{\mathrm{anon},0}_{\mathcal{S}',\mathcal{M},\mathcal{D}}(n)$ and $\mathbf{Exp}^{\mathrm{anon},1}_{\mathcal{S}',\mathcal{M},\mathcal{D}}(n)$ must be computationally indistinguishable.

Note that the proof still works if $\mathcal{D}$ knows the signing keys since we merely need the pseudorandomness of the extractor. This shows that the scheme remains anonymous with respect to full key exposure. □

Some remarks follow. First, note that our proof actually shows that signatures in our scheme are *pseudorandom*, even when knowing the signing keys. Clearly, such pseudorandom signatures imply anonymity (with respect to full key exposure), because it is hard to tell such signatures apart from random strings.

Second, we can modify our signature scheme to get a strongly unforgeable scheme, given that the starting scheme is strongly unforgeable. To this end we let the signature algorithm sign $\mathsf{H}(K, m; r)||r||u$ instead of the hash value only. It follows similarly to the unforgeability proof above that the scheme is strongly unforgeable.

As a proof outline of the strong unforgeability of our modified scheme, as-sume that the adversary outputs a valid forgery $(m^*, \tau^*||r^*||u^*)$ such that the values (m^*, r^*, u^*) have never appeared before. Then this would contradict the unforgeability of the original signature scheme. Assume, on the other hand, that such values have appeared before (in which case there is a unique signature reply $\tau||r^*||u^*$ in which they appear, with overwhelming probability over the random choices of r, u in the signing process). This implies that the adversary has only modified τ to a different τ^*. But then the validity of the forgery attempt would imply that $\sigma^* \leftarrow \tau^* \oplus \mathsf{Ext}(E, m^*; u^*)$ is different from σ in the original signature, and that this value σ^* together with "message" $\mathsf{H}(K, m^*; r^*)||r^*||u^*$ contradicts the strong unforgeability of the underlying scheme. And this modified scheme is still anonymous with respect to full key exposure.

Third, we finally notice that our result extends to classes $\mathcal{C}_\mathcal{M}$ of message distributions, if the underlying extractor is pseudorandom with respect to this class. Hence, we get a provably secure construction assuming that $\mathcal{C}_\mathcal{M}$ only contains distributions of min-entropy at least $\lambda(n)$, where the fixed bound $\lambda(n)$ depends on the extractor in question (see Section 3).

References

1. Adam Bender, Jonathan Katz, and Ruggero Morselli. *Ring Signatures: Stronger Definitions, and Constructions Without Random Oracles.* Theory of Cryptography Conference (TCC) 2006, Volume 3876 of Lecture Notes in Computer Science, pages 60–79. Springer-Verlag, 2006.

2. Ran Canetti. *Towards Realizing Random Oracles: Hash Functions That Hide All Partial Information.* Advances in Cryptology — Crypto'97, Volume 1294 of Lecture Notes in Computer Science, pages 455–469. Springer-Verlag, 1997.
3. Ran Canetti, Daniele Micciancio, and Omer Reingold. *Perfectly One-Way Probabilistic Hash Functions.* Proceedings of the Annual Symposium on the Theory of Computing (STOC)'98, pages 131–140. ACM Press, 1998.
4. Yevgeniy Dodis, Aggelos Kiayias, Antonio Nicolosi, and Victor Shoup. *Anonymous Identification in Ad Hoc Groups.* Advances in Cryptology — Eurocrypt 2004, Volume 3027 of Lecture Notes in Computer Science, pages 609–626. Springer-Verlag, 2004.
5. Noam Nisan and Amnon Ta-Shma. *Extracting Randomness: A Survey and New Constructions.* Journal of Computer and System Science, 58(1):148–173, 1999.
6. Noam Nisan and David Zuckerman. *Randomness is Linear in Space.* Journal of Computer and System Science, 52(1):43–52, 1996.
7. Ronald Rivest, Adi Shamir, and Yael Tauman. *How to Leak a Secret.* Advances in Cryptology — Asiacrypt 2001, Volume 2248 of Lecture Notes in Computer Science, pages 552–565. Springer-Verlag, 2001.
8. Ronen Shaltiel. *Recent Developments in Extractors — a Survey.* Bulletin of the European Association for Theoretical Computer Science, 77:67–95, 2002.
9. Guomin Yang, Duncan Wong, Xiaotie Deng, and Huaxiong Wang. *Anonymous Signature Schemes.* Public-Key Cryptography (PKC) 2006, Volume 3958 of Lecture Notes in Computer Science, pages 347–363. Springer-Verlag, 2006.

On the Generic and Efficient Constructions of Secure Designated Confirmer Signatures

Guilin Wang[1], Joonsang Baek[1], Duncan S. Wong[2], and Feng Bao[1]

[1] Institute for Infocomm Research (I^2R)
21 Heng Mui Keng Terrace, Singapore 119613
{glwang, jsbaek, baofeng}@i2r.a-star.edu.sg
[2] City University of Hong Kong, Hong Kong
duncan@cityu.edu.hk

Abstract. For controlling the public verifiability of ordinary digital signatures, designated confirmer signature (DCS) schemes were introduced by Chaum at Eurocrypt 1994. In such schemes, a signature can be verified only with the help of a semi-trusted third party, called the designated confirmer. The confirmer can further selectively convert individual designated confirmer signatures into ordinary signatures so that anybody can check their validity. In the last decade, a number of DCS schemes have been proposed. However, most of those schemes are either inefficient or insecure. At Asiacrypt 2005, Gentry, Molnar and Ramzan presented a generic transformation to convert any signature scheme into a DCS scheme, and proved the scheme is secure in their security model. Their DCS scheme not only has efficient instantiations but also gets rid of both random oracles and general zero-knowledge proofs. In this paper, we first show that their DCS transformation does not meet the desired security requirements by identifying two security flaws. Then, we point out the reasons that cause those flaws and further propose a secure improvement to fix the flaws. Finally, we present a new generic and efficient DCS scheme without using any public key encryption and prove its security. To the best of our knowledge, this is the first secure DCS scheme that does not require public key encryption.

Keywords: Designated Confirmer Signature, Digital Signature, Fair Exchange.

1 Introduction

As an important cryptographic primitive, digital signatures are employed to achieve the integrity and authenticity of digital documents. In some scenarios, however, the public verifiability of ordinary signatures is not desired, since the signer may wish the recipient of a digital signature could not show the signature to a third party at will. To control the public verifiability, Chaum and van Antwerpen [12] introduced the concept of *undeniable signatures*. Different from ordinary signatures, undeniable signatures cannot be verified without the help

T. Okamoto and X. Wang (Eds.): PKC 2007, LNCS 4450, pp. 43–60, 2007.

of the signer. Naturally, the signer can only confirm valid signatures or disavow invalid signatures.

However, undeniable signatures will not be verifiable if the signer is unavailable or unwilling to help a verifier. To overcome this weakness, *designated confirmer signature* (DCS) schemes were suggested by Chaum at Eurocrypt 1994 [13]. In a DCS scheme, the ability of verifying signatures is delegated to a semi-trusted third party, called *the designated confirmer*. If necessary, the confirmer can further selectively convert individual designated confirmer signatures into ordinary signatures in such a way that anybody can check their validity. In the last decade, a number of DCS schemes [33,30,14,10,28,32,25] have been proposed. However, most of those schemes are either inefficient or insecure.

Okamoto [33] presented the first formal model for DCS and proved that the notion of DCS is in fact equivalent to that of public key encryption. But Michels and Stadler [30] showed that in Okamoto's concrete DCS schemes the confirmer can forge valid signatures on behalf of the signer. Realizing this problem, they further proposed a new security model and constructed efficient DCS schemes secure in their model. However, Camenisch and Michels [10] identified an attack against the DCS schemes proposed in [13,33,30] such that the validity of a DCS issued by a signer S can be linked to that of a DCS issued by another signer S'. Therefore, those schemes are insecure if multiple signers share the same confirmer, though this seems to be natural in e-commerce applications, such as fair exchange of digital signatures [1,2,3,4], fair e-payment schemes [8,14], and fair contract signing [22]. Based on this observation, a new model that covers this kind of attacks was proposed in [10]. At the same time, Camenisch and Michels also suggested a generic DCS scheme, which is realized by encrypting an ordinary signature under the confirmer's public key. This construction is provably secure, but inefficient since proving the correctness of such an encryption usually relies on general zero-knowledge proofs for NP statements. In [28], Goldwasser and Waisbard proposed several DCS schemes without appealing to either random oracles [5] or generic zero-knowledge proofs. They achieved this goal by weakening the security requirements of Okamoto [33] and exploiting *strong witness hiding proofs of knowledge*, instead of zero-knowledge proof of knowledge. But their Disavowal protocol (used to disavow an invalid DCS) is still inefficient since it requires general ZK proofs. Monnerat and Vaudenay [32] naturally extended Chaum's DCS scheme [13], but the resulting scheme is provably secure only under non-adaptive chosen-message attack.

At Asiacrypt 2005, Gentry, Molnar and Ramzan [25] presented a generic transformation to convert *any* secure signature scheme into a DCS scheme. Their basic idea is to add "a layer of indirection" in the signature generation procedure. More precisely, in their scheme the signer generates a DCS by issuing an ordinary signature on the commitment of a message and encrypting the randomness used for commitment separately. They proved the DCS scheme constructed in this manner is secure in their security model, which is an enhancement of the model proposed in [28]. Their transformation is interesting, since it gives rise to an efficient and generic DCS scheme without appealing to both random oracles and general zero-knowledge proofs.

In this paper, we first identify two security flaws in Gentry et al's DCS transformation [25] by showing that their scheme does not meet two essential security requirements under their security model. Specifically, we present two attacks against their DCS scheme, in which (a) the confirmer and the signer can collude together to cheat a verifier by issuing a confirmable but invalid signature, and (b) an adaptive attacker can check the validity of a DCS without directly asking for the confirmer's help on this signature. We then point out the reasons causing those flaws and propose an improvement to fix the flaws. Finally, we propose a new generic and efficient DCS scheme without using public key encryption and prove its security. To the best of our knowledge, this is the first generic and secure DCS scheme that does not rely on any public key encryption.

Table 1 gives a brief comparison between our DCS constructions and other existing efficient DCS schemes. Similar to the comparison made in [25], we also compare those DCS schemes in three categories, i.e., whether the scheme relies on the random oracle model [5], which kinds of the basic underlying signatures are used, and how about the computational efficiency. Actually, most items are adopted from [25]. A difference is that in Table 1, we also compare the efficiency of ConfirmedSign protocols in those schemes, which is not discussed in [25]. In Table 1, we list the estimated numbers of exponentiations needed in each interactive protocol. Note that those numbers include the computational overheads introduced by the transformation from a SHVSK protocol to a CZK protocol (See Section 2). In addition, as we shall see in Section 4.2, to achieve the soundness of Confirm protocol both the GW [28] and GMR [25] schemes should be updated. Naturally, this will introduce additional overheads. Due to this reason, an asterisk (*) is marked to the corresponding Confirm protocols. From this comparison, we can see that both of our improved GMR scheme and new DCS scheme have comparable efficiency with the original GMR scheme. Especially, our new DCS scheme without using public key encryption has a very efficient Disavowal protocol, though its security relies on the random oracle. According to our analysis in Section 4.2, however, the GMR scheme suffers two security weaknesses.

Table 1. Comparison of DCS Schemes

	Random Oracle	Underlying Signature	ConfirmedSign Protocol	Confirm Protocol	Disavowal Protocol
CM [10]	Yes	RSA-FDH	-	24λ	60λ
GW [28]	No	CS [17]	5λ	2λ *	generic ZK
GW [28]	No	GMR [27]	5λ	2λ *	generic ZK
GW [28]	No	GHR [23]	5λ	2λ *	generic ZK
GMR [25]	No	Any	20	10 *	41
Improved GMR	No	Any	15	25	60
Our New DCS	yes	Any	15	15	16

The rest of this paper is organized as follows. In Section 2, we introduce notations and some primitives. Section 3 describes the security model of a DCS scheme. Section 4 reviews and analyzes Gentry et al.'s DCS scheme (called GMR scheme for simplicity). We then improve the GMR scheme in Section 5 and propose a new DCS scheme without any public key encryption in Section 6.

2   Preliminaries

Notations. Throughout the paper, λ denotes the security parameter, which is a positive integer. We use $\mathsf{negl}(\lambda)$ to denote a *negligible function* in λ. For a positive integer a, $[a]$ is defined as the set of $\{0, 1, \cdots, a-1\}$. For three integers a, b and c with $c > 0$, $a = b$ rem c denotes the *balanced remainder* of b modulo c. Namely, $a = b + kc \in [-c/2, c/2)$ for some integer k. If $\mathsf{Alg}(\cdot, \cdot, \cdots)$ is a probabilistic algorithm, then $x \leftarrow \mathsf{Alg}(x_1, x_2, \cdots)$ denotes the output x of algorithm Alg on inputs $x_1, x_2, \cdots$, according to the probabilistic distribution determined by Alg's random choices.

Zero-Knowledge Proof. In the setting of DCS schemes, we usually need *concurrent zero-knowledge* (CZK) protocols rather than *special honest-verifier zero-knowledge* (SHVZK) protocols [15]. The reason is that an adversary in DCS schemes may act as an arbitrary cheating verifier during the execution of protocols that confirm or disavow an alleged designated confirmer signature. Briefly speaking, an interactive proof (P, V) for a language L is a CZK protocol if (a) There is a simulator that can simulate transcripts of interaction between Prover P and Verifier V; (b) There is a probabilistic polynomial-time (PPT) knowledge extractor E who can extract a witness (knowledge) given oracle access to Prover P, where E could be rewound if necessary; and (c) Prover P can execute the protocol with one or multiple verifiers in any concurrent way.

Fortunately, there are well known approaches [26,18,19,24] that can efficiently transform SHVZK protocols to CZK protocols. Specifically, Gennaro's approach [24] based on multi-trapdoor commitments has simple structure, while Cramer-Damgård-MacKenzie (CDM) approach [18] can be realized without introducing additional intractability assumptions. In [25], the CDM approach is suggested to use. In our constructions, we would like to select Gennaro's approach due to its simplicity in structure. In any case, the signer or the confirmer (in the GMR scheme and our DCS constructions) will use such CZK protocols to convince a verifier that an alleged message-signature pair is either valid or invalid. However, the verifier (or a number of colluding verifiers) cannot convince the same fact to a third party, even if he/she (or they) executes those verification protocols in any concurrent way as many polynomial times as possible.

CS-Paillier Cryptosystem. An efficient instance of the GMR DCS scheme [25] uses an adaptation of Paillier-based encryption scheme [34] proposed by Camenisch and Shoup in [11]. For simplicity, we call this encryption scheme "CS-Paillier cryptosystem", which can be exploited to realize verifiable encryption of discrete logarithms conveniently. The CCA2 security of this scheme relies on the *decisional composite residuosity assumption* (DCRA) in $\mathbb{Z}^*_{n^2}$, where $n = pq$ is the product of two Sophie-Germain primes p and q (i.e., there exist two primes p' and q' such that $p = 2p' + 1$ and $q = 2q' + 1$). Informally, the DCRA states that it is infeasible to distinguish random elements from $\mathbb{Z}^*_{n^2}$ and random elements from the subgroup consisting of all n-th powers of elements in $\mathbb{Z}^*_{n^2}$.

Now, we briefly review this encryption scheme (refer to [11] for details). The user generates a composite modulus $n = pq$ as above. The user's public key includes a collision-resistant hash function H, $h = 1 + n$, a random $g' \in \mathbb{Z}^*_{n^2}$, and values $g = g'^{2n}$, $y_1 = g^{x_1}$, $y_2 = g^{x_2}$, and $y_3 = g^{x_3}$, where $x_1, x_2, x_3 \in_R [n^2/4]$ constitute the private key. Define a function $\mathsf{abs}(\cdot) : \mathbb{Z}_{n^2} \to \mathbb{Z}_{n^2}$ as $\mathsf{abs}(a) = a$ if $0 \le a \le n^2/2$, or $\mathsf{abs}(a) = n^2 - a \bmod n^2$ if $n^2/2 < a < n^2$.

To encrypt a value $r \in [n]$ with a label $L \in \{0,1\}^*$, the sender picks $t \in_R [n/4]$ and computes a triple (u, e, v) by $u = g^t$, $e = y_1^t h^r$, and $v = \mathsf{abs}((y_2 y_3^{H(u,e,L)})^t)$. The resulting ciphertext (u, e, v) with label L can be decrypted follows. First, the user checks whether $\mathsf{abs}(v) \equiv v$ and $u^{2(x_2 + H(u,e,L) \cdot x_3)} \equiv v^2$. If any check fails, output $\bot$. Otherwise, the user computes $\hat{r} = (e/u^{x_1})^{2k}$ for $k = 2^{-1} \bmod n$. If $\hat{r}$ is of form h^r for some $r \in [n]$ (i.e., $\hat{r} - 1$ is divisible by n), then output $r = (\hat{r} - 1)/n \in [n]$. Otherwise, output $\bot$.

3   Security Model and Definitions of DCS

We now review the security model and definitions of designated confirmer signatures (DCS) following Gentry et al.'s exposition in [25]. Specifically, the syntax of DCS is the same as given in [25], while the security definitions are improved in some minor ways mainly for readability. A DCS scheme has three different roles of parties: a signer S, a verifier V, and a designated confirmer C.

Definition 1 (Syntax). A **designated confirmer signature** (DCS) scheme consists of a tuple of probabilistic polynomial-time (PPT) algorithms and interactive protocols, $(\mathsf{DCGen}, \mathsf{Sign}, \mathsf{Verify}, \mathsf{Extract}, \mathsf{ConfirmedSign}_{(S,V)}, \mathsf{Confirm}_{(C,V)}, \mathsf{Disavowal}_{(C,V)})$, as described below.

- DCGen: As the key generation algorithm of DCS, it takes as input the security parameter 1^λ, and outputs two pairs of keys (sk_S, pk_S) and (sk_C, pk_C). Here, (sk_S, pk_S) are the signer S's signing and verification keys respectively, while (sk_C, pk_C) the confirmer C's private and public keys respectively[1].
- Sign: takes as input a message m and a signing key sk_S, and outputs a basic signature σ such that $\mathsf{Verify}(m, \sigma, pk_S) = \mathsf{Accept}$.
- Verify: takes as input a triple (m, σ, pk_S), and outputs Accept if σ is an output of $\mathsf{Sign}(m, sk_S)$ *or* $\bot$ otherwise.
- $\mathsf{Extract}$: takes as input (m, σ', sk_C, pk_S), and outputs a string σ such that $\mathsf{Verify}(m, \sigma, pk_S) = \mathsf{Accept}$ if σ is an output of $\mathsf{Sign}(m, sk_S)$, or $\bot$ otherwise.

---

[1] As pointed in [25], for simplicity DCGen is here denoted as a single algorithm. In a real implementation, the signer S and confirmer C would generate their key pairs separately, using two distinct algorithms SGen and CGen, so that C does not learn sk_S and S does not learn sk_C.

- ConfirmedSign$_{(S,V)}$: an interactive protocol between the signer S (with private input sk_S) and a verifier V with common input (m, pk_S, pk_C). The output of V is a pair (b, σ') where $b \in \{\mathsf{Accept}, \bot\}$ and σ' is S's designated confirmer signature on message m. For some verifier V, the ConfirmedSign protocol should be complete and sound.
    - **Completeness:** There is some signer S such that for any (valid) signer and confirmer keys, any message m, the ConfirmedSign protocol outputs $(\mathsf{Accept}, \sigma')$, where $\mathsf{Verify}(m, \mathsf{Extract}(m, \sigma', sk_C, pk_S), pk_S) = \mathsf{Accept}$.
    - **Soundness:** For any signer S', if ConfirmedSign$_{(S',V)}(m, pk_S, pk_C) = (\mathsf{Accept}, \sigma')$, then
    $$\Pr[\mathsf{Verify}(m, \mathsf{Extract}(m, \sigma', sk_C, pk_S), pk_S) = \bot] < \mathsf{negl}(\lambda). \qquad (1)$$

    In other words, even a cheating signer S' cannot convince an honest verifier V that an "un-extractable" DCS σ' is valid.
- Confirm$_{(C,V)}$: an interactive protocol between the confirmer C and a verifier V to confirm a valid DCS σ'. The common input is (m, σ', pk_S, pk_C), and C's private input is sk_C, while the output is $b \in \{\mathsf{Accept}, \bot\}$. For some verifier V, the Confirm protocol must be both complete and sound.
    - **Completeness:** There is some C such that if $\mathsf{Verify}(m, \mathsf{Extract}(m, \sigma', sk_C, pk_S), pk_S) = \mathsf{Accept}$ then Confirm$_{(C,V)}(m, \sigma', pk_S, pk_C) = \mathsf{Accept}$.
    - **Soundness:** For any confirmer C', if $\mathsf{Verify}(m, \mathsf{Extract}(m, \sigma', sk_C, pk_S), pk_S) = \bot$, then
    $$\Pr[\mathsf{Confirm}_{(C',V)}(m, \sigma', pk_S, pk_C) = \mathsf{Accept}] < \mathsf{negl}(\lambda). \qquad (2)$$

    That is, even a cheating confirmer C' cannot convince an honest verifier V that an "un-extractable" DCS σ' is valid.
- Disavowal$_{(C,V)}$: an interactive protocol between the confirmer C and a verifier V to disavow an invalid DCS σ'. Given the common input (m, σ', pk_S, pk_C) and C's private input sk_C, the Disavowal protocol outputs $b \in \{\mathsf{Accept}, \bot\}$. For some verifier V, the protocol must be complete and sound.
    - **Completeness:** There is a confirmer C such that if $\mathsf{Verify}(m, \mathsf{Extract}(m, \sigma', sk_C, pk_S), pk_S) = \bot$, then Disavowal$_{(C,V)}(m, \sigma', pk_S, pk_C) = \mathsf{Accept}$.
    - **Soundness:** For any PPT confirmer C', if $\mathsf{Verify}(m, \mathsf{Extract}(m, \sigma', sk_C, pk_S), pk_S) = \mathsf{Accept}$, then
    $$\Pr[\mathsf{Disavowal}_{(C',V)}(m, \sigma', pk_S, pk_C) = \mathsf{Accept}] < \mathsf{negl}(\lambda). \qquad (3)$$

    In other words, even a cheating confirmer C' cannot convince an honest verifier V that an "extractable" DCS σ' is invalid. $\qquad\Box$

We consider three security requirements of a designated confirmer signature scheme, each of which is from the view point of a different role in a DCS scheme. More specifically, a DCS should be: (a) *secure for verifiers*, i.e., confirmed DCS should be extractable and disavowed DCS should be un-extractable; (b) *secure for the signer*, i.e., anybody else (including the confirmer) should be unable to forge a DCS on a new message unsigned by the signer; and (c) *secure for the confirmer*, i.e., only the confirmer can confirm or disavow an alleged DCS.

For the purposes of the security model, a two-move protocol $\mathsf{OutputDCS}_{(S,V)}$ is also introduced, which is the stunted version of $\mathsf{ConfirmedSign}_{(S,V)}$ in which V queries m and S outputs a DCS σ' on m without confirming its correctness. In the following, the adversary $\mathcal{A}$ is allowed to access a collection of oracles $\mathcal{O} = \{\mathsf{ConfirmedSign}_{(S,\mathcal{A})}, \mathsf{Confirm}_{(C,\mathcal{A})}, \mathsf{Disavowal}_{(C,\mathcal{A})}, \mathsf{Extract}\}$ for: 1) receiving a confirmed signature on a message of its choice (via the $\mathsf{ConfirmedSign}_{(S,\mathcal{A})}$ oracle); 2) executing the interactive $\mathsf{Confirm}_{(C,\mathcal{A})}$ protocol in the verifier role; 3) executing the interactive protocol $\mathsf{Disavowal}_{(C,\mathcal{A})}$ in the verifier role; and 4) getting a basic signature from a designated confirmer signature via the $\mathsf{Extract}$ oracle. Furthermore, since we consider the security of a DCS scheme with multiple signers, any adversary in the following definitions is allowed at any time to generate additional signature pairs $(sk_{S'}, pk_{S'})$ (not necessary by running the key generation algorithm DCGen) and to interact with the confirmer C with respect to those keys.

Informally, security for verifiers requires that even if the adversary $\mathcal{A}$ compromises the private keys of both the confirmer C and the signer S simultaneously, it is still unable to create a pair (m, σ') that will be confirmed (via either ConfirmedSign or Confirm) even though (m, σ') is un-extractable, or that will be disavowed (via Disavowal) even though (m, σ') is extractable. For simplicity, in the following descriptions we use π to denote the public parameters $(1^\lambda, pk_S, pk_C)$.

Definition 2 (Unfoolability: Security for Verifiers). Formally, we say a DCS scheme is *secure for verifiers* if for any PPT algorithm $\mathcal{A}$ involved in the experiment $\mathtt{Exp1\text{-}UnFoolVerifier}$, its advantage $\mathsf{Adv}^{\mathsf{fool}}(\mathcal{A}) := \Pr[b_{\mathsf{fool}} = 1] < \mathsf{negl}(\lambda)$, where b_{fool} is the one bit information returned by the experiment.

$\mathtt{Exp1\text{-}UnFoolVerifier}$:
1. $(sk_S, pk_S, sk_C, pk_C) \leftarrow \mathsf{DCGen}(1^\lambda)$
2. $(m, \sigma', \tau_1, \tau_2, \tau_3) \leftarrow \mathcal{A}_0^{\mathcal{O}}(sk_S, sk_C, \pi)$
3. $(b_1, \sigma') \leftarrow \mathsf{ConfirmedSign}_{(\mathcal{A}_1(\tau_1), V)}(m, \pi)$ in Case 1
4. $b_2 \leftarrow \mathsf{Confirm}_{(\mathcal{A}_2(\tau_2), V)}(m, \sigma', \pi)$ in Case 1
5. $b_3 \leftarrow \mathsf{Disavowal}_{(\mathcal{A}_3(\tau_3), V)}(m, \sigma', \pi)$ in Case 2
6. Return $b_{\mathsf{fool}} = (b_1 = \mathsf{Accept} \lor b_2 = \mathsf{Accept} \lor b_3 = \mathsf{Accept})$.

Note that here "Case 1" and "Case 2" refer to the restraint conditions on the adversary's output (m, σ'):

- Case 1: $\mathsf{Verify}(m, \mathsf{Extract}(m, \sigma', sk_C, pk_S), pk_S) = \bot$, i.e., σ' is un-extractable.
- Case 2: $\mathsf{Verify}(m, \mathsf{Extract}(m, \sigma', sk_C, pk_S), pk_S) = \mathsf{Accept}$, i.e., σ' is extractable.

□

Security for the signer informally requires that an adversary $\mathcal{A}$ (including the confirmer C) must be unable to forge a valid DCS pair (m, σ') for a new message m, though it may be able to create an extractable or confirmable (via either ConfirmedSign or Confirm) (m, σ'') for a signed message m.

For each DCS scheme, we can specify an efficiently computable equivalence relation R, and say (m, σ') and (m, σ'') are *equivalent* if and only if $R(m, \sigma', \sigma'') = 1$. For example, if a DCS scheme is assumed to be *strongly existentially unforgeable*, it may be appropriate to define $R(m, \sigma', \sigma'') = 1$ iff $\sigma' = \sigma''$. However, the relation R depending on the concrete implementation may need not be so restrictive.

Definition 3 (Unforgeability: Security for the Signer). We formally say a DCS scheme is *secure for the signer* if for any PPT adversary $\mathcal{A}$ involved in the following experiment Exp2-UnForge, its advantage $\mathsf{Adv}^{\mathsf{forge}}(\mathcal{A}) := \Pr[b_{\mathsf{forge}} = 1] < \mathsf{negl}(\lambda)$, where b_{forge} is the one bit information returned by the experiment. Note that in the experiment, L_{sig} denotes the list of all message-signature pairs (m_i, σ'_i) output by the ConfirmedSign oracle in Step 2 and all (m_i, σ''_i) such that $R(m_i, \sigma'_i, \sigma''_i) = 1$.

Exp2-UnForge:
1. $(sk_S, pk_S, sk_C, pk_C) \leftarrow \mathsf{DCGen}(1^\lambda)$
2. $(m, \sigma') \leftarrow \mathcal{A}^{\mathcal{O}}(\pi, sk_C)$
3. $b \leftarrow \mathsf{Verify}(m, \sigma, pk_S)$ for $\sigma = \mathsf{Extract}(m, \sigma', sk_C, pk_S)$
4. Return $b_{\mathsf{forge}} = (b = \mathsf{Accept} \wedge (m, \sigma') \notin L_{sig})$. $\square$

Security for the confirmer informally requires that the evidences of confirmation or disavowal of a DCS σ' should be *non-transferable*. Namely, the transcript of a proof of knowledge in $\mathsf{Confirm}_{(C, V_1)}(m, \sigma', pk_S, pk_C)$ or $\mathsf{ConfirmedSign}_{(C, V_1)}$ (m, σ', pk_S, pk_C) should not convince V_2 ($\neq V_1$) that σ' signs m, while the transcript of a proof of knowledge in $\mathsf{Disavowal}_{(C, V_1)}(m, \sigma', pk_S, pk_C)$ should not convince V_2 ($\neq V_1$) that σ' does not sign m. To guarantee that a DCS scheme satisfies non-transferability, i.e., the transcripts in those protocols are unconvincing, we require that those transcripts be simulatable. In a DCS scheme with non-transferability, even if verifier V_1 already knew the validity of a message-signature pair (m, σ') (via interacting with the signer or the confirmer), it cannot convince verifier V_2 to believe this fact, since all the evidences provided by V_1 could be simulated, i.e., not true transcripts from real executions of the ConfirmedSign, Confirm or Disavowal protocols.

In the following formal definition, algorithms $\mathcal{A}_1$, $\mathcal{A}_2$ and $\mathcal{A}'_1$ represent verifier V_1, verifier V_2 and a simulation algorithm, respectively. If $\mathcal{A}_2$ has only negligible advantage to guess whether its input τ came from $\mathcal{A}_1$ or $\mathcal{A}'_1$, this suggests that $\mathcal{A}_1$'s potentially authentic transcript showing that m_0 was signed is no more convincing or informative than $\mathcal{A}'_1$'s simulated transcript (falsely) showing that m_1 was signed. In the security proof, $\mathcal{A}'_1$ will use $\mathcal{A}_1$ as a subroutine, and will simulate correct answers to $\mathcal{A}_1$'s oracle queries.

Definition 4 (Transcript Simulatability: Security for the Confirmer). Formally, we say a DCS scheme is *secure for the confirmer* if for any PPT adversary $\mathcal{A} = (\mathcal{A}_0, \mathcal{A}_1, \mathcal{A}_2)$ involved in the following experiment Exp3-Transcript Simulatability, there exists a PPT algorithm $\mathcal{A}'_1$ such that $\mathcal{A}$'s advantage respect to $\mathcal{A}_1'$ is negligible in the security parameter. Namely, $\mathsf{Adv}^{\mathsf{trans}}(\mathcal{A}, \mathcal{A}_1') :=$ $|\Pr[b_{\mathsf{trans}} = 1] - 1/2| < \mathsf{negl}(\lambda)$, where b_{trans} is the one bit information returned by the experiment. In the experiment, $\mathcal{A}_0$ with sk_S first outputs two messages m_0 and m_1 and some state s. Then, a DCS σ' on m_0 or m_1 is output randomly by ConfirmedSign. After that, $\mathcal{A}_1$, $\mathcal{A}_1'$ and $\mathcal{A}_2$ play a game in which $\mathcal{A}_1'$ tries to make its output (when m_1 is signed) look indistinguishable from $\mathcal{A}_1$'s output (when m_0 is signed); $\mathcal{A}_2$ attempts to distinguish whether its input τ came from $\mathcal{A}_1$ or $\mathcal{A}_1'$. In the experiment, $\mathcal{A}_1$ gets oracle accesses $\mathcal{O}_1$, i.e., all oracles in $\mathcal{O}$ under the restriction that $(m_0, \sigma'), (m_1, \sigma') \notin L_{ext}$, where L_{ext} is a list consisting of each (m_i, σ_i') that has been queried by $\mathcal{A}_1$ to the Extract oracle, as well all (m_i, σ_i'') for which $R(m_i, \sigma_i', \sigma_i'') = 1^2$. On the other hand, $\mathcal{A}_1'$ is given very limited oracle accesses, i.e., it can make only q OutputDCS queries as long as $\mathcal{A}_1$ makes at most q ConfirmedSign queries. $\mathcal{A}_2$ is given access to oracles in $\mathcal{O}_2$, i.e., all oracles in $\mathcal{O}$ with the restriction that $\mathcal{A}_2$ cannot make any oracle query on (m_0, σ'') if $R(m_0, \sigma', \sigma'') = 1$ or on (m_1, σ'') if $R(m_1, \sigma', \sigma'') = 1$ (Otherwise, the distinguishing task of $\mathcal{A}_2$ will become trivial.). Finally, $\mathcal{A}_2$ outputs one bit information b' as its guess to the value of b, i.e., whether m_0 or m_1 is signed.

Exp3-TranscriptSimulatability:
1. $(sk_S, pk_S, sk_C, pk_C) \leftarrow \mathsf{DCGen}(1^\lambda)$
2. $(m_0, m_1, s) \leftarrow \mathcal{A}_0^{\mathcal{O}}(\pi, sk_S)$
3. $b \leftarrow_R \{0, 1\}$
4. $(\mathsf{Accept}, \sigma') \leftarrow \mathsf{ConfirmedSign}(\pi, m_b)$
5. If $b = 0$, $\tau \leftarrow \mathcal{A}_1^{\mathcal{O}_1}(\pi, b, m_0, m_1, s, \sigma')$;
    else, $\tau \leftarrow \mathcal{A}_1'^{\mathsf{OutputDCS}}(\pi, b, m_0, m_1, s, \sigma')$
6 $b' \leftarrow \mathcal{A}_2^{\mathcal{O}_2}(\pi, m_0, m_1, \tau, \sigma')$
7. Return $b_{\mathsf{trans}} = ((b' = b) \wedge ((m_0, \sigma') \notin L_{ext}) \wedge ((m_1, \sigma') \notin L_{ext}))$.   □

Note that the above transcript simulatability is not the strongest requirement, but it is strong enough, as pointed out in [25] and further explained below. On the one hand, the transcript is not *perfectly* simulatable in the sense that σ' may convince verifier $\mathcal{A}_2$ that the signer indeed signed some message m, though $\mathcal{A}_2$ cannot tell which specific message (i.e. m_0 or m_1) was signed. So this security requirement is weaker than that given in [33]. On the other hand, the above security model actually prevents *confirmer impersonation*. Namely, even if an adversary $\mathcal{B}$ controls sk_S it cannot impersonate the confirmer by executing Extract, Confirm, Disavowal, or ConfirmedSign associated to a pair $(m, \sigma') \in L_{sig} \backslash L_{ext}$ (See the discussions provided in [25]).

Moreover, we would like to point out that the above transcript simulatability also implies the property of *invisibility*, whose formal definition is given by Camenisch and Michels in [10][3]. Informally, invisibility requires that an adaptively chosen message attacker $\mathcal{A}$ cannot correctly guess a newly issued DCS σ'

---

[2] Otherwise, $\mathcal{A}_1$ could trivially give $\mathcal{A}_2$ explicit proof that m_0 was signed by revealing the extraction of σ'.

[3] Galbraith and Mao [21] formally specified another definition of invisibility, which is a little stronger than the version given in [10]. For many real life applications, however, it seems (weak) invisibility is enough.

is for m_0 or m_1 with probability better than $1/2$ non-negligibly. It is not difficult to see that the corresponding experiment for invisibility can be obtained from Exp3-TranscriptSimulatability by deleting algorithms $\mathcal{A}_1$ and $\mathcal{A}'_1$ (i.e. Step 5), and deleting τ in the input of algorithm $\mathcal{A}_2$. From this observation, we know that invisibility is implied by transcript simulatability. However, note that according to the result in [10], the DCS schemes in [13,33,30] *do not* satisfy invisibility.

Definition 5 (Security of a DCS Scheme). We say a designated confirmer signature scheme is **secure**, if it satisfies security for verifiers, the signer, and the confirmer. That is, the DCS scheme meets the formal requirements given in definitions 2, 3 and 4 simultaneously. □

4   The GMR Scheme and Its Security

4.1   Review of the GMR Scheme

This section reviews the GMR scheme [25], which is a generic construction that transforms any existentially unforgeable signature scheme [27] into a DCS scheme. In this transformation, the following two primitives are required: an IND-CCA2 secure encryption scheme PKE [20], and a statistically hiding computationally binding commitment scheme $\mathsf{Com}(m, r)$. The basic idea is to issue a DCS on a message m the signer signs on a commitment $\mathsf{Com}(m, r)$ instead of m itself. To guarantee that the confirmer can open a commitment $\mathsf{Com}(m, r)$ with respect to m, the randomness r used in commitment is encrypted under the confirmer's public key and the resulting ciphertext c is attached as a component of DCS. To prove the validity of such a DCS, the signer or the confirmer convinces a verifier that ciphertext c is properly prepared by exploiting zero knowledge proofs secure against cheating verifiers. The following is the high-level descriptions of the GMR scheme.

- DCGen: The signer S uses a secure digital signature scheme DSS=(SGen, Sig, Ver), and creates a key pair $(sk_S, pk_S) \leftarrow \mathsf{SGen}(1^\lambda)$. The confirmer C uses an IND-CCA2 encryption scheme PKE=(CGen, Enc, Dec), and creates key pair $(sk_C, pk_C) \leftarrow \mathsf{CGen}(1^\lambda)$. Note that C need not participate in any setup other than creating and publishing a key pair.
- Sign: To sign a message m with auxiliary information c, the signer S creates a statistically hiding and computationally binding commitment $\psi = \mathsf{Com}(m, r)$ to the message m by selecting randomness r and creates $\sigma^* = \mathsf{Sig}((\psi, c, pk_S), sk_S)$. The basic signature is $\sigma = (\sigma^*, c, r)$.
- Extract: On input $\sigma' = (\sigma^*, \psi, c)$ and m, it outputs r if $\sigma^* = \mathsf{Sig}((\psi, c, pk_S), sk_S)$ and the confirmer C can derive $r = \mathsf{Dec}(sk_C, c)$ so that $\psi = \mathsf{Com}(m, r)$. Otherwise, it outputs $\bot$.
- ConfirmedSign: In addition to the above steps in the Sign procedure, the signer S also computes the ciphertext $c = \mathsf{Enc}(pk_C, r)$. The designated confirmer signature is $\sigma' = (\sigma^*, \psi, c)$, where $\sigma^* = \mathsf{Sig}((\psi, c, pk_S), sk_S)$. The signer also performs a ZK proof of knowledge of a value r such that $\psi = \mathsf{Com}(m, r)$ and $c = \mathsf{Enc}(pk_C, r)$.

- Confirm: The confirmer C first checks that (ψ, c, pk_S) has been signed with sk_S using the provided pk_S, and aborts if the check fails. Then, C performs a ZK proof of knowledge of a value r such that $\psi = \mathsf{Com}(m, r)$.
- Disavowal: To disavow a purported signature $\sigma' = (\sigma^*, \psi, c)$ on message m, the confirmer C does the following. C first checks if c is a valid encryption of some r. If not, it performs a ZK proof of knowledge that the string c is not a well-formed encryption. Otherwise, C computes $r' = \mathsf{Dec}(sk_C, c)$. If $\psi \neq \mathsf{Com}(m, r')$, then C provides a ZK proof of knowledge that there is a value r' such that $\psi \neq \mathsf{Com}(m, r')$ and $r' = \mathsf{Dec}(sk_C, c)$.

Gentry et al. pointed out that all the above statements involving ZK proofs can be expressed as NP statements (with short witnesses). Therefore, in theory the above generic DCS scheme can be implemented in polynomial time from any suitably secure encryption scheme, commitment scheme, and signature scheme. Since generic ZK proofs for NP-statements are not very practical, they suggested that an efficient instantiation can be obtained by selecting the CS-Paillier encryption scheme [11], and the Pedersen commitment scheme [35] over a prime order group Γ. However, in [25] this instantiation was just given in a high-level description without implementation details.

4.2 Security of the GMR Scheme

The GMR scheme reviewed above is an interesting designated signature scheme, since it is a generic transformation with efficient implementations. In this section, however, we shall identify two security flaws in the GMR scheme. Namely, it *does not* satisfy the unfoolablility and the invisibility.

According to the definition of security for verifiers, an adversary $\mathcal{A}$ should not be able to create confirmable but un-extractable DCS message-signature pair (m, σ') or disavowable but extractable pair (m, σ'), even if the adversary $\mathcal{A}$ compromises both sk_S and sk_C, i.e. the private keys of the confirmer S and the signer C. However, according to the specification of the GMR scheme, such an adversary $\mathcal{A}$ can fool a verifier as follows. $\mathcal{A}$ first picks two random numbers r and c (with proper lengths), then computes $\psi = \mathsf{Com}(m, r)$ for an arbitrary message m and issues $\sigma^* = \mathsf{Sig}((\psi, c, pk_S), sk_S)$ using sk_S. The resulting DCS message-signature pair is (m, σ'), where $\sigma' = (\sigma^*, \psi, c)$. Note that σ' can be confirmed by running the Confirm protocol, since σ^* is S's valid signature on (ψ, c, pk_S) and the adversary $\mathcal{A}$ with the randomness r can provide a ZK proof of knowledge showing that there is a value r such that $\psi = \mathsf{Com}(m, r)$. In the experiment UnFoolVerifier, this attack allows V to output $b_2 = 1$ with probability 1.

In their security claim (Theorem 1 in [25]), Gentry et al. pointed out that security for verifiers follows the soundness of ConfirmedSign, Confirm and Disavowal protocols. This is a correct reasoning, but in the context of their DCS scheme the assumption is not true. Because their Confirm protocol is actually not sound, as demonstrated by the above attack. Based on this observation, we can simply get a sound Confirm protocol by requiring the confirmer C to prove in ZK that it knows a value r such that $\psi = \mathsf{Com}(m, r)$ and $r = \mathsf{Dec}(sk_C, c)$.

Remark 1. Note that a similar attack applies to the GW generic DCS scheme proposed by Goldwasser and Waisbard in [28], since their Confirmation Protocol *does not* satisfy the soundness too (For detail, please check the first paragraph of page 91 [28]). That is, a verifier can be fooled by an un-extractable DCS signature, if the signer and the confirmer collude together or their private keys are compromised by an adversary. Naturally, we could repair the GW scheme as suggested above. By doing so, however, the resulting Confirmation Protocol will become less efficient than the original one.

Informally, *invisibility* means that an (adaptively chosen message) adversary $\mathcal{A}$ cannot distinguish whether a DCS σ' is on message m_0 or message m_1 with non-negligible advantage better than $1/2$, even if $\mathcal{A}$ is given the signer's private key sk_S. The formal definition of this version of invisibility can be found in [10]. Now, we present an attack that breaches invisibility and then breaks transcript simulatability, since the latter implies the former, as we mentioned before.

Our attack is based on the observation that in the GMR DCS scheme, the ciphertext c of randomness r could be re-used in different signatures. For simplicity, let us demonstrate the attack in the scenario where Pedersen commitment scheme [35] and Cramer-Shoup CCA2 secure encryption scheme [16] are used in the GMR scheme. That is, we compute $\psi = \mathsf{Com}(m, r) := \delta^m \gamma^r$, where δ and γ are two random generators of a group Γ with prime order ρ. Let $\sigma' = (\sigma^*, \psi, c)$ be a valid DCS for message m_0 or message m_1 with exact probability $1/2$. So, there exists $b \in \{0,1\}$ and a value r such that $\sigma^* = \mathsf{Sig}((\psi, c, pk_S), sk_S)$, $\psi = \delta^{m_b} \gamma^r$, and $c = \mathsf{Enc}(pk_C, r)$. The goal of an adversary $\mathcal{A}$ is to tell whether the bit b equals 1 or 0. To this end, the adversary $\mathcal{A}$ first picks an arbitrary message m' ($m' \neq m_0$ and $m' \neq m_1$), and computes $\psi' = \psi \delta^{m'} \delta^{-m_0}$ ($= \delta^{m'+m_b-m_0} \gamma^r$). Then, $\mathcal{A}$ asks the signing oracle of the underlying signature scheme to get a signature σ^{**} on (ψ', c, pk_S), i.e., $\sigma^{**} = \mathsf{Sig}((\psi', c, pk_S), sk_S)$. After that, $\mathcal{A}$ asks the Extract oracle by enquiring $(m', \sigma'' = (\sigma^{**}, \psi', c))$. Finally, $\mathcal{A}$ outputs $b = 0$ if a value r is received from the Extract oracle; otherwise (i.e., the Extract oracle reveals $\perp$), $\mathcal{A}$ outputs $b = 1$. Note that to correctly guess the random bit b, $\mathcal{A}$ can alternatively run Confirm or Disavowal protocol on the same pair (m', σ'') with the confirmer. It is not difficult to see that $\mathcal{A}$ wins the above game with probability 1.

Actually, in the setting of multiple signers, the above adversary $\mathcal{A}$ can also check the validity of signer S's DCS $\sigma' = (\sigma^*, \psi, c)$ on message m by interacting with the confirmer C on another message-signature pair (m', σ'') from signer S''s (different from S). The reason is that $\mathcal{A}$ can collude with S' so that S' issues his DCS σ'' on a new message m' by re-using c similarly, i.e., $\sigma^{**} = \mathsf{Sig}((\psi', c, pk_{S'}), sk_{S'})$, where $\psi' = \psi \delta^{m'} \delta^{-m}$.

In the scenarios of fair exchange, the above attacks may allow one party to cheat the other. In addition, the above attack also implies that the signer is *coercible* [10,32]. That is, even if the signer S erases the intermediate results (i.e. randomness r etc.) after the computation of a DCS σ', S may still be coerced since a third party can prove the fact that S indeed issued σ'.

5   Improved GMR Scheme

To enhance the transcript simulatability of the GMR scheme, we should let the confirmer know the "context" of the ciphertext c meaning that c is created with respect to which message m and which verification key pk_S. We notice that this can be achieved if the underlying IND-CCA2 secure encryption scheme supports the use of labels. Namely, we can define a label $L = m||pk_S$ so that the confirmer is aware of the context of c. In the following, we describe our improvement on the GMR DCS scheme in the setting of exploiting CS-Paillier encryption scheme [11] and Pedersen commitment [35]. Such a treatment could be helpful to readers who want to know (and apply) a concrete DCS implementation with clearly technical details. At the same time, note that this concrete DCS scheme can be straightforwardly generalized by using any IND-CCA2 secure encryption with labels and any perfectly hiding and computationally binding commitment.

To obtain a verifiable encryption scheme from the CS-Paillier cryptosystem, we assume that there is an additional composite modulus $n_2 = p_2 q_2$, where $p_2 = 2p_2'+1$ and $q_2 = 2q_2'+1$ are two safe primes, along with elements $g_2, h_2 \in \mathbb{Z}_{n_2}^*$ of order $p_2' q_2'$. In addition, we select a third group Γ of prime order ρ, along with two random generators δ and γ. In the group Γ, the discrete logarithm problem is assumed to be hard. In our DCS scheme, a message digest m (the hashed value of a real message) shall be committed by $\mathsf{Com}(m, r) = \delta^m \gamma^r$, where $r \in_R [\rho]$. We require $n_2 \neq n$, $\rho = |\Gamma| < n \cdot 2^{-k-k'-3}$, and $2^k < \min\{p', q', p_2', q_2'\}$ for two further security parameters k and k'. Actually, $\{0,1\}^k$ defines the "challenge space" of the verifier V, while k' controls the quality of the ZK property [11]. In addition, it is required that the prover (a signer S or the confirmer C) does not know the factorization of n_2. So, for simplicity, we just assume that $(n_2, g_2, h_2, \Gamma, \gamma, \delta)$ are generated by a trusted party and viewed as a common reference string.

- DCGen: The signer S generates a key pair $(sk_S, pk_S) \leftarrow \mathsf{SGen}(1^\lambda)$ for any secure digital signature scheme DSS=$(\mathsf{SGen}, \mathsf{Sig}, \mathsf{Ver})$. The confirmer C generates a key pair $(sk_C, pk_C) \leftarrow \mathsf{CGen}(1^\lambda)$ for the CS-Paillier encryption scheme. Namely, we assume $sk_C = (x_1, x_2, x_3)$ and $pk_C = (n, g, h, y_1, y_2, y_3, H)$.
- Sign: To sign a message $m \in [\rho]$, the signer S first selects a random number $r \in_R [\rho]$, then computes $\psi = \mathsf{Com}(m, r) = \delta^m \gamma^r$ and $\sigma^* = \mathsf{Sig}((\psi, pk_S), sk_S)$. The basic signature for message m is $\sigma = (\sigma^*, r)$.
- Verify: On input an extracted DCS signature $\sigma = (\sigma^*, r)$ for a message m, it returns the output of $\mathsf{Ver}((\psi, pk_S), \sigma^*, pk_S)$, where $\psi = \mathsf{Com}(m, r)$.
- Extract: On input $\sigma' = (\sigma^*, \psi, c)$ and message m, it outputs r if $\sigma^* = \mathsf{Sig}((\psi, pk_S), sk_S)$ and the confirmer C can derive $r = \mathsf{Dec}(sk_C, c)$ w.r.t. label $L = m||pk_S$ such that $\psi = \mathsf{Com}(m, r)$. Otherwise, it outputs $\bot$.
- ConfirmedSign: In addition to the above steps in the Sign procedure, the signer S also computes the ciphertext $c := (u, e, v) = \mathsf{Enc}(pk_C, r)$ under the label $L = m||pk_S$ (recall Section 2). The designated confirmer signature is $\sigma' = (\sigma^*, \psi, c)$, where $\sigma^* = \mathsf{Sig}((\psi, pk_S), sk_S)$. Then, the signer runs a CZK protocol with a verifier to show that c and ψ are properly prepared. That is, the signer provides the following ZK proof of knowledge of values (t, r, s), where $s \in_R [n_2/4]$ and $\alpha = \psi \delta^{-m}$:

$$PK\{(t,r,s) : u^2 = g^{2t} \wedge e^2 = y_1^{2t} h^{2r} \wedge v^2 = (y_2 y_3^{H(u,e,L)})^{2t} \wedge$$
$$\alpha = \gamma^r \wedge \ell = g_2^r h_2^s \wedge -n/2 < r < n/2\}. \tag{4}$$

- Confirm: Upon receiving a message-signature pair $(m, \sigma' = (\sigma^*, \psi, c))$ with respect to pk_S, the confirmer C first checks whether σ^* is S's signature on (ψ, pk_S). C aborts if the check fails. Otherwise, C decrypts $c = (u, e, v)$ using label $L = m \| pk_S$ to get a value r, and then checks that $\psi \equiv \mathsf{Com}(m, r)$. If any step of this procedure fails, C performs the Disavowal protocol. Otherwise, C needs to show that there is such an r in ZK. That is, the signer provides the following ZK proof of knowledge of values (x_1, x_2, x_3, r, s), where $s \in_R [n_2/4]$ and $\alpha = \psi \delta^{-m}$:

$$PK\{(x_1, x_2, x_3, r, s) : y_1 = g^{x_1} \wedge y_2 = g^{x_2} \wedge y_3 = g^{x_3} \wedge e^2 = u^{2x_1} h^{2r} \wedge$$
$$v^2 = u^{2x_2} u^{2H(u,e,L)x_3} \wedge \alpha = \gamma^r \wedge \ell = g_2^r h_2^s \wedge -n/2 < r < n/2\}. \tag{5}$$

- Disavowal: To disavow a purported signature $\sigma' = (\sigma^*, \psi, c)$ on message m, the confirmer C does the following. C first checks if c is a valid encryption of some r. If not, it performs a ZK proof of knowledge that the string c is not well-formed. Otherwise, C computes $r = \mathsf{Dec}(sk_C, c)$ and proves in ZK that $\psi \neq \mathsf{Com}(m, r)$. That is, the confirmer C provides a ZK proof for the following statement:

$$[c \text{ is invalid w.r.t. } L = m \| pk_S] \text{ OR}$$
$$[\exists\, r \text{ s.t. } r = \mathsf{Dec}(sk_C, c) \text{ AND } \psi \neq \mathsf{Com}(m, r)]. \tag{6}$$

Compared with the original GMR scheme, there are three main changes in the above improvement. First, our basic signature is a pair (σ^*, r) instead of a triple (σ^*, c, r) in GMR scheme, where c is treated as auxiliary information in [25]. Our proposal not only becomes simpler, but also avoids the potential question whether a proof should be provided to show that c indeed encrypts r. We also remark that the algorithm Verify is not specified in the GMR scheme [25]. Second, the Confirm protocol is enhanced to guarantee the soundness, as we mentioned before. Third, we explicitly specify how to use labels in the DCS scheme. In contrast, the authors of [25] claimed that *any* IND-CCA2 secure encryption scheme [20] can be used by the confirmer without mentioning how to use the labels in their instantiation, where CS-Paillier cryptosysem is exploited.

In addition, a practical implementation should guarantee that the Extract algorithm is performed correctly. To this end, we can require that the confirmer first runs Confirm or Disavowal protocol with a verifier, and then outputs a correct value r or $\perp$ respectively. Alternatively, the confirmer can provide some non-interactive proof to show that it did this properly. For example, the confirmer can perform the non-interactive version of Confirm or Disavowal protocol with additional output r or $\perp$ correspondingly.

The implementation details and the security proof of the improved GMR scheme can be found in the full version [37]. The following theorem summarizes the security result on this DCS scheme.

Theorem 1. *Let DSS = (SGen, Sig, Ver) be any signature scheme which is existentially unforgeable against chosen message attack, and PKE = (CGen, Enc, Dec) be any IND-CCA2 secure encryption scheme supporting labels, and Com(m, r) be any statistically-hiding computationally-binding commitment scheme. Then the improved GMR scheme is a secure designated confirmer signature scheme, i.e., it satisfies the security requirements for verifiers, the signer, and the confirmer as specified in definitions 2, 3 and 4.*

6 A New DCS Scheme Without Public Key Encryption

In this section, we propose a new generic DCS scheme, which is not only more efficient but also does not rely on any public key encryption. The basic idea is to exploit a *confirmer commitment* scheme, first introduced by Michels and Stadler in [30]. The difficulty, however, lies in realizing the invisibility in this setting, since Michels-Stadler DCS schemes were broken by Camenisch and Michels [10]. In our construction, we take a new approach to this problem by requiring the signer to issue a partial proof showing that a confirmer commitment is delegated to a specific signature and signer. To confirm or disavow an alleged signature, we extensively exploit the zero-knowledge protocols proposed by Korusawa and Heng [29] for their undeniable signatures.

Again, our scheme is just described for a short message digest $m \in [\rho]$, where ρ is a prime. To sign an arbitrary message $M \in \{0,1\}^*$ we can exploit a collision-free hash function $H_1 : \{0,1\}^* \to [\rho]$ and then use $H_1(M)$ to replace m in the following description.

- DCGen: The signer S generates a key pair $(sk_S, pk_S) \leftarrow \mathsf{SGen}(1^\lambda)$ for any secure digital signature scheme DSS=(SGen, Sig, Ver). The confirmer C chooses a group Γ of prime order ρ with a generator δ, and generates a key pair $(sk_C = x, pk_C = \gamma = \delta^x)$ by selecting a random number $x \in_R [\rho]$.
- Sign: To sign a message $m \in [\rho]$, the signer S first selects a random number $r \in [\rho]$, then computes $d_1 = \delta^r$, $d_2 = \gamma^{r+m}$, and $\sigma^* = \mathsf{Sig}(d_1||d_2||pk_S||pk_C, sk_S)$. After that, S with randomness r provides a non-interactive proof π_0 showing that $(\delta, d_1, \gamma, d_2\gamma^{-m})$ is a Diffie-Hellman (DH) tuple. That is,

$$\pi_0 = SPK\{(r,x) : (d_1 = \delta^r \wedge d_2\gamma^{-m} = \gamma^r) \vee (\gamma = \delta^x \wedge d_2\gamma^{-m} = d_1^x)\}(pk_S||pk_C).$$

  The basic signature is $\sigma = (\sigma^*, d_1, d_2, \pi_0)$.
- Verify: On input a basic signature $\sigma = (\sigma^*, d_1, d_2, \pi_0)$ and a message m, it outputs Accept if σ^* is the signer's valid signature on (d_1, d_2, pk_S, pk_C) and π_0 is a valid proof showing that $(\delta, \gamma, d_1, d_2\gamma^{-m})$ is a DH-tuple. Otherwise, it outputs $\perp$.
- Extract: On input an alleged DCS message-signature pair $(m, \sigma' = (\sigma^*, d_1, d_2, \pi_1))$ w.r.t. pk_S and pk_C, it outputs a non-interactive proof π_0 using the confirmer's private key x, if $(\delta, \gamma, d_1, d_2\gamma^{-m})$ is a DH-tuple. Otherwise, it outputs $\perp$.

- ConfirmedSign: To generate a DCS $\sigma' = (\sigma^*, d_1, d_2, \pi_1)$ for message $m \in [\rho]$, the signer first produces d_1, d_2 and σ^* as in the Sign procedure by selecting a random number r. Then, the signer S provides a non-interactive proof π_1 showing that he or she knows the discrete logarithm of d_1 to the base δ. That is,

$$\pi_1 = SPK\{r : d_1 = \delta^r\}(d_2||pk_S||pk_C).$$

We call $(m, \sigma' = (\sigma^*, d_1, d_2, \pi_1))$ is an *alleged* DCS message-signature pair w.r.t. pk_S and pk_C, if σ^* is a valid signature on $d_1||d_2||pk_S||pk_C$ w.r.t. public key pk_S, and π_1 is a valid signature proof of knowledge (SPK) [9] for $d_1 = \delta^r$ w.r.t. message $d_2||pk_S||pk_C$. Finally, S performs the interactive version of π_0 with a verifier V to show that $(\delta, d_1, \gamma, , d_2\gamma^{-m})$ is a DH-tuple, i.e.,

$$\pi_0' = PK\{(r, x) : (d_1 = \delta^r \wedge d_2\gamma^{-m} = \gamma^r) \vee (\gamma = \delta^x \wedge d_2\gamma^{-m} = d_1^x)\}.$$

- Confirm: For an alleged DCS message-signature pair $(m, \sigma' = (\sigma^*, d_1, d_2, \pi_1))$ with respect to pk_S and pk_C, the confirmer C checks if $(\delta, d_1, \gamma, , d_2\gamma^{-m})$ is a DH-tuple. If not, C performs Disavowal protocol. If yes, using its private key x the confirmer C runs the interactive protocol π_0' (see above) with a verifier V.
- Disavowal: To disavow an alleged DCS message-signature pair $(m, \sigma' = (\sigma^*, d_1, d_2, \pi_1))$ w.r.t. pk_S and pk_C, where $(\delta, d_1, \gamma, , d_2\gamma^{-m})$ is *not* a DH-tuple, using its private key x the confirmer C performs the following interactive protocol with a verifier V:

$$\pi_2' = PK\{(r, x) : (d_1 = \delta^r \wedge d_2\gamma^{-m} \neq \gamma^r) \vee (\gamma = \delta^x \wedge d_2\gamma^{-m} \neq d_1^x)\}.$$

Note that in the above specification, $d_2||pk_S||pk_C$ is particularly embedded in the partial proof π_1. The purpose is to prevent another signer from re-using (d_1, d_2, π_1). Otherwise, invisibility may be compromised. The implementation details and the security proof of the above DCS scheme can be found in the full version of this paper [37]. The following theorem summarizes the security result on this DCS scheme.

Theorem 2. *Let DSS = (SGen, Sig, Ver) be any signature scheme which is existentially unforgeable against chosen message attack, and $\Gamma = \langle \delta \rangle$ be a group in which the Decisional Diffie-Hellman (DDH) problem is intractable. Then the above DCS scheme without public key encryption is a secure designated confirmer signature scheme, i.e., it satisfies the security requirements for verifiers, the signer, and the confirmer as specified in definitions 2, 3 and 4.*

References

1. N. Asokan, V. Shoup, and M. Waidner. Optimistic Fair Exchange of Digital Signatures. In: *Proc. of Advances in Cryptology - EUROCRYPT '98*, LNCS 1403, pp. 591-606. Springer-Verlag, 1998.
2. N. Asokan, V. Shoup, and M. Waidner. Optimistic Fair Exchange of Digital Signatures. *IEEE Journal on Selected Areas in Communications*, 18(4): 591-606, 2000.

3. G. Ateniese. Efficient Verifiable Encryption (and Fair Exchange) of Digital Signature. In: *Proc. of ACM Conference on Computer and Communications Security* (*CCS '99*), pp. 138-146. ACM Press, 1999.
4. F. Bao, R.H. Deng, and W. Mao. Efficient and Practical Fair Exchange Protocols with Off-line TTP. In: *Proc. of IEEE Symposium on Security and Privacy*, pp. 77-85, 1998.
5. M. Bellare and P. Rogaway. Random Oracles Are Practical: A Paradigm for Designing Efficient Protocols. In: *Proc. of the 1st ACM Conf. on Computer and Communications Security* (*CCS '93*), pp. 62-73. ACM press, 1993.
6. F. Boudot. Efficient Proofs that a Committed Number Lies in an Interval. In: *Proc. of Advances in Cryptology - EUROCRYPT '00*, LNCS 1807, pp. 431-444. Springer-Verlag, 2000.
7. J. Boyar, D. Chaum, I. Damgard and T. Pedersen. Convertible Undeniable Signatures. In: *Proc. of Advances in Cryptology - CRYPTO'90*, LNCS 537, pp. 189-208, Springer-Verlag, 1990.
8. C. Boyd and E. Foo. Off-line Fair Payment Protocols Using Convertible Signatures. In: *Proc. of Advances in Cryptology - ASIACRYPT '98*, LNCS 1514, pp. 271-285. Springer-Verlag, 1998.
9. J. Camenisch and M. Stadler. Efficient Group Signature Schemes for Large Groups (Extended Abstract). In: *Proc. of Advances in Cryptology - CRYPTO '97*, LNCS 1294, pp. 410-424. Springer-Verlag, 1997.
10. J. Camenisch and M. Michels. Confirmer Signature Schemes Secure against Adaptive Adversaries. In: *Proc. of Advances in Cryptology - EUROCRYPT '00*, LNCS 1870, pp. 243-258. Springer-Verlag, 2000.
11. J. Camenisch and V. Shoup. Practical Verifiable Encryption and Decryption of Discrete Logarithms. In: *Proc. of Advances in Cryptology - CRYPTO '03*, LNCS 2729, pp. 126-144. Springer-Verlag, 2003. Full version of this paper is available at http://shoup.net/papers/.
12. D. Chaum and H. van Antwerpen. Undeniable Signatures. In: *Proc. of Advances in Cryptology - CRYPTO'89*, LNCS 435, pp. 212-216, Springer-Verlag, 1989.
13. D. Chaum. Designated Confirmer Signatures. In: *Proc. of Advances in Cryptology - EUROCRYPT '94*, LNCS 950, pp. 86-91, Springer-Verlag, 1994.
14. L. Chen. Efficient Fair Exchange with Verifiable Confirmation of Signatures. In: *Proc. of Advances in Cryptology - ASIACRYPT '98*, LNCS 1514, pp. 286-299. Springer-Verlag, 1998.
15. R. Cramer, I. Damgård, and B. Schoenmakers. Proofs of Partial Knowledge and Simplied Design of Witness Hiding Protocols. In: *Proc. of Advances in Cryptology - CRYPTO '94*, LNCS 839, pp. 174-187. Springer-Verlag, 1994.
16. R. Cramer and V. Shoup. A Practical Public Key Cryptosystem Provably Secure Against Adaptive Chosen Ciphertext Attack. In: *Proc. of Advances in Cryptology - CRYPTO '98*, LNCS 1462, pp. 13-25. Springer-Verlag, 1998.
17. R. Cramer and V. Shoup. Signature Schemes based on the Strong RSA Assumption. In: *Proc. of the 6th ACM Conf. on Computer and Communications Security* (*CCS '99*), pp. 46-51. ACM press, 1999.
18. R. Cramer, I. Damgård, and P. MacKenzie. Efficient Zero-Knowledge Proofs of Knowledge Without Intractability Assumptions. In: *Proc. of PKC '00*, LNCS 1751, pp. 354-373. Springer-Verlag, 2000.
19. I. Damgård. Efficient Concurrent Zero-Knowledge in the Auxiliary String Model. In: *Proc. of Advances in Cryptology - EUROCRYPT '00*, LNCS 1807, pp. 418-430, Springer-Verlag, 2000.

20. D. Dolev, D. Dwork, and N. Naor. Non-meallleable cryptography. In: *SIAM Journal on Computing*, 2000, 30(2): 391-437.
21. S. D. Galbraith and W. Mao. Invisibility and Anonymity of Undeniable and Confirmer Signatures. In: *Proc. of CT-RSA '03*, LNCS 2612, pp. 80-97. Springer-Verlag, 2003.
22. J. Garay, M. Jakobsson, and P. MacKenzie. Abuse-free Optimistic Contract Signing. In: *Proc. of Advances in Cryptology - CRYPTO '99*, LNCS 1666, pp. 449-466. Sprnger-Verlage, 1999.
23. R. Gennaro, S. Halevi, and T. Rabin. Secure Hash-and-Sign Signatures without the Random Oracle. In: *Proc. of Advances in Cryptology - EUROCRYPT '99*, LNCS 1592, pp. 123-139. Springer-Verlag, 1999.
24. R. Gennaro. Multi-trapdoor Commitments and Their Applications to Proofs of Knowledge Secure Under Concurrent Man-in-the-Middle Attacks. In: *Advances in Cryptology - CRYPTO '04*, LNCS 3152, pp. 220-236. Springer-Verlag, 2004.
25. C. Gentry, D. Molnar, and Z. Ramzan. Efficient Designated Confirmer Signatures without Random Oracles or General Zero-knowledge Proofs. In: *Advances in Cryptology - ASIACRYPT 2005*, LNCS 3788, pp. 662-681. Springer-Verlag, 2005.
26. O. Goldreich and A. Kahan. How to Construct Constant-Round Zeroknowledge Proof Systems for NP. *Journal of Cryptology*, 9(3): 167-189, 1996.
27. S. Goldwasser, S. Micali, and R. Rivest. A Digital Signature Scheme Secure against Adaptive Chosen-message Attack. *SIAM Journal of Computing*, 17(2): 281-308, 1988.
28. S. Goldwasser and E. Waisbard. Transformation of Digital Signature Schemes into Designated Confirmer Signature Schemes. In: *Proc. of Theory of Cryptography TCC '04*, LNCS 2951, pp. 77-100, Springer-Verlag, 1996.
29. K. Kurosawa and S.-H. Heng. 3-Move Undeniable Signature Scheme. In: *Proc. of Advances in Cryptology - EUROCRYPT '05*, LNCS 3494, pp.181-197. Springer-Verlag, 2005.
30. M. Michels and M. Stadler. Generic Constructions for Secure and Efficient Confirmer Signature Schemes. In: *Proc. of Advances in Cryptology - EUROCRYPT '98*, LNCS 1403, pp. 406-421. Springer-Verlag, 1998.
31. M. Michels and M. Stadler. Efficient Convertible Undeniable Signature Schemes. In: *Proc. of 4th Annual Workshop on Selected Areas in Cryptography (SAC '97)*, pp. 231-244, 1997.
32. J. Monnerat and S. Vaudenay. Chaum's Designated Confirmer Signature Revisited. In: *Proc. of Information Security (ISC '05)*, LNCS 3650, pp. 164-178. Springer-Verlag, 2005.
33. T. Okamoto. Designated Confirmer Signatures and Public Key Encryption Are Equivalent. In: *Proc. of Advances in Cryptology - CRYPTO '94*, LNCS 839, pp. 61-74. Springer-Verlag, 1994.
34. P. Paillier. Public Key Cryptosystems based on Composite Degree Residuosity Classes. *Proc. of Advances in Cryptology - EUROCRYPT '99*, LNCS 1592, pp. 223-238. Springer-Verlag, 1999.
35. T.P. Pedersen. Non-interactive and Information-theoretic Secure Verifiable Secret Sharing. In: *Proc. of Advances in Cryptology - CRYPTO '91*, LNCS 576, pp. 129-140. Springer-Verlag, 1992.
36. C.P. Schnorr. Efficient Signature Generation by Smart Cards. *Journal of Cryptology*, 4(3): 161-174, 1991.
37. G. Wang, J. Baek, D.S. Wong, and F. Bao. On the Generic and Efficient Constructions of Secure Designated Confirmer Signatures. Full version of this paper is available from the authors or Cryptology ePrint Archive.

Cryptanalysis of Group-Based Key Agreement Protocols Using Subgroup Distance Functions

Dima Ruinskiy, Adi Shamir, and Boaz Tsaban

The Weizmann Institute of Science, Rehovot, Israel

Abstract. We introduce a new approach for cryptanalysis of key agreement protocols based on noncommutative groups. Our approach uses functions that estimate the distance of a group element to a given subgroup. We test it against the Shpilrain-Ushakov protocol, which is based on Thompson's group F, and show that it can break about half the keys within a few seconds on a single PC.

Keywords: Key agreement, Cryptanalysis, Thompson's group, Shpilrain-Ushakov, Subgroup distance function.

1 Introduction

Key agreement protocols have been the subject of extensive studies in the past 30 years. Their main task is to allow two parties (in the sequel, Alice and Bob) to agree on a common secret key over an insecure communication channel. The best known example of such a protocol is the Diffie-Hellman protocol, which uses a (commutative) cyclic group. Over the last few years, there was a lot of interest in key agreement protocols based on noncommutative groups, and much research was dedicated to analyzing these proposals and suggesting alternative ones (see, e.g., [1,4,5,6,7,8,10,11,12], and references therein).

A possible approach for attacking such systems is the *length-based cryptanalysis*, which was outlined in [6]. This approach relies on the existence of a good length function on the underlying group, i.e., a function $\ell(g)$ that tends to grow as the number of generators multiplied to obtain g grows. Examples of groups known to have such length functions are the *braid group B_N* [2] and *Thompson's group F* [3]. For these groups, several practical realizations of length-based attacks were demonstrated [4,5,9]. These attacks can achieve good success rates, but usually only when we allow the algorithm to explore many suboptimal partial solutions, which greatly increases both the time and space complexities (see [5] for more details).

We introduce a novel approach to cryptanalysis of such key agreement protocols, which relies on the notion of *subgroup distance functions*, i.e., functions that estimate, for an element $g \in G$ and a subgroup $H \leq G$, the distance from g to H. The motivation for these distance-based attacks is the fact that several families of public key agreement protocols suggest predefined pairs of subgroups of the main group to be used for key generation, and their security depends on

T. Okamoto and X. Wang (Eds.): PKC 2007, LNCS 4450, pp. 61–75, 2007.

the ability of the adversary to generate any elements in these subgroups, which are in some way equivalent to the originals (see [9,11]). We construct the theoretical framework for *distance-based attacks* and demonstrate its applicability using the Shpilrain-Ushakov protocol in Thompson's group F [12] as an example. Although it has recently been shown by Matucci [8] that the implementation of the proposed protocol in F can be broken deterministically using a specialized attack based on the structural properties of the group, it is still an interesting test case for more generic attacks, such as the one proposed here.

The paper is organized as follows: in Section 2 we present the protocol in its general form. We then introduce in Section 3 the notion of subgroup distance function and a general attack scheme based on it. Section 4 describes the setting for the protocol in Thompson's group F. In Section 5 we introduce several subgroup distance functions in F. Section 6 describes our experimental cryptanalytic results.

2   The Shpilrain-Ushakov Key Agreement Protocol

The protocol below was suggested by Shpilrain and Ushakov in [12]. The authors suggested to use Thompson's group F for its implementation. Before we focus on that example, we'll discuss the general case.

(0) Alice and Bob agree (publicly) on a group G and subgroups $A, B \leq G$, such that $ab = ba$ for each $a \in A$ and each $b \in B$.
 1. A public word $z \in G$ is selected.
 2. Alice selects privately at random elements $a_1 \in A$ and $b_1 \in B$, computes $u_1 = a_1 z b_1$, and sends u_1 to Bob.
 3. Bob selects privately at random elements $a_2 \in A$ and $b_2 \in B$, computes $u_2 = b_2 z a_2$, and sends u_2 to Alice.
 4. Alice computes $K_A = a_1 u_2 b_1 = a_1 b_2 z a_2 b_1$, whereas Bob computes $K_B = b_2 u_1 a_2 = b_2 a_1 z b_1 a_2$.

As $a_1 b_2 = b_2 a_1$ and $a_2 b_1 = b_1 a_2$, $K_A = K_B = K$ and so the parties share the same group element, from which a secret key can be derived.

2.1   Breaking the Protocol

The goal of the adversary is to obtain the secret group element K from the publicly known elements u_1, u_2 and z. For this it suffices to solve the following problem:

Definition 1 (Decomposition problem). *Given $z \in G$ and $u = azb$ where $a \in A$ and $b \in B$, find some elements $\tilde{a} \in A$ and $\tilde{b} \in B$, such that $\tilde{a} z \tilde{b} = azb$.*

Indeed, assume that the attacker, given $u_1 = a_1 z b_1$, finds $\tilde{a}_1 \in A$ and $\tilde{b}_1 \in B$, such that $\tilde{a}_1 z \tilde{b}_1 = a_1 z b_1$. Then, because $u_2 = b_2 z a_2$ is known, the attacker can compute
$$\tilde{a}_1 u_2 \tilde{b}_1 = \tilde{a}_1 b_2 z a_2 \tilde{b}_1 = b_2 \tilde{a}_1 z \tilde{b}_1 a_2 = b_2 u_1 a_2 = K_B \ .$$

Alternatively, the attacker can break the protocol by finding a valid decomposition of $u_2 = b_2 z a_2$.

For any given $\tilde{a} \in A$ we can compute its *complement* $\tilde{b} = z^{-1}\tilde{a}^{-1}u = z^{-1}\tilde{a}^{-1}(azb)$, which guarantees that $\tilde{a}z\tilde{b} = azb$. The pair $\tilde{a}, \tilde{b}$ is a solution to this problem if, and only if, $\tilde{b} \in B$. A similar comment applies if we start with $\tilde{b} \in B$. This involves being able to solve the *group membership problem*, i.e., to determine whether $\tilde{b} \in B$ (or $\tilde{a} \in A$ in the second case).

It should be stressed that solving the decomposition problem is sufficient, but not necessary in order to cryptanalyze the system. All that is required in practice is finding some pair $\tilde{a}, \tilde{b}$ that succeeds in decrypting the information passed between Alice and Bob. Any pair $\tilde{a} \in A$ and $\tilde{b} \in B$ will work, but there can be other pairs, which are just as good. This observation can be useful in cases where the group membership problem is difficult or in groups where the centralizers of individual elements are considerably larger than the centralizers of the subgroups (which is not the case in F, see [9]). For simplicity, in the sequel we will restrict ourselves to solutions where $\tilde{a} \in A$ and $\tilde{b} \in B$.

3 Subgroup Distance Functions

Definition 2 (Subgroup distance function). *Let G be a group, $H \leq G$ a subgroup. A function $d_H : G \to \mathbb{R}^+$ is a subgroup distance function if it satisfies the following two axioms:*

1. *Validity: $d_H(h) = 0$ for all $h \in H$.*
2. *Non-triviality: $d_H(g) > 0$ for all $g \notin H$.*

It is an invariant *subgroup distance function if it also satisfies:*

(3) Invariance: $d_H(gh) = d_H(hg) = d_H(g)$ for all $g \in G$ and $h \in H$.

Clearly, if it is possible to evaluate a subgroup distance function d_H on all elements of G, then the membership decision problem for H is solvable: $g \in H \iff d_H(g) = 0$. Conversely, if one can solve the membership decision problem, a trivial distance function can be derived from it, e.g., $d_H(g) = 1 - \chi_H(g)$, where χ_H is the characteristic function of H.

Obviously, this trivial distance function is not a good example. For the subgroup distance function to be useful, it has to somehow measure how close a given element g is to H, that is, if $d_H(g_1) < d_H(g_2)$, then g_1 is closer to H than g_2. This concept of "closeness" can be hard to define, and even harder to evaluate. The notion of what's considered a good distance function may vary, depending on the subgroups and on the presentation. In the sequel we will discuss concrete examples of subgroup distance function in Thompson's group F.

Assuming the existence of such functions, consider the following algorithm for solving the decomposition problem:

Algorithm 1 (Subgroup distance attack)
We are given words $z, xzy \in G$, where $x \in X$ and $y \in Y$, X, Y are commuting subgroups of G and S_X, S_Y are their respective (finite) generating sets. The goal it to find some $\tilde{x} \in X$ and $\tilde{y} \in Y$, such that $xzy = \tilde{x}z\tilde{y}$. The algorithm runs at most a predefined number of iterations N.

1. *Let $\tilde{x} \leftarrow 1$.*
2. *For each $g_i \in S_X^{\pm 1}$ compute $x_i = \tilde{x}g_i$, its complement $y_i = z^{-1}x_i^{-1}xzy$ and evaluate $d_Y(y_i)$. If $d_Y(y_i) = 0$, let $\tilde{x} = x_i$, $\tilde{y} = y_i$ and halt.*
3. *Let j be the index of the minimum $d_Y(y_i)$ (if several such j are possible, choose one arbitrarily).*
4. *If the maximal number of iterations N has been reached, terminate. Otherwise, let $\tilde{x} \leftarrow x_j$ and return to step 2.*

Observe that if the algorithm halts in step 2, then the pair $\tilde{x}, \tilde{y}$ is a solution of the decomposition problem.

Algorithm 1 is very similar to the length-based attacks described in [4,9]. The difference is that it uses the subgroup distance function, instead of the length function to evaluate the quality of candidates. As such, any extensions applicable to the length-based algorithms (such as memory, lookahead, etc.) can be used with the distance-based attack as well. Refer to [5,9] for more information.

3.1   Attacking the Shpilrain-Ushakov Protocol

The adversary is given the common word z and the public elements u_1, u_2. These can be translated into four equations in the group:

$$
\begin{aligned}
u_1 &= a_1 z b_1 \\
u_2 &= b_2 z a_2 \\
u_1^{-1} &= b_1^{-1} z^{-1} a_1^{-1} \\
u_2^{-1} &= a_2^{-1} z^{-1} b_2^{-1}
\end{aligned}
\tag{1}
$$

Algorithm 1 (with or without possible extensions) can be applied to each of the four equations separately, thus attacking each of the four private elements $a_1, a_2, b_1^{-1}, b_2^{-1}$. A single success out of the four attempts is sufficient to break the cryptosystem (see Section 2.1).

4   Thompson's Group

Thompson's group F is the infinite noncommutative group defined by the following generators and relations:

$$
F = \langle\, x_0, x_1, x_2, \ldots \mid x_i^{-1} x_k x_i = x_{k+1} \; (k > i) \,\rangle
\tag{2}
$$

Remark 1. *From Equation (2) it's evident that the elements x_0, x_1 and their inverses generate the entire group, because $x_k^{\pm 1} = x_0^{1-k} x_1^{\pm 1} x_0^{k-1}$ for every $k \geq 2$.*

Definition 3. *A basic generator* $x_i^{\pm 1}$ *of* F *is called a* letter. *A generator* x_i *is a* positive *letter. An* inverse x_i^{-1} *is a* negative *letter. A* word *in* F *is a sequence of letters. We define* $|w|$ *as the* length *of the word* w , *i.e., the number of letters in it.*

Definition 4. *A word* $w \in F$ *is said to be in* normal form, *if*

$$w = x_{i_1} \cdots x_{i_r} x_{j_t}^{-1} \cdots x_{j_1}^{-1} \tag{3}$$

and the following two conditions hold:

(NF1) $i_1 \leq \cdots \leq i_r$ *and* $j_1 \leq \cdots \leq j_t$
(NF2) If both x_i, x_i^{-1} *occur in* w, *then at least one of* x_{i+1}, x_{i+1}^{-1} *occurs too.*

A word is said to be in seminormal form *if only (NF1) holds.*

While a seminormal form is not necessarily unique, a normal form is, i.e., two words represent the same group element if and only if they have the same normal form [3]. The following rewriting rules can be used to convert any word to its seminormal form [12]:
For all non-negative integers $i < k$:

$$
\begin{aligned}
(R1) \ & x_k x_i && \to x_i x_{k+1} \\
(R2) \ & x_k^{-1} x_i && \to x_i x_{k+1}^{-1} \\
(R3) \ & x_i^{-1} x_k && \to x_{k+1} x_i^{-1} \\
(R4) \ & x_i^{-1} x_k^{-1} && \to x_{k+1}^{-1} x_i^{-1}
\end{aligned}
$$

For all non-negative integers i:

$$(R5) \ x_i^{-1} x_i \quad \to 1$$

The seminormal form can be subsequently converted to a normal form by searching for pairs of indices violating (NF2), starting from the boundary between the positive and negative parts, and applying the inverses of rewriting rules (R1) and (R4) to eliminate these pairs [12]:
Suppose that $(x_{i_a}, x_{j_b}^{-1})$ is a pair of letters violating (NF2) and that a and b are maximal with this property (i.e., there exists no violating pair $(x_{i_k}, x_{j_l}^{-1})$ with $k > a$ and $l > b$). Then $i_a = j_b$ and all indices in $x_{i_{a+1}} \cdots x_{i_r} x_{j_t}^{-1} \cdots x_{j_{b+1}}^{-1}$ are higher than $i_a + 1$ (by definition of (NF2)). Applying the inverse of (R1) to x_{i_a} and the inverse of (R4) to $x_{j_b}^{-1}$ we get:

$$w = x_{i_1} \cdots x_{i_a} \underbrace{\left(x_{i_{a+1}} \cdots x_{i_r} x_{j_t}^{-1} \cdots x_{j_{b+1}}^{-1}\right)}_{c} x_{j_b}^{-1} \cdots x_{j_1}$$

$$\to x_{i_1} \cdots x_{i_{a+1}-1} \cdots x_{i_r-1} \underbrace{\left(x_{i_a} x_{j_b}^{-1}\right)}_{cancel} x_{j_t-1}^{-1} \cdots x_{j_{b+1}-1}^{-1} \cdots x_{j_1}$$

$$\to x_{i_1} \cdots x_{i_a-1} \underbrace{\left(x_{i_{a+1}-1} \cdots x_{i_r-1} x_{j_t-1}^{-1} \cdots x_{j_{b+1}-1}^{-1}\right)}_{c'} x_{j_b-1} \cdots x_{j_1}$$

The violating pair $(x_{i_a}, x_{j_b}^{-1})$ is cancelled and the subword c' obtained from c by index shifting contains no violating pairs (by the assumption of maximality on (a, b)). Thus, we can continue searching for bad pairs, starting from $a - 1$ and $b - 1$ down. Thus we are guaranteed to find and remove all the violating pairs and reach the normal form.

Definition 5 (Normal form length). *For $w \in F$, whose normal form is $\hat{w}$, define the* normal form length *as $\ell_{NF}(w) = |\hat{w}|$.*

The following lemma shows the effect multiplication by a single letter has on the normal form of the word. This result will be useful in the following sections.

Lemma 1. *Let $w \in F$ and $x = x_t^{\pm 1}$ be a basic generator of F in the presentation (2). Then $\ell_{NF}(xw) = \ell_{NF}(w) \pm 1$ (and due to symmetry, $\ell_{NF}(wx) = \ell_{NF}(w) \pm 1$).*

Proof. We'll concentrate on the product xw (obviously, the case of wx is similar) and observe what happens to the normal form of w when it's multiplied on the left by the letter x. Without loss of generality, $w = x_{i_1} \cdots x_{i_k} x_{j_l}^{-1} \cdots x_{j_1}^{-1}$ is in normal form. Denote the positive and negative parts of w by w_p and w_n respectively.

Assume that $x = x_t$ is a positive letter. Then bw is converted to a seminormal form by moving x into its proper location, while updating its index, using repeated applications of (R1). Assuming m applications of (R1) are necessary, the result is of the form:

$$\overline{bw} = x_{i_1} \cdots x_{i_m} \boldsymbol{x_{t+m}} x_{i_{m+1}} \cdots x_{i_k} x_{j_l}^{-1} \cdots x_{j_1}^{-1} \ ,$$

where $i_m < t + m - 1$ and $i_{m+1} \geq t + m$.

Remark 2. *Observe that it is not possible that $i_m = t + m - 1$, because in order to apply (R1): $x_{t+m-1} x_{i_m} \to x_{i_m} x_{t+m}$, one must have $i_m < t + m - 1$.*

Example 1. *$w = x_3 x_7 x_{11} x_9^{-1} x_4^{-1}$, $b = x_8$. $bw = x_8 \cdot x_3 x_7 x_{11} x_9^{-1} x_4^{-1}$ is converted to $\overline{bw} = x_3 x_7 \boldsymbol{x_{10}} x_{11} x_9^{-1} x_4^{-1}$, by 2 applications of (R1).*

Obviously, $\overline{bw}$ is a seminormal form and $|\overline{bw}| = |w| + 1$. If $\overline{bw}$ is in normal form (as in the above example), we're done. The only situation where it's not in normal form, is if it contains pairs violating (NF2). Since x_{t+m} is the only letter introduced, the only violating pair can be (x_{t+m}, x_{t+m}^{-1}). This may occur, if w contained x_{t+m}^{-1}, but neither x_{t+m}, nor $x_{t+m+1}^{\pm 1}$.

Example 2. *$w = x_3 x_7 x_{11} x_9^{-1} x_4^{-1}$, $b = x_7$. $bw = x_7 \cdot x_3 x_7 x_{11} x_9^{-1} x_4^{-1}$ is converted to $\overline{bw} = x_3 x_7 \boldsymbol{x_9} x_{11} x_9^{-1} x_4^{-1}$. In this case (x_9, x_9^{-1}) violates (NF2). The inverse of (R1) is applied to rewrite $x_9 x_{11} \to x_{10} x_9$, and $x_9 x_9^{-1}$ are canceled out, yielding the (normal) word $\widehat{bw} = x_3 x_7 x_{10} x_4^{-1}$.*

Whenever a situation occurs as described above, the pair (x_{t+m}, x_{t+m}^{-1}) is cancelled, according to the procedure described in Section 4. This causes all indices above $t + m$ to be decreased by 1. The resulting word is

$$\widehat{bw} = x_{i_1} \cdots x_{i_m} x_{i_{m+1}-1} \cdots x_{i_k-1} x_{j_l-1}^{-1} \cdots x_{j_{n+1}-1}^{-1} x_{j_n}^{-1} \cdots x_{j_1}^{-1} \ ,$$

where $i_m < t + m - 1$, $i_{m+1} \geq t + m + 2$, $j_n \leq t + m$ and $j_{n+1} \geq t + m + 2$. We have $|\widehat{bw}| = |w| - 1$ and, in fact, $\widehat{bw}$ is in normal form. Indeed, once the pair (x_{t+m}, x_{t+m}^{-1}) is cancelled, the only new pair violating **(NF2)** that can be introduced is $(x_{t+m-1}, x_{t+m-1}^{-1})$, but this is not possible, because x_{t+m-1} does not appear in $\widehat{bw}$, due to Remark 2. This completes the proof for positive letters.

Now, consider the case where $x = x_t^{-1}$, a negative letter. bw is converted to a seminormal form by moving x_t^{-1} to the right, while updating its index, using the different rewriting rules. There are two possible outcomes:

(1) After m applications of (R2) the resulting word is

$$\overline{bw} = x_{i_1} \cdots x_{i_m} \boldsymbol{x_{t+m}^{-1}} x_{i_{m+1}} \cdots x_{i_k} x_{j_l}^{-1} \cdots x_{j_1}^{-1} \ ,$$

where $i_{m+1} = t + m$, and so the pair is cancelled by applying (R5). Now, because $i_m < t + m - 1$, the elimination of the pair (x_{t+m}, x_{t+m}^{-1}) does not introduce pairs that violate **(NF2)**, and so $\overline{bw}$ is in normal form and has $|\overline{bw}| = |w| - 1$.

Example 3. $w = x_3 x_7 x_9^{-1} x_4^{-1}$, $b = x_6^{-1}$. $bw = \boldsymbol{x_6^{-1}} x_3 x_7 x_9^{-1} x_4^{-1}$ is converted to $x_3 \boldsymbol{x_7^{-1}} \boldsymbol{x_7} x_9^{-1}$ and the pair of inverses is cancelled out to obtain $x_4^{-1} \rightarrow x_3 x_9^{-1} x_4^{-1}$.

(2) x_t^{-1} is moved to its proper place among the negative letters, updating its index if necessary. This is completed through m applications of (R2), followed by $k - m$ applications of (R3) and finally, $l - n$ applications of (R4), to obtain

$$\overline{bw} = x_{i_1} \cdots x_{i_m} \boldsymbol{x_{t+m}^{-1}} x_{i_{m+1}+1} \cdots x_{i_k+1} x_{j_l+1}^{-1} \cdots x_{j_{n+1}+1}^{-1} \boldsymbol{x_{t+m}^{-1}} x_{j_n}^{-1} \cdots x_{j_1}^{-1} \ ,$$

where $i_m < t + m - 1$, $i_{m+1} > t + m$, $j_{n+1} > t + m$ and $j_n \leq t + m$. Because the letter x_{t+m} is not present in $\overline{bw}$ (otherwise the previously described situation would occur), the newly introduced letter x_{t+m}^{-1} cannot violate **(NF2)**, and therefore $\overline{bw}$ is in fact in normal form and $|\overline{bw}| = |w| + 1$.

Example 4. $w = x_3 x_7 x_9^{-1} x_4^{-1}$, $b = x_5^{-1}$. $bw = \boldsymbol{x_5^{-1}} x_3 x_7 x_9^{-1} x_4^{-1}$ is rewritten as: $\boldsymbol{x_6^{-1}} x_7 x_9^{-1} x_4^{-1} \rightarrow x_3 x_8 \boldsymbol{x_6^{-1}} x_9^{-1} x_4^{-1} \rightarrow x_3 x_8 x_{10}^{-1} \boldsymbol{x_6^{-1}} x_4^{-1}$.

This completes the proof for negative letters.

□

4.1 The Shpilrain-Ushakov Protocol in Thompson's Group

For a natural number $s \geq 2$ let $S_A = \{x_0 x_1^{-1}, \ldots, x_0 x_s^{-1}\}$, $S_B = \{x_{s+1}, \ldots, x_{2s}\}$ and $S_W = \{x_0, \ldots, x_{s+2}\}$. S_W generates F (see Remark 1). Denote by A_s and B_s the subgroups of F generated by S_A and S_B, respectively.

All of the following facts are shown in [12]: A_s is exactly the set of elements whose normal form is

$$x_{i_1} \cdots x_{i_m} x_{j_m}^{-1} \cdots x_{j_1}^{-1} \ ,$$

i.e, has positive and negative parts of the same length m, and additionally satisfies $i_k - k < s$ and $j_k - k < s$ for every $k = 1, \ldots, m$. B_s is the set of all elements of F whose normal form consists only of letters with indices $\geq s + 1$. Additionally, A_s and B_s commute elementwise, which makes them usable for implementing the protocol in Section 2.

Key generation. Let $s \geq 2$ and L be positive integers. The words $a_1, a_2 \in A_s$, $b_1, b_2 \in B_s$, and $w \in F$ are all chosen of normal form length L, as follows: Let X be A, B, or W. Start with the empty word, and multiply it on the right by a generator (or inverse) selected uniformly at random from the set S_X. Continue this procedure until the normal form of the word has length L.

For practical and (hopefully) secure implementation of the protocol, it is suggested in [12] to use $s \in \{3, 4, \ldots, 8\}$ and $L \in \{256, 258, \ldots, 320\}$.

5   Subgroup Distance Functions in Thompson's Group

In this section we'll suggest several natural distance functions from the subgroups $A_s, B_s \leq F$ defined in Section 4.1. These distance functions can be used to implement the attack outlined by Algorithm 1.

5.1   Distance Functions from B_s

For $w \in F$ define $P_i(w)$ and $N_i(w)$ as the number of occurrences of x_i and x_i^{-1} in the normal form $\hat{w}$ of w.

Definition 6 (Distance from B_s). *Let $s \leq 2$ be an integer. For $w \in F$ the distance from B_s is defined as*

$$d_{B_s}(w) = \sum_{i=0}^{s} (P_i(w) + N_i(w))$$

Claim 1. d_{B_s} *is a distance function.*

Proof. This is immediate, since an element is in B_s if and only if its normal form does not contain generators with indices below $s + 1$ (see Section 4.1). □

Claim 2. d_{B_s} *is an invariant distance function.*

Proof. It is enough to consider only the generators of B_s. Indeed, if multiplication by a single generator of B_s does not change the distance of a word w, neither does multiplication by a sequence of these generators.

Let $w \in F$. Let $b = x_{s+\alpha}^{\pm 1}$, where $\alpha > 0$. By Lemma 1, we know that b is either moved to its proper position (and $\ell_{NF}(bw) = \ell_{NF}(w) + 1$) or it is cancelled with its inverse, either by (R5) or as part of a pair violating (NF2), in which case $\ell_{NF}(bw) = \ell_{NF}(w) - 1$. The index of b is initially above s, and may only increase when the rewriting rules are applied. Therefore, if b is cancelled at some point, the index of its inverse is also above s. Furthermore, when pairs of elements are rewritten, the lower-indexed element is not affected, so any letters with indices $\leq s$ will not be affected by moving b. Finally, if b is cancelled out due to violating (NF2), the process again only affects letters with indices higher than b's (see the proof of Lemma 1). In all cases, the generators with indices $\leq s$ are not affected at all, and so $d_{B_s}(bw) = d_{B_s}(w)$.

□

One can intuitively feel that d_{B_s} is a natural distance function, because it counts the number of "bad" letters in w (letters that do not belong to the subgroup B_s). Indeed, if w is in normal form, $w = w_p w_c w_n$, where w_p and w_n are the "bad" positive and negative subwords, respectively, then $d_{B_s}(w) = |w_p| + |w_n|$ and $w_p^{-1} w w_n^{-1} \in B$.

We now introduce another natural function that measures distance from B_s.

Definition 7 (Weighted distance from B_s). *Let $s \leq 2$ be an integer. For $w \in F$ the weighted distance from B_s is defined as*

$$\overline{d_{B_s}}(w) = \sum_{i=0}^{s} (s + 1 - i) (P_i(\hat{w}) + N_i(\hat{w}))$$

$\overline{d_{B_s}}$ does not only count the "bad" letters, but assigns a score for each letter, depending on how far below $s + 1$ it is (in particular, $d_{B_s}(w) \leq \overline{d_{B_s}}(w)$ for all $w \in F$. The following claim is straightforward.

Claim 3. $\overline{d_{B_s}}$ *is an invariant distance function.*

Proof. The proof of Claim 2 shows that multiplication by b does not alter any letters below $s+1$ in w. Therefore, the weight of each such letter is also preserved. $\square$

5.2   Distance Functions from A_s

We will now describe a number of natural distance functions from the subgroup A_s. Recall (Section 4.1) that A_s is the set of all elements in F, whose normal form is of the type $x_{i_1} \cdots x_{i_m} x_{j_m}^{-1} \cdots x_{j_1}^{-1}$, i.e, has positive and negative parts of the same length m, and additionally satisfies $i_k - k < s$ and $j_k - k < s$ for every $k = 1, \ldots, m$.

Definition 8 (Distance from A_s). *Let $s \geq 2$ be an integer. Let $w \in F$, such that its normal form is $\hat{w} = x_{i_1} \cdots x_{i_p} x_{j_n}^{-1} \cdots x_{j_1}^{-1}$. The distance from A_s is defined as*

$$d_{A_s}(w) = |\{k : i_k - k \geq s\}| + |\{l : j_l - l \geq s\}| + |p - n|$$

$d_{A_s}(w)$ is the number of "bad" letters in $\hat{w}$, i.e., letters that violate the A_s property, plus the difference between the lengths of the positive or negative parts. d_{A_s} is clearly a distance function. However, it is not invariant, as shown by the following example:

Similarly we can define a weighted distance function from A_s, which not only counts the number of bad letters, but gives a score to each such letter, based on the difference $i_k - k$ (or $j_k - k$).

Definition 9 (Weighted distance from A_s). *Let $s \geq 2$ be an integer. Let $w \in F$, such that its normal form is $\hat{w} = x_{i_1} \cdots x_{i_p} x_{j_n}^{-1} \cdots x_{j_1}^{-1}$. The weighted distance from A_s is defined as*

$$\overline{d_{A_s}}(w) = \sum_{\substack{k=1\ldots p}}^{i_k - k \geq s} (i_k - k - s + 1) + \sum_{\substack{k=1\ldots n}}^{j_k - k \geq s} (j_k - k - s + 1) + |p - n|$$

For each bad letter x_{i_k} or $x_{j_k}^{-1}$, $\overline{d_{A_s}}$ adds a positive integer. As such, it's a distance function, which is again not invariant (the example above works here too).

A somewhat different approach to defining distance from A_s arises from the observation that the number of bad letters can be less important than the maximum value of the differences $i_k - k$ and $j_k - k$ across the word, which measures the size of the violation. The difference between the two distance functions roughly corresponds to the difference between the L_1 and L_∞ norms.

Let $\hat{w} = x_{i_1} \cdots x_{i_p} x_{j_n}^{-1} \cdots x_{j_1}^{-1}$. Suppose that for some integer k we have $i_k - k - s + 1 = m_p > 0$ and that m_p is the maximum for all i_k. By multiplying the word by $x_0^{m_p}$ we shift the position for all the original positive letters of w by m_p, and so all of the positive letters, including the first m x_0's have $i_k - k < s$. Similarly, if m_n is the maximum violation in the negative subword, multiplication by $x_0^{-m_n}$ on the right eliminates all violations among negative letters. However, this still does not mean that the word is in A_s, because the positive and negative lengths may differ. Let $\hat{w}'$ be the normal form obtained from $\hat{w}$ through multiplication by $x_0^{m_p}$ and $x_0^{-m_n}$ on the left and right, respectively. Let l_p and l_n be the corresponding lengths of the positive and negative parts of $\hat{w}'$. If $l_p - l_n > 0$, then $\hat{w}' x_0^{l_n - l_p} \in A_s$. If $l_p - l_n < 0$, then $x_0^{l_n - l_p} \hat{w}' \in A_s$. Altogether, any word can be changed to a word in A_s through multiplication by $m_p + m_n + |l_p + l_n|$ indices (when l_p and l_n are evaluated *after* multiplying by $x_0^{m_p}$ and $x_0^{-m_n}$).

This observation suggests the following distance function:

Definition 10 (Maximum-based distance from A_s). *Let $s \geq 2$ be an integer. Let $w \in F$, such that its normal form is $\hat{w} = x_{i_1} \cdots x_{i_p} x_{j_n}^{-1} \cdots x_{j_1}^{-1}$. Let*

$$m_p = \max\left(\{0\} \cup \{i_k - k - s + 1 : k = 1 \ldots p\}\right)$$

and

$$m_n = \max\left(\{0\} \cup \{j_k - k - s + 1 : k = 1 \ldots n\}\right) .$$

The maximum-based distance from A_s is defined as

$$d_{A_s}^m(w) = m_p + m_n + |(p + m_p) - (n + m_n)|$$

For every $w \in A_s$ m_p, m_n and $|p - n|$ are 0 by definition, while for every $w \notin A_s$ at least one of them has to be positive, so the $d_{A_s}^m$ is a distance function. It turns out that, unlike the two previously defined distance functions, $d_{A_s}^m$ is also invariant.

Claim 4. *$d_{A_s}^m$ is an invariant distance function.*

Proof. As with Claim 2, it's sufficient to prove that multiplication by a single generator of A_s does not change the distance from any word w to A_s. We will consider multiplications on the left by generators and their inverses. The multiplication on the right follows symmetrically.

Let $w = x_{i_1} \cdots x_{i_p} x_{j_n}^{-1} \cdots x_{j_1}^{-1}$, without loss of generality, in normal form. Consider the generator $x_0 x_t^{-1}$, where $1 \leq t \leq s$. Define w' as the normal form of $x_0 x_t^{-1} w$. For the parameters p, n, m_p, m_n of w, denote by p', n', m_p', m_n' their corresponding values in w'.

From Lemma 1 it follows that each of the letters x_t^{-1} and x_0 can either be cancelled out with the appropriate inverse, decreasing the length by 1, or placed in its appropriate location, increasing the length by 1. There is a total of 4 possible options:

(1) x_t^{-1} is cancelled out, but x_0 is not: $w' = x_0 x_{i_1} \cdots x_{i_m} x_{i_{m+2}} \cdots$ $x_{i_p} x_{j_n}^{-1} \cdots x_{j_1}^{-1}$, where x_{t+m}^{-1} is cancelled out with $x_{i_{m+1}}$ after m applications of (R2). It follows that $p' = p$, $n' = n$ and $m_n' = m_n$ (because the negative letters are unaffected). Observe also that there can be no bad letters among the first m: indeed, (R2) is applied m times, for each $k = 1 \ldots m$ rewriting $x_{t+k-1}^{-1} x_{i_k} \to x_{i_k} x_{t+k}^{-1}$, so necessarily $i_k < t + k - 1$ for all k, or equivalently, $i_k - k < t - 1 < s$. The multiplication by x_0 on the left only increases their relative positions, thus decreasing $i_k - k$. Now, any possible bad letters above i_m are unchanged, and neither is their relative position, so $m_p' = m_p$ and overall $d_{A_s}^m(w') = d_{A_s}^m(w)$.

(2) Both x_t^{-1} and x_0 are cancelled out: $w' = x_{i_1-1} \cdots x_{i_m-1} x_{i_{m+2}-1} \cdots$ $x_{i_p-1} x_{j_n-1}^{-1} \cdots x_{j_{q+1}-1}^{-1} x_0^{1-q}$. Here $p' = p-1$, $n' = n-1$ and $m_n' = m_n$ because all negative letters $x_{j_k}^{-1}$ with $j_k > 0$ had both their indices and their relative positions decreased by 1. The same thing applies to positive letters above i_m, which are the only positive letters that may be bad. So again, $m_p' = m_p$ and $d_{A_s}^m(w') = d_{A_s}^m(w)$.

(3) Neither x_t^{-1}, nor x_0 are cancelled out: $w' = x_0 x_{i_1} \cdots x_{i_m} x_{i_{m+1}+1} \cdots$ $x_{i_p+1} x_{j_n+1}^{-1} \cdots x_{j_{q+1}+1}^{-1} \boldsymbol{x_{t+m}^{-1}} x_{j_q}^{-1} \cdots x_{j_1}^{-1}$. Here $p' = p + 1$ and $n' = n + 1$. Due to the former observation, bad positive letters may only exist beyond the first m. All these letters had their indices i_k and their relative positions k increased by 1, so the difference is preserved and $m_p' = m_p$. Among the negative letters, only the letters whose indices increased, also had their relative position increased, so $j_k - k$ is preserved for all the original letters of w. Hence, $m_n' \geq m_n$ and the only situation when it may actually increase is when the new maximum is attained at the new letter, i.e., $m_n' = (t + m) - (q + 1) - s + 1 > m_n$. Because $t \leq s$, $m \leq p$ and $q \leq n$, we have $m_n' \leq p - q$, from which it follows that

$$(p' + m_p') - (n' + m_n') = (p' - n') + (m_p' - m_n') = (p + 1) - (n + 1) + m_p - m_n' \geq$$

$$\geq m_p + (p - n) - (p - q) = m_p + q - n \geq 0$$

Assuming $m_n' > m_n$, it's obvious that

$$(p - n) + (m_p - m_n) > (p' - n') + (m_p' - m_n') \geq 0 \ ,$$

and so if m_n increases, $|(p + m_p) - (n + m_n)|$ decreases by the same amount, and overall $d_{A_s}^m(w') = d_{A_s}^m(w)$.

(4) x_t^{-1} is not cancelled out, but x_0 is: $w' = x_{i_1-1} \cdots x_{i_m-1} x_{i_{m+1}} \cdots$ $x_{i_p} x_{j_n}^{-1} \cdots x_{j_{q+1}}^{-1} \boldsymbol{x_{t+m-1}^{-1}} x_{j_q-1}^{-1} \cdots x_{j_{r+1}-1}^{-1} x_0^{1-r}$, where $p' = p$, $n' = n$, $m_p' = m_p$ (because the first m positive letters, whose indices have changed, contained no bad letters), and m'_n again may only increase, if it's attained at x_{t+m-1}^{-1}. Repeating the same calculations shows that $d_{A_s}^m(w') = d_{A_s}^m(w)$ in this case too.

Now consider the inverse $x_t x_0^{-1}$ and denote $w' = x_t x_0^{-1} w$. The four possible outcomes are:

(1) x_0^{-1} is cancelled out, but x_t is not: x_0^{-1} can only be cancelled out if $i_1 = 0$, and the resulting word is: $w' = x_{i_2} \cdots x_{i_m} \boldsymbol{x_{t+m-1}} x_{i_{m+1}} \cdots x_{i_p} x_{j_n}^{-1} \cdots x_{j_1}^{-1}$. Here $p' = p$, $n' = n$, $m'_n = m_n$ (negative part is not affected) and $m'_p = m_p$ because the letters x_{i_2} to x_{i_m} cannot be bad and the relative position of other positive letters has not changed.

(2) Both x_0^{-1} and x_t are cancelled out: Assuming x_t is cancelled out (due to violation of **(NF2)**) with $x_{j_q}^{-1}$, $w' = x_{i_2} \cdots x_{i_m} x_{i_{m+1}-1} \cdots x_{i_p-1} x_{j_n-1}^{-1} \cdots x_{j_{q+1}-1}^{-1} x_{j_{q-1}}^{-1} \cdots x_{j_1}^{-1}$. Here $p' = p - 1$, $n' = n - 1$, $m'_p = m_p$, because x_{i_2} to x_{i_m} cannot be bad and the relative position of other positive letters has not changed, and $m'_n = m_n$, because the letters whose positions shifted also had their indices decreased.

(3) Neither x_0^{-1}, nor x_t are cancelled out. $w' = x_{i_1+2} \cdots x_{i_m+2} \boldsymbol{x_{t+m}} x_{i_{m+1}+1} \cdots x_{i_p+1} x_{j_n+1}^{-1} \cdots x_{j_q+1}^{-1} \boldsymbol{x_0^{-q}}$. Here $p' = p + 1$, $n' = n + 1$, $m'_p = m_p$, because indices above i_m grew by 1, as did their positions, and indices $i_1, \ldots, i_m$ cannot be bad, and also $m'_n = m_n$, because all letters whose indices increased (j_q and above) shifted in position accordingly.

(4) x_0^{-1} is not cancelled out, but x_t is: $w' = x_{i_1+2} \cdots x_{i_m+2} x_{i_{m+1}} \cdots x_{i_p} x_{j_n}^{-1} \cdots x_{j_{q+1}}^{-1} x_{j_{q-1}+1}^{-1} \cdots x_{j_r+1}^{-1} \boldsymbol{x_0^{-r}}$, the cancelled pair being $(x_{t+m}, x_{j_q}^{-1})$, where $j_q = t + m$. In this case, any positive letters that can be bad kept their indices and positions, the negative letters $j_{r+1}, \ldots, j_{q-1}$ had their indices and positions shifted, while the letters $j_{q+1}, \ldots, j_n$ kept their indices and positions. So $m'_p = m_p$ and $m'_n = m_n$ and obviously $p' = p$ and $n' = n$.

We see that in all the possible cases, $d_{A_s}^m(w') = d_{A_s}^m(w)$. This completes the proof. □

6   Experimental Results

To test the applicability of the subgroup distance functions to cryptanalysis, we tested Algorithm 1 against the Shpilrain-Ushakov protocol in the settings of Thompson's group. Initially, each of the five distance functions presented in the previous section was tested separately: we generated a public element azb and tried to recover a single private element a or b from it. For the recovery of a, the functions d_{B_s} and $\overline{d_{B_s}}$ were used to assess the quality of the complements. Similarly, for the recovery of b, we tried d_{A_s}, $\overline{d_{A_s}}$ and $d_{A_s}^m$.

For each distance function, the experiment was run at least 1000 times, each time with new, randomly generated keys, with the minimum recommended parameters of $s = 3, L = 256$. The bound $N = 2L$ was chosen on the number of iterations, since preliminary experiments have shown that the success rates do not increase beyond that. The results are summarized in Table 1. It can be seen that the distance functions d_{B_s} and $d_{A_s}^m$ noticeably outperform the other

Table 1. Success rates for the different subgroup distance functions

	d_{B_s}	$\overline{d_{B_s}}$	d_{A_s}	$\overline{d_{A_s}}$	$d_{A_s}^m$
Recovery probability	11.7%	3.4%	3.7%	3.4%	23.3%

distance functions, in recovering a and b, respectively. The fact that $d_{A_s}^m$ clearly outperforms its counterparts suggests that the notion of invariance may be useful for assessing the suitability of a given distance function.

Preliminary experiments have shown that, regardless of the settings, the success probability of finding a_1 given $a_1 z b_1$ is similar to that of finding a_2^{-1} given $a_2^{-1} z^{-1} b_2^{-1}$. A similar assertion holds for b_2 and b_1^{-1}. Therefore, in order to estimate the overall success rate against an actual instance of the cryptosystem, it's sufficient to try to recover one of the four a's and b's. If we denote by p_a and p_b the probability of successfully recovering a and b, respectively, and assume that all probabilities are independent, then, the expected total success rate is roughly $1 - (1 - p_a)^2 (1 - p_b)^2$ (because each instance of the protocol contains two elements of type a and two of type b).

When the success rates of the two best distance functions, d_{B_s} for a and $d_{A_s}^m$ for b, are combined, the expected overall success probability, according to the above, is between 50% and 54%, which was experimentally verified. Note that this attack is very efficient, since it involves no backtracking, no lookahead, and no analysis of suboptimal partial results: it tries to peel off the generators by a greedy algorithm, which considers only locally optimal steps. Attacking each key required only a few seconds on a single PC, and it is very surprising that such a simple attack succeeds about half the time. These results are much better than those achieved by length-based attacks of similar complexity on this cryptosystem (see [9]).

It is interesting to note that possible extensions of the attack, such as memorizing many suboptimal partial solutions or using significant lookahead (which require much higher time and space complexities) have different effects on length-based and distance-based attacks. While it was shown in [9] that these extensions greatly improve the success rates of the length-based attack, experiments with the distance-based attack, with similar values of the memory and lookahead parameters, showed almost no improvement. However, the situation may be very different for other cryptosystems and other subgroup distance functions.

To further test the performance of the distance functions, several experiments were run with different values of the parameters (s, L). We used the combina-

Table 2. Success rates for different combinations of (s, L)

	$L = 128$	$L = 256$	$L = 320$	$L = 512$	$L = 640$	$L = 960$
$s = 3$	51.7%	47.9%	55.5%	51.2%	50.4%	52.6%
$s = 5$	46.0%	47.1%	48.4%	51.1%	48.2%	48.3%
$s = 8$	36.2%	42.8%	41.3%	46.5%	42.4%	50.3%

tion of d_{B_s} and $d_{A_s}^m$, which was established as the best in the former experiment. Table 2 shows the overall success probability, for $L \in \{128, 256, 320, 512, 640, 960\}$ and $s \in \{3, 5, 8\}$. The success rates stay remarkably consistent across different lengths for a given s, and even increasing s does not cause a significant drop. The time complexity of the attack grows linearly with s and roughly quadratically with L, with most of the time being spent on computing normal forms of elements in the group. For the largest parameters presented here, the attack still required under a minute in most cases. This suggests that for the Shpilrain-Ushakov cryptosystem the distance-based attack remains a viable threat, even when the security parameters s and L are increased beyond the original recommendations.

7   Conclusion

We introduced a novel form of heuristic attacks on public key cryptosystems that are based on combinatorial group theory, using functions that estimate the distance of group elements to a given subgroup. Our results demonstrate that these distance-based attacks can achieve significantly better success rates than previously suggested length-based attacks of similar complexity, and thus they are a potential threat to any cryptosystem based on equations in a noncommutative group, which takes its elements from specific subgroups. It will be interesting to test this approach for other groups and other protocols.

References

1. I. Anshel, M. Anshel and D. Goldfeld, *An algebraic method for public-key cryptography*, Mathematical Research Letters **6** (1999), 287–291.
2. E. Artin, *Theory of Braids*, Annals of Mathematics **48** (1947), 127–136.
3. J.W. Cannon, W.J. Floyd and W.R. Parry, *Introductory notes on Richard Thompson's groups*, L'Enseignement Mathematique (2) **42** (1996), 215–256.
4. D. Garber, S. Kaplan, M. Teicher, B. Tsaban, and U. Vishne, *Length-based conjugacy search in the Braid group*, Contemporary Mathematics **418** (2006), 75–87.
5. D. Garber, S. Kaplan, M. Teicher, B. Tsaban, and U. Vishne, *Probabilistic solutions of equations in the braid group*, Advances in Applied Mathematics **35** (2005), 323–334.
6. J. Hughes and A. Tannenbaum, *Length-based attacks for certain group based encryption rewriting systems*, Workshop SECI02 Sécurité de la Communication sur Internet (2002).
7. K.H. Ko, S.J. Lee, J.H. Cheon, J.W. Han, J. Kang and C. Park, *New Public-Key Cryptosystem Using Braid Groups*, Lecture Notes in Computer Science **1880** (2000), 166–183.
8. F. Matucci, *The Shpilrain-Ushakov Protocol for Thompson's Group F is always breakable*, e-print arxiv.org/math/0607184 (2006).
9. D. Ruinskiy, A. Shamir and B. Tsaban, *Length-based cryptanalysis: The case of Thompson's group*, e-print arxiv.org/cs/0607079 (2006).

10. V. Shpilrain, *Assessing security of some group based cryptosystems*, Contemporary Mathematics **360** (2004), 167–177.
11. V. Shpilrain and A. Ushakov, *The conjugacy search problem in public key cryptography: unnecessary and insufficient*, Applicable Algebra in Engineering, Communication and Computing **17** (2006), 291–302.
12. V. Shpilrain and A. Ushakov, *Thompson's group and public key cryptography*, ACNS 2005, Lecture Notes in Computer Science **3531** (2005), 151–164.

Length Based Attack and Braid Groups: Cryptanalysis of Anshel-Anshel-Goldfeld Key Exchange Protocol

Alex D. Myasnikov and Alexander Ushakov

Department of Mathematical Sciences, Stevens Institute of Technology,
Hoboken, New Jersey, USA, 07030
{amyasnik,aushakov}@stevens.edu

Abstract. The length based attack on Anshel-Anshel-Goldfeld commutator key-exchange protocol [1] was initially proposed by Hughes and Tannenbaum in [9]. Several attempts have been made to implement the attack [6], but none of them had produced results convincing enough to believe that attack works. In this paper we show that accurately designed length based attack can successfully break a random instance of the simultaneous conjugacy search problem for certain parameter values and argue that the public/private information chosen uniformly random leads to weak keys.

1 Introduction

Braid group cryptography has attracted a lot of attention recently due to several suggested key exchange protocols (see [1], [10]) using braid groups as a platform. We refer to [2], [5] for more information on braid groups.

In this paper we discuss the so-called Length Based Attack on the Anshel-Anshel-Goldfeld key exchange protocol [1] (subsequently called the AAG protocol). The Length Based Attack, LBA for short, was first introduced by Hughes and Tannenbaum in [9], however no actual experiments were performed and the real threat of the attack has not been evaluated. Since then there were several implementations of LBA published [6] but none of them produced a convincing evidence that LBA, indeed, breaks AAG. Finally, the authors of [6] make conclusion that AAG protocol is invulnerable to LBA.

We need to mention here that successful attacks on AAG were proposed in [7,11,14]. It is common believe now that AAG with original parameters is not secure. However, the scalability of the attacks has not been completely realized. This leads to speculations that AAG protocol may still be secure with a different set of parameters such as longer private keys, for example.

In the paper we analyze the reasons behind the failure of the previous implementations of LBA. We show that for slightly increased values of parameters LBA can be modified so it breaks AAG protocol with a very high rate of success. We also present an evidence that the keys generated uniformly randomly are not secure and suggest that a more cautious approach in selecting private

T. Okamoto and X. Wang (Eds.): PKC 2007, LNCS 4450, pp. 76–88, 2007.

information is necessary for AAG protocol to be immune to the length based attack.

Here we start out by giving a brief description of the Anshel-Anshel-Goldfeld key exchange protocol [1] (subsequently called the AAG protocol). Let B_n be the group of braids on n strands and $X_n = \{x_1, \ldots, x_{n-1}\}$ the set of standard generators. Thus,

$$B_n = \langle x_1, \ldots, x_{n-1}; \; x_i x_{i+1} x_i = x_{i+1} x_i x_{i+1}, \; x_i x_j = x_j x_i \text{ for } |i - j| > 1 \rangle.$$

Let $N_1, N_2 \in \mathbb{N}$, $1 \leq L_1 \leq L_2$, and $L \in \mathbb{N}$ be preset parameters. The AAG protocol [1] is the following sequence of steps:

(1) Alice randomly generates an N_1-tuple of braid words $\bar{a} = (a_1, \ldots a_{N_1})$, each of length between L_1 and L_2, such that each generator of B_n non-trivially occurs in $\bar{a}$. The tuple $\bar{a}$ is called *Alice's public set*.
(2) Bob randomly generates an N_2-tuple of braid words $\bar{b} = (b_1, \ldots b_{N_2})$, each of length between L_1 and L_2, such that each generator of B_n is non-trivially involved in $\bar{b}$. The tuple $\bar{b}$ is called *Bob's public set*.
(3) Alice randomly generates a product $A = a_{s_1}^{\varepsilon_1} \ldots a_{s_L}^{\varepsilon_L}$, where $0 < s_i < N_1$ and $\varepsilon_i = \pm 1$ (for each $1 \leq i \leq L$). The word A is called *Alice's private key*.
(4) Bob randomly generates a product $B = b_{t_1}^{\delta_1} \ldots b_{t_L}^{\delta_L}$, where $0 < t_i < N_1$ and $\delta_i = \pm 1$ (for each $1 \leq i \leq L$). The word B is called *Bob's private key*.
(5) Alice computes $b_i' = D(A^{-1} b_i A)$ $(1 \leq i \leq N_2)$ and transmits them to Bob. Here $D(w)$ denotes Dehornoy handle free form of a braid word w (see [4] for the definition of Dehornoy form of a braid).
(6) Bob computes $a_i' = D(B^{-1} a_i B)$ $(1 \leq i \leq N_1)$ and transmits them to Alice.
(7) Alice computes $K_A = A^{-1} a_{s_1}'^{\varepsilon_1} \ldots a_{s_L}'^{\varepsilon_L}$. It is straightforward to see that $K_A = A^{-1} B^{-1} A B$ in the group B_n.
(8) Bob computes $K_B = b_{t_L}'^{-\delta_L} \ldots b_{t_1}'^{-\delta_1} B$. Again, it is easy to see that $K_B = A^{-1} B^{-1} A B$ in the group B_n.

Thus, Alice and Bob obtain the same element $K = K_A = K_B = A^{-1} B^{-1} A B$ of the group B_n. This K is now their *shared secret key*.

In the steps (5) and (6) of the protocol the so-called Dehronoy form is used do diffuse the public commutators. It is out of scope of this paper to define the Dehornoy form in detail. Informally, the Dehornoy form is a reduced braid word obtained as a result of a particular rewriting procedure. It is believed that Dehornoy forms are linearly computable and it is computationally infeasible to reconstruct the original braid from its Dehornoy form. For more details on the definition and the procedure to compute the Dehornoy form we refer to [4].

Note that for an intruder to get the shared secret key K, it is sufficient to find:

- an element $A' \in \langle a_1, \ldots, a_{N_1} \rangle$ such that $\bar{b}' = A'^{-1} \bar{b} A'$ in B_n;
- an element $B' \in \langle b_1, \ldots, n_{N_2} \rangle$ such that $\bar{a}' = B'^{-1} \bar{a} B'$ in B_n.

Such elements A' and B' successfully substitute Alice's and Bob's private keys A and B, in particular, $[A, B] = [A', B']$. For more information see [16]. Finding an element A' (and B') is an instance of the *subgroup-restricted simultaneous conjugacy search problem* (abbreviated SR-SCSP) which is a variation of *simultaneous conjugacy search problem* (SCSP) where it is required to find any conjugator for two conjugated tuples.

Therefore, we say that the security of AAG protocol is partially based (but not equivalent) on the assumption that SR-SCSP is hard. Below we describe several types of attacks on variations of simultaneous conjugacy problem.

A. There is only one attack aiming to break SR-SCSP directly – the length-based attack (initially proposed in [9]). It is a heuristic descend method for solving SR-SCSP. We discuss it at length in Section 2.
B. All other attacks are aiming at SCSP:
   1) *Summit Set Attack* [11]. This method starts by reducing conjugates to the minimal level with respect to the canonical length (called the summit set) and then performs the exhaustive search in that level.
   2) *Hofheinz-Stainwandt Attack* [7] which has the same first step as in the summit set attack and then uses a heuristic to obtain a solution in the minimal level.
   3) *Linear Attack* which uses presentations of braids by matrices, e.g., Burau or Kramer presentations (see [8]). This attack produces a conjugator in a matrix form and further lifting to braids is required.

A different type of heuristic attacks which is called *the subgroup attack* was presented in [14]. It does not solve any variation of the conjugacy problem. Instead it reduces the original problem to the one with shorter generators simplifying the conjugacy problem. In particular, using the subgroup attack it was shown that for parameters originally proposed by Anshel-Anshel-Goldfeld

– SCSP and SR-SCSP are equivalent for majority of random public sets;
– the majority of random public sets define the same subgroup which coincides with the whole group;

which justifies the success of attacks B.1), B.2), and B.3) which perform well, although with different success rates, on the original parameters suggested in [1]:

$$n = 80, \quad N_1 = N_2 = 20, \quad L_1 = 5, \quad L_2 = 8, \quad L = 100$$

It is well accepted now that these values of parameters do not provide good level of security. In this paper we increase values of parameters L_1 and L_2 to

$$n = 80, \quad N_1 = N_2 = 20, \quad L_1 = 20, 30, 40, \quad L_2 = L_1 + 3, \quad L = 50.$$

and show that accurately designed LBA can crack a random instance of the SR-SCSP generated using these values of parameters. Notice that we increase lengths of generators of the public sets but decrease lengths of decompositions of the private keys to keep the size of private keys A and B within practical bounds. To be more precise we got the following results in our experiments:

L_1, L_2	10,13	20,23	30,33	40,43
Success rate	00%	51%	97%	96%

See Table 1 for more details.

The rest of the paper is organized as follows. In Section 2 we describe the idea of the length based attack and its variations. We give examples of potentially hard instances and explain what prevents LBA from being successful. We conclude Section 2 by showing that it is unlikely that a private key taken at random will be hard to break when values of L_1 and L_2 are sufficiently large. We argue that a naive approach of increasing the size of the key will not guarantee increase in the security of the protocol. In Section 3 we describe our version of the generalized length based attack for breaking AAG and present experimental results.

All the algorithms described in this paper are available at [3].

2   The Length Based Attack

The length based attack is a heuristic procedure for finding the Alice's (symmetrically Bob's) private key A (B). Following the notation of Section 1 let $\bar{a} = \{a_1, \ldots, a_{N_1}\}$, $\bar{b} = \{b_1, \ldots, b_{N_2}\}$, $A = a_{s_1}^{\varepsilon_1} \ldots a_{s_L}^{\varepsilon_L}$, and $\bar{b}' = \{b_1', \ldots, b_{N_2}'\}$, where $b_i' = D(A^{-1}b_i A)$. Essentially each b_i' is a result of a sequence of conjugations of b_i by the factors of A:

$$
\begin{array}{c}
b_i \\
\downarrow \\
a_{s_1}^{-\varepsilon_1}\ b_i\ a_{s_1}^{\varepsilon_1} \\
\downarrow \\
a_{s_2}^{-\varepsilon_2}a_{s_1}^{-\varepsilon_1}\ b_i\ a_{s_1}^{\varepsilon_1}a_{s_2}^{\varepsilon_2} \\
\downarrow \\
\ldots \\
\downarrow \\
b_i' = a_{s_L}^{-\varepsilon_L} \ldots a_{s_2}^{-\varepsilon_2}a_{s_1}^{-\varepsilon_1}\ b_i\ a_{s_1}^{\varepsilon_1}a_{s_2}^{\varepsilon_2} \ldots a_{s_L}^{\varepsilon_L}
\end{array}
\tag{1}
$$

A conjugating sequence is the same for each b_i and is defined by the private key A. The main goal of the attack is to reverse the sequence (1) and going back from the bottom to the top recover each conjugating factor. If successful the procedure will result in the actual conjugator as a product of elements from $\bar{a}$.

2.1   LBA as a Minimization Problem

To achieve the goal outlined above we need some efficiently computable function whose values would guide us on the way from the bottom to the top of (1). The most natural idea is to find a function l such that

$$
\text{for the majority of elements } a, b \in B_n\ l(a^{-1}ba) > l(b).
\tag{2}
$$

If such function exists then LBA can be set as a minimization problem and solved using some heuristic optimization methods.

The choice of the function l is crucial for the success of the attack. In the original paper [9] it was proposed to use a length function. There are several length functions available for braids. In [9] the authors do not specify the function explicitly, although their arguments are based on the work of Vershik et al. [17] where the length defined as the geodesic length, i.e. the length of the shortest path in the corresponding Cayley graph of a group.

Unfortunately there are no practically useful length functions are known in braid groups which satisfy the criteria (2). The geodesic length of a braid denoted by $|\cdot|$ seems to be the best candidate. However, there is no known efficient algorithm for computing $|\cdot|$. Moreover, it was shown in [15] that the set of geodesic braids in B_∞ is co-NP complete.

Some of length functions such as the canonical length of the Garside normal form $|\cdot|_\Delta$ and the canonical length of the Birman-Ko-Lee normal form $|\cdot|_\delta$ are efficiently computable but very crude, in a sense that many braids consisting of many crossings have very small lengths. For instance, permutation braids contain up to $1/2n(n-1)$ crossings but have canonical length $|\cdot|_\Delta$ equal 1.

In this paper we use the method to approximate geodesic length proposed in [14]. It does not guarantee the optimal result, although a series of experiments show that for braids used in AAG the results of the approximation satisfy the desired property given by the relation (2). From now on we denote by $|\cdot|$ the result of the approximation function. The experiments suggest that our approximation function $|\cdot|$ satisfies $|a^{-1}ba| > |b|$ for almost all a and b. Moreover, as the length of a and b grows we have $2|a| + |b| - |a^{-1}ba|$ significantly smaller than $2|a|$ which means that $|a^{-1}ba| > |b|$ and the difference is large. Figure 1 shows the distribution of $2|a| + |b| - |a^{-1}ba|$ in B_{80} for $|b| = 400$, $|a| = 5, 10, 20, 30, 40$. In particular, for $|a| = 5$ we see that in 90% of the cases cancellation in $|a^{-1}ba|$ is limited by 4 symbols which means that in 90% of the cases conjugation by the element of length 5 increases the length by at least 6. The small fraction of elements which do not satisfy $|a^{-1}ba| > 2|a| + |b|$ (negative values in the distribution) are caused by the errors of the approximation.

2.2 Variations of LBA

In this section we discuss heuristic approaches to be used with the length function $|\cdot|$. All the algorithms in this section have the following input/output:

- INPUT: Tuples $\bar{a} = (a_1, \ldots, a_{N_1})$, $\bar{b} = (b_1, \ldots, b_{N_2})$, and $\bar{b}' = (b'_1, \ldots, b'_{N_2})$ such that $\bar{b}$ and $\bar{b}'$ are conjugate by an element from $\langle a_1, \ldots, a_{N_1} \rangle$.
- OUTPUT: An element $x \in \langle a_1, \ldots, a_{N_1} \rangle$ such that $\bar{b}^x = \bar{b}'$ or $FAIL$ if algorithm is unable to find such x.

For an arbitrary tuple of braids $\bar{c} = (c_1, \ldots, c_k)$ denote by $|\bar{c}|$ its *total length* $\sum_{i=1}^{k} |c_i|$. Algorithm 1 (*LBA with backtracking*) enumerates all possible sequences of conjugations decreasing the length of a tuple. We maintain set S which contains tuples in work.

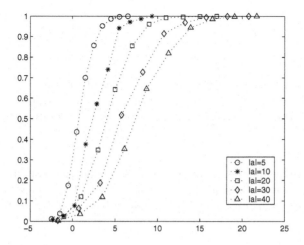

Fig. 1. Distribution of $2|a| + |b| - |a^{-1}ba|$ in B_{80} for $|b| = 400$, $|a| = 5, 10, 20, 30, 40$

Algorithm 1. *(LBA with backtracking)*

A. *Initialize a set $S = \{(\overline{b}', e)\}$, where e is the identity of B_n.*
B. *If $S = \emptyset$ then output $FAIL$.*
C. *Choose a pair $(\overline{c}, x) \in S$ with a minimal $|\overline{c}|$. Remove $(\overline{c}, x)$ from S.*
D. *For each $i = 1, \ldots, N_1$, $\varepsilon = \pm 1$ compute $\delta_{i,\varepsilon} = |\overline{c}| - |\overline{c}^{a_i^{\varepsilon}}|$.*
E. *If $\delta_{i,\varepsilon} > 0$ then add $(\overline{c}^{a_i^{\varepsilon}}, xa_i^{\varepsilon})$ into S.*
F. *If $\overline{c}^{a_i^{\varepsilon}} = \overline{a}$ them output xa_i^{ε}.*
G. *Otherwise goto B.*

Algorithm 2 (*best descend LBA*) is a version of a length based attack where on each step we choose conjugator which gives the maximal decrease among all currently available tuples. It is weaker than Algorithm 1 but works well for certain parameter values as our experiments show. It has the same steps as Algorithm 1, except that on step E we add only the tuple corresponding to the maximal positive $\delta_{i,\varepsilon}$ to the set S. Thus at each time the set S contains at most 1 pair and no backtracking.

Algorithm 2. *(Best Descend)*

E. *Choose the greatest positive $\delta_{i,\varepsilon} > 0$ (if exists) and add $(\overline{c}^{a_i^{\varepsilon}}, xa_i^{\varepsilon})$ into S.*

The next version of the length based attack is so called *generalized LBA*. This is an LBA with backtracking in which we extend the set of elements in Bob's (respectively Alice's) public sets. It was conjectured in [9] that generalized length based attack can break the multiple conjugacy search problem for any parameter values. We need to mention here that one has to be cautious about the choice of the new elements as the complexity of each iteration of LBA depends on the number of elements in the public set $\overline{a}$.

Algorithm 3. *(Generalized LBA)*

A. *Extend $\bar{a}$ with products $a_{i_1}^{\varepsilon_1} \ldots a_{i_j}^{\varepsilon_j}$ where j is limited by some constant.*
B. *Run Algorithms 1 or 2 with the obtained tuple $\bar{a}$ and tuples $\bar{b}$, $\bar{b}'$.*

Algorithms 1-3 always halt because only tuples of total lengths smaller than the lengths of the public sets are considered. Note that all of the algorithms above are heuristic in their nature and may halt without producing the solution.

2.3   Peaks

In this section we define the notion of a peak and show that condition (2) on the length function in the platform group B_n is not enough for the success of LBA. We give examples of instances of AAG invulnerable to the length based attacks 2 and 1.

Example 1. (Hard instance) Consider B_{80} and two braids

$$a_1 = x_{39}^{-1} x_{12} x_7 x_3^{-1} x_1^{-1} x_{70} x_{25} x_{24}^{-1}$$

and

$$a_2 = x_{42} x_{56}^{-1} x_8 x_{18}^{-1} x_{19} x_{73} x_{33}^{-1} x_{22}^{-1}$$

which we think of as elements from Alice's public set. It is easy to check that

$$a_1^{-1} a_2^{-1} a_1 = x_7^{-1} \cdot a_2^{-1} \cdot x_7 = x_7^{-1} x_{22} x_{33} x_{73}^{-1} x_{19}^{-1} x_{18} x_8^{-1} x_{56} x_{42}^{-1} x_7$$

and

$$a_1^{-1} a_2^{-1} a_1 a_2 = x_7 x_8^{-1}.$$

Hence $|a_1| = 8$, $|a_1^{-1} a_2^{-1}| = 16$, $|a_1^{-1} a_2^{-1} a_1| = 10$, and $|a_1^{-1} a_2^{-1} a_1 a_2| = 2$. Now let $\bar{b} = (b_1, \ldots, b_N)$ be a random tuple of braids thought of as Bob's public set. As we saw, for the majority of braids conjugation increases the length by almost twice the length of a conjugator. Hence, for generic tuple $\bar{b}$ the following length growth would be expected:

$$\bar{b}$$
$$\downarrow$$
$$|a_{s_1}^{-\varepsilon_1} \bar{b} \, a_{s_1}^{\varepsilon_1}| \qquad\qquad \approx |\bar{b}| + 8N$$
$$\downarrow$$
$$|a_{s_2}^{-\varepsilon_2} a_{s_1}^{-\varepsilon_1} \bar{b} \, a_{s_1}^{\varepsilon_1} a_{s_2}^{\varepsilon_2}| \qquad\qquad \approx |\bar{b}| + 16N \qquad\qquad (3)$$
$$\downarrow$$
$$|a_{s_3}^{-\varepsilon_3} a_{s_2}^{-\varepsilon_2} a_{s_1}^{-\varepsilon_1} \bar{b} \, a_{s_1}^{\varepsilon_1} a_{s_2}^{\varepsilon_2} a_{s_3}^{\varepsilon_3}| \qquad\qquad \approx |\bar{b}| + 10N$$
$$\downarrow$$
$$|a_{s_4}^{-\varepsilon_4} a_{s_3}^{-\varepsilon_3} a_{s_2}^{-\varepsilon_2} a_{s_1}^{-\varepsilon_1} \bar{b} \, a_{s_1}^{\varepsilon_1} a_{s_2}^{\varepsilon_2} a_{s_3}^{\varepsilon_3} a_{s_4}^{\varepsilon_4}| \approx |\bar{b}| + 2N$$

Clearly, the length based attacks 2 and 1 fail for such element A because to guess the first correct conjugator it is required to increase the length of the tuple substantially (from $|\bar{b}| + 2N$ to $|\bar{b}| + 10N$).

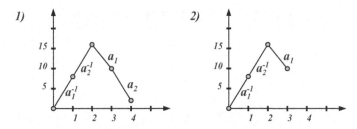

Fig. 2. 1) Commutator-type 4-peak $[a_1, a_2]$ from Example 1. 2) Conjugator-type 2-peak as in Example 1 for $a_1^{-1} a_2^{-1} a_1$

The reason for the attack failure in the previous example is that Alice's private key $[a_1, a_2]$ forms a peak (*commutator-type peak*):

Definition 1. *(Peak) Let $G = \langle X; R \rangle$, l_G a length function on G, and $H = \langle w_1, \ldots, w_k \rangle$. We say that a word $w = w_{i_1} \ldots w_{i_n}$ is an n-peak in H relative to l_G if there is no $1 \le j \le n-1$ such that*

$$l_G(w_{i_1} \ldots w_{i_n}) \ge l_G(w_{i_1} \ldots w_{i_j}).$$

We say that $w = w_{i_1} \ldots w_{i_n}$ is m-hard if there exist $s \in \{1, \ldots, n\}$ such that for each $j = 1, \ldots, k$

$$l_G(w_{i_1} \ldots w_{i_{s+k-1}}) \ge l_G(w_{i_1} \ldots w_{i_{s+k-j}})$$

and m is maximal with such property.

Note that according to the definition of m-hardness each product $w_{i_1} \ldots w_{i_n}$ is at least 1-hard. To see the hardness of the word $w = w_{i_1} \ldots w_{i_n} \in H$ (given as a product of generators of H) it is often convenient to depict the function $k \mapsto l_G(w_{i_1} \ldots w_{i_k})$ for $k = 0, \ldots, n$. See Figure 2 for the words from Example 1. The graphs explain the choice of term peak. On the other hand given $w \in H$ we do not know any way to compute its hardness other than to compute the decomposition of w in a product of generators, which is a very hard problem for some subgroups of a braid group.

After making lots of experiments we strongly believe that the computational hardness of SR-SCSP in braid groups is not an intrinsic property of conjugation, but comes from the structure of the corresponding subgroup. To defend against LBA it is necessary to choose a public set and m-hard private keys, where m is large compared to N_1, N_2. One can generate such keys using the Mihailova construction [12].

However, generating keys that are immune just to LBA is not sufficient for the security of the protocol. A generating procedure which provides keys secure against all known attacks is a difficult task and is a current research objective.

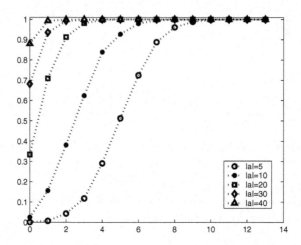

Fig. 3. Distribution of the number of peaks in private keys

2.4   Peaks in Randomly Chosen Private Keys

Even though it is not hard to construct instances invulnerable to LBA, such instances are quite rare and it is very unlikely to generate one uniformly for certain parameter values. Figure 3 shows the distribution of the number of peaks in private keys for B_{80} and $L_1 = 5, 10, 20, 30, 40$, $L_2 = L_1 + 3$. Figure 4 shows the distribution of the maximal size of peaks in private keys for B_{80} and $L_1 = 5, 10, 20, 30, 40$, $L_2 = L_1 + 3$. The distributions shown in Figures 3 and 4 are obtained experimentally using the approximation of the geodesic length.

According to Figures 3 and 4 the greater length of the generators the shorter and rarer the peaks are. Intuitively, we can distinguish 3 types of distribution of peaks depending on the parameter L_1 (for B_{80}):

1) *Short generators ($L_1 \in [5, 20]$).* A random private key contains several peaks, one or two of which are relatively long. The probability of a success of Algorithm 1 in this case is very low. To make Algorithm 3 work it requires extending the basis with a lot of elements, which suggests using subgroup attack. Note that this case is in the ballpark of the parameters suggested in [1]. LBA fails in this case.

2) *Long generators ($L_1 > 40$).* With probability 90% random private key contains no peaks. The LBA is expected to work smoothly.

3) *Middle sized generators ($L_1 \in [20, 40]$).* A random private key with probability 90% contains at most two short peaks. Experiments showed that almost all peaks are conjugator-type peaks $a_i^\varepsilon a_j^\delta a_i^{-\varepsilon}$ (for some indices i, j and powers $\varepsilon, \delta = \pm 1$). Also there are a few commutator-type peaks $a_i^\varepsilon a_j^\delta a_i^{-\varepsilon} a_j^{-\delta}$.

In other ranks experiments show similar behavior with different interval values of L_1.

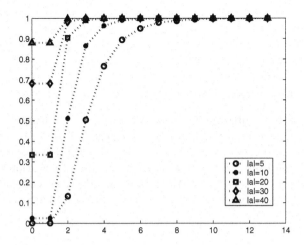

Fig. 4. Distribution of the size of maximal peaks in private keys

3   The Attack

Based on our observations from Section 2.4 on the structure of peaks we introduce a modification of the generalized length based attack which breaks the instances of AAG with middle to high lengths of generators.

The main idea behind the generalized LBA is to add elements from the corresponding subgroup to "cut" the peaks inside the private key as in the following example. Consider Alice's public tuple (a_1, a_2) from Example 1 and choose her private key to be $a_1^{-1}a_2^{-1}a_1$. Extending (a_1, a_2) with the product $a_2^{-1}a_1$ cuts the peak in Figure 2.(2) making the descend possible. Obviously any peak in the private key A can be cut by extending the tuple $\bar{a}$ with all the products of the length up to the length of the decomposition L. However, this is equivalent to breaking the system by the brute force approach. The number of such products depends exponentially on the product length L with respect to the rank of braid group. With the parameters considered in this paper the number of all such products is of order 20^{50}. Our goal is to introduce a relatively small set of short products which will eliminate most of the frequently occurring peaks.

As we discussed in Section 2.4 most of the peaks in a randomly generated word are of lengths 2 and 3, and most of them are of conjugator-type. Indeed, the expected number of conjugators $E[C_L]$, given that the factors are sampled uniformly and independently, is estimated about $1/2N_2(L - 2)$. For values $L = 50$ and $N_2 = 20$ we have $E[C_{50}] \approx 1.2$, i.e. a conjugator is expected to occur at least once. It is also easy to see that the probability of a long peak to occur in a uniform random word is very small.

Hence, it is a natural idea to extend $\bar{a}$ with all conjugators and commutators of its elements (observe that this quadratically increases the size of the tuple). In general the decision of extending the input tuple with a set of products is based on the balancing of the tradeoff between the frequency of occurrences of corresponding peaks and the increase of complexity on each iteration. In our implementation we choose to add only conjugators as they seem to be inevitable, whereas commutators as well as other types of longer peaks are very rare in the key generated uniformly randomly.

3.1 Most Significant Generator Heuristic

Adding all products of subgroup generators up to a certain length increases the size of a generating set by a polynomial with respect to the subgroup rank (N_1 or N_2). Although theoretically feasible, this introduces practical problems even in the case of small ranks. The following experimental observation can be used as a heuristic which helps to reduce the number of operations on each iteration.

Let δ_{k,ε_k} be the maximal length reduction obtained during an iteration I (see step D of Algorithm 1):

$$\delta_{k,\varepsilon_k} = \max\{\delta_{i,\varepsilon} \mid i = 1, \ldots, N_1\}.$$

The corresponding generator $a_k^{\varepsilon_k}$ is called the *most significant generator* of the iteration I. According to our experiments, the most significant generators almost always are either the correct generators, or are contained in corresponding peaks. The simple heuristic suggests to vary the tuple $\bar{a}$ on each iteration and extend it with elements which are the products containing the current most significant generator. In this case the number of operations performed during one iteration is still linear with respect to the subgroup rank N_1.

3.2 Algorithms

Based on the heuristics given above we introduce two new attacks on AAG protocol. Both procedures have the same input and output as described in Section 2.2.

The first attack is a relatively straightforward implementation of the generalized length based attack where the set of generators $\bar{a}$ is extended by adding all conjugations of the original generators.

Algorithm 4. *(Generalized LBA with conjugation)*

A. *Extend $\bar{a}$ with all conjugators:* $\bar{a} = \bar{a} \cup \{x_i x_j x_i^{-1} \mid x_i, x_j \in \bar{a}^{\pm 1}, i \neq j\}$.
B. *Run Algorithm 1 with the obtained tuple.*

The second attack uses the dynamic extension set based on the products containing the most significant generator. These products include conjugators and products of two generators from $\bar{a}$. It is possible that none of the generators a_i cause length reduction on the step D of the LBA procedure 1. In such situation we introduce all conjugators and two generator products, hoping to either cut a peak or reduce the length function approximation error.

Algorithm 5. *(LBA with dynamic set)*

A. *Initialize a set $S = \{(\overline{b}', e)\}$, where e is the identity of B_n.*
B. *If $S = \emptyset$ then output $FAIL$.*
C. *Choose a pair $(\overline{c}, x) \in S$ with a minimal $|\overline{c}|$. Remove $(\overline{c}, x)$ from S.*
D. *For each $i = 1, \ldots, N_1$, $\varepsilon = \pm 1$ compute $\delta_{i,\varepsilon} = |\overline{c}| - |\overline{c}^{a_i^\varepsilon}|$.*
E. *If $\forall i$ $\delta_{i,\varepsilon} \leq 0$ then define $\overline{a}_{ext} = \overline{a} \cup \{x_i x_j x_i^{-1}, x_i x_j, x_i^2 \mid x_i, x_j \in \overline{a}^{\pm 1}, i \neq j\}$*
F. *Else define $\overline{a}_{ext} = \overline{a} \cup \{x_j x_m x_j^{-1}, x_m x_j, x_j x_m, x_m^2 \mid x_j \in \overline{a}^{\pm 1}, m \neq j\}$, where x_m s.t. $\delta_m = \max\{\delta_{i,\varepsilon} \mid i = 1, \ldots, N_1\}$.*
G. *For all $w \in \overline{a}_{ext}$ compute $\delta_w = |\overline{c}| - |\overline{c}^w|$, if $\delta_w > 0$ add $(\overline{c}, xw)$ to S.*
H. *If $\overline{c}^w = \overline{b}$ them output xw.*
I. *Otherwise goto B.*

3.3 Experiments

We performed a series of experiments to test the heuristic approaches described in the previous sections. The following parameters were chosen: $B_n = B_{80}$, $N_1 = N_2 = 20$, $L = 50$ and parameters L_1, L_2 were varied to demonstrate the better success rate of the length based attack for instances with longer subgroup generators. There were 100 problems generated for each set of parameters.

Table 1. Success rate of the length based attack (%)

L_1, L_2	10,13	20,23	30,33	40,43
Algorithm 2	00	05	45	60
Algorithm 4	00	51	80	64
Algorithm 5	00	30	97	96

The attack was considered unsuccessful if an algorithm stopped and produced $FAIL$ or it has not terminated after 24 hours of execution. Experiments were performed on Dual 1 GHz Pentium III processors with 2GB of RAM.

The percentages of successful attacks are given in Table 1. According to the experiments Algorithms 4 and 5 almost never produce $FAIL$ indicating that the success rate could be improved by using more powerful computing or extending the termination time.

As expected, none of the attacks were successful on instances with short generators. However, keys obtained from long generators in many cases can be reconstructed successfully even using the naive best descend procedure (see Algorithm 2). The heuristics described in Section 3.1 seem to work well in cutting peaks contained in uniformly randomly generated keys, showing over 50% success rate even for instances with middle length generators.

Acknowledgments. We are grateful to the Algebraic Cryptography Center at Stevens Institute of Technology for support of our research. Also, we would like to thank anonymous reviewers for their valuable comments and suggestions on the paper.

References

1. I. Anshel, M. Anshel, D. Goldfeld, *An algebraic method for public-key cryptography*, Math. Res. Lett. **6** (1999), 287–291.
2. J. S. Birman, *Braids, links and mapping class groups*, Ann. Math. Studies **82**, Princeton Univ. Press, 1974.
3. CRyptography And Groups (CRAG), C++ and Python Library for computations in groups and group based cryptography, available at http://www.acc. stevens.edu/downloads.php.
4. P.Dehornoy, *A fast method for comparing braids*, Advances in math. 125, (1997), 200-235.
5. D. B. A. Epstein, J. W. Cannon, D. F. Holt, S. V. F. Levy, M. S. Paterson, W. P. Thurston, *Word processing in groups.* Jones and Bartlett Publishers, Boston, MA, 1992.
6. D. Garber, S. Kaplan, M. Teicher, B. Tsaban, U. Vishne, "Length-based conjugacy search in the Braid group", http://arxiv.org/abs/math.GR/0209267.
7. D. Hofheinz, R. Steinwandt. *A Practical Attack on Some Braid Group Based Cryptographic Primitives.* In Public Key Cryptography, 6th International Workshop on Practice and Theory in Public Key Cryptography, PKC 2003 Proceedings, Y.G. Desmedt, ed., vol. 2567 of Lecture Notes in Computer Science, pp. 187-198, Springer, 2002.
8. J. Hughes, "A Linear Algebraic Attack on the AAFG1 Braid Group Cryptosystem", ACISP 2002, Lecture Notes in Computer Science, vol. 2384, (2002), 176–189.
9. J. Hughes, A. Tannenbaum, *Length-based attacks for certain group based encryption rewriting systems.* In: Workshop SECI02 Securitè de la Communication sur Intenet, September 2002, Tunis, Tunisia.
10. K. H. Ko, S. J. Lee, J. H. Cheon, J. W. Han, J. Kang, C. Park, *New public-key cryptosystem using braid groups.* In: Advances in cryptology – CRYPTO 2000 (Santa Barbara, CA), 166–183 (Lecture Notes Comp. Sc., vol. 1880) Berlin Heidelberg New York Tokyo: Springer 2000.
11. S. J. Lee, E. Lee, *Potential Weaknesses of the Commutator Key Agreement protocol Based on Braid Groups.* In: Advances in cryptology – Eurocrypt 2002, 14-28 (Lecture Notes Comp. Sc., vol. 2332) Berlin Heidelberg New York Tokyo: Springer 2002.
12. K. A. Mihailova, "The occurrence problem for free products of groups", Math USSR-Sbornik 70, (1966), 241-251.
13. A. G. Myasnikov, V. Shpilrain, A. Ushakov. *A practical attack on some braid group based cryptographic protocols.* In CRYPTO 2005, Lecture Notes Comp. Sc. 3621 (2005), 86-96.
14. A. G. Myasnikov, V. Shpilrain, A. Ushakov. *Random subgroups of braid groups: an approach to cryptanalysis of a braid group based cryptographic protocol.* In PKC 2006, Lecture Notes Comp. Sc. 3958 (2006), 302-314.
15. M. Paterson, A. Razborov, *The set of minimal braids in co-NP-complete* J. Algorithms, **12** (1991), 393-408.
16. V. Shpilrain and A. Ushakov, *The conjugacy search problem in public key cryptography: unnecessary and insufficient*, Applicable Algebra in Engineering, Communication and Computing, to appear. http://eprint.iacr.org/2004/321/
17. A. Vershik, S. Nechaev, R. Bikbov. *Statistical properties of braid groups in locally free approximation.* In Communications in Mathematical Physics, vol. 212, 2000, pp. 469–501.

New Chosen-Ciphertext Attacks on NTRU

Nicolas Gama[1] and Phong Q. Nguyen[2]

[1] École normale supérieure, DI, 45 rue d'Ulm, 75005 Paris, France
nicolas.gama@ens.fr
[2] CNRS/École normale supérieure, DI, 45 rue d'Ulm, 75005 Paris, France
http://www.di.ens.fr/~pnguyen

Abstract. We present new and efficient key-recovery chosen-ciphertext attacks on NTRUENCRYPT. Our attacks are somewhat intermediate between chosen-ciphertext attacks on NTRUENCRYPT previously published at CRYPTO '00 and CRYPTO '03. Namely, the attacks only work in the presence of decryption failures; we only submit valid ciphertexts to the decryption oracle, where the plaintexts are chosen uniformly at random; and the number of oracle queries is small. Interestingly, our attacks can also be interpreted from a provable security point of view: in practice, if one had access to a NTRUENCRYPT decryption oracle such that the parameter set allows decryption failures, then one could recover the secret key. For instance, for the initial NTRU-1998 parameter sets, the output of the decryption oracle on a single decryption failure is enough to recover the secret key.

1 Introduction

NTRU [8] is one of the fastest public-key cryptosystems known, offering both encryption (under the name NTRUENCRYPT) and digital signatures (under the name NTRUSIGN [7]) using inexpensive operations on polynomials with small coefficients. Besides efficiency, another interesting feature of NTRU compared to traditional public-key cryptosystems based on factoring or discrete logarithm is its potential resistance to quantum computers: no efficient quantum algorithm is known for the NP-hard lattice problems related to the security of NTRU. The security and insecurity of NTRU primitives has been an active research topic in the past 10 years, and NTRU is now being considered by the *IEEE P1363.1* standards [12].

While cryptanalysis has been rather successful on NTRU signatures (the basic version of NTRUSIGN has recently been broken in [14], and all the versions of its ancestor NSS were successfully attacked [4,5]), it can be argued that no significant weakness has ever been found on NTRU encryption. To date, the most dangerous attacks on NTRUENCRYPT are perhaps key-recovery chosen-ciphertext attacks. The first key-recovery chosen-ciphertext attacks were found by Jaulmes and Joux [13] at CRYPTO '00, and used few oracle queries. However, the attacks used invalid ciphertexts of very special shape, and do not seem to work for all NTRU instantiations. In particular, they can easily be thwarted by an appropriate padding scheme (as is often the case in public-key encryption),

T. Okamoto and X. Wang (Eds.): PKC 2007, LNCS 4450, pp. 89–106, 2007.

which is anyway necessary to achieve strong security notions. At CRYPTO '03, Howgrave-Graham et al. [11] realized that an unusual property of NTRUEN-CRYPT known as *decryption failure* gave rise to much more powerful chosen-ciphertext attacks. Until the publication of [11] (and even [10]), all parameter sets proposed by NTRU allowed decryption failures: the ciphertext of a randomly chosen message could fail to decrypt correctly when using the NTRU decryption algorithm. Although the probability of decryption failures was small, it was significant enough (ranging from 2^{-12} to 2^{-40}) not to be ignored in practice: an attacker might realistically collect decryption failures. The most powerful chosen-ciphertext attack of [11] then allowed to attack any instantiation of NTRU, independently of the padding scheme, and using only a weak decryption oracle which asserts if a given (valid) ciphertext failed to decrypt or not. However, this attack required a large number of decryption failures (estimated to be about a million by [11]), and had not been fully implemented. In particular, the attack uses in the final stage a sophisticated algorithm by Gentry and Szydlo [5] (designed to attack the NSS signature scheme), which is polynomial time, but has to the best of our knowledge not been fully implemented.

Our results. In this paper, we present new and efficient chosen-ciphertext attacks on NTRUENCRYPT. Our attacks are somewhat intermediate between the attacks of Jaulmes and Joux [13], and those of Howgrave-Graham et al. [11]. Like [11], the attacks are based on decryption failures and only query the decryption oracle on valid ciphertexts. However, unlike [11], we do not only ask whether a given (valid) ciphertext fails to decrypt, we ask for the full output of the NTRU decryption algorithm on that (valid) ciphertext, like in an usual chosen-ciphertext attack: when there is a decryption failure, this will provide additional information. As a result, the number of decryption failures required to make the attack successful is much lower than in [11], which makes it possible to fully implement the attack in practice and check its efficiency. For instance, for the initial NTRU-1998 parameter sets, a decryption query on a single decryption failure is enough to recover the private key. For more recent parameter sets, the number of required decryption failures increases but is at most a few hundreds. The efficiency of our attacks seems to confirm the importance of removing decryption failures in NTRUENCRYPT, as was first suggested in [11]: it should be noted that the latest version [10] of NTRUENCRYPT modifies the NTRU parameters so that no decryption failure can ever occur. Furthermore, because we query the decryption oracle on random ciphertexts of messages uniformly chosen at random, our attacks can also be interpreted from a security point of view. If one could simulate the NTRU decryption algorithm, one would be able to recover the NTRU secret key in practice.

Road map. The paper is organized as follows. In Section 2, we provide background on NTRUENCRYPT, and we introduce the model of our attacks. In Section 3, we study the probability distributions of the coefficients of the polynomials used during decryption, and we analyze the information obtained in the presence of decryption failures. In Section 4, we derive a first chosen-ciphertext attack against the initial instantiation NTRU-1998 of NTRUENCRYPT, which can recover the secret key using a single decryption failure. Finally, in Section 5, we present a general chosen-ciphertext attack against all instantiations of NTRU allowing decryption failures. It is perhaps worth noting that our attacks make no use of lattices.

2   Background

2.1   Definitions and Notation

NTRUENCRYPT operations take place in the quotient ring of polynomials $\mathcal{P} = \mathbb{Z}[X]/(X^N - 1)$, where N is an integer. If $f(X)$ is a polynomial in $\mathcal{P}$, for all $k \in [0, N-1]$, f_k denotes the coefficient of X^k and for all $x \in \mathbb{C}$, $f(x)$ represents the evaluation of f at x. The convolution product $h = f * g$ of two polynomials f and g in $\mathcal{P}$ is given by $h_k = \sum_{i+j \equiv k \bmod N} f_i \cdot g_j$. Several different measures of the size of a polynomial will be useful. We define the *norm* of a polynomial f in the usual way, as the square root of the sum of the squares of its coefficients: $\|f\| = \left(\sum_{i=0}^{N-1} f_i^2 \right)^{1/2}$. We also define the *"standard deviation"* of a polynomial f as $\sigma(f) = \left(\sum_{i=1}^{N} \left(f_i - \frac{f(1)}{N} \right)^2 \right)^{1/2}$. Note that $\|f\| = \sigma(f)$ if the average value $\frac{f(1)}{N}$ of the coefficients of the polynomial is equal to zero.

2.2   The NTRU Encryption Scheme

The NTRU [8] cryptosystem has many possible instantiations. It uses a set of parameters whose values will be given later:

- An integer N. This fundamental parameter in NTRUENCRYPT is taken to be prime to prevent attacks due to Gentry [3], and sufficiently large to prevent lattice attacks.
- Two relatively prime integers p and q, or alternatively the polynomial $p = X + 2$ and a prime number q (which does not divide $2^N + 1$), so that the elements p and q generate prime ideals in $\mathcal{P}$. Standard practice is to take q to be close to a power of 2 between $N/2$ and N, and p to be either the integer 2, 3 or the polynomial $2 + X$ [1,2].
- Four subsets $\mathcal{L}_f, \mathcal{L}_g, \mathcal{L}_r, \mathcal{L}_m$ of $\mathcal{P}$ used for key generation and encryption. The polynomials in all these subsets have very small coefficients and may further be sparse.
- A bijection ψ between $\mathcal{L}_m \bmod p$ and $\mathcal{L}_m$. The set of plaintexts is $\mathcal{L}_m$.

The key generation, encryption and decryption primitives are as follows:

Key generation
1: Choose $f \in \mathcal{L}_f$ and $g \in \mathcal{L}_g$ uniformly at random such that f is invertible in $\mathcal{P}$ modulo q and modulo p.
2: Set $F_q = f^{-1} \bmod q$ and $F_p = f^{-1} \bmod p$.
3: The private key is (f, F_p).
4: The public key is $H = p \cdot g * F_q \bmod q$.

Note that in NTRUENCRYPT, the polynomial g is not necessary for decryption, and therefore is not included in the private key. However, g could easily be deduced from f thanks to $H * f = p \cdot g \bmod q$.

Encryption. The encryption algorithm $\mathfrak{E}$ is probabilistic.

Input: A message $m \in \mathcal{L}_m$, and a public key H.
Output: A ciphertext $e \in \mathfrak{E}(m)$.
  1: Select $r \in \mathcal{L}_r$ uniformly at random.
  2: **return** $e = r * H + m \bmod q$.

To achieve strong security notions, NTRU implementations additionally use paddings: the message m is preprocessed and r might depend on m and hash functions. In this paper, for any $m \in \mathcal{L}_m$ we denote by $\mathfrak{E}(m)$ the set of all possible ciphertexts of the plaintext m, and by $\mathfrak{E}(\mathcal{L}_m)$ their union over all plaintexts m. These sets take possible paddings into account, hence $\mathfrak{E}(\mathcal{L}_m)$ is also the set of all validly generated ciphertexts.

Decryption. The decryption algorithm $\mathfrak{D}$ provided by NTRU is very efficient, but may not work correctly on all inputs, depending on the parameter set.

Input: A ciphertext $e \in \mathfrak{E}(\mathcal{L}_m)$ and a private key (f, F_p).
Output: A plaintext $\mathfrak{D}(e) = m \in \mathcal{L}_m$.
  1: Compute $a \bmod q = e * f \bmod q$.
  2: Using a centering procedure, try to recover the integer polynomial $a = p \cdot r * g + f * m \in \mathcal{P}$ from $a \bmod q$.
  3: Compute $m \bmod p = a * F_p \bmod p$.
  4: **return** The plaintext $m = \psi(m \bmod p)$.

Note that the operations performed by the decryption algorithm could in theory be applied to any polynomial in $\mathcal{P} \bmod q$, not only ciphertexts in $\mathfrak{E}(\mathcal{L}_m)$, and this would still output a polynomial in $\mathcal{L}_m$. The chosen-ciphertext attacks of [13] relied on this extra-functionality: they used invalid ciphertexts which do not belong to $\mathfrak{E}(\mathcal{L}_m)$.

   For all the NTRU parameter sets proposed until 2005 [10], the centering procedure used in Step 2 could fail to recover a. Thus, there may exist valid ciphertexts $e \in \mathfrak{E}(m)$ whose decryption $\mathfrak{D}(e)$ is not equal to m. Such events have been called *decryption failures* in [11]. Note that the decryption algorithm could also perform additional checks: for instance, it can extract the random polynomial r used by $\mathfrak{E}$ from the formula $r * H = (e - \mathfrak{D}(e)) \bmod q$, thanks to the notion of pseudo-inverse (see [16]). Then, it can check whether r is really in $\mathcal{L}_r$, or whether the potential paddings requirements are met. In particular, we have a plaintext-checking oracle: given a ciphertext and a plaintext, we can check whether the ciphertext corresponds to the plaintext.

2.3   Instantiations of NTRU

One difficulty with analyzing NTRU is the significant number of variants. Different choices of parameters can completely transform the security of NTRU: an attack against a particular instantiation of NTRU may not work against other instantiations. In this section, we recall the three main instantiations of NTRU which have been proposed in the past eight years.

NTRU-1998. In the initial instantiation of NTRU [8], p is equal to 3 and q is a power of 2 (for example $q = 128$). The subset $\mathcal{L}_m$ is the set of ternary polynomials with coefficients in $\{-1, 0, 1\}$, and the bijection ψ between $\mathcal{L}_m \bmod p$ and $\mathcal{L}_m$ is defined by selecting the representative $-1, 0$ or 1 of each coefficient mod 3. The set $\mathcal{L}_f$ is defined as $\mathcal{T}(d_f, d_f - 1)$ where $\mathcal{T}(i, j)$ is the subset of ternary polynomials containing exactly i times 1 and j times -1. Finally, $\mathcal{L}_g = \mathcal{T}(d_g, d_g)$ and $\mathcal{L}_r = \mathcal{T}(d_r, d_r)$. Naturally, one drawback with this instantiation is the conversion between binary messages and their ternary representation in $\mathcal{L}_m$. As an example, the parameters $N = 263$, $q = 128$, $d_f = 50$, $d_g = 24$ and $d_r = 16$ were recommended for high security. Each parameter set in [8] leads to a decryption failure every 2^{15} encryptions of random messages, experimentally.

NTRU-2001. In the standards [1,2], a new instantiation is proposed, where p is the polynomial $X + 2$ and q is a prime number. The subset $\mathcal{L}_m$ is the set of binary polynomials with coefficients in $\{0, 1\}$, and $\mathcal{L}_f$ is the subset of polynomials of the form $1 + p * F$ with $F \in \mathcal{B}(d_F)$, where $\mathcal{B}(d_F)$ denotes the set of binary polynomials with exactly d_F coefficients equal to 1. The other subsets are $\mathcal{L}_g = \mathcal{B}(d_g)$ and $\mathcal{L}_r = \mathcal{B}(d_r)$. The bijection ψ between a plaintext m and its representative modulo $X + 2$ (which is the evaluation at $X = -2$) is non-trivial. Mathematically, the function ψ computes the binary decomposition $\sum_{i=0}^{N-1} \nu_i 2^i$ of $m(-2)$, and identifies it with the polynomial $\sum_{i=0}^{N-1} \nu_i X^i \in \mathcal{L}_m$. More details for an efficient implementation are given in [9]. The main advantage of having the private key f of the form $1 + p * F$ is that the inverse F_p modulo p is equal to 1, so the final multiplication by F_p in the decryption process disappears. The average number of encryptions of random messages leading to a decryption failure ranges from 2^{12} to 2^{25}, depending on the parameter set [1,2]. (see [11] for more information).

NTRU-2005. In the last standard [10], the polynomial $p = X + 2$ disappears and is replaced by the integer $p = 2$. Furthermore, the use of product-form polynomials (introduced in [9]) is recommended as a replacement of binary polynomials: so f has the form $1 + p \cdot F$ with $F \in \mathcal{X}(d_f)$, which means that $F = f_1 * f_2 + f_3$ with each $f_1, f_2, f_3 \in \mathcal{B}(d_f)$. The other subsets are $\mathcal{L}_g = \mathcal{B}(N/2)$, $\mathcal{L}_r = \mathcal{X}(d_r)$ and $\mathcal{L}_m$ is the set of binary polynomials. Generally, d_F and d_r are equal and are very small (*e.g.* between $N/25$ and $N/20$). More importantly, since it had been discovered [11] that decryption failures could be a threat, the prime number q has been multiplied by a factor of at least 2 so that no decryption failure can ever happen: one drawback is that the resistance to lattice attacks is weakened. But it is interesting to analyze what would happen if q had the same size as in previous instantiations. In this case, the problem of finding the private key from the public key seems as hard as in previous instantiations. But the proportion of decryption failures would also be the same as in the previous instantiations.

In this paper, we want to analyze attacks based on decryption failures, so when we refer to NTRU-2005, we actually mean a modified version with a smaller q.

2.4   The Attack Model, and Comparison with Previous Attacks

In a chosen-ciphertext attack, a decryption oracle is given to an attacker. As a precomputation, the attacker can submit as many ciphertexts as he wants to the oracle. Then using the collected information, he must either recover a private key or be able to decrypt a challenge ciphertext. For NTRU, the notion of decryption oracle is ambiguous because of decryption failures. Here, like [11], by decryption oracle, we do not mean an ideal algorithm which would extract m from a ciphertext in $\mathfrak{E}(m)$ without any failure, but the decryption algorithm $\mathfrak{D}$ provided by NTRU. In the following, we only consider key-recovery chosen-ciphertext attacks.

The majority of previous chosen-ciphertext attacks against NTRU work by running the algorithm $\mathfrak{D}$ on special polynomials in $\mathcal{P} \bmod q$, which are generally not valid ciphertexts in $\mathfrak{E}(\mathcal{L}_m)$. Following our terminology, these attacks do not use decryption failures. For example, the article of Jaulmes and Joux at CRYPTO'00 [13] presents two chosen-ciphertext attacks on NTRU-1998. By sending roughly ten special polynomials to the oracle, an attacker recovers the product of the key F_p and a low hamming-weight polynomial. After an exhaustive search which takes a couple of minutes for the highest security parameters, the attacker recovers F_p and deduces the private key f. Note that the bijection between F_p and f only exists in the NTRU-1998 instantiation.

The second attack of [13] queries the decryption oracle N times on very close inputs. Again, the input polynomials are in general not validly generated ciphertexts in $\mathfrak{E}(\mathcal{L}_m)$. If f is binary or ternary, the output of the decryption oracle then discloses the value and the position of many coefficients of f. Thus, with less than a thousand calls to the decryption oracle, the private key f is fully recovered. This attack can be rewritten and remains valid for NTRU-2001, but fails on NTRU-2005, when f is in product form.

Other papers, like Han *et al.*'s paper [6], present chosen-ciphertext attacks with the assumption that the user has power on m and r, which is not compatible with the strongest paddings.

The first paper to introduce and use decryption failures in a chosen-ciphertext attack is Howgrave-Graham *et al.*'s paper [11] at CRYPTO'03, where the authors present (among others) a key-recovery chosen-ciphertext attack against NTRU-2001 working with any padding scheme. The oracle is weak: it only accepts valid ciphertexts in $\mathfrak{E}(\mathcal{L}_m)$ and only indicates whether or not there is a decryption failure. The authors of [11] claim that if they are given a million decryption failures, they can recover the polynomial $X^N f(X) f(\frac{1}{X})$, and then recover the private key thanks to an algorithm of Gentry and Szydlo [5], which was introduced to break a former version of NTRU signatures. The main advantage of this attack is that since all messages are validly generated, it is compatible with any padding, including the very restrictive ones. However, the number 1,000,000 is only a heuristic estimate, and the algorithm of Gentry and Szydlo [5] recovering

f from $X^N f(X) f(\frac{1}{X})$ is proved polynomial time, but has to our knowledge not yet been fully implemented in practice.

In this paper, we also use decryption failures. Our attack model is intermediate between the restrictive chosen-ciphertext attack of Jaulmes and Joux [13], and the realistic model in Howgrave-Graham et al.'s attack [11]. The oracle is only queried during the search for decryption failures, which is performed by Algorithm 1. With this description, we clearly see that the decryption oracle is

---

Algorithm 1. Find a random decryption failure

Input: A NTRU parameter set, a public key H and the decryption oracle $\mathfrak{D}$.
Output: A decryption failure as (m, r, m') where $\mathfrak{D}(m + r * H) = m' \neq m$.
1: **repeat**
2:     Generate a random message $m \in \mathcal{L}_m$ and encrypt it with $\mathfrak{E}$ to obtain a valid ciphertext e.
3:     Remember (or recover) the random polynomial r used by $\mathfrak{E}$.
4:     Submit the ciphertext e to the decryption oracle $\mathfrak{D}$.
5: **until** there is a decryption failure $(m' = \mathfrak{D}(e) \neq m)$
6: **return** the triplet (m, r, m').

---

only used on validly generated ciphertexts. Furthermore, these ciphertexts are not even chosen by the attacker, but are randomly generated. For these reasons, the attacker is less powerful than in Jaulmes and Joux' attack [13]. However, the attacker has access to the output m', which gives more information than in Howgrave-Graham et al.'s attack [11]. We will see in the next sections the number of decryption failures which is necessary to recover the private key.

3   Analysis of Decryption Failures

3.1   The Decryption Process

In Section 2.2, we only gave a sketch of the decryption primitive. In this section, we give a detailed implementation (see Algorithm 2), in order to explain decryption failures. In the first step of the decryption algorithm $\mathfrak{D}$, when calculating $a \bmod q = f * e \bmod q$, one actually computes

$$a \bmod q = f * e = f * (r * h + m) = p \cdot r * g + f * m \bmod q$$

The polynomials r, g, f and m have very small coefficients, so heuristically the coefficients of the integer polynomial $a = p \cdot r * g + f * m$ satisfy:

$$\forall i \in [0..N-1], \ a_i \in \left[\frac{a(1)}{N} - \frac{q}{2}; \frac{a(1)}{N} + \frac{q}{2} \right[. \tag{1}$$

Note that all the parameter sets of NTRU given in Section 2.3 make it possible to compute $\frac{a(1)}{N}$ without knowing r or m. If Condition (1) holds, a may be recovered exactly from $a \bmod q$ in the ring $\mathcal{P}$ (using Step 9 of Algorithm 2).

Algorithm 2. Decryption oracle $\mathfrak{D}$

Input: A validly generated ciphertext e and the instantiation of NTRU (and a hidden private key (p, f, F_p)).

Output: The decryption of e (which might be incorrect).

1: compute $a \bmod q = f * e \bmod q$.
2: **if** instantiation=NTRU-1998 **then**
3:     Select the representative $a_{\text{est}} \in \mathcal{P}$ of $a \bmod q$ which has all its coefficients in $[-\frac{q}{2}; \frac{q}{2}[$.
4: **else**
5:     Compute $r1 = r(1), f1 = f(1)$, and $g1 = g(1)$ using the definition of $\mathcal{L}_r, \mathcal{L}_f$ and $\mathcal{L}_g$.
6:     Compute $m(1) \bmod q = e(1) - r1 * H(1) \bmod q$,
7:     Choose $m1$ in $[\frac{N}{2} - \frac{q}{2}; \frac{N}{2} + \frac{q}{2}[$ so that $m1 \equiv m(1) \bmod q$.
8:     Compute $a1 = p \cdot r1 \cdot g1 + f1 \cdot m1$.
9:     Select the representative $a_{\text{est}} \in \mathcal{P}$ of $a \bmod q$ which has all its coefficients in $[\frac{a1}{N} - \frac{q}{2}; \frac{a1}{N} + \frac{q}{2}[$
10: **end if**
11: Compute $m' = a_{\text{est}} * F_p \bmod p$.
12: **return** $\psi(m')$.

In the NTRU-1998 instantiation, the mean value $\frac{a(1)}{N}$ of the coefficients of a is equal to $\frac{m(1)}{N}$, and is therefore between -1 and 1. For this reason, it is equivalent to choose every coefficient of a in $[-\frac{q}{2}; \frac{q}{2}[$ at Step 3. Finally $a \bmod p$ is equal to $f * m \bmod p$ and the multiplication by F_p at Step 11 recovers $m \bmod p$, and therefore the plaintext m.

Decryption only works if the condition (1) is fulfilled. Unfortunately, this condition does not always hold: depending on the choice of $\mathcal{L}_m$ and $\mathcal{L}_r$, it may happen for some rare m and r, that some coefficients of a lie outside the centering range. In this case, the output $m' = \mathfrak{D}(e)$ will (almost always) differ from the original plaintext m. These events are the so-called *decryption failures* [11], which will be reused in this paper to construct key-recovery attacks on NTRUENCRYPT.

We now analyze the probability distribution of the coefficients of a in the particular case of a decryption failure. In order to simplify Condition (1), it is possible to translate the polynomials so that the average value of their coefficients is always zero. We say that a polynomial a is zero-centered if $a(1) = 0$, where $a(1)$ is the evaluation of the polynomial at 1, that is, the sum of the coefficients of a. Given any polynomial in $\mathcal{P}$ or $\mathcal{R}$, we can recenter this polynomial by subtracting an appropriate multiple of the polynomial $(1 + X + \cdots + X^{N-1})$, as shown in the following elementary lemma:

Lemma 1. *The following function is an algebra homomorphism:*

$$\mathbb{R}[X]/\left(X^N - 1\right) \to \mathbb{R}[X]/\left(X^N - 1\right)$$

$$A \to \check{A} = A - \frac{A(1)}{N}(1 + X + \cdots + X^{N-1})$$

Then Condition (1) can be rewritten as: there is a decryption failure if and only if the polynomial $\breve{a} = p \cdot \breve{r} * \breve{g} + \breve{f} * \breve{m}$ satisfy:

$$\exists i \in [0..N-1], \ |\breve{a}_i| > \frac{q}{2}. \tag{2}$$

3.2 Probability Assumptions

In the following, we will often need to assume that certain objects are random. More precisely, for any deterministic function φ from $\mathcal{L}_m \times \mathcal{L}_r$ (e.g. the encryption function $(m, r) \rightarrow m + r * H$ or the function $(m, r) \rightarrow p \cdot r * g + f * m$ implicitly used in the decryption process), we say that a polynomial $z = \varphi(m, r)$ is randomly chosen in the image of φ if m and r are uniformly and independently chosen in the finite subsets $\mathcal{L}_m$ and $\mathcal{L}_r$. Here, we focus on the particular case of the centered polynomials $\breve{a}$, which are computed from m and r with the deterministic formula $\breve{a} = p \cdot \breve{r} * \breve{g} + \breve{f} * \breve{m}$. In order to analyze the distribution of their coefficients, we need to make two simplifying assumptions:

Assumption 1. *If $z \in \mathcal{P}$ is a binary or ternary polynomial uniformly chosen at random, then the coefficients of the zero-centered polynomial $\breve{z}$ are all independent.*

Assumption 2. *If a and b are randomly and independently drawn from finite sets of zero-centered polynomials and if their coefficients are all independent, then the coefficients of the product $c = a * b$ are all independent.*

These assumptions are rather strong. However, one can hope that it is not that far from the reality, due to the following: the average value of the coefficients of a zero-centered polynomial is constant and equal to zero, so when a coefficient is bigger than expected, the others will tend to be smaller. For this reason, there is a small anti-correlation between different coefficients: the paper [17] shows a correlation $\text{Corr}(c_i, c_j) = -\frac{1}{N-1}$ if i and j are distinct indexes. There is a small inaccuracy due to this anti-correlation, but the effect is very small when N grows. Furthermore, we will see that experimentally, if one coefficient has not the expected size, then the others behave correctly. Thus the effect of the anti-correlation is in fact very limited.

3.3 Shape of Decryption Failures

In the decryption algorithm $\mathfrak{D}$, since r and m are randomly chosen independently of the keys f and g, the coefficients of the polynomial $\breve{a}$ are assumed to be independent by Assumptions 1 and 2. As we saw in Section 3.1, a decryption failure only occurs if Condition (2) holds. In this case, at least one coefficient of the polynomial $\breve{a} = p \cdot \breve{g}\breve{r} + \breve{f}\breve{m}$ is outside the range $[-\frac{q}{2}; \frac{q}{2}[$. Using these assumptions, we deduce two heuristics:

Heuristic 1. *In case of a decryption failure, then with extremely high probability, there is exactly one coefficient $\breve{a}_k$ of $\breve{a}$ which is outside $[-\frac{q}{2}; \frac{q}{2}[$*

Explanation. We denote by p_e the probability to choose (r, m) leading to a decryption failure. Because of the independence assumption, the probability for one coefficient of $\breve{a}$ to be outside the range $[-\frac{q}{2}; \frac{q}{2}[$ is $p_a = 1 - (1 - p_e)^{\frac{1}{N}} \approx \frac{1}{N} p_e$. The probability that exactly one coefficient of $\breve{a}$ is too big, is $p_{one} = \binom{N}{1} \cdot p_a (1 - p_a)^{N-1} \approx p_e(1 - \frac{N-1}{N} p_e)$. Thus in case of a decryption error, the probability that only one coefficient of $\breve{a}$ is too big is $p_{one}/p_e \approx (1 - \frac{N-1}{N} p_e)$. Since the probability of decryption failure p_e is always very small, the last probability is almost equal to 1. $\square$

When a decryption failure occurs, all the coefficients except one are in the correct interval. The second heuristic guesses the value of this *overflowing coefficient*.

Heuristic 2. *In case of a decryption failure, the overflowing coefficient of $\breve{a}_k$ defined by Condition (2) is very close to $\pm \frac{q}{2}$. More precisely, for standard NTRU parameters, we expect that $\breve{a}_k = \pm \left(\frac{q}{2} + \varepsilon \right)$ where $\varepsilon \leq 5$.*

Explanation. The distribution of a coefficient $\breve{a}_k$ should be a discrete hypergeometric distribution whose mean is 0, and whose standard deviation is smaller than $\frac{q}{4}$. If so, it would decrease much faster than a geometric distribution for the rare values greater than $\frac{q}{2}$. Then the expectation of the value of the overflowing coefficient of $\breve{a}$ would be very close to $\frac{q}{2}$. $\square$

3.4   Experiments

To check the validity of our heuristics, we performed experiments on the main NTRU instantiations: NTRU-1998, NTRU-2001 and the slightly modified version of NTRU-2005 seen in Section 2.3. We obtained approximately one decryption failure every 25,000 messages, and we collected about 4,000 decryption failures for each parameter set. For every decryption failure, we obtained exactly one overflowing coefficient in $\breve{a}$, and in more than 90% of the cases, the absolute value of this coefficient was lower than $\frac{q}{2} + 5$. So the two heuristics seem to be verified in practice.

However, in our experiments, the distribution of overflowing coefficients in case of a decryption failure does not decrease as fast as was announced in the explanation of Heuristic 2 (see Figure 1). Heuristic 2 is nevertheless true for every parameter set tested, but this is only an experimental fact.

The two graphs in Figure 1 represent the experimental distribution of the coefficients of a random polynomial $\breve{a} = p \cdot \breve{r} * \breve{g} + \breve{f} * \breve{m}$ satisfying Condition (2). The black bars represent the distribution of the overflowing coefficient (whose absolute value is greater than $\frac{q}{2}$), and the grey boxes represent the distribution of the other coefficients. The two curves are based on the NTRU-2005 instantiation, the first one with $p = 2, q = 67, N = 127$ and binary polynomials, and the second one with $p = 2, q = 67, N = 127$ and product-form polynomials. When the polynomial $\breve{a}$ contains an overflowing coefficient, there exists a rotation of $\breve{m}$ (resp. $\breve{r}$) which is either positively or negatively correlated with the key $\breve{f}$ (resp. $p \cdot \breve{g}$), depending on whether the overflowing coefficient is positive or negative

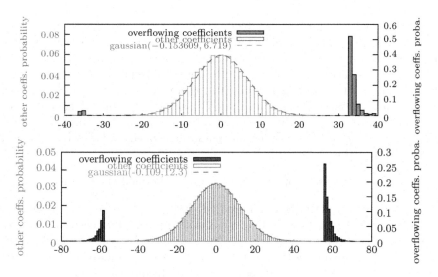

Fig. 1. Experimental densities

(see Section 5). In these two particular examples, there are more positive correlations, but this is not the general case.

4   A New Chosen-Ciphertext Attack Against NTRU-1998

We will now describe chosen-ciphertext attacks on NTRU which only require few decryption failures to recover the private key. In this section, we consider the special case of NTRU-1998. The first attack uses the fact that a single decryption failure is enough to recover F_p up to a shift. It turns out that in NTRU-1998, the choice of $p = 3$ and f a ternary polynomial makes it possible to recover f from $f \bmod p$ or $F_p \bmod p$. Thus, one can recover a circular shift of the private key f in the quotient ring $\mathcal{P}$, which is enough to decrypt. The attack is summarized in Algorithm 3.

Algorithm 3. A key-recovery chosen-ciphertext attack on NTRU-1998

Input: A public key H of NTRU-1998.
Output: A private key (f, F_p).
1: Find a decryption failure (m, r, m') using Algorithm 1.
2: compute $F'_p \leftarrow (m' - m) \bmod p$ **where** $p = 3$.
3: $f' \leftarrow F_p^{-1} \bmod p$ (chose the coefficients of f' in $\{-1, 0, 1\}$.
4: **if** $g' = (f' * H * p^{-1}) \bmod q \notin \mathcal{L}_g$ **restart;**.
5: **return** (f', F'_p).

4.1   Description of the Attack

The parameters sets of [8] give rise to a decryption failure every 25,000 encryptions, independently of the security level. Thus, after say 50,000 calls to the decryption oracle, we may reasonably assume that we were able to find a message $m \in \mathcal{L}_m$ and a blinding polynomial $r \in \mathcal{L}_r$ leading to a decryption failure, and we know the polynomial $m' \neq m$ returned by the decryption oracle. Then if Heuristic 1 is satisfied, there is exactly one coefficient a_k of $a = prg + fm$ which is not in the centering range. Thus, there exists an integer $\alpha \in \mathbb{Z}$ such that $a - \alpha q X^k$ satisfies Condition (1), and it is precisely this polynomial which is computed instead of a during the decryption algorithm. In the last step of the decryption, $a - \alpha q \cdot X^k$ is taken modulo p and multiplied by F_p, so the incorrect plaintext returned is:

$$m' = F_p * (fm - \alpha q \cdot X^k) \bmod p = m - (\alpha q \bmod p) \cdot X^k * F_p.$$

Since there was a decryption failure and since $p = 3$, we are sure that $\alpha' = \alpha q \bmod p$ is equal to ± 1. Therefore, by considering the difference $m - m'$, we recover a rotation (up to a sign) $F'_p = \alpha' X^k * F_p$ of the polynomial F_p from the private key. It is then easy to invert $F'_p \bmod p$ in order to find the second part of the key $f' = \alpha' X^{N-k} * f$. As we saw at the beginning of the section, the computed polynomials (f', F'_p) form a secret key equivalent to (f, F_p), so it is not necessary to find the value of k.

4.2   Experiments

We have implemented the attack described by Algorithm 3. In practice, the first decryption failure is found before 40,000 calls to the oracle $\mathfrak{D}$. As seen previously, the probability for (f', F'_p) computed in steps 2 and 3 to be a valid private key is higher than $1 - p_e \approx \frac{24999}{25000}$. In this case, the polynomial g' computed in step 4 is a rotation of g, and the algorithm ends. We chose 4 keys at random in each parameter set of [8], and we collected 50 decryption failures per key. Instead of stopping the execution once a circular shift of the key had been found, we ran the attack on all the decryption failures obtained on the NTRU-1998 instantiation. Each one disclosed a rotation (up to a sign) of the private key, which is an equivalent private key.

5   A General Attack Against All NTRU Instantiations

The attack on NTRU-1998 seen in the last section cannot be applied to more recent instantiations of NTRU. Indeed, in the original implementation of NTRU, the choice of $p = 3$ and a ternary key f made it possible to recover entirely f from F_p. But in recent optimizations, the choice of $f = 1 + p \cdot F$ implies that F_p is always equal to 1, and does not leak any information about f. However, it is still possible to construct a key-recovery algorithm, using this time a few hundreds of decryption failures. Our attack builds on [11], where it was noticed that each decryption failure gave rise to an approximation of an (unknown) rotation of f and g. Here, we further notice that the full output of the decryption oracle enables us to find out which rotation it is. In other words, the output of the oracle on each decryption failure discloses two polynomials, which have a majority of coefficients in common with the secret keys f and g (without any rotation). Unfortunately, the approximation provided by the decryption oracle does not reveal the exact position of the correct coefficients. In this attack, we therefore average many approximations of f deduced from independent decryption failures, in order to compute a more accurate approximation, until f can be recovered by rounding. The attack will be described with p being an integer. However it works on every instantiation of NTRU, even if p is the polynomial $X + 2$. In this case, the only difference is that we have to replace the multiplication $p \cdot g$ by the convolution product $p * g$. The attack is summarized by Algorithm 4.

Algorithm 4. A general key-recovery chosen-ciphertext attack

Input: A public key H.
Output: A secret key (f, F_p).
1: $p \leftarrow 0$; $\boldsymbol{S} \leftarrow \boldsymbol{0}$.
2: estimate $\alpha \leftarrow \dfrac{2}{2\left(\|\check{f}\|^2 + \|p\cdot\check{g}\|^2\right)}$ using NTRU parameters.
3: **loop**
4:    Find a decryption failure (m, r, m') using Algorithm 1.
5:    Find the integer k such that $m_k \neq m'_k$.
6:    $\boldsymbol{V} \leftarrow (m_k, m_{k-1}, \ldots, m_{k-N+1} \bmod N, r_k, r_{k-1}, \ldots, r_{k-N+1} \bmod N)$.
7:    $\epsilon \leftarrow \text{sign}(\langle \boldsymbol{V}, \boldsymbol{S} \rangle)$ or $+1$ if $\langle \boldsymbol{V}, \boldsymbol{S} \rangle = 0$.
8:    $\boldsymbol{S} \leftarrow \boldsymbol{S} + \epsilon \boldsymbol{V}$; $z \leftarrow z + 1$.
9:    let $f = \sum_{i=0}^{N-1} \text{round}(\frac{1}{\alpha z}\boldsymbol{S}_1 + \frac{f(1)}{N})X^i$.
10:    **if** $f * H * p^{-1} \bmod q \in \mathcal{L}_g$, **then return** $(f, f^{-1} \bmod p)$.
11:    let $f' = \sum_{i=0}^{N-1} \text{round}(-\frac{1}{\alpha z}\boldsymbol{S}_1 + \frac{f(1)}{N})X^i$.
12:    **if** $f' * H * p^{-1} \bmod q \in \mathcal{L}_g$, **then return** $(f', f'^{-1} \bmod p)$.
13: **end loop**.

5.1   Description of the Attack

Again, we assume that we were able to find $m \in \mathcal{L}_m$ and $r \in \mathcal{L}_r$ such that the ciphertext $m + rH$ is decrypted as $m' \neq m$. This time, m and r are not zero-centered, so it is necessary to use the centering homomorphism in order to use Condition (1). From Heuristic 1, we know that there exists $\epsilon = \pm 1$ and $k \in [0, N-1]$ such that $p \cdot \check{r} * \check{g} + \check{m} * \check{f} - \epsilon q \cdot X^k$ has all its coefficients in $[-\frac{q}{2}; \frac{q}{2}[$. Thus, the output of the decryption algorithm is $m' = m + X^k \bmod p$, and k is therefore the only index where the coefficients m and m' differ. Hence, the value of k is disclosed and the kth coefficient is the overflowing coefficient, so:

$$\left| \sum_{j=0}^{N-1} \check{m}_{k-j} \bmod N \check{f}_j + \sum_{j=0}^{N-1} \check{r}_{k-j} \bmod N p\check{g}_j \right| \geq \frac{q}{2}$$

If we call $\boldsymbol{V}$ the vector $(\check{m}_{(k-0) \bmod N}, \ldots, \check{m}_{(k-N+1) \bmod N}, \check{r}_{(k-0) \bmod N}, \ldots, \check{r}_{(k-N+1) \bmod N})$ and $\boldsymbol{K}$ the vector $(\check{f}_0, \ldots, \check{f}_{N-1}, p\cdot\check{g}_0, \ldots, p\cdot\check{g}_{N-1})$ representing the private key, the previous inequality can be rewritten as $|\langle \boldsymbol{V}, \boldsymbol{K} \rangle| \geq \frac{q}{2}$. Thus, either V is very correlated with K or it is strongly anti-correlated. And K is in one-to-one correspondence with the private key. Note that since the sum of the coefficients of V is equal to zero, the squared norm $\|V\|^2$ is the sum of the variance of m and r. It is a constant σ^2 depending only on the NTRU parameter set. Likewise, $\|K\|^2$ is the sum of the variances of the keys f and g, and it depends only on the parameter set. For instance, in NTRU-2005 with binary polynomials, the private key f is equal to $1 + 2F$ where F is binary and contains exactly d_F ones. Therefore $\|f\|^2 = \sum_{j=0}^{N-1} f_j^2 = 1 + 4d_F$. After centering the polynomial, $\left\|\check{f}\right\|^2 = \|f\|^2 - \frac{1}{N}f^2(1)$ where $f(1) = 1 + 2d_F$, so $\left\|\check{f}\right\|^2 = 4 \cdot \frac{d_F(N - d_F - 1)}{N}$. Using the same kind of arguments for $\|p \cdot \check{g}\|^2$, we show that $\|K\|^2 = \frac{4}{N} \cdot (d_F(N - d_F - 1) + 2d_g(N - d_g))$ in NTRU-2005.

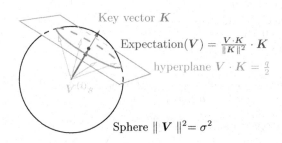

Fig. 2. Simplified case

Simplified case. In the simplified case, only positive correlations occur, and Heuristic 2 suggests that the inequality $|\langle V, K \rangle| \geq \frac{q}{2}$ is in fact almost an equality. Then, as shown in Figure 2, such a vector V is located on the hypersphere at the intersection of the sphere of equation $\|V\|^2 = \sigma^2$ and the hyperplane of equation $|\langle V, K \rangle| = \frac{q}{2}$. If we gather many independent decryption failures, we will obtain many $V^{(i)}$'s in this hypersphere. Their expectation is the center of the hypersphere, which is the multiple $\frac{q}{2\|K\|^2} \cdot K$ of the private key vector. Therefore if we consider n vectors $V^{(i)}$s coming from independent decryption failures, then their mean value $\frac{1}{n} \sum_{i=1}^n V^{(i)}$ shall converge to $\frac{q}{2\|K\|^2} \cdot K$ when n grows. In practice, $\frac{q}{2\|K\|^2}$ seems to be greater than $\frac{1}{16}$ in every instantiation of NTRU containing decryption failures. For this reason, if n is of the order of N, we expect to have enough accuracy to recover the full key K.

Real case. In reality, there may be both positive and negative correlations between V and K. Therefore, V is located on the union of two opposite hyperspheres $\|V\|^2 = \sigma^2 \cap \langle V, K \rangle = \pm\frac{q}{2}$ (see Figure 3). Unfortunately, the proportion of positive and negative correlations (which depends on the fractional part of $\frac{a(1)}{N}$) may be equal to $\frac{1}{2}$ in the worst case. In this case, the expectation of V is zero. We must be able to decide whether the correlation between V and K is positive or not. The best test would be to compute directly the dot product $\langle V, K \rangle$, but we do not know K. Therefore, in our algorithm, we

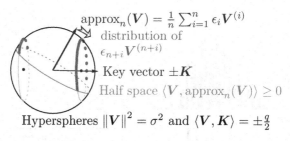

Hyperspheres $\|V\|^2 = \sigma^2$ and $\langle V, K \rangle = \pm\frac{q}{2}$

Fig. 3. Real case

try to guess for each $V^{(i)}$, a sign $\epsilon_i = \pm 1$ such that $\langle \epsilon_i V^{(i)}, K \rangle \geq \frac{q}{2}$ for all i, or $\langle \epsilon_i V^{(i)}, K \rangle \leq -\frac{q}{2}$ for all i. In order to do that, we arbitrarily set $\epsilon_1 = 1$, and recursively set $\epsilon_{n+1} = \text{sign}(\langle V^{(n+1)}, \sum_{i=1}^{n} \epsilon_i {}^i V \rangle)$, hoping that $\sum_{i=1}^{n} \epsilon_i V^{(i)}$ is not orthogonal to K (as shown in Figure 3). Then, as suggested on the figure, the sum $\sum_{i=1}^{n} \epsilon_i V^{(i)}$ will slowly take the direction of K or $-K$, and like in the simple case, the average vector $\frac{1}{n} \sum_{i=1}^{n} \epsilon_i V^{(i)}$ will converge to $\pm\frac{q}{2\|K\|^2} \cdot K$.

5.2 Experiments

We have implemented the attack described by Algorithm 4. Both the encryption, decryption algorithms and the attack were implemented using the NTL library [15] without any running-time optimization. Indeed, since the attack only consists of adding a few hundreds of vectors, its running time is negligible compared to the time of collecting the required number of decryption failures. We refer to [8,10,9] for the actual running time of an efficient implementation of the encryption and the decryption algorithm.

As shown in Table 1, the number of decryption failures needed in order to fully recover the private key (even for highest parameters) is a few hundreds. Recall that there is a decryption failure every 2^{15} encryptions: this means that the total number of calls to the decryption oracle is about 2^{23}, which takes less than two days with an unoptimized version of the encryption and decryption algorithms. As shown in Figure 4, the main idea of the algorithm is to build an approximation of the private key vector. The more decryption failures we use, the more accurate the approximation. Since the secret key has integer coefficients, the approximation eventually reaches a precision level where a simple rounding procedure is enough to fully recover the key.

These two graphs represent the distribution of the coefficients of the estimation of the key (that is the vector S/z of Algorithm 4 line 9) for NTRU-2005 with product-form keys with $N = 251$, $q = 113$. The different levels of grey represent the value of the corresponding key coefficient. The attack works only if the different colors are well separated (by the dotted vertical lines). The first graph is obtained after gathering 150 decryption failures, and the second after 250 decryption failures. In the first graph, there is only one black bar which is misplaced (in the $f_i = 2$ area, so after 150 decryption failures, we have recovered

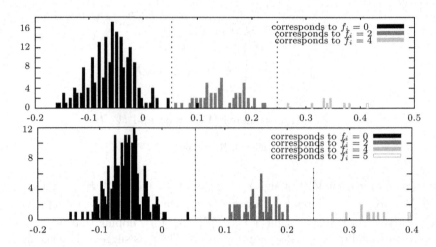

Fig. 4. Coefficients of the estimation of the key in the algorithm

Table 1. Experiments

type NTRU	N	p	q	d_F	number of decryption failures used	number of digits of f recovered
NTRU-1998	167	3	128	32	50	N-3
					100	N (all)
NTRU-2001	251	X+2	127	40	80	N-1
					140	N (all)
NTRU-2005 binary (using a smaller q)	251	2	127	64	80	N-2
					130	N (all)
NTRU-2005 product form (using a smaller q)	251	2	113	9	100	N-3
					150	N-1
					250	N (all)

all bits of f with exactly 1 error. In the second graph, the colors are well separated, so the private key is fully recovered.

5.3   Potential Improvements

Here, we discuss potential improvements which might further lower the number of required decryption failures.

Exhaustive search. The number of errors in Table 1 between the private key and the estimation is very small during the last half of the algorithm. If we assume that there are less than three errors of at most one unit in our estimation, then the number of possible keys is bounded by $8\binom{N}{2}+4\binom{N}{2}+2N$. Even with $N = 251$, it is possible to perform this exhaustive search in practice. In Table 1, the number of decryption failures needed to recover the private key up to 3 errors is half of the number required to fully recover the key. Hence, exhaustive search would divide the number of calls to the decryption oracle by a factor 2.

Lattice attack. Instead of performing an exhaustive search, we may use a lattice reduction algorithm. Once we get a sufficiently accurate approximation of the vector $K = (f, p \cdot g)$, the distance between this approximation of K and the lattice generated by the NTRU public basis should be extremely small compared to its shortest vector. In this case, we may hope that lattice reduction algorithms can recover the whole private key from this approximation in practice.

Acknowledgements. Part of this work is supported by the Commission of the European Communities through the IST program under contract IST-2002-507932 ECRYPT.

References

1. Consortium for Efficient Embedded Security. Efficient embedded security standards #1: Implementation aspects of NTRU and NSS, 2001.
2. Consortium for Efficient Embedded Security. Efficient embedded security standards #1: Implementation aspects of NTRUEncrypt and NTRUSign, 2002.
3. C. Gentry. Key recovery and message attacks on NTRU-composite. In *Proc. of Eurocrypt '01*, volume 2045 of *LNCS*. IACR, Springer-Verlag, 2001.
4. C. Gentry, J. Jonsson, J. Stern, and M. Szydlo. Cryptanalysis of the NTRU signature scheme (NSS) from Eurocrypt 2001. In *Proc. of Asiacrypt '01*, volume 2248 of *LNCS*. Springer-Verlag, 2001.
5. C. Gentry and M. Szydlo. Cryptanalysis of the revised NTRU signature scheme. In *Proc. of Eurocrypt '02*, volume 2332 of *LNCS*. Springer-Verlag, 2002.
6. D. Han, J. Hong, J. W. Han, and D. Kwon. Key recovery attacks on NTRU without ciphertext validation routine. *ACISP 2003*, LNCS 2727:pages 274–284, 2003.
7. J. Hoffstein, N. A. Howgrave-Graham, J. Pipher, J. H. Silverman, and W. Whyte. NTRUSIGN: Digital signatures using the NTRU lattice. In *Proc. of CT-RSA*, volume 2612 of *LNCS*. Springer-Verlag, 2003.
8. J. Hoffstein, J. Pipher, and J. Silverman. NTRU: a ring based public key cryptosystem. In *Proc. of ANTS III*, volume 1423 of *LNCS*, pages 267–288. Springer-Verlag, 1998. First presented at the rump session of Crypto '96.
9. J. Hoffstein and J. H. Silverman. Optimizations for NTRU. In *Public-key Cryptography and Computational Number Theory*. DeGruyter, 2000. available at http://www.ntru.com.
10. N. Howgrave-Graham, J. H. Silverman, and W. Whyte. Choosing parameter sets for NTRUEncrypt with NAEP and SVES-3.
11. N. A. Howgrave-Graham, P. Q. Nguyen, D. Pointcheval, J. Proos., J. H. Silverman, A. Singer, and W. Whyte. The impact of decryption failures on the security of NTRU encryption. In *Proc. of the 23rd Cryptology Conference (Crypto '03)*, volume 2729 of *LNCS*, pages 226–246. IACR, Springer-Verlag, 2003.
12. IEEE. *P1363.1 Public-Key Cryptographic Techniques Based on Hard Problems over Lattices*, June 2003. IEEE., Available from http://grouper.ieee.org/groups/1363/lattPK/index.html.
13. E. Jaulmes and A. Joux. A chosen ciphertext attack on NTRU. In *Proc. of Crypto '00*, volume 1880 of *LNCS*. IACR, Springer-Verlag, 2000.

14. P. Q. Nguyen and O. Regev. Learning a parallelepiped: cryptanalysis of GGH and NTRU signatures. In S. Vaudenay, editor, *Proc. of Eurocrypt '06*, volume 4004 of LNCS, pages 271–288. Springer, 2006.
15. V. Shoup. Number Theory C++ Library (NTL) version 5.4. Available at `http://www.shoup.net/ntl/`.
16. J. H. Silverman. Invertibility in truncated polynomial rings. Technical report, NTRU Cryptosystems, 2003. Technical reports available at `http://www.ntru.com`.
17. J. H. Silverman and W. Whyte. Technical report n. 18, version 1: Estimating decryption failure probabilities for ntruencrypt. Technical report, NTRU Cryptosystems, 2005.

Cryptanalysis of the Paeng-Jung-Ha Cryptosystem from PKC 2003

Daewan Han[1], Myung-Hwan Kim[2,*], and Yongjin Yeom[1]

[1] National Security Research Institute,
161 Gajeong-dong, Yuseong-gu, Daejeon, 305-350, Korea
{dwh,yjyeom}@etri.re.kr
[2] Department of Mathematical Science and ISaC-RIM,
Seoul National University, Seoul, 151-747, Korea
mhkim@math.snu.ac.kr

Abstract. At PKC 2003 Paeng, Jung, and Ha proposed a lattice based public key cryptosystem(PJH). It is originated from GGH, and designed as a hybrid of GGH and NTRUEncrypt in order to reduce the key size. They claimed that PJH is secure against all possible attacks, especially against lattice attacks. However, in this paper, we present a key recovery attack, based on lattice theory, against PJH. The running time of our attack is drastically short. For example, we could recover all secret keys within 10 minutes even for the system with $n = 1001$ on a single PC. Unlike other lattice attacks against NTRUEncrypt and GGH, the attack may be applied well to the system with much larger parameters. We present some clues why we believe so. Based on this belief, we declare that PJH should not be used in practice.

Keywords: Paeng-Jung-Ha cryptosystem, GGH, NTRUEncrypt, Lattice attack.

1   Introduction

Since Ajtai's seminal work [1], some lattice-based public-key cryptosystems [2,4,5] have been suggested inspired by his work. Among them GGH [4] and NTRU [5] attracted much attention because both systems seemed to be practical with fast encryption/decryption and reasonable key size. GGH is a lattice version of the previously well-known code-based cryptosystems [9]. Though its key size is somewhat large, the system is fast. The proposers claimed that the system with practically usable parameters would be secure. A few years later, however, Nguyen presented a powerful lattice attack against it [12]. In order for GGH to be secure against Nguyen's attack, its key size should be too large to be practical. Thus, GGH has been regarded as a broken system since then. NTRU, more precisely NTRUEncrypt, is another lattice-based system widely reviewed. The system is very efficient and unbroken till now. From the lattice-theoretic point of view, NTRUEncrypt is a special instance of GGH in the sense that the

---

* The second author was partially supported by KRF(2005-070-C00004).

T. Okamoto and X. Wang (Eds.): PKC 2007, LNCS 4450, pp. 107–117, 2007.

former uses a circulant matrix for a public key while the latter uses a random square matrix. As a result, the key size of NTRUEncrypt is $O(n)$ while that of GGH is $O(n^2)$, where n is the dimension of the matrix.

A few years after Nguyen's attack, Paeng, Jung, and Ha proposed a variant [18] of GGH, which we will call PJH in this paper. Motivations of developing such a variant are as follows: Firstly, one-way function of GGH has still merits since it is simple and faster than other systems using modular exponentiations. Secondly, at the time that PJH was suggested, it seemed to be easier to design a natural signature scheme based on GGH than on NTRUEncrypt, although both signature schemes turned out to be insecure recently [13]. Thirdly, it seems to be possible to overcome Nguyen's attack by choosing lattices more carefully. With these in mind, they designed PJH as a hybrid type of GGH and NTRUEncrypt: PJH looks similar to GGH except that it takes a partially circulant matrix for a public key. As a result, its key size reduces down to $O(n)$, which is same as that of NTRUEncrypt. Concerning the security of PJH, the proposers claimed that it would be secure against all possible attacks with practical key sizes. Because GGH was broken by a lattice attack, they presented extensive analysis on the security against lattice attacks, and concluded that their system would be secure on the basis of various simulation results.

However, in this paper, we present a key recovery attack against PJH with a lattice technique. In order to recover the secret keys, we induce a linear equation from the public information on key pairs. Then, we construct a lattice from the equation and obtain some of the secret keys by applying lattice reduction algorithms to the lattice. The remaining secret keys can be recovered simply by solving a few linear equations. We could recover secret keys within 10 minutes even for the system with $n = 1001$, where n is a system parameter which will be described in the next section. Unlike other lattice attacks against NTRUEncrypt and GGH, our attack may be applied well to the system of much larger n's. We present some clues why we believe so. Based on this belief, we declare that PJH should not be used in practice.

The rest of this paper is organized as follows. In the next section, we briefly introduce PJH and describe basic principles of general lattice attacks against public key cryptosystems. In Section 3, we present our key recovery attack, simulation results, and applicability of our attack against the system with much larger parameters. Finally, we conclude in Section 4.

2   Preliminaries

2.1   Overview of PJH Cryptosystem

Notations and Parameters. Let n be a prime integer, and consider a polynomial ring

$$\mathcal{R} = \mathbb{Z}[x]/\langle x^n - 1 \rangle.$$

We identify a polynomial $f(x) = a_0 + a_1 x + \cdots + a_{n-1} x^{n-1} \in \mathcal{R}$ with a vector $(a_0, a_1, \cdots, a_{n-1}) \in \mathbb{Z}^n$. We will denote both by f. Note that the multiplication $f \cdot g$ of f and g is computed by the convolution product of them, that is,

$$h = f \cdot g, \qquad c_k = \sum_{i+j=k \bmod n} a_i b_j,$$

where $g = b_0 + b_1 x + \cdots + b_{n-1} x^{n-1}$ and $h = c_0 + c_1 x + \cdots + c_{n-1} x^{n-1}$. For $f = a_0 + a_1 x + \cdots + a_{n-1} x^{n-1} \in \mathcal{R}$ let $\Phi(f)$ be the $n \times n$ circulant matrix

$$\begin{pmatrix} a_0 & a_1 & \cdots & a_{n-1} \\ a_{n-1} & a_0 & \cdots & a_{n-2} \\ \vdots & \vdots & \ddots & \vdots \\ a_1 & a_2 & \cdots & a_0 \end{pmatrix}.$$

Then, it is easy to verify the following:

$$f \cdot g = g \cdot f = f \Phi(g) = g \Phi(f).$$

Finally, we remark that we will use row-oriented notations in matrix representations of lattices while PJH adopts column-oriented rotations in [18].

Key Generation. In order to generate a private key, PJH generates 4 polynomials $f_1, f_2, h_1, h_2 \in \mathcal{R}$ which have the following properties:

- $f_1(x) = \alpha_0 + \alpha_1 x^1 + \cdots + \alpha_{n-1} x^{n-1}$ and $f_2(x) = \beta_0 + \beta_1 x^1 + \cdots + \beta_{n-1} x^{n-1}$, where $|\alpha_0|, |\beta_0| \approx \sqrt{2n}$ and the other coefficients are elements in $\{-1, 0, 1\}$.
- The coefficients of h_1 and h_2 are elements in $\{-1, 0, 1\}$.

The private key R is defined by

$$R := \begin{pmatrix} \Phi(f_1) & \Phi(h_2) \\ \Phi(h_1) & \Phi(f_2) \end{pmatrix}.$$

Let p be a positive integer. In [18] p is a 10-bit or 80-bit integer which need not be prime. Proposers recommended that p is kept secret although it does not affect the security. In order to generate public keys, PJH chooses $g \in \mathcal{R}$ with coefficients in $(-p/2, p/2]$ such that g is invertible in $\mathbb{Z}_p[x]/\langle x^n - 1 \rangle$. Then there exists g_p with coefficients in $(-p/2, p/2]$ and Q in $\mathcal{R}$ such that

$$g \cdot g_p - 1 = pQ \in \mathcal{R}.$$

Now, four public polynomials $P_1, P_2, P_3, P_4 \in \mathcal{R}$ are defined as follows:

$$\begin{aligned} P_1 &:= f_1 \cdot g + h_1 \cdot Q, \\ P_2 &:= p f_1 + h_1 \cdot g_p, \\ P_3 &:= h_2 \cdot g + f_2 \cdot Q, \\ P_4 &:= p h_2 + f_2 \cdot g_p. \end{aligned} \tag{1}$$

The public key B is defined by

$$B := \begin{pmatrix} \Phi(P_1) & \Phi(P_3) \\ \Phi(P_2) & \Phi(P_4) \end{pmatrix}.$$

The pair (R, B) constructed in this way have the same properties as that in GGH. That is, R and B are different bases of a same lattice and have low and high dual-orthogonality defects, respectively. For more details, we refer the readers to [18].

Table 1. Comparison of key sizes(KB) of PJH and GGH

rank of B	PJH(10-bit p)	PJH(80-bit p)	GGH	GGH(HNF)
200	0.85	4.4	330	32
300	1.4	6.6	990	75
400	1.8	8.8	2370	140
500	2.3	11		

Encryption and Decryption. For a message $m = (m_1, m_2) \in \mathcal{R}^2$, the cipher-text c is calculated by

$$c = (c_1, c_2) = mB + e \in (\mathbb{Q}[x]/\langle x^n - 1 \rangle)^2$$

for an error vector $e = (e_1, e_2) \in (\mathbb{Q}[x]/\langle x^n - 1 \rangle)^2$, where the coefficients of e_i are elements in $\{-1/2, 1/2\}$.

Let T be a matrix defined by

$$T := \begin{pmatrix} \Phi(g) & \Phi(Q) \\ pI & \Phi(g_p) \end{pmatrix}^{-1}.$$

Then, c can be decrypted as follows:

$$m = (m_1, m_2) = \lceil cR^{-1} \rfloor T.$$

The decryption works similarly to that of GGH. Since we don't have to understand thoroughly how the decryption works in order to explain our attack, we omit the details.

Efficiency and Security. Since the public matrix B is determined by four polynomials in $\mathcal{R}$, key size of PJH is $O(n)$ while that of GGH is $O(n^2)$. The comparison of key sizes of PJH with GGH in [18] is given in Table 1. The values in the last column are the key size of GGH when it uses Micciancio's HNF expression [10].

Concerning the security of PJH, the proposers claimed that the system is secure against all possible attacks even if the parameter p is disclosed. Because GGH was broken by a lattice attack, they presented extensive analysis on the security against lattice attacks. We briefly describe their analysis. Because the equations in (1), which are the only public information on secret keys and public keys, are quadratic of unknown variables in $\mathcal{R}$, they expected that no key

Table 2. Running times to break PJH estimated by the proposers

n	expected run time
211	1.46×10^9 seconds ≈ 46 years
257	1.45×10^{11} seconds $\approx 4.6 \times 10^3$ years
373	1.58×10^{16} seconds $\approx 5 \times 10^8$ years
503	5.18×10^{21} seconds $\approx 1.6 \times 10^{14}$ years

recovery attack using lattice techniques would be feasible. On the other hand, a message recovery attack seems to be feasible. However, they claimed that the reduction algorithm would work badly because they made *expected-gaps*, which is defined in the next subsection, small. Running times to break PJH estimated by the authors of [18] are given in Table 2.

2.2 Lattice Attacks

A *Lattice* $\mathcal{L}$ is defined to be a discrete subgroup of $\mathbb{R}^n$. It consists of all integral linear combinations of a set of some linearly independent vectors $\mathbf{b}_1, \mathbf{b}_2, \cdots, \mathbf{b}_d \in \mathbb{R}^n$. Such a set of vectors is called a lattice *basis*. All the bases of a lattice have the same number of elements, and this number is called the *dimension* of the lattice, denoted by $\dim(\mathcal{L})$. There are infinitely many bases for $\mathcal{L}$ when $\dim(\mathcal{L}) \geq 2$. Any two bases of a lattice $\mathcal{L}$ are related to each other by some unimodular matrix (integral matrix of determinant ± 1), and therefore all the bases share the same Gramian determinant $\det_{1 \leq i,j \leq d} \langle \mathbf{b}_i, \mathbf{b}_j \rangle$, where $\{\mathbf{b}_1, \mathbf{b}_2, \ldots, \mathbf{b}_d\}$ is a basis of $\mathcal{L}$. The *volume* $\mathrm{vol}(\mathcal{L})$ of $\mathcal{L}$ is defined by the square root of the Gramian determinant, which is the d-dimensional volume of the parallelepiped spanned by the $\mathbf{b}_i$'s. Since a lattice is discrete, it has a shortest non-zero vector. The Euclidean length of a shortest vector of $\mathcal{L}$ is called the *first minimum*, denoted by $\lambda_1(\mathcal{L})$. More generally, for all $1 \leq i \leq \dim(\mathcal{L})$, the *i-th minimum* $\lambda_i(\mathcal{L})$ is defined by the minimum of $\max_{1 \leq j \leq i} \|\mathbf{v}_j\|$, where $\{\mathbf{v}_1, \cdots, \mathbf{v}_i\}$ runs over all possible sets of linearly independent vectors $\mathbf{v}_1, \cdots, \mathbf{v}_i \in \mathcal{L}$. The ratio λ_2/λ_1 is called *lattice gap*, which is useful in estimating the feasibility of lattice attacks.

Given a basis for a lattice $\mathcal{L}$, the problem of finding a shortest vector of $\mathcal{L}$ is called the *shortest vector problem* (SVP). Another famous problem related to lattices is the *closest vector problem* (CVP), the problem of finding a vector $\mathbf{v} \in \mathcal{L}$ which is closest to a given vector $\mathbf{t} \in \mathbb{R}^n$. The CVP in ℓ_p-norm is proved to be NP-hard for all p, and the SVP is also believed to be hard [11]. Indeed, there are no known polynomial time algorithms to solve even the approximated versions of them, if approximation factors are polynomials in $\dim(\mathcal{L})$. However, if the dimension of a lattice is less than a few hundreds, we can solve them in practice using lattice reduction algorithms such as LLL [8] and its variants [19].

For a given lattice basis $\{\mathbf{b}_1, \cdots, \mathbf{b}_n\}$, LLL outputs a reduced basis $\{\mathbf{b}_1^*, \cdots, \mathbf{b}_n^*\}$ satisfying $\|\mathbf{b}_1^*\| \leq 2^{(n-1)/2} \lambda_1(\mathcal{L})$ within $O(n^4 \log B)$ integer arithmetic operations, where B is the maximum of $\|\mathbf{b}_i\|^2$'s. The fastest LLL variant known has bit-complexity essentially $O(n^5 \log^2 B)$ [14]. However, the real performances of LLL and its variants are more better than what are expected from the theory, both in terms of the running time and the output quality [15]. Thus, we can find a genuine shortest vector of a given lattice using the algorithms when the dimension of the lattices are less than a few hundreds.

Lattices have been widely used in attacking public-key cryptosystems. Readers are referred to [16] for well-written summary of the various results about them. Here we briefly describe basic principles to attack systems using lattices. The attacks are accomplished by reducing the problem of finding a secret information in the system to a specific instance of SVP or CVP. We describe the SVP case here. First, one constructs a lattice from public information such as system parameters and public keys. Then, one shows that a relatively short vector $\mathbf{v}$ of the lattice includes the secret information we want to obtain, and finds such $\mathbf{v}$ by solving SVP with lattice reduction algorithms. However, in most cases, one cannot prove that $\mathbf{v}$ is a genuine shortest vector of the lattice. Instead, one can infer that it is a shortest vector by using Gaussian heuristic: Given a random lattice $\mathcal{L}$ of dimension n, the first minimum $\lambda_1(\mathcal{L})$ of $\mathcal{L}$ will be

$$\sqrt{\frac{n}{2\pi e}}\mathrm{vol}(\mathcal{L})^{\frac{1}{n}} \leq \lambda_1(\mathcal{L}) \leq \sqrt{\frac{n}{\pi e}}\mathrm{vol}(\mathcal{L})^{\frac{1}{n}}.$$

One use $\sigma(\mathcal{L})$ as the estimation of $\lambda_1(\mathcal{L})$, where $\sigma(\mathcal{L})$ (briefly σ) is defined by

$$\sigma(\mathcal{L}) := \sqrt{\frac{n}{2\pi e}}\mathrm{vol}(\mathcal{L})^{\frac{1}{n}}.$$

If $\|\mathbf{v}\|$ is less than σ, one may expect that $\mathbf{v}$ is a shortest vector. In practice, the larger the ratio $\sigma/\|\mathbf{v}\|$ is, the easier we can find $\mathbf{v}$. We call this ratio an *expected-gap* of $\mathcal{L}$ with respect to $\mathbf{v}$.

3   Key Recovery Attack Against PJH

3.1   Volume of the Lattice Generated by $\Phi(P_2)$

For a polynomial $f \in \mathcal{R}$, let's define $V(f)$ by the volume of the lattice generated by the circulant matrix $\Phi(f)$. In our attack, $V(P_2)$ is used essentially: More precisely, we need to estimate a reasonable lower bound of $\delta_n(P_2)$, which is defined for randomly chosen P_2 by

$$\delta_n(P_2) := p^{-1}\sqrt{\frac{1}{2\pi e}}V(P_2)^{\frac{1}{n+1}}.$$

In this subsection we present a heuristic on the asymptotic estimation of $\delta_n(P_2)$.

To our knowledge, it is difficult to understand asymptotic behavior of $V(f)$ theoretically. For simplicity, suppose that the lattice is of full rank. In that case, $V(f)$ is equal to the determinant of the circulant matrix $\Phi(f)$. So, we can infer intuitively

$$V(f) = \det(\Phi(f)) = \frac{\|f\|^n}{\mathrm{orth\text{-}defect}(\Phi(f))} \sim O(\|f\|^n).$$

However, if there are no conditions on n and f, there are no known theoretical results on asymptotic properties of $V(f)$. Moreover, we could not find meaningful characteristics even from simulations.

Now, turn to our attention to $\delta_n(P_2)$ in PJH. Because PJH uses prime n and P_2 is obtained by special formulas, $V(P_2)$ and $\delta_n(P_2)$ behave regularly as n increases. We could verify this by simulations. We calculated $\delta_n(P_2)$ in randomly

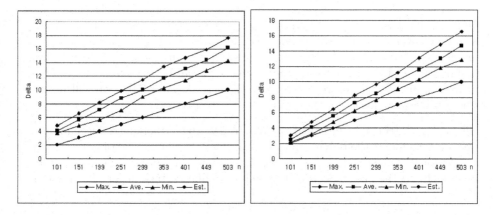

Fig. 1. Experimental estimation of $\delta_n(P_2)$ for 10-bit p(left) and 80-bit p(right)

constructed PJH for several n's and for several 10-bit or 80-bit p's. We tested 100 times for each n and p. The experimental results are shown in Figure 1. The upper three curves in the figure show the simulated maximum, average, and minimum values of $\delta_n(P_2)$, respectively. They tend to increase linearly as n increases. If the bit-size of p increases, the value of $\delta_n(P_2)$ decreases a little bit. However, as one can see in Figure 1, the slopes of $\delta_n(P_2)$ do not change much as the bit-size of p increases.

From our simulations, we estimate a lower bound of $\delta_n(P_2)$ for large n and for $p \leq 2^{80}$ very conservatively as follows:

$$\delta_n(P_2) \geq 0.02n \quad \text{for } n \geq 100. \tag{2}$$

The lowest line in the figure shows the lower bound in (2). In the next subsections, we will use this estimation for theoretical analysis of our attack against PJH.

3.2   A Linear Relation Between Key Pairs

Let's recall some of equations in (1).

$$P_1 = f_1 \cdot g + h_1 \cdot Q \tag{3}$$

$$P_2 = pf_1 + h_1 \cdot g_p \tag{4}$$

By multiplying g to (4), we induce the following equation in $\mathcal{R}$:

$$
\begin{aligned}
g \cdot P_2 &= pf_1 \cdot g + h_1 \cdot g_p \cdot g \\
&= pf_1 \cdot g + h_1 \cdot (1 + pQ) \\
&= p(f_1 \cdot g + h_1 \cdot Q) + h_1 \\
&= pP_1 + h_1.
\end{aligned}
\tag{5}
$$

In (5), g, p and h_1 are unknown variables. However, note that the equation is linear while those in (1) are quadratic. Suppose we can recover h_1 and p. Then, g can be recovered by solving the linear equation (5). From g and p we can obtain g_p and Q easily. Then, (1) becomes a system of four linear equations of four unknown variables so that the other secret keys can be recovered easily. Thus, if we can find h_1 and p, we can recover all secret keys of PJH. We will recover them using a lattice technique in the following subsections.

Remark 1. PJH can be designed flexibly. In [18], the authors introduced another scheme which uses the polynomial ring $\mathbb{Z}[x]/\langle x^n - x - 1\rangle$ instead of $\mathbb{Z}[x]/\langle x^n - 1\rangle$ in Section 4.4, and one more in the appendix. However, our attack can be applied identically to the one in Section 4.4, and a modified attack, using the equation

$$g \cdot P_{12} = pP_{11} + h_1$$

instead of (5), can be applied to the one in the appendix.

3.3   Finding h_1 with a Lattice Technique

The Case When p is not Secret. Consider a lattice $\mathcal{L}_1$ generated by rows of the following $(n+1) \times (n+1)$ matrix L_1:

$$L_1 = \begin{pmatrix} \Phi(P_2) & 0_n \\ pP_1 & 1 \end{pmatrix},$$

where 0_n is a column vector of dimension n whose entries are all 0. Then, a vector

$$\mathbf{v}_1 = (h_1, -1) = (g \cdot P_2 - pP_1, -1) = (g, -1)L_1$$

is contained in $\mathcal{L}_1$ and its length satisfies

$$\|\mathbf{v}_1\| = \sqrt{\|h_1\|^2 + 1} \leq \sqrt{n+1}.$$

According to Gaussian heuristic we can expect

$$\sigma_1 \sim \sqrt{\frac{n+1}{2\pi e}} \mathrm{vol}(\mathcal{L}_1)^{\frac{1}{n+1}} = \delta_n(P_2)p\sqrt{n+1},$$

where σ_1 is the length of a shortest vector in $\mathcal{L}_1$. Using the approximation of $\delta_n(P_2)$ in (2), we can estimate σ_1 as follows:

$$\sigma_1 \geq 0.02np\sqrt{n+1} \quad \text{for } n \geq 100.$$

Thus, the expected-gap of $\mathcal{L}_1$ with respect to $\mathbf{v}_1$ is bigger than or equal to $0.02np$, i.e.,

$$\frac{\sigma_1}{\|\mathbf{v}_1\|} \geq 0.02np \quad \text{for } n \geq 100. \tag{6}$$

Since this is very large in PJH parameters, where p is a 10-bit or 80-bit prime, $\mathbf{v}_1$ will be a shortest vector of $\mathcal{L}_1$ with high probability. So, we can easily find $\mathbf{v}_1$ (and hence h_1) by using lattice reduction algorithms.

Table 3. Breaking times (in seconds) of PJH for 80-bit public p

Dimension of lattice	$n = 211$	$n = 257$	$n = 373$	$n = 503$	$n = 1001$
Time(Seconds)	< 1	< 1	< 10	< 10	< 100

We simulated the above attack on a Pentium IV 3.2 GHz PC using the floating-point variant of LLL algorithm (LLL_FP) with default parameters implemented in NTL package [17]. We tested our attack against PJH with different n's for 10-bit and 80-bit randomly selected p's. For each n and p, 10 different instances were tested against. We could obtain $\mathbf{v}$ for all instances. For 10-bit p's, the running times for lattice reduction were too short to be described. The running times for 80-bit p's are given in Table 3. Even for $n = 1001$, we could find the solutions within 100 seconds.

The Case When p is Secret. If p is secret, we cannot construct the lattice $\mathcal{L}_1$. Instead, we consider a lattice $\mathcal{L}_2$ generated by the following matrix L_2:

$$L_2 = \begin{pmatrix} \Phi(P_2) & 0_n \\ P_1 & 1 \end{pmatrix}.$$

Then, a vector $\mathbf{v}_2 = (h_1, -p)$ is contained in $\mathcal{L}_2$ and its length is smaller than or equal to $\sqrt{p^2 + n^2}$. The σ_2 corresponding to $\mathcal{L}_2$ is equal to σ_1, and hence $\sigma_2 \geq 0.02np\sqrt{n+1}$. Thus, we get

$$\frac{\sigma_2}{\|\mathbf{v}_2\|} \geq \frac{0.02np\sqrt{n+1}}{\sqrt{p^2 + n^2}} \sim 0.02n\sqrt{n}. \tag{7}$$

Although this value is smaller than the expected-gap when p is public, it is still large (see Table 5). So, we can find $\mathbf{v}_2$ (and hence h_1, and p) by using lattice reduction algorithms.

We also simulated the above attack on the same machine using the same algorithm as in the previous case. The results for 80-bit p's are given in Table 4. The running times for lattice reduction in this case were more longer than those in case of public p. This was expected because the expected-gap of the former is smaller than that of the latter. Still, we could find the solutions within 500 seconds even for $n = 1001$.

Remark 2. We can use another lattice in our attack to get larger expected-gap. Let d_p be the bit-length of p, and consider a vector $\mathbf{v}_3 = (2^{d_p} h_1, -p)$ and a lattice $\mathcal{L}_3$ generated by the following matrix L_3:

$$L_3 = \begin{pmatrix} 2^{d_p}\Phi(P_2) & 0_n \\ 2^{d_p}P_1 & 1 \end{pmatrix}.$$

Then, $\mathbf{v}_3$ is a short vector of $\mathcal{L}_3$ and the expected-gap of $\mathcal{L}_3$ with respect to $\mathbf{v}_3$ is about $\delta_n(P_2)p$. However, since the entries of L_3 is larger than those of L_2, it takes more time in lattice reduction for $\mathcal{L}_3$ than for $\mathcal{L}_2$. Thus, using L_2 is more efficient in practice.

Table 4. Breaking times (in seconds) of PJH for 80-bit secret p

Dimension of lattice	$n =211$	$n =257$	$n =373$	$n =503$	$n = 1001$
Times(second)	< 20	< 30	< 60	< 100	< 500

Table 5. Expected-gaps in attacks against NTRUEncrypt, GGH, and PJH

Dimension of the lattice	200	250	300	350	400	450	500
GGH [12]	9.7	9.4	9.5	9.4	9.6		
NTRUEncrypt [7]	5.7	6.3	6.9	7.5	8.0	8.5	8.9
PJH(secret p) [From (7)]	56.6	79.1	103.9	131.0	160.0	190.9	223.6
PJH(public p) [From (6)]	$4p$	$5p$	$6p$	$7p$	$8p$	$9p$	$10p$

3.4 Attack Against PJH with Larger Parameters

In attack against GGH, expected-gaps are small and do not increase as the lattice dimension n increases [12], and in attack against NTRUEncrypt, they increase but are bounded by about $0.25\sqrt{n}$ [7]. On the other hand, the efficiency of reduction algorithm becomes worse as n increases. These two facts cause the difficulty in attacking GGH and NTRUEncrypt when n is sufficiently large [3,6,12]. The attacks are not possible practically when n is more than 400 ~ 500.

However, expected-gaps in our attack against PJH are much large and increase very fast as n increases. The comparison of expected-gaps in attacks against GGH, NTRUEncrypt, and PJH are given in Table 5. The large expected-gaps explains why breaking times of PJH are shorter compared to other systems. Moreover, the fact that the expected-gaps increases fast compensates the inefficiency of reduction algorithms for large n. Thus, we expect that we can break PJH until n grows too large to be used practically.

4   Conclusion

We have shown that Paeng-Jung-Ha cryptosystem proposed at PKC 2003 is not secure against a lattice attack contrary to proposer's expectation. From the relations between public keys and secret keys, we could induce a linear equation useful for a lattice attack. Because the breaking times for suggested parameters are drastically short and the feasibility of our attack against the system with larger parameters is high, we may declare that the system should not be used practically.

It seems to be hard to modify PJH to be secure against our attack without worsening the efficiency. Our result shows that, although lattice-based cryptosystems look attractive, it is difficult to design a practical system other than NTRUEncrypt.

Acknowledgements. The authors would like to thank the anonymous referees for pointing out some errors of this paper and giving valuable comments.

References

1. M. Ajtai. Generating Hard Instances of Lattice Problems. In Proc. of 28th ACM STOC, 99-108, 1996.
2. M. Ajtai and C. Dwork. A Public-key Cryptosystem with Worst-case/Average-case Equivalence. In Proc. of 29th ACM STOC, 284-293, 1997.
3. D. Coppersmith and A. Shamir. Lattice Attacks on NTRU. In Proc. of Eurocrypt'97, LNCS 1233, 52-61, Springer-Verlag, 1997.
4. G. Goldreich, S. Goldwasser, and S. Halevi. Public-key Cryptosystems from Lattice Reduction Problems. In Proc. of Crypto '97, LNCS 1294, 112-131, Springer-Verlag, 1997.
5. J. Hoffstein, J. Pipher, and J. H. Silverman. NTRU: A Ring-Based Public Key Cryptosystem. In Proc. of ANTS III, LNCS 1423, 267-288, Springer-Verlag, 1998.
6. J. Hoffstein, J. H. Silverman, and W. Whyte. Estimated Breaking Times for NTRU Lattices. Technical Report #12(Version 2), NTRU Cryptosystems, 2003.
7. N. Howgrave-Graham, J. H. Silverman, and W. Whyte. Choosing Parameter Sets for NTRUEncrypt with NAEP and SVES-3. In Proc. of CT-RSA 2005, LNCS 3376, 118-135, Springer-Verlag, 2005.
8. A. K. Lenstra, H. W. Lenstra Jr, and L. Lovász. Factoring Polynomials with Rational Coefficients. Mathematische Ann. 261, 513-534, 1982.
9. R. J. McEliece. A public-key Cryptosystem Based on Algebraic Coding Theory. DSN Prog. Rep., Jet Prop. Lab., California Inst. Technol., Pasadena, CA, pages 114–116, January 1978.
10. D. Micciancio. Improving Lattice Based Cryptosystems Using the Hermite Normal Form. In Proc. of CaLC 2001, LNCS 2146, 126-145, Springer-Verlag, 2001.
11. D. Micciancio and S. Goldwasser. *Complexity of lattice problems : A Cryptographic perspective*. Kluwer Academic Publishers, 2002.
12. P. Q. Nguyen. Cryptanalysis of the Goldreich-Goldwasser-Halevi Cryptosystem from Crypto '97. In Proc. of Crypto '99, LNCS 1666, 288-304, Springer-Verlag, 1999.
13. P. Q. Nguyen and O. Regev. Learning a Parallelepiped: Cryptanalysis of GGH and NTRU Signatures. In Proc. of Eurocrypt'06, LNCS 4004, 271-288, Springer-Verlag, 2006.
14. P. Q. Nguyen and D. Stehlé. Floating-point LLL revisited. In Proc. of Eurocrypt 2005, LNCS 3494, 215-233, Springer-Verlag, 2005.
15. P. Q. Nguyen and D. Stehlé. LLL on the Average. In Proc. of ANTS VII, LNCS 4076, 238-256, Springer-Verlag, 2006.
16. P. Q. Nguyen and J. Stern. The Two Faces of Lattices in Cryptology. In Proc. of CaLC 2001, LNCS 2146, 146-180, Springer-Verlag, 2001.
17. NTL - A Number Theory Library. Available at http://shoup.net/ntl.
18. S. Paeng, B. E. Jung, and K. Ha. A Lattice Based Public Key Cryptosystem Using Polynomial Representations. In the Proc. of PKC 2003, LNCS 2567, 292-308, Springer-Verlag, 2003.
19. C. P. Schnorr. A Hierarchy of Polynomial Time Lattice Basis Reduction Algorithms. Theoretical Computer Science 53, 201-224, 1987.

Optimistic Fair Exchange
in a Multi-user Setting

Yevgeniy Dodis[1], Pil Joong Lee[2,*], and Dae Hyun Yum[2,*]

[1] Department of Computer Science, New York University, NY, USA
dodis@cs.nyu.edu
[2] Department of Electronic and Electrical Eng., POSTECH, Pohang, Korea
{pjl,dhyum}@postech.ac.kr

Abstract. This paper addresses the security of *optimistic fair exchange* in a *multi-user* setting. While the security of public key encryption and public key signature schemes in a single-user setting guarantees the security in a multi-user setting, we show that the situation is different in the optimistic fair exchange. First, we show how to break, in the multi-user setting, an optimistic fair exchange scheme provably secure in the single-user setting. This example separates the security of optimistic fair exchange between the single-user setting and the multi-user setting. We then define the formal security model of optimistic fair exchange in the multi-user setting, which is the first complete security model of optimistic fair exchange in the multi-user setting. We prove the existence of a generic construction meeting our multi-user security based on one-way functions in the random oracle model and trapdoor one-way permutations in the standard model. Finally, we revisit two well-known methodologies of optimistic fair exchange, which are based on the verifiably encrypted signature and the sequential two-party multisignature, respectively. Our result shows that these paradigms remain valid in the multi-user setting.

1 Introduction

MULTI-USER SECURITY. In the early stage of modern cryptography, public key cryptography was usually studied in the single-user setting and the security model assumed only one public key [20,21]; one receiver in the public key encryption and one signer in the public key signature. However, there are many users in the real world and the security in the single-user setting does not guard against the attacks by colluding dishonest users. The security in the multi-user setting was formally studied only recently [4,18]. Fortunately, these researches show that the security of encryption schemes in the single-user setting is preserved in the multi-user setting [4] and the same result holds good for signature schemes [18]. Therefore, we only have to deal with the single-user security and need not consider the multi-user security in the public key encryption and signature schemes.

---

* The research of the second author and the third author was supported by the MIC of Korea, under the ITRC support program (IITA-2006-C1090-0603-0026) and BK21.

T. Okamoto and X. Wang (Eds.): PKC 2007, LNCS 4450, pp. 118–133, 2007.

While the security of public key encryption and public key signature schemes in the single-user setting guarantees the security in the multi-user setting, there are other cryptosystems (e.g. identity-based encryption schemes) where the single-user security is not enough.

OPTIMISTIC FAIR EXCHANGE. A fair exchange scheme is a protocol by which two parties Alice and Bob swap items or services without allowing either party to gain an advantage by quitting prematurely or otherwise misbehaving. For instance, Alice signs some statement (e.g., e-cash) and Bob fulfills some obligation (e.g., delivery of goods). However, each party will play the role only if he (or she) is sure that the other party will keep the appointment. Of course, one could use an online trusted third party in every transaction to act as a mediator; each party sends the item to the trusted third party, who upon verifying the correctness of both items, forwards each item to the other party. A drawback of this approach is that the trusted third party is always involved in the exchange even if both parties are honest and no fault was occurred. In practice, sending messages via a trusted third party can lead to performance problems.

A more desirable approach is that a semi-trusted arbitrator involves only in cases where one party attempts to cheat or simply crashes. We call such a fair exchange protocol *optimistic*. In this model, Alice first issues a verifiable "partial signature" σ' to Bob. Bob verifies the validity of the partial signature and fulfills his obligation, after which Alice sends her "full signature" σ to complete the transaction. Thus, if no problem occurs, the arbitrator does not participate in the protocol. However, if Alice refuses to send her full signature σ at the end, Bob will send σ' (and proof of fulfilling his obligation) to the arbitrator who will convert σ' into σ, sending σ to Bob.

Optimistic fair exchange was introduced by Asokan et al. [1] and formally studied in [2,3] where several solutions were presented based on *verifiably encrypted signatures*. The approach of [2,3] was later generalized by [9], but all these schemes involve expensive and highly interactive zero-knowledge proofs in the exchange phase. The first *non-interactive* verifiably encrypted signature was built by Boneh et al. [8] under a form of the computational Diffie-Hellman assumption over special elliptic curve groups.

A different approach for building non-interactive optimistic fair exchange based on *sequential two-party multisignatures* was proposed by Park et al. [24], which was broken and repaired by Dodis and Reyzin [14]. While the schemes in [14] are very efficient, one important drawback of the approach based on the sequential two-party multisignature is that it is *setup-driven* [32]; the registration is required between the user and the arbitrator.

OUR CONTRIBUTION. There have been attempts to formally define the security of optimistic fair exchange. The first formal security model was proposed by Asokan et al. [2,3] but was not complete as their model did not consider a dishonest arbitrator. A more generalized and unified model for non-interactive optimistic fair exchange was suggested by Dodis and Reyzin [14]. Their model, called *verifiably committed signatures*, incorporates all aspects of non-interactive optimistic fair exchange but was defined in a single-user setting. If the security of optimistic fair exchange in the single-user setting guarantees the multi-user security, the model of [14] is satisfactory. Otherwise, we should extend the model to the multi-user setting.

In this paper, we show that the single-user security of optimistic fair exchange does not guarantee multi-user security. We present a simple counterexample based on a signature scheme and a trapdoor permutation. We then define the multi-user security model of optimistic fair exchange, extending the model of [14]. While the single-user model of [14] is setup-driven, our multi-user model is *setup-free* [32], which we feel is a more natural and advantageous realization of "optimistic" fair exchange in the multi-user setting; (1) If every fair exchange is performed normally (i.e., every user behaves honestly), it is desirable that users need not contact the arbitrator even for the registration purpose. (2) The arbitrator in setup-driven schemes should be semi-online to respond to registration requests, even when no dispute between users occurs. (3) If there are several arbitrators, the user in setup-free schemes can decide on a particular arbitrator in run-time.

After defining security notions, we address our attention to the basic theoretical question, namely whether or not a scheme satisfying the security notions exists, and, if so, what are the minimal computational complexity assumptions under which this existence can be proven. We answer this by providing a generic setup-free construction which relies on one-way functions in the random oracle model and trapdoor one-way permutations in the standard model. While the construction in the standard model is of theoretic interest, some specific instantiations in the random oracle model are efficient enough for practical use. Finally, we revisit two well-known techniques of optimistic fair exchange; the verifiably encrypted signature and the sequential two-party signature. Fortunately, our result shows that these paradigms remain valid in the multi-user setting if the underlying primitives satisfy some security properties. Furthermore, the construction based on the verifiably encrypted signature shows that trapdoor permutations imply optimistic fair exchange schemes that are *stand-alone* as well as setup-free; a fair exchange scheme is stand-alone if the full signature is the same as it were produced by an ordinary signature scheme only [32].

2 Preliminaries

2.1 NP-Relations and Σ-Protocols

An **NP**-relation R is a subset of $\{0,1\}^* \times \{0,1\}^*$ for which there is an efficient algorithm to decide whether $(\alpha, \beta) \in R$ or not in time polynomial in $|\alpha|$. The **NP**-language $\mathcal{L}_R$ associated with R is the set of α for which there exists β such that $(\alpha, \beta) \in R$, i.e., $\mathcal{L}_R = \{\alpha \mid \exists \beta \ [(\alpha, \beta) \in R]\}$.

A Σ-protocol [12] for an **NP**-relation R is an efficient 3-move two-party protocol between the prover and the verifier on a common input $\alpha \in \mathcal{L}_R$. Besides α, a valid **NP**-witness β for α, meaning $(\alpha, \beta) \in R$, is also given to the prover as a private input. The prover first sends a commitment message c to the receiver. After receiving the commitment message c, the verifier sends a challenge message e to the prover. Finally, the prover sends a response message s to the verifier who decides to output 1 (accept) or 0 (reject) based on the input α and the transcript $\pi = \{c, e, s\}$. The transcript π is valid if the verifier outputs 1 (accept).

A Σ-protocol should satisfy three properties: correctness, special soundness, and special (honest-verifier) zero-knowledge. Correctness property states that for all $\alpha \in \mathcal{L}_R$ and all valid witnesses β for α, if the prover and the verifier follow the protocol honestly, the verifier must output 1 (accept). Special soundness property states that there is an efficient extraction algorithm (called a knowledge extractor) that on input $\alpha \in \mathcal{L}_R$ and two valid transcripts π_1, π_2 with the same commitment message c outputs β such that $(\alpha, \beta) \in R$. Special zero-knowledge property states that there is an efficient simulation algorithm (called a simulator) that on input $\alpha \in \mathcal{L}_R$ and any challenge message e, outputs a valid transcript $\pi' = \{c', e, s'\}$. Moreover, the distribution of (c', s') is computationally indistinguishable from the corresponding distribution on (c, s) produced by the prover knowing a valid witness β for α and the verifier.

A function $f : \{0, 1\}^* \to \{0, 1\}^*$ is a one-way function, if there exists a polynomial time algorithm which computes $f(x)$ correctly for all x and the following probability is negligible for all PPT algorithm A: $\Pr[f(x') = y \mid x \leftarrow \{0, 1\}^k; y = f(x); x' \leftarrow A(y, 1^k)]$. A one-way function f is called a trapdoor (one-way) permutation, if f is a permutation (that is, every $f(x)$ has a unique pre-image x) and there exists a polynomial-length trapdoor td such that the inverse of f can efficiently be computed with td. For simplicity, we let f^{-1} be an inverse algorithm of f with the trapdoor td. It is known that any language in **NP** has a Σ-protocol if one-way functions exist.

Theorem 1 ([15,19]). *A Σ-protocol for any* **NP***-relation can be constructed if one-way functions exist.*

While the Σ-protocol for any **NP**-relation can be constructed in generic ways [15,19], there exist very efficient Σ-protocols for specific cases; for example, GQ protocol [22] and Schnorr protocol [31].

A Σ-protocol can be transformed into a signature scheme by using the Fiat-Shamir heuristic [17]. To sign a message m, the legal signer produces a valid transcript $\pi = \{c, e, s\}$ of the Σ-protocol, where $e = H(c, m)$ and $H(\cdot)$ is a cryptographic hash function modeled as a random function. The signature scheme obtained by applying the Fiat-Shamir heuristic to the Σ-protocol is secure in the random oracle model [5,26]. It is also known that the Fiat-Shamir heuristic provides a non-interactive proof of knowledge in the random oracle model (i.e., the witness can be extracted by rewinding the adversary).

If there are two Σ-protocols, i.e., Σ_1 for R_1 and Σ_2 for R_2, we can construct another Σ-protocol Σ_{OR} (called OR-proof) [12] which allows the prover to show that given two inputs x_1, x_2, he knows w such that either $(x_1, w) \in R_1$ or $(x_2, w) \in R_2$ without revealing which is the case (called the witness indistinguishability property [16]). By applying the Fiat-Shamir heuristic to the

OR-proof Σ_{OR}, we obtain a signature scheme $\mathcal{S}_{OR}$ (called the OR-signature) secure in the random oracle model such that a valid signature can be generated by the signer who knows a valid witness w corresponding to either of the two inputs x_1, x_2. It is known that the Fiat-Shamir heuristic does not affect the witness indistinguishability property of the Σ-protocol.

2.2 Signatures

A signature scheme $\mathcal{S}$ consists of three efficient algorithms: $\mathcal{S} = $ (Sig-Gen, Sign, Vrfy). We consider *existential unforgeability under adaptive chosen message attacks*, denoted by UF-CMA [21]. The adversary $\mathcal{A}$ is given oracle access to the signing oracle O_{Sign}. Naturally, $\mathcal{A}$ is considered successful only if it forges a valid signature σ of a message m which has not been queried to O_{Sign}. Quantitatively, we define

$$\mathsf{Adv}^{\mathcal{S}}_{\mathcal{A}}(k) = \Pr[\mathsf{Vrfy}_{vk}(m, \sigma) = 1 \mid (sk, vk) \leftarrow \mathsf{Sig\text{-}Gen}(1^k), \ (m, \sigma) \leftarrow \mathcal{A}^{O_{\mathsf{Sign}}}(vk)]$$

where m should not be queried to the signing oracle O_{Sign}. An adversary $\mathcal{A}$ is said to (t, q_s, ε)-break $\mathcal{S}$, if $\mathcal{A}$ runs in time at most t, makes at most q_s signing queries to O_{Sign}, and succeeds in forgery with probability at least ε. $\mathcal{S}$ is said to be (t, q_s, ε)-secure, if no adversary can (t, q_s, ε)-break it. Asymptotically, $\mathcal{S}$ is UF-CMA-secure if $\mathsf{Adv}^{\mathcal{S}}_{\mathcal{A}}(k)$ is negligible for any PPT adversary $\mathcal{A}$.

2.3 Encryption

An encryption scheme $\mathcal{E}$ consists of three algorithms: $\mathcal{E} = $ (Enc-Gen, Enc, Dec). We consider *indistinguishability against adaptive chosen ciphertext attacks*, denoted by IND-CCA [27]. For an efficient algorithm $\mathcal{A}$, which runs in two stages of find and guess, we define the adversary's advantage $\mathsf{CCA\text{-}Adv}^{\mathcal{E}}_{\mathcal{A}}(k)$ as

$$\left| \Pr\left[b = \tilde{b} \ \middle| \ \begin{array}{l} (ek, dk) \leftarrow \mathsf{Enc\text{-}Gen}(1^k), \ (m_0, m_1, \alpha) \leftarrow \mathcal{A}^{O_{\mathsf{Dec}}}(ek, \mathsf{find}), \\ b \leftarrow \{0, 1\}, \ c_b \leftarrow \mathsf{Enc}_{ek}(m_b), \ \tilde{b} \leftarrow \mathcal{A}^{O_{\mathsf{Dec}}}(c_b, \alpha, \mathsf{guess}) \end{array} \right] - \frac{1}{2} \right|$$

where the challenge ciphertext c_b should not be queried to the decryption oracle in the guess stage. An adversary $\mathcal{A}$ is said to (t, q_d, ε)-break $\mathcal{E}$, if $\mathcal{A}$ runs in time at most t, makes at most q_d decryption queries to O_{Dec}, and succeeds in distinguishing the challenge ciphertext with advantage at least ε. The encryption scheme $\mathcal{E}$ is said to be (t, q_d, ε)-secure, if no adversary can (t, q_d, ε)-break it. Asymptotically, $\mathcal{E}$ is CCA-secure if $\mathsf{CCA\text{-}Adv}^{\mathcal{E}}_{\mathcal{A}}(k)$ is negligible for any efficient adversary $\mathcal{A}$.

3   Optimistic Fair Exchange in a Single-User Setting

3.1 Definition

We review the single-user model of optimistic fair exchange [14].

Definition 1. *A non-interactive optimistic fair exchange involves the signer Alice, the verifier Bob and the arbitrator Charlie, and is given by the following efficient algorithms:*

- Setup. *This is a registration protocol between Alice and Charlie, by the end of which Alice learns her secret signing key* SK, *Charlie learns his secret arbitration key* ASK, *and they publish Alice's public verification key* PK *and Charlie's partial verification key* APK.
- Sig *and* Ver. *These are similar to conventional signing and verification algorithms of an ordinary digital signature scheme.* Sig(m, SK, APK) — *run by Alice* — *outputs a signature* σ *on* m, *while* Ver(m, σ, PK, APK) — *run by Bob (or any verifier)* — *outputs* 1 *(accept) or* 0 *(reject).*
- PSig *and* PVer. *These are partial signing and verification algorithms.* PSig *together with* Res *is functionally equivalent to* Sig. PSig(m, SK, APK) — *run by Alice* — *outputs a partial signature* σ', *while* PVer(m, σ', PK, APK) — *run by Bob (or any verifier)* — *outputs* 1 *(accept) or* 0 *(reject).*
- Res. *This is a resolution algorithm run by Charlie in case Alice refuses to open her signature* σ *to Bob, who in turn possesses a valid partial signature* σ' *on* m *(and a proof that he fulfilled his obligation to Alice). In this case,* Res(m, σ', ASK, PK) *should output a legal signature* σ *on* m.

Correctness property states that

- Ver$(m, Sig(m, SK, APK), PK, APK) = 1,$ PVer$(m, $PSig$(m, SK, APK), PK, APK)$ $= 1,$ *and* Ver$(m, Res(m, $PSig$(m, SK, APK), ASK, PK), PK, APK) = 1.$

Ambiguity property states that

- *Any "resolved signature"* Res$(m, $PSig$(m, SK, APK), ASK, PK)$ *is computationally indistinguishable from the "actual signature"* Sig$(m, SK, APK).$

In a meaningful application, Charlie runs Res to produce a full signature σ from σ' only if Bob's obligation to Alice has been fulfilled. The security of non-interactive optimistic fair exchange consists of ensuring three aspects: security against the signer, security against the verifier, and security against the arbitrator. In the following, we denote by O_{PSig} an oracle simulating the partial signing procedure PSig, and by O_{Res} an oracle simulating the resolution procedure Res.

SECURITY AGAINST ALICE. We require that any PPT adversary A succeeds with at most negligible probability in the following experiment.

$$\mathsf{Setup}^*(1^k) \rightarrow (\mathsf{SK}^*, \mathsf{PK}, \mathsf{ASK}, \mathsf{APK})$$
$$(m, \sigma') \leftarrow A^{O_{\mathsf{Res}}}(\mathsf{SK}^*, \mathsf{PK}, \mathsf{APK})$$
$$\sigma \leftarrow \mathsf{Res}(m, \sigma', \mathsf{ASK}, \mathsf{PK})$$
$$\text{success of } A = [\mathsf{PVer}(m, \sigma', \mathsf{PK}, \mathsf{APK}) \overset{?}{=} 1 \ \wedge \ \mathsf{Ver}(m, \sigma, \mathsf{PK}, \mathsf{APK}) \overset{?}{=} 0]$$

where Setup* denotes the run of Setup with dishonest Alice (run by A) and SK* is A's state after this run. In other words, Alice should not be able to produce partial signature σ', which looks good to Bob but cannot be transformed into her full signature by honest Charlie.

SECURITY AGAINST BOB. We require that any PPT adversary B succeeds with at most negligible probability in the following experiment.

$$\mathsf{Setup}(1^k) \rightarrow (\mathsf{SK}, \mathsf{PK}, \mathsf{ASK}, \mathsf{APK})$$
$$(m, \sigma) \leftarrow B^{O_{\mathsf{PSig}}, O_{\mathsf{Res}}}(\mathsf{PK}, \mathsf{APK})$$
$$\text{success of } B = [\mathsf{Ver}(m, \sigma, \mathsf{PK}, \mathsf{APK}) \stackrel{?}{=} 1 \ \wedge \ (m, \cdot) \notin Query(B, O_{\mathsf{Res}})]$$

where $Query(B, O_{\mathsf{Res}})$ is the set of valid queries of B has asked to the resolution oracle O_{Res} (i.e., (m, σ') such that $\mathsf{PVer}(m, \sigma', \mathsf{PK}, \mathsf{APK}) = 1$). In other words, Bob should not be able to complete any partial signature σ' that he received from Alice into a complete signature σ, without explicitly asking Charlie to do so. Note that there is no need to provide B with access to the signing oracle O_{Sig}, since it could be simulated by O_{PSig} and O_{Res}. Finally, we remark that we also want Bob to be unable to generate a valid partial signature σ' which was not produced by Alice (via a query to O_{PSig}). However, this guarantee will follow from a stronger security against Charlie, which is defined below.

SECURITY AGAINST CHARLIE. We require that any PPT adversary C succeeds with at most negligible probability in the following experiment.

$$\mathsf{Setup}^*(1^k) \rightarrow (\mathsf{SK}, \mathsf{PK}, \mathsf{ASK}^*, \mathsf{APK})$$
$$(m, \sigma) \leftarrow C^{O_{\mathsf{PSig}}}(\mathsf{ASK}^*, \mathsf{PK}, \mathsf{APK})$$
$$\text{success of } C = [\mathsf{Ver}(m, \sigma, \mathsf{PK}, \mathsf{APK}) \stackrel{?}{=} 1 \ \wedge \ m \notin Query(C, O_{\mathsf{PSig}})]$$

where Setup^* denotes the run of Setup with dishonest Charlie (run by C), ASK^* is C's state after this run, and $Query(C, O_{\mathsf{PSig}})$ is the set of queries of C asked to the partial signing oracle O_{PSig}. In other words, Charlie should not be able to produce a valid signature on m without explicitly asking Alice to produce a partial signature on m (which Charlie can complete into a full signature by himself using ASK).

3.2 Single-User Security $\nRightarrow$ Multi-user Security

We show that the single-user security of optimistic fair exchange does not imply the multi-user security by presenting a counter-example.

SCHEME. Let $f(\cdot)$ be a trapdoor permutation and $\mathcal{S} = (\mathsf{Sig\text{-}Gen}, \mathsf{Sign}, \mathsf{Vrfy})$ be a signature scheme.

- Setup. Charlie generates a trapdoor permutation (f, f^{-1}) and publishes $\mathsf{APK} = f$, while he keeps $\mathsf{ASK} = f^{-1}$ secret. Alice generates $(sk, vk) \leftarrow \mathsf{Sig\text{-}Gen}(1^k)$ and publishes $\mathsf{PK}_A = vk$ and keeps $\mathsf{SK}_A = sk$ secret.
- Sig and Ver. To sign a message m, Alice chooses a random number r_A, and computes $y_A = f(r_A)$ and $\delta_A = \mathsf{Sign}_{sk}(m\|y_A)$. The signature of m is $\sigma_A = (r_A, \delta_A)$. To verify Alice's signature $\sigma_A = (r_A, \delta_A)$ of m, Bob computes $y_A = f(r_A)$ and checks $\mathsf{Vrfy}_{vk}(m\|y_A, \delta_A) \stackrel{?}{=} 1$.

- PSig and PVer. To generate a partial signature, Alice chooses a random number r_A and computes $y_A = f(r_A)$ and $\delta_A = \text{Sign}_{sk}(m\|y_A)$. The partial signature of m is $\sigma'_A = (y_A, \delta_A)$. Bob verifies $\sigma'_A = (y_A, \delta_A)$ by checking $\text{Vrfy}_{vk}(m\|y_A, \delta_A) \stackrel{?}{=} 1$.
- Res. Given a partial signature (m, y_A, δ_A), the arbitrator Charlie first verifies its validity by checking $\text{Vrfy}_{vk}(m\|y_A, \delta_A) \stackrel{?}{=} 1$. If valid, he computes $r_A = f^{-1}(y_A)$ and returns $\sigma_A = (r_A, \delta_A)$.

THE SINGLE-USER SECURITY. The above scheme is secure in the single-user setting, which can easily be shown following the proofs in [14].

ATTACK SCENARIO. We observe that y_A can be re-used by a dishonest user without knowing the corresponding r_A, which causes the scheme to be insecure in the multi-user setting. Dishonest users Bob and Eve attack Alice as follows:

1. Alice gives a partial signature (m_A, y_A, δ_A) to Bob, where $y_A = f(r_A)$ and $\delta_A = \text{Sign}_{\text{SK}_A}(m_A\|y_A)$.
2. Bob gives (m_B, y_B, δ_B) to his dishonest friend Eve, where $m_B \neq m_A$, $y_B = y_A$ and $\delta_B = \text{Sign}_{\text{SK}_B}(m_B\|y_B)$.
3. Eve comes to the arbitrator with (m_B, y_B, δ_B) and claims that Bob refuses to open his signature (and maybe gives a proof to the arbitrator that Eve fulfilled her obligation to Bob).
4. The arbitrator does not suspect anything and completes this signature by giving $r_A = f^{-1}(y_B)$ to Eve.
5. Eve gives r_A to Bob, who now has completed the signature of Alice, (m_A, r_A, δ_A), although Alice never intended to open this and Bob did not fulfill his duty to Alice.

Therefore, the above optimistic fair exchange scheme is secure in the single-user setting but insecure in the multi-user setting. This counterexample entails the following theorem.

Theorem 2. *The single-use security of optimistic fair exchange does not imply the multi-user security.*

4 Optimistic Fair Exchange in a Multi-user Setting

4.1 Definition

Instead of defining the syntax and security from scratch, we extend the model of [14] to the multi-user setting. Firstly, we separate the Setup algorithm of the single-user setting into two algorithms Setup^{TTP} and Setup^{User} to model the setup-free optimistic fair exchange. By running Setup^{User}, each user U_i generates his own key pair $(\text{SK}_{U_i}, \text{PK}_{U_i})$.

Definition 2. *A non-interactive optimistic fair exchange involves the users (signers and verifiers) and the arbitrator, and is given by the following efficient algorithms:*

- Setup^{TTP}. *The arbitrator setup algorithm takes as input a security parameter and returns a secret arbitration key* ASK *and a public partial verification key* APK.
- Setup^{User}. *The user setup algorithm takes as input a security parameter and (optionally)* APK. *It returns a private signing key* SK *and a public verification key* PK.
- Sig *and* Ver. *These are similar to conventional signing and verification algorithms of an ordinary digital signature scheme.* Sig$(m, \mathsf{SK}_{U_i}, \mathsf{APK})$ — *run by a signer* U_i — *outputs a signature* σ_{U_i} *on* m, *while* Ver$(m, \sigma_{U_i}, \mathsf{PK}_{U_i}, \mathsf{APK})$ — *run by a verifier* — *outputs* 1 *(accept) or* 0 *(reject).*
- PSig *and* PVer. *These are partial signing and verification algorithms.* PSig *together with* Res *is functionally equivalent to* Sig. PSig$(m, \mathsf{SK}_{U_i}, \mathsf{APK})$ — *run by a signer* U_i — *outputs a partial signature* σ'_{U_i}, *while* PVer$(m, \sigma'_{U_i}, \mathsf{PK}_{U_i}, \mathsf{APK})$ — *run by a verifier* — *outputs* 1 *(accept) or* 0 *(reject).*
- Res. *This is a resolution algorithm run by the arbitrator in case a signer* U_i *refuses to open his signature* σ_{U_i} *to a user* U_j, *who possesses a valid partial signature* σ'_{U_i} *on* m *(and a proof that* U_j *fulfilled his obligation to* U_i). *In this case,* Res$(m, \sigma'_{U_i}, \mathsf{ASK}, \mathsf{PK}_{U_i})$ *should output a legal signature* σ_{U_i} *on* m.

Correctness property states that

- Ver$(m, \mathsf{Sig}(m, \mathsf{SK}_{U_i}, \mathsf{APK}), \mathsf{PK}_{U_i}, \mathsf{APK}) = 1$,
  PVer$(m, \mathsf{PSig}(m, \mathsf{SK}_{U_i}, \mathsf{APK}), \mathsf{PK}_{U_i}, \mathsf{APK}) = 1$, *and*
  Ver$(m, \mathsf{Res}(m, \mathsf{PSig}(m, \mathsf{SK}_{U_i}, \mathsf{APK}), \mathsf{ASK}, \mathsf{PK}_{U_i}), \mathsf{PK}_{U_i}, \mathsf{APK}) = 1$.

Ambiguity property states that

- *Any "resolved signature"* Res$(m, \mathsf{PSig}(m, \mathsf{SK}_{U_i}, \mathsf{APK}), \mathsf{ASK}, \mathsf{PK}_{U_i})$ *is computationally indistinguishable from the "actual signature"* Sig$(m, \mathsf{SK}_{U_i}, \mathsf{APK})$.

We do not deal with the subtle issue of timely termination addressed by [2,3]. We remark, however, that the technique of [2,3] can easily be added to our solutions to resolve this problem. The security of non-interactive optimistic fair exchange is composed of ensuring three aspects: security against signers, security against verifiers, and security against the arbitrator. To clarify the identity of the signer, we hereinafter assume that the message m (implicitly) includes the identity of the signer. One simple and trivial solution is to include the signer's identity inside the message. If the included signer's identity does not correspond to the subject of the alleged signer's public key, we consider the signature (or the partial signature) is invalid. We also remark that it is a good practice to include an enforcing resolution policy κ inside the message, as suggested in [3].

In order to consider the collusion attack of dishonest users, we modify the resolution oracle O_{Res}. In the single-user setting, the input to O_{Res} is (m, σ'), assuming that σ' is the partial signature value of the single signer Alice and the oracle checks the validity of σ' by using Alice's public key. In the multi-user setting, we define the input to O_{Res} as $(m, \sigma', \mathsf{PK}_{U_i})$ where PK_{U_i} is the public key of the alleged signer U_i. As usual, we assume that the authenticity of public keys can be verified and each user should show his knowledge of the legitimate private key in the public key registration stage to defend against key substitution attacks.

For simplicity but without loss of generality, when we model either the dishonest verifier or the dishonest arbitrator, we suppose that the adversary attacks an honest user Alice and the adversary can collude with all other (dishonest) users. Therefore, the dishonest verifier or the dishonest arbitrator has access to private keys of all users except Alice, and the partial signing oracle O_{PSig}, taking as input a message m, always returns Alice's partial signature σ'_A on m.

SECURITY AGAINST SIGNERS. We require that any PPT adversary A, who models the dishonest signer Alice, succeeds with at most negligible probability in the following experiment.

$$\mathsf{Setup}^{\mathsf{TTP}}(1^k) \rightarrow (\mathsf{ASK}, \mathsf{APK})$$
$$(m, \sigma', \mathsf{PK}_A) \leftarrow A^{O_{\mathsf{Res}}}(\mathsf{APK})$$
$$\sigma \leftarrow \mathsf{Res}(m, \sigma', \mathsf{ASK}, \mathsf{PK}_A)$$
$$\text{success of } A = [\mathsf{PVer}(m, \sigma', \mathsf{PK}_A, \mathsf{APK}) \stackrel{?}{=} 1 \ \wedge \ \mathsf{Ver}(m, \sigma, \mathsf{PK}_A, \mathsf{APK}) \stackrel{?}{=} 0]$$

In the single-user setting, the signer Alice wins if she comes up with a partial signature (m, σ') which is valid with respect to her public key but cannot be transformed into her full signature by the honest arbitrator. In the multi-user setting, Alice wins if she comes up with $(m, \sigma', \mathsf{PK}_A)$ where σ' is a valid partial signature with respect to PK_A but cannot be completed to the full signature (w.r.t. PK_A) by the honest arbitrator. Note that there is no need to provide A with access to any kind of the partial signing oracle, since she has access to private keys of all users and can simulate all partial signing oracles by herself.

SECURITY AGAINST VERIFIERS. We require that any PPT adversary B succeeds with at most negligible probability in the following experiment.

$$\mathsf{Setup}^{\mathsf{TTP}}(1^k) \rightarrow (\mathsf{ASK}, \mathsf{APK})$$
$$\mathsf{Setup}^{\mathsf{User}}(1^k) \rightarrow (\mathsf{SK}_A, \mathsf{PK}_A)$$
$$(m, \sigma) \leftarrow B^{O_{\mathsf{PSig}}, O_{\mathsf{Res}}}(\mathsf{PK}_A, \mathsf{APK})$$
$$\text{success of } B = [\mathsf{Ver}(m, \sigma, \mathsf{PK}_A, \mathsf{APK}) \stackrel{?}{=} 1 \ \wedge \ (m, \cdot, \mathsf{PK}_A) \notin Query(B, O_{\mathsf{Res}})]$$

where $Query(B, O_{\mathsf{Res}})$ is the set of valid queries of B has asked to the resolution oracle O_{Res} (i.e., $(m, \sigma', \mathsf{PK}_{U_i})$ such that $\mathsf{PVer}(m, \sigma', \mathsf{PK}_{U_i}, \mathsf{APK}) = 1$). Even though the adversary B is not allowed to ask a valid query $(m, \cdot, \mathsf{PK}_A)$ with the target message m, it can freely ask $(\cdot, \cdot, \mathsf{PK}_{U_i})$ to the resolution oracle O_{Res} as long as PK_{U_i} is not Alice's public key. This very property was used to attack the scheme of Section 3.2. Note that there is no need to provide B with access to the signing oracle O_{Sig}, since it can be simulated by O_{PSig} and O_{Res}.

SECURITY AGAINST THE ARBITRATOR. We require that any PPT adversary C succeeds with at most negligible probability in the following experiment.

$$\mathsf{Setup}^{\mathsf{TTP}^*}(1^k) \rightarrow (\mathsf{ASK}^*, \mathsf{APK})$$
$$\mathsf{Setup}^{\mathsf{User}}(1^k) \rightarrow (\mathsf{SK}_A, \mathsf{PK}_A)$$
$$(m, \sigma) \leftarrow C^{O_{\mathsf{PSig}}}(\mathsf{ASK}^*, \mathsf{PK}_A, \mathsf{APK})$$
$$\text{success of } C = [\mathsf{Ver}(m, \sigma, \mathsf{PK}_A, \mathsf{APK}) \stackrel{?}{=} 1 \,\wedge\, m \notin Query(C, O_{\mathsf{PSig}})]$$

where $\mathsf{Setup}^{\mathsf{TTP}^*}$ denotes the run of $\mathsf{Setup}^{\mathsf{TTP}}$ with the dishonest arbitrator (run by C), ASK^* is C's state after this run, and $Query(C, O_{\mathsf{PSig}})$ is the set of queries of C asked to the partial signing oracle O_{PSig}.

4.2   Generic Construction

We present a generic construction of non-interactive setup-free[1] optimistic fair exchange based on the OR-proof where the signer has one witness and the arbitrator has the other witness. We use the Fiat-Shamir heuristic in the random oracle model and the non-interactive witness indistinguishable proof of knowledge in the standard model.

SCHEME. Let $\mathcal{S} = (\mathsf{Sig\text{-}Gen}, \mathsf{Sign}, \mathsf{Vrfy})$ be an ordinary signature scheme.

- $\mathsf{Setup}^{\mathsf{TTP}}$. The arbitrator chooses (sk, vk) by running $\mathsf{Sig\text{-}Gen}(1^k)$ and sets $(\mathsf{ASK}, \mathsf{APK}) = (sk, vk)$.
- $\mathsf{Setup}^{\mathsf{User}}$. Each user U_i chooses (sk_i, vk_i) by running $\mathsf{Sig\text{-}Gen}(1^k)$ and sets $(\mathsf{SK}_{U_i}, \mathsf{PK}_{U_i}) = (sk_i, vk_i)$.
- Sig. When a user U_i wants to sign a message m, the signer generates an ordinary signature s_1 on "$0||m$" (i.e., $s_1 = \mathsf{Sign}_{sk_i}(0||m)$) and then generates an OR-signature s_2 on "$1||m$" for the knowledge of sk_i or $\mathsf{Sign}_{sk}(1||m)$. Since the signer U_i knows sk_i, he can generate the valid OR-signature s_2. The signature value on m is $\sigma_{U_i} = (s_1, s_2)$.
- Ver. To verify the signature $\sigma_{U_i} = (s_1, s_2)$ on m, a verifier checks that (1) $\mathsf{Vrfy}_{vk_i}(0||m, s_1) \stackrel{?}{=} 1$ and (2) s_2 is a valid OR-signature on "$1||m$" for the knowledge of sk_i or $\mathsf{Sign}_{sk}(1||m)$.
- PSig and PVer. The same as Sig and Ver except that the partial signature σ'_{U_i} on m is s_1.
- Res. For the user U_i's partial signature $\sigma'_{U_i} = s_1$ on m, the arbitrator first checks that $\mathsf{Vrfy}_{vk_i}(0||m, s_1) \stackrel{?}{=} 1$ and then computes an OR-signature s_2 on "$1||m$" for the knowledge of sk_i or $\mathsf{Sign}_{sk}(1||m)$. Since the arbitrator knows sk, he can compute an ordinary signature $\mathsf{Sign}_{sk}(1||m)$ and then the valid OR-signature s_2. The arbitrator outputs $\sigma_{U_i} = (s_1, s_2)$.

The correctness property of the scheme is obvious and the ambiguity property follows from the witness indistinguishability of the OR-signature s_2.

Theorem 3. *The generic construction of the optimistic fair exchange is multi-user secure in the random oracle model if the underlying signature is secure.*

---

[1] If we allow the registration between the signer and the arbitrator, there are trivial setup-driven solutions.

Proof. See [13].

Theorem 4. *If there are one-way functions, we can build the setup-free optimistic fair exchange schemes that are multi-user secure in the random oracle model.*

Proof. Secure signatures exist if and only if one-way functions exist [23,28]. Together with Theorem 3, we obtain Theorem 4 .

The proof of Theorem 3 only requires two properties from the Fiat-Shamir proofs: (1) witness indistinguishability and (2) proof of knowledge. Hence, we can use the straight-line extractable witness indistinguishable proof [25] instead of the Fiat-Shamir proof. Like the Fiat-Shamir heuristic, the construction of the straight-line extractable witness indistinguishable proof starts with the Σ-protocol but the length of the resulting proof is much longer. However, non-programmable random oracle is used and better exact security can be obtained.

Instead of the Fiat-Shamir proof, we can also use the non-interactive witness indistinguishable proofs of knowledge for sk_i or $\mathsf{Sign}_{sk}(m)$. In this case, we do not need the random oracle and can instead use a common reference string (which could be generated by the arbitrator).[2] The construction of non-interactive witness indistinguishable proofs of knowledge requires the existence of trapdoor permutations [30] and this observation leads to the following theorem.

Theorem 5. *If there are trapdoor permutations, we can build the setup-free optimistic fair exchange schemes that are multi-user secure in the standard model.*

Remark 1. While the construction using non-interactive witness indistinguishable proofs of knowledge in the standard model is mainly of theoretic interest, the construction using the Fiat-Shamir heuristic in the random oracle is efficient for specific cases, as there are efficient Σ-protocols for the knowledge of a signature value and for the knowledge of a secret key corresponding to a given public key (e.g., [22,31,10,11,7]).

5   Previous Paradigms Revisited

5.1   Optimistic Fair Exchange from Verifiably Encrypted Signature

Suppose Alice wants to show Bob that she has signed a message. Alice first encrypts her signature using the public encryption key of the arbitrator, and sends the ciphertext to Bob with proof that she has given him a valid encryption of her signature. Bob can verify that Alice has signed the message, but cannot deduce any information on her signature. Later in the protocol, if Alice is unable or unwilling to reveal her signature, Bob can ask the arbitrator to decrypt the ciphertext of Alice's signature.

---

[2] We use a common "reference" string rather than a common "random" string. The arbitrator can indeed publish the common reference string because in our particular scheme cheating in OR-signature or NIZK does not help the arbitrator.

SCHEME. Let (P, V) be a non-interactive zero-knowledge (NIZK) proof system for the NP-language $L = \{(c, m, ek, vk) \mid \exists s \ [c = \mathsf{Enc}_{ek}(s) \wedge \mathsf{Vrfy}_{vk}(m, s) = 1]\}$, where $\mathcal{E} = (\mathsf{Enc\text{-}Gen}, \mathsf{Enc}, \mathsf{Dec})$ is an encryption scheme and $\mathcal{S} = (\mathsf{Sig\text{-}Gen}, \mathsf{Sign}, \mathsf{Vrfy})$ is a signature scheme.[3]

- $\mathsf{Setup}^{\mathsf{TTP}}$. The arbitrator chooses (dk, ek) by running $\mathsf{Enc\text{-}Gen}(1^k)$ and sets $(\mathsf{ASK}, \mathsf{APK}) = (dk, ek)$.
- $\mathsf{Setup}^{\mathsf{User}}$. Each user U_i chooses (sk_i, vk_i) by running $\mathsf{Sig\text{-}Gen}(1^k)$ and sets $(\mathsf{SK}_{U_i}, \mathsf{PK}_{U_i}) = (sk_i, vk_i)$.
- Sig. When a user U_i wants to sign a message m, the signer generates a signature $s = \mathsf{Sign}_{sk_i}(m)$. The signature value of m is $\sigma_{U_i} = s$.
- Ver. To verify the signature $\sigma_{U_i} = s$ of m, a verifier checks $\mathsf{Vrfy}_{vk_i}(m, s) \overset{?}{=} 1$.
- PSig. When a user U_i wants to generate a partial signature of m, the signer first computes a signature $s = \mathsf{Sign}_{sk_i}(m)$ and then encrypts s with APK, i.e., $c = \mathsf{Enc}_{ek}(s)$. The partial signature of m is $\sigma'_{U_i} = (c, \pi)$, where π is a proof showing $(c, m, ek, vk_i) \in L$.
- PVer. To verify the partial signature $\sigma'_{U_i} = (c, \pi)$ of m, a verifier checks that π is an accepting proof for the statement $(c, m, ek, vk_i) \in L$. If so, 1 is returned and otherwise, 0 is returned.
- Res. For the user U_i's partial signature $\sigma'_{U_i} = (c, \pi)$ of m, the arbitrator first checks that π is an accepting proof for the statement $(c, m, ek, vk_i) \in L$ and then decrypts $s = \mathsf{Dec}_{dk}(c)$. The arbitrator outputs $\sigma_{U_i} = s$.

Theorem 6. *The optimistic fair exchange scheme based on a verifiably encrypted signature is secure if the underlying $\mathcal{E}$ is CCA-secure, $\mathcal{S}$ is UF-CMA-secure, and (P, V) is a simulation-sound NIZK proof system.*

Proof. See [13].

We observe that the full signature $\sigma_{U_i} = s$ is a signature value of the underlying ordinary signature scheme $\mathcal{S}$, which means that the fair exchange scheme is stand-alone. In addition, CCA-secure encryption $\mathcal{E}$, UF-CMA-secure signature $\mathcal{S}$, and simulation-sound NIZK proof system (P, V) can be built from trapdoor permutations [29,23,28]. Hence, we obtain the following existence theorem of setup-free and stand-alone fair exchange schemes.

Theorem 7. *If there are trapdoor permutations, we can build the optimistic fair exchange schemes that are setup-free and stand-alone.*

5.2   Optimistic Fair Exchange from Sequential Two-Party Multisignature

A multisignature scheme allows any subgroup of users to jointly sign a document such that a verifier is convinced that each user of the subgroup participated in

---

[3] For brevity's sake, we omit the description of a common reference string, which could be generated by the arbitrator.

signing. To construct an optimistic fair exchange, we can use a simple type of multisignature, which is called a sequential two-party multisignature.

A sequential two-party multisignature $\mathcal{MS}$ consists of five efficient algorithms: $\mathcal{MS} = $ (Sig-Gen, Sign, Vrfy, MSign, MVrfy). Key generation algorithm Sig-Gen, signing algorithm Sign, and verification algorithm Vrfy are similar to the conventional algorithms of an ordinary signature scheme. MSign takes as input (m, s_i, vk_i, sk_j) and returns a multisignature s_{ij}, where $m \in \mathcal{M}$ is a message, sk_j is a signing key, s_i is a valid signature w.r.t. a verification key vk_i, and s_{ij} is a multisignature w.r.t. verification keys vk_i and vk_j. MVrfy takes (m, s_{ij}, vk_i, vk_j) as input and returns 1 (accept) or 0 (reject). Correctness property requires that $\mathsf{Vrfy}_{vk_i}(m, \mathsf{Sign}_{sk_i}(m)) = 1$ and $\mathsf{MVrfy}(m, \mathsf{MSign}(m, s_i, vk_i, sk_j), vk_i, vk_j) = 1$, for any $m \in \mathcal{M}$. A multisignature scheme is *symmetric* if s_{ij} and s_{ji} are computationally indistinguishable.

For security consideration, we allow the adversary $\mathcal{A}$, who tries to forge a multisignature w.r.t. a given verification key, to have access to the signing oracle O_{Sign} and the multi-signing oracle O_{MSign}. $\mathcal{A}$'s query to O_{Sign} is (m, vk_i) and O_{Sign} returns $\mathsf{Sign}_{sk_i}(m)$. $\mathcal{A}$'s query to O_{MSign} is (m, s_i, vk_i, vk_j) and O_{MSign} returns s_{ij} if $\mathsf{Vrfy}_{vk_i}(m, s_i) = 1$. While the adversary $\mathcal{A}$ is allowed to create arbitrary keys for corrupted users, we require $\mathcal{A}$ to prove knowledge of secret keys during the public key registration. For simplicity, we follow the model of [6] which asks $\mathcal{A}$ to output the public key and secret key of a corrupted user in the key registration stage. Let $Query(\mathcal{A}, O_{\mathsf{Sign}})$ and $Query(\mathcal{A}, O_{\mathsf{MSign}})$ be the set of valid queries of $\mathcal{A}$ to O_{Sign} and O_{MSign}, respectively. We define $\mathcal{A}$'s advantage $\mathsf{Adv}_{\mathcal{A}}^{\mathcal{MS}}(k)$ of attacking $\mathcal{MS}$ as follows.

$$\Pr[\mathsf{MVrfy}(m, s, vk_i, vk_j) = 1 \vee \mathsf{MVrfy}(m, s, vk_j, vk_i) = 1 \mid$$
$$(sk_i, vk_i) \leftarrow \mathsf{Sig\text{-}Gen}(1^k), (m, s, vk_j) \leftarrow \mathcal{A}^{O_{\mathsf{Sign}}, O_{\mathsf{MSign}}}(vk_i)]$$

Definition 3. *Let $\mathcal{MS} = $ (Sig-Gen, Sign, Vrfy, MSign, MVrfy) be a sequential two-party signature scheme. An adversary $\mathcal{A}$ is said to $(t, q_s, q_{ms}, \varepsilon)$-break $\mathcal{MS}$, if $\mathcal{A}$ runs in time at most t, makes at most q_s signing queries to O_{Sign} and q_{ms} multi-signing queries to O_{MSign}, and succeeds in forgery with probability at least ε. $\mathcal{MS}$ is said to be $(t, q_s, q_{ms}, \varepsilon)$-secure, if no adversary can $(t, q_s, q_{ms}, \varepsilon)$-break it. Asymptotically, $\mathcal{MS}$ is UF-CMA-secure if $\mathsf{Adv}_{\mathcal{A}}^{\mathcal{MS}}(k)$ is negligible for any PPT adversary $\mathcal{A}$.*

By relaxing the definition of optimistic fair exchange to allow interactive registration during setup (i.e., setup-driven), we can have much simpler (almost trivial) schemes based on the sequential two-party multisignature. Each user U_i generates four keys $\mathsf{SK}_{U_i}, \mathsf{PK}_{U_i}, \mathsf{ASK}_{U_i}, \mathsf{APK}_{U_i}$ and sends $\mathsf{PK}_{U_i}, \mathsf{ASK}_{U_i}, \mathsf{APK}_{U_i}$ to the arbitrator, who checks if the keys were properly generated. The arbitrator will then store ASK_{U_i} and certify APK_{U_i}. A verifier will accept partial signatures from U_i only if they are valid w.r.t. APK_{U_i}.

SCHEME.   Let $\mathcal{MS} = $ (Sig-Gen, Sign, Vrfy, MSign, MVrfy) be a sequential two-party multisignature scheme.

- Setup^{TTP} and Setup^{User}. Each user U_i chooses $(sk_{U_i}^0, vk_{U_i}^0)$ and $(sk_{U_i}^1, vk_{U_i}^1)$ by running Sig-Gen(1^k) twice, and sends $(vk_{U_i}^0, sk_{U_i}^1, vk_{U_i}^1)$ to the arbitrator. After checking validity of the keys, the arbitrator stores $sk_{U_i}^1$ and certifies $vk_{U_i}^1$. If we use a simplified notation such as $sk_{i_0} = sk_{U_i}^0$, $vk_{i_1} = vk_{U_i}^1$, the output is $(\mathsf{SK}_{U_i}, \mathsf{PK}_{U_i}, \mathsf{ASK}_{U_i}, \mathsf{APK}_{U_i}) = ((sk_{i_0}, sk_{i_1}), (vk_{i_0}, vk_{i_1}), sk_{i_1}, vk_{i_0})$.
- Sig. When a user U_i wants to sign a message m, the signer computes $s_{i_0} = \mathsf{Sign}_{sk_{i_0}}(m)$ and a multisignature $s_{i_0 i_1} = \mathsf{MSign}(m, s_{i_0}, vk_{i_0}, sk_{i_1})$. The signature value of m is $\sigma_{U_i} = s_{i_0 i_1}$.
- Ver. A verifier checks $\mathsf{MVrfy}(m, s_{i_0 i_1}, vk_{i_0}, vk_{i_1}) \overset{?}{=} 1$.
- PSig. When a user U_i wants to generate a partial signature of a message m, the signer computes $s_{i_0} = \mathsf{Sign}_{sk_{i_0}}(m)$. The partial signature is $\sigma'_{U_i} = s_{i_0}$.
- PVer. To verify the partial signature $\sigma'_{U_i} = s_{i_0}$ of m w.r.t. PK_{U_i}, a verifier checks $\mathsf{Vrfy}_{vk_{i_0}}(m, s_{i_0}) \overset{?}{=} 1$. If so, 1 is returned and otherwise, 0 is returned.
- Res. For the user U_i's partial signature $\sigma'_{U_i} = s_{i_0}$ of m, the arbitrator first checks $\mathsf{Vrfy}_{vk_{i_0}}(m, s_{i_0}) \overset{?}{=} 1$ and then generates a multisignature $s_{i_0 i_1} = \mathsf{MSign}(m, s_{i_0}, vk_{i_0}, sk_{i_1})$. The arbitrator outputs $\sigma_{U_i} = s$.

Remark 2. Specific instantiations could be very efficient by directly using the combined signing key $sk_{U_i} = sk_{U_i}^0 \diamond sk_{U_i}^1$ to generate multisignatures and the combined verification key $pk_{U_i} = pk_{U_i}^0 \circ pk_{U_i}^1$ to verify multisignatures.

Theorem 8. *The setup-driven optimistic fair exchange scheme based on a sequential two-party multisignature is secure if the underlying multisignature is UF-CMA-secure.*

Proof. See [13].

References

1. N. Asokan, M. Schunter, and M. Waidner. Optimistic protocols for fair exchange. *ACM CCS*, pages 7–17. ACM, 1997.
2. N. Asokan, V. Shoup, and M. Waidner. Optimistic fair exchange of digital signatures (extended abstract). *EUROCRYPT 1998*, pages 591–606, 1998.
3. N. Asokan, V. Shoup, and M. Waidner. Optimistic fair exchange of digital signatures. *IEEE Journal on Selected Areas in Communication*, 18(4):593–610, 2000.
4. M. Bellare, A. Boldyreva, and S. Micali. Public-key encryption in a multi-user setting: Security proofs and improvements. *EUROCRYPT 2000*, pages 259–274.
5. M. Bellare and P. Rogaway. Random oracles are practical: A paradigm for designing efficient protocols. *ACM CCS*, pages 62–73, 1993.
6. A. Boldyreva. Threshold signatures, multisignatures and blind signatures based on the gap-Diffie-Hellman-group signature scheme. *PKC 2003*, pages 31–46, 2003.
7. D. Boneh, X. Boyen, and H. Shacham. Short group signatures. *CRYPTO 2004*, pages 41–55, 2004.
8. D. Boneh, C. Gentry, B. Lynn, and H. Shacham. Aggregate and verifiably encrypted signatures from bilinear maps. *EUROCRYPT 2003*, pages 416–432, 2003.

9. J. Camenisch and I. Damgård. Verifiable encryption, group encryption, and their applications to separable group signatures and signature sharing schemes. *ASIACRYPT 2000*, pages 331–345, 2000.
10. J. Camenisch and A. Lysyanskaya. A signature scheme with efficient protocols. In *SCN 2002*, pages 268–289, 2002.
11. J. Camenisch and A. Lysyanskaya. Signature schemes and anonymous credentials from bilinear maps. *CRYPTO 2004*, pages 56–72, 2004.
12. R. Cramer, I. Damgård, and B. Schoenmakers. Proofs of partial knowledge and simplified design of witness hiding protocols. *CRYPTO 1994*, pages 174–187, 1994.
13. Y. Dodis, P.J. Lee, and D.H. Yum. Optimistic fair exchagne in a multi-user setting. *IACR ePrint Archive*, http://eprint.iacr.org/, 2007.
14. Y. Dodis and L. Reyzin. Breaking and repairing optimistic fair exchange from PODC 2003. *2003 ACM Workshop on Digital Rights Management*, pages 47–54.
15. U. Feige and A. Shamir. Zero knowledge proofs of knowledge in two rounds. *CRYPTO 1989*, pages 526–544, 1989.
16. U. Feige and A. Shamir. Witness indistinguishable and witness hiding protocols. *the 22nd STOC*, pages 416–426. ACM, 1990.
17. A. Fiat and A. Shamir. How to prove yourself: Practical solutions to identification and signature problems. *CRYPTO 1986*, pages 186–194, 1986.
18. S. D. Galbraith, J. Malone-Lee, and N. P. Smart. Public key signatures in the multi-user setting. *Inf. Process. Lett.*, 83(5):263–266, 2002.
19. O. Goldreich, S. Micali, and A. Wigderson. Proofs that yield nothing but their validity or all languages in NP have zero-knowledge proof systems. *J. ACM*, 38(3):691–729, 1991.
20. S. Goldwasser and S. Micali. Probabilistic encryption. *J. Comput. Syst. Sci.*, 28(2):270–299, 1984.
21. S. Goldwasser, S. Micali, and R. L. Rivest. A digital signature scheme secure against adaptive chosen-message attacks. *SIAM J. Comput.*, 17(2):281–308, 1988.
22. L. C. Guillou and J.-J. Quisquater. A "paradoxical" indentity-based signature scheme resulting from zero-knowledge. *CRYPTO 1988*, pages 216–231, 1988.
23. M. Naor and M. Yung. Universal one-way hash functions and their cryptographic applications. *the 21st STOC*, pages 33–43. ACM, 1989.
24. J. M. Park, E. K. P. Chong, and H. J. Siegel. Constructing fair-exchange protocols for e-commerce via distributed computation of RSA signatures. *PODC 2003*, pages 172–181. ACM, 2003.
25. R. Pass. On deniability in the common reference string and random oracle model. *CRYPTO 2003*, pages 316–337, 2003.
26. D. Pointcheval and J. Stern. Security proofs for signature schemes. *EUROCRYPT 1996*, pages 387–398, 1996.
27. C. Rackoff and D. R. Simon. Non-interactive zero-knowledge proof of knowledge and chosen ciphertext attack. *CRYPTO 1991*, pages 433–444, 1991.
28. J. Rompel. One-way functions are necessary and sufficient for secure signatures. *the 22nd STOC*, pages 387–394. ACM, 1990.
29. A. Sahai. Non-malleable non-interactive zero knowledge and adaptive chosen-ciphertext security. *the 40th FOCS*, pages 543–553. IEEE, 1999.
30. A. D. Santis and G. Persiano. Zero-knowledge proofs of knowledge without interaction. *the 33rd FOCS*, pages 427–436. IEEE, 1992.
31. C.-P. Schnorr. Efficient identification and signatures for smart cards. *CRYPTO 1989*, pages 239–252, 1989.
32. H. Zhu and F. Bao. Stand-alone and setup-free verifiably committed signatures. *CT-RSA 2006*, pages 159–173, 2006.

Multi-party Stand-Alone and Setup-Free Verifiably Committed Signatures

Huafei Zhu[1], Willy Susilo[2], and Yi Mu[2]

[1] Cryptography Lab, Institute for Infocomm Research, A-star, Singapore
huafei@i2r.a-star.edu.sg
[2] School of Computer Science and Software Engineering,
University of Wollongong, Australia
{wsusilo,ymu}@uow.edu.au

Abstract. In this paper, we first demonstrate a gap between the security of verifiably committed signatures in the two-party setting and the security of verifiably committed signatures in the multi-party setting. We then extend the state-of-the-art security model of verifiably committed signatures in the two-party setting to that of multi-party setting. Since there exists trivial setup-driven solutions to multi-party verifiably committed signatures (e.g., two-signature based solutions, we propose solutions to the multi-party stand-alone verifiably committed signatures in the setup-free model, and show that our implementation is provably secure under the joint assumption that the underlying Zhu's signature scheme is secure against adaptive chosen-message attack, Fujisaki-Okamoto's commitment scheme is statistically hiding and computationally binding and Paillier's encryption is semantically secure and one-way as well as the existence of collision-free one-way hash functions.

Keywords: multi-party, setup-free, stand-alone, verifiably committed signatures.

1 Introduction

Optimistic fair-exchange protocols was first introduced by Asokan et al, in [1] and formally studied in [2], [3] and [14] in the context of verifiably encrypted signatures. Very recently, Dodis and Reyzin[11] have formalized a unified model for fair-exchange protocols as a new cryptographic primitive called verifiably committed signatures in the two-party setting. Zhu and Bao[20] have shown that the existence of verifiably encrypted signatures implies the existence of the verifiably committed signatures while the existence of verifiably committed signatures does not imply the existence of verifiably encrypted signatures. As a result, the notion of verifiably committed signatures is a general extension of the notion of verifiably encrypted signatures.

A verifiably committed signature can be setup-driven or setup-free[19]. A verifiably committed signature is called setup-driven if an initial key setup protocol between a primary signer and its trusted third party (TTP) must be involved

T. Okamoto and X. Wang (Eds.): PKC 2007, LNCS 4450, pp. 134–149, 2007.

such that at the end of the key setup protocol, the primary signer and its TTP share a prior auxiliary string. This shared auxiliary information enables TTP to convert any valid partial signature into the corresponding full signature if a conflict occurs between the primary signer and its verifier. A verifiably committed signature is called setup-free if an individual participant needs not to contact his/her arbitrator(s) even for the registration purpose. Namely, no initial key setup procedure between a primary signer and his/her TTP is involved except for one requirement that the primary signer can obtain and verify TTP's certificate and vice versa.

A verifiably committed signature can be stand-alone[19] or not[18]. A verifiably committed signature is called stand-alone if on input a valid partial signature scheme, the distribution of outputs of a resolution algorithm is identical with the distribution of signatures generated by a full signing algorithm. A verifiably committed signature is called non-stand-alone if it is not stand-alone.

The state-of-the-art verifiably committed signatures are only considered in the two-party setting (a primary signer and a verifier, together with an off-line arbitrator). We are interested in studying stand-alone and setup-free verifiably committed signatures in the multi-party setting throughout the paper by demonstrating that the security of two-party setup-free verifiably committed signatures does not guarantee the security of multi-party setup-free verifiably committed signatures.

We stress that the existence of multi-party verifiably committed signatures in the setup-driven model is obvious assuming that the underlying signatures are secure in the sense of [13]. That is, suppose a primary signer's public and secret key pair (pk_1, sk_1) is the public key and secret key pair for the first signature scheme, and at the same time the prime signer and its TTP share another public/secret key (pk_2, sk_2) of the second signature scheme. By $pk= (pk_1, pk_2)$ we denote the public key of the entire signature scheme, and by $sk=(sk_1, sk_2)$, we denote the corresponding secret keys. Now given a message m, the primary signer produces its partial signature σ_1 on the message m. A full signature of the message m is defined as $\sigma =(\sigma_1, \sigma_2)$, where σ_2 is the signature of m corresponding the public/secret key pair (pk_2, sk_2). It is easy to verify that this two-signature based solution is a multi-party verifiably committed signature scheme since the security of public key signatures in the two-party setting is preserved in the multi-party setting[6]. This leaves an interesting research problem: *how to implement multi-party stand-alone and setup-free verifiably committed signatures in the standard complexity model?*

The contribution of this paper is of three-fold. In the first fold, we demonstrate that there is a gap between the security of two-party verifiably committed signatures and multi-party verifiably committed signatures. In the second fold, we extend the state-of-the-art security definition of verifiably committed signatures in the two-party setting to that of the multi-party case. In the third fold, we propose an efficient implementation of multi-party stand-alone and setup-free verifiably committed signatures. We are able to show that our implementation is provably secure under the joint assumption that the underlying Zhu's signature scheme is secure against adaptive chosen-message attack, Fujisaki-Okamoto's commitment scheme is statistically hiding and computationally binding and Paillier's encryption is semantically secure and one-way as well as the existence of collision-free one-way hash functions. To the best of our knowledge, this is the first implementation of stand-alone and setup-free verifiably committed signature scheme which is provably secure in the multi-party setting.

The rest of this paper is organized as follows: in Section 2, a gap between the security of two-party verifiably committed signatures and multi-party verifiably committed signatures is demonstrated. In Section 3, syntax and security definitions of stand-alone and setup-free verifiably committed signatures in the multi-party setting are introduced and formalized. In Section 4, building blocks on which our implementation is based are briefly sketched. An efficient implementation of multi-party stand-alone and setup-free verifiably committed signatures is proposed in Section 5, and we conclude our work in Section 6.

2   A Gap Between Two-Party and Multi-party Verifiably Committed Signatures

A stand-alone and setup-free verifiably committed signature in the two-party setting based on Cramer and Shoup's signature scheme has been presented in [19]. We are about to demonstrate that although this scheme is provably secure in the two-party setting, it is not secure in the multi-party setting. To show this gap, we first sketch their scheme below:

- primary signer's key generation algorithm KG_A: on input k_A, a primary signer Alice runs KG_A to generate two large safe primes p_A and q_A such that $p_A - 1 = 2p'_A$ and $q_A - 1 = 2q'_A$, where p'_A, q'_A are two l'-bit primes. KG_A also chooses two random elements x_A and h_B from QR_{n_A}, where $n_A = p_A q_A$ and QR_{n_A} is the quadratic residue of $Z^*_{n_A}$. Finally, KG_A outputs a description of a group G of order s, and two random elements g_1 and g_2 of G with order s. We stress that in the Cramer and Shoup's signature scheme the choice of group G is independent with n_A (see [8] for more details).

  The public key of Alice is $(n_A, h_A, x_A, g_1, g_2, H)$, along with an appropriate description of G including s, where H is a collision-free cryptographic hash function with output length l-bit (say, $l=160$). The private key is (p_A, q_A). The primary signer Alice now proves to her CA that all values are correctly generated and then obtains her certificate $Cert_A$ from her CA;

- arbitrator's key generation algorithm KG: on input k', an arbitrator runs KG to generate a k'-bit RSA modulus $N = p_c q_c$, where p_c, q_c are two large safe primes.

  The public key of the arbitrator is $APK=((1 + N), N)$. The private key is $ASK=(p_c, q_c)$. The arbitrator should prove to his CA that the public and secret key pair is correctly generated and then obtains his certificate $Cert_B$ from his CA;

- full signing algorithm Sig: To sign a message m, Alice runs Sig to choose at random a $(l + 1)$-bit prime number e, a string $t \in Z_s$. The equation $y^e = x_A h_A{}^{H(g_1^t g_2^{H(m)})}$ modn_A is solved for y. The corresponding signature σ of the message m is (e, t, y).
- full verification algorithm Vf: given a putative triple (e, t, y), a verifier Bob runs Vf to check whether e is an odd $(l + 1)$-bit number. If so, Bob further checks the validation of the equation $x_A = y^e h_A{}^{-H(g_1^t g_2^{H(m)})}modn_A$. If the equation is valid, then Bob accepts, otherwise, he rejects.
- partial signing algorithm PSig: on input a message m, Alice runs PSig to choose a $(l + 1)$-bit prime e and a string $t \in Z_s$. The equation $y^e = x_A h_A{}^{H(g_1^t g_2^{H(m)})}$ modn_A is solved for y.

  Alice then computes $u = g_1^t$ and $c = (1 + N)^t r^N$ modN^2 together with a proof pr that she knows that u contains the same number as the encryption and $t \in I$ using Boudot's protocol [4]. The partial signature σ' of message m is defined by $(e, y, u, c, \mathsf{pr})$.
- partial verification algorithm PVf: given a putative signature $\sigma' = (e, y, u, c, \mathsf{pr})$, Bob runs PVf to check whether e is an odd $(l + 1)$-bit number. Second PVf checks the validity of the equation $x_A = y^e h_A{}^{-H(u g_2^{H(m)})}$ modn_A. If the equation is valid, then PVf further checks the validity of proof pr that u contains the same number as the encryption, and then uses Boudot's protocol to verify that the encrypted value $t \in I$. If it is valid then the verifier accepts, otherwise, it rejects.
- resolution algorithm Res: given $\sigma' = (e, y, u, c, \mathsf{pr})$ and a proof that Bob fulfilled his obligation to the primary signer. The arbitrator first checks validity of the request message. If so, the arbitrator then runs Res to output a valid full signature of (e, y, t) using his decryption key, otherwise, Res rejects the request.

Suppose now an adversary Eve generates two large safe primes p_E and q_E such that $p_E = 2p'_E + 1$ and $q_E = 2q'_E + 1$, where p'_E, q'_E are two l'-bit primes. Eve also chooses two random elements $x_E, h_E \in QR_{n_E}$, where $n_E = p_E q_E$ and QR_{n_E} is the quadratic residue of $Z^*_{n_E}$. Eve's now reuses Alice's partial public key (G, s, g_1, g_2). We stress that the reuse of Alice's partial public key is not a problem since the public data (G, s, g_1, g_2, H) can be chosen independently with the private key (n_A, p_A, q_A). We now can show how the malicious verifier Bob and Eve attack Alice below:

- Alice gives her partial signature $(e, y, u, c, \mathsf{pr}_A)$ to Bob, where pr_A is Alice's proof that u contains the same number as that of c and the encrypted value $t \in I$;
- Bob gives his partial signature $(e', y', u, c, \mathsf{pr}_B)$ to the malicious Eve, where $\mathsf{pr}_B \leftarrow \mathsf{pr}_A$. We stress that although the malicious Bob does not know the exactly hiding value $t \in I$, he can provide a valid proof pr_B by copying Alice's pr_A.
- Eve asks TTP to open Bob's signature by forwarding partial signature $(e', y', u, c, \mathsf{pr}_B)$ and a proof that Eve fulfilled her obligation to Bob;

- TTP opens t such that $u = g^t$ and $c = E(t, r)$ if and only if $(e', y', u, c, \mathrm{pr}_B)$ and a proof that Eve fulfilled her obligation to Bob are valid; Finally, TTP sends t back to Eve;
- Eve gives t to Bob, who now has the full signature of Alice.

The counterexample shows that the security of verifiably committed signatures in the single setting does not imply the security of verifiably committed signatures in the multi-party setting. We stress that in the above counterexample, the common reference string (the description of G is shared between Alice and Eve) is reused. This is possible since the description of G is independent with APK.

3 Multi-party Stand-Alone and Setup-Free Verifiably Committed Signatures: Syntax and Security Definitions

3.1 Syntax

We now extend (stand-alone and setup-free) two-party verifiably committed signatures [11], [19] and [20] to the multi-party verifiably committed signatures setting.

Definition 1. *A multi-party stand-alone and setup-free verifiably committed signature scheme consists of the following algorithms:*

- *arbitrator key generation algorithm KG: on input a security parameter k, it returns a public key and secret key pair (pk, sk);*
- *individual key generation algorithms IKG: on input a security parameter k_i, it returns a public key and secret key pair (pk_i, sk_i).*
- *full signing and verification algorithms(Sig, Vf): these are conventional signing and verification algorithms. on input a message m_j, pk_i and sk_i, Sig outputs a full signature $\sigma_{i,j}$ on m_j; on input a putative signature $(m_j, \sigma_{i,j}, pk_i)$, Vf will output 1 (accept) or 0 (reject);*
- *partial signing and verification algorithms(PSig, PVf): these are partial signing and verification algorithms, which are similar to ordinary signing and verification algorithms, except they can depend on the public arbitration key pk. That is, on input a message (m_j, sk_i, pk_i, pk), PSig outputs a partial signature $\sigma'_{i,j}$; on input a putative partial signature $(m_j, \sigma'_{i,j}, pk_i, pk)$, PVf outputs 1 (accept) or 0 (reject);*
- *resolution algorithm Res: this is a resolution algorithm run by the arbitrator in case the primary signer pk_i refuses to open her signature $\sigma_{i,j}$ to the verifier, who in turn possesses a valid partial signature $\sigma'_{i,j}$ on m_j and a proof that he fulfilled his obligation to the primary signer[1]. In this case, Res(m_j, $\sigma'_{i,j}$, pk_i, sk, pk) should output a valid full signature $\sigma_{i,j}$ of m_j.*

---

[1] The definition does not deal with any specific question of how a verifier proves to the arbitrator that he/she fulfilled his/her obligation to the primary signer.

Correctness. The correctness property of a multi-party verifiably committed signatures states that:

- $\mathsf{Vf}(m_j, \mathsf{Sig}(m_j, sk_i, pk_i)) = 1$ ($\forall j, \forall i$);
- $\mathsf{PVf}(m_j, \mathsf{PSig}(m_j, sk_i, pk_i, pk), pk_i, pk) = 1$ ($\forall j, \forall i$);
- $\mathsf{Vf}(m_j, \mathsf{Res}(\mathsf{PSig}(m_j, sk_i, pk_i, pk), sk, pk, pk_i), pk_i) = 1$ ($\forall j, \forall i$).

3.2   The Definitions of Security

We extend the security definition of Dodis and Reyzin[11] in the two party setting to the multi-party setting. The security definition of multi-party stand-alone and setup-free verifiably committed signatures consists of the following three aspects: security against any primary signer, security against any verifier and security against any arbitrator/TTP.

Security against malicious primary signer: Intuitively, an individual primary signer should not provide a partial signature which is valid both from the viewpoints of a verifier and an arbitrator but which will not be opened into the primary signer's full signature by the honest arbitrator. More precisely, By k_i, we denote the system security parameter of individual user i; By $\mathcal{O}^{\mathsf{PSig}(pk_i, sk_i, \cdots)}$, we denote an oracle of the partial signing procedure $\mathsf{PSig}(pk_i, sk_i, \cdots)$ and by $\mathcal{O}^{\mathsf{Res}(pk_i, pk, sk, \cdots)}$ an oracle of the resolution procedure $\mathsf{Res}(pk_i, pk, sk, \cdots)$. We require that any probabilistic polynomial time Adv succeeds with at most negligible probability in the following game.

- arbitrator key generation algorithm KG: on input a security parameter k, it outputs (sk, pk);
- individual key generation algorithm IKG: on input a security parameter k_i, it outputs (sk_i^*, pk_i), where $\mathsf{IKG}^*(k_i)$ denotes the run of key generator IKG with the corrupted primary signer pk_i by the adversary, and sk_i^* denotes the adversary's states.

    The honest primary signer j ($j \neq i$) runs IKG on input k_j and obtains a public and secret key pair (pk_j, sk_j). The adversary obtains (pk_j, sk_j) and pk_i but not sk_i^* ($1 \leq i, j \leq t(k')$ and $j \neq i$).
- resolution oracle query $\mathcal{O}^{\mathsf{Res}(pk_i, pk, sk, \cdots)}$: for each adaptively chosen message m_j, the adversary computes its partial signature $\sigma'_{i,j}$ for m_j and forwards $\sigma'_{i,j}$ to the oracle $\mathcal{O}^{\mathsf{Res}(pk_i, pk, sk, \sigma'_{i,j})}$ to obtain full signature $\sigma_{i,j}$ of message m_j, where $1 \leq j \leq t(k_i)$, and $t(\cdot)$ is a polynomial.
- at the end of $\mathcal{O}^{\mathsf{Res}(pk_i, pk, sk, \cdots)}$ oracle query, the adversary produces a message and its full signature pair $(m_*, \sigma_{i,*})$, i.e.,

$$(m_*, \sigma'_{i,*}) \leftarrow Adv^{\mathcal{O}^{\mathsf{Res}(pk_i, pk, sk, \cdots)}}(sk_i^*, pk_i, pk); m_* \neq m_j, 1 \leq j \leq t(k')$$

$$\sigma_{i,*} \leftarrow Adv(m_*, \sigma'_{i,*}, sk^*, pk, pk_i)$$

- success of $succ = [\mathsf{PVf}(m_*, \sigma'_{i,*}, pk, pk_i) = 1 \wedge \mathsf{Vf}(m_*, \sigma_{i,*}, pk_i) = 0]$.

Definition 2. *A multi-party verifiably committed signature is secure against malicious primary signer pk_i, if any probabilistic polynomial time adversary Adv associated with resolution oracle, succeeds with at most negligible probability, where the probability takes over coin tosses in* $\mathsf{IKG}^*(k_i, \cdot)$, $\mathsf{PSig}(pk_i, \cdot)$ *and* $\mathcal{O}^{\mathsf{Res}(pk_i, pk, sk, \cdots)}$.

Security against malicious verifier: Suppose a primary signer pk_i and a verifier v are trying to exchange signature in a fair way. The primary signer pk_i wants to commit to the transaction by providing his/her partial signature. Of course, it should be computationally infeasible for the verifier v to compute the corresponding full signature from any partial signature[2]. More formally, we require that any probabilistic polynomial time adversary Adv succeeds with at most negligible probability in the following game:

- arbitrator key generation algorithm KG: on input a security parameter k, it outputs (sk, pk);
- individual key generation IKG: on input a security parameter k_j, it outputs (sk_j, pk_j), where $\mathsf{IKG}(k_j)$ denotes the run of key generator IKG with the corrupted primary signer pk_j by the adversary, and sk_j denotes the adversary's states. The honest primary signer i $(i \neq j)$ runs $\mathsf{IKG}(k_i)$, obtains a public and secret key pair (pk_i, sk_i). The adversary obtains (pk_j, sk_j) and pk_i but not sk_i $(1 \leq i, j \leq t(k')$ and $j \neq i)$.
- $\mathcal{O}^{\mathsf{PSig}(pk_i, sk_i, pk, \cdot)}$ and $\mathcal{O}^{\mathsf{Res}(pk_i, sk, pk, \cdots)}$ oracle queries: for each adaptively chosen message m_j, the adversary obtains a partial signature $\sigma'_{i,j}$ of message m_j by querying the partial signing oracle $\mathcal{O}^{\mathsf{PSig}(i, m_j)}$. The adversary forwards $\sigma'_{i,j}$ to the resolution oracle $\mathcal{O}^{\mathsf{Res}(pk_i, sk, pk, \sigma'_{i,j})}$ to obtain the full signature $\sigma_{i,j}$ of message m_j, where $1 \leq j \leq t(k_i)$, and $t(\cdot)$ is a polynomial.
- at the end of oracle queries to $\mathcal{O}^{\mathsf{PSig}(pk_i, sk_i, pk, \cdots)}$ and $\mathcal{O}^{\mathsf{Res}(pk_i, sk, pk, \cdots)}$, the adversary outputs a message-partial signature pair $(m_*, \sigma'_{i,*})$. On input $(m_*, \sigma'_{i,*})$, the adversary further outputs a message-full signature pair $(m_*, \sigma_{i,*}) \leftarrow Adv^{\mathcal{O}^{\mathsf{PSig}(pk_i, sk_i, pk, \sigma'_{i,*})}, \mathcal{O}^{\mathsf{Res}(pk_i, sk, pk, \sigma'_{i,*})}}$.
- success of adversary $succ$: $= [\mathsf{Vf}(m_*, \sigma_{i,*}, pk_i) = 1 \wedge m_* \notin Query\,(Adv, \mathcal{O}^{\mathsf{Res}(pk_i, sk, pk, \cdots)})]$, where $Query(\,Adv, \mathcal{O}^{\mathsf{Res}(pk_i, sk, pk, \cdots)})$ is the set of valid queries the adversary Adv asked to the resolution oracle $\mathcal{O}^{\mathsf{Res}(pk_i, sk, pk, \cdots)}$, i.e., $(m_*, \sigma'_{i,*})$ such that $\mathsf{Vf}(m_*, \sigma'_{i,*}) = 1$.

Definition 3. *A multi-party verifiably committed signature is secure against a malicious verifier, if any probabilistic polynomial time adversary Adv which is associated with a partial signing oracle* $\mathcal{O}^{\mathsf{PSig}(pk_i, sk_i, pk, \cdots)}$ *and a resolution oracle* $\mathcal{O}^{\mathsf{Res}(pk_i, sk, pk, \cdots)}$, *succeeds with at most negligible probability, where the probability takes over coin tosses in* $(pk_i, sk_i) \leftarrow \mathsf{IKG}(k_i)$ *and* $(pk, sk) \leftarrow \mathsf{KG}(k)$, $\mathcal{O}^{\mathsf{PSig}(pk_i, sk_i, pk, \cdots)}$ *and* $\mathcal{O}^{\mathsf{Res}(pk_i, sk, pk, \cdots)}$.

---

[2] The security preventing a malicious third party from forging valid partial signatures is stated as security against any malicious arbitrator below as a malicious arbitrator is the most powerful adversary in the security model.

Security against semi-trusted arbitrator: Even though the arbitrator is semi-trusted, a primary signer does not want this arbitrator to produce a valid signature which the primary signer do not intend on producing. To achieve this goal, we require that any probabilistic polynomial time adversary Adv associated with partial signing oracle $\mathcal{O}^{\mathsf{PSig}(pk_i, sk_i, pk, \cdots)}$, succeeds with at most negligible probability in the following game:

- key generation algorithm KG^*: on input security parameter k, $\mathsf{KG}^*(k)$ outputs (sk^*, pk), where $\mathsf{KG}^*(k)$ is run by the dishonest arbitrator.
- individual key algorithm IKG: on input a security parameter k_j, it outputs (sk_j, pk_j), where $\mathsf{IKG}(k_j)$ denotes the run of key generator IKG with the corrupted primary signer pk_j by the adversary, and sk_j denotes the adversary's states. The honest primary signer i $(i \neq j)$ runs $\mathsf{IKG}(k_i)$, obtains a public and secret key pair (pk_i, sk_i). The adversary obtains (pk_j, sk_j) and pk_i but not sk_i $(1 \leq i, j \leq t(k'))$ and $j \neq i$).
- $\mathcal{O}^{\mathsf{PSig}(pk_i, sk_i, pk, \cdots)}$ oracle query: for each adaptively chosen message m_j, the adversary obtains the partial signature $\sigma'_{i,j}$ for m_j from the oracle $\mathcal{O}^{\mathsf{PSig}(pk_i, sk_i, pk, m_j)}$, where $1 \leq j \leq t(k')$.
- at the end of the partial partial signing oracle query, the adversary produces a message-full signature pair $(m_*, \sigma_{i,*})$, i.e.,

$$(m_*, \sigma_{i,*}) \leftarrow Adv^{\mathcal{O}^{\mathsf{PSig}(pk_i, sk_i, pk, m_*)}}(sk^*, pk, pk_i).$$

- success of adversary is defined as follows:

$$succ = [\mathsf{Vf}(m, \sigma, pk_i) = 1 \wedge m_* \notin Query(Adv, \mathcal{O}^{\mathsf{PSig}(pk_i, sk_i, pk, \cdots)})]$$

where $Query(Adv, \mathcal{O}^{\mathsf{PSig}(pk_i, sk_i, pk, \cdots)}$ is the set of valid queries Adv asked to the partial oracle such that $\mathsf{PVf}(m_j, \sigma'_{i,j}) = 1$.

Definition 4. *A multi-party verifiably committed signature is secure against malicious arbitrator, if any probabilistic polynomial time adversary Adv associated with partial signing oracle P, succeeds with at most negligible probability, where the probability takes over coin tosses in $(pk_i, sk_i) \leftarrow \mathsf{IKG}(k_i)$ and $(pk, sk^*) \leftarrow \mathsf{KG}^*(k)$, $\mathcal{O}^{\mathsf{PSig}(pk_i, sk_i, pk, \cdots)}$.*

Definition 5. *A multi-party verifiably committed signature is secure if it is secure against any malicious primary signer, malicious verifier and malicious arbitrator.*

4   Building Blocks

Before we propose our implementation, we would like to sketch the following building blocks on which our protocol is based.

4.1 Paillier's Cryptographic System

Paillier investigated a novel computational problem, called Composite Residuosity Class Problem, and its applications to public key cryptography in [15]. Our construction of multi-party verifiably committed signatures will heavily rely on this probabilistic encryption scheme sketched below.

- the public key is a κ-bit RSA modulus $N = PQ$, where P, Q are two large safe primes, where $|P|=|Q| =2\kappa$. the private key is (P,Q);
- the plain-text space is Z_N and the cipher-text space is $Z_{N^2}^*$;
- to encrypt $\alpha \in Z_N$, one chooses $R_a \in Z_N^*$ uniformly at random and computes the cipher-text as $E_{PK}(a, R_a) = (1 + N)^a R_a^N \mod N^2$.
- given $c =(1 + N)^a R_a^N \mod N^2$, and trapdoor information (P,Q), one can first computes c_1 $(=c \mod N)$, and then compute R_a from the equation R_a $= c_1^{N^{-1}\mod\phi(N)} \mod N$; Finally, one can compute a from the equation cR_a^{-N} $\mod N^2 =1 + aN$.
- the encryption function is homomorphic, i.e., $E_{PK}(a_1, R_1) \times E_{PK}(a_2, R_2)$ $\mod N^2 = E_{PK}(a_1 + a_2 \mod N, R_1 \times R_2 \mod N)$.

4.2 Fujisaki-Okamoto Commitment Scheme

Let τ be a security parameter. The public key is a τ-bit RSA modulus $n=pq$, where p, q are two large safe primes. We assume that neither a committer nor a receiver knows factorization n. Let g_1 be a generator of QR_n and g_2 be an element of large order of the group generated by g_1 such that both discrete logarithm of g_1 in base g_2 and the discrete logarithm of g_2 in base g_1 are unknown by the committer or the receiver. We denote $C(a, r_a) = g_1^a g_2^{r_a} \mod n$ a commitment to a in bases (g_1, g_2), where r_a is randomly selected over $\{0, 2^s n\}$, where s is a security parameter. This commitment scheme first appeared in [12] and reconsidered by Damgård and Fujisaki [10] is statistically hiding and computationally binding, i.e.,

- a committer is unable to commit itself to two values a_1, a_2 such that $a_1 \neq a_2$ in Z by the same commitment unless the committed can factor n or solves the discrete logarithm of g_1 in base g_2 or the the discrete logarithm of g_2 in base g_1;
- $C(a, r_a)$ statistically reveals no information to the receiver, i.e., there is a simulator which outputs simulated commitments to a which are statistically indistinguishable from true ones.
- this commitment is homomorphic, i.e., $C(a+b, r_a+r_b) = C(a, r_a) \times C(b, r_b)$.

4.3 Boudot's Protocol

With the help of Fujisaki-Okamoto commitment scheme, an efficient protocol allows Alice to prove to Bob that a committed number $x \in [a, b]$ belongs to the desired interval $[a, b]$ $(0 < a \in Z$ and $a < b \in Z)$, has been proposed by Boudot [4]. The idea behind Boudot's protocol is that to achieve a proof of membership without tolerance, the size of x is first enlarged, and then Alice proves to Bob that the value $2^T x$ lies in interval $< 2^T a - 2^T, 2^T b + 2^T >$ with tolerance (a proof with tolerance is easier than a proof without tolerance, we refer the reader to [4] for further reference), and thus $x \in [a, b]$. Boudot's protocol is zero-knowledge proof of knowledge and it is sound assuming that the underlying Fujisaki-Okamoto commitment scheme is statistically hiding and computationally binding.

4.4 Proof Equality of a Committed Number and an Encryption in Different Moduli

An efficient implementation for proving the equality of a committed number and an encryption has been proposed by Damgård and Jurik[9]:

- let λ be maximum bit length of x. Let C be a commitment $C(x, r_x) = g_1^x g_2^{r_x}$ mod$n$ computed from Fujisaki-Okamoto commitment scheme and E be a cipher-text $E(x, R_x) = (1 + N)^x R_x{}^N$ modN^2 computed from Paillier's encryption scheme, a prover should provide a proof that C and E hide the same value x.
- the prover chooses at random $\omega \in \{0, 1\}^{\lambda + 2l}$, where l is a security parameter. The prover sends $C' = g_1^\omega g_2^{r_\omega}$ and $E' = E(\omega, R_\omega)$ to the verifier. Here we assume that the security parameter κ of Paillier's system is larger than $(\lambda + 2l)$
- the verifier chooses a l-bit challenge f;
- the prover opens the encryptions $C' C^f$ mod$n$ and $E' E^f$ modN^2, to reveal in both cases the number $z = \omega + xf$ defined over the integer domain. The verifier checks the opening were correct.

The protocol can be made non-interactive in the standard way using a hash function $\mathcal{RO}$ and the Fiat-Shamir technique. It is also statistically zero-knowledge in the random oracle mode.

4.5 Proof Equality of a Committed Number and a Discrete Logarithm in Different Moduli

Let l, t and s be three security parameters. Assume that a prover Alice holds a secret value $x \in \{0, T\}$. We denote by $E_1 = g_1^x g_2^r$ modn_1, be a commitment computed from Fujisaki-Okamoto commitment scheme and $E_2 = g^x$ modn_2 be a discrete logarithm of QR_{n_2} modulo n_2, where $n_2 = p_2 q_2$, $p_2 = 2p_2' + 1$, $q_2 = 2q_2' + 1$ and $QR_{n_2} = < g >$. A prover Alice wants to prove to a verifier Bob that she knows x and $r \in \{-2^s n_1 + 1, 2^s n_1 - 1\}$ such that $E_1 = g_1^x g_2^r$ modn_1 and $E_2 = g^x$ modn_2.

- Alice picks random strings $\omega \in \{1, \cdots, 2^{l+t}T - 1\}$ and $\rho \in \{1, \cdots, 2^{l+t+s}n - 1\}$. Alice then computes $\pi_1 = g_1^\omega g_2^\rho$ modn_1 and $\pi_2 = g^\omega$ modn_2; Finally, Alice sends (π_1, π_2) to Bob;
- Bob sends $f \in \{0, 1\}^{2t}$ to Alice;
- Alice computes $\tau_1 = \omega + fx$ and $\tau_2 = \rho + fr$ (over the integer domain Z);
- Bob checks whether $g_1^{\tau_1} g_2^{\tau_2} = \pi_1 E_1^f$ modn_1 and $g^{\tau_1} = \pi_2 E_2^f$ modn_2.

This protocol originally appeared in [5] and independently in [7] is a zero-knowledge proof of equality of a committed number and a discrete logarithm in different moduli. Again, the protocol can be made non-interactive in the standard way using a hash function $\mathcal{RO}$ and the Fiat-Shamir technique. It is also statistically zero-knowledge in the random oracle mode.

4.6   Zhu's Signature Scheme

Our multi-party verifiably committed signatures is built on the top of Zhu's signature (see [16], [17] and [18] for more details).

- Key generation algorithm: Let p, q be two large safe primes (i.e., $p - 1 = 2p'$ and $q - 1 = 2q'$, where p', q' are two primes with length $(l' + 1)$). Let $n = pq$ and QR_n be the quadratic residue of Z_n^*. Let $X, g, h \in QR_n$ be three generators chosen uniformly at random. The public key is (n, g, h, X, H), where H is a collision free hash function with output length l. The private key is (p, q).
- Signature algorithm: To sign a message m, a $(l + 1)$-bit prime e and a string $t \in \{0, 1\}^l$ are chosen at random. The equation $y^e = Xg^t h^{H(m)} \bmod n$ is solved for y. The corresponding signature of the message m is (e, t, y).
- Verification algorithm: Given a putative triple (e, t, y), the verifier checks that e is an $(l + 1)$-bit odd number. Then it checks the validity of $X = y^e g^{-t} h^{-H(m)} \bmod n$. If the equation is valid, then the signature is valid. Otherwise, it is rejected.

Zhu's signature scheme is provably secure against adaptive chosen-message attack under joint assumptions that the strong RSA problem is hard and the discrete logarithm defined over QR_n is hard as well as the underlying hash function H is collision free.

5   Stand-Alone, Setup-Free Verifiably Committed Signatures in Multi-party Setting

5.1   Implementation

With the help of these building blocks listed above, we can now describe our implementation of multi-party stand-alone, setup-free verifiably committed signatures below.

- arbitrary key generation algorithms $(\mathsf{KG}_E, \mathsf{KG}_C)$: on input a security parameter κ, an arbitrary runs KG_E (it is a key generator of Paillier's encryption algorithm) to generate κ-bit RSA modulus $N = PQ$, where P, Q are two large safe primes. The plain-text space is Z_N and the cipher-text space is $Z_{N^2}^*$.

  On input τ, the arbitrator runs KG_C (it is a key generator of Okamot-Fujisaki's commitment scheme) to generate τ-bit RSA modulus $N_c = P_c Q_c$, where P_c and Q_c are two large prime numbers. KG_C also outputs two random elements $g, h \in QR_{N_c}$.

The public key $pk = (pk_E, pk_C)$, where $pk_E = (1 + N, N)$ and $pk_C = (N_c, g, h)$. The secret keys $sk = (sk_E, sk_C)$, where $sk_E = (P, Q)$ and $sk_C = (P_c, Q_c)$.

– individual key generation algorithm IKG: on input a security parameter (k_i, l_i, l_i'), the ith user runs IKG (it is a key generation algorithm of Zhu's signature scheme) to generate two large primes p_i and q_i such that $p_i - 1 = 2p_i'$ and $q_i - 1 = 2q_i'$, where p_i', q_i' are two $(l_i' + 1)$-bit strings.

Let $n_i = p_i q_i$ and QR_{n_i} be the quadratic residue of $Z_{n_i}^*$. Let g_i, h_i be two generators of QR_{n_i} chosen uniformly at random. The public key is the ith user is $(n_i, g_i, h_i, x_i, H_i)$, where $x_i \in QR_{n_i}$ and H_i is a collision free hash function with output length l_i. The private key is (p_i, q_i).

– full signature algorithm Sig: to sign a message m_j, a $(l_i + 1)$-bit prime $e_{i,j}$ and a l_i bit string $t_{i,j}$ are chosen at random. The equation $y_{i,j}^{e_{i,j}} = x_i g_i^{t_{i,j}} h_i^{H_i(m_j)} \bmod n_i$ is solved for y_j. The corresponding signature $\sigma_{i,j}$ of the message m_j is $(e_{i,j}, t_{i,j}, y_{i,j})$.

– verification algorithm Vf: given a putative triple $(e_{i,j}, t_{i,j}, y_{i,j})$, Vf first checks that $e_{i,j}$ is an odd $(l_i + 1)$-bit number. Second it checks the validation that $x_i = y_{i,j}^{e_{i,j}} g_i^{-t_{i,j}} h_i^{-H_i(m_j)} \bmod n_i$. If the equation is valid, then Vf accepts, otherwise, it rejects.

– partial signing algorithm PSig: on input a message m_j, $(l_i + 1)$-bit prime $e_{i,j}$ and a l_i string $t_{i,j}$ are chosen at random. The equation $y_{i,j}^{e_{i,j}} = x_i g_i^{t_{i,j}} h_i^{H_i(m_j)}$ $\bmod n_i$ is solved for y_j. Then the ith user (say Alice) further performs the following computations:

- $u_{i,j} \leftarrow g_i^{t_{i,j}}$;
- $E_{i,j} \leftarrow E(pk_E, t_{i,j})$, where $E(pk_E, t_{i,j}) = (1 + N)^{t_{i,j}} R_{i,j}^N \bmod N^2$;
- $C_{i,j} \leftarrow C(pk_c, t_{i,j})$, where $C(pk_C, t_{i,j}) = g^{t_{i,j}} h^{r_{i,j}} \bmod N_c$;
- a proof $\mathsf{pr}_{i,j}$ that she knows that $u_{i,j}$ contains the same number as that hidden by $E(pk_E, t_{i,j})$ as well as $t_{i,j}$ is a l_i-bit string. More precisely, the proof $\mathsf{pr}_{i,j}$ consists of the following three statements:
  * the prover runs the protocol specified in Section 4.4 and proves to the verifier Bob the equality of the committed number by $C_{i,j}$ and the encrypted number by $E_{i,j}$;
  * the prover runs the protocol specified in Section 4.5 and proves to the verifier Bob the equality of the committed number by $C_{i,j}$ and the discrete logarithm by $u_{i,j}$ on base g_i;
  * the prover runs the protocol specified in Section 4.3 and proves to the verifier Bob that the committed number by $C_{i,j}$ lies in the interval $\{0, 2^{l_i} - 1\}$.

The partial signature is denoted by $\sigma_{i,j}' = (e_{i,j}, y_{i,j}, u_{i,j}, c_{i,j}, \mathsf{pr}_{i,j})$.

– The corresponding partial signature verification algorithm PVf: given a putative signature $\sigma_{i,j}' = ((e_{i,j}, y_{i,j}, u_{i,j}, c_{i,j}, \mathsf{pr}_{i,j}))$, the verifier Bob performs the following checks:

- checking $e_{i,j}$ is an odd $(l_i + 1)$-bit number.
- checking the validity of the equation $x_i = y_{i,j}^{e_{i,j}} g_i^{-t_{i,j}} h_i^{-H_i(m_j)} \bmod n_i$.
- checking the validity of proof $\mathsf{pr}_{i,j}$;
- if all checks are valid then the verifier accepts, otherwise, it rejects.

– resolution algorithm Res: given $\sigma'_{i,j} = ((e_{i,j}, y_{i,j}, u_{i,j}, c_{i,j}\ \mathsf{pr}_{i,j}))$, and a proof that Bob fulfilled his obligation to the primary signer pk_i. If the verification is passed, then the arbitrator outputs a valid full signature $(e_{i,j}, y_{i,j}, t_{i,j})$ using his decryption key sk_E, otherwise, it rejects.

This ends the description of our protocol. We stress that the technique presented in this section can be easily extended to the case where the underlying signature scheme is Cramer-Shoup's hash signature such that individual group G_i is chosen independently.

5.2   The Proof of Security

The proof of security follows that presented in [19]. We also stress that the technique presented in this section can be applied to the case where the underlying signature scheme is Cramer-Shoup's hash signature with the restriction that individual group G_i is chosen independently and is never reused.

Lemma 1. *The verifiably committed signature is secure against malicious primary signer in the multi-party setting.*

Proof. Suppose the ith user Alice is able to provide a valid partial signature $\sigma'_{i,j} = (e_{i,j}, y_{i,j}, u_{i,j}, E_{i,j}, C_{i,j}, \mathsf{pr}_{i,j})$ corresponding to a message m_j, where the valid proof $\mathsf{pr}_{i,j}$ means that she knows that $u_{i,j}$ contains the same number as the encryption $E_{i,j}$ and the encrypted value $t_{i,j} \in I$, $I = \{0, 2^{l_i} - 1\}$. Since $\sigma'_{i,j}$ is valid from the viewpoints of its verifier and TTP, by rewinding Alice, both verifier and cosigner can extract $t_{i,j} \in I$ such that

$$u_{i,j} = g_1^{t_{i,j}}, E_{i,j} = E(pk_E, t_{i,j}), y_{i,j}^{e_{i,j}} = x_i g_i^{t_{i,j}} h_i^{H_i(m_j)}, t_{i,j} \in I.$$

It follows that the designated TTP can always transform any valid partial signature scheme into the correspondenting valid signature $\sigma_{i,j} = (e_{i,j}, y_{i,j}, t_{i,j})$.

Lemma 2. *Our construction is secure against malicious verifier under the joint assumptions that Fujisaki-Okamoto's commitment scheme is statistically hiding and computationally binding and Paillier's encryption scheme is semantically secure and one-way.*

Proof. We convert any attacker $\mathcal{B}$ that attacks our verifiably committed signature scheme into an inverter $\mathcal{B}'$ of the underlying encryption scheme. That is, given a random cipher-text $E_{i,j}$, $\mathcal{B}'$ will obtain the corresponding plain-text m_j with non-negligible probability with the help of the attacker $\mathcal{B}$. This can be done as follows:

– $\mathcal{B}'$ runs IKG to generate the ith primary signer's public/secret key (pk_i, sk_i) as that in the real verifiably committed signature scheme and obtains the public and secret key pair (pk_i, sk_i).
– $\mathcal{B}'$ then runs KG to generate the arbitrator's public/secret key (pk, sk) as that in the real verifiably committed signature scheme and obtains pk but not sk from the arbitrator.

Given the target cipher-text $E_{i,j}$, we first describe a simulator of the partial signature oracle $\mathcal{O}^{\mathsf{PSig}(pk_i,sk_i,pk,\cdots)}$ as follows:

Let q_{PSig} be the total number of queries made by $\mathcal{B}$, and let ι be a random number chosen from $\{1, q_{\mathsf{PSig}}\}$ by $\mathcal{B}'$.

- If $i \in \{1, q_{\mathsf{PSig}}\}$ and $i \neq \iota$, then $\mathcal{B}'$ runs the partial signing oracle as the real partial signature scheme;
- If $i \in \{1, q_{\mathsf{PSig}}\}$ and $i = \iota$, for the given target cipher-text $E_{i,j}$, $\mathcal{B}'$ chooses a random string $f_{i,j}$, $z_{i,j}$ and $u_{i,j}$ in the correct interval specified in the real protocol and then $\mathcal{B}'$ computes $E'_{i,j}$ from the equation $E(pk_E, z) = E'_{i,j}$ $E_{i,j}^{f_{i,j}}$. At the same time, it computes $u'_{i,j}$ from the equation $g_i^{z_{i,j}} = u'_{i,j} u_{i,j}^{f_{i,j}}$.
- Given $u_{i,j}$, $\mathcal{B}'$ computes $(e_{i,j}, y_{i,j})$ from the equation $y_{i,j}^{e_{i,j}} = x_i u_{i,j} h_i^{H_i(m_j)}$, this is possible since $\mathcal{B}'$ knows the secret key sk_i (notice that $\mathcal{B}'$ assigns $f_{i,j}$ to be the hash value of the random oracle $\mathcal{RO}$ if the specified protocol in Section 4.5 is non-interactive).

  Similarly, for the given $u_{i,j}$, there exists a simulator that can simulate views for the following proofs:
  - a proof of equality of the committed number $C_{i,j}$ and the discrete logarithm $\log_{g_i}(u_{i,j})$, where $C_{i,j}$ is a forgery commitment;
  - a proof of equality of the committed number by $C_{i,j}$ and the encrypted number by $E_{i,j}$;
  - a proof that the committed number by $C_{i,j}$ lies in the correct interval.

  Such a simulator can be defined by the concatenation of individual simulators for the above zero-knowledge proof systems since Boudot's protocol, Damgård and Jurik's protocol, as well as Boudot, and Camenisch and Michels' protocols are zero-knowledge proof systems (see Section 4.3, Section 4.4 and Section 4.5 for more details). As a result, the existence of such a simulator following the definition of the zero-knowledge proof system immediately.

$\mathcal{B}'$ simulates $\mathcal{O}^{\mathsf{Res}(pk_i,sk,pk,\cdots)}$ oracle queries as follows:

- If $(m_j, \sigma'_{i,j})$ that is in the partial signature query list and if $j \neq \iota$, then $\mathcal{O}^{\mathsf{Res}(pk_i,sk,pk,\cdots)}$ outputs t_i;
- If $(m_j, \sigma'_{i,j})$ that is in the partial signature query list and if $j = \iota$, then $\mathcal{O}^{\mathsf{Res}(pk_i,sk,pk,\cdots)}$ outputs $\perp$;
- If $(m_j, \sigma'_{i,j})$ that is not in the partial signature query list, then $\mathcal{O}^{\mathsf{Res}(pk_i,sk,pk,\cdots)}$ outputs $\perp$.

Notice that the probability that the simulator outputs $\perp$ is $1 - 1/q_{\mathsf{PSig}}$ for the queries whose partial signatures are listed in the $\mathcal{O}^{\mathsf{PSig}(pk_i,sk_i,pk,\cdots)}$ oracle query. Thus when the adversary outputs a valid full signature (m^*, σ^*) whose partial signature is in the list of $\mathcal{O}^{\mathsf{PSig}(pk_i,sk_i,pk,\cdots)}$ oracle query, the probability that $\mathcal{B}'$ can invert the target cipher-text $E_{i,j}$ with probability at least $\epsilon/q_{\mathsf{PSig}}$, where ϵ stands for the probability that $\mathcal{B}$ can break our verifiably committed signature scheme.

Lemma 3. *Our construction is secure against malicious arbitrator under the joint assumptions that the underlying Zhu's signature scheme is secure against adaptive chosen-message attack, Fujisaki-Okamoto's commitment scheme is statistically hiding and computationally binding and Paillier's encryption scheme is semantically secure.*

Proof. Suppose an arbitrator is able to forgery partial signature $\sigma'_{i,j}$ with non-negligible probability, then by rewinding the arbitrator, we can extract $t_{i,j}$ from the valid proof $\mathsf{pr}_{i,j}$. It follows that the arbitrator is able to output a valid forgery signature from Zhu's signature scheme with non-negligible probability. Since the underlying Zhu's signature scheme signature has proved to be secure against adaptive chosen-message attack under joint assumptions of the strong RSA problem as well as the existence of collision free hash function. It follows that our construction is secure against semi-trusted arbitrator under joint assumptions that the hardness of the strong-RSA problem and the existence of collision free hash functions.

In summary, we have proved the main result below:

Theorem 1. *The stand-alone, setup-free verifiably committed signature scheme constructed above is provably secure under the joint assumption that the underlying Zhu's signature scheme is secure against adaptive chosen-message attack, Fujisaki-Okamoto's commitment scheme is statistically hiding and computationally binding and Paillier's encryption is semantically secure and one-way.*

6   Conclusion

In this paper, we have demonstrated a gap between the security of a two-party verifiably committed signatures and the security of multi-party verifiably committed signatures. We also have extended Dodis and Leyzin's security model for the two-party verifiably committed signatures to the multi-party setting. Finally, we have implemented an efficient stand-alone and setup-free verifiably committed signatures in the multi-party setting and shown that our implementation is provably secure under the joint assumptions that the underlying Zhu's signature scheme is secure against adaptive chosen-message attack, Fujisaki-Okamoto's commitment scheme is statistically hiding and computationally binding and Paillier's encryption is semantically secure and one-way.

References

1. N.Asokan, M.Schunter and M.Waidner: Optimistic Protocols for Fair Exchange. ACM Conference on Computer and Communications Security 1997: 7 - 17.
2. N.Asokan, V.Shoup and M.Waidner: Optimistic Fair Exchange of Digital Signatures (Extended Abstract). EUROCRYPT 1998: 591 - 606.

3. D.Boneh, C.Gentry, B.Lynn and H.Shacham: Aggregate and Verifiably Encrypted Signatures from Bilinear Maps. EUROCRYPT 2003: 416 -432
4. F.Boudot: Efficient Proofs that a Committed Number Lies in an Interval. Proc. of EUROCRYPT 2000: 431 - 444, Springer Verlag.
5. F.Boudot and J.Traore: Efficient Publicly Verifiable Secret Sharing Schemes with Fast or Delayed Recovery. ICICS'99, 87- 102.
6. Ran Canetti: Universally Composable Signature, Certification, and Authentication. CSFW 2004, 219.
7. J.Camenisch and M.Michels: Proving in Zero-Knowledge that a Number Is the Product of Two Safe Primes. EUROCRYPT 1999: 107-122.
8. R.Cramer and V.Shoup. Signature scheme based on the Strong RAS assumption. 6th ACM Conference on Computer and Communication Security, Singapore, ACM Press, November 1999.
9. I.Damgård and M.Jurik: Client/Server Tradeoffs for Online Elections. Proc. of Public Key Cryptography 2002: 125 - 140. Springer Verlag.
10. I.Damgård and E.Fujisaki: A Statistically-Hiding Integer Commitment Scheme Based on Groups with Hidden Order. Proc. of ASIACRYPT 2002: 125 - 142, Springer Verlag.
11. Y.Dodis and L.Reyzin. Breaking and Repairing Optimistic Fair Exchange from PODC 2003, ACM Workshop on Digital Rights Management (DRM), October 2003.
12. E.Fujisaki and T.Okamoto. Statistically zero knowledge protocols to prove modular polynomial relations. Crypto'97. 16 - 30, 1997.
13. S.Goldwasser, S.Micali and R.L.Rivest: A Digital Signature Scheme Secure Against Adaptive Chosen-Message Attacks. SIAM J. Comput. 17(2): 281 - 308 (1988).
14. S.Lu, R.Ostrovsky, A.Sahai, H.Shacham and B.Waters: Sequential Aggregate Signatures and Multisignatures Without Random Oracles. EUROCRYPT 2006: 465-485
15. P.Paillier: Public-Key Cryptosystems Based on Composite Degree Residuosity Classes. Proc. of EUROCRYPT 1999: 223 - 238, Springer Verlag.
16. H.Zhu. New Digital Signature Scheme Attaining Immunity to Adaptive Chosen-message attack. Chinese Journal of Electronics, Vol.10, No.4, Page 484-486, Oct, 2001.
17. H. Zhu. A formal proof of Zhu's signature scheme, http://eprint.iacr.org/, 2003/155.
18. H.Zhu: Constructing Committed Signatures from Strong-RSA Assumption in the Standard Complexity Model. Public Key Cryptography 2004: 101-114.
19. H.Zhu and F.Bao: Stand-Alone and Setup-Free Verifiably Committed Signatures. CT-RSA 2006: 159-173.
20. H.Zhu and F.Bao: More on Stand-Alone and Setup-Free Verifiably Committed Signatures. ACISP 2006: 148 -158.

Knowledge-Binding Commitments with Applications in Time-Stamping

Ahto Buldas[1,2,3,*] and Sven Laur[4,**]

[1] Cybernetica AS, Akadeemia tee 21, 12618 Tallinn, Estonia
[2] Tallinn University of Technology, Raja 15, 12618 Tallinn, Estonia
[3] University of Tartu, Liivi 2, 50409 Tartu, Estonia
Ahto.Buldas@ut.ee
[4] Helsinki University of Technology, Laboratory for Theoretical Computer Science,
P.O.Box 5400, FI-02015 TKK, Finland
slaur@tcs.hut.fi

Abstract. We prove in a non-black-box way that every bounded list and set commitment scheme is *knowledge-binding*. This is a new and rather strong security condition, which makes the security definitions for time-stamping much more natural compared to the previous definitions, which assume *unpredictability* of adversaries. As a direct consequence, list and set commitment schemes with partial opening property are sufficient for secure time-stamping if the number of elements has an explicit upper bound N. On the other hand, white-box reductions are in a sense strictly weaker than black-box reductions. Therefore, we also extend and generalize the previously known reductions. The corresponding new reductions are $\Theta(\sqrt{N})$ times more efficient, which is important for global-scale time-stamping schemes where N is very large.

1 Introduction

Commitment schemes are basic building blocks in numerous cryptographic protocols. The most important properties of commitment schemes are binding and hiding. A commitment is hiding if it reveals no information about the committed message and binding if it is impossible to change the committed message afterwards without detection. First such schemes for committing a single bit were proposed by Blum [4] and by Brassard *et al* [5] and were proven secure under the hardness of factoring assumption. Later works have significantly improved their efficiency and weakened the underlying complexity theoretic assumptions, see [14,10] for further references. Here, we study the so called *partially releasable* commitments, in which one can compute a commitment (also called *digest*) for a list $\mathfrak{X} = (x_1, \ldots, x_N)$ of bit-strings, so that it is possible to partially open the commitment for every $x_i \in \mathfrak{X}$ without disclosing the other elements of $\mathfrak{X}$. For opening x_i it is sufficient to present a decommitment string s_i (also called *certificate*). Achieving the hiding property is somewhat trivial, as one can always add

---

* Partially supported by Estonian SF grant no. 6944, and by EU FP6-15964: "AEOLUS".
** Partially supported by Finnish Academy of Sciences, and by Estonian Doctoral School in Information and Communication Technologies.

T. Okamoto and X. Wang (Eds.): PKC 2007, LNCS 4450, pp. 150–165, 2007.

another layer of commitments. Hence, our main emphasis is on the binding property. List commitments [3,1,17] that are only binding are known as *one-way accumulators*.

In particular, we analyze the security of a *time-stamping* protocol, where clients send their requests $x_1, \ldots, x_N$ to a Time-Stamping Server (TSS) who computes the commitment c and sends the corresponding certificates $s_1, \ldots, s_N$ back to the clients. If c is published in an authentic way then everybody can verify that x_i was generated before c was published. This principle is used in practical time-stamping schemes [12] where c is computed as the root of a hash tree. List commitment schemes were believed to be exactly what one needs for such kind of time-stamping. However, Buldas *et al* [7] pointed out a flaw in the security proof of [12]. By giving a carefully crafted oracle separation they showed that pure collision-resistance is insufficient to prove that the hash tree time-stamping schemes [12] are secure. In other words, either there are collision-resistant functions that are still insecure for time-stamping, or the security of time-stamping schemes follows from currently unknown complexity-theoretic results. The key point of this paradoxical result is that the number of committed elements is potentially unbounded. In Sec. 4, we prove that all list and set commitments, where the cardinality of $\mathcal{X}$ has an explicit bound $|\mathcal{X}| \leq N$, are suitable for time-stamping. The proof is given in the exact security framework and is $\Theta(\sqrt{N})$ times more efficient than the previous reduction [7]. This improvement is especially valuable for global-scale time-stamping schemes in which N is very large.

In Sec. 5, we show that all binding bounded list and set commitments are *knowledge-binding*. This is a new and extremely strong security requirement inspired from the security of time-stamping schemes. Its strength is comparable to the *plaintext awareness* property, which is defined for public key encryption. The knowledge-binding property is also much more intuitive requirement for time-stamping schemes than the previous ones [7,9], which use unpredictable probability distributions to model the stream of "new documents" sent to a TSS. Roughly, the knowledge-binding property states that for every efficient TSS, it is possible (by observing the commitment procedure) to efficiently extract the list $\mathcal{X}$ of all documents that can be opened by the TSS in the future. The dedicated extractor must know only the internal coin tosses of TSS and some public parameters. Consequently, even if the TSS is malicious, it must *know* the whole list $\mathcal{X}$ before the corresponding commitment is published. This allows to prove the security in the classical *ideal vs real world* comparison framework [11, pp.622–631,697–700].

Moreover, the notion of knowledge-binding commitments can be useful in other cryptographic protocols, because the ability to open a commitment does not change in time and we may skip the proofs of knowledge in the commitment phase. On the other hand, the corresponding security proofs are not black box. This means that once we have an efficient adversary A that breaks the knowledge-binding condition *we know that there exists* an efficient adversary A' that breaks the binding property of the corresponding commitment scheme. However, we may have no efficient ways to construct A'. Therefore, in reality the knowledge-binding property can be violated but the commitment scheme may still be practically binding—the efficient breaking procedure exists but is not known. Black-box security proofs in turn give an efficient procedure for constructing A' from A. In this sense, Theorems 1–4 give substantially stronger security guarantees for a fixed hash function (e.g. SHA-1) than Theorems 5 and 6.

In Sec. 6, we briefly discuss about other possible applications of knowledge-binding such as distributed and fine-grained time-stamping.

Some of the details of this work have been omitted because of space limitations. The missing details will be published in the IACR ePrint Archive.

2 Preliminaries and Notation

We use a non-uniform model of computations, where each algorithm A is specified as an input of a universal multi-tape Turing machine U that first copies the code of A to its working-tape and then starts to interpret it. A is a *t-time algorithm* if U performs at most t elementary operations to interpret the code of A independent of the input of A.

By $x \leftarrow \mathcal{D}$ we mean that x is chosen randomly according to a distribution $\mathcal{D}$. In particular, if A is an algorithm, then $x \leftarrow A(y)$ means that x is chosen according to the output distribution of A on an input y. Finite sets are identified with the corresponding uniform distributions, e.g., $x \leftarrow \{0,1\}^\ell$ means that x is a uniformly chosen ℓ-bit string. If $\mathcal{D}_1, \ldots, \mathcal{D}_m$ are distributions and $F(x_1, \ldots, x_m)$ is a predicate, then $\Pr[x_1 \leftarrow \mathcal{D}_1, \ldots, x_m \leftarrow \mathcal{D}_m : F(x_1, \ldots, x_m)]$ denotes the probability that $F(x_1, \ldots, x_m)$ is true after the ordered assignment of $x_1, \ldots, x_m$.

By a *cryptographic primitive* $\mathfrak{P}$ we mean a set of computable functions associated with the advantage function $\mathrm{Adv}_{\mathfrak{P}}(\cdot)$, such that for every adversarial algorithm A, the advantage $\mathrm{Adv}_{\mathfrak{P}}(A)$ is a positive real number. Mostly, $\mathrm{Adv}_{\mathfrak{P}}(A)$ is defined as the non-trivial success (scaled probability) in certain game sec that captures the desired properties of $\mathfrak{P}$. A primitive $\mathfrak{P}$ is said to be (t, ε)-secure in terms of sec if $\mathrm{Adv}_{\mathfrak{P}}^{\mathrm{sec}}(A) \leq \varepsilon$ for every t-time adversary A. For example, by a (t, ε)-secure *collision-resistant hash function* we mean a pair $\mathcal{H} = (\mathsf{Gen}, h)$ of algorithms such that if $\mathsf{pk} \leftarrow \mathsf{Gen}$ is an arbitrary output of the generation function then $h(\mathsf{pk}, \cdot) = h_{\mathsf{pk}}(\cdot)$ is a function of type $\{0,1\}^\ell \to \{0,1\}^m$ where $\ell > m$; and for every t-time adversary A :

$$\mathrm{Adv}_{\mathcal{H}}^{\mathrm{coll}}(A) = \Pr[\mathsf{pk} \leftarrow \mathsf{Gen}, (x_1, x_2) \leftarrow A(\mathsf{pk}) : x_1 \neq x_2 \wedge h_{\mathsf{pk}}(x_1) = h_{\mathsf{pk}}(x_2)] \leq \varepsilon .$$

Time-success ratio. Quite often it is suitable for adversaries to find a trade-off between plausible attacking-time t and the corresponding advantage $\varepsilon(t)$ against $\mathfrak{P}$. If the minimum *time-success ratio* for $\mathfrak{P}$ is $\alpha_{\mathfrak{P}}$, then $\varepsilon(t) \leq \frac{t}{\alpha_{\mathfrak{P}}}$ by definition. Often, we cannot estimate anything else about $\mathfrak{P}$ than $\alpha_{\mathfrak{P}}$. Now, any black- or white-box reduction introduces a *change ratio* $\gamma = \frac{\alpha_1}{\alpha_0}$ where α_0 is the time-success ratio of the basic primitive and α_1 is the ratio of the derived primitive, i.e., we have established a new approximate bound $\varepsilon_1(t) \leq \frac{t}{\gamma \alpha_0}$. Therefore, large values of γ provide better approximating bounds.

Sampling bounds. Our proofs use several standard statistical bounds. Let $X_1, \ldots, X_m$ be identically distributed independent zero-one random variables with $\mu = \Pr[X_i = 1]$ and let $X = \sum_{i=1}^m X_i$. Then for any $0 \leq \theta \leq 1$ the Chernoff bounds [13]

$$\Pr[X \leq (1 - \theta)\mu m] \leq e^{-\theta^2 m\mu/2} , \quad \text{and} \quad \Pr[X \geq (1 + \theta)\mu m] \leq e^{-\theta^2 m\mu/3} .$$

We also need a Birthday bound to determine the collision probability. Let $Y_1, \ldots, Y_m$ be identically but arbitrarily distributed independent random variables with possible values $\{1, \ldots, N\}$. Then the probability p that all Y_i-s are different satisfies $p \leq e^{-\frac{m(m-1)}{2N}}$. In particular, if $m \geq 1.5\sqrt{N}$ and $N \geq 9$ then $p \leq \frac{1}{2}$.

3   Partially Releasable Commitment Schemes

Set and List Commitments. Most commitment schemes for ℓ-bit strings facilitate only complete disclosure of the committed input. In the context of time-stamping, the complete input can be several gigabytes long whereas we actually need to disclose only a few hundred bits. Therefore, we study commitment schemes that facilitate partial disclosure of inputs. *List commitments* are order-preserving: committed strings are ordered tuples. *Set commitments* in turn do not provide any ordering. Like ordinary commitment schemes, these commitments are specified by four basic algorithms: Gen, Com, Cert and Ver. Initialization algorithm Gen generates public parameters pk. Elements $(m_1, \ldots, m_n)$ are committed by computing $(c, d) \leftarrow \mathsf{Com}_{\mathsf{pk}}(m_1, \ldots, m_n)$, where the commitment c is sent to the receiver and d is kept by the sender for later use. To prove that m_i was indeed used to compute the commitment c, the sender generates a certificate[1] $s \leftarrow \mathsf{Cert}_{\mathsf{pk}}(d, m_i)$ the validity of which can be tested with the Ver algorithm.

The commitment scheme is *functional* if for any $(c, d) \leftarrow \mathsf{Com}_{\mathsf{pk}}(m_1, \ldots, m_n)$ and $s \leftarrow \mathsf{Cert}_{\mathsf{pk}}(d, m_i)$, the verification result $\mathsf{Ver}_{\mathsf{pk}}(c, n, m_i, s) = \mathsf{true}$ with overwhelming probability. For list commitments, the certificate s contains also the exact location i of the decommitted element, denoted as $\mathsf{loc}(s) = i$. We explicitly assume that a decommitment certificate for a set $\mathcal{X} = \{x_1, \ldots, x_r\}$ is a union of the corresponding element certificates $s_1, \ldots, s_r$ denoted by $s_1 \cup \ldots \cup s_r$. Consequently, certificates can be freely joined together and split into sub-certificates. For many commitment schemes such lists can further be compressed but this is only an implementation detail.

We omit the formal definition of the hiding property, since we study only the features related to the binding property. The binding property is different for set and list commitments. For list commitments, the binding property is violated if an adversary can open the i-th element in two different ways:

$$\mathrm{Adv}^{\mathsf{bind}}(\mathsf{A}) = \Pr \left[\begin{array}{l} \mathsf{pk} \leftarrow \mathsf{Gen}, \ (c, n, x_0, s_0, x_1, s_1) \leftarrow \mathsf{A}(\mathsf{pk}) : \\ x_0 \neq x_1 \wedge \mathsf{loc}(s_0) = \mathsf{loc}(s_1) \\ \wedge \ \mathsf{Ver}_{\mathsf{pk}}(c, n, x_0, s_0) = \mathsf{Ver}_{\mathsf{pk}}(c, n, x_1, s_1) = \mathsf{true} \end{array} \right] , \quad (1)$$

where the probability is taken over the coin tosses of all relevant algorithms. Since certificates are closed under union and there is no ordering for set commitments, the only way to misbehave is to exceed the size of $\mathcal{X}$:

$$\mathrm{Adv}^{\mathsf{bind}}(\mathsf{A}) = \Pr \left[\begin{array}{l} \mathsf{pk} \leftarrow \mathsf{Gen}, \ (c, n, \mathcal{X}, s) \leftarrow \mathsf{A}(\mathsf{pk}) : \\ \mathsf{Ver}_{\mathsf{pk}}(c, n, \mathcal{X}, s) = \mathsf{true} \wedge |\mathcal{X}| > n \end{array} \right] , \quad (2)$$

where $\mathsf{Ver}_{\mathsf{pk}}(c, n, \mathcal{X}, s)$ first splits $\mathcal{X}$ and s into components and then verifies each component $x_i \in \mathcal{X}$ separately by using the corresponding component-certificate $s_i \in s$. We say that the commitment scheme is (τ, ε)-binding if for all τ-time adversaries $\mathrm{Adv}^{\mathsf{bind}}(\mathsf{A}) \leq \varepsilon$. For unbounded adversaries, we speak about *statistical ε-binding*.

Note that set and list commitments must explicitly specify the number n of the committed elements. Indeed, if the certificates do not reveal the size of the commitment,

---

[1] To be precise, Cert should return a vector of certificates for each location of m_i in the list.

a malicious adversary can just hide some committed elements and receivers can never be sure if the commitment is fully opened. A commitment scheme is *N-bounded* if $\mathsf{Ver}_{\mathsf{pk}}(c, n, x, s) = \mathsf{false}$ for all $n > N$.

List commitment schemes that satisfy only the binding properties are known as *one-way accumulators* [1,3,17]. One-way accumulators that in addition to positive statements $x \in X$ also allow to (compactly) prove negative statements $x \notin X$ are called *undeniable attesters* [6]. The commonly used binding requirement for one-way accumulators is *n-times collision-freeness* [1], which is equivalent to the binding property of set commitments.

Time-Stamping Schemes. Time-stamping protocols process documents in batches X_1, $X_2, X_3, \ldots$ that we call *rounds*. The rounds correspond to time periods of fixed duration (one hour, one day, etc.) After the i-th period, a short commitment c_i of the corresponding batch X_i is published. A document $x \in X_i$ precedes document y, if there is $j > 0$ such that $y \in X_{i+j}$. Obviously, for a fixed commitment c_i there must be an efficient way to prove that $x \in X_i$. However, for documents $y \notin X_i$ such proofs must be infeasible to create. Note that c_i can be viewed as a classical set or list commitment to the set X_i and the corresponding proof of $x \in X_i$ as a certificate. Therefore, time-stamping schemes share the same functionality and algorithmic description as the set and list commitment schemes. Such a structural similarity is indeed remarkable. Still, careful studies of the security requirements reveal considerable differences between time-stamping and commitment schemes. Different security definitions exist for time-stamping schemes [7,8,9,12]. In this paper, we adapt the strongest[2] definition [9] for the non-uniform precise security framework with minor modifications in notations.

Formal definitions of time-stamping schemes do not require that n is explicitly given as an argument to the verification algorithm Ver, but negative results in [7] suggest that time-stamping schemes (at least those without additional third parties) must be bounded, i.e., n has to be at least implicitly specified.

Intuitively, time-stamping schemes must be secure against "back-dating" and this itself raises a subtle issue: How to model the future? Most works [7,8,9] have taken an approach based on computational entropy. Document generation is modeled as an efficient randomized procedure and the security guarantees are given for document distributions with high enough computational entropy. More formally, an adversary $A = (A_1, A_2)$ is (τ, δ)-*unpredictable* if for every τ-time predictor Π :

$$\mathsf{Adv}_A^{\mathsf{upr}}(\Pi) = \Pr \left[\begin{array}{l} \omega_1 \leftarrow \Omega, \mathsf{pk} \leftarrow \mathsf{Gen}, \hat{x} \leftarrow \Pi(\mathsf{pk}, \omega_1), \\ (c, n, \phi) \leftarrow A_1(\mathsf{pk}; \omega_1), (x, s) \leftarrow A_2(\phi) : \hat{x} = x \end{array} \right] \leq \delta \ ,$$

where ω_1 denotes the random coins of A_1 and the probability is taken over the coin tosses of all relevant algorithms. The second stage A_2 of the adversary models an efficient document generation (back-dating) procedure.

Definition 1 (Entropy based security). *A time-stamping scheme is $(t, \tau, \delta, \varepsilon)$-secure if for every (τ, δ)-unpredictable t-time A :*

---

[2] There exist stronger security definitions for time-stamping schemes with additional (auditing) parties [8]. The main drawback of those schemes is a large amount of extra communication.

$$\mathrm{Adv}^{\mathsf{ts}}(A) = \Pr \begin{bmatrix} \omega_1 \leftarrow \Omega, \mathsf{pk} \leftarrow \mathsf{Gen}, (c, n, \phi) \leftarrow \mathsf{A}_1(\mathsf{pk}; \omega_1), \\ (x, s) \leftarrow \mathsf{A}_2(\phi) : \mathsf{Ver}_{\mathsf{pk}}(c, n, x, s) = \mathsf{true} \end{bmatrix} \leq \varepsilon . \qquad (3)$$

Here, δ quantifies a trivial advantage. Indeed, consider the next adversary $A = (A_1, A_2)$:

- $A_1(\mathsf{pk}; \omega_1)$ computes $(c, d) \leftarrow \mathsf{Com}_{\mathsf{pk}}(\hat{x})$ and the corresponding valid certificate $s \leftarrow \mathsf{Cert}_{\mathsf{pk}}(c, \hat{x})$ and outputs a tuple $(c, 1, (\hat{x}, s))$.
- $A_2(\hat{x}, s)$ generates a random x so that $x = \hat{x}$ with probability δ, and outputs (x, s).

For every τ the adversary A is (τ, δ)-unpredictable. However, no matter how the time-stamping scheme is defined, the advantage $\mathrm{Adv}^{\mathsf{ts}}(A)$ of A is at least δ. Hence, it is reasonable to assume that $\delta \ll \varepsilon$. Moreover, as $\log \frac{1}{\delta}$ is an upper bound for the computational Rényi entropy, we implicitly assume that the computational Shannon entropy of the future documents is at least $\log \frac{1}{\delta}$ w.r.t. the time-bound τ.

The biggest drawback of the entropy based definition is non-uniformity. The security definition is natural in the polynomial model but has some flaws when adapted to the exact model. It only offers protection against (τ, δ)-unpredictable adversaries! Hence, it does not exclude extremely successful adversaries that are just *not quite so unpredictable*. In theory, a time-stamping scheme could be protected against (τ, δ)-unpredictable adversaries but still be totally insecure against $(\tau, \delta + \delta^{100})$-unpredictable adversaries. This flaw can be fixed by requiring strong uniformity in the definition:

Definition 2 (Black-box security). *A time-stamping scheme is (t, τ, ε)-secure if there exists a τ-time black-box extractor machine $\mathcal{K}$ such that for every t-time A :*

$$\mathrm{Adv}^{\mathsf{ts}}(A) = \Pr \begin{bmatrix} \omega_1 \leftarrow \Omega, \mathsf{pk} \leftarrow \mathsf{Gen}, \hat{\mathcal{X}} \leftarrow \mathcal{K}^{A(\mathsf{pk};\omega_1,\cdot)}(\mathsf{pk}), \\ (c, n, \phi) \leftarrow \mathsf{A}_1(\mathsf{pk}; \omega_1), (x, s) \leftarrow \mathsf{A}_2(\phi) : \\ (\mathsf{Ver}_{\mathsf{pk}}(c, n, x, s) = \mathsf{true} \wedge x \notin \hat{\mathcal{X}}) \vee |\hat{\mathcal{X}}| > n \end{bmatrix} \leq \varepsilon , \qquad (4)$$

where ω_1 denotes random coins of A_1 and $\mathcal{K}$ gets a black-box access to $A_1(\mathsf{pk}; \omega_1)$ and $A_2(\phi; \cdot)$. The working time of $\mathcal{K}^{A(\mathsf{pk};\omega_1,\cdot)}$ includes the time needed to execute all oracle calls. For list commitments, we treat $\hat{\mathcal{X}}$ as a list and write $x \in \hat{\mathcal{X}}$ iff $x = \hat{\mathcal{X}}[\mathsf{loc}(s)]$.

Intuitively, we state that malicious time-stamping servers cannot issue valid certificates for unknown documents, as there exists a well known algorithm $\mathcal{K}^{A(\mathsf{pk};\omega_1,\cdot)}$ for efficiently reconstructing the list of all valid documents $\hat{\mathcal{X}}$. This algorithm can be automatically constructed for every t-time adversary.

It is straightforward to see that (t, τ, ε)-secure time-stamping scheme is always $(t, \tau, \delta, \varepsilon + N\delta)$ secure where $N \geq |\mathcal{X}|$, as one can use $\mathcal{K}$ in prediction. In Sec. 4, we prove that every binding N-bounded list commitment scheme is also a secure time-stamping scheme. Still, there are quantitative differences between these two notions.

Practical constructions based on hash trees. Merkle trees [15] and count-certified hash trees [16] (described below) constructed from collision-resistant hash functions are binding but not hiding even if the hash function is modeled as a random oracle—a release of an element (a leaf node) also reveals one neighboring element (the sibling leaf node). Nevertheless, if we use Merkle trees to compute a short commitment from hiding and binding commitments, we get binding and hiding list and set commitments.

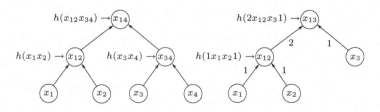

Fig. 1. Merkle hash tree for $\{x_1, x_2, x_3, x_4\}$ and a count-certified hash tree for $\{x_1, x_2, x_3\}$

A *Merkle hash tree* for a list $\mathcal{X}$ is a binary tree the leaves of which are the elements of $\mathcal{X}$ and each non-leaf node is a hash of its two children (Fig. 1, left). Nodes with a single child can be avoided. Hence, every non-leaf node is assumed to have two children.

A *count-certified hash tree* (Fig. 1, right) is a binary tree which is similar to a Merkle tree, except that its arcs are labeled with *counters* each of which equal to the number of leaves in the corresponding subtree. Each non-leaf vertex v is a hash $h(n_L x_L x_R n_R)$, where n_L and n_R are the counters of the left- and the right subtree respectively. The counter c of the unique outgoing arc of v is the sum $n_v = n_L + n_R$.

Each hash tree can be represented as a commitment function $(c, \mathcal{X}) \leftarrow \mathsf{Com}_{pk}(\mathcal{X})$, where c is the root hash value of the corresponding tree and pk denotes the public parameters associated with the collision-resistant hash function h. By the certificate $\mathsf{Cert}_{pk}(\mathcal{X}, x_i)$ for $x_i \in \mathcal{X}$ we mean the smallest amount of data needed to recompute the root hash value. For example, in the Merkle hash tree (Fig. 1, left) the certificate s_2 for x_2 is $s_2 = ((x_1, \_), (\_, x_{34}))$ which represents a sequence of hashing steps starting from the leaf x_2 and ending with the root hash value, whereas $\_$ denotes an *empty slot* which during the verification is filled with the hash of the previous pair. Similarly, in the count-certified hash tree (Fig. 1, right) the certificate for x_2 is $s_2 = ((1, x_1, \_, 1), (2, \_, x_3, 1))$. The verification function $\mathsf{Ver}_{pk}(c, n, x, s)$ simply recomputes the root hash value by using s and compares it with c. It also checks whether $n \leq N$. The verification algorithm for count-certified trees also recomputes the intermediate counter values to verify the certificate s, in particular if the counter of the root vertex is n.

Collision-Extraction Property. For hash trees with a fixed shape and count-certified hash trees there is a straight and precise reduction of the binding property to the collision-resistance of h because of the following property: If $x_0 \neq x_1$, $\mathsf{Ver}_{pk}(c, n, x_0, s_0) = \mathsf{Ver}_{pk}(c, n, x_1, s_1) = \mathsf{true}$, and $\mathsf{loc}(s_0) = \mathsf{loc}(s_1)$, then the internal h-calls of these two verifications comprise a collision for h. Moreover, if the tree is balanced, then the collision can be extracted in $O(|s_0| + |s_1|) = O(\log_2 N)$ time.

4   Bounded Commitments Are Sufficient for Time-Stamping

In this section, we prove that bounded commitment schemes with partial opening are sufficient to construct secure time-stamping schemes. The new security reductions use a simple black-box certificate extractor (Fig. 2) and in the proofs we just show that a big enough set of valid decommitments $\mathcal{V}$ allows to break the binding property.

---

1. Execute A_1 in a black-box way and store $(c, n, \phi) \leftarrow A_1(\mathsf{pk}; \omega_1)$.
2. Generate m independent samples $(x_1, s_1) \leftarrow A_2(\phi), \ldots, (x_m, s_m) \leftarrow A_2(\phi)$.
3. Output (c, n) and a set of valid pairs $\mathcal{V} = \{(x_i, s_i) : \mathsf{Ver}_{\mathsf{pk}}(c, n, x_i, s_i) = \mathsf{true}\}$.

Fig. 2. Black-box certificate extractor $\mathcal{K}^{\mathsf{A}}_{\mathsf{cert}}(m)$

Our proofs do not only generalize the existing ones [7] but are also more efficient. Presented theorems together with the previous separation results [7,9] provide a clear border between the well studied classical binding properties like collision-freeness and the properties needed for time-stamping. For bounded commitment schemes the binding property implies time-stamping security. Otherwise, these notions are independent—binding properties are not necessary [9] nor sufficient [7].

To clarify the presentation, we have omitted a small $O(N \log N + t)$ term that counts the computational effort needed to manage the list $\mathcal{V}$ of valid decommitments, as the contribution to the total working time is irrelevant for all reasonable values of ε. To be absolutely precise, one has to increase the time-bounds for the binding property by $O(N \log N + t)$ in Theorems 1–4.

Theorem 1 (Entropy based security). *Every* $\left(\frac{6t\sqrt{N}}{\varepsilon}, \frac{\varepsilon}{8}\right)$*-binding and N-bounded list commitment scheme is also a* $\left(t, t, \frac{\varepsilon^3}{432 \cdot N}, \varepsilon\right)$*-secure time-stamping scheme for $N \geq 9$.*

Proof. Let $A = (A_1, A_2)$ be a t-time adversary that violates $\left(t, t, \frac{\varepsilon^3}{432 \cdot N}, \varepsilon\right)$-security promise, i.e., $\mathrm{Adv}^{\mathsf{ts}}(A) \geq \varepsilon$ and A_2 is sufficiently unpredictable (even for itself):

$$\Pr[\mathsf{Coll}] := \Pr\left[\begin{array}{l} \mathsf{pk} \leftarrow \mathsf{Gen}, (c, n, \phi) \leftarrow A_1(\mathsf{pk}; \omega), \\ (x_0, s_0) \leftarrow A_2(\phi), (x_1, s_1) \leftarrow A_2(\phi) : x_0 = x_1 \end{array}\right] \leq \frac{\varepsilon^3}{432N} \ .$$

If $m = \frac{6\sqrt{N}}{\varepsilon}$ then the black-box certificate extractor $\mathcal{K}^{\mathsf{A}}_{\mathsf{cert}}(m)$ runs in time $\frac{6t\sqrt{N}}{\varepsilon}$ and provides enough certificates to reveal a double opening. Let Coll^* denote that two equal messages $x_i = x_j$ are produced internally by $\mathcal{K}^{\mathsf{A}}_{\mathsf{cert}}(m)$. Then by the union bound

$$\Pr[\mathsf{Coll}^*] \leq \sum_{\mathsf{pk}, \omega_1} \Pr[\mathsf{pk}, \omega_1] \cdot \frac{m(m-1)}{2} \cdot \Pr[\mathsf{Coll}|\mathsf{pk}, \omega_1]$$

$$\leq \frac{m(m-1)}{2} \cdot \Pr[\mathsf{Coll}] \leq \frac{m^2}{2} \cdot \frac{\varepsilon^3}{432N} \leq \frac{\varepsilon}{24} \ .$$

Next, we estimate the number of valid document-certificate pairs created by $\mathcal{K}^{\mathsf{A}}_{\mathsf{cert}}(m)$. Let $\varepsilon_{\mathsf{pk}, \omega_1} = \mathrm{Adv}^{\mathsf{ts}}(A|\mathsf{pk}, \omega_1)$ denote the probability that A is successful for fixed pk and ω_1. As $\Pr\left[\mathsf{pk} \leftarrow \mathsf{Gen}, \omega_1 \leftarrow \Omega : \varepsilon_{\mathsf{pk}, \omega_1} \geq \frac{\varepsilon}{2}\right] \geq \frac{\varepsilon}{2}$, we apply the Chernoff bound for these (pk, ω_1) pairs with $\theta = \frac{1}{2}$ and X_i indicating $(x_i, s_i) \in \mathcal{V}$, and get

$$\Pr\left[|\mathcal{V}| \leq 1.5\sqrt{N}|\varepsilon_{\mathsf{pk}, \omega_1} \geq \frac{\varepsilon}{2}\right] \leq e^{-\frac{3\sqrt{N}}{8}} < 1/3 \ .$$

Since $\mathcal{V}$ consists of identically distributed independent variables, we apply the Birthday bound. If $|\mathcal{V}| \geq 1.5\sqrt{N}$ then $\mathsf{loc}(s_i) = \mathsf{loc}(s_j)$ for some i, j with probability $> \frac{1}{2}$. Let

C be an adversary that runs $\mathcal{K}^A_{cert}(m)$ and then tries to find a double opening in $\mathcal{V}$. Then

$$\mathrm{Adv}^{bind}(C) \geq \frac{\varepsilon}{2} \cdot \left(1 - e^{-\frac{3\sqrt{N}}{8}}\right) \cdot \frac{1}{2} - \Pr\left[\mathsf{Coll}^*\right] > \frac{\varepsilon}{6} - \frac{\varepsilon}{24} = \frac{\varepsilon}{8}$$

for $N \geq 9$ and we have obtained a desired contradiction.   □

Theorem 2 (Entropy based security). *Every $\left(\frac{4Nt}{\varepsilon}, \frac{\varepsilon}{8}\right)$-binding and N-bounded set commitment scheme is a $\left(t, t, \frac{\varepsilon^3}{64N^2}, \varepsilon\right)$-secure time-stamping scheme for $N \geq 6$.*

Proof. Similarly to the previous proof, let $A = (A_1, A_2)$ be a t-time adversary that violates a $\left(t, t, \frac{\varepsilon^3}{64N^2}, \varepsilon\right)$-time-stamping security promise. In other words, $\mathrm{Adv}^{ts}(A) \geq \varepsilon$ and $\Pr\left[\mathsf{Coll}\right] \leq \frac{\varepsilon^3}{64(N+1)^2}$. Fix $m = \frac{4N}{\varepsilon}$. Then the black-box certificate extractor $C := \mathcal{K}^A_{cert}(m)$ then runs in time $\frac{4Nt}{\varepsilon}$. The Chernoff bound with $\theta = \frac{1}{2}$ yields

$$\Pr\left[|\mathcal{V}| \leq N \big| \varepsilon_{pk,\omega_1} \geq \tfrac{\varepsilon}{2}\right] \leq e^{-\frac{N}{4}} < 1/2 .$$

Again, $\Pr\left[pk \leftarrow \mathsf{Gen}, \omega_1 \leftarrow \Omega : \varepsilon_{pk;\omega} \geq \tfrac{\varepsilon}{2}\right] \geq \tfrac{\varepsilon}{2}$ and we have obtained a contradiction: $\mathrm{Adv}^{bind}(C) \geq \tfrac{\varepsilon}{2} \cdot \left(1 - e^{-\frac{N}{4}}\right) - \Pr\left[\mathsf{Coll}^*\right] > \tfrac{\varepsilon}{4} - \tfrac{m^2}{2} \cdot \tfrac{\varepsilon^3}{64N^2} = \tfrac{\varepsilon}{8}.$ □

Theorem 3 (Uniform security). *Every $\left(\frac{2Nt}{\varepsilon}, \frac{\varepsilon}{2}\right)$-binding and N-bounded list commitment scheme is also a $(t, \frac{2Nt}{\varepsilon}, \varepsilon)$-black-box secure time-stamping scheme.*

Proof. For the proof we have to fix a canonical black-box extractor machine $\mathcal{K}^A$:

1. First run A_1 and store $(c, n, \phi) \leftarrow A_1(pk; \omega_1)$ and set $\hat{\mathcal{X}}[i] = \perp$ for $i \in \{1, \ldots, n\}$.
2. Fix $m = \frac{2N}{\varepsilon}$ and for $k \in \{1, \ldots, m\}$ do
   - Compute an independent sample $(x_k, s_k) \leftarrow A_2(\phi)$.
   - If $\mathsf{Ver}_{pk}(c, n, x_k, s_k) = \mathsf{true}$ and $\hat{\mathcal{X}}[\mathsf{loc}(s_k)] = \perp$ then set $\hat{\mathcal{X}}[\mathsf{loc}(s_k)] = x_k$.
3. Output the last snapshot of $\hat{\mathcal{X}}$.

Clearly, for every t-time adversary $A = (A_1, A_2)$, the extraction algorithm $\mathcal{K}^A$ runs in time $\frac{2Nt}{\varepsilon}$ and the extractor $\mathcal{K}$ is valid for the definition.

For the sake of contradiction, assume that a t-time adversary $A = (A_1, A_2)$ violates the security promise (4) w.r.t. $\mathcal{K}$. Let a pair (x_k, s_k) be *revealing* if $x_k \neq \hat{\mathcal{X}}[\mathsf{loc}(s_k)]$ in Step 2 of $\mathcal{K}^A$. Then the probability that (x_k, s_k) is revealing must be larger than ε for every $k \in \{1, \ldots, m\}$, since the previous state of $\hat{\mathcal{X}}$ can be viewed as a partial output of $\mathcal{K}^A$. Let X_k be the corresponding zero-one indicator variable, i.e., $X_k = 1$ if (x_k, s_k) is revealing. Then $\varepsilon_k = \mathbf{E}[X_k] > \varepsilon$ and the average of $S_m = \sum_{k=1}^m X_k$ is

$$\mathbf{E}[S_m] = \mathbf{E}\left[X_1 + \cdots + X_m\right] = \varepsilon_1 + \cdots \varepsilon_m > m\varepsilon = 2N .$$

On the other hand, $\mathbf{E}[S_m] \leq N + \Pr\left[S_m > N\right] \cdot \frac{2N}{\varepsilon}$ and thus $\Pr\left[S_m > N\right] > \frac{\varepsilon}{2}$. Therefore, with probability strictly more than $\frac{\varepsilon}{2}$ there are $N+1$ revealing pairs (x_k, s_k) computed by $\mathcal{K}^A$. As the commitment scheme is N-bounded, revealing pairs exist only if $n \leq N$. Hence, at least one slot must be overwritten if there are $N+1$ revealing pairs and we have found a double opening with probability strictly more than $\frac{\varepsilon}{2}$.   □

Theorem 4 (Uniform security guarantee). *Every* $(\frac{2Nt}{\varepsilon}, \frac{\varepsilon}{2})$-*binding* N-*bounded set commitment scheme is also* $(t, \frac{2Nt}{\varepsilon}, \varepsilon)$-*black-box secure time-stamping scheme.*

Proof. The construction given above is also valid for set commitments.   □

Comparison with previous results. Our reductions are not completely novel. A similar proof with a different reduction was given in [7] for hash trees. Therefore, we compare the time-success ratios. Recall that the minimal time-success ratio α implies $\varepsilon(t) \leq \frac{t}{\alpha}$ and hence large ratios $\gamma = \frac{\alpha_1}{\alpha_0}$ lead to better security bounds.

In Thm. 1 we constructed a double opener with running time $t_0 \approx \frac{6t\sqrt{N}}{\varepsilon}$ and with advantage $\varepsilon_0 \approx \frac{\varepsilon}{8}$, based on a back-dating adversary with running time t and advantage ε. Thus the change ratio is $\gamma \approx \frac{\varepsilon}{48\sqrt{N}}$ for our reduction. If we adapt the reduction presented in [7] for the exact security model we obtain a ratio $\gamma \approx \frac{\varepsilon}{2N}$, which is significantly smaller for $N \geq 600$. In *global-scale* time-stamping services, N can be very large (say millions or even billions) and our new reduction by far supersedes the previous one [7].

Similarly, one can verify that $\gamma \approx \frac{\varepsilon}{4N}$ for Thm. 3 and Thm. 4 but the security guarantees are much stronger. To break the black-box security an adversary can produce valid document-certificate pairs with low computational Rényi entropy, which makes it impossible to use the birthday paradox. It is easy to see that the extractor must work in time $\Theta(\frac{Nt}{\varepsilon})$ and $\sqrt{N}$ in the denominator is not achievable.

5   All Bounded Commitment Schemes Are Knowledge-Binding

Both security definitions for time-stamping (Def. 1,2) are based on heuristic assumptions. Namely, the future is modeled as a *computationally efficient stochastic process*. Such an assumption has two major drawbacks. Firstly, it is philosophically questionable and causes practical problems in the classical framework of secure computations [11]: due to the non-uniform nature of such model, future documents may have arbitrary distributions. Secondly, the success of back-dating adversaries is computed as an average over the distribution of future documents and it might still be easy to "backdate" a fixed document. To overcome these problems, we propose a new security notion where the future is modeled as an advice string that is independent of pk. The independence assumption is essential. Otherwise, no computationally binding commitment scheme can be secure, since the advice may contain explicit double-openings.

Definition 3. *A commitment scheme is* (t, τ, ε)-*knowledge-binding if for every* t-*time adversary* $\mathsf{A} = (\mathsf{A}_1, \mathsf{A}_2)$ *there exist a dedicated* τ-*time extractor machine* $\mathcal{K}_\mathsf{A}$ *such that*

$$\mathrm{Adv}^{\mathsf{k\text{-}bind}}(\mathsf{A}) = \max_{\mathsf{adv}} \Pr \left[\begin{array}{l} \mathsf{pk} \leftarrow \mathsf{Gen}, \ \omega_1 \leftarrow \Omega, \ \hat{\mathcal{X}} \leftarrow \mathcal{K}_A(\mathsf{pk}; \omega_1), \\ (c, n, \phi) \leftarrow \mathsf{A}_1(\mathsf{pk}; \omega_1), (x, s) \leftarrow \mathsf{A}_2(\phi, \mathsf{adv}) : \\ (\mathsf{Ver}_{\mathsf{pk}}(c, n, x, s) = \mathsf{true} \wedge x \notin \hat{\mathcal{X}}) \vee |\hat{\mathcal{X}}| > n \end{array} \right] \leq \varepsilon \ ,$$

where adv *varies over all advices of length* t *and the probability is taken over the coins of* Gen, A_1 *and* A_2. *For list commitments,* $\hat{\mathcal{X}}$ *is a list and write* $x \in \hat{\mathcal{X}}$ *iff* $x = \hat{\mathcal{X}}[\mathsf{loc}(s)]$.

The new definition explicitly states that there exists an efficient *extraction strategy* $\mathcal{K}_A$ that is able (by observing the internal computations of the committing algorithm A_1) to predict any bit-string x that is later "back-dated" by A_2. I.e, in some sense x already existed before the commitment and no real back-dating attacks were performed.

But there is an even more intuitive interpretation. When an adversary publishes a commitment c, he implicitly fixes his level of knowledge about the commitment and no future actions can change it. As the level of knowledge does not change in time, a successful opening "proves" that the adversary already "knew" the committed element when the commitment was created. Hence, we can omit proofs of knowledge at the commitment stage and reduce the number of rounds in various protocols. Thus, the new notion is very similar to plaintext-awareness of public-key encryption schemes.

Finally, note that knowledge-binding is a necessary condition for the multi-party security of time-stamping schemes. In the ideal implementation, TSS gives a list $\mathcal{X}$ to a trusted party who will later serve partial release queries $x \in \mathcal{X}$? Hence, there must be an efficient way to extract all documents that TSS can potentially open as a response for any future message that is independent of pk, i.e., the extractor machine $\mathcal{K}_A$ must exist. To get multi-party security in the malicious model, we must also protect a honest TSS against malicious clients. This can be done in an obvious way by using digital signatures, but due to the space limitations we defer the discussion to follow-up articles.

Clearly, the knowledge-binding property can be established only by using white-box reductions. In other words, we cannot efficiently construct the code of $\mathcal{K}_A$ given only the code of A, although $\mathcal{K}_A$ itself is an efficient algorithm. Such reductions provide substantially weaker security guarantees for *fixed hash functions* like SHA-1, since we know *a priori* that efficient collision finders must exist for SHA-1. Therefore, the claims of existence without efficient construction strategies provide no new information. As a result, we can only talk about the security of hash function families, i.e., we have to consider SHA-1 as a "typical" representative of a collision-free hash function family.

The proofs consist of two main steps. First we analyze the behavior of A and construct a dedicated knowledge extractor $\mathcal{K}_A$. Next we show that $\mathcal{K}_A$ is efficient and $\mathrm{Adv}^{\mathrm{k\text{-}bind}}(A)$ is sufficiently small. To construct $\mathcal{K}_A$, we run A on all possible inputs and find suitable triggering messages adv that force A to reveal most of the valid certificates. Next, we construct $\mathcal{K}_A$ from A and the triggering messages. As the knowledge-binding condition only requires the *existence* of $\mathcal{K}_A$, the construction time is not an issue.

Theorem 5. *For every $t > 0$ and $\delta > 0$, there exists $\tau = (\frac{N}{\delta} + 1) \cdot O(t)$ such that every (τ, ε)-binding list commitment scheme is $(t, \tau, \varepsilon + \delta)$-knowledge binding.*

Proof. Fix a t-time adversary A and consider a giant status matrix $W[\mathrm{pk}, \omega_1; \mathrm{adv}, \omega_2]$ the rows of which are indexed by public keys pk and random coins ω_1 of A_1, whereas the columns are indexed by t-bit advices adv and random coins ω_2 of A_2. Define

$$W[\mathrm{pk}, \omega_1; \mathrm{adv}, \omega_2] = \begin{cases} 0, & \text{if } \mathrm{Ver}_{\mathrm{pk}}(c, n, x, s) = \text{false} , \\ \mathrm{loc}(s), & \text{if } \mathrm{Ver}_{\mathrm{pk}}(c, n, x, s) = \text{true} , \end{cases}$$

where $(c, n, \phi) \leftarrow A_1(\mathrm{pk}; \omega_1)$ and $(x, s) \leftarrow A_2(\phi, \mathrm{adv}; \omega_2)$. Note that few columns of W cover most of the rows containing non-zero elements. Namely, Lemma 1 from

App. A assures the existence of $\mathcal{I} = \{(\mathsf{adv}_1, \omega_2^1), \ldots, (\mathsf{adv}_k, \omega_2^k)\}$ such that $|\mathcal{I}| \leq \frac{N}{\delta}$ and for any fixed advice-randomness pair (adv, ω_2):

$$\Pr\left[(\mathsf{pk}, \omega_1) : 0 \neq \mathsf{W}[\mathsf{pk}, \omega_1; \mathsf{adv}, \omega_2] \notin \mathcal{L}[\mathsf{pk}, \omega_1] \wedge |\mathcal{L}[\mathsf{pk}, \omega_1]| < N\right] \leq \delta \ , \qquad (5)$$

where $\mathcal{L}[\mathsf{pk}, \omega_1] = \{\mathsf{W}[\mathsf{pk}, \omega_1; \mathsf{adv}, \omega_2] : (\mathsf{adv}, \omega_2) \in \mathcal{I}\}$ is a set of revealed locations. Now the construction[3] of $\mathcal{K}_{\mathsf{A}}$ is evident:

1. Given (pk, ω_1) store $(c, n, \phi) \leftarrow \mathsf{A}_1(\mathsf{pk}; \omega_1)$ and set $\hat{\mathcal{X}}[i] = \perp$ for $i \in \{1, \ldots, n\}$.
2. For each $(\mathsf{adv}, \omega_2) \in \mathcal{I}$ do
   - Compute $(x, s) \leftarrow \mathsf{A}_2(\phi, \mathsf{adv}; \omega_2)$.
   - If $\mathsf{Ver}_{\mathsf{pk}}(c, n, x, s) = \mathsf{true}$ then set $\hat{\mathcal{X}}[\mathsf{loc}(s)] \leftarrow x$.
3. Output the last snapshot of $\hat{\mathcal{X}}$.

To analyze the advantage of $\mathcal{K}_{\mathsf{A}}$, we fix a pair (adv, ω_2). Let $(c, n, \phi) \leftarrow \mathsf{A}_1(\mathsf{pk}; \omega_1)$ and $(x, s) \leftarrow \mathsf{A}_2(\phi, \mathsf{adv}; \omega_2)$ as before. For valid decommitment value s, the entry $\hat{\mathcal{X}}[\mathsf{loc}(s)] = \perp$ only if $|\mathcal{L}[\mathsf{pk}, \omega_1]| < N$ and thus the inequality (5) given above yields $\Pr\left[(\mathsf{pk}, \omega_1) : \mathsf{Ver}_{\mathsf{pk}}(c, n, x, s) = \mathsf{true} \wedge \hat{\mathcal{X}}[\mathsf{loc}(s)] = \perp\right] \leq \delta$. Alternatively, $\mathcal{K}_{\mathsf{A}}$ can fail if $\mathsf{Ver}_{\mathsf{pk}}(c, n, x, s) = \mathsf{true}$ but $\hat{\mathcal{X}}[\mathsf{loc}(s)] \neq x$. However, we can naturally combine A_1, A_2 and $\mathcal{K}_{\mathsf{A}}$ into an adversary B that outputs these double openings and performs $(\frac{N}{\delta} + 1) \cdot O(t)$ elementary operations. Consequently, $\mathrm{Adv}^{\mathsf{bind}}(\mathsf{B}) \leq \varepsilon$ and thus

$$\Pr\left[(\mathsf{pk}, \omega_1) : \mathsf{Ver}_{\mathsf{pk}}(c, n, x, s) = \mathsf{true} \wedge x \neq \hat{\mathcal{X}}[\mathsf{loc}(s)] \neq \perp\right] \leq \varepsilon \ .$$

As a result, we have obtained that for any pair (adv, ω_2):

$$\Pr\left[(\mathsf{pk}, \omega_1) : \mathsf{Ver}_{\mathsf{pk}}(c, n, x, s) = \mathsf{true} \wedge x \neq \hat{\mathcal{X}}[\mathsf{loc}(s)]\right] \leq \delta + \varepsilon$$

and the claim follows. $\qquad\qquad\qquad\qquad\qquad\qquad\qquad\qquad\qquad\qquad\qquad\qquad\square$

Theorem 6. *For every $t > 0$ and $\delta > 0$, there exists $\tau = (\frac{N}{\delta} + 1) \cdot O(t)$ such that every (τ, ε)-binding set commitment scheme is $(t, \tau, \varepsilon + \delta)$-knowledge-binding.*

Proof. Fix a t-time adversary A and consider a status matrix $\mathsf{W}[\mathsf{pk}, \omega_1; \mathsf{adv}, \omega_2]$ that is indexed identically to the previous proof but the entries are defined differently:

$$\mathsf{W}[\mathsf{pk}, \omega_1; \mathsf{adv}, \omega_2] = \begin{cases} 0, & \text{if } \mathsf{Ver}_{\mathsf{pk}}(c, n, x, s) = \mathsf{false} \ , \\ x, & \text{if } \mathsf{Ver}_{\mathsf{pk}}(c, n, x, s) = \mathsf{true} \ , \end{cases}$$

where $(c, n, \phi) \leftarrow \mathsf{A}_1(\mathsf{pk}; \omega_1)$ and $(x, s) \leftarrow \mathsf{A}_2(\phi, \mathsf{adv}; \omega_2)$. Then Lemma 1 from App. A assures the existence of $\mathcal{I} = \{(\mathsf{adv}_1, \omega_2^1), \ldots, (\mathsf{adv}_k, \omega_2^k)\}$ such that $|\mathcal{I}| \leq \frac{N}{\delta}$ and for every fixed advice-randomness pair (adv, ω_2):

$$\Pr\left[(\mathsf{pk}, \omega_1) : 0 \neq \mathsf{W}[\mathsf{pk}, \omega_1; \mathsf{adv}, \omega_2] \notin \mathcal{L}[\mathsf{pk}, \omega_1] \wedge |\mathcal{L}[\mathsf{pk}, \omega_1]| < N\right] \leq \delta \ , \qquad (6)$$

where $\mathcal{L}[\mathsf{pk}, \omega_1] = \{\mathsf{W}[\mathsf{pk}, \omega_1; \mathsf{adv}, \omega_2] : (\mathsf{adv}, \omega_2) \in \mathcal{I}\}$ is a set of revealed elements. Now the construction of $\mathcal{K}_{\mathsf{A}}$ is straightforward:

---

[3] Note that all elements of the set $\mathcal{I}$ are hardwired as explicit constants into the code of $\mathcal{K}_{\mathsf{A}}$, i.e., $\mathcal{K}_{\mathsf{A}}$ *does not* compute $\mathcal{I}$. As $\mathcal{K}_{\mathsf{A}}$ runs on a universal Turing machine, it must rewind the code of A_2 and thus $\mathcal{K}_{\mathsf{A}}$ performs at most $O(t)$ extra steps to complete the loop of Step 2.

1. Given (pk, ω_1) store $(c, n, \phi) \leftarrow \mathsf{A}_1(\mathsf{pk}; \omega_1)$ and set $\hat{\mathcal{X}} \leftarrow \emptyset$.
2. For each $(\mathsf{adv}, \omega_2) \in \mathcal{I}$ do
   - Compute $(x, s) \leftarrow \mathsf{A}_2(\phi, \mathsf{adv}; \omega_2)$.
   - If $\mathsf{Ver}_{\mathsf{pk}}(c, n, x, s) = \mathsf{true}$ then add x to $\hat{\mathcal{X}}$.
3. Output the last snapshot of $\hat{\mathcal{X}}$.

To analyze the advantage of $\mathcal{K}_{\mathsf{A}}$, fix (adv, ω_2). Let $(c, n, \phi) \leftarrow \mathsf{A}_1(\mathsf{pk}; \omega_1)$ and $(x, s) \leftarrow \mathsf{A}_2(\phi, \mathsf{adv}, \omega_2)$ as before. As $\hat{\mathcal{X}}[\mathsf{pk}, \omega_1] = \mathcal{L}[\mathsf{pk}, \omega_1]$ by the construction (see Lemma 1), the inequality (6) yields $\Pr[\mathsf{Ver}_{\mathsf{pk}}(c, n, x, s) = \mathsf{true} \wedge x \notin \hat{\mathcal{X}} \wedge |\hat{\mathcal{X}}| < n \leq N] \leq \delta$. The extractor $\mathcal{K}_{\mathsf{A}}$ can also fail when $\mathsf{Ver}_{\mathsf{pk}}(c, n, x, s) = \mathsf{true}$ but $x \notin \hat{\mathcal{X}}$ and $|\hat{\mathcal{X}}| \geq n$. Again, we can naturally combine $\mathsf{A}_1, \mathsf{A}_2$ and $\mathcal{K}_{\mathsf{A}}$ into an adversary B with running-time $(\frac{N}{\delta} + 1) \cdot O(t)$ that runs all algorithms and extracts all valid openings. Consequently, the restriction $\mathsf{Adv}^{\mathsf{bind}}(\mathsf{B}) \leq \varepsilon$ yields $\Pr[\mathsf{Ver}_{\mathsf{pk}}(c, n, x, s) = \mathsf{true} \wedge x \notin \hat{\mathcal{X}} \wedge |\hat{\mathcal{X}}| \geq n] \leq \varepsilon$ and we have obtained that for any pair (adv, ω_2):

$$\Pr[\mathsf{Ver}_{\mathsf{pk}}(c, n, x, s) = \mathsf{true} \wedge x \notin \hat{\mathcal{X}}] \leq \delta + \varepsilon$$

and the claim follows. $\square$

Efficiency of the New Reduction. Again, we compute time-success ratios to compare the efficiency of the new white-box reduction to the previous black-box ones. To have a fair comparison we take $\delta \approx \varepsilon$. Then Theorems 5 and 6 provide attacks against the binding property with parameters $t_0 \approx (\frac{N}{\delta} + 1)t$ and $\varepsilon_0 = \varepsilon$, provided that there exist a t-time adversary achieving $\varepsilon + \delta$ success. As a result, we obtain a change ratio $\gamma = \frac{\alpha_1}{\alpha_0} \approx (\frac{N}{\delta} + 1)^{-1} \cdot \frac{\varepsilon}{\varepsilon + \delta} \approx \frac{\varepsilon}{2N}$, which is better than the change ratio $\gamma \approx \frac{\varepsilon}{4N}$ provided by Thm. 3 and Thm. 4. The difference is not essential rather it comes from slightly loose success bounds in Thm. 3 and Thm. 4.

6   Applications of Knowledge-Binding Commitments

Here, we briefly describe how knowledge-binding count-certified hash trees can be used and why knowledge-binding property is important. Knowledge-binding property can be viewed as an indifference against outside advices. Similar to the plaintext-awareness, the knowledge-binding property allows one to combine commitments with other cryptographic primitives without a fear of unwanted interference. Such interference often makes it hard or impossible to prove the security of new constructions. If the secret or public parameters of other primitives are independent of the commitment parameters pk, then the rest of the protocol can be interpreted as an external advice. Hence, one can use the standard hybrid argument technique even if the primitives are used concurrently.

Distributed and fine-grain time-stamping. Knowledge-binding commitments give rise to a secure time-stamping service where a central time-stamping authority (TSS) computes and publishes the round commitment (c, n) and distributes the respective certificates s_i to the clients. But such service is susceptible to denial-of-service attacks. Hence, it is more natural to consider a distributed service where k independent servers compute sub-commitments (c_i, n_i) and at the end of the round the master commitment

(c, n) is compiled. Therefore, it is advantageous to use knowledge-binding commitments that facilitate fast merging of sub-commitments and mostly local certificate computations. Count-certified hash trees have the following important property: every root node (c_i, n_i) of a hash subtree forms a correct commitment. Moreover, given two root nodes (c_L, n_L) and (c_R, n_R) it is straightforward to compute the commitment of the merged tree and update the corresponding certificates.

In a way, a set commitment scheme provides a really coarse-grain time-stamping service. It is impossible to order the events inside the round $\mathcal{X}$. List commitment provides only a partial solution, as clients have to trust that the TSS orders documents correctly in a single round. Tree-shaped list commitments that preserve knowledge-binding w.r.t. the root of each subtree allow also fine-grained time-stamping even if the TSS acts maliciously. Essentially, TSS has to send to a Client all root commitments (c_i, n_i) of all preceding computations, then the Client has strong guarantees that after submitting his query the TSS cannot insert any messages in the prefix of the list without getting caught. Hence, count-certified hash trees could be used for fine-grain time-stamping.

Non-malleable partially releasable commitments. To show that knowledge-binding commitments have other applications outside of the domain of time-stamping, we give a construction of partially releasable non-malleable commitments form non-malleable string commitments and knowledge-binding commitments. It is just an informal example, we do not formalize the claim due to the lack of space.

Recall that a commitment scheme is non-malleable if given a commitment c it is infeasible to construct a new commitment $c' \neq c$ such that after seeing a certificate s for x it is infeasible to output a valid certificate s' for x' such that x and x' are related. Let $\mathcal{L} = \{c_1, \ldots, c_n\}$ be a list of non-malleable commitments for $x_1, \ldots, x_n$ and $(C, D) \leftarrow \mathsf{Com}_{\mathsf{pk}}(\mathcal{L})$ is computed by using a knowledge-binding commitment scheme. Then the resulting commitment scheme is non-malleable. From the knowledge-binding property it follows that after seeing a proof that c_i was computed by using x_i, adversary's ability to output certificates (c, s) such that $\Pr[\mathsf{Ver}(C, n, c, s) = \mathsf{true}]$ does not increase. Hence, the adversary knows all valid commitment-certificate pairs (c_i, s_i) essentially before any commitment is opened. Therefore, non-malleability directly follows from the non-malleability of the lower-level commitment.

References

1. N. Barić and B. Pfitzmann. Collision-free accumulators and fail-stop signature schemes without trees. In Proc. of *EUROCRYPT'97, LNCS 1233*, pages 480–494, 1997.
2. D. Bayer, S. Haber, and W.-S. Stornetta. Improving the efficiency and reliability of digital time-stamping. In *Sequences II: Methods in Communication, Security, and Computer Science*, pages 329-334, Springer-Verlag, New York 1993.
3. J. Benaloh and M. de Mare. One-way accumulators: a decentralized alternative to digital signatures. In Proc. of *EUROCRYPT'93, LNCS 765*, pages 274–285, 1994.
4. M. Blum. Coin flipping by telephone: a protocol for solving impossible problems. In Proc. of *CompCon*, pages 133–137, 1982.
5. G. Brassard, D. Chaum, and C. Crépeau. Minimum disclosure proofs of knowledge. *JCSS*, vol.37, pages 156–189, 1988.

6. A. Buldas, P. Laud, H. Lipmaa. Eliminating counterevidence with applications to accountable certificate management. *Journal of Computer Security*, 10(3), pages 273–296, 2002.
7. A. Buldas and M. Saarepera. On provably secure time-stamping schemes. In Proc. of *ASIACRYPT 2004, LNCS 3329*, pages 500–514, 2004.
8. A. Buldas, P. Laud, M. Saarepera, and J. Willemson. Universally composable time-stamping schemes with audit. In *ISC05, LNCS 3650*, pages 359–373, 2005.
9. A. Buldas, S. Laur. Do broken hash functions affect the security of time-stamping schemes? In Proc. of *ACNS'06, LNCS 3989*, pages 50–65, 2006.
10. I. Damgård. Commitment schemes and zero knowledge protocols. In *Lectures on Data Security: modern cryptology in theory and prectice, LNCS 1561*, pages 63–86, 1999.
11. O. Goldreich. *Foundations of Cryptography II: Basic Applications*, Cambridge University Press, 2004.
12. S. Haber and W.-S. Stornetta. Secure Names for Bit-Strings. In Proc. of *ACM Conference on Computer and Communications Security*, pages 28–35, 1997.
13. T. Hagerup and C. Rüb. A Guided Tour of Chernoff Bounds. *Information Processing Letters*, 33, pages 305–308, 1990.
14. S. Halevi and S. Micali. Practical and provably-secure commitment schemes from collision-free hashing. In *CRYPTO'96, LNCS 1109*, pages 201–215, 1996.
15. R. C. Merkle. Protocols for public-key cryptosystems. *Proceedings of the 1980 IEEE Symposium on Security and Privacy*, pages 122–134, 1980.
16. G. Nuckolls, C. U. Martel, and S. G. Stubblebine. Certifying Data from Multiple Sources. In Proc. of the *DBSec 2003*, pages 47–60, 2003.
17. K. Nyberg. Fast accumulated hashing. In Proc. of *FSE'96, LNCS 1039*, pages 83–87, 1996.

A   Combinatorial Extraction Lemma

Consider a finite matrix $W[r; c]$ the rows of which are indexed by $r \in \mathcal{R}$ and the columns are indexed by $c \in \mathcal{C}$. Moreover, assume that a certain probability measure $\Pr[\cdot]$ is defined over the row indices $\mathcal{R}$. Then it is straightforward to state and prove a combinatorial lemma that we used for proving the knowledge-binding property.

Lemma 1. *For any $\delta > 0$ and $N \in \mathbb{N}$, there exist a set of column indices $\emptyset \subseteq \mathcal{I} \subseteq \mathcal{C}$ such that $0 \leq |\mathcal{I}| \leq \frac{N}{\delta}$ and for every column $c \in \mathcal{C}$:*

$$\Pr[r \leftarrow \mathcal{R} : W[r; c] \neq 0 \wedge W[r; c] \notin \mathcal{L}[r] \wedge |\mathcal{L}[r]| < N] \leq \delta ,$$

where $\mathcal{L}[r] = \{W[r, c] : c \in \mathcal{I}\} \setminus \{0\}$ is the set of nonzero elements revealed by $\mathcal{I}$.

Proof. Consider following iterative procedure:

1. Set $\mathcal{I} = \emptyset$ and initialise row counters $\text{cnt}[r] = N$ for $r \in \mathcal{R}$.
2. While exists $c \in \mathcal{C}$ such that $\Pr[r : W[r; c] \neq 0] \geq \delta$ do
   (a) Choose c such that $\Pr[r : W[r; c] \neq 0] \geq \delta$ and insert c into $\mathcal{I}$.
   (b) For each row $r \in \mathcal{R}$ such that $W[r; c] \neq 0$ do
       – Store $w \leftarrow W[r; c]$.
       – Remove w entries from the row.
         If $W[r; c'] = w$ then $W[r, c'] \leftarrow 0$ for $c' \in \mathcal{C}$.
       – Decrease counter $\text{cnt}[r] \leftarrow \text{cnt}[r] - 1$.
   (c) Zero all rows where $\text{cnt}[r] = 0$.

- If $cnt[r] = 0$, set $W[r; c'] \leftarrow 0$ for $c' \in \mathcal{C}$.

Let $\mathcal{N} = \{r : \exists W[r; c] \neq 0\}$ denote nonzero rows and $\mathcal{N}_{old}, \mathcal{N}_{new}$ denote the value of $\mathcal{N}$ before and after update at Step 2. Let

$$\mu[\mathcal{N}] = \sum_{r \in \mathcal{N}} \Pr[r]\, cnt[r]$$

be the average counter value. Then by the construction $\mu[\mathcal{N}_{new}] \leq \mu[\mathcal{N}_{old}] - \delta$ after a single iteration of Step 2. As initially $\mu[\mathcal{N}] \leq N$, then after $\lfloor N/\delta \rfloor$ iterations $\Pr[\mathcal{N}] \leq \mu[\mathcal{N}] < \delta$. Note that the algorithm nullifies the elements $W[r, c']$ only if they already belong to $\mathcal{L}[r]$ or $|\mathcal{L}[r]| \geq N$. In the end, each column c contains at most a δ-fraction of elements that satisfy the predicate $W[r; c] \neq 0 \wedge W[r; c] \notin \mathcal{L}[r] \wedge |\mathcal{L}[r]| < N$ and the claim follows. Note that $\mathcal{I}$ can be empty. □

$\mathcal{I} = \emptyset$					$\mathcal{L}$
1	2	0	1	1	$\emptyset$
1	0	3	0	2	$\emptyset$
2	0	1	2	3	$\emptyset$ ⇒
0	0	0	1	0	$\emptyset$
0	0	0	0	2	$\emptyset$

$\mathcal{I} = \{1\}$					$\mathcal{L}$
0	2	0	0	**0**	$\{1\}$
0	0	3	0	2	$\{1\}$
0	0	1	**0**	3	$\{2\}$ ⇒
0	0	0	1	0	$\emptyset$
0	0	0	0	2	$\emptyset$

$\mathcal{I} = \{1,3\}$					$\mathcal{L}$
0	2	**0**	0	0	$\{1\}$
0	0	**0**	0	**0**	$\{1,3\}$
0	0	**0**	0	**0**	$\{2,1\}$ ⇒
0	0	0	1	0	$\emptyset$
0	0	0	0	2	$\emptyset$

$\mathcal{I} = \{1,3\}$					$\mathcal{L}$
1	2	0	1	1	$\{1\}$
1	0	3	0	2	$\{1,3\}$
2	0	1	2	3	$\{1,2\}$
0	0	0	1	0	$\emptyset$
0	0	0	0	2	$\emptyset$

Fig. 3. Illustration of Lemma 1. The first three sub-figures show how the columns are selected for the uniform distribution over the rows and for parameter values $N = 2$, $\delta = 0.3$, boldface symbols denote the changed values. The last sub-figure shows the final result. Boldface symbols denote the revealed entries. Underlined symbols denote the entries that satisfy the predicate.

Efficient Ring Signatures
Without Random Oracles

Hovav Shacham[1,*] and Brent Waters[2,**]

[1] Weizmann Institute of Science
`hovav.shacham@weizmann.ac.il`
[2] SRI International
`bwaters@csl.sri.com`

Abstract. We describe the first efficient ring signature scheme secure, without random oracles, based on standard assumptions. Our ring signatures are based in bilinear groups. For l members of a ring our signatures consist of $2l + 2$ group elements and require $2l + 3$ pairings to verify. We prove our scheme secure in the strongest security model proposed by Bender, Katz, and Morselli: namely, we show our scheme to be anonymous against full key exposure and unforgeable with respect to insider corruption. A shortcoming of our approach is that all the users' keys must be defined in the same group.

1 Introduction

Ring signatures were introduced by Rivest, Shamir, and Tauman [18, 19]. Each user in the system generates and publishes a public key. (This key can be, for example, the description of an RSA permutation.) In generating a ring signature, a user can choose, arbitrarily, some other users to implicate in the signature. The public keys of these implicated users, along with the signer's public key, are said to form the ring for that signature. A verifier is convinced that someone in the ring is responsible for the signature, but cannot tell who.

In this paper we present the first efficient ring signature scheme secure, without random oracles, based on standard assumptions. Our scheme gives $O(l)$ signatures, with no a priori bound on ring size. Our ring signatures are based in bilinear groups. In particular, for l members of a ring our signatures consist of $2l + 2$ group elements and require $2l + 3$ pairings to verify. We now outline our approach.

In our ring signature scheme each user generates her own public-private key-pair from the Waters [21] signature scheme defined over a group G of a composite order n, where the group is set up by a trusted authority. When a user wants to sign a message M on a ring R she first creates a ciphertext C, which is a BGN [9] encryption of her public signing key. Next, she proves that C is an encryption

---

* Supported by a Koshland Scholars Program fellowship.
** Supported by NSF CNS-0524252 and the US Army Research Office under the CyberTA Grant No. W911NF-06-1-0316.

T. Okamoto and X. Wang (Eds.): PKC 2007, LNCS 4450, pp. 166–180, 2007.

of exactly one of the public keys in the the ring R. We use proofs similar to that of Groth, Ostrovsky, and Sahai [16] to do this efficiently. Finally, she gives an encrypted signature of the message M using her private signing key and proves that the signature verifies under the encrypted key.

A shortcoming of our approach is that all the users' keys must be defined in the group G. This is unlike the generic construction of Bender, Katz, and Morselli [4], which does not place restrictions on the user keys, and also unlike some of the random-oracle–based schemes (discussed below) that allow for independently generated RSA user keys. In compensation, however, we obtain an efficient scheme provably secure, without random oracles, in the strongest security model proposed by Bender, Katz, and Morselli [4]: namely, we show our scheme to be anonymous against full key exposure and unforgeable with respect to insider corruption.

Related Work. The construction of Rivest, Shamir, and Tauman, requires that the users' public keys be for trapdoor-permutation–based schemes, i.e., include descriptions of a trapdoor permutation. Subsequently, ring signature constructions were presented where the underlying keys are discrete-log–based [17], discrete-log–based in the bilinear map setting [8], factoring-based [15], or a mix of trapdoor-permutation–type and discrete-log–type [1].

Ring signatures are also related to group signatures, which were introduced by Chaum and Van Heyst [13] and are themselves the subject of much subsequent research. The two concepts differ in two main ways. First, the ring is determined by the signer and can be different for each signatures; in a group signature, group membership is controlled by a group manager and, at any given time, is fixed.[1] Second, no one can determine which member of a ring generated a signature; in a group signature, a tracing party possesses a special trapdoor that allows it to determine which group member is responsible for a signature.

Applications. The canonical application for ring signatures is secret leaking: A signature by the ring of all cabinet ministers on a leaked memo is credible, but doesn't incriminate any particular minister for the leak. Other applications have been proposed [4, 19].

Ring Signatures in the Standard Model. The security of the ring signatures proposed by Rivest, Shamir, and Tauman and in most subsequent papers holds in the random oracle model [2].[2] Some recent papers have considered how to construct ring signatures that are provably secure in the standard model.

Xu, Zhang, and Feng [22] describe a ring signature secure in the standard model, but the proof presented is not rigorous and is apparently flawed [4, n. 1]. Chow et al. [14] give a ring signature scheme with proof in the standard model,

---

[1] Dodis et al. [15, Sect. 6.3] describe ad-hoc group signatures, a primitive for which this difference is less pronounced.

[2] More precisely, Rivest, Shamir, and Tauman analyzed their construction in the ideal-cipher model; Bresson, Stern, and Szydlo [11] later showed that random oracles suffice for proving its security.

but based on a strong new assumption. Bender, Katz, and Morselli present a ring signature secure in the standard model assuming trapdoor permutations exist, but the scheme uses generic ZAPs for NP as a building block, and is thus impractical. In addition, they give two ring signature schemes secure in the standard model but which allow only two-signer rings: one based on the Waters signature [21], a second based on the Camenisch-Lysyanskaya signature [12].

Our ring signature scheme is related to a recent group signature secure without random oracles due to Boyen and Waters [10]. One important difference is that in their group signature paper the master public key, which belongs to the group manager, is in the clear and the first level message, which corresponds to the user's identity, is encrypted and then proved to be well formed. In our scheme, on the other hand, the message to be signed is public, but the verification key – which belongs to the user who generated the signature – is encrypted and then a proof is given that *it* is well formed. (In our case, "well-formed" means "in the ring.") The Boyen-Waters group signature is itself based on two lines of research: the identity-based encryption scheme in the standard model due to Waters [21], which follows up on earlier schemes by Boneh and Boyen [5, 6]; and the perfect non-interactive zero knowledge proofs of Groth, Ostrovsky, and Sahai [16], which are based on the homomorphic encryption scheme proposed by Boneh, Goh, and Nissim [9].

2   Mathematical Setting

Like Boyen and Waters, we make use of bilinear groups of composite order. These were introduced by Boneh, Goh, and Nissim [9]. Let n be a composite with factorization $n = pq$. We have:

- G is a multiplicative cyclic group of order n;
- G_p is its cyclic order-p subgroup, and G_q is its cyclic order-q subgroup;
- g is a generator of G, while h is a generator of G_q;
- G_T is a multiplicative group of order n;
- $e : G \times G \to G_T$ is an efficiently computable map with the following properties:
  - Bilinear: for all $u, v \in G$ and $a, b \in \mathbb{Z}$, $e(u^a, v^b) = e(u, v)^{ab}$;
  - Non-degenerate: $\langle e(g, g) \rangle = G_T$ whenever $\langle g \rangle = G$;
- $G_{T,p}$ and $G_{T,q}$ are the G_T-subgroups of order p and q, respectively;
- the group operations on G and G_T can be performed efficiently; and
- bitstrings corresponding to elements of G (and of G_T) can be recognized efficiently.

In our ring signature scheme, the description of such a group G, including the generators g and h, is given in the common reference string generated by the setup authority.

2.1   Complexity Assumptions

For our ring signature, we assume that two problems are difficult to solve in the setting described above: computational Diffie-Hellman in G_p and the Subgroup Decision Problem.

Computational Diffie-Hellman in G_p**.** Given the tuple (η, η^a, η^b), with $\eta \xleftarrow{\text{R}} G_p$ and $a, b \xleftarrow{\text{R}} \mathbb{Z}_p$, compute and output η^{ab}. In the composite setting one is additionally given the description of the larger group G, including the factorization (p, q) of its order n.

Subgroup Decision. Given w selected at random either from G (with probability $1/2$) or from G_q (with probability $1/2$), decide whether w is in G_q. For this problem one is given the description of G, but *not* given the factorization of n.

The assumptions are formalized by measuring an adversary's success probability for computational Diffie-Hellman and an adversary's guessing advantage for the subgroup decision problem. Note that if CDH in G_p as we have formulated it is hard then so is CDH in G. The assumption that the subgroup decision problem is hard is called the Subgroup Hiding (SGH) assumption, and was introduced by Boneh, Goh, and Nissim [9].

3 Underlying Signature

The underlying signature scheme is the Waters signature [21]. This signature was adapted for composite order groups by Boyen and Waters [10]. The variant we describe differs from theirs in retaining the original Waters formulation for the public key: $g_1, g_2 \in G$ rather than $e(g_1, g_2) \in G_T$.

Suppose that messages to be signed are encoded as elements of $\{0, 1\}^k$ for some k. (For example, as the output of a k-bit collision-resistant hash function.) In addition to the system parameters of Sect. 2 above, the Waters scheme makes use of random generators $u', u_1, u_2, \ldots, u_k$ in G.

The scheme is as follows.

WC.Kg. Pick random $\alpha, \beta \xleftarrow{\text{R}} \mathbb{Z}_n$ and set $g_1 \leftarrow g^\alpha$ and $g_2 \leftarrow g^\beta$. The public key pk is $(g_1, g_2) \in G^2$. The private key sk is (α, β).

WC.Sig(sk, M)**.** Parse the user's private key sk as $(\alpha, \beta) \in \mathbb{Z}_n^*$ and the message M as a bitstring $(m_1, \ldots, m_k) \in \{0, 1\}^k$. Pick a random $r \xleftarrow{\text{R}} \mathbb{Z}_n$ and compute

$$S_1 \leftarrow g^{\alpha\beta} \cdot \left(u' \prod_{i=1}^{k} u_i^{m_i}\right)^r \qquad \text{and} \qquad S_2 \leftarrow g^r \ .$$

The signature is $\sigma = (S_1, S_2) \in G^2$.

WC.Vf(pk, M, σ)**.** Parse the user's public key pk as $(g_1, g_2) \in G^2$, the message M as a bitstring $(m_1, \ldots, m_k) \in \{0, 1\}^k$, and the signature σ as $(S_1, S_2) \in G^2$. Verify that

$$e(S_1, g) \cdot e\left(S_2^{-1}, u' \prod_{i=1}^{k} u_i^{m_i}\right) \stackrel{?}{=} e(g_1, g_2) \tag{1}$$

holds; if so, output `valid`; if not, output `invalid`.

This signature is existentially unforgeable if computational Diffie-Hellman holds on G.

The Waters Signature in G_p. One can also restrict the Waters signature to the subgroup G_p, obtaining a signature scheme to which we refer as $\mathcal{WP}$. In this case, the generator g is replaced by a generator η of G_p, and exponents are drawn from $\mathbb{Z}_p$ rather than $\mathbb{Z}_n$. In particular, the verification equation is

$$e(\hat{S}_1, \eta) \cdot e\left(\hat{S}_2^{-1}, \hat{u}' \prod_{i=1}^{k} \hat{u}_i^{m_i}\right) \stackrel{?}{=} e(\eta_1, \eta_2) \ . \tag{2}$$

This variant is secure assuming CDH is hard in G_p, and is used in our reductions.

4   Ring Signature Definitions

Informally, a ring signature scheme should satisfy two security properties. First, it should be anonymous: an adversary should not be able to determine which member of a ring generated a signature. Second, it should be unforgeable: an adversary should be able to construct a valid signature on a ring of public keys only if he knows the secret key corresponding to one of them. Formalizing this intuition is tricky. Rivest, Shamir, and Tauman [18] gave a formalization which has been used in much subsequent work. Recently, Bender, Katz, and Morselli [4] described several possible stronger formulations of each notion.

Below, we show our scheme to be anonymous against full key exposure and unforgeable with respect to insider corruption. For both anonymity and unforgeability these are the strongest formulations considered by Bender, Katz, and Morselli. We now recall these formulations; see [4] for additional details and motivation.

RS.Kg. This randomized algorithm outputs a public verification key pk and a private signing key sk.

RS.Sig(pk, sk, R, M). This algorithm takes as input a keypair (pk, sk) and a set of public keys R that constitutes the ring, along with a message M in some message space to be signed. It is required that $pk \in R$ hold. The algorithm returns a signature σ on M for the ring R.

RS.Vf(R, M, σ). The verification algorithm takes as input a set of public keys R that constitutes the ring and a purported signature σ on a message M. It returns either `valid` or `invalid`.

Anonymity. Anonymity against full key exposure for a ring signature scheme $\mathcal{RS}$ is defined using the following game between a challenger and an adversary $\mathcal{A}$:

Setup. The challenger runs algorithm Kg l times to obtain public-private keypairs $(pk_1, sk_1), \ldots, (pk_l, sk_l)$. In addition, the challenger records the random coins $\{\omega_i\}$ used in generating each keypair. Here l is a game parameter. The adversary $\mathcal{A}$ is given the public keys $\{pk_i\}$.

Signing Queries. Algorithm $\mathcal{A}$ is allowed to make ring signing queries of the form (s, R, M). Here M is the message to be signed, R is a set of public keys, and s is an index such that $pk_s \in R$ holds. (The other keys in R need not be keys in the set $\{pk_i\}$.) The challenger responds with $\sigma = \text{Sig}(pk_s, sk_s, R, M)$.

Challenge. Algorithm $\mathcal{A}$ requests a challenge by sending to the challenger the values (i_0, i_1, R, M). Here M is to be signed with respect to the ring R, and i_0 and i_1 are indices such that $pk_{i_0}, pk_{i_1} \in R$. (The other keys in R need not be keys in the set $\{pk_i\}$.) The challenger chooses a bit $b \xleftarrow{\text{R}} \{0,1\}$, computes the challenge signature $\sigma \leftarrow \text{Sig}(pk_{i_b}, sk_{i_b}, R, M)$, and provides $\mathcal{A}$ with σ. In addition, the challenger provides $\mathcal{A}$ with the coins $\{\omega_i\}$ used to generate the keys; from these, $\mathcal{A}$ can recompute $\{sk_i\}$.

Output. Algorithm $\mathcal{A}$ finally outputs its guess b' for b, and wins if $b = b'$.

We define $\mathbf{Adv}^{\text{rsig-anon-ke}}_{\mathcal{RS}, \mathcal{A}}$ to be the advantage over $1/2$ of $\mathcal{A}$ in the above game.

Unforgeability. Unforgeability with respect to insider corruption for a ring signature scheme $\mathcal{RS}$ is defined using the following game between a challenger and an adversary $\mathcal{A}$:

Setup. The challenger runs algorithm Kg l times to obtain public-private keypairs $(pk_1, sk_1), \ldots, (pk_l, sk_l)$. Here l is a game parameter. The adversary $\mathcal{A}$ is given the public keys $\{pk_i\}$. The challenger also initializes the set C of corrupted users as $C \leftarrow \emptyset$.

Queries. Algorithm $\mathcal{A}$ is allowed to make ring signing queries and corruption queries. A ring signing query is of the form (s, R, M). Here M is the message to be signed, R is a set of public keys, and s is an index such that $pk_s \in R$ holds. (The other keys in R need not be keys in the set $\{pk_i\}$.) The challenger responds with $\sigma = \text{Sig}(pk_s, sk_s, R, M)$. A corruption query is of the form s, where s is again an index. The challenger provides sk_s to $\mathcal{A}$ and adds pk_s to C.

Output. Eventually, $\mathcal{A}$ outputs a tuple (R^*, M^*, σ^*) and wins the game if (1) it never made a ring signing query (s, R^*, M^*) for any s; (2) $R^* \subseteq \{pk_i\} \setminus C$; and (3) $\text{Vf}(R^*, M^*, \sigma^*) = \texttt{valid}$.

We define $\mathbf{Adv}^{\text{rsig-uf-ic}}_{\mathcal{RS}, \mathcal{A}}$ to be the probability that $\mathcal{A}$ wins in the above game.

Trusted Setup. In our model we allow for a trusted global setup by an authority. This is a stronger setup assumption than what was used in previous results. However, this setup allows us to realize the benefits of an efficient scheme provably secure in the standard model. In practice the authority role can be split amongst several parties. For example, using techniques like those of Boneh and Franklin [7] several parties could generate a shared modulus n and group description efficiently for our scheme.

5 On Bender, Katz, and Morselli's Two-User Ring Signatures

Bender, Katz, and Morselli propose a ring signature secure without random oracles based on the Waters signature. This ring signature allows only two-signer rings, but this suffices for some applications of ring signatures, in particular designated-verifier signatures. Unlike the scheme we present, the BKM ring signature is proven unforgeable only against chosen-subring attacks. In this section, we recall the BKM ring signature and show that it is, in fact, insecure with respect to insider corruption.

We stress that Bender, Katz, and Morselli do not claim that their scheme is secure with respect to insider corruption. They prove security against chosen-subring attacks, a weaker notion, and this proof is correct. Our contribution in this section is to demonstrate a practical attack against the scheme in the more general model.

Consider a group G of prime order p, together with a bilinear map $e : G \times G \to G_T$, where G_T is also of size p. (This is unlike the composite-order setup of our paper.) Each user has a private key $\alpha \in \mathbb{Z}_p$ and a public key that includes $g_1 = g^\alpha$ and her own Waters hash generators $u', u_1, \ldots, u_k \in G$. Now, if Alice wishes to sign a message $M = (m_1, \ldots, m_k)$ in a ring that comprises her and Bob, whose public key is $(\bar{g}_1, \bar{u}', \bar{u}_1, \ldots, \bar{u}_k)$, she picks $r \xleftarrow{\text{R}} \mathbb{Z}_p$ and computes

$$S_1 \leftarrow (\bar{g}_1)^\alpha \cdot \left(u' \prod_{i=1}^k u_i^{m_i}\right)^r \cdot \left(\bar{u}' \prod_{i=1}^k \bar{u}_i^{m_i}\right)^r \qquad \text{and} \qquad S_2 \leftarrow g^r \ .$$

For any two users, the values $(g_1, \bar{g}_1)$ act like the Waters public key (g_1, g_2); the value $g^{\alpha\bar{\alpha}}$ acts as a shared signing key. Since either user is capable of computing this value, anonymity is unconditional. Unforgeability against chosen-subring attacks follows from the security of the underlying Waters signature.

This scheme has the advantage that it requires no shared setup beyond the group description. This justifies making each signer generate and publish her own Waters hash generators, since a third party trusted with generating them for all users could use its knowledge of their discrete logs to recover the shared signing key $g^{\alpha\bar{\alpha}}$ from any signature.

The unforgeability condition under which Bender, Katz, and Morselli prove their scheme secure does not allow for adversarially generated keys. We show that the scheme is in fact insecure against such attacks, which, for a two-user ring signature, have the following form: Alice and Bob publish their public keys. Then Veronica publishes her key and tricks Alice into signing a message for the Alice-Veronica ring; what she learns from this signature allows her to forge an Alice-Bob ring signature.

Suppose Alice's public key is $(g_1, u', u_1, \ldots, u_k)$ and Bob's public key is $(\bar{g}_1, \bar{u}', \bar{u}_1, \ldots, \bar{u}_k)$. In our attack, Veronica picks $s, t', t_1, \ldots, t_k \xleftarrow{\text{R}} \mathbb{Z}_p$ and sets

$$\hat{g}_1 \leftarrow \bar{g}_1 \cdot g^s \qquad \text{and} \qquad \hat{u}' \leftarrow g^{t'}/u' \qquad \text{and} \qquad \hat{u}_i \leftarrow g^{t_i}/u_i \quad 1 \le i \le k \ .$$

Now when Alice generates an Alice-Veronica ring signature on a message $M = (m_1, \ldots, m_k)$ we will have

$$S_1 = (\hat{g}_1)^\alpha \cdot \left(u'\hat{u}' \prod_{i=1}^k (u_i\hat{u}_i)^{m_i}\right)^r = (\bar{g}_1)^\alpha (g^s)^\alpha (g^t)^r$$

where $t = t' + \sum_{i=1}^k m_i t_i$, and Veronica recovers the shared Alice-Bob signing key $g^{\alpha\bar{\alpha}}$ as $S_1/(g_1^s S_2^t)$.

Note that Veronica need not know the discrete logarithms of all her Waters generators. It suffices for her to pick $\hat{u}'$ specially while letting the rest be globally specified. In this variant, Veronica picks ahead of time a message $M^* = (m_1^*, \ldots, m_k^*)$ that she thinks she can trick Alice into signing. She then chooses $s, t' \xleftarrow{R} \mathbb{Z}_p$, and computes

$$\hat{g}_1 \leftarrow \bar{g}_1 \cdot g^s \cdot \qquad \text{and} \qquad \hat{u}' \leftarrow g^{t'} / \left(u' \prod_{i=1}^{k} (u_i \hat{u}_i)^{m_i^*} \right) .$$

Now, when Alice generates an Alice-Veronica ring signature on M^*, we have $S_1 = (\bar{g}_1)^\alpha (g^s)^\alpha (g^{t'})^r$, from which Veronica can recover $g^{\alpha \bar{\alpha}}$.

The attack described above is prevented if all users share the same Waters generators $(u', u_1, \ldots, u_k)$; but even in this case Veronica can still obtain from Alice an Alice-Bob ring signature when Alice thinks she is generating an Alice-Veronica ring signature. To achieve this, Veronica chooses $s \xleftarrow{R} \mathbb{Z}_p$ and sets $\hat{g}_1 \leftarrow (\bar{g}_1)^s$. Now an Alice-Veronica ring signature on $M = (m_1, \ldots, m_k)$ will have the form

$$S_2 = g^r \qquad \text{and} \qquad S_1 = (\hat{g}_1)^\alpha \cdot \left(u' \prod_{i=1}^{k} u_i^{m_i} \right)^r = (\bar{g}_1^\alpha)^s \cdot \left(u' \prod_{i=1}^{k} u_i^{m_i} \right)^r ,$$

and therefore $(S_1^{1/s}, S_2^{1/s})$ is an Alice-Bob ring signature on M with randomness r/s.

Attack on the Camenisch-Lysyanskaya–Based Scheme. In the full version of their paper [3], Bender, Katz, and Morselli also give a two-user ring signature based on Camenisch-Lysyanskaya signatures [12]. As with their Waters-based scheme, they claim and prove security against chosen-subring attacks. Here, we show an attack on this ring signature similar to the attack above, again with respect to insider corruption. We stress once more that Bender, Katz, and Morselli do not claim security in this stronger model.

Suppose that Alice and Bob have respective secret keys x and y, and public keys $X = g^x$ and $Y = g^y$. Their ring signature on a message $m \in \mathbb{Z}_p$ is (a, a^y, a^{x+mxy}), where a is random in G. If $a = g^r$ with $r \in \mathbb{Z}_p$ then Alice computes the ring signature as $(a, Y^r, a^x Y^{mxr})$ and Bob as (a, a^y, X^{r+mry}). If Veronica plays the part of Alice, she publishes as her key $\hat{X} = X^s$ for $s \xleftarrow{R} \mathbb{Z}_p$. Bob then generates the Veronica-Bob signature $(S_1, S_2, S_3) = (a, a^y, a^{sx+msxy})$, from which Veronica can produce an Alice-Bob ring signature on m as $(S_1, S_2, S_3^{1/s})$. If Veronica plays the part of Bob, she publishes as her key $\hat{Y} = Y^s$ for $s \xleftarrow{R} \mathbb{Z}_p$. Alice then generates the Alice-Veronica signature $(S_1, S_2, S_3) = (a, a^{sy}, a^{x+mxsy})$, from which Veronica can produce an Alice-Bob ring signature on $m' = ms$ as $(S_1, S_2^{1/s}, S_3)$.

Implications for Designated-Verifier Signatures. The attack described above demonstrates a trade-off between our Waters-based ring signature and the BKM one. Our scheme requires a trusted setup, but achieves security even in the presence of adversarially generated keys. This is important for designated-verifier signatures, the main proposed application for two-user ring signatures, since there is no reason that Alice will only wish to designate as verifiers users whose keys she trusts to have been properly generated.

6   Our Ring Signature Construction

In this section, we describe our ring signature scheme. As noted in the introduction, in our ring signature all the users' keys must be defined in a group G of composite order. That group must be set up by a trusted authority, since the factorization of its order n must be kept secret. In addition to setting up the group G, the setup authority must also set up some additional parameters, using a global setup algorithm we now describe.

Global Setup. The trusted ring signing setup algorithm first constructs a group G of composite order $n = pq$ as described in Sect. 2 above. It then chooses exponents $a, b_0 \xleftarrow{\text{R}} \mathbb{Z}_n$ and sets

$$A \leftarrow g^a \qquad \text{and} \qquad B_0 \leftarrow g^{b_0} \qquad \text{and} \qquad \hat{A} \leftarrow h^a \ .$$

Let $H : \{0,1\}^* \rightarrow \{0,1\}^k$ be a collision-resistant hash function. The setup algorithm picks Waters hash generators

$$u', u_1, u_2, \ldots, u_k \xleftarrow{\text{R}} G \ .$$

The published common reference string includes a description of the group G and of the collision-resistant hash H, along with $(A, B_0, \hat{A})$ and $(u', u_1, \ldots, u_k)$. The factorization of n is not revealed. Note that anyone can use the pairing to verify that the pair $(A, \hat{A})$ is properly formed.

The Scheme. Individual users now use the public parameters published by the setup algorithm in generating their keys, signing, and verifying. The algorithms they use are as follows.

LRS.Kg. Choose a random exponent $b \xleftarrow{\text{R}} \mathbb{Z}_n$; set $pk \leftarrow g^b \in G$ and $sk \leftarrow A^b \in G$.

Recall that in the variant of the Water's signature scheme that we use a public key is a pair of group elements in G. Here, one of the two group elements for a user's key is always the global setup value A. In effect the user's public key is like the Water's public key A, g^b. However, all users share the element A.

LRS.Sig(pk, sk, R, M). The signing algorithm takes as input a message $M \in \{0,1\}^*$, a ring R of public keys, and a keypair $(pk, sk) \in G^2$. No key may appear twice in R, and R must include pk.

Compute $(m_1, \ldots, m_k) \leftarrow H(M, R)$. Let $l = |R|$; parse the elements of R as $v_i \in G$, $1 \le i \le l$. Let i^* be the index such that $v_{i^*} = pk$. Define $\{f_i\}_{i=1}^l$ as

$$f_i = \begin{cases} 1 & \text{if } i = i^*, \\ 0 & \text{otherwise.} \end{cases}$$

Now for each i, $1 \leq i \leq l$, choose a random exponent $t_i \xleftarrow{\text{R}} \mathbb{Z}_n$ and set

$$C_i \leftarrow (v_i/B_0)^{f_i} h^{t_i} \quad \text{and} \quad \pi_i \leftarrow \left((v_i/B_0)^{2f_i-1} h^{t_i}\right)^{t_i} .$$

As in the papers of Groth, Ostrovsky, and Sahai [16] and Boyen and Waters [10], the value π_i acts as a proof that C_i is well-formed – here, specifically, that $f_i \in \{0, 1\}$. Let $C \leftarrow \prod_{i=1}^{l} C_i$ and $t \leftarrow \sum_{i=1}^{l} t_i$. Observe that, when there is exactly one non-zero value amongst $\{f_i\}$, viz., f_{i*}, we have $B_0 C = (v_{i*})(h^t)$, so C serves as an encryption of the user's public key. (The role of B_0 is discussed below.) Finally, choose $r \xleftarrow{\text{R}} \mathbb{Z}_n$ and compute

$$S_1 \leftarrow \text{sk} \cdot \left(u' \prod_{j=1}^{k} u_j^{m_j}\right)^r \cdot \hat{A}^t \quad \text{and} \quad S_2 \leftarrow g^r$$

The signature is output as $\sigma = \left((S_1, S_2), \{(C_i, \pi_i)\}_{i=1}^{l}\right) \in G^{2l+2}$.

LRS.Vf(R, M, σ). Compute $(m_1, \ldots, m_k) \leftarrow H(M, R)$. Let $l = |R|$; parse the elements of R as $v_i \in G$, $1 \leq i \leq l$. Verify that no element is repeated in R and reject otherwise. Parse the signature σ as $\left((S_1, S_2), \{(C_i, \pi_i)\}_{i=1}^{l}\right) \in G^{2l+2}$. (If this parse fails, reject.) Check first that the proofs $\{\pi_i\}$ are valid: for each i, $1 \leq i \leq l$, that

$$e\left(C_i, \, C_i/(v_i/B_0)\right) \stackrel{?}{=} e(h, \pi_i) \tag{3}$$

holds. If any of the proofs is invalid, reject. Otherwise, set $C \leftarrow \prod_{i=1}^{l} C_i$. Accept if the following equation is satisfied:

$$e(A, B_0 C) \stackrel{?}{=} e(S_1, g) \cdot e\left(S_2^{-1}, u' \prod_{j=1}^{k} u_j^{m_j}\right) . \tag{4}$$

Discussion. As outlined in the introduction, in our ring signature scheme we wish to prove that the value C which is computed by multiplying all C_i values together contains an encryption of exactly one key from the ring. This can be done by both using GOS proofs to show that each C_i is either an encryption of the proper public key or the identity element and that exactly one of these is not the identity element. (If every C_i were an encryption of the identity element everywhere, the public key encrypted in C would be the identity element and trivial for the adversary to forge under.)

Instead of directly proving this, which would require larger – though still $O(l)$-sized[3] – proofs, we have the user prove that each C_i is an encryption of the identity element or the i-th public key in the ring times some group element B_0 given by the setup algorithm. Thus, C will be an encryption of a public key times B_0. Now a signer will instead prove that the signature verifies under the encrypted key divided by B_0, which is the signers original public key.. In this way if a forger attempts to forge by letting all C_i be encryptions of the identity element, he will need to forge under the public key B_0.

---

[3] A possible circuit is as follows. Let $\{f_i\}$ be the indicator variables. Let $c_0^1 = c_0^2 = 0$, and for $i \geq 1$ compute c_i^1 and c_i^2 as $c_i^1 \leftarrow c_{i-1}^1 \vee f_i$ and $c_i^2 \leftarrow c_{i-1}^2 \vee (f_i \wedge c_{i-1}^1)$. Finally, prove that $c_l^1 = 1$ and $c_l^2 = 0$.

7 Security

We now prove that our ring signature scheme is anonymous against full key exposure and unforgeable with respect to insider corruption.

7.1 Anonymity

The anonymity proof closely follows that given by Boyen and Waters for their group signature [10].

Theorem 1. *Our ring signature scheme is anonymous against full key exposure if SGH is hard.*

Proof. The proof proceeds in games. We define Games 0 and 1 as follows. In Game 0, h is chosen uniformly from G_q; in Game 1, h is chosen uniformly from G.

Games 0 and 1. Algorithm $\mathcal{B}$ is given: the group order n (but not its factorization); the description of the group G, together with generators g of G and h; in Game 0, h is chosen from G_q; in Game 1, h is chosen from all of G. Algorithm $\mathcal{B}$ chooses a collision resistant hash function $H : \{0,1\}^* \to \{0,1\}^k$. It follows the setup algorithm above to obtain system parameters $(A, B_0, \hat{A})$ and $(u', u_1, \ldots, u_k)$. Algorithm $\mathcal{B}$ then runs Kg l times to obtain public-private key-pairs $\{(pk_i, sk_i)\}_{i=1}^l$, recording in addition the randomnesses $\{b_i\}$ used in each run.

Algorithm $\mathcal{B}$ runs $\mathcal{A}$, providing to it the following: the description of the group G, including its order n and the generators g and h; the common parameters $(A, B_0, \hat{A})$ and $(u', u_1, \ldots, u_k)$, along with the description of the hash function H; and the challenge public keys $\{pk_i\}_{i=1}^l$. When $\mathcal{A}$ makes a signing query of the form (s, R, M), $\mathcal{A}$ responds with $\sigma = \mathsf{Sig}(pk_s, sk_s, R, M)$. Finally, $\mathcal{A}$ requests a challenge with the values (i_0, i_1, R, M). Algorithm $\mathcal{B}$ chooses a bit $b \xleftarrow{\text{R}} \{0,1\}$, computes the challenge signature $\sigma \leftarrow \mathsf{Sig}(pk_{i_b}, sk_{i_b}, R, M)$, and provides $\mathcal{A}$ with σ. In addition, the challenger provides $\mathcal{A}$ with the random coins $\{b_i\}$ used to generate the private keys. Algorithm $\mathcal{A}$ finally outputs its guess b' for b; $\mathcal{B}$ outputs 1 if $b = b'$, 0 otherwise.

Discussion. Denote by $\mathbf{Adv}_{\mathcal{B}}^{\text{game-0}}$ the advantage $\mathcal{B}$ has over $1/2$ in Game 0, and by $\mathbf{Adv}_{\mathcal{B}}^{\text{game-1}}$ the advantage over $1/2$ it has in Game 1. Clearly, we have

$$\mathbf{Adv}_{\mathcal{B}}^{\text{game-0}} = \mathbf{Adv}_{\mathcal{LRS}, \mathcal{A}}^{\text{rsig-anon-ke}} \ , \tag{5}$$

since in Game 0 $\mathcal{A}$'s environment is exactly as specified in the anonymity game. Moreover, suppose that $\mathcal{B}$'s output were different in the two games. Then we could use $\mathcal{B}$, with $\mathcal{A}$ as a subroutine, to solve SGH: given generators (g, h) to test, we provide them to $\mathcal{B}$ and output 1 if $\mathcal{B}$ does. This gives a new algorithm $\mathcal{C}$ for which we have

$$\mathbf{Adv}_{\mathcal{C}}^{\mathrm{sgh}} = \left| \Pr\!\left[\mathcal{B} = 1 \mid h \xleftarrow{\mathrm{R}} G_p\right] - \Pr\!\left[\mathcal{B} = 1 \mid h \xleftarrow{\mathrm{R}} G\right] \right|$$

$$= \frac{1}{2}\left|\left(2\Pr\!\left[\mathcal{B} = 1 \mid h \xleftarrow{\mathrm{R}} G_p\right] - 1\right) - \left(2\Pr\!\left[\mathcal{B} = 1 \mid h \xleftarrow{\mathrm{R}} G\right] - 1\right)\right|$$

$$= \frac{1}{2}\left|\mathbf{Adv}_{\mathcal{B}}^{\mathrm{game\text{-}0}} - \mathbf{Adv}_{\mathcal{B}}^{\mathrm{game\text{-}1}}\right| . \tag{6}$$

But now, we argue that $\mathbf{Adv}_{\mathcal{B}}^{\mathrm{game\text{-}1}} = 0$, even if $\mathcal{A}$ is computationally unbounded. Consider the distinguishing challenge $\left((S_1, S_2), \{(C_i, \pi_i)\}_{i=1}^{l'}\right) \in G^{2l'+2}$. For each i, we have $C_i = (v_i/B_0)^{f_i} h^{t_i}$ with $f_i \in \{0, 1\}$ and $t_i \in \mathbb{Z}_n$. But when h is a generator of G there exist $\tau_{i0}, \tau_{i1} \in \mathbb{Z}_n$ such that $C_i = (v_i/B_0)h^{\tau_{i1}} = h^{\tau_{i0}}$ and, moreover, denoting by $(\pi_i \mid f_i = b)$ the value which π_i is assigned if f_i is set to $b \in \{0, 1\}$, we have

$$(\pi_i \mid f_i = 1) = ((v_i/B_0)^1 h^{\tau_{i1}})^{\tau_{i1}} = (h^{\tau_{i0}})^{\tau_{i1}} = (h^{\tau_{i1}})^{\tau_{i0}}$$
$$= ((v_i/B_0)^{-1} h^{\tau_{i0}})^{\tau_{i0}} = (\pi_i \mid f_i = 0) ,$$

so for each i the pair (C_i, π_i) is consistent with either $f_i = 0$ or $f_i = 1$, and $\mathcal{A}$ can gain no information from this part of the signature. The value $S_2 = g^r$ is unrelated to the choice of signer. Thus if $\mathcal{A}$ can gain information, it is only from S_1. But, having fixed S_2 and $\{(C_i, \pi_i)\}$, S_1 is the unique value satisfying (4). Specifically, letting $A = g^a$, $S_2 = g^r$, and $C/B_0 = g^c$ (all of which a computationally unbounded adversary can calculate), we have $S_1 = g^{ac} \cdot \left(u' \prod_{j=1}^{k} u_j^{m_j}\right)^r$. Thus this value gives no information about whether sk_{i_0} or sk_{i_1} was used to generate the challenge signature, and $\mathcal{A}$ can do no better than guess b. This establishes

$$\mathbf{Adv}_{\mathcal{B}}^{\mathrm{game\text{-}1}} = 0 \tag{7}$$

Putting equations (5), (6), and (7) together, we see that

$$\mathbf{Adv}_{\mathcal{LRS}, \mathcal{A}}^{\mathrm{rsig\text{-}anon\text{-}ke}} \leq 2\mathbf{Adv}_{\mathcal{C}}^{\mathrm{sgh}} .$$

To interpret this result concretely, we note that the algorithm $\mathcal{B}$ used in the reduction took $O(1)$ operations to set up and obtain the result, and $O(1)$ time to answer each of $\mathcal{A}$'s queries. To interpret it asymptotically, we introduce the security parameter that we have suppressed, note that the reduction is polynomial-time in that parameter, and observe that if $\mathbf{Adv}_{\mathcal{LRS}, \mathcal{A}}^{\mathrm{rsig\text{-}anon\text{-}ke}}$ is non-negligible, then so is $\mathbf{Adv}_{\mathcal{C}}^{\mathrm{sgh}}$. Either interpretation implies the result stated informally in the theorem.

7.2   Unforgeability

We show that our ring signature scheme is unforgeable. We present a proof sketch here, with the proof relegated to the full version of the paper [20].

Theorem 2. *Our ring signature scheme is unforgeable with respect to insider corruption if H is collision resistant and CDH is hard in G_p.*

Proof (sketch). The algorithm that makes the reduction is given the factorization of n. Using this and standard Chinese Remaindering techniques, it can decompose an element of G into its G_p and G_q constituents. This allows it to undo BGN blinding with h^t terms, and to recover from a signature the values f_i used in generating it. Each of these must be in the set $\{0, 1\}$ by the perfect soundness of GOS proofs.

First, we ensure that any forgery (M^*, R^*) is such that $H(M^*, R^*)$ is not equal to $H(M, R)$ for any previous signing query (M, R) made by the adversary. This is easy: an adversary for which this is not true would break the collision resistance of H.

Having disposed of this possibility, we distinguish between two types of adversaries. Consider the values $\{f_i\}$ that we recover from the forgery. For the first type of adversary, the number of i's such that $f_i = 0$ is either 0 or more than 1. For the second type, exactly one f_i equals 1.

For the first type of adversary, we note that each C_i such that $f_i = 1$ contributes a (v_i/B_0) term to the encrypted Waters key $C = \prod C_i$. Thus the Waters key under which the encrypted signature (S_1, S_2) is verified, $B_0 C$, will include a B_0^{1-f} term, where $f = \sum f_i \neq 1$ for this type of adversary. Thus if we embed a CDH challenge in A and B_0, but construct the Waters hash generators $(u', u_1, \ldots, u_k)$ and user keys $\{v_i\}$ so that we know their discrete logarithms, we will obtain from the forgery values (S_1, S_2) such that $e(A, B_0^{1-f} \cdot \eta^r) = e(S_1, \eta) \cdot e(S_2^{-1}, \eta^x)$, where r and x are numbers we compute. From this we easily obtain the CDH solution. (Because we must project into G_p to recover the f_i's, we obtain a CDH solution in G_p rather than G, which is why the generator η of G_p has replaced g in the verification equation above.)

For the second type of adversary, we obtain a Waters signature forgery. Given the challenge Waters public key (η_1, η_2), which again is in G_p, and the Waters hash generators $(\hat{u}', \hat{u}_1, \ldots, \hat{u}_k)$, we place η_1 in A, adding a random G_q component so that A spans G, and pick B_0 arbitrarily. We similarly extend the challenge waters hash generators to G. We pick all the user keys arbitrarily except one, which we instantiate using η_2, properly extended to G. Now we can handle corruption queries for every user except the special one. Signing queries we can answer directly for the normal users, and can answer for the special user using our Waters signing oracle. This oracle returns a signature $(\hat{S}_1, \hat{S}_2) \in G_p^2$; extending this to a properly-blinded signature in G takes a bit of work, but isn't terribly difficult. The index of the special user is kept hidden from the adversary, so with probability $1/l$ he doesn't make a corruption query for that user but then does make his forgery for that user. (Recall that this type of adversary always has exactly one user for which $f_i = 1$.) We convert the adversary's forgery to a Waters signature forgery in G_p. Because $H(M^*, R^*)$ is different for this forgery than for previous signing queries, the forgery is nontrivial.

Thus we obtain from a ring signature forging adversary a break of either the collision resistance of H or the CDH hardness of G_p or (with a $1/l$ loss of advantage) to the unforgeability of the Waters signature in G_p. However, the

Waters signature in G_p is unforgeable if CDH is hard in G_p, and the theorem statement follows.

8 Conclusions and Open Problems

We presented the first efficient ring signatures that are provably secure without random oracles under standard assumptions. Signatures in our scheme are of size $2l + 2$ group elements for l members in a ring. We showed our signatures to be secure for the strongest definitions of security. Two interesting open problems remain: to obtain a ring signature secure without random oracles where (1) user keys need not be generated in a particular shared group; or (2) signature length is independent of the number of signers implicated in the ring.

References

[1] M. Abe, M. Ohkubo, and K. Suzuki. 1-out-of-n signatures from a variety of keys. In Y. Zheng, editor, *Proceedings of Asiacrypt 2002*, volume 2501 of *LNCS*, pages 415–32. Springer-Verlag, Dec. 2002.

[2] M. Bellare and P. Rogaway. Random oracles are practical: A paradigm for designing efficient protocols. In D. Denning, R. Pyle, R. Ganesan, R. Sandhu, and V. Ashby, editors, *Proceedings of CCS 1993*, pages 62–73. ACM Press, Nov. 1993.

[3] A. Bender, J. Katz, and R. Morselli. Ring signatures: Stronger definitions, and constructions without random oracles. Cryptology ePrint Archive, Report 2005/304, 2005. http://eprint.iacr.org/.

[4] A. Bender, J. Katz, and R. Morselli. Ring signatures: Stronger definitions, and constructions without random oracles. In S. Halevi and T. Rabin, editors, *Proceedings of TCC 2006*, volume 3876 of *LNCS*, pages 60–79. Springer-Verlag, Mar. 2006.

[5] D. Boneh and X. Boyen. Efficient selective-ID secure identity based encryption without random oracles. In C. Cachin and J. Camenisch, editors, *Proceedings of Eurocrypt 2004*, volume 3027 of *LNCS*, pages 223–38. Springer-Verlag, May 2004.

[6] D. Boneh and X. Boyen. Secure identity based encryption without random oracles. In M. Franklin, editor, *Proceedings of Crypto 2004*, volume 3152 of *LNCS*, pages 443–59. Springer-Verlag, Aug. 2004.

[7] D. Boneh and M. Franklin. Efficient generation of shared RSA keys. *J. ACM*, 48(4):702–22, July 2001.

[8] D. Boneh, C. Gentry, B. Lynn, and H. Shacham. Aggregate and verifiably encrypted signatures from bilinear maps. In E. Biham, editor, *Proceedings of Eurocrypt 2003*, volume 2656 of *LNCS*, pages 416–32. Springer-Verlag, May 2003.

[9] D. Boneh, E.-J. Goh, and K. Nissim. Evaluating 2-DNF formulas on ciphertexts. In J. Kilian, editor, *Proceedings of TCC 2005*, number 3378 in LNCS, pages 325–41. Springer-Verlag, Feb. 2005.

[10] X. Boyen and B. Waters. Compact group signatures without random oracles. In S. Vaudenay, editor, *Proceedings of Eurocrypt 2006*, volume 4004 of *LNCS*, pages 427–44. Springer-Verlag, May 2006.

[11] E. Bresson, J. Stern, and M. Szydlo. Threshold ring signatures and applications to ad-hoc groups. In M. Yung, editor, *Proceedings of Crypto 2002*, volume 2442 of *LNCS*, pages 465–80. Springer-Verlag, Aug. 2002.

[12] J. Camenisch and A. Lysyanskaya. Signature schemes and anonymous credentials from bilinear maps. In M. Franklin, editor, *Proceedings of Crypto 2004*, volume 3152 of *LNCS*, pages 56–72. Springer-Verlag, Aug. 2004.

[13] D. Chaum and E. van Heyst. Group signatures. In D. W. Davies, editor, *Proceedings of Eurocrypt 1991*, volume 547 of *LNCS*, pages 257–65. Springer-Verlag, Apr. 1991.

[14] S. Chow, J. Liu, V. Wei, and T. H. Yuen. Ring signatures without random oracles. In S. Shieh and S. Jajodia, editors, *Proceedings of ASIACCS 2006*, pages 297–302. ACM Press, Mar. 2006.

[15] Y. Dodis, A. Kiayias, A. Nicolosi, and V. Shoup. Anonymous identification in ad hoc groups. In C. Cachin and J. Camenisch, editors, *Proceedings of Eurocrypt 2004*, volume 3027 of *LNCS*, pages 609–26. Springer-Verlag, May 2004.

[16] J. Groth, R. Ostrovsky, and A. Sahai. Perfect non-interactive zero knowledge for NP. In S. Vaudenay, editor, *Proceedings of Eurocrypt 2006*, volume 4004 of *LNCS*, pages 339–58. Springer-Verlag, May 2006.

[17] J. Herranz and G. Sáez. Forking lemmas for ring signature schemes. In T. Johansson and S. Maitra, editors, *Proceedings of Indocrypt 2003*, volume 2904 of *LNCS*, pages 266–79. Springer-Verlag, Dec. 2003.

[18] R. Rivest, A. Shamir, and Y. Tauman. How to leak a secret. In C. Boyd, editor, *Proceedings of Asiacrypt 2001*, volume 2248 of *LNCS*, pages 552–65. Springer-Verlag, Dec. 2001.

[19] R. Rivest, A. Shamir, and Y. Tauman. How to leak a secret: Theory and applications of ring signatures. In O. Goldreich, A. Rosenberg, and A. Selman, editors, *Essays in Theoretical Computer Science: in Memory of Shimon Even*, volume 3895 of *LNCS Festschrift*, pages 164–86. Springer-Verlag, 2006.

[20] H. Shacham and B. Waters. Efficient ring signatures without random oracles. Cryptology ePrint Archive, Report 2006/289, 2006. http://eprint.iacr.org/.

[21] B. Waters. Efficient identity-based encryption without random oracles. In R. Cramer, editor, *Proceedings of Eurocrypt 2005*, volume 3494 of *LNCS*, pages 114–27. Springer-Verlag, May 2005.

[22] J. Xu, Z. Zhang, and D. Feng. A ring signature scheme using bilinear pairings. In C. H. Lim and M. Yung, editors, *Proceedings of WISA 2004*, volume 3325 of *LNCS*, pages 160–9. Springer-Verlag, Aug. 2004.

Traceable Ring Signature

Eiichiro Fujisaki and Koutarou Suzuki

NTT Information Sharing Platform Laboratories, NTT Corporation,
1-1 Hikari-no-oka, Yokosuka, Kanagawa, 239-0847 Japan
{fujisaki.eiichiro,suzuki.koutarou}@lab.ntt.co.jp

Abstract. The ring signature allows a signer to leak secrets anonymously, without the risk of identity escrow. At the same time, the ring signature provides great flexibility: No group manager, no special setup, and the dynamics of group choice. The ring signature is, however, vulnerable to malicious or irresponsible signers in some applications, because of its anonymity. In this paper, we propose a traceable ring signature scheme. A traceable ring scheme is a ring signature except that it can restrict "excessive" anonymity. The traceable ring signature has a *tag* that consists of a list of ring members and an *issue* that refers to, for instance, a social affair or an election. A ring member can make any signed but anonymous opinion regarding the issue, but only once (per tag). If the member submits another signed opinion, possibly pretending to be another person who supports the first opinion, the identity of the member is immediately revealed. If the member submits the same opinion, for instance, voting "yes" regarding the same issue twice, everyone can see that these two are linked. The traceable ring signature can suit to many applications, such as an anonymous voting on a BBS. We formalize the security definitions for this primitive and show an efficient and simple construction in the random oracle model.

1 Introduction

A ring signature scheme allows a signer to sign a message while preserving anonymity behind a group, called a "ring," which is selected by the signer. A verifier can check the validity of the signature, but cannot know who generated it among all possible ring members. In addition, two signatures generated by the same singer are unlinkable. Namely, it is infeasible for the verifier to determine whether the signatures are generated by the same signer. This notion was first formally introduced by Rivest, Shamir, and Tauman [24], and since then, this topic has been studied extensively in [19,6,1,17,16,4], for instance. The ring signature is related to the notion of group signature, due to [10]. In the group signature, however, there is a group manager that has the power to revoke the anonymity of any signer if necessary. The group manager must also establish a special type of key assignment to create a group, and hence it is difficult to change the group dynamically. Some people say that the group manager is too strong because he can even revoke the anonymity of a honest signer. On the other hand, a ring signature scheme has no group manager, no special setup,

T. Okamoto and X. Wang (Eds.): PKC 2007, LNCS 4450, pp. 181–200, 2007.

and allows ad-hoc group formation. In addition, a ring signature scheme is free from the risk of identity escrow.

Anonymity is not always good, however. While the group signature has too strong a traceability characteristic, an ordinary ring signature scheme has nothing at all to restrict anonymity. In this paper, we consider a ring signature scheme with a "gentle" anonymity restriction, which only prohibits "excessive" anonymity in some applications. Informally, we consider "one-more unforgeability" and "double-spending traceability" in the context of a ring signature.

Initially, these two notions appeared in the context of a blind signature scheme and a restricted blind signature scheme, as in [7] and [9], respectively. In the blind signature scheme, a user interacts with a signer a number of times and has the signer sign a blind message (In this stage, the signer may know the identity of the user, but not know the contents of the message). After the user transformed it to a "blind" signature, it cannot be traced to the user even by the signer. However, the user who obtained the blind signature from the signer cannot generate a "one-more" new signature. This property is called one-more unforgeability. The restricted blind signature has an additional property called double-spending, so that if a user "spends" a signature twice, he can be traced later [9,22,5]. Such a property can be used in the "off-line" anonymous e-cash systems. Note that the identity of a honest user is not threatened, even by the signer.

We incorporate these properties into the ring signature by introducing formal security requirements.

1.1   Our Contribution: Formalization and Construction

In this paper, we introduce the concept of a traceable ring signature. It preserves the flexibility of the ring signature: No group manager, no special setup for sharing secrets among members in a group, and the dynamics of group choice. It implies that the identity of a signer is never escrowed by a special person or group. A traceable ring signature has a *tag* $L = (issue, pk_N)$, where pk_N is the set of public keys of the ring members and *issue* refers to, fo r instance, an id of an election or some social issue. A ring member can sign a message using his own secret key and the verifier can verify the signature on the message with respect to tag L, but cannot know who generated the signature among all the possible ring members in L. If the signer signed the same message again with the same tag, everyone can see that the two signatures are linked, whereas if he signed a different message with the same tag, then not only is it evident that they are linked, but the anonymity of the signer is revoked. Informally, the security requirements we provide for this primitive are as follows:

- **Public Traceability** - Anyone who creates two signatures for different messages with respect to the same tag can be traced, where the trace can be done only with pairs of message/signature pairs and the tag.
- **Tag-Linkability (One-more unforgeability)** - Every two signatures generated by the same signer with respect to the same tag are linked, that is, the total number of signatures with respect to the same tag cannot exceed the total number of ring members in the tag, if every any two signatures are not linked.

- **Anonymity** - As long as a signer does not sign on two different messages with respect to the same tag, the identity of the signer is indistinguishable from any of the possible ring members. In addition, any two signatures generated with respect to two distinct tags are always unlinkable. Namely, it is infeasible for anyone to determine whether they are generated by the same signer.
- **Exculpability** - A honest ring member cannot be accused of signing twice with respect the same tag — Namely, an adversary cannot produce a traceable ring signature such that, along with one generated by the target, it can designate the target member in the presence of the publicly traceable mechanism. This should be infeasible even after the attacker has corrupted all ring members but the target.

The above security goals must be preserved under the so-called *adversarially-chosen key and sub-ring attack*, which Bender, Katz, and Morselli have formally addressed in [4]. In addition, our security model follows [4] in the sense that the role of PKI is minimal, namely it only maintains the global public-key list properly, which implies that malicious PKI can't harm a honest signer.

On one hand, our security goals are related to those of the group signature [3]. We stress that the standard unforgeability requirement (as in an ordinary ring signature) is unnecessary for the traceable ring signature because the combined requirements for tag-linkability and exculpability imply unforgeability. We discuss this issue later.

We show how to construct an efficient and conceptually-simple traceable ring signature scheme on an ordinary Abelian group, on which the DDH and discrete logarithm problems are hard, by using the Fiat-Shamir transformation.

1.2   Applications

There are several applications for the traceable ring signature.

An anonymous voting on a BBS - Suppose that some group of people is discussing some issue on a bulletin board via the Internet and wish to vote anonymously among themselves on that issue. They could write to the bulletin board anonymously; however, they do not want to engage a trusted party or establish a heavy setup protocol just for this vote. In addition, it is expected that some people in the group won't vote. An ordinary ring signature cannot be used here because it cannot restrict a member to only one vote. A traceable ring signature however can be applied to this case [1].

---

[1] We are aware of the fact that public traceability makes any anonymous signature primitive lose the deniability property as discussed in Sec. 2.3. However, it is sometimes more problematic to establish a trusted authority in some realistic situation. In case of pursuiting deniability, we can incorporate the technique of a receipt-free voting scheme [21] into a traceable ring signature scheme. In that case, a trusted party is necessary but only for the receipt-freeness. The other security properties of the traceable ring signature mentioned above hold true even against a dishonest trusted party.

An unclonable group identification "without the group manager" - Recently, Damgård, Dupont, and Pedersen proposed the notion of the unclonable group identification [12]. The traceable ring signature can be applied to this application. The original unclonable group identification requires a group manager, but the traceable ring signature does not.

A traceable ring signature scheme is "functionally" related to a restricted blind signature. Hence, it can be applied to a very primitive "off-line" anonymous e-cash system.

Another possible application is, for instance, k-times anonymous authentication [25]. Any traceable ring signature scheme can be efficiently transformed into a traceable ring signature scheme with k-times anonymity defined as in [25], but see also Sec. 6.2.

1.3   Related Works

Linkable ring signatures [17,27,18,26,2] are closely related to the traceable ring signature. A linkable ring signature scheme is a ring signature scheme with the property that two signatures generated by the same signer with respect to the same ring can be linked, although it doesn't need satisfy the anonymity revocation property. The earlier papers about linkable ring signatures [17,18] didn't consider a realistic threat that a dishonest signer makes a honest signer accused of "double-spending" (The schemes in [17,18] are vulnerable to the attack. See Sec. 3, where our first-step protocol is substantially the same as the schemes in [17,18]). The recent papers [27,2] take care of this problem, which makes the security conditions more complicated. Our security definitions of the traceable ring signature works also on the linkable ring signature, if the tracing algorithm is appropriately modified, which implies that the unforgeability requirement is unnecessary also for a linkable ring signature scheme[2]. Recently, Tsang and Wei proposed a short linkable ring signature [26], based on a short group identification from [13], which allows for a shorter length of communication than our proposed scheme as the number of the ring members grows huge. Their scheme is, however, not a ring signature in our sense, because a trusted party must set up the parameter of an accumulator and the scheme is vulnerable to a dishonest trusted party[3]. In addition, it doesn't seem to provide public traceability. To our knowledge, only the proposal in [27] seems to be able to incorporate into itself the anonymity revocation property, but our scheme is simpler and more efficient than that scheme.

The restricted blind signature [9,22,5,20], including its variant [25], is functionally related to the traceable ring signature. In the restricted blind signature, however, the user must interact with the signer (corresponding to the group manager) to obtain a blind signature, which corresponds to a special setup with the group manager. This setup may seem somehow similar to the registration

---

[2] In [2], this implication has been suggested.

[3] The accumulater used in [26] is based on factoring where an RSA modulus n is a system parameter, while the factoring should be kept secret.

to PKI. In particular, the k-times anonymous authentication [25] is closer, because it allows a user to use the "blind signature" permanently (similar to a public-key), once he obtained it from the signer. However, the (restricted) blind signature, including the k-times anonymous authentication, cannot allow ad-hoc group formation. After the signer issues the blind signatures to the user, an arbitrary subgroup including the user cannot be selected as a ring and the services cannot be exclusively restricted to the subgroup.

Recently, Damgård, Dupont, and Pedersen proposed unclonable group identification [12]. It is functionally very close to the k-times anonymous authentication in the sense that after a user obtains a "coin" from the group manager, he can utilize it permanently. However, it does not allow for ad-hoc group formation, either.

A traceable signature scheme [15] is a group signature scheme with traceability (in particular, from a signature to a user), but it requires a group manager.

2   Traceable Ring Signature: Definitions

2.1   Notations and Syntax

For probabilistic algorithm A, we write $y \leftarrow A(x_1, \ldots, x_n)$ to denote the experiment of running A for given $(x_1, \ldots, x_n)$, selecting r uniformly from an appropriate domain, and assigning the result of this experiment to the variable y, i.e., $y := A(x_1, \ldots, x_n; r)$. For probability spaces, $X_1, \ldots, X_k$, and k-ary predicate ϕ, we write $\Pr[x_1 \leftarrow X_1; x_2 \leftarrow X_2; \cdots : \phi(x_1, \ldots, x_k)]$ to denote the probability that the predicate $\phi(x_1, \ldots, x_k)$ is true after the experiments, "$x_1 \leftarrow X_1; x_2 \leftarrow X_2; \cdots$", are executed in that order. Let $\epsilon, \tau : \mathbb{N} \to [0, 1](\subset \mathbb{R})$ be positive $[0, 1]$-valued functions. We say that $\epsilon(k)$ is negligible in k if, for any constant $c > 0$, there exists a constant, $k_0 \in \mathbb{N}$, such that $\epsilon(k) < (1/k)^c$ for any $k > k_0$. We say that $\tau(k)$ is overwhelming in k if $\epsilon(k) \triangleq 1 - \tau(k)$ is negligible in k. For ordered finite set S, we denote by a_S vector $(a_i)_{i \in S}$. For $n \in \mathbb{N}$, we often write N to denote an ordered set $(1, \ldots, n)$.

We refer to an ordered public key set $pk_N = (pk_1, \ldots, pk_n)$ as a ring. We define a traceable ring signature scheme as indicated below.

Syntax. A traceable ring signature scheme is a tuple of algorithms, $\Sigma = (\mathbf{Gen}, \mathbf{Sig}, \mathbf{Ver}, \mathbf{Trace})$, such that, for $k \in \mathbb{N}$, the following is true.

- **Gen:** A probabilistic polynomial-time (in k) algorithm that takes security parameter $k \in \mathbb{N}$ and outputs a public/secret-key pair (pk, sk).
- **Sig:** A probabilistic polynomial-time (in k) algorithm that takes a secret key, sk_i, where $i \in N$, tag $L = (issue, pk_N)$, and message $m \in \{0, 1\}^*$, and that outputs signature σ.
- **Ver:** A deterministic polynomial-time (in k) algorithm that takes tag $L = (issue, pk_N)$, message $m \in \{0, 1\}^*$, and signature σ, and outputs a bit.

- **Trace:** A deterministic polynomial-time (in k) algorithm that takes tag $L = (issue, pk_N)$, and two message/signature pairs, $\{(m, \sigma), (m', \sigma')\}$, and outputs one of the following strings: "indep," "linked," or pk, where $pk \in pk_N$.

For simplicity, we often write $(pk_N, sk_N) \leftarrow \mathbf{Gen}(1^k)$ to denote the experiment of $(pk_i, sk_i) \leftarrow \mathbf{Gen}(1^k)$ for $i \in N$ and assigning $(pk_N, sk_N) := (pk_i, sk_i)_{i \in N}$.

As an ordinary signature scheme, a traceable ring signature scheme must satisfy the following correctness conditions: For every $k \in \mathbb{N}$, every $n \in \mathbb{N}$, every $i \in N := \{1, \ldots, n\}$, every $issue \in \{0,1\}^*$, and every $m \in \{0,1\}^*$, if $(pk_N, sk_N) \leftarrow \mathbf{Gen}(1^k)$, and $\sigma \leftarrow \mathbf{Sig}_{sk_i}(L, m)$, where $L = (issue, pk_N)$, it holds with an overwhelming probability (in k) that $\mathbf{Ver}(L, m, \sigma) = 1$.

Public Traceability - A traceable ring signature scheme requires that the following condition must hold: For every $k \in \mathbb{N}$, every $n \in \mathbb{N}$, every $i, i' \in N := \{1, \ldots, n\}$, every $issue \in \{0,1\}^*$, and every $m, m' \in \{0,1\}^*$, if $(pk_N, sk_N) \leftarrow \mathbf{Gen}(1^k)$, $\sigma \leftarrow \mathbf{Sig}_{sk_i}(L, m)$, where $L = (issue, pk_N)$, and $\sigma' \leftarrow \mathbf{Sig}_{sk_{i'}}(L, m')$, it holds with an overwhelming probability (in k) that

$$\mathbf{Trace}(L, m, \sigma, m', \sigma') = \begin{cases} \text{``indep''} & \text{if } i \neq i', \\ \text{``linked''} & \text{else if } m = m', \\ pk_i & \text{otherwise .} \end{cases}$$

In addition, if $m \neq m'$, **Trace** never output "linked." Public traceability is a correctness condition, that is, it does not assure that the opposite holds. However, if a traceable signature scheme has tag-linkability (along with public traceability), $\mathbf{Trace}(L, m, \sigma, m', \sigma') =$ "indep" implies that these two signatures are generated by different signers. If it has exculpability, $\mathbf{Trace}(L, m, \sigma, m', \sigma') = pk_i$ implies that they are signed by the same signer i. Note that $\mathbf{Trace}(L, m, \sigma, m, \sigma') =$ "linked" doesn't mean that they are always generated by the same signer (because anyone can make a "dead" copy of any signature).

2.2   Security Definitions

In this section, we describe the formal security definitions for the traceable ring signature. We give three requirements: *tag-linkability*, *anonymity*, and *exculpability*. As mentioned earlier, the "standard unforgeability" requirement is unnecessary for the traceable ring signature. We discuss this issue later in Sec. 2.3.

The tag-linkability is significantly different from the other two requirements in the sense that it is to defend the system, not the users. Hence, we assume all users (signers) are potential cheaters, which leads to the model that a central adversary generates all the public/secret keys for the users. On the other hand, anonymity and exculpability are to protect user(s) from the rest of players, including the system provider and the adversarial users. In these settings, an adversary is given the target public key(s) and allowed to append a polynomial number (in total) of new public keys to the global public-key list in any timing. Possibly, these public-keys can be related to the given target key(s). We assume that the global public-key list is maintained properly: A public-key should be referred to only one user and vice versa. The adversary is basically allowed to choose an arbitrary subring in the global public-key list, when it accesses the signing oracle(s) with respect to the target user(s). We call such an attack *the adversarially-chosen-key-and-sub-ring attack*, which Bender, Katz, and Morselli have formally addressed in [4]. In our security model, as in [4], the role of PKI is minimal, namely it only maintains the global public-key list properly, which implies that security requirements hold true against malicious PKI.

We give the formal definitions of the security requirements as follows.

Tag-Linkability - Let F be an adversary modeled as a probabilistic algorithm. It takes security parameter $k \in \mathbb{N}$ and outputs $L = (issue, pk_N)$ and $(n + 1)$ message/signature pairs, $\{(m^{(1)}, \sigma^{(1)}), \ldots, (m^{(n+1)}, \sigma^{(n+1)})\}$, where $pk_N = (pk_1, \ldots, pk_n)$. We define the advantage of F against Σ to be

$$\mathbf{Adv}_{\Sigma}^{\text{forge}}(F)(k) \triangleq \Pr[\mathbf{Expt}^F(k) = 1]$$

where $\mathbf{Expt}^F(k)$ are:

1. $\left(L, \{(m^{(1)}, \sigma^{(1)}), \ldots, (m^{(n+1)}, \sigma^{(n+1)})\}\right) \leftarrow F(1^k)$;
2. Return 1 iff
   - $\mathbf{Ver}(L, m^{(i)}, \sigma^{(i)}) = 1$ for all $i \in \{1, \ldots, n+1\}$, and
   - $\mathbf{Trace}(L, m^{(i)}, \sigma^{(i)}, m^{(j)}, \sigma^{(j)}) = $ "indep" for all $i, j \in \{1, \ldots, n+1\}$, where $i \neq j$.

Definition 1. *We say that Σ is tag-linkable if for any probabilistic polynomial-time (in k) algorithm F, $\mathbf{Adv}_{\Sigma}^{\text{forge}}(F)(k)$ is negligible in k.*

Anonymity - Let D be an adversary modeled as a probabilistic algorithm. Let (pk_0, pk_1) be the two target public keys, where (pk_0, sk_0) and (pk_1, sk_1) are generated by $\mathbf{Gen}(1^k)$. Let $b \in \{0, 1\}$ be a random hidden bit. D starts the game with target (pk_0, pk_1). D may do the following things polynomial number of times in an arbitrary order: D may append new public keys to the global public-key list and may access three signing oracles, $\mathbf{Sig}_{sk_b}$, $\mathbf{Sig}_{sk_0}$, and $\mathbf{Sig}_{sk_1}$, where

- $\mathbf{Sig}_{sk_b}$ is the challenge signing oracle with respect to sk_b for signing (L, m), and
- $\mathbf{Sig}_{sk_0}$ (resp. $\mathbf{Sig}_{sk_1}$) is the signing oracle with respect to sk_0 (resp. sk_1) for signing (L, m).

Here we assume that L should include both pk_0, pk_1; that is, $pk_0, pk_1 \in pk_N$ for $L = (issue, pk_N)$. In addition, the following condition must hold:

- If (L, m) and (L, m') are two queries of D to the challenge signing oracle $\mathbf{Sig}_{sk_b}$, then $m = m'$.
- If (L, m) is a query of D to $\mathbf{Sig}_{sk_b}$ and $(\tilde{L}, \tilde{m})$ is a query of D to $\mathbf{Sig}_{sk_0}$ or $\mathbf{Sig}_{sk_1}$, then $L \neq \tilde{L}$.

Finally, D outputs a bit b'. We define the advantage of D against Σ as

$$\mathbf{Adv}_{\Sigma}^{\mathrm{anon}}(D)(k) \triangleq \Pr \left[\begin{array}{l} (pk_0, sk_0), (pk_1, sk_1) \leftarrow \mathbf{Gen}(1^k); \\ b \leftarrow \{0,1\}; \\ b' \leftarrow D^{\mathbf{Sig}_{sk_b},\mathbf{Sig}_{sk_0},\mathbf{Sig}_{sk_1}}(pk_0, pk_1) \end{array} : \quad b = b' \right] - \frac{1}{2}.$$

Definition 2. *We say that Σ is anonymous if, for every probabilistic polynomial-time (in k) adversary D, the advantage $\mathbf{Adv}_{\Sigma}^{\mathrm{anon}}(D)(k)$ is negligible in k.*

Remark 1. Our anonymity definition corresponds to Definition 3 in [4], which is not the strongest among their three definitions. It is, however, impossible for a traceable ring signature scheme to satisfy the strongest definition in [4], because the strongest definition requires that an adversary cannot distinguish which target generated the signature even when the adversary is given one of the target secrets; namely, all but one secret key in the ring is exposed. This condition and the public traceability cannot hold simultaneously.

Exculpability - Let A be a probabilistic algorithm as an adversary. Let pk be the target public key where (pk, sk) is generated by $\mathbf{Gen}(1^k)$. A starts the game with the target pk. A may do the following things a polynomial number of times in an arbitrary order. A may append new public keys to the global public-key list and may ask the signing oracle with respect to sk, $\mathbf{Sig}_{sk}$, to sign any $(\tilde{L}, \tilde{m})$, where $\tilde{L} = (is\tilde{s}ue, pk_{\tilde{N}})$, only with the restriction that $pk \in pk_{\tilde{N}}$. Finally, A outputs two pairs, (L, m, σ) and (L, m', σ'), where $L = (issue, pk_N)$. Here they should satisfy $pk \in pk_N$, $\mathbf{Ver}(L, m, \sigma) = 1$, and $\mathbf{Ver}(L, m', \sigma') = 1$. In addition, it must hold that at least one of (L, m, σ) or (L, m', σ') is not linked to any $(L, \hat{m}, \hat{\sigma})$ in the query/answer list between A and $\mathbf{Sig}_{sk}$ [4]. It is, however, allowed that one of them is linked to one in the query/answer list.

We say that A entraps a player with respect to pk if $\mathbf{Trace}(L, m, \sigma, m', \sigma') = pk$. We define the advantage of A against Σ, to be $\mathbf{Adv}_{\Sigma}^{\mathrm{entrap}}(A)(k) \triangleq$

$$\Pr \left[\begin{array}{l} (pk, sk) \leftarrow \mathbf{Gen}(1^k); \\ (L, m, \sigma), (L, m', \sigma') \leftarrow A^{\mathbf{Sig}_{sk}}(pk) \end{array} : \mathbf{Trace}(L, m, \sigma, m', \sigma') = pk \right].$$

Definition 3. *We say that Σ is exculpable if, for any probabilistic polynomial-time adversary A, $\mathbf{Adv}_{\Sigma}^{\mathrm{entrap}}(A)(k)$ is negligible in k.*

Remark 2. **In relation to the adaptively-chosen insider corruption attack:** One might think that the exculpability definition could be stronger when there are not only one but polynomially-many targets and the adversary can adaptively request the corruption of the target signers and finally attack one of the remaining uncorrupted targets. However, it is obvious that if an traceable ring signature satisfies this version of exculpability, then it also satisfies

---

[4] It implies two-fold. Our definition doesn't care for strong unforgeability. In addition, A is allowed to output a signature originally forged by himself with a copy (or linked one) from the query/answer list.

the improved definition, because the number of the ring members are at most polynomial (in security parameter k).

2.3 Discussion

As mentioned earlier, the standard unforgeability requirement (as defined in an ordinary ring signature) is inessential for a traceable ring signature scheme. We define unforgeability as the inability of an adversary that takes all public-key $pk_{\overline{N}}$ and, after having access to the signing oracle with (L, m, i), outputs (L', m', σ'), $L' = (issue', pk_{N'})$ and $N' \subset \overline{N}$, such that (L', m') never asked to the signing oracle. Here, for query (L, m, i), where $L = (issue, pk_N)$ and $i \in N \subset \overline{N}$, the signing oracle returns $\mathbf{Sig}_{sk_i}(L, m)$. We then have the following result.

Theorem 1. *If a traceable ring signature scheme is tag-linkable and exculpable, then it is unforgeable.*

Proof. Suppose for contradiction that there is an adversary A' against unforgeability. Let (L, m, σ) be the output of A', where $L = (issue, pk_N)$. Then, consider n independent pairs $\{(L, m^{(1)}, \sigma^{(1)}), \ldots, (L, m^{(n)}, \sigma^{(n)})\}$, such that $m^{(i)} \neq m$ and $\mathbf{Ver}(L, m^{(i)}, \sigma^{(i)}) = 1$ for all $i \in \{1, \ldots, n\}$. If every $n + 1$ pairs are independent, then it contradicts tag-linkability. Therefore, there is an $i \in \{1, \ldots, n\}$ such that $\mathbf{Trace}(L, m, \sigma, m^{(i)}, \sigma^{(i)}) = pk \in pk_N$, because $m^{(i)} \neq m$ (Remember that $\mathbf{Trace}$ never outputs "linked" if $m^{(i)} \neq m$). This case, however, contradicts the exculpability requirement, because we can construct adversary A against exculpability, by using A' as a black box oracle as follows. For simplicity, we assume, without loss of generality, that A takes all public-keys as the targets, as discussed in Remark 2. A feeds all public-keys to A'. For any query of A', A asks the signing oracle the answer and returns it to A'. A' finally outputs (L, m, σ), where $L = (issue, pk_N)$. Then, A asks for n queries and obtains $(L, m^{(1)}, \sigma^{(1)}), \ldots, (L, m^{(n)}, \sigma^{(n)})$, where $m^{(i)} \neq m$ for all i. Since there is an i such that $\mathbf{Trace}(L, m, \sigma, m^{(i)}, \sigma^{(i)}) = pk \in pk_N$, A outputs (L, m, σ) and $(L, m^{(i)}, \sigma^{(i)})$, which contradicts exculpability. $\square$

We note that a traceable ring signature always provides efficient confirmation and disavowal protocols (where we don't assume that these protocol are zero-knowledge). If a member of the ring wants to prove that a signature has been generated by himself, he can make another signature for a different message with the same tag, which would reveal his identity. Similarly, if a member of the ring wants to prove that a signature has not been generated by himself, he can submit another signature for an arbitrary message with the same tag, which shows that the second one is independent of the previous one. In some application it is undesirable, but *any* anonymous authentication primitive with public traceability (or linkability) cannot avoid this property.

3   Towards Our Scheme

Although our proposal is not very complicated, we construct our scheme step by step to understand more easily the concept behind our design.

Let us keep in mind the undeniable signature scheme proposed by Chaum [8]: Letting $y_i = g^{x_i} \in G$ be a public key of player i, the Chaum's undeniable signature on message M is $\sigma_i = H(M)^{x_i} \in G$, where H denotes a hash function. Now let $M = issue\|pk_N$ where $pk_N = (pk_1, \ldots, pk_n)$ are a vector of n public-keys. Pick up at random $(n-1)$ elements, σ_j's, from G, where $j \neq i$. Then, set a NP-language

$$\mathcal{L} \triangleq \{(y_N, h, \sigma_N)) \mid \exists i \in N \text{ such that } \log_g(y_i) = \log_h(\sigma_i).\},$$

where $h = H(issue\|y_N)$ and $\sigma_N = (\sigma_1, \ldots, \sigma_n)$.

Then, consider a zero-knowledge based signature (using secret x_i) on this language. It is well-known that such a signature can be constructed by applying the technique of Cramer et al. [11] (one-out-of n honest-verifier zero-knowledge) to the Fiat-Shamir technique. The signature on m is then (σ_N, p), where $p = (c, z)$ is a (non-interactive) proof on $\mathcal{L}$ and $c = H(\sigma_N, a, m)$, where a is computed by p. We call this our first-step construction.

Suppose now that this scheme is applied to anonymous voting on BBS, where each user can write on BBS anonymously. Let $L = (issue, pk_N)$, where $issue$ denotes the vote id number and pk_N corresponds to the authorized voters. Each voter simply sends message "yes" or "no" along with signature (σ_N, p) to a bulletin board via a sender-anonymous channel (such as the Internet in practice). If proof p is sound, a cheating player, say i, could not vote twice because it turns out $\sigma_i = \sigma_i' = h^{x_i}$, which takes the risk of revealing his identity.

However, this construction does not work well when an adversary is one of the voters. The problem is that an adversarial player, say j, can entrap an innocent player, say i, or at least void the first vote, with a significant probability. Player j waits for someone to send the first vote, say ("yes," (σ_N, p)), to the bulletin board. After seeing this signature, he generate a valid signature (σ_N', p') on message "no," using secret key x_j, following a valid signing procedure, except that he sets $\sigma_i' = \sigma_i$ and $\sigma_k' \neq \sigma_k$ for all $k \neq i$. He then sends ("no," σ_N', p') to the board. If the first vote is really generated by player i, player i cannot deny the second vote, because the second vote is a valid signature potentially generated by player i. At least, player i would lose his first vote, because he cannot prove which of two votes are valid.

Our solution is to make signer i fix every σ_j, $j \neq i$, depending on (L, m) and σ_i. More precisely, each point $(j, \log_h(\sigma_j))$ is forced to be on the line defined by $(i, \log_h(\sigma_i))$ and $(0, \log_h(H(L, m)))$. Intuitively, to generate a signature that will pass verification, player i must set $\sigma_i = h^{x_i}$, while to entrap player j, he must set at the same time that $(j, \log_h(\sigma_j))$ lies on the line defined by $(i, \log_h(\sigma_i))$ and $(0, \log_h(H(L, m)))$, which seems intractable. On the other hand, suppose that signer i generates two signatures, σ_N and σ_N', on m and m', $m \neq m'$, with respect to the same tag L. Every $(j, \log_h(\sigma_j))$ derived from the first σ_N lies on the line defined by $(i, \log_h(\sigma_i))$ and $(0, \log_h(H(L, m)))$, whereas every $(j, \log_h(\sigma_j'))$ derived from the second σ_N' does on the line defined by $(i, \log_h(\sigma_i))$ and $(0, \log_h(H(L, m')))$. Since the first line intersects with the second line at $(i, \log_h(\sigma_i))$ and these are not the same line (because $H(L, m) \neq H(L, m')$), it holds that $\sigma_i = \sigma_i'$ and $\sigma_j \neq \sigma_j'$ for all $j \neq i$, which implies that the identity of the cheating player is traced. We formally prove in Sec. 5 that this approach successfully works. Interestingly, this scheme is more efficient than the first-step construction described above in terms of communication traffic.

4 An Efficient Traceable Ring Signature Scheme

In this section, we describe our proposal.

Let G be a multiplicative group of prime order q and let g be a generator of G. Let $H : \{0,1\}^* \to G$, $H' : \{0,1\}^* \to G$, and $H'' : \{0,1\}^* \to \mathbb{Z}_q$ be distinct hash functions (modeled as random oracles in the security statements below). These above are public parameters. The key generation for player i is as follows: Player i picks up random element x_i in $\mathbb{Z}_q$ and computes $y_i = g^{x_i}$. The public key of i is $pk_i = \{g, y_i, G\}$ and the corresponding secret key is $sk_i = \{pk_i, x_i\}$. The player i registers his public-key to PKI. We denote by $N = \{1, \dots, n\}$ an ordered list of n players. We let $pk_N = (pk_1, \dots, pk_n)$ be an ordered public-key list for set N. Let *issue* be an arbitrary string in $\{0,1\}^*$.

Signing protocol: To sign message $m \in \{0,1\}^*$ with respect to tag $L = (issue, pk_N)$, using the secret-key sk_i, proceed as follows:

1. Compute $h = H(L)$ and $\sigma_i = h^{x_i}$, using $x_i \in \mathbb{Z}_q$.
2. Set $A_0 = H'(L, m)$ and $A_1 = \left(\frac{\sigma_i}{A_0}\right)^{1/i}$.
3. For all $j \neq i$, compute $\sigma_j = A_0 A_1^j \in G$. Notice that every $(j, \log_h(\sigma_j))$ is on the line defined by $(0, \log_h(A_0))$ and (i, x_i), where $x_i = \log_h(\sigma_i)$.
4. Generate signature (c_N, z_N) on (L, m), based on a (non-interactive) zero-knowledge proof of knowledge for the relation derived from language

$$\mathcal{L} \triangleq \{(L, h, \sigma_N)) \mid \exists i' \in N \text{ such that } \log_g(y_{i'}) = \log_h(\sigma_{i'}).\},$$

   where $\sigma_N = (\sigma_1, \dots, \sigma_n)$, as follows:
   (a) Pick up random $w_i \leftarrow \mathbb{Z}_q$ and set $a_i = g^{w_i}, b_i = h^{w_i} \in G$.
   (b) Pick up at random $z_j, c_j \leftarrow \mathbb{Z}_q$, and set $a_j = g^{z_j} y_i^{c_j}, b_j = h^{z_j} \sigma_j^{c_j} \in G$ for every $j \neq i$.
   (c) Set $c = H''(L, A_0, A_1, a_N, b_N)$ where $a_N = (a_1, \dots, a_n)$ and $b_N = (b_1, \dots, b_n)$.
   (d) Set $c_i = c - \sum_{j \neq i} c_j \pmod q$ and $z_i = w_i - c_i x_i \pmod q$. Return (c_N, z_N), where $c_N = (c_1, \dots, c_n)$ and $z_N = (z_1, \dots, z_n)$, as a proof of $\mathcal{L}$.
5. Output $\sigma = (A_1, c_N, z_N)$ as the signature on (L, m).

Verification protocol: To verify signature $\sigma = (A_1, c_N, z_N)$ on message m with respect to tag L, check the following:

1. Parse L as $(issue, pk_N)$. Check $g, A_1 \in G$, $c_i, z_i \in \mathbb{Z}_q$ and $y_i \in G$ for all $i \in N$. Set $h = H(L)$ and $A_0 = H'(L, m)$, and compute $\sigma_i = A_0 A_1^i \in G$ for all $i \in N$.

2. Compute $a_i = g^{z_i} y_i^{c_i}$ and $b_i = h^{z_i} \sigma_i^{c_i}$ for all $i \in N$.
3. Check that $H''(L, m, A_0, A_1, a_N, b_N) \equiv \sum_{i \in N} c_i \pmod{q}$, where $a_N = (a_1, \ldots, a_n)$ and $b_N = (b_1, \ldots, b_n)$.
4. If all the above checks are successfully completed, accept, otherwise reject.

Tracing protocol: To check the relation between (m, σ) and (m', σ'), with respect to the same tag L where $\sigma = (A_1, c_N, z_N)$ and $\sigma' = (A_1', c_N', z_N')$, check the following:

1. Parse L as $(issue, pk_N)$. Set $h = H(L)$ and $A_0 = H'(L, m)$, and compute $\sigma_i = A_0 A_1^i \in G$ for all $i \in N$. Do the same thing for σ' and retrieve σ_i', for all $i \in N$.
2. For all $i \in N$, if $\sigma_i = \sigma_i'$, store pk_i in **TList**, where **TList** is initially an empty list.
3. Output pk if pk is the only entry in **TList**; "linked" else if **TList** $= pk_N$; "indep" otherwise (i.e., **TList** $= \emptyset$ or $1 < \#\textbf{TList} < n$).

5   Security

In this section, we give security proofs for our traceable ring signature scheme.

Before proving tag-linkability for our scheme, we prove the following useful lemmas. We consider adversary A against our signature scheme above. A is given 1^k and allowed to access the random oracles, H' and H'', at most $q_{H'}$ and $q_{H''}$ times, respectively. Here it is not necessary that A is polynomial-time bounded. Then, we have the following lemmas.

Lemma 1. *Suppose that A outputs valid pair (L, m, σ).*

1. *The probability that $\#\{i \in N | \log_h(\sigma_i) = \log_g(y_i)\} < 1$ is at most $\frac{q_{H''}}{q}$, whereas*
2. *The probability that $\#\{i \in N | \log_h(\sigma_i) = \log_g(y_i)\} > 1$ is at most $\frac{q_{H'}}{q}$,*

where the probability is taken over the choices of H', H'' and the inner coin tosses of A.

Proof. Case 1 ($\#\{i \in N | \log_h(\sigma_i) = \log_g(y_i)\} < 1$): $\textbf{Ver}(L, m, \sigma) = 1$ implies that $a_i = g^{z_i} y_i^{c_i} \in G$ and $b_i = h^{z_i} \sigma_i^{c_i} \in G$ for $i \in N$, which means that $\log_g(a_i) = z_i + c_i \cdot \log_g(y_i)$ and $\log_h(b_i) = z_i + c_i \cdot \log_h(\sigma_i)$ for $i \in N$. Note that if $\log_g(y_i) \neq \log_h(\sigma_i)$, c_i is determined. Hence, Case 1 implies that all c_i's, where $i \in N$, are uniquely determined. Since H'' is a random oracle, for any given $(L, m, A_0, A_1, a_N, b_N)$, the probability that $H''(L, m, A_0, A_1, a_N, b_N) = \sum_{i \in N} c_i \pmod{q}$, is at most q^{-1}. Therefore, for any A with at most $q_{H''}$ queries to random oracle H'', the probability of Case 1 is at most $\frac{q_{H''}}{q}$.

Case 2 ($\#\{i \in N | \log_h(\sigma_i) = \log_g(y_i)\} > 1$): Since $\sigma_i = A_0 A_1^i \in G$ for $i \in N$, every point $(i, \log_h(\sigma_i))$, $i \in N$, is on line $y = \log_h(A_1)x + \log_h(A_0)$. Case 2 implies that at least two points, $(i, \log_g(y_i))$'s, are on the line, which means, when pk_N are fixed, the line is determined, so $\log_h(A_0)$ and $\log_h(A_1)$ are determined. However, we also need $\log_h(A_0) = \log_h(H'(L(issue, pk_N), m))$, where $H'(L, m)$ is determined independently of the above line, because H' is a random oracle. Actually, the probability that $\log_h(H'(L, m)) = \log_h(A_0)$ is at most q^{-1} for given (L, m). Hence, for any adversary A with at most $q_{H'}$ number of queries to random oracle H', the probability of Case 2 is at most $\frac{q_{H'}}{q}$.   □

Lemma 2. *Suppose A is defined above and it outputs $(L, m^{(1)}, \sigma^{(1)})$ and $(L, m^{(2)}, \sigma^{(2)})$, such that $\mathbf{Trace}(L, m^{(1)}, \sigma^{(1)}, m^{(2)}, \sigma^{(2)}) =$ "indep". Let $\mathbf{TList}$ be the list defined above in our tracing protocol. Then, the probability that $1 < \#\mathbf{TList}$ is $\frac{q_{H'}^2}{2q}$, where the probability is taken over the choices of H' and the inner coin tosses of A.*

Proof. By $1 < \#\mathbf{TList}$, the line defined by $\sigma^{(1)}$ intersects with the line defined by $\sigma^{(2)}$ at least at two points, which means that the two lines coincide. Hence, $A_0^{(1)} = H'(L, m^{(1)})$ and $A_0^{(2)} = H'(L, m^{(2)})$, because $\log_h A_0^{(1)} = \log_h A_0^{(2)}$ where $h = H(L)$. Therefore, the advantage of A is bounded by the probability that A can find a collision of outputs of H', which is $\frac{q_{H'}^2}{2q}$.   □

Theorem 2 (Tag-Linkability). *Our proposed scheme is tag-linkable in the random oracle model.*

Proof. Suppose for contradiction that there is adversary F that takes 1^k and successfully outputs tag $L = (issue, pk_N)$ and $\{(m^{(1)}, \sigma^{(1)}), \ldots, (m^{(n+1)}, \sigma^{(n+1)})\}$.

Based on lemma 2, $\mathbf{Trace}(L, m^{(i)}, \sigma^{(i)}, m^{(j)}, \sigma^{(j)}) =$ "indep," for all i, j, means that, (with an overwhelming (i.e., $1 - \frac{q_{H'}^2}{2q}$) probability), $\sigma_k^{(i)} \neq \sigma_k^{(j)}$ holds, for all i, j, k, where $1 \leq i, j \leq n+1$, $i \neq j$, and $1 \leq k \leq n$. On the contrary, by Case 1 of Lemma 1, for every i, where $1 \leq i \leq n+1$, there exist $k \in N$ such that $\log_g(y_k) = \log_h(\sigma_k^{(i)})$ (with at least $(1 - \frac{(n+1)q_{H''}}{q})$ probability). Since $1 \leq k \leq n$, there exist i, j, k such that $\sigma_k^{(i)} = \sigma_k^{(j)}$, which contradicts the assumption (if the advantage of F exceeds $\max(\frac{q_{H'}^2}{2q}, \frac{(n+1)q_{H''}}{q})$).

Therefore, the probability that F can forge the proposed scheme above is at most $\max(\frac{q_{H'}^2}{2q}, \frac{(n+1)q_{H''}}{q})$, where $q_{H'}$ and $q_{H''}$ denotes the number of queries of F to random oracles, H' and H'', respectively.   □

Before proceeding other theorems, we define a protocol, commonly used in some of the following proofs.

Procedure of SimNIZK.
On input: (L, m, h, A_0, A_1).
Output: (c_N, z_N).

1. For all $i \in N$, pick up at random $z_i, c_i \xleftarrow{}_U \mathbb{Z}_q$, and set $a_i = g^{z_i} y_i^{c_i}, b_i = h^{z_i} \sigma_i^{c_i} \in G$, where $\sigma_i = A_0 A_1^i$.
2. Set $H''(L, m, A_0, A_1, a_N, b_N)$ as $c := \sum_{i \in N} c_i$, where $a_N = (a_1, \ldots, a_n)$ and $b_N = (b_1, \ldots, b_n)$. If $H''(L, m, A_0, A_1, a_N, b_N)$ has been already booked as a different value in query/answer list $Q_{H''}$, then output "failure," otherwise

3. Output (c_N, z_N), where $c_N = (c_1, \ldots, c_n)$ and $z_N = (z_1, \ldots, z_n)$.

We now show the following theorem.

Theorem 3 (Anonymity). *Our proposed scheme is anonymous under the decisional Diffie-Hellman assumption in the random oracle model.*

Proof. Suppose that there is an adversary D with advantage ϵ, which means that, by definition, D can correctly guess b with probability $\epsilon + \frac{1}{2}$. We now construct an algorithm A to solve the decisional Diffie-Hellman problem. Let (g_1, g_2, u, v) be a given instance, where $g_1, g_2, u, v \in G$. When (g_1, g_2, u, v) is a DDH tuple, $\log_{g_1}(u) = \log_{g_2}(v)$ holds. We construct A as follows:

1. A is given instance (g_1, g_2, u, v).
2. A picks up at random $b \leftarrow \{0, 1\}$.
3. A sets $g := g_1$, $y_b := u$ and, picking up at random $t \in \mathbb{Z}_q$, $y_{1-b} := y_b g^t$.
4. A feeds y_0, y_1 to D.
5. In case D submits a fresh query to random oracles, H' and H'', A picks up random elements in G and $\mathbb{Z}_q$ respectively, to reply with. Then, A stores the query/answer pairs in the lists, $Q_{H'}$ and $Q_{H''}$, respectively.
6. In case D submits a fresh query to random oracle H, A picks up at random $r_1, r_2 \leftarrow \mathbb{Z}_q$ and returns $g_1^{r_1} g_2^{r_2}$. Then, A stores the value as well as (r_1, r_2) in query/answer list Q_H.

   In this simulation, if A picks up the same $g_1^{r_1} g_2^{r_2}$ again, namely, $H(L) = H(L')$ happens for $L \neq L'$, A aborts. However, such an event happens at most $\frac{q_H}{q}$, which is negligible in k, where q_H denotes the total number of queries of D to H.
7. In case D submits a query (L, m) to $\mathbf{Sig}_{sk_b}$, A sets $g_1^{r_1} g_2^{r_2}$ as $h := H(L)$ and $\sigma_b := u^{r_1} v^{r_2}$, picking up at random $r_1, r_2 \in \mathbb{Z}_q$. Then, A picks up a random element A_0 as $H'(L, m)$. If $H(L)$ and $H'(L, m)$ have been already stored in Q_H and $Q_{H'}$, respectively, A uses these stored values. A sets A_1 and σ_N, by using A_0 and σ_b. Then, A simulates a NIZK proof on language

$$\mathcal{L} \triangleq \{(L, h, \sigma_N)) \mid \quad \exists i' \in N \text{ such that } \log_g(y_{i'}) = \log_h(\sigma_{i'}).\},$$

   following procedure **SimNIZK** described above to get (c_N, z_N), where $c_N = (c_1, \ldots, c_n)$ and $z_N = (z_1, \ldots, z_n)$. If **SimNIZK** succeeds, A returns $\sigma = (A_1, c_N, z_N)$ to D, otherwise A halts.
8. In case D submits a query (L, m) to $\mathbf{Sig}_{sk_0}$, if $b = 0$ do the same thing as in Step 7. Otherwise, A sets $g_1^{r_1} g_2^{r_2}$ as $h := H(L)$ and $\sigma_0 := u^{r_1} v^{r_2} (g_1^{r_1} g_2^{r_2})^t$, picking up at random $r_1, r_2 \in \mathbb{Z}_q$. Then, A picks up a random element A_0 as $H'(L, m)$. If $H(L)$ and $H'(L, m)$ have been already stored in Q_H and $Q_{H'}$, respectively, A uses these stored values. A sets A_1 and σ_N, by using A_0 and σ_0. Then, A simulates a NIZK proof on language

$$\mathcal{L} \triangleq \{(L, h, \sigma_N)) \mid \quad \exists i' \in N \text{ such that } \log_g(y_{i'}) = \log_h(\sigma_{i'}).\},$$

   following procedure **SimNIZK** described below to get (c_N, z_N), where $c_N = (c_1, \ldots, c_n)$ and $z_N = (z_1, \ldots, z_n)$. If **SimNIZK** succeeds, A returns $\sigma = (A_1, c_N, z_N)$ to D, otherwise A halts.

9. In case D submits a query (L, m) to $\mathbf{Sig}_{sk_1}$, do the same thing as in Step 8.
10. Finally, D outputs b'. If $b = b'$, A output 1, otherwise A flips a coin $b'' \in \{0, 1\}$ to output.

The advantage of A against the DDH problem is defined as

$$\Pr[A(g_1, g_2, u, v) = 1 \mid (g_1, g_2, u, v) \in \mathrm{DDH}] - \Pr[A(g_1, g_2, u, v)$$
$$= 1 \mid (g_1, g_2, u, v) \notin \mathrm{DDH}].$$

We say that A succeeds in simulation if no collision happens in simulating random oracle H and $\mathbf{SimNIZK}$ succeeds in simulating proofs for all queries of D to the signing oracles. $\mathbf{SimNIZK}$ fails in generating a proof with at most probability $\frac{q_{H''}}{q}$, where $q_{H''}$ denotes the total number of queries of D to H''. Hence, the probability that $\mathbf{SimNIZK}$ fails at least once in this game is bounded by $\frac{q_{\mathbf{Sig}} \cdot q_{H''}}{q}$, where $q_{\mathbf{Sig}}$ denotes the total number of queries of D to the signing oracles.

We evaluate the following probabilities on the condition that A succeeds in simulation.

Notice that if (g_1, g_2, u, v) is a DDH tuple and a reply of the signing oracles, $\mathbf{Sig}_{sk_b}$, $\mathbf{Sig}_{sk_0}$, and $\mathbf{Sig}_{sk_1}$, is identical to the real signature using sk_b, sk_0, and sk_1, respectively (on the condition that $\mathbf{SimNIZK}$ succeeds in simulating a proof).

On the other hand, if it is a random tuple, hidden bit b is perfectly independent of the adversary's view.

Hence, we have $\Pr[b = b' \mid (g_1, g_2, u, v) \in \mathrm{DDH}] = \epsilon + \frac{1}{2}$ by assumption and $\Pr[b = b' \mid (g_1, g_2, u, v) \notin \mathrm{DDH}] = \frac{1}{2}$.

Therefore, $\Pr[A(g_1, g_2.u, v) = 1 \mid (g_1, g_2, u, v) \in \mathrm{DDH}] = \Pr[b = b' \mid (g_1, g_2, u, v) \in \mathrm{DDH}] + \Pr[b \neq b' \mid (g_1, g_2, u, v) \in \mathrm{DDH}] \cdot \Pr[b'' = 1 \mid (g_1, g_2, u, v) \in \mathrm{DDH} \wedge b \neq b'] = \left(\epsilon + \frac{1}{2}\right) + \left(1 - \left(\epsilon + \frac{1}{2}\right)\right) \cdot \frac{1}{2} = \frac{\epsilon}{2} + \frac{3}{4}$.

On the other hand, $\Pr[A(g_1, g_2, u, v) = 1 \mid (g_1, g_2, u, v) \notin \mathrm{DDH}] = \Pr[b = b' \mid (g_1, g_2, u, v) \notin \mathrm{DDH}] + \Pr[b \neq b' \mid (g_1, g_2, u, v) \notin \mathrm{DDH}] \cdot \Pr[b'' = 1 \mid (g_1, g_2, u, v) \notin \mathrm{DDH} \wedge b \neq b'] = \frac{1}{2} + \frac{1}{2} \cdot \frac{1}{2} = \frac{3}{4}$.

Based on this estimation, the advantage of A is $\frac{1}{2} \cdot \epsilon$, if A succeeds in simulation. Therefore, the advantage of A is bounded by

$$\frac{1}{2} \cdot \epsilon - \frac{q_H}{q} - \frac{q_{\mathbf{Sig}} \cdot q_{H''}}{q}.$$

To suppress the advantage of A to be negligible in k, ϵ must be negligible in k. □

Before proceeding to the exculpability statement, we prove the following lemma. Let A be an adversary against exculpability for our scheme. Let $q_{H'}, q_{H''}$ denote the total number of queries to the random oracles, H', H'', respectively. Here it is not necessary that A is polynomial-time bounded. Then, we have the following.

Lemma 3. *When A entraps player i, the probability that $\log_h(\sigma_i) \neq \log_g(y_i)$ is at most $\frac{(n-1)(n-2)q_{H'}^2}{2q} + \frac{q_{H''}}{q}$. The probability is taken over the choices of H', H'' and the inner coin tosses of A.*

Proof. Assume that $\log_h(\sigma_i) \neq \log_g(y_i)$. Based on lemma 1, if $\mathbf{Ver}(L, m, \sigma) = 1$, the probability that $\#\{i \in N \mid \log_h(\sigma_i) = \log_g(y_i)\} < 1$ is at most $\frac{q_{H''}}{q}$. Hence, for σ and σ' that A outputs, there are $j, k \in N$, with an overwhelming probability, such that $\log_h(\sigma_j) = \log_g(y_j)$ and $\log_h(\sigma'_k) = \log_g(y_k)$, which implies that

$$\log_h(y_j) = \log_h(A_1) \cdot j + \log_h(A_0) \tag{1}$$

$$\log_h(y_k) = \log_h(A'_1) \cdot k + \log_h(A'_0). \tag{2}$$

Since $\log_h(\sigma_i) \neq \log_g(y_i)$, it holds that $j, k \neq i$.

By assumption, line $y = \log_h(A_1) \cdot x + \log_h(A_0)$ intersects with line $y = \log_h(A'_1) \cdot x + \log_h(A'_0)$ at $x = i$. Hence, we have

$$\log_h(A_1) \cdot i + \log_h(A_0) = \log_h(A'_1) \cdot i + \log_h(A'_0). \tag{3}$$

By (1), (2), and (3), we have

$$A \cdot \log_h(A_0) + B \cdot \log_h(A'_0) = C, \tag{4}$$

where A, B, C are fixed when i, j, k, $\log_g(y_j)$ and $\log_g(y_k)$ are fixed. Remember that $A_0 = H'(L, m)$ and $A'_0 = H'(L, m')$ must hold, where $L = (issue, pk_N)$. Note that $H'(L, m), H'(L, m')$ are fixed *after* i, j, k, $\log_g(y_j)$ and $\log_g(y_k)$ are fixed. Hence, the probability that A_0 and A'_0 satisfy (4) is at most $\frac{q^2_{H'}}{2q}$, because H' is a random oracle.

The probability that A_0, A'_0 satisfy (4) is the same in every $j, k \in N - \{i\}$, $j \neq k$; Hence, the probability that $\log_h(\sigma_i) \neq \log_g(y_i)$ is at most $\frac{(n-1)(n-2)q^2_{H'}}{2q} + \frac{q_{H''}}{q}$.
$\square$

When adversary A entraps player i, there are two possibilities: One is the case that A really forges the signature of player i (possibly, after seeing her/his real signature). Namely, it is the case that $\log_h(\sigma_i) = \log_h(\sigma'_i) = \log_g(y_i)$. The other case $\log_h(\sigma_i) = \log_h(\sigma'_i) \neq \log_g(y_i)$, means that A does not forge the signatures of player i but, letting σ, σ' be generated by A, the i-th entries of them, σ_i and σ'_i, are the same. This lemma implies that if A entraps player i, it is the case, with an overwhelming probability, that A has really forged a signature of player i.

Theorem 4 (Exculpability). *Our proposed scheme is exculpable under the discrete logarithm assumption in the random oracle model.*

A very rough strategy for proving the theorem is as follows: Based on lemma 3, we know that if an adversary A against exculpability for our scheme can entraps the target player i, then it is the case with an overwhelming probability that A has actually forged a signature of player i, i.e., $\log_h \sigma_i = \log_g y_i$. In addition, by lemma 1, we realize that that it is "never" a potential signature of any other player at the same time, i.e., $\log_h \sigma_j \neq \log_g y_j$, for $j \neq i$ (with an overwhelming probability). This implies that by the standard rewinding, we have $c_i \neq c''_i$ for the target i, which breaks the discrete log of the target y_i and leads to the contradiction.

Proof. Suppose that there is adversary A that takes pk and entraps the player with respect to pk. Then, we can construct algorithm A' that solves the discrete logarithm problem. Let $g, Y \in G$ be a given instance of discrete logarithm problem. The goal of A' is to output $\log_g Y$. We construct A' as follows.

Without loss of generality, we assume that the id number of the target player is i. Hence, A' sets $y_i := Y$ and feeds $pk_i = \{y_i, g\}$ to adversary A.

A may access the random oracles, H, H', H'', and the signing oracle, at most $q_H, q_{H'}, q_{H''}$ and $q_{\mathbf{Sig}}$ times, respectively. In case A submits a fresh query to random oracles, H' and H'', A' picks up random elements in G and $\mathbb{Z}_q$ respectively, to use as a reply, maintaining the query/answer lists, $Q_{H'}$ and $Q_{H''}$, respectively. In case A submits a fresh query to random oracle H, A' picks up random $v \in \mathbb{Z}_q$ and return g^v to A, maintaining query/answer list Q_H. In case A submits query $(\tilde{L}, \tilde{m})$, to the signing oracle, A' returns σ as follows.

1. Pick up random $v \in \mathbb{Z}_q$, to set value $\tilde{h} := H(\tilde{L})$ as g^v. Pick up random $\tilde{A}_0$ as $H'(\tilde{L}, \tilde{m})$. If $H(\tilde{L})$ and $H'(\tilde{L}, \tilde{m})$ have been already booked in Q_H and $Q_{H'}$, respectively, use these stored values. Set $\tilde{\sigma}_i := y_i^v$.
2. Compute $\tilde{A}_1$ and $\tilde{\sigma}_N$. Then use **SimNIZK** on input $(\tilde{L}, \tilde{m}, \tilde{h}, \tilde{A}_0, \tilde{A}_1)$. **SimNIZK** returns $(\tilde{c}_N, \tilde{z}_N)$ except for a negligible probability $\frac{q_{H''}}{q}$. If **SimNIZK** fails in simulating a proof, then A' aborts.

   The probability that **SimNIZK** fails at least once in this game is bounded by $\frac{q_{\mathbf{Sig}} \cdot q_{H''}}{q}$.
3. Return $\tilde{\sigma} = (\tilde{A}_1, \tilde{c}_N, \tilde{z}_N)$ and store the query/answer pair in the list $Q_{\mathbf{Sig}}$.

Finally, A outputs (L, m, σ) and (L, m', σ'). A entraps player i with probability ϵ, which is the advantage of A. Then, A' works as follows. Since at least one of (L, m, σ) and (L, m', σ') is not an entry in $Q_{\mathbf{Sig}}$, A' renames the value (L, m, σ) and rename the other (L, m', σ') (If both are not an entry in $Q_{\mathbf{Sig}}$, A' swaps the names at random). Then, A' picks up a new random element $c'' \in Z_q$, where if c'' is identical to the first $H''(L, m, A_0, A_1, a_N, b_N)$, A' halts. However, this occurs only with probability q^{-1}. Then, A' runs A again on the same random coins except that $c'' := H''(L, m, A_0, A_1, a_N, b_N)$. There is some probability that A finally outputs (L, m, σ'') (and another pair $(L, ., .)$) such that $\sigma'' = (A_1, c''_N, z''_N)$. As studied in [23], such an event happens with probability $\frac{1}{q_{H''}}\epsilon$, on the condition that A succeeds in the first run. Then, A' checks that $c_i \neq c''_i$. If $c_i = c''_i$, A' halts, otherwise output $\frac{z''_i - z_i}{c_i - c''_i}$, which implies that A' outputs $\log_g(Y)$ on input (g, Y, G), because $a_i = g^{z_i} y_i^{c_i} = g^{z''_i} y_i^{c''_i}$ and $y_i = Y$.

We now claim that the probability that $c_i \neq c''_i$ is overwhelming in k: By lemma 3, if adversary A entraps player i, it is the case with an overwhelming probability that A has really forged the signature of player i; namely, $\log_h(\sigma_i) = \log_g(y_i)$. On one hand, since $c \neq c''$, there is at least a $t \in N$, such that $c_t \neq c''_t$. By lemma 1, however, the possibility that $\#\{i \in N | \log_h(\sigma_i) = \log_g(y_i)\} > 1$ is at most $\frac{q_{H'}}{q}$. Therefore, we conclude $t = i$ because at least, $\log_h(\sigma_i) = \log_g(y_i)$.

To sum up, the success probability of A' is bounded by

$$\frac{\epsilon^2}{q_{H''}} - \frac{1}{q} - \frac{q_{\mathrm{Sig}}q_{H''}}{q} - \frac{(n-1)(n-2)q_{H'}^2}{2q} - \frac{q_{H''}}{q} - \frac{q_{H'}}{q}.$$

To suppress the advantage of A' to be negligible in k, ϵ, the advantage of A, must be negligible in k.   □

Remark 3 (On-Line Extractor). The standard rewinding strategy works well on our scheme in the game of exculpability but it only provides a loose security reduction. Actually, for adversary A that runs in time T with advantage ϵ, we construct algorithm A' breaking the discrete-log problem in time $T' \approx 2T$ with probability $\epsilon' \approx \frac{\epsilon^2}{q_H}$ in the proof of Theorem 4. Based on Fischlin's technique [14], we can replace, at a small efficiency cost, our non-interactive zero-knowledge part in the signing protocol with one for which there is an on-line extractor; that is, one can extract the secret witness from the adversary without rewinding. Here, if A attacks the new scheme in time T with advantage ϵ, then there is algorithm A' breaking the discrete-log problem in time $T' = O(T)$ with probability $\epsilon' \approx \epsilon$.

6   Some Other Remarks

6.1   Threshold Version of Traceable Ring Signature

The extension of our proposal to a t-out-of-n traceable ring signature is straightforward. Let S be the set of t signers. First of all, each signer in S makes signature his own $\sigma_i = h^{x_i}$, where $h = H(L)$, and distributes σ_i to the other signers. Then, each signer in S computes every other signature σ_i, $i \notin S$, as point $(i, \log_h \sigma_i)$ lies on a polynomial curve of degree t, $y = \alpha(x)$, uniquely defined from $(t+1)$ points, $(0, \log_h A_0)$, $(k_1, x_{k_1}), \ldots, (k_t, x_{k_t})$, where $A_0 = H'(L, m)$ and $S = \{k_1, \ldots, k_t\}$. Actually, each signer in S can locally compute σ_i, $i \notin S$, as $\sigma_i = \prod_{j=0}^{t}(A_j)^{i^j} \in G$ for all $i \notin S$, where $A_0 = H(L, m) \in G$, and $A_j = \prod_{k \in S}(\sigma_k/A_0)^{m_{j,k}} \in G$ for $j = 1, \ldots, t$, where

$$\begin{pmatrix} m_{1,k_1} & \cdots & m_{1,k_t} \\ \vdots & \ddots & \vdots \\ m_{t,k_1} & \cdots & m_{t,k_t} \end{pmatrix} = \begin{pmatrix} k_1^{\;1} & \cdots & k_1^{\;t} \\ \vdots & \ddots & \vdots \\ k_t^{\;1} & \cdots & k_t^{\;t} \end{pmatrix}^{-1}$$

is the inverse matrix of van der Monde matrix. Notice that there exists a polynomial of degree t, $\alpha(x) \in \mathbb{Z}_q[x]$, such that $A_0 = h^{\alpha(0)} \in G$ and $\sigma_i = h^{\alpha(i)} \in G$ for every i. Then they collaborate and generate a NIZK based signature on (L, m), p, by applying the technique of [11], with respect to the language

$$\mathcal{L} \triangleq \{(L, h, \sigma_N)) \mid \exists S \subset N \text{ such that } \#S \geq t \text{ and } \log_g(y_i) = \log_h(\sigma_i) \text{ for } i \in S\}.$$

Finally, the signers output signature $\sigma = (A_1, \ldots, A_t, p)$, where $p = (\beta(x), z_N)$ and $\beta(x)$ is a polynomial of degree $(n-t)$ in $\mathbb{Z}_q[x]$.

6.2 k-Times Anonymity on the Same Tag

Any traceable ring signature scheme can be efficiently transformed into a traceable ring signature scheme with k-times anonymity in the sense of [25], where the k-times anonymity means that a signer is allowed to sign messages with respect to the same tag at most k times without being traced. It is simply obtained by regarding $(i, \mathbf{Sig}_{sk}((L, i), m))$ as a signature on m, with respect to tag L, where the verifier checks if $\mathbf{Ver}((L, i), m) = 1$ and $1 \leq i \leq k$ (Here the signer need not publish i in order). It is obvious that the identity of a signer is not revealed if the signer is enough careful not to issue the same index twice on the same tag. We, however, remark that this implementation has a weakness in the unlinkability property, while it satisfies the condition of the k-time anonymity defined in [25], because whether or not the two signatures have been generated by the different signers can be easily determined, if the two signatures have the same tag and index. The scheme appeared in [25], too, substantially has the same problem.

References

1. M. Abe, M. Ohkubo, and K. Suzuki. Efficient threshold signer-ambiguous signatures from variety of keys. *IEICE Trans. Fund.*, vol.E87-A, no.2:471–479, 2004.
2. M. H. Au, S. S. M. Chow, W. Susilo, and P. P. Tsang. Short linkable ring signatures revisited. In *EUROPKI 2006*, LNCS 4043, pages 101–115, 2006.
3. M. Bellare, H. Shi, and C. Zhang. Foundations of group signatures: The case of dynamic groups. In *CT-RSA '05*, 2005.
4. A. Bender, J. Katz, and R. Morselli. Ring signatures:stronger definitions, and constructions without random oracles. In S. Halevi and T. Rabin, editors, *TCC 2006*, LNCS 3876, pages 60–79. Springer-Verlag, 2006.
5. S. Brands. Untraceable off-line cash in wallet with observers. In D. Stinson, editor, *CRYPTO '93*, LNCS 773, pages 302–318. Springer-Verlag, 1993.
6. E. Bresson, J. Stern, and M. Szydlo. Threshold ring signatures and applications to ad-hoc groups. In Moti Yung, editor, *CRYPTO 2002*, LNCS 2442, pages 465–480. Springer-Verlag, 2002.
7. D. Chaum. Blind signatures for untraceable payments. In D. Chaum, R. Rivest, and A. Sherman, editors, *CRYPTO '82*, pages 199–204. Prenum Publishing Corporation, 1982.
8. D. Chaum. Zero-knowledge undeniable signatures. In *EUROCRYPT 1990*, pages 458–464, 1990.
9. D. Chaum, A. Fiat, and M. Naor. Untraceable electronic cash. In S. Goldwasser, editor, *CRYPTO '88*, LNCS 403, pages 319–327. Springer-Verlag, 1990.
10. D. Chaum and E. Van Heyst. Group signatures. In D. W. Davies, editor, *EUROCRYPT '91*, LNCS 547, pages 257–265. Springer-Verlag, 1991.
11. R. Cramer, I. Damgård, and B. Schoenmakers. Proofs of partial knowledge and simplified design of witness hiding protocols. In *CRYPTO 1994*, pages 174–187, 1994.
12. I. Damgard, K. Dupont, and M. Pedersen. Unclonable group identification. In S. Vaudenay, editor, *EUROCRYPT 2006*, LNCS 4004, pages 555–572. Springer-Verlag, 2006.

13. Y. Dodis, A. Kiayias, A. Nicolosi, and V. Shoup. Anonymous identification in ad hoc groups. In C. Cachin and J. Camenisch, editors, *EUROCRYPT 2004*, LNCS 3027, pages 609–626. Springer-Verlag, 2004.
14. M. Fischlin. Communication-efficient non-interactive proofs of knowledge with online extractor. In *CRYPTO 2005*, LNCS 3621. Springer-Verlag, 2005.
15. A. Kiayias, Y. Tsiounis, and M. Yung. Traceable signatures. In C. Cachin and J. Camenisch, editors, *EUROCRYPT 2004*, LNCS 3027. Springer-Verlag, 2004.
16. Y. Komano, K. Ohta, A. Shimbo, and S. Kawamura. Toward the fair anonymous signatures: Deniable ring signatures. In D. Pointcheval, editor, *CT-RSA '06*, LNCS 3860, pages 174–191. Springer-Verlag, 2006.
17. J. K. Liu, V. K. Wei, and D. S. Wong. Linkable spontaneous anonymous group signature for ad hoc groups (extended abstract). In *ACISP 2004*, LNCS 3108, pages 325–335, 2004.
18. J. K. Liu and D. S. Wong. Linkable ring signatures: Security models and new schemes. In *ICCSA 2005*, LNCS 3481, pages 614–623, 2005.
19. M. Naor. Deniable ring authentication. In *CRYPTO 2002*, pages 481–498, 2002.
20. T. Okamoto. An efficient divisible electronic cash scheme. In D. Coppersmith, editor, *CRYPTO'95*, LNCS 963, pages 438–451. Springer-Verlag, 1995.
21. T. Okamoto. Receipt-free electronic voting schemes for large scale elections. In *Security Protocols Workshop*, pages 25–35, Paris, 1997.
22. T. Okamoto and K. Ohta. Universal electronic cash. In *CRYPTO '91*, LNCS 576, pages 324–337. Springer-Verlag, 1992.
23. D. Pointcheval and J. Stern. Security arguments for digital signatures and blind signatures. *Journal of Cryptology*, 2000.
24. R. Rivest, A. Shamir, and Y. Tauman. How to leak a secret. In C. Boyd, editor, *Asiacrypt 2001*, LNCS 2248, pages 552–565. Springer-Verlag, 2001.
25. I. Teranishi, J. Furukawa, and K. Sako. k-times anonymous authentication. In P.J. Lee, editor, *Asiacrypt 2004*, LNCS 3329, pages 308–322. Springer-Verlag, 2004.
26. P. P. Tsang and V. K. Wei. Short linkable ring signatures for e-voting, e-cash and attestation. In *IPSEC 2005*, 2005.
27. P. P. Tsang, V. K. Wei, T. K. Chan, M. H. Au, J. K. Liu, and D. S. Wong. Separable linkable threshold ring signatures. In *INDCRYPT 2004*, LNCS 3348, pages 389–398, 2004.

Two-Tier Signatures, Strongly Unforgeable Signatures, and Fiat-Shamir Without Random Oracles

Mihir Bellare and Sarah Shoup

Department of Computer Science and Engineering, University of California San Diego, 9500 Gilman Drive, La Jolla, CA 92093-0404
mihir@cs.ucsd.edu, sshoup@cs.ucsd.edu
www-cse.ucsd.edu/users/mihir, www-cse.ucsd.edu/users/sshoup

Abstract. We provide a positive result about the Fiat-Shamir (FS) transform in the standard model, showing how to use it to convert three-move identification protocols into *two-tier signature schemes* with a proof of security that makes a standard assumption on the hash function rather than modeling it as a random oracle. The result requires security of the starting protocol against *concurrent* attacks. We can show that numerous protocols have the required properties and so obtain numerous efficient two-tier schemes. Our first application is a two-tier scheme based transform of any unforgeable signature scheme into a strongly unforgeable one. (This extends Boneh, Shen and Waters [8] whose transform only applies to a limited class of schemes.) The second application is new one-time signature schemes that, compared to one-way function based ones of the same computational cost, have smaller key and signature sizes.

1 Introduction

Recall that the Fiat-Shamir (FS) transform [18] is a way to obtain a signature scheme from a three-move identification protocol by "collapsing" the interaction via a hash function. (Briefly, the signature consists of the two prover moves corresponding to a verifier challenge set to be the hash of the first prover move and the message being signed.) There are lots of protocols to which the transform can be applied, and the resulting signature schemes include some of the most efficient known (eg. [35,24,23]). Furthermore, due to their algebraic properties, FS-transform-derived signature schemes lend themselves nicely to extensions such as to blind [33], multi [28] or group [7] signatures to name just a few. For these reasons, the transform is popular and widely used.

Naturally, one would like that the constructed signature scheme meets the standard notion of unforgeability under chosen-message attack (uf-cma) of [22]. Results of [33,30,1] say this is true in the random oracle (RO) model (meaning, if the hash function is a random oracle) as long as the starting protocol is itself secure (we will discuss in what sense later). However, Goldwasser and Tauman-Kalai [21] show the existence of a protocol that, under the FS transform, yields a

T. Okamoto and X. Wang (Eds.): PKC 2007, LNCS 4450, pp. 201–216, 2007.
© International Association for Cryptologic Research 2007

signature scheme that is uf-cma secure when the hash function is a RO but is not uf-cma secure for *any* "real" implementation of the hash function. This means that the transform (at least in general) does not yield uf-cma secure schemes in the standard model.

The question we ask is whether the FS transform can, however, yield weaker-than-uf-cma but still useful types of signature schemes in the standard model. We answer this in the affirmative. We show how the FS transform yields *two-tier signature schemes* which are secure assuming only that the hash function is collision-resistant and the starting protocol is secure. We exhibit some applications of two-tier signatures in general and FS-derived ones in particular, namely for an efficient and general transform of uf-cma to strongly unforgeable (suf-cma) signature schemes and to implement one-time signatures that are much shorter than conventional ones of the same computational cost. Let us now look at all this in more detail.

TWO-TIER SCHEMES. In a two-tier scheme, a signer has a primary public key and matching primary secret key. Each time it wants to sign, it generates a fresh pair of secondary public and secret keys and produces the signature as a function of these, the primary keys and the message. Verification requires not only the primary public key but also the secondary one associated to the message. Security requires that it be computationally infeasible to forge relative to the primary public key and any secondary public key that was generated by the signer, even under a chosen-message attack.

As the reader might rightfully note, two-tier signatures are not well suited for direct signing in the standard PKI, because not just the primary but also the secondary public keys would need to be certified. However, we do not propose to use them in this direct way. Instead what we will see is that they are useful tools in building other primitives.

BUILDING TWO-TIER SIGNATURES VIA FS. We adapt the FS transform in a natural way to convert a three-move identification protocol into a two-tier signature scheme. (Briefly, the first prover move, rather than being in the signature, is now the secondary public key. See Section 4 for details.) We show (cf. Theorem 2) that the constructed two-tier scheme is secure assuming the protocol is secure (we will see exactly what this means below) and the hash function is collision-resistant. So security of FS-based two-tier signatures is guaranteed in the standard model unlike security of FS-based regular signatures which is guaranteed only in the RO model.

Both the security of regular FS-based signatures (in the RO model) [30,1] and the security of our FS-based two-tier signatures (in the standard model) are based on some security assumption about the starting protocol. (Naturally, since otherwise there is no reason for the constructs to be secure.) There is, however, a difference in the two cases. Recall that security of this class of protocols can be considered under three different types of attack: passive, where the adversary merely observes interactions between the prover and honest verifier; active [18,16], where the adversary plays a cheating verifier and engages in sequential interactions with the honest prover; or concurrent [4], where, as a cheating verifier, the adversary can interact concurrently with different prover clones. For (uf-cma) security of FS-based regular signatures in the RO model, it suffices that the protocol be secure against passive (i.e. eavesdropping) attack [30,1]. Our result showing security of FS-based two-tier signatures requires however that the protocol be secure against *concurrent* attack. Thus, part of what makes it possible to dispense with random oracles is to start from protocols with a stronger property. However, we show that the property is in fact possessed by the bulk of example protocols, so that we lose very little in terms of actual constructions. Specifically it is easy to show appropriate security under concurrent attack for the Schnorr [35], Okamoto [31], and GQ [24,23] protocols as well as others, using techniques from the original papers and more recent analyses [4,2]. Thereby we obtain numerous specific and efficient constructions of two-tier signatures via the FS transform.

We think this is an interesting application of concurrent security of protocols. The latter is usually motivated as being important for certain communication environments such as the Internet, while we are saying it is relevant to the security of a protocol-based signature.

FROM UF-CMA TO SUF-CMA. Returning again to regular (rather than two-tier) signatures, recall that strong unforgeability (suf-cma) is a stronger requirement than the usual uf-cma of [22], requiring not only that the adversary can't produce a signature of a new message but also that it can't produce a new signature of an old message (i.e. one whose signature it has already obtained via its chosen-message attack). The problem we are interested in is to convert a uf-cma scheme into a suf-cma one without using random oracles. Our work is motivated by Boneh, Shen and Waters [8] who turn Waters' uf-cma scheme [38] into an suf-cma one via a transform that applies to a subclass of signature schemes that they call *partitioned*. Unfortunately, there seem to be hardly any schemes in this class besides Waters', so their transform is of limited utility. We, instead, provide a general transform that applies to *any* uf-cma scheme. The transform uses as a tool any two-tier scheme. Instantiating the latter with a FS-based two-tier scheme we obtain efficient, standard model transforms. For example, using the Schnorr scheme, our transform confers suf-cma while adding just one exponentiation to the signing time and increasing the signature size by only two group elements. Briefly, the idea of the transform is to have two signatures, one from the original uf-cma scheme and the other from the two-tier scheme, mutually authenticate each other. This application exploits the fact that our FS-based two-tier signatures are themselves strongly unforgeable due to properties of the starting protocols. (That is, if the adversary has seen the signature of m relative to a secondary public key, it can produce neither a different signature of m nor a signature of some $m' \neq m$ relative to the same secondary key.)

NEW ONE-TIME SIGNATURES. A two-tier signature scheme yields a one-time signature scheme as a special case. (Restrict to a single secondary key.) Thus we obtain FS-based strongly unforgeable one-time signatures. These turn out to be interesting because they have smaller key and signature sizes than conventional one-way function based one-time schemes of the same computational cost. Specifically, say we are signing a 160-bit message (which is the hash of the real message). Our Schnorr-instantiated FS-based one-time scheme implemented over a 160-bit elliptic curve group has key size 480 bits, signature size 160 bits, key-generation time 2 exponentiations, signing time 1 multiplication, and verifying time 1 exponentiation. Let us contrast this with what is achieved by the best one-way function based one-time signature schemes, namely those of [15,6]. Unforgeability is proved by [15] under the assumption that the one-way function is quasi-one-way. We observe that the scheme is strongly unforgeable under the additional assumption that the function is collision-resistant. So, let us use SHA-1 as the one-way function. The resulting schemes exhibit the following size to computation tradeoff. For any positive integer t dividing 160, there is a one time scheme with key and signature size $(1 + 160/t) \cdot 160$ and key-generation, signing and verifying time $(160/t) \cdot 2^t$ hash computations. An implementation with the crypto++ library [12] indicates that an exponentiation in a 160-bit group costs about $3,300$ hashes. To match the key-generation time of 2 exponentiations (which is the largest of the computation times in our algebraic scheme) we thus want to choose t such that $(160/t) \cdot 2^t \approx 6,600$. Let us (generously) set $t = 10$. The key and signature size now becomes $2,720$ bits, which is much more than in our scheme. (And at this point, while key-generation time in the one-way function scheme is essentially the same as in our scheme, signing time is much more.) Note we would get the same efficiency gains using the standard Schnorr [35] scheme instead of our scheme, but the proof of the former uses random oracles [32].

Our new one-time signature scheme is interesting for applications like the DDN and Lindell constructions of IND-CCA public-key encryption schemes [14,27], the IBE-based constructions of IND-CCA schemes of [9], and the composition of encryption schemes [13]. All of these make use of strongly unforgeable one-time signatures, and the reduced key size of the latter results in reduced ciphertext size for the encryption schemes they build.

ALTERNATIVE TWO-TIER SCHEMES AND THEIR IMPLICATIONS. We noted above that two-tier schemes yield (strongly unforgeable) one-time ones as a special case. Conversely, however, one can also construct a two-tier scheme from any strongly unforgeable one-time scheme. (Set the primary keys to empty, and use a new instance of the one-time scheme for each secondary key. See [5] for details.)

One implication of this observation is that we can obtain one-way function based constructions of the primitives we have been discussing, thereby answering the main foundational question about their existence. Specifically, as we discuss in more detail in [5], it is easy to build UOWHF [29] based strongly unforgeable one-time schemes. Since UOWHFs exist given any one-way function [34], we obtain one-way function based two-tier schemes. We also obtain a one-way function based transform of uf-cma signature schemes into suf-cma ones. This yields a somewhat simpler construction of a one-way function based suf-cma signature scheme than given by Goldreich in [19].

However, the above observation (that strongly unforgeable one-time schemes yield two-tier schemes) also raises some questions. The first of these is, what is the point of FS-based two-tier schemes given that there are other ways to build two-tier schemes? However, the same question can be asked about the use of the FS transform to build regular signatures, for of course regular signatures can be built in other ways too. In both cases the point is that FS-based constructs have efficiency or other properties not provided by other constructs. (Specifically, FS-based two-tier schemes have smaller key and signature sizes than two-tier schemes of the same computational cost built from any known strongly unforgeable one-time schemes.) One might also ask what is the point of introducing two-tier schemes at all. Indeed, we could have based our transform (of uf-cma schemes into suf-cma ones) on strongly unforgeable one-time schemes rather than on two-tier schemes, and we could have built FS-based strongly unforgeable one-time schemes directly rather than building two-tier schemes. Two-tier schemes however have the advantage over using one-time schemes that any key information that is long-lived across multiple instances of a one-time scheme can be re-used, resulting in shorter keys. This results in shorter signatures for the suf-cma schemes built by our transform. Another advantage is improved concrete security: the reduction from suf-cma signatures to two-tier and uf-cma signatures is tight, whereas if we had used one-time signatures, we would incur a factor of the number of signing queries. Furthermore our reductions from identification protocols to two-tier schemes derived via the FS transform are tight too. Overall it seemed simple and worthwhile enough to make the optimization (meaning to introduce and use two-tier signatures) and hence we have done so.

RELATED WORK. Cramer and Damgård [11] present a non-RO transform of protocols with certain properties into signature schemes. Their transform is not the FS one (it is more complex and less efficient) but they obtain regular unforgeable signature schemes while we obtain only two-tier schemes.

Independently of our work, others have extended [8] to provide general transforms of unforgeable signature schemes into strongly unforgeable ones. The transform of Huang, Wong and Zhao [26] is similar to the special case of ours with a two-tier signature scheme built from a collision-resistant hash function based one-time signature scheme. However, this yields large signatures. Teranishi, Oyama and Ogata [37] present a discrete log, chameleon commitment based transform that is very efficient.

2 Definitions

NOTATION AND CONVENTIONS. We denote by $a_1 \| \cdots \| a_n$ a string encoding of $a_1, \ldots, a_n$ from which the constituent objects are uniquely recoverable. We denote the empty string by ε. Unless otherwise indicated, an algorithm may be randomized. A collision for a function h is a pair x, y of distinct points in its domain such that $h(x) = h(y)$. If A is a randomized algorithm then $y \xleftarrow{\$} A(x_1, \ldots)$ denotes the operation of running A with fresh coins on inputs $x_1, \ldots$ and letting y denote the output. If S is a (finite) set then $s \xleftarrow{\$} S$ denotes the operation of picking s uniformly at random from S.

SIGNATURES. A (digital) signature scheme $\mathsf{DS} = (\mathsf{KG}, \mathsf{SGN}, \mathsf{VF})$ is specified as usual by three algorithms. Via $(PK, SK) \xleftarrow{\$} \mathsf{KG}$ a prospective signer can generate its public and associated secret key. Via $\sigma \xleftarrow{\$} \mathsf{SGN}(SK, M)$ the signer can produce a signature σ on a message $M \in \{0, 1\}^*$. Via $d \leftarrow \mathsf{VF}(PK, M, \sigma)$, a verifier can run the deterministic verification algorithm to get a decision bit $d \in \{0, 1\}$. We require perfect consistency, meaning that

$$\Pr\left[\, \mathsf{VF}(PK, M, \sigma) = 1 \ : \ (PK, SK) \xleftarrow{\$} \mathsf{KG} \,;\, \sigma \xleftarrow{\$} \mathsf{SGN}(SK, M) \,\right] = 1$$

for all messages M. To define security consider the following game involving an adversary A:

$$(PK, SK) \xleftarrow{\$} \mathsf{KG} \,;\, (M, \sigma) \xleftarrow{\$} A^{\mathsf{SGN}(SK, \cdot)}(PK) \,.$$

The adversary is given a signing oracle and the public key, and outputs a message and candidate signature. Let $M_1, \ldots, M_q$ denote the messages queried by A to its oracle in its chosen-message attack, and let $\sigma_1, \ldots, \sigma_q$ denote the signatures returned by the oracle, respectively. We say that A forges if $\mathsf{VF}(PK, M, \sigma) = 1$ and $M \notin \{M_1, \ldots, M_q\}$. We say that A strongly forges if $\mathsf{VF}(PK, M, \sigma) = 1$ and $(M, \sigma) \notin \{(M_1, \sigma_1), \ldots, (M_q, \sigma_q)\}$. We let $\mathbf{Adv}_{\mathsf{DS}}^{\mathrm{uf\text{-}cma}}(A)$ and $\mathbf{Adv}_{\mathsf{DS}}^{\mathrm{suf\text{-}cma}}(A)$ denote, respectively, the probability that A forges and the probability that it strongly forges. The first measure represents the standard uf-cma notion of [22], while the second represents strong unforgeability (suf-cma).

SYNTAX OF TWO-TIER SIGNATURE SCHEMES. A two-tier signature scheme $\mathsf{ds} = (\mathsf{pkg}, \mathsf{skg}, \mathsf{sgn}, \mathsf{vf})$ is specified by four algorithms. They are called the primary key-generation, secondary key-generation, signing and verifying algorithms, respectively, and the last is deterministic. Via $(ppk, psk) \xleftarrow{\$} \mathsf{pkg}$, a prospective signer generates a primary public key ppk and associated primary secret key psk. Think of these as the keys at the first tier of the two-tier scheme. The signer may then at any time generate a secondary public key spk and associated secondary secret key ssk via $(spk, ssk) \xleftarrow{\$} \mathsf{skg}(ppk, psk)$. These will be the second tier keys, and there can be many of them. Via $s \xleftarrow{\$} \mathsf{sgn}(psk, ssk, m)$ the signer can generate a signature of a message m. Via $d \leftarrow \mathsf{vf}(ppk, spk, m, s)$, a verifier can produce a decision bit $d \in \{0, 1\}$ indicating whether or not s is a valid signature of m relative to ppk, spk. We require perfect consistency, meaning that for all messages m, $\mathsf{vf}(ppk, spk, m, s) = 1$ with probability 1 in the following experiment:

$$(ppk, psk) \xleftarrow{\$} \mathsf{pkg} \,;\, (spk, ssk) \xleftarrow{\$} \mathsf{skg}(ppk, psk) \,;\, s \xleftarrow{\$} \mathsf{sgn}(psk, ssk, m) \,.$$

In usage, a signer will have a single primary key pair. It will, however, use a fresh secondary key pair for each message, meaning the secondary key pairs are one-time. Since generation of a secondary key pair does not require knowing the message, this generation can either be done when the message to be signed arrives, or off-line, in advance.

SECURITY OF TWO-TIER SIGNATURE SCHEMES. To define security, consider the following game. We let $(ppk, psk) \xleftarrow{\$} \mathsf{pkg}$, initialize a set U to $\emptyset$ and initialize

Oracle SPKO()	Oracle SIGNO(j, m)
$i \leftarrow i + 1$	If $j > i$ OR $j \in U$ then return $\perp$
$(spk_i, ssk_i) \stackrel{\$}{\leftarrow} \mathsf{skg}(ppk, psk)$	$U \leftarrow U \cup \{j\}$; $m_j \leftarrow m$
Return spk_i	$s_j \stackrel{\$}{\leftarrow} \mathsf{sgn}(psk, ssk_j, m_j)$
	Return s_j

Fig. 1. Oracles for adversary attacking two-tier scheme $\mathsf{ds} = (\mathsf{pkg}, \mathsf{skg}, \mathsf{sgn}, \mathsf{vf})$

a counter i to 0. We then run an adversary A on input ppk with access to the oracles shown in Figure 1. A can obtain a fresh secondary public key at any time by calling its secondary public-key oracle SPKO. A can obtain a signature of a message m of its choice under an already generated secondary public key spk_j by calling the signing oracle SIGNO on inputs j, m, where $j \geq 1$. However, A cannot obtain more than one signature under a particular secondary public key. (This restriction is enforced by the oracle via the set U.) Finally A outputs a forgery, which must be a triple of the form (l, m, s). Let $(j_1, m_1), \ldots, (j_q, m_q)$ denote the queries made by A to its SIGNO oracle in its chosen-message attack, and let $s_1, \ldots, s_q$ denote the signatures returned by the oracle, respectively. We say that A wins if $\mathsf{vf}(ppk, spk_l, m, s) = 1$ and $1 \leq l \leq i$ but $(l, m, s) \notin \{(j_1, m_1, s_1), \ldots, (j_q, m_q, s_q)\}$. Here i is the final value of the counter, meaning the number of queries A made to SPKO. The probability that A wins is denoted $\mathbf{Adv}_{\mathsf{ds}}^{\mathsf{suf\text{-}cma}}(A)$.

Notice that this definition is of strong unforgeability, meaning this has been built in as a requirement. We do this because it is what the applications need and also what the FS-based constructs naturally provide.

DISCUSSION. Two-tier schemes are hybrids of regular and one-time schemes. If the secondary keys are empty, we have a regular scheme. If the primary keys are empty, we have multiple instances of a one-time scheme.

3   From uf-cma to suf-cma

Suppose we are given a uf-cma signature scheme DS and want to transform it into a suf-cma signature scheme $\overline{\mathsf{DS}}$, efficiently and without random oracles. This problem was recently considered by [8] who provided a transform that works under the assumption that the starting uf-cma scheme is what they call "partitioned." However, there are few examples of partitioned schemes. In this section, we provide a general transform, namely one that applies to any starting uf-cma scheme. It uses an arbitrary two-tier scheme as an auxiliary tool. The transform does not use random oracles, and, when instantiated with appropriate FS-based two-tier schemes, matches that of [8] in computational overhead while providing signatures that are longer by only one group element.

THE TRANSFORM. Let $\mathsf{DS} = (\mathsf{KG}, \mathsf{SGN}, \mathsf{VF})$ be the given uf-cma scheme. Let $\mathsf{ds} = (\mathsf{pkg}, \mathsf{skg}, \mathsf{sgn}, \mathsf{vf})$ be a (any) given two-tier scheme. We associate to these the signature scheme $\overline{\mathsf{DS}} = (\overline{\mathsf{KG}}, \overline{\mathsf{SGN}}, \overline{\mathsf{VF}})$ defined as follows. The key-generation algorithm $\overline{\mathsf{KG}}$ runs KG to get (PK, SK), runs pkg to get (ppk, psk), and returns $\overline{PK} = PK\|ppk$ as the public key and $\overline{SK} = SK\|psk$ as the secret key. The new signing and verifying algorithms are as follows:

Algorithm $\overline{\mathsf{SGN}}(\overline{SK}, \overline{M})$	Algorithm $\overline{\mathsf{VF}}(\overline{PK}, \overline{M}, \overline{S})$
Parse $\overline{SK}$ as $SK\|psk$	Parse $\overline{PK}$ as $PK\|ppk$
$(spk, ssk) \xleftarrow{\$} \mathsf{skg}(ppk, psk)$	Parse $\overline{S}$ as $S\|spk\|s$
$M \leftarrow spk\|\overline{M}$	$M \leftarrow spk\|\overline{M}$
$S \xleftarrow{\$} \mathsf{SGN}(SK, M)$	If $\mathsf{VF}(PK, M, S) = 0$ then return 0
$s \xleftarrow{\$} \mathsf{sgn}(psk, ssk, S)$	If $\mathsf{vf}(ppk, spk, S, s) = 0$ then return 0
$\overline{S} \leftarrow S\|spk\|s$	Return 1
Return $\overline{S}$	

The following implies that the constructed scheme $\overline{\mathsf{DS}}$ is strongly unforgeable if DS is unforgeable and the two-tier scheme ds is strongly unforgeable. The proof may be found in [5].

Theorem 1. *Let $\overline{\mathsf{DS}}$ be the signature scheme associated to signature scheme DS and two-tier signature scheme ds as described above. Let $\overline{F}$ be an adversary attacking the strong unforgeability of $\overline{\mathsf{DS}}$ and making at most q signing queries. Then there exist adversaries F, f attacking the unforgeability of DS and the strong unforgeability of ds, respectively, such that*

$$\mathbf{Adv}_{\overline{\mathsf{DS}}}^{\mathrm{suf\text{-}cma}}(\overline{F}) \leq \mathbf{Adv}_{\mathsf{DS}}^{\mathrm{uf\text{-}cma}}(F) + \mathbf{Adv}_{\mathsf{ds}}^{\mathrm{suf\text{-}cma}}(f) .$$

Furthermore F and f make at most q signing queries, and their running times are that of $\overline{F}$ plus an overhead that is linear in q. ∎

4   Constructions of Two-Tier Schemes

CANONICAL IDENTIFICATION PROTOCOLS. The FS transform applies to a class of protocols we call canonical identification protocols [1]. We need to have a general syntax for these protocols since the transform and its proof will refer to this. The protocol can be described as a tuple $\mathsf{ID} = (\mathcal{K}, P, \mathrm{ChSet}, V)$. Via $(pk, sk) \xleftarrow{\$} \mathcal{K}$, the (honest) prover generates its public and secret keys. Now the public key pk is viewed as an input for the verifier, while sk is a private input to the honest prover. The prover can now convince the verifier of its identity via a three move interaction as depicted in Figure 2. We refer to the moves as commitment, challenge, and response. The (honest) prover maintains a state St whose initial value is its secret key sk. In its first move, it applies P to the current conversation (which is ε) and current state (St $= sk$) to get a commitment CM and an updated state St. The former is sent to the verifier, who now draws its challenge CH at random from ChSet and sends this to the prover. The (honest) prover now lets RP $\xleftarrow{\$} P(\mathrm{CM}\|\mathrm{CH}, \mathrm{St})$ and sends RP back to the verifier. The latter applies the deterministic function V to pk and the transcript CM$\|$CH$\|$RP to output the decision DEC $\in \{0, 1\}$. We require *perfect completeness*, meaning

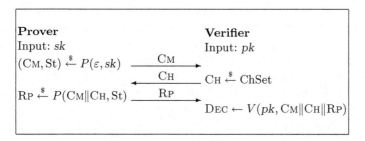

Fig. 2. Canonical Protocol. Keys pk and sk are produced using key generation algorithm $\mathcal{K}$.

that for all (pk, sk) that can be output by $\mathcal{K}$ we have $V(pk, \text{CM}\|\text{CH}\|\text{RP}) = 1$ with probability 1 in the following experiment:

$$(\text{CM}, \text{St}) \stackrel{\$}{\leftarrow} P(\varepsilon, sk)\,;\ \text{CH} \stackrel{\$}{\leftarrow} \text{ChSet}\,;\ \text{RP} \stackrel{\$}{\leftarrow} P(\text{CM}\|\text{CH}, \text{St})\,. \tag{1}$$

Examples of canonical identification protocols include the Schnorr protocol [35] illustrated in Figure 3 and the Okamoto protocol [31] illustrated in Figure 4.

SECURITY NOTIONS. The "master" property of protocols in this domain is *special soundness*. We will consider it under different forms of attack, namely passive, active and concurrent. (We only use the last in our results but for discussions it is useful to see them all.) To define these consider the following game involving an attacker I. The game begins by picking keys via $(pk, sk) \stackrel{\$}{\leftarrow} \mathcal{K}$. Then there are two phases. In the first phase, adversary I gets to mount its attack on the honest prover. In a passive attack, it gets an oracle that upon being invoked (with no arguments) returns a random transcript of an interaction between the honest prover (given input sk) and the verifier (given input pk). In an active or concurrent attack, I gets to play the role of verifier and interact with "clones" of the honest prover. We can imagine a sequence P_j $(j \geq 1)$ of potential clones. Each clone maintains a state St_j and has its own random coins. The game maintains a counter a, initially 0, and a set A of clones that are *activated*, initially empty. Adversary I can ask for a new clone to be activated, in which case the game increments a, computes $(\text{CM}_a, \text{St}_a) \stackrel{\$}{\leftarrow} P(\varepsilon, sk)$, and returns CM_a to I. If the attack is concurrent, it adds a to A, but if the attack is active, it replaces A by $\{a\}$, meaning that only one clone can be activated at any time. If $j \in A$ then I can send clone P_j a message CH_j representing the verifier move. Adversary I can pick this value any way it wishes, in particular not necessarily at random like the honest verifier. The game computes $\text{RP}_j \stackrel{\$}{\leftarrow} P(\text{CM}_j\|\text{CH}_j, \text{St}_j)$, returns RP_j to I, and removes j from A. (Which means no further interaction with P_j is possible.) Note that the difference between an active and concurrent attack is that in the former, the adversary is allowed to have only one clone (namely P_a) activated at any time, corresponding to sequential interactions with the honest prover, while in a concurrent attack, any number of clones may simultaneously be activated, and I can choose a challenge sent to one of them as a function of all communications it has received from all clones so far. Note that in either case, the adversary does not see or control the internal state of a prover clone. In no case can it reset or backup a clone. After it has completed its attack (of whatever form), we enter the second phase. The adversary outputs a pair $(\mathrm{CM}, \mathrm{CH}_1, \mathrm{RP}_1), (\mathrm{CM}, \mathrm{CH}_2, \mathrm{RP}_2)$ of transcripts where the commitment is the same. It wins if these transcripts are accepting but $(\mathrm{CH}_1, \mathrm{RP}_1) \neq (\mathrm{CH}_2, \mathrm{RP}_2)$. The probability that it wins is denoted $\mathbf{Adv}_{\mathsf{ID}}^{\text{ss-atk}}(I)$, where atk = pa if the attack is passive; atk = aa if the attack is active; and atk = ca if the attack is concurrent.

DISCUSSION. The typical formulation of special soundness is that given a pair $(\mathrm{CM}, \mathrm{CH}_1, \mathrm{RP}_1), (\mathrm{CM}, \mathrm{CH}_2, \mathrm{RP}_2)$ of accepting transcripts where the commitment is the same but $\mathrm{CH}_1 \neq \mathrm{CH}_2$, one can easily find a matching secret key sk. This implies in particular that the protocol is a proof of knowledge of the secret key which in turn is crucial to proving security against impersonation under passive, active or concurrent attack. (Impersonation means that after its attack, meaning in the second phase, rather than outputting a pair of transcripts, the adversary plays the role of prover in an interaction with the honest verifier and wins if it can convice the latter to accept.) For our purposes, however, we work directly with special soundness rather than any of its derivative properties. We directly require that the probability of finding transcripts of the appropriate type is negligible rather than relating this to finding the secret key. This is similar to the security requirement used in [11], though they apply it to a different protocol-based transform. Note we weaken the condition under which the adversary wins from $\mathrm{CH}_1 \neq \mathrm{CH}_2$ to $(\mathrm{CH}_1, \mathrm{RP}_1) \neq (\mathrm{CH}_2, \mathrm{RP}_2)$. We will have to prove that the resulting stronger security requirement is met by the constructs.

A Σ protocol is one that has special soundness and honest-verifier zero-knowledge. We do not explicitly require the latter as part of special soundness, although in establishing special soundness of particular protocols we might use it. Note none of the example protocols in this domain are full (i.e. even against cheating verifiers) zero-knowledge. Indeed, this is ruled out under blackbox simulation [20].

Special soundness is usually considered as a stand-alone property, but it is natural to consider it under the three forms of attack that exist for identification protocols as we have done.

For our particular transform, we require special soundness under concurrent attack, rather than active or passive. This is necessary for our proof due to the nature of two-tier signatures and our security definition. In our transform, each request for a new secondary key will require the instantiation of a new clone. Each clone will be required for a signature using its corresponding key, and since the adversary is not required to sign on a key immediately after acquiring it, it is necessary to have multiple clones active at a time. For this reason, we require security under concurrent attack.

THE TRANSFORM. We now describe how to turn a canonical identification protocol $\mathsf{ID} = (\mathcal{K}, P, \mathsf{ChSet}, V)$ into a two-tier signature scheme $\mathsf{ds} = (\mathsf{pkg}, \mathsf{skg}, \mathsf{sgn}, \mathsf{vf})$ via the Fiat-Shamir transform. We do not use a random oracle but instead a family $H : \{0,1\}^k \times \{0,1\}^* \to \mathsf{ChSet}$ of collision-resistant (CR) hash functions where each k-bit key K specifies a particular hash function $H(K, \cdot)$ with range the challenge set ChSet. (The keys will be random but public.) The primary key generation algorithm pkg lets $K \xleftarrow{\$} \{0,1\}^k$ and $(pk, sk) \xleftarrow{\$} \mathcal{K}$, and returns $(ppk, psk) \leftarrow (K\|pk, K\|sk)$. The skg, sgn, and vf algorithms are as follows:

skg(ppk, psk)	sgn(psk, ssk, m)	vf(ppk, spk, m, s)
Parse ppk as $K\|pk$	Parse psk as $K\|sk$	Parse ppk as $K\|pk$
Parse psk as $K\|sk$	Parse ssk as $\text{CM}\|\text{St}$	$\text{CM} \leftarrow spk$
$(\text{CM}, \text{St}) \xleftarrow{\$} P(\varepsilon, sk)$	$\text{CH} \leftarrow H(K, \text{CM}\|m)$	$\text{CH} \leftarrow H(K, \text{CM}\|m)$
$spk \leftarrow \text{CM}$	$\text{RP} \xleftarrow{\$} P(\text{CM}\|\text{CH}, \text{St})$	$\text{RP} \leftarrow s$
$ssk \leftarrow \text{CM}\|\text{St}$	$s \leftarrow \text{RP}$	$\text{DEC} \leftarrow V(pk, \text{CM}\|\text{CH}\|\text{RP})$
Return (spk, ssk)	Return s	Return DEC

Note that in generating s, algorithm P will be executed with a challenge that, unlike the one the honest prover expects to receive, is not random. The implications for security are dealt with by the theorem that follows, but at this point we need to first check that it does not lead to a violation of the perfect consistency requirement of two-tier schemes. This is true because the protocol has perfect completeness as per Equation (1), which means for *all* values of the verifier challenge, the prover returns a response that leads the verifier to accept.

SECURITY OF THE TRANSFORM. Recall that the cr-advantage of an adversary F attacking H is $\mathbf{Adv}_H^{\text{cr}}(F)$, defined as follows:

$$\Pr\left[H(K, x_1) = H(K, x_2) \wedge x_1 \neq x_2 \;:\; K \xleftarrow{\$} \{0,1\}^k \;;\; (x_1, x_2) \xleftarrow{\$} F(K) \right] .$$

The following says that if H is CR and ID is secure against concurrent attack then the two-tier scheme derived via the FS transform is secure. The proof may be found in [5].

Theorem 2. *Let* ds $=$ (pkg, skg, sgn, vf) *be the two-tier signature scheme associated to canonical identification protocol* ID $= (\mathcal{K}, P, \text{ChSet}, V)$ *and hash function* $H \colon \{0,1\}^k \times \{0,1\}^* \to \text{ChSet}$ *via the Fiat-Shamir transform as described above. Let f be an adversary attacking the strong unforgeability of* ds *and making at most q signing queries. Then there exists an adversary I attacking the special soundness of* ID *under concurrent attack, and an adversary F attacking the collision-resistance of H, such that*

$$\mathbf{Adv}_{\text{ds}}^{\text{suf-cma}}(f) \leq \mathbf{Adv}_{\text{ID}}^{\text{ss-ca}}(I) + \mathbf{Adv}_H^{\text{cr}}(F) .$$

Furthermore I initiates at most $q + 1$ prover clones, and the running time of I and F is that of f plus a constant amount of overhead. ∎

To instantiate the above we now seek efficient protocols for which we can prove special soundness under concurrent attack. There are actually several such protocols. We illustrate by looking at a pair of examples that are representative due to the proof techniques.

DEFINITIONS. In what follows, G denotes a group whose order p is a prime. (For example an appropriate elliptic curve group, or a subgroup of the group of integers modulo some prime q such that p divides $q - 1$.) Let $G^* = G - \{1\}$ be

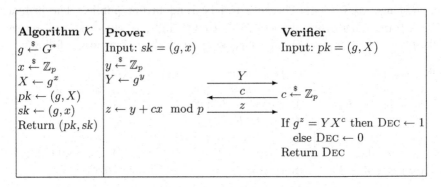

Fig. 3. Schnorr Protocol. Above, G is a group of prime order p, and $\text{ChSet} = \mathbb{Z}_p$.

the set of generators of G, where 1 is the identity element of G. We let $\text{DLog}_g(h)$ denote the discrete logarithm of $h \in G$ to base a generator $g \in G^*$. We assume G, p are fixed and known to all parties. Let

$$\mathbf{Adv}_G^{\text{dl}}(A) \;=\; \Pr\left[\, x' = x \;:\; g \xleftarrow{\$} G^* \,;\, x \xleftarrow{\$} \mathbb{Z}_p \,;\, x' \xleftarrow{\$} A(g, g^x) \,\right]$$

denote the advantage of an adversary A in attacking the discrete logarithm (dl) problem. An adversary A for the one more dl (omdl) problem [3] is given input a generator $g \in G^*$ and has access to two oracles. The first is a challenge oracle $\text{CHO}()$ that takes no inputs and, every time it is invoked, returns a random element of G. The second is a dl oracle $\text{DLog}_g(\cdot)$ that, given any $W \in G$, returns $\text{DLog}_g(W)$. Let $W_1, \ldots, W_q$ denote the responses to A's queries to its challenge oracle. A's goal is to compute the discrete logarithms of all challenges, meaning output $w_1, \ldots, w_q \in \mathbb{Z}_p$ satisfying $g^{w_i} = W_i$ for all $1 \le i \le q$. Of course this is easy because it has a $\text{DLog}_g(\cdot)$ oracle. To make the task non-trivial, however, we restrict A to make strictly less queries to its $\text{DLog}_G(\cdot)$ oracle than it does to its challenge oracle. Let $\mathbf{Adv}_G^{\text{omdl}}(A)$ be the probability that A wins.

SCHNORR IDENTIFICATION PROTOCOL. The Schnorr identification protocol [35] shown in Figure 3 is probably the most "canonical" example of a canonical identification protocol. It is secure against impersonation under passive attack under the dl assumption [35]. Security against impersonation under active (and concurrent) attack, however, remained an open question for a while. Indeed, it does not seem possible to prove this under the dl assumption. Eventually, however, security against impersonation under active and concurrent attack was proved by [4] under the one more dl (omdl) assumption. However, we need special soundness rather than security under impersonation. Also, we need to show that our strong form of special soundness holds, namely that the adversary not only cannot find a pair of accepting transcripts $(\text{CM}, \text{CH}_1, \text{RP}_1), (\text{CM}, \text{CH}_2, \text{RP}_2)$ with $\text{CH}_1 \ne \text{CH}_2$ but cannot even find such transcripts with $\text{CH}_1 = \text{CH}_2$ as long as $\text{RP}_1 \ne \text{RP}_2$. We revisit the proof to establish these things. We make use of the fact that the protocol has a "unique answer" property. The proof of the following may be found in [5].

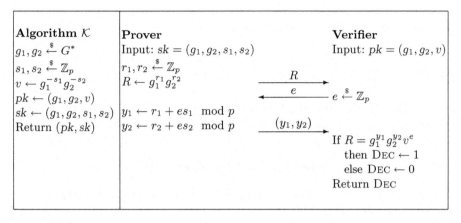

Fig. 4. Okamoto Protocol. Above, G is a group of prime order p, and ChSet $= \mathbb{Z}_p$.

Proposition 1. *Let* $\mathsf{ID} = (\mathcal{K}, P, \mathrm{ChSet}, V)$ *be the Schnorr identification protocol described in Figure 3. Let I be an adversary against the special soundness of* ID *under concurrent attack. Then there exists an omdl adversary A such that*

$$\mathbf{Adv}^{\mathrm{ss-ca}}_{\mathsf{ID}}(I) \leq \mathbf{Adv}^{\mathrm{omdl}}_{G}(A) .$$

Furthermore the running time of A is that of I plus some overhead to compute an inverse and product modulo p, and if I activates q clones, then A makes $q+1$ challenge queries.

We remark that the reduction is tight. In contrast, in the reductions showing security against impersonation [4], $\mathbf{Adv}^{\mathrm{omdl}}_{G}(A)$ is proportional to the *square* of the probability that I succeeds in impersonation. This is an advantage to working directly with special soundness rather than with impersonation. We now sketch a proof based on the ideas of [4].

The two-tier scheme resulting from our FS-based transform instantiated with the Schnorr protocol is very efficient. Generating a secondary key pair takes just one group exponentiation, while signing only requires a multiplication modulo p. In the context of our uf-cma to suf-cma transform of Section 3, this means that the computational overhead for signing (added cost of signing in the suf-cma scheme versus the uf-cma scheme) is just one group exponentiation and the bandwidth overhead (added length of a signature in the suf-cma scheme compared to that in the uf-cma scheme) is one group element and one integer modulo p.

OKAMOTO IDENTIFICATION PROTOCOL. Okamoto's protocol [31] is illustrated in Figure 4. Its advantage is that security can be proved under the standard dl assumption rather than the omdl assumption. (Yet in fact the efficiency is not much different as we will see below.) The idea is that there are many secret keys corresponding to a single public key and witness-indistinguishability [17] can be used in the simulation. The protocol was proved in [31] to be secure against impersonation under active attack assuming hardness of the dl problem, and the proof extends to concurrent attacks. However, again, we need special soundness rather than security under impersonation, and in our new, strong form. The Okamoto protocol, however, does not have the unique answer property. But we can still prove the security we need. We now state the result. The proof may be found in [5].

Proposition 2. *Let* $\mathsf{ID} = (\mathcal{K}, P, \mathrm{ChSet}, V)$ *be the Okamoto identification proto-col described in Figure 4. Let I be an adversary against the special soundness of* ID *under concurrent attack. Then there exists a dl adversary A such that*

$$\mathbf{Adv}_{\mathsf{ID}}^{\mathrm{ss-ca}}(I) \;\leq\; \frac{1}{p} + \mathbf{Adv}_{G}^{\mathrm{dl}}(A) \;.$$

Furthermore the running time of A is that of I plus the time to compute three inverses and three products modulo p. ∎

Again, the reduction is essentially tight due to working with special soundness, whereas the reduction of [31] to establish security against impersonation incurs the square loss we discussed in the context of Schnorr.

   In the two-tier scheme resulting from our FS-transform instantiated with the Okamoto protocol, generating a secondary key pair takes one group exponenti-ation. (It is a multi-exponentiation, which has the same cost as a single one.) Signing requires a couple of multiplications modulo p. So the computational cost is the same as for Schnorr although security relies only on dl rather than omdl. In the context of our uf-cma to suf-cma transform of Section 3, this means that the computational overhead for signing is again just one group exponentiation. But the bandwidth overhead is one group element and two integers modulo p, slightly more than when we used the Schnorr scheme.

ADDITIONAL PROTOCOLS. Above we have discussed two protocols that meet our ss-ca security requirement. We have however identified several more with the property in question. We omit proofs since they are similar to the ones given here, and instead provide a brief discussion. We exclude the Fiat-Shamir protocol from this discussion, as it does not seem to meet our requirements.

   The GQ protocol [24] was proved secure against impersonation under concur-rent attack in [4] under the assumption that RSA is secure against one more inversion [3]. We can extend this proof to show it is ss-ca under the same as-sumption in the same way that we extended the proof of the Schnorr scheme. This protocol has Fiat-Shamir like efficiency yet has small key sizes.

   Shamir presented an identity-based identification scheme in [36]. A corre-sponding standard (i.e. not identity-based) version was presented in [2], along with a variant they called Sh* and proved secure against impersonation under concurrent attack assuming security of RSA under one more inversion. This too can be proved ss-ca under the same assumption. The protocol is however a mirror image of GQ and has the same efficiency attributes as the latter.

   Then there are pairings-based schemes. Both Hs-SI [2] and ChCh-SI [2] are ss-ca secure under the one more computational Diffie-Hellman assumption. These schemes were presented in [2] and are based upon existing identity-based signature schemes, namely those of Hess [25] and Cha and Cheon [10]. Again, the proof of ss-ca extends the proofs of security against impersonation of [2].

Acknowledgements

The first author was supported in part by NSF grant CNS-0524765 and a gift from Intel Corporation. The second author was supported by a UCSD Powell fellowship and the above mentioned grants of the first author.

References

1. M. Abdalla, J. H. An, M. Bellare, and C. Namprempre. From identification to signatures via the Fiat-Shamir transform: Minimizing assumptions for security and forward-security. In *EUROCRYPT 2002*, volume 2332 of *LNCS*. Springer-Verlag.
2. M. Bellare, C. Namprempre, and G. Neven. Security proofs for identity-based identification and signature schemes. In *EUROCRYPT 2004*, volume 3027 of *LNCS*. Springer-Verlag.
3. M. Bellare, C. Namprempre, D. Pointcheval, and M. Semanko. The one-more-RSA-inversion problems and the security of Chaum's blind signature scheme. *Journal of Cryptology*, 16(3):185–215, 2003.
4. M. Bellare and A. Palacio. GQ and Schnorr identification schemes: Proofs of security against impersonation under active and concurrent attacks. In *CRYPTO 2002*, volume 2442 of *LNCS*. Springer-Verlag.
5. M. Bellare and S. Shoup. Two-tier signatures, strongly unforgeable signatures, and fiat-shamir without random oracles. Full version of current paper. Available from authors' web pages.
6. D. Bleichenbacher and U. Maurer. On the efficiency of one-time digital signatures. In *ASIACRYPT'96*, volume 1163 of *LNCS*. Springer-Verlag.
7. D. Boneh, X. Boyen, and H. Shacham. Short group signatures. In *CRYPTO 2004*, volume 3152 of *LNCS*. Springer-Verlag.
8. D. Boneh, E. Shen, and B. Waters. Strongly unforgeable signatures based on computational diffie-hellman. In *PKC 2006*, volume 3958 of *LNCS*. Springer-Verlag.
9. R. Canetti, S. Halevi, and J. Katz. Chosen-ciphertext security from identity-based encryption. In *EUROCRYPT 2004*, volume 3027 of *LNCS*. Springer-Verlag.
10. J. C. Cha and J. H. Cheon. An identity-based signature from gap Diffie-Hellman groups. In *PKC 2003*, volume 2567 of *LNCS*. Springer-Verlag.
11. R. Cramer and I. Damgård. Secure signature schemes based on interactive protocols. In *CRYPTO'95*, volume 963 of *LNCS*. Springer-Verlag.
12. W. Dai. Crypto++ Library. http://www.cryptopp.com/
13. Y. Dodis and J. Katz. Chosen-ciphertext security of multiple encryption. In *TCC 2005*, volume 3378 of *LNCS*. Springer-Verlag.
14. D. Dolev, C. Dwork, and M. Naor. Nonmalleable cryptography. *SIAM Journal on Computing*, 30(2):391–437, 2000.
15. S. Even, O. Goldreich, and S. Micali. On-line/off-line digital signatures. *Journal of Cryptology*, 9(1):35–67, 1996.
16. U. Feige, A. Fiat, and A. Shamir. Zero knowledge proofs of identity. *Journal of Cryptology*, 1(2):77–94, 1988.

17. U. Feige and A. Shamir. Witness indistinguishable and witness hiding protocols. In *22nd ACM STOC*, 1990. ACM Press.
18. A. Fiat and A. Shamir. How to prove yourself: Practical solutions to identification and signature problems. In *CRYPTO'86*, volume 263 of *LNCS*. Springer-Verlag.
19. O. Goldreich. *Foundations of Cryptography: Basic Applications*, volume 2. Cambridge University Press, Cambridge, UK, 2004.
20. O. Goldreich and H. Krawczyk. On the composition of zero-knowledge proof systems. *SIAM Journal on Computing*, 25(1):169–192, Feb. 1996.
21. S. Goldwasser and Y. T. Kalai. On the (in)security of the Fiat-Shamir paradigm. In *44th FOCS*, 2003. IEEE Computer Society Press.
22. S. Goldwasser, S. Micali, and R. L. Rivest. A digital signature scheme secure against adaptive chosen-message attacks. *SIAM Journal on Computing*, 17(2):281–308, Apr. 1988.
23. L. C. Guillou and J.-J. Quisquater. A practical zero-knowledge protocol fitted to security microprocessor minimizing both transmission and memory. In *EURO-CRYPT'88*, volume 330 of *LNCS*. Springer-Verlag.
24. L. C. Guillou and J.-J. Quisquater. A "paradoxical" indentity-based signature scheme resulting from zero-knowledge. In *CRYPTO'88*, volume 403 of *LNCS*. Springer-Verlag.
25. F. Hess. Efficient identity based signature schemes based on pairings. In *SAC 2002*, volume 2595 of *LNCS*. Springer-Verlag.
26. Q. Huang, D. S. Wong, and Y. Zhaoe. Generic transformation to strongly unforgeable signatures. Cryptology ePrint Archive, Report 2006/346, 2006. http://eprint.iacr.org/2006/346.
27. Y. Lindell. A simpler construction of cca2-secure public-key encryption under general assumptions. *Journal of Cryptology*, 19(3):359–377, 2006.
28. S. Micali, K. Ohta, and L. Reyzin. Accountable-subgroup multisignatures. In *ACM CCS 01*, 2001. ACM Press.
29. M. Naor and M. Yung. Universal one-way hash functions and their cryptographic applications. In *21st ACM STOC*, 1989. ACM Press.
30. K. Ohta and T. Okamoto. On concrete security treatment of signatures derived from identification. In *CRYPTO'98*, volume 1462 of *LNCS*. Springer-Verlag.
31. T. Okamoto. Provably secure and practical identification schemes and corresponding signature schemes. In *CRYPTO'92*, volume 740 of *LNCS*. Springer-Verlag.
32. D. Pointcheval and J. Stern. Security proofs for signature schemes. In *EURO-CRYPT'96*, volume 1070 of *LNCS*. Springer-Verlag.
33. D. Pointcheval and J. Stern. Security arguments for digital signatures and blind signatures. *Journal of Cryptology*, 13(3):361–396, 2000.
34. J. Rompel. One-way functions are necessary and sufficient for secure signatures. In *22nd ACM STOC*, 1990. ACM Press.
35. C.-P. Schnorr. Efficient signature generation by smart cards. *Journal of Cryptology*, 4(3):161–174, 1991.
36. A. Shamir. Identity-based cryptosystems and signature schemes. In *CRYPTO'84*, volume 196 of *LNCS*. Springer-Verlag.
37. I. Teranishi, T. Oyama, and W. Ogata. General conversion for obtaining strongly existentially unforgeable signatures. In *INDOCRYPT 2006*, LNCS.
38. B. R. Waters. Efficient identity-based encryption without random oracles. In *EUROCRYPT 2005*, volume 3494 of *LNCS*.

Improved On-Line/Off-Line Threshold Signatures

Emmanuel Bresson[1], Dario Catalano[2,*], and Rosario Gennaro[3]

[1] DCSSI Crypto Lab, 51 bd de La Tour-Maubourg, 75700 PARIS 07 SP, France
emmanuel.bresson@polytechnique.org
[2] Dipartimento di Matematica e Informatica, Università di Catania, Viale Andrea
Doria 6, 95125 Catania, Italy
catalano@dmi.unict.it
[3] I.B.M. T.J.Watson Research Center, P.O.Box 704, Yorktown Heights, NY 10598
rosario@us.ibm.com

Abstract. At PKC 2006 Crutchfield, Molnar, Turner and Wagner proposed a generic threshold version of on-line/off-line signature schemes based on the "hash-sign-switch" paradigm introduced by Shamir and Tauman. Such a paradigm strongly relies on *chameleon hash functions* which are collision-resistant functions, with a secret trapdoor which actually allows to find arbitrary collisions efficiently. The "hash-sign-switch" paradigm works as follows. In the off-line phase, the signer hashes and signs a random message s. When, during the on-line phase, he is given a message m to sign the signer uses its knowledge of the hash trapdoor to find a second preimage and "switches" m with the random s. As shown by Crutchfield *et al.* adapting this paradigm to the threshold setting is not trivial. The solution they propose introduces additional computational assumptions which turn out to be implied by the so-called one-more discrete logarithm assumption.

In this paper we present an alternative solution to the problem. As in the previous result by Crutchfield *et al.*, our construction is *generic* and can be based on any threshold signature scheme, combined with a chameleon hash function based on discrete log. However we show that, by appropriately modifying the chameleon function, our scheme can be proven secure based *only* on the traditional discrete logarithm assumption. While this produces a slight increase in the cost of the off-line phase, the efficiency of the on-line stage (the most important when optimizing signature computation) is unchanged. In other words the *efficiency* is essentially preserved. Finally, we show how to achieve *robustness* for our scheme. Compared to the work by Crutchfield *et al.*, our main solution tolerates at most $\lceil n/4 \rceil$ (arbitrarily) malicious players instead of $\lceil n/3 \rceil$ however we stress that we do not rely on random oracles in our proofs. Moreover we briefly present a variant which can achieve robustness in the presence of $\lceil n/3 \rceil$ malicious players.

---

* Work partially done while CNRS Researcher at the Laboratoire d'Informatique de l'Ecole Normale Superieure, Paris, France.

T. Okamoto and X. Wang (Eds.): PKC 2007, LNCS 4450, pp. 217–232, 2007.

1 Introduction

In a threshold signature scheme [6], digital signatures can be produced by a group of n players (rather than by one party) who hold the secret key in a shared form among them. In order to produce a valid signature on a given message m, the individual players engage in a communication protocol that has the signature as its output: a simplified way to think about this is that each player produces a *partial signature* on the message, and then the players combine them into a full signature on m. A threshold signature scheme achieves threshold $t < n$, if no coalition of t (or less) players can produce a new valid signature, even after the system has produced many signatures on different messages. Threshold signatures are mainly motivated by the need to protect signature keys from the attack of internal and external adversaries: by keeping these keys shared, the adversary must compromise at least $t+1$ servers to learn the private signing key. Threshold signatures have found many practical applications, not only in the area of protecting high-security keys (such as the signature key of a certification authority), but also as a tool implementing secure distributed protocols, such as large-scale distributed data storage systems [17,19].

The most serious obstacle in the practical deployment of threshold signatures is the time needed to compute signatures, since the "normal" costs of public-key operations required by a "centralized" digital signature are magnified by the communication and computations required by the distributed protocol that computes threshold signatures. As pointed out in [4], Pond (a prototype for OceanStore a large-scaled distributed data storage system [17]) spends 86% of its time computing threshold signatures. Thus it is important to look for ways of speeding up signature computation, without compromising security.

The idea proposed in [4] (the inspiration for our work) is to use *on-line/off-line signatures* (introduced in [8]). In these signatures the signing process is divided in two parts: a computationally intensive part which is done off-line, i.e. before the message being signed is known. This off-line part produces some temporary data which is stored and then used at the time the message to be signed is known. At that point, the computation of the actual signature requires very little effort. Such signatures can be constructed starting from any regular digital signature, via combination with one-time signatures (as in [8]) or chameleon hashing ([15,21]). It is also worth pointing out that some digital signature schemes (e.g. the Digital Signature Standard [16]) are intrinsically on-line/off-line.

What we need then, is an *on-line/off-line threshold digital signature*. We should point out that the threshold DSS signatures presented in [12] is an example of such signature. What we are interested however is a *generic* solution: a way to convert any threshold signature into an on-line/off-line one. The work by Crutchfield *et al.* in [4] is the first example of that. They showed how to combine any threshold signature with a threshold version of a specific chameleon hash function based on the discrete logarithm problem (the well known Pedersen commitment [18]). The final result is a reasonably efficient scheme whose security holds under the security of the original signature scheme together with the *one-more discrete-log assumption* (recalled below), which is stronger than the traditional assumption of computational infeasibility of the discrete log function.

OUR RESULTS. We present a new and improved generic on-line/off-line threshold signature scheme. As in [4] we combine any threshold signature scheme, with a chameleon hash function based on discrete log. However our scheme can be proven secure based only on the traditional discrete log assumption. The price to pay is a slight increase in the cost of the off-line signature computation component, but the efficiency of the on-line part remains unchanged with respect to [4]. Thus we present a scheme that without compromising the overall level of efficiency improves [4] on the security assumption.

1.1 The Approach in a Nutshell

First we describe the so-called "hash-sign-switch" paradigm as introduced by Shamir-Tauman [21], that uses chameleon hashing [15] to construct on-line/off-line signatures. Then we discuss the threshold version in [4] and finally our improvement on it.

A chameleon hash function is defined by a public key CH (we use the public key to denote the actual function) and a secret trapdoor T. It takes two arguments a message m and a random string r. The function is collision-resistant, unless one knows the trapdoor T. But knowledge of T allows to find arbitrary collisions, i.e. given $c = CH(m, r)$ and an arbitrary message m', the holder of the trapdoor can find r' such that $c = CH(m', r')$. For many chameleon hash functions, this collision-finding procedure is very efficient, requiring only a single modular multiplication. The Shamir-Tauman [21] idea is to construct on-line/off-line signatures as follows. The off-line part would consists of computing $c = CH(a, r')$ for some arbitrary a, r' and then computes s the signature of c under an ordinary signature scheme. On input the actual message m the signer (who knows the trapdoor T as part of the signing key) computes r such that $c = CH(m, r)$ and outputs r, s. The verifier computes c and verifies s on it.

The contribution of Crutchfield *et al.* is to build a way to compute the values c and r distributively, i.e. by servers who hold T in a shared form. They use Pedersen's commitment [18] as the chameleon hash function: $CH(m, r) = g^r h^m$ in a cyclic group of prime order. To "thresholdize" CH they use techniques developed in the context of discrete-log based threshold cryptography (e.g. [12]). The proof of their scheme has, however, a subtle issue. The proof of security of the threshold scheme in [4] is carried out via simulation: an adversary forging the threshold scheme is transformed via a simulation of the distributed environment into a forger for the centralized scheme, or a collision-finder for CH. In the [4] protocol the value c is revealed to the adversary (who may have corrupted up to t of the signing servers) *before* the final signature is computed (as opposed to the centralized Shamir-Tauman solution where the adversary sees c only after the signature is issued). This in turns means that the simulation of the on-line phase is constrained to use a specific c generated in a simulation performed before m was known. This is why the proof in [4] must use the stronger one-more discrete log assumption.

Our contribution is an alternative way to get around the above problem, so that we do not require this stronger assumption. The basic idea is to use a variation of Pedersen's commitment for the chameleon hashing. We define $CH(m, r, s) = g^m h_1^r h_2^s$. The crucial property of this chameleon hash function is that it has two "independent" trapdoors ($\log_g h_1$ and $\log_g h_2$), and we can give a random one to the simulator to help in performing the simulation[1]. On the other hand if the adversary finds a collision for CH, with probability $1/2$ this collision will reveal the other trapdoor, thus allowing us to solve the discrete log problem.

ON THE DIFFERENCE BETWEEN THE ASSUMPTIONS. Our proof relies on the standard discrete log assumption: given a cyclic group G of prime order q, a generator g, and a random value $y \in G$, find $z \in Z_q$ such that $y = g^x$. This assumption has been widely used and it's the basis of many of the cryptographic schemes used in practice. The assumption used in [4] is stronger since the adversary is given access to an oracle that computes discrete logs: on input y the oracle returns x such that $y = g^x$. The task is then: given k random values in G, $y_1, y_2, \ldots, y_k$, find *all* the discrete logs x_i s.t. $y_i = g^{x_i}$, while being allowed to query the oracle at most $k - 1$ times. This assumption is newer and not as established as the traditional discrete log assumption.

ON THE ROBUSTNESS GUARANTEES. It is desirable in a distributed environment to be able to guarantee robustness. Informally, this means that, even if up to t players behave dishonestly, the remaining honest ones are still able to perform the computation correctly. The scheme proposed in [4] enables such property, either in the random oracle model, or by using a technique pointed out by Damgård and Dupont [5], and provided that $n > 3t + 1$. As a comparison, our technique allows to deal with up to $n/3$ players that can be either *halting* at any time, or arbitrarily *malicious* except during the on-line signing phase. If we want to tolerate malicious players at any step of the protocol, we have to[2] restrict the threshold to $t < n/4$.

1.2   Related Work

As we pointed out, Even *et al.* introduced the notion of on-line/off-line signatures in [8] and constructed them combining regular signatures with efficient one-time signatures. However the length of the signatures is an issue in this approach. Shorter signatures can be obtained by using chameleon hashing [15] combined with regular signatures as pointed out by Shamir and Tauman [21].

---

[1] The idea of using two independent trapdoors to construct a secure digital signature scheme is not new, as it goes back to the seminal paper of Goldwasser, Micali and Rivest [14].

[2] More precisely, it would be possible to tolerate one third of the players behaving maliciously at any time, by using general techniques such as non-interactive zero-knowledge proofs in order to enhance every protocol step with robustness. However, the obtained scheme would have become highly inefficient; we decided to maintain practicability rather than optimizing threshold.

Threshold signature schemes were introduced by Desmedt and Frankel [6]. We point out that threshold DSS signatures (constructed in [12]) are intrinsically on-line/off-line and do not require the extra steps described in this paper or [4]. On the other hand the techniques in this paper allow the underlying signature to be any desired scheme. RSA-based threshold signatures (which can be used as the underlying scheme in our construction) are presented in [11,22].

2   Definitions and Notation

A function $f : \mathbb{N} \to \mathbb{R}$ is said to be negligible if for any $c > 0$, there exists an index $k_c \in \mathbb{N}$ such that $f(k) < k^{-c}$ for all $k > k_c$. PPT stands for Probabilistic Polynomial-Time. In several points in this paper we make use of a cyclic subgroup of prime order in a finite field $\mathbb{Z}_p$. To fix the notations, we denote by p and q two prime numbers such that $q|p-1$ and q is sufficiently large. Moreover, we will denote by G a subgroup of $\mathbb{Z}_p^\star$ with order q and by g a generator of G.

Definition 1 (Discrete logarithm assumption). *Let $k = |q|$ be a security parameter. The Discrete Logarithm (DLOG) Assumption in G states that for any PPT algorithm $\mathcal{A}$, the probability that $\mathcal{A}$ outputs x on input (p, q, g, g^x) is negligible in k (the probability space is on the random choice of p, q, g and $x \in \mathbb{Z}_q$ and the internal coins tosses of $\mathcal{A}$).*

For lack of space we omit the definition of digital signature schemes.

Definition 2 (On-line/off-line signature scheme). *An on-line/off-line signature scheme $\Sigma^{\mathsf{on,off}} = (\mathsf{KeyGen}, \mathsf{Sign}, \mathsf{Ver})$ is a signature scheme in which the signing algorithm Sign can be divided into two phases:*

- *Off-line phase: an algorithm $\mathsf{Sign}^{\mathsf{off}}$ that takes as input the private key and generates a signature token σ^{off},*
- *On-line phase: an algorithm $\mathsf{Sign}^{\mathsf{on}}$ which on input a message m and a signature token σ^{off}, together with the private signing key, produces a signature σ on m.*

For this definition to be of practical interest, it is required that the cost of the on-line phase is as small as possible.

Definition 3 (Threshold signature scheme). *A threshold signature scheme $\mathsf{T}\text{-}\Sigma$ consists of the following PPT algorithms $(\mathsf{T\text{-}KeyGen}, \mathsf{T\text{-}Sign}, \mathsf{Ver})$:*

- *the key generation algorithm $\mathsf{T\text{-}KeyGen}(1^\ell)$ is a distributed key generation algorithm that generates a public key pk and provides each party with a share sk_i of the secret key sk;*
- *the threshold signing protocol $\mathsf{T\text{-}Sign}$ runs in two phases:*
  - *the signature share generation $\mathsf{T\text{-}Sign}^{\mathsf{share}}(m, \{sk_i\})$ is run interactively so that each party obtains a share σ_i of a signature on the message m,*

- the signature reconstruction $\mathsf{T\text{-}Sign}^{\mathsf{combine}}(\{\sigma_i\})$ builds the full signature σ given the generated signature shares σ_i;
- the verification algorithm $\mathsf{Ver}(pk, m, \sigma)$ is unchanged.

It is required that such scheme is simulatable, in the sense of [10]. Also it is worth noticing that the notion is independent of the on-line/off-line feature. Here, we are going to consider "threshold" on-line/off-line signatures. In this case, the signature share generation coincides with the off-line phase of the scheme: the obtained "shares" are generated without knowing the message to be signed; and the signature reconstruction coincides with the on-line phase. For completeness, we provide below a formal definition for such scenario.

Definition 4 (On-line/off-line threshold signature). *An on-line/off-line threshold signature* $\mathsf{T\text{-}\Sigma}^{\mathsf{on,off}}$ *is made of the following components:*

- $\mathsf{T\text{-}KeyGen}(1^\ell)$ *is the distributed key generation algorithm that generates* pk *and provides each party with a share* sk_i;
- $\mathsf{T\text{-}Sign}^{\mathsf{share,off}}$ *is the off-line signature share generation that generates a signature token* σ^{off} *and provides each party with a signature share* σ_i;
- $\mathsf{T\text{-}Sign}^{\mathsf{combine,on}}$ *is the on-line reconstruction phase that, given the message* m *to be signed, produces the final signature* σ *from the token* σ^{off} *and the private signature shares* σ_i;
- Ver *is the verification algorithm (unchanged).*

Security of a threshold signature scheme can be defined in several ways, but the strongest definition (see [12]) requires the protocols to be *simulatable*, which guarantees that the threshold signature scheme is as secure as its centralized version. If the protocol is secure even in the presence of t arbitrarily malicious players, then the protocol is called *robust*.

3   Building Blocks

In this section we briefly discuss some basic protocols that are going to be useful in the sequel. In the following we will denote by n the number of players involved in the protocol (in particular we assume $n \ll q$). We assume that the players are connected through point-to-point private channels and by a broadcast channel. We model failures on the network by allowing the existence of an adversary who is allowed to corrupt up to $t < n/3$ players[3]. The adversary is assumed to be *static*, meaning that the set of corrupted players is chosen at the beginning of the protocol.

All the basic protocols presented in this section require $O(1)$ rounds of communication. We assume that all secrets are shared through a secret sharing scheme *à la Shamir* [20], using polynomials of degree t and, throughout this section, we assume that $t < n/3$. We remark that, for these choices of parameters, all the

---

[3] For the protocols described in the next section, however, we will require $t < n/4$ to guarantee robustness.

following protocols already provide robustness (or they can easily be modified to do so using very standard techniques).

MULTIPLYING TWO SHARED SECRETS. For this task we adopt the well known protocol by Ben-Or et al. [2]. In what follows we denote $\texttt{MUL}[a_i, b_i] \rightarrow [c_i]$ an execution of this protocol, where a_i and b_i are the original shares held by player P_i and c_i is the share obtained after the additional communication round.

We stress that it is well known [2], how to modify the above protocols in order to achieve robustness against a static adversary controlling up to $t < n/3$ players.

PEDERSEN'S VSS. Pedersen's Verifiable Secret Sharing protocol [18], extends Shamir secret sharing scheme [20] in order to tolerate a malicious adversary corrupting up to $n/2$ players, including the dealer. Moreover the scheme preserves the security of the secret in a strong information theoretic sense. In a nutshell the scheme goes as follows. Let h be another generator of G, such that the discrete logarithm of h in base g is unknown and assumed to be hard to compute. In the sharing phase, the dealer $\mathcal{D}$ starts the protocol by choosing two (random) polynomials $f(\cdot)$ and $g(\cdot)$ of degree t, such that $f(0) = a$, where a is the secret being shared. Next, it gives the values $(a_i, r_i) = (f(i), g(i))$ to each participants P_i. Moreover it broadcasts the verification values $V_j = g^{\alpha_j} h^{\beta_j} \bmod p$ where α_j (resp. β_j) is the j-th coefficient of $f(\cdot)$ (resp. $g(\cdot)$). By these positions, each player is allowed to verify the validity of the received shares by simply checking that $g^{a_i} h^{r_i} = \prod_{j=0}^{t} V_j^{i^j} \bmod p$.

If some player holds shares that do not satisfy the equation above, he broadcasts a complain against the dealer. If more than t players do so, the dealer is disqualified. Otherwise the dealer publishes the values $f(i), g(i)$ matching the equation above for each complaining party P_i.

In the reconstruction phase each player P_i is required to reveal both $f(i)$ and $g(i)$. This is to make sure that players provide the (correct) shares they originally received. Notice that a dishonest player can provide incorrect shares that are consistent with the equation above if and only if it can compute the discrete logarithm of h in base g. Thus, Pedersen's VSS guarantees soundness only with respect to polynomially bounded adversaries.

We denote by $\texttt{Ped-VSS}[a, r](g, h, p, q, t, n) \rightarrow [a_i, r_i](V)$ an execution of Pedersen's VSS protocol where the dealer distributes a secret a, using the additional random value r, with public parameters (g, h, p, q, t, n). Moreover, a_i, r_i denote the local (secret) shares received by player P_i at the end of the distribution phase. $V = \{V_j\}$ denotes the set of commitments broadcasted by the dealer during the execution of the protocol.

JOINT PEDERSEN'S VSS. The sharing phase of Pedersen's VSS can be easily generalized to the case where no special dealer is required and where the players jointly generate a random shared secret. We denote with $\texttt{Joint-RPed-VSS}(g, h, p, q, t, n) \rightarrow [a_i, r_i, T_S, a](V, Q)$ the execution of the protocol with public parameters g, h, p, q, t, n and where each player P_i gets as local output the shares a_i, r_i, with a_i referring to the final secret a. Q denotes the subset of $\{1, \ldots, n\}$ of the indexes of the players that have not been disqualified during the execution of the protocol. Finally T_S denotes the transcript produced by the n VSS's executed by the players.

COMPUTING SHARES OF THE INVERSE OF A SHARED SECRET. Let a be an *invertible* element in $\mathbb{Z}_q$. Assume that a is shared among the players and denote with a_i the share held by player P_i. The following protocol, due to Bar-Ilan and Beaver [1], allows to compute shares of b, such that $ab \equiv 1 \bmod q$ from shares of a. The basic idea is as follows. First the players jointly generate a shared random value r (using the protocol described above), then they multiply the two shared secrets a and r by means of the (full) multiplication protocol. To conclude this phase, the players reveal the shares obtained after the execution of the multiplication protocol and they jointly reconstruct the value $u \equiv ar \bmod q$. If $u \equiv 0 \bmod q$ the protocol is restarted. Otherwise u is invertible modulo q and every player can locally compute his share of $a^{-1} \bmod q$ by setting $b_i = r_i \cdot u^{-1} \bmod q$. We denote this protocol by $\texttt{INV}[a_i] \rightarrow [b_i]$.

SHARED EXPONENTIATION OF SECRETS [7]. This allows to compute $g^a h_1^b h_2^c$ when a, b, c are shared secrets. For lack of space the description of this protocol is omitted. The interested reader can find full details in [7]. In the following we will refer to this protocol as $\texttt{Share-Exp}(g, h_1, h_2) \rightarrow (g^a h_1^b h_2^c)$.

DISCRETE LOG-BASED DISTRIBUTED KEY GENERATION [10]. This protocol allows a set of user to securely generate private keys for discrete log based encryption schemes (see [10] for details). In the following we will refer to this protocol as $\texttt{DL-DKG}(g, h, p, q, t, n) \rightarrow [x_i](y, V, Q)$.

4   The New Scheme

We now describe our generic on-line/off-line threshold signature scheme. This scheme can be based on any threshold signature $\mathsf{T}\text{-}\Sigma = (\mathsf{T\text{-}KGen}, \mathsf{T\text{-}Sig}, \mathsf{Ver})$. We will focus on an *optimistic* version of it where, instead of verifying correctness each time a new signature is generated, verification occurs only if a signature happens to be invalid.

Recall that a generic threshold on-line/off-line signature scheme $\mathsf{T}\text{-}\Sigma^{\mathsf{off},\mathsf{on}}$ is composed of the following algorithms

$$\mathsf{T}\text{-}\Sigma^{\mathsf{off},\mathsf{on}} = (\mathsf{T\text{-}KeyGen}, \mathsf{T\text{-}Sign}^{\mathsf{share},\mathsf{off}}, \mathsf{T\text{-}Sign}^{\mathsf{combine},\mathsf{on}}, \mathsf{Ver})$$

In what follows we assume that $t < n/4$.

KEY GENERATION. This protocol is performed only once. The full description is given in Figure 1. We assume that the primes p, q and two generators g, g_1 of a subgroup G of order q in $\mathbb{Z}_p^*$ are given as public parameters to the players. Note that such an assumption can be relaxed using standard techniques: for example it is possible to consider a more general key generation protocol where the parties jointly choose the primes p and q as well as the generators g and g_1. However we believe that such a formulation would only make the presentation

---

On-line/Off-line Threshold Key Generation Protocol

Public Parameters: a set of n players $P_1, \ldots, P_n$, a security parameter k, two
primes p, q such that $q|p - 1$ and $|q| = k$, two elements g, g_1 of order q in $\mathbb{Z}_p^*$, a
threshold parameter $t < n/4$ and a threshold signature scheme T-Σ. We denote
by G the subgroup of $\mathbb{Z}_p^*$ generated by g;
Common Output: the public key of the scheme;
Private Output (for player P_j): a share of the signing secret key.

1. The players jointly run the T-KGen algorithm, on input 1^k. This produces a
   public verification key vk. Moreover each player privately receives a share sk_i
   of the corresponding signing key.
2. The players jointly run the DL-DKG(g, g_1, p, q, t, n) algorithm twice (with parameters g, p, q) in order to obtain two public values h_1, h_2. We denote with y_i
   and z_i the shares of the two secret keys y, z (such that $g^y = h_1$ and $g^z = h_2$)
   held by player P_i.
3. The players run the INV(y_i) protocol to get shares Y_i of the inverse Y of y.
4. The public key is set as $PK = (g, p, q, g_1, vk, h_1, h_2)$, while each player P_i
   retains the quadruple $SK_i = (sk_i, y_i, z_i, Y_i)$ as its own local secret key.

Fig. 1. The Key Generation Protocol for our On-line/off-line Threshold Signature
Scheme

more intricate, thus distracting the reader from the focus of this paper, which
are the protocols for threshold on-line/off-line threshold signatures.

OFF-LINE SIGNING. The signing protocol for the off-line phase is described in
Figure 3. We remark here that every time the Joint-RPed-VSS protocol is executed, the sharing polynomial is tacitly assumed to have degree t.

ON-LINE SIGNING. The signing protocol for the on-line phase is described in
Figure 2. We remark here that no signature share verification is explicitly required by the protocol. This is because we decided to follow an optimistic approach (in general it is reasonable to assume that the signature shares are going
to be correct almost all the time). Still, in order to guarantee robustness, we need
to make sure that, even if some players sent incorrect shares, honest participants
should be able to reconstruct a valid signature. Later we describe how to achieve
that for the case $n > 4t$.

VERIFICATION. Given a purported signature $(\mathsf{Com}, \rho, r, s)$ on a message m, one
accepts it as valid if the following relation is true

$$\mathsf{Ver}(vk, \mathsf{Com}, \rho) \stackrel{?}{=} 1 \quad \wedge \quad \mathsf{Com} \stackrel{?}{=} g^m h_1^r h_2^s$$

ACHIEVING ROBUSTNESS. If the verification procedure $\mathsf{Ver}(vk, \mathsf{Com}, \rho)$ fails, then
some of the participants are providing incorrect shares. In principle, one can
always reconstruct the correct signature as our assumption that $n > 4t$ assures
us enough points to correctly interpolate s' and r'. The trivial approach of trying

---

On-line Threshold Signing Protocol

Public Parameters: A set of n players $P_1, \ldots, P_n$, a security parameter k, two primes p, q such that $q|p-1$ and $|q| = k$, two generators g, g_1 of G, a threshold parameter $t < n/4$ and a threshold signature scheme T-Σ;

Public Input: a message m' to be signed;

Private Input (for player P_j): the signing key $SK_j = (sk_j, y_j, z_j, Y_j)$, together with the signature token $\sigma^{\text{off}} = (\text{Com}, \rho)$ and the signature share $\sigma_i = (\omega_i, \tau_i, s_i')$ produced during the off-line stage;

Public Output: a signature σ for m'

1. Each player broadcasts the share s_i'. This allows the player to locally interpolate the value s'.
2. Each player P_i locally computes the following share

$$r_i' = (\tau_i - m' - s' \cdot z_i) \cdot Y_i + \omega_i \bmod q$$

3. Finally the players broadcast their shares r_i', in order to reconstruct r'.
4. The signature for m' is given by

$$\sigma = (\text{Com}, \rho, r', s')$$

Fig. 2. The signing algorithm for the on-line stage

all the possible subsets of $2t + 1$ shares, however, does not work, as the number of such subsets is in general exponential (in n). Here we suggest the following two-phases approach.

First Phase: In the first phase, the correctness of the s_i''s is verified. This is done though the commitment materials produced during round 6 of the off-line threshold signing protocol. If t shares turn out to be incorrect, this allow us to identify and remove all the dishonest players immediately (and then there is no need to proceed to phase two).

Second Phase: If less than t incorrect shares have been identified in phase one, in round 3 of the on-line phase, the players interpolate the correct r' using the Berlekamp-Welch decoder [3]. The correctness of this approach follows from the error correcting capabilities of polynomial interpolation. Since we are interpolating a polynomial of degree $d = 2t$ and we have up to $f = t$ erroneous points, using the Berlekamp-Welch bound we get that the number of points needed to correctly interpolate is $d + 2f + 1$, which, in our case, means, $2t + 2t + 1 = 4t + 1$ (this is why we required $n > 4t$).

Remark 1. We stress that, the key generation and the off-line signing protocols, can achieve robustness even with respect to an adversary controlling up to $n/3-1$ players (rather than the more restrictive setting $t < n/4$). This is because, as observed in Section 3, all the protocols we are using as building blocks (i.e. those described in Section 3) are already robust against such kind of adversaries, or they can easily be modified to achieve robustness. By contrast, the on-line signing

---

Off-line Threshold Signing Protocol

Public Parameters: a set of n players $P_1, \ldots, P_n$, a security parameter k, two primes p, q such that $q | p - 1$, $|q| = k$, two generators g, g_1 of G, a threshold parameter $t < n/4$ and a threshold signature scheme T-Σ;

Private Input (for player P_j): the local signing key $SK_j = (sk_j, y_j, z_j, Y_j)$;

Private Output (for player P_j): a signature token σ^{off} and a signature share σ_j.

1. The players jointly run the Joint-RPed-VSS(g, g_1, p, q, t, n) protocol three times to produce three shared random values m, r, s. Let m_i, r_i, s_i be the shares obtained by player P_i after participating to the three Joint-RPed-VSS.

2. The players execute the Share-Exp protocol, each holding local inputs m_i, r_i, s_i. Let Com $= g^m h_1^r h_2^s$ be the public output.

3. The players run the (entire) T-Sig algorithm to compute a signature ρ on the message Com.

4. The players run (a simplified version of) the Joint-RPed-VSS algorithm (with parameters g, p, q) to generate shares ω_i of a $2t$-degree (random) polynomial p_0, such that $p_0(0) = 0$.

5. The players run the full multiplication protocol MUL twice to compute shares of the products $r \cdot y$ and $s \cdot z$. Finally they (non interactively) compute shares of the quantity $m + r \cdot y + s \cdot z$. Let τ_i be the share held by player P_i.

6. The players jointly run the Joint-RPed-VSS(g, g_1, p, q, t, n) protocol in order to produce a shared random value s'. Let s_i' be the share obtained by player P_i as a local output.

7. The output signature token is $\sigma^{\text{off}} = (\text{Com}, \rho)$ while the signature share for P_i is $\sigma_i = (\omega_i, \tau_i, s_i')$

Fig. 3. The signing algorithm for the off-line stage

protocol makes use of a reconstruction phase for values that are shared over $2t$-degree polynomials and thus, requires the threshold to be bounded by $n/4$.

5 Security Proof

Theorem 1. *Assuming that* T-Σ = (T-KGen, T-Sig, Ver) *is a threshold signature scheme secure against adaptive chosen message attack and the discrete logarithm assumption holds, the On-Line/Off-line Threshold Signature scheme presented above is existentially unforgeable against an adaptive chosen message attack, mounted by a static adversary controlling up to one fourth of the n participants.*

Proof (Sketch). The proof goes by contradiction, we assume that there exists an adversary $\mathcal{A}$ that breaks the existential unforgeability of the proposed scheme and we show how to exploit it to break either the unforgeability of the underlying signature scheme T-Σ or the discrete logarithm assumption. In other words, we build an efficient algorithm $\mathcal{B}$ that, using $\mathcal{A}$ as a black box, succeeds in the above mentioned tasks.

Notice that, any valid forgery must be of one of the following types

- **Type I:** $(\mathtt{Com}, \rho, s', r')$ on a message m' such that $\mathtt{Com} \neq \mathtt{Com}_i$ for all previously issued signatures $(\mathtt{Com}_i, \rho_i, s'_i, r'_i)$ on messages m'_i,
- **Type II:** $(\mathtt{Com}, \rho, s', r')$ on m' such that $\mathtt{Com} = \mathtt{Com}_i$ for some previously issued signature $(\mathtt{Com}_i, \rho_i, s'_i, r'_i)$ on a message m'_i, but at least two of the following conditions must hold
  1. $m' \neq m'_i$
  2. $s' \neq s'_i$
  3. $r' \neq r'_i$

It is easy to get convinced that the above (mutually exclusive) conditions cover the entire spectrum of possibilities.

TYPE I FORGERIES. We show how to build an algorithm $\mathcal{B}$ against the existential unforgeability of T-Σ using an adversary $\mathcal{A}$ that produces this type of forgeries with non-negligible probability. To do so we start with $\mathcal{B}$ receiving as input, in a preliminary phase, the public key material of a secure threshold signature scheme T-$\Sigma = (\mathsf{T\text{-}KGen}, \mathsf{T\text{-}Sig}, \mathsf{Ver})$. His goal is to use the forgery produced by $\mathcal{A}$ to contradict the existential unforgeability of T-Σ. This means that, after having received a number of signatures $\mathtt{Sig}_i$ for messages M_i of its own choice, $\mathcal{B}$ should be able to produce a couple $(M, \mathtt{Sig})$ such that $\mathtt{Sig}$ is a valid signature for the message M with respect to the given public key (and, of course, $(M, \mathtt{Sig}) \neq (M_i, \mathtt{Sig}_i)$ for all i's).

First note that, being T-Σ a secure threshold signature scheme scheme we require that it is simulatable, in the sense of [10]. In particular this means (see [10]) that:

1. The algorithm T-KGen is simulatable, meaning with this that there exists a simulator S_1 that, on input the verification key and the public output generated by an execution of T-KGen, can simulate the view of the adversary on that execution.
2. The protocol T-Sig is simulatable, meaning with this that there exists a simulator S_2 that, on input the public input of T-Sig, t shares, and the produced signature σ, can simulate the view of the adversary on an execution of T-Sig that outputs σ.

With this in mind we show how to simulate the three protocols presented in the previous section.

On-line/Off-line Threshold Key Generation: $\mathcal{B}$ performs rounds 2, 3 and 4 exactly as in the real game, meaning with this that it plays the role of each honest player exactly as prescribed by the protocol.

Round 1 is done by running the simulator S_1 on input the relevant values $\mathcal{B}$ has received in the preliminary phase.

Thus, by the simulatability property of T-KGen, the entire simulation of T-KeyGen is indistinguishable from a real execution of the protocol.

Off-line Threshold Signing Protocol: $\mathcal{B}$ executes the following variant of the T-Sign$^{\text{share,off}}$ protocol.

Steps 1, 2, 4, 5 and 6 are done exactly as in the original protocol, thus we focus on step 3. At that point $\mathcal{B}$ queries his signing oracle (which is relative to T-Sig) in order to get a signature ρ_i on the computed Com$_i$. Then $\mathcal{B}$ executes the simulator S_2 on input the public parameters, the shares of the controlled players and the value of ρ_i in order to produce the corresponding view. By the simulatability of T-Sig this is indistinguishable from a real execution.

On-line Threshold Signing Protocol: Whenever $\mathcal{A}$ asks the i-th signature query on a message m'_i, $\mathcal{B}$ executes the protocol exactly as prescribed in the previous section.

Now assume that, once $\mathcal{A}$ is done with its signing queries, it produces a forgery of type I $(\rho, \text{Com}, s', r')$ on a message m'. Type I forgery means that Com differs from all Com$_i$ and thus was never queried by $\mathcal{B}$ to its signing oracle. Then $\mathcal{B}$ produces its own forgery against T-Σ by setting $M = \text{Com}$ and $\text{Sig} = \rho$.

TYPE II FORGERIES. We show how to build an algorithm $\mathcal{B}$ that breaks the discrete logarithm assumption using an adversary $\mathcal{A}$ that produces this type of forgeries with non-negligible probability. To do so we start with $\mathcal{B}$ receiving as input, in a preliminary phase, a couple $(g, h) \in G^2$. His goal is to use the forgery produced by $\mathcal{A}$ to determine the discrete log of h in base g.

We assume that $\mathcal{B}$ is allowed to program the common parameters g, g_1, in the sense that it is allowed to set g as the g received in the preliminary phase and to choose g_1 according to a distribution that is perfectly indistinguishable from the distribution according to which g_1 has to be chosen. In particular, notice that this allows $\mathcal{B}$ to choose g_1 in a way such that it knows the discrete log of g_1 in base[4] g. In what follows we assume, for simplicity, that $m' \neq m'_i$ always holds. It is straightforward to extend the proof to the more general case where m' (the forged message) may be equal to m'_i (the message queried for signing).

First, $\mathcal{B}$ flips a coin β. If $\beta = 0$ it bets on the fact that $\mathcal{A}$ will provide a forgery of type II where conditions 1 and 3 above hold true, that is $m' \neq m'_i$ and $r' \neq r'_i$. If $\beta = 1$ $\mathcal{B}$ bets on the fact that the forgery will satisfy $m' \neq m'_i$ and $s' \neq s'_i$. Informally the proof goes in two stages. In the first one $\mathcal{B}$ will simulate a real execution of the protocol, playing the role of non-corrupted parties. In this phase we have to make sure that the simulated protocol is perfectly indistinguishable from the real one. In the second part of the proof, we show how $\mathcal{B}$ can exploit the provided forgery to solve the received discrete logarithm challenge.

As for the first part of the proof, we describe in detail the simulation of the three protocols, described in the previous section.

On-line/Off-line Threshold Key Generation: $\mathcal{B}$ performs steps 1 and 4 exactly as in the real game, meaning with this that it plays the role of each honest player exactly as prescribed by the protocol.

---

[4] Formally this is equivalent to assume that all the public parameters are part of a shared random string, that the simulator is allowed to "program" in the proof.

Step 2 is done as follows. The first execution of the DL-DKG protocol (i.e. the one leading to the generation of h_1) is replaced by a execution of the simulator S for DL-DKG, as given in [10], on input (g, h). As a result, this produces the public value $h_1 = h$ and properly distributed values for the parties controlled by $\mathcal{A}$. In particular the simulation looks to $\mathcal{A}$ perfectly indistinguishable from the real execution of the protocol, however the players will share some secret value $\hat{y}$ that does not correspond to the actual discrete log of h_1 in base g. The second execution of the DL-DKG protocol is done as in the real game.

Step 3. $\mathcal{B}$ runs an execution of the INV protocol, but with each of the honest players holding a share $\hat{y}_i$ of $\hat{y}$. Notice that such an execution looks perfectly indistinguishable (with respect to the real one) to $\mathcal{A}$, as the latter is static and controls only up to $t < n/4$ players.

Hence the simulation provides the adversary with a view (public outputs + controlled players' private outputs) which is perfectly indistinguishable from a real execution.

Off-line Threshold Signing Protocol: Steps 1, 2, 3, 4 and 6 are done exactly as in the real game, thus we focus on step 5. Here the only difference with respect to the real protocol is that the (full) multiplication protocol MUL used to compute $r \cdot y$ is run by $\mathcal{B}$ using the shares $\hat{y}_i$ for the honest players. Once again, this results in a protocol which looks perfectly indistinguishable to the real one, from $\mathcal{A}$'s perspective.

On-line Threshold Signing Protocol: $\mathcal{B}$ first recovers the value s' shared during the off-line phase. Notice that it can do this as it controls $n - t > 3n/4 > t$ parties. Next, once m' is known, it sets $r' = r$ and and computes a value $\hat{s}'$ such that $r' = (m + r\hat{y} + sz - m' - \hat{s}'z)\hat{Y} \bmod q$, where $\hat{Y}$ is the (known) inverse computed in the key generation protocol. Notice that this means that $\hat{s}' = (m - m')z^{-1} + s \bmod q$. We stress that, since $\mathcal{B}$ controls more than $2t$ players it can easily compute all the values above. Next, $\mathcal{B}$ uses its knowledge of the discrete log of g_1 in base g to cheat and interpolate s' as $\hat{s}'$ (in a way that remains consistent with the previously broadcasted commitments). The rest of the protocol is done as in the real execution.

Note that the simulation is perfectly indistinguishable from the real one. This means that the adversary cannot know if the simulator knows both the values y and z or only z, as in our case. Thus if the adversary produces a forgery of type II such that $m'_i \neq m'$ and $r'_i \neq r'$ one can easily break the received discrete logarithm challenge. Indeed, since $\text{Com}' = \text{Com}_i$ we have that

$$g^{m'_i + zs'_i} h_1^{r'_i} = g^{m' + zs'} h_1^{r'}$$

and thus the required value is $((m'_i - m') + z(s'_i - s'))(r' - r'_i)^{-1} \bmod q$.

If $\beta = 1$ $\mathcal{B}$ bets on the fact that $\mathcal{A}$ will provide a forgery of type II where conditions 1 and 2 hold, that is, $m' \neq m'_i$ and $s' \neq s'_i$. Again, we describe the simulation of the three protocols, focusing on the differences with the case $\beta = 0$.

On-line/Off-line Threshold Key Generation: This time, the simulation of DL-DKG is used to generate h_2 and thus $\mathcal{B}$ knows y and a value $\hat{z}$ that differs from $\log_g h_2$.

Note, this change influences step 3, which, this time, is done exactly as in a real execution of the protocol (with $\mathcal{B}$ controlling the honest players).

Off-line Threshold Signing Protocol: Everything is done as before, by just switching the roles of z and y.

On-line Threshold Signing Protocol: In this simulation $\mathcal{B}$ uses its knowledge of the discrete logarithm of g_1 in base g to interpolate s' as the value s shared in round 1 of Off-line Threshold Signing Protocol. The rest of the protocol is done exactly as in the real game.

Again, note that the simulation is perfectly indistinguishable from the real one. Thus if the adversary produces a forgery of type II on a message m' such that $m_i' \neq m'$ and $s_i' \neq s'$ one can easily break the received discrete logarithm challenge in a way that is basically identical to what described for the case $\beta = 0$.

Remark 2 (Achieving robustness for up to $t < n/3$ faults). Notice that the protocol presented in previous section can be modified in order to tolerate up to $t < n/3$ malicious players. The modification is as follows. The key generation algorithm remains more or less unchanged: we add one additional round on which the players compute shares $\lambda_i = Y_i \cdot z_i$. In the off-line signing algorithm we add one additional execution of the (full) multiplication to create shares μ_i of the product $\tau \cdot Y$. Finally, in the on-line signing algorithm, step 2 is modified by setting $r_i' = \mu_i - m'Y_i - s'\lambda_i + \omega_i \bmod q$.

It is easy to check that the proof goes through in basically the same way. Notice that this modified protocol is less efficient than the proposed one, but the efficiency loss involves the off/line components only (i.e. key generation and off-line signing).

References

1. J. Bar-Ilan and D. Beaver. Non cryptographic fault tolerant computing in a constant number of rounds of interaction. In *Proceedings of the ACM Symposium on Principles of Distributed Computation*, pp.201–209, 1989.
2. M. Ben-or, S. Goldwasser and A. Widgerson Completeness Theorems for non-cryptographic fault tolerant distributed computation. In *Proc. of 20th Annual Symposium on Theory of Computing*, 1988.
3. E. Berlekamp and L. Welch Error correction of algebraic block codes. US Patent 4,633,470.
4. C. Crutchfield, D. Molnar, D. Turner and D. Wagner Generic On-Line/Off-Line Threshold Signatures In *Proc. of PKC '06*, pp.58–74, Lecture Notes in Computer Science vol.3958, Springer-Verlag, 2006.
5. I. Damgård and K. Dupont. Efficient Threshold RSA Signatures with General Moduli and No Extra Assumptions. In *Proc. of PKC '05*, pp 346–361, Springer-Verlag, 2005.
6. Y. Desmedt and Y. Frankel. *Threshold Cryptosystems*. CRYPTO'89, LNCS vol.435 pp.307–315, Springer 1990.

7. M. Di Raimondo and R. Gennaro Provably Secure Threshold Password-Authenticated Key Exchange. In *Proc. of Eurocrypt'03*, 2003.
8. S. Even, O. Goldreich and S. Micali. *On-Line/Off-Line Digital Signatures*. J. Cryptology 9(1): 35-67, Springer 1996.
9. P. Feldman A Practical Scheme for Non-Interactive Verifiable Secret Sharing. In *Proc. 28th FOCS*, pp. 427–437, 1987.
10. R. Gennaro, S. Jarecki, H. Krawczyk, and T. Rabin. Secure Distributed Key Generation for Discrete-Log Public-Key Cryptosystems. *Eurocrypt'99*, pp.295–310, Lecture Notes in Computer Science vol.1592, Springer-Verlag, 1999.
11. R. Gennaro, S. Jarecki, H. Krawczyk and T. Rabin. *Robust and Efficient Sharing of RSA Functions*. J. Cryptology 13(2): 273-300, Springer 2000.
12. R. Gennaro, S. Jarecki, H. Krawczyk and T. Rabin. : *Robust Threshold DSS Signatures*. Inf. Comput. 164(1): 54-84 (2001).
13. R. Gennaro, M. Rabin and T. Rabin. Simplified VSS and fast-track multi-party computations with applications to threshold cryptography. In *Proc. 17th ACM Symposium on Principle of Distributed Computing*, 1998.
14. S. Goldwasser, S. Micali and R. Rivest. A digital signature scheme secure against adaptive chosen message attacks. *SIAM J. on Computing* 17(2):281-308 1988.
15. H. Krawczyk and T. Rabin. *Chameleon Signatures*. 2000 NDSS Symposium, pp.143-154.
16. National Institute for Standards and Technology. Digital Signature Standard (DSS). Technical Report 169, August 30 1991.
17. J.Kubiatowicz, D.Bindel, Y.Chen, S. Czerwinski, P. Eaton, D. Geels, R. Gummadi, S. Rhea, H. Weatherspoon, W. Weimer, C. Wells and B. Zhao. *OceanStore: An architecture for GlobalScale Persistent Storage*. 2000 ACM Architectural Support for Programming Languages and Operating Systems Conference.
18. T. Pedersen. Non-interactive and information-theoretic secure verifiable secret sharing. *Crypto'91*, pp.129-140, Lecture Notes in Computer Science vol.576, Springer-Verlag, 1992.
19. S. Rhea, P. Eaton, D. Geels, H. Weatherspoon, B. Zhao and J. Kubiatowicz. *Pond: The OceanStore prototype*. 2003 USENIX Conference on File and Storage Technologies.
20. A. Shamir, "How to share a secret," *Comm. of the ACM*, vol. 22, no. 11, pp. 612–613, November 1979.
21. A. Shamir and Y. Tauman. Improved On-line/Off-line Signature Schemes. *Crypto'01*, pp.355-367, Lecture Notes in Computer Science vol.2139, Springer-Verlag, 2001.
22. V. Shoup. *Practical Threshold Signatures*. EUROCRYPT 2000, LNCS vol.1807, pp.207–220, Springer 2000.

High Order Linearization Equation (HOLE) Attack on Multivariate Public Key Cryptosystems

Jintai Ding[1,*], Lei Hu[2,**], Xuyun Nie[2], Jianyu Li[2], and John Wagner[1]

[1] Department of Mathematical Sciences, University of Cincinnati, Fachbereich
Informatik, Technische Universität Darmstadt,
Cincinnati, OH, 45220, USA
[2] State Key Laboratory of Information Security, Graduate School of Chinese
Academy of Sciences, Beijing 100049, China
ding@math.uc.edu, {hu, nxy04b, ljy}@is.ac.cn, wagnerjh@email.uc.edu

Abstract. In the CT-track of the 2006 RSA conference, a new multivariate public key cryptosystem, which is called the Medium Field Equation (MFE) multivariate public key cryptosystem, is proposed by Wang, Yang, Hu and Lai. We use the second order linearization equation attack method by Patarin to break MFE. Given a ciphertext, we can derive the plaintext within 2^{23} $\mathbb{F}_{2^{16}}$-multiplications, after performing once for any given public key a computation of complexity less than 2^{52}. We also propose a high order linearization equation (HOLE) attack on multivariate public key cryptosystems, which is a further generalization of the (first and second order) linearization equation (LE). This method can be used to attack extensions of the current MFE.

Keywords: multivariate public key cryptosystem, quadratic polynomial, algebraic cryptanalysis, high order linearization equation.

1 Introduction

For the last three decades, public key cryptosystems, as a revolutionary breakthrough in cryptography, have developed into an indispensable element of our modern communication system. For RSA and other number theory based cryptosystems, their security depends on the assumption about the difficulty of certain number theory problems, such as the Integer Prime Factorization Problem or the Discrete Logarithm Problem. However, due to the quantum computer attack by Shor [Sho99] and the demand for more efficient cryptosystems for small devices, there is a great challenge to build new public key cryptosystems, in particular ones that could survive future attacks utilizing quantum computers [PQ].

* The work of this author is partially supported by the Charles Phelps Taft Research Center and the Alexander von Humboldt Foundation.
** The work of this author is supported by NSFC (60573053) and National 863 Project of China (2006AA01Z416).

T. Okamoto and X. Wang (Eds.): PKC 2007, LNCS 4450, pp. 233–248, 2007.

One such research direction utilizes a set of multivariate polynomials over a finite field, in particular, quadratic polynomials, as the public key of the cipher, which are called multivariate public key cryptosystems (MPKC). This method is based on the proven theorem that solving a set of multivariate quadratic polynomial equations over a finite field generally is an NP-complete problem. Note, however, this does not guarantee that these new cryptosystems are secure. In the last decade, there has been tremendous amount of work devoted to this area. In 2004, one such cryptosystem, Sflash [ACDG03] [PCG01a], was accepted as one of the final selections in the New European Schemes for Signatures, Integrity, and Encryption: IST-1999-12324. A more efficient family of Rainbow signature schemes was also proposed in the last years [DS05] [YC05] [WHLCY05].

In the development of MPKC, one particular interesting and important new area is the development of the so-called algebraic attack. This new attack method started from the linearization equation (LE) attack by Patarin [Pat95], which is used to break Matsumoto-Imai cryptosystems. A linearization equation is an equation in the form: $\sum a_{ij}u_iv_j + \sum b_iu_i + \sum c_jv_j + d = 0$, where the u_i are components of the plaintext and the v_j are components of the ciphertext.

Later, Patarin, Courtois, Shamir, and Kipnis generalized this method by multiplying high order terms $u_1^{\alpha_1} \cdots u_n^{\alpha_n}$ of the plaintext variables but using only linear terms of ciphertext variables (v_j), which is called the XL method [CKPS00]. The method is closely related to the new Gröbner basis method by Faugere [Fau99] [AFIKS04]. Furthermore, this new algebraic method was used to attack symmetric ciphers like AES and others [CPi02]. One can see that algebraic attacks are becoming increasingly important in cryptography.

Another generalization of LE also by Patarin [Pat96, PCG01a, C00], which is not as well-known, is the type of equations in the form:

$$\sum a_{ijk}u_iv_jv_k + \sum b_{ij}u_iv_j + \sum c_iu_i + \sum d_{jk}v_jv_k + \sum e_jv_j + f = 0.$$

As a further extension, we propose to call the equations that use high order terms of the ciphertext variables (v_j) while using only linear terms of plaintext variables (u_i), high order linearization equations (HOLE). The total degree of the highest order of the ciphertext variables (v_j) is called the order of the HOLE and the equation above is thus called a second order linearization equation (SOLE). For any MPKC, if we can derive such equations, then for any given ciphertext, we can insert it into the HOLEs, producing linear equations satisfied by the plaintext and these equations can be used to attack the system.

It turns out that the SOLEs can be used efficiently to break the Medium Field Equation (MFE) multivariate public key cryptosystem proposed by Wang, Yang, Hu and Lai in the CT-track of the 2006 RSA conference [WYH06].

MFE is an encryption scheme. Many encryption schemes of MPKC have been proposed, and many of them have been broken, for example, the TTM cryptosystem family [Moh99] [GC00] [CM01] [DS03a] [DS03b] [MCY04]. A very different direction goes along the idea started by Matsumoto and Imai [MI88], which can be generally called the "Big Field" idea.

Given a multivariate public key cryptosystem, the public key is defined as a map over the vector space $\mathbb{K}^n$, where $\mathbb{K}$ is a small finite field with q elements. However from the theory of finite fields, $\mathbb{K}^n$ can also be identified with a "big" finite field $\mathbb{E}$, which is a degree n extension of $\mathbb{K}$. That is, there is a standard $\mathbb{K}$-linear vector space isomorphism that identifies $\mathbb{E}$ with $\mathbb{K}^n$. The idea of the "Big Field" is that we can find a map, say ϕ_2, that is easy to invert on $\mathbb{E}$. Under the isomorphism we can build a map $\tilde{\phi}_2 \colon \mathbb{K}^n \to \mathbb{K}^n$ as:

$$\tilde{\phi}_2(u_1, ..., u_n) \mapsto (g_1(u_1, ..., u_n), \cdots, g_n(u_1, ..., x_n)).$$

Then we use ϕ_1 and ϕ_3, two randomly chosen invertible affine linear maps over $\mathbb{K}^n$ which are the key part of the private key to "hide" ϕ_2. The public key is given by

$$\bar{\phi}_2(u_1, ..., u_n) = \phi_3 \circ \tilde{\phi}_2 \circ \phi_1(u_1, ..., u_n)$$
$$= (h_1(u_1, ..., u_n), h_2(u_1, ..., u_n), \cdots, h_n(u_1, ..., u_n)).$$

The Matsumoto-Imai (MI) cryptosystem was broken by Patarin [Pat95], and later Patarin developed the HFE cryptosystem [Pat96]. The only difference between HFE and the MI is that they choose different ϕ_2. Currently the more promising cryptosystems are new variants of the MI and the HFE through Oil-Vinegar constructions and internal perturbations [Din04a] [FGS05] [DG05] [DS04a]. The idea to put several "big fields" together to build a cryptosystem is also used [MI88] [Pat96]. The new MFE cryptosystem [WYH06] uses what the designers call "Medium Field Encryption". The non-linear critical part of the public key is a function over an extension of the base field $\mathbb{K}$ of degree smaller than what would be called the "big field". Another key difference between MFE and HFE is that MFE uses functions derived from a matrix structure while the MI and the HFE use only polynomials of a single variable.

In the attack on MFE, we first use second order linearization equations (SOLEs), which we derive from the special algebraic structure of the crucial nonlinear map in MFE. This is the most essential step in our attack. Any given ciphertext can be inserted into the SOLEs to produce a set of equations linear in the plaintext variables. Solutions to these equations are finally plugged back into the original public key polynomial equations, providing a set of new quadratic equations that could be easily solved. The complexity of our break is less than 2^{52} one-time multiplications over $\mathbb{K}$ for any given public key, and the practical complexity of recovering a ciphertext is less than 2^{23} $\mathbb{K}$-operations.

The current MFE is based on matrices of size 2×2 and one may extend it to a construction using matrices of bigger size. The HOLEs of higher order can be extended to attack such an extension of the current MFE and the order of HOLE corresponds exactly to the size of the matrices.

We organize the paper as follows. We introduce the MFE cryptosystem in Section 2, and present our attack in Section 3. In Section 4, we discuss the connection of HOLE with the XL method. In the final section, we present the conclusion.

2   MFE Public Key Cryptosystem

Let $\mathbb{K}$ be a finite field, generally $\mathbb{F}_{2^{16}}$. Let $\mathbb{L}$ be its degree r extension field; $\mathbb{L}$ is considered the "Medium Field". In MFE, we always identify $\mathbb{L}$ with $\mathbb{K}^r$ by a $\mathbb{K}$-linear isomorphism $\pi : \mathbb{L} \rightarrow \mathbb{K}^r$. Namely we take a basis of $\mathbb{L}$ over $\mathbb{K}$, $\{\theta_1, \cdots, \theta_r\}$, and define π by $\pi(a_1\theta_1 + \cdots + a_r\theta_r) = (a_1, \cdots, a_r)$ for any $a_1, \cdots, a_r \in \mathbb{K}$. It is natural to extend π to two $\mathbb{K}$-linear isomorphisms $\pi_1 : \mathbb{L}^{12} \rightarrow \mathbb{K}^{12r}$ and $\pi_2 : \mathbb{L}^{15} \rightarrow \mathbb{K}^{15r}$.

A private key of MFE consists of two invertible affine transformations ϕ_1 and ϕ_3; and ϕ_1 is defined on $\mathbb{K}^{12r}$, and ϕ_3 on $\mathbb{K}^{15r}$. Let $\phi_2 : \mathbb{L}^{12} \rightarrow \mathbb{L}^{15}$ be the central nonlinear quadratic map of MFE. Note ϕ_2 is fixed except for the three components Q_1, Q_2, and Q_3, which have randomly chosen coefficients. The corresponding public key is $15r$ quadratic polynomials $h_1(u_1, ..., u_{12r}), h_2(u_1, ..., u_{12r}), \cdots$, and $h_{15r}(u_1, ..., u_{12r})$ given by

$$(h_1(u_1, ..., u_{12r}), \cdots, h_{15r}(u_1, ..., u_{12r})) = \phi_3 \circ \pi_2 \circ \phi_2 \circ \pi_1^{-1} \circ \phi_1(u_1, ..., u_{12r}). \quad (1)$$

Let $\phi_2(X_1, \cdots, X_{12}) = (Y_1, \cdots, Y_{15})$. The expressions of the Y_i are given by

$$\begin{cases} Y_1 = X_1 + X_5X_8 + X_6X_7 + Q_1; \\ Y_2 = X_2 + X_9X_{12} + X_{10}X_{11} + Q_2; \\ Y_3 = X_3 + X_1X_4 + X_2X_3 + Q_3; \\ Y_4 = X_1X_5 + X_2X_7; \qquad Y_5 = X_1X_6 + X_2X_8; \\ Y_6 = X_3X_5 + X_4X_7; \qquad Y_7 = X_3X_6 + X_4X_8; \\ Y_8 = X_1X_9 + X_2X_{11}; \qquad Y_9 = X_1X_{10} + X_2X_{12}; \\ Y_{10} = X_3X_9 + X_4X_{11}; \qquad Y_{11} = X_3X_{10} + X_4X_{12}; \\ Y_{12} = X_5X_9 + X_7X_{11}; \qquad Y_{13} = X_5X_{10} + X_7X_{12}; \\ Y_{14} = X_6X_9 + X_8X_{11}; \qquad Y_{15} = X_6X_{10} + X_8X_{12}. \end{cases} \quad (2)$$

Here Q_1, Q_2, and Q_3 form a triple (Q_1, Q_2, Q_3) which is a triangular map from $\mathbb{K}^{3r}$ to itself as follows. Let $\pi(X_1) = (x_1, \cdots, x_r)$, $\pi(X_2) = (x_{r+1}, \cdots, x_{2r})$, $\pi(X_3) = (x_{2r+1}, \cdots, x_{3r})$, and let $q_i \in \mathbb{K}[x_1, \cdots, x_{i-1}]$ for $2 \leq i \leq 3r$. Then

$$\begin{cases} Q_1(X_1) = \sum_{i=2}^{r} q_i(x_1, \cdots, x_{i-1})\theta_i, \\ Q_2(X_1, X_2) = \sum_{i=r+1}^{2r} q_i(x_1, \cdots, x_{i-1})\theta_{i-r}, \\ Q_3(X_1, X_2, X_3) = \sum_{i=2r+1}^{3r} q_i(x_1, \cdots, x_{i-1})\theta_{i-2r}. \end{cases}$$

The q_i can be any randomly chosen quadratic polynomials. A specific "tower"-structural choice for them is given in §5 of [WYH06].

The encryption of MFE is the evaluation of public key polynomials, namely given a plaintext $(u_1, \cdots, u_{12r})$, its ciphertext is

$$(v_1, \cdots, v_{15r}) = (h_1(u_1, \cdots, u_{12r}), \cdots, h_{15r}(u_1, \cdots, u_{12r})).$$

Given a valid ciphertext $(v_1, \cdots, v_{15r})$, the decryption of MFE is to calculate in turn $\phi_1^{-1} \circ \pi_1 \circ \phi_2^{-1} \circ \pi_2^{-1} \circ \phi_3^{-1}(v_1, \cdots, v_{15r})$. Here the point is how to invert ϕ_2, its basic idea is to use the triangular structure of ϕ_2. Relating to our cryptanalysis, the method of computing ϕ_2^{-1} is listed as follows, see §4.2 and Appendix B of [WYH06].

Write $X_1, \cdots, X_{12}, Y_4, \cdots, Y_{15}$ as six 2×2 matrices:

$$M_1 = \begin{pmatrix} X_1 & X_2 \\ X_3 & X_4 \end{pmatrix}, M_2 = \begin{pmatrix} X_5 & X_6 \\ X_7 & X_8 \end{pmatrix}, M_3 = \begin{pmatrix} X_9 & X_{10} \\ X_{11} & X_{12} \end{pmatrix},$$

$$Z_3 = M_1 M_2 = \begin{pmatrix} Y_4 & Y_5 \\ Y_6 & Y_7 \end{pmatrix}, Z_2 = M_1 M_3 = \begin{pmatrix} Y_8 & Y_9 \\ Y_{10} & Y_{11} \end{pmatrix}, \tag{3}$$

$$Z_1 = M_2^T M_3 = \begin{pmatrix} Y_{12} & Y_{13} \\ Y_{14} & Y_{15} \end{pmatrix}.$$

Then

$$\begin{cases} \det(M_1) \cdot \det(M_2) = \det(Z_3), \\ \det(M_1) \cdot \det(M_3) = \det(Z_2), \\ \det(M_2) \cdot \det(M_3) = \det(Z_1). \end{cases}$$

When M_1, M_2, and M_3 are all invertible, we can get values of $\det(M_1)$, $\det(M_2)$, and $\det(M_3)$ from $\det(Z_1)$, $\det(Z_2)$, and $\det(Z_3)$, for instance, $\det(M_1) = (\det(Z_2) \cdot \det(Z_3) / \det(Z_1))^{1/2}$. The square root operation is easy to handle over a field of characteristic 2.

With values of $\det(M_1)$, $\det(M_2)$, and $\det(M_3)$, we solve the following triangular map over $\mathbb{K}^{3r}$

$$\begin{cases} Y_1 = X_1 + Q_1 + \det(M_2) \\ Y_2 = X_2 + Q_2 + \det(M_3) \\ Y_3 = X_3 + Q_3 + \det(M_1) \end{cases} \tag{4}$$

to get in turn $x_1, \cdots, x_r, x_{r+1}, \cdots, x_{2r}, x_{2r+1}, \cdots$, and x_{3r}. Thus, we recover X_1, X_2, and X_3. From $X_1 X_4 + X_2 X_3 = \det(M_1)$ we then get X_4 provided $X_1 \neq 0$. The $X_5, \cdots, X_{12}$ are consequently solved from the 4th to 11th equations of (2). Appendix B of [WYH06] presents a method of computing the X_i in the case when $X_1 = 0$. It is slightly easier than the case of $X_1 \neq 0$.

If there is a non-invertible matrix among M_1, M_2, and M_3, then the decryption mentioned above will not work. This decryption failure exists in MFE [WYH06]. We call a plaintext **singular** if its corresponding M_1, M_2, and M_3 are not all invertible, otherwise it is called **nonsingular**. The ciphertext of a nonsingular plaintext is called a nonsingular ciphertext.

It is easy to prove that the ratio of singular plaintexts to all possible plaintexts is at most $4|\mathbb{L}|^{-1}$; when $\mathbb{L} = \mathbb{F}_{2^{64}}$, the ratio is at most 2^{-62}, which is quite small. In the next section we only consider how to recover nonsingular ciphertext.

There are two typical instances of MFE proposed by the designers of MFE.

1) MFE-1, where $\mathbb{K} = \mathbb{F}_{2^{16}}$ and $r = 4$. The public key has 60 polynomials with 48 variables.

2) MFE-1', where $\mathbb{K} = \mathbb{F}_{2^{16}}$ and $r = 5$. The public key has 75 polynomials and 60 variables.

There is also a mini-version of MFE (MFE-0) using $\mathbb{K} = \mathbb{F}_{2^8}$ and $r = 4$, which has the same number of polynomials and variables as MFE-1.

3   Cryptanalysis on MFE

The designers of MFE noted they should avoid the linearization attack of Patarin (§6.2 of [WYH06]), and this is indeed the case. In the design of MFE, the last equations of (2) in MFE are defined such that $Z_1 = M_2^T M_3$ (see (2)), instead of $Z_1 = M_2 M_3$. Otherwise we would have $Z_3 M_3 = M_1 Z_1 (= M_1 M_2 M_3)$; this would have produced linearization equations for the cryptosystem. However we can use the HOLE, in particular the SOLE, to attack this cryptosystem.

3.1   Second Order Linearization Equations

First, we will show algebraically why the MFE has second order linearization equations. Denote by M^* the associated matrix of a square matrix; for $M = \begin{pmatrix} a & b \\ c & d \end{pmatrix}$, its associated matrix is $M^* = \begin{pmatrix} d & -b \\ -c & a \end{pmatrix}$. From (3), we have

$$Z_3 = M_1 M_2, \qquad Z_2 = M_1 M_3. \tag{5}$$

From these, we can derive

$$M_3 M_3^* M_1^* M_1 M_2 = M_3 (M_1 M_3)^* (M_1 M_2) = M_3 Z_2^* Z_3,$$

$$M_3 M_3^* M_1^* M_1 M_2 = (M_3 M_3^*)(M_1 M_1^*) M_2 = \det(M_3)\det(M_1) M_2 = \det(Z_2) M_2,$$

and hence,

$$M_3 Z_2^* Z_3 = \det(Z_2) M_2, \tag{6}$$

that is,

$$\begin{pmatrix} X_9 & X_{10} \\ X_{11} & X_{12} \end{pmatrix} \begin{pmatrix} Y_{11} & -Y_9 \\ -Y_{10} & Y_8 \end{pmatrix} \begin{pmatrix} Y_4 & Y_5 \\ Y_6 & Y_7 \end{pmatrix} = (Y_8 Y_{11} - Y_9 Y_{10}) \begin{pmatrix} X_5 & X_6 \\ X_7 & X_8 \end{pmatrix}. \tag{7}$$

Expanding (7), we get four equations of the form

$$\sum a'_{ijk} X_i Y_j Y_k = 0, \tag{8}$$

which hold for any corresponding pair $(X_1, \cdots, X_{12}, Y_1, \cdots, Y_{15})$. For any non-singular plaintext, if we substitute all the Y_i by its corresponding value in the four equations of the form (8) derived from (7), we would get four linear equations with X_i as its . These four equations are linearly independent, since the matrices $\begin{pmatrix} Y_{11} & Y_9 \\ Y_{10} & Y_8 \end{pmatrix}$ and $\begin{pmatrix} Y_4 & Y_5 \\ Y_6 & Y_7 \end{pmatrix}$ are invertible.

Substituting $(X_1, \cdots, X_{12}) = \pi_1^{-1} \circ \phi_1(u_1, \cdots, u_{12r})$ and $(Y_1, \cdots, Y_{15}) = \pi_2^{-1} \circ \phi_3^{-1}(v_1, \cdots, v_{15r})$ into (8), we get $4r$ equations of the form

$$\sum_i u_i \left(\sum_{j \leq k} a_{ijk} v_j v_k + \sum_j b_{ij} v_j + c_i \right) + \sum_{j \leq k} d_{jk} v_j v_k + \sum_j e_j v_j + f = 0, \quad (9)$$

where the coefficients $a_{ijk}, b_{ij}, c_i, d_{jk}, e_j, f \in \mathbb{K}$, and the summations are respectively over $1 \leq i \leq 12r$, $1 \leq j \leq k \leq 15r$ and $1 \leq j \leq 15r$. These equations, which are linear in plaintext components u_i and quadratic in ciphertext components v_j, are **second order linearization equations (SOLEs)**. It is easy to show that when all the v_j are substituted by any nonsingular ciphertext, the $4r$ SOLEs derived from (9) become linearly independent linear equations in u_i.

Similarly to (6), we can deduce from (5) another equation

$$M_2 Z_3^* Z_2 = \det(Z_3) M_3, \quad (10)$$

or in its matrix form,

$$\begin{pmatrix} X_5 & X_6 \\ X_7 & X_8 \end{pmatrix} \begin{pmatrix} Y_7 & -Y_5 \\ -Y_6 & Y_4 \end{pmatrix} \begin{pmatrix} Y_8 & Y_9 \\ Y_{10} & Y_{11} \end{pmatrix} = (Y_4 Y_7 - Y_5 Y_6) \begin{pmatrix} X_9 & X_{10} \\ X_{11} & X_{12} \end{pmatrix}. \quad (11)$$

The $4r$ SOLEs resulted from (11) are clearly different from the ones corresponding to (9). Furthermore, we can show that the $8r$ SOLEs obtained from (9) and (11) are all linearly independent. However, we note that when the v_i in these $8r$ SOLEs derived from (7) and (11) are assigned any nonsingular ciphertext, we will get only $4r$ linearly independent linear equations in u_i. In other words, once the values of v_i are given, as linear equations in X_i, (10) is completely equivalent to (6), and one can deduce (10) directly from (6) and vice versa. One can see this by the fact that multiplying from the right the both sides of (6) by $Z_3^* Z_2 / \det(Z_2)$ (this is a constant invertible matrix if the y_i values are given) gives (10).

Now, it is obvious that there are more SOLEs. We apply the above trick that results (6) and (10) from (5) to obtain

$$M_2 (Z_1^T)^* Z_2^T = \det(Z_1) M_1^T, \quad (12)$$

$$M_1^T (Z_2^T)^* Z_1^T = \det(Z_2) M_2, \quad (13)$$

from $Z_2 = M_1 M_3$ and $Z_1 = M_2^T M_3$. We can also obtain

$$M_1^T (Z_3^T)^* Z_1 = \det(Z_3) M_3, \quad (14)$$

$$M_3 (Z_1)^* Z_3^T = \det(Z_1) M_1^T, \quad (15)$$

from $Z_3 = M_1 M_2$ and $Z_1 = M_2^T M_3$. It is not hard to check that the polynomial equations derived from (6), (10), and (12)-(15) in terms of X_i and Y_j are all linearly independent. Thus, we get at least $24r$ linearly independent SOLEs in u_i and v_i over $\mathbb{K}$.

To find all SOLEs, we need to evaluate sufficiently many plain/cipher-texts in (9) to get a system of linear equations on the $a_{ijk}, b_{ij}, \cdots, f$. Let s be the dimension of its solution space and $(a^{(l)}_{ijk}, b^{(l)}_{ij}, \cdots, f^{(l)})$, $1 \le l \le s$, be its s linearly independent solutions. As mentioned above, we know $s \ge 24r$. For attack purposes, we only need to do the computation to get all the SOLEs once for any given public key.

Similarly to the relation between (6) and (10), as linear equations in X_i, (12) is equivalent to (13), and (14) is equivalent to (15) provided that the Y_i are assigned a nonsingular ciphertext value.

In addition, we can show that if we are given the values of v_i of a nonsingular ciphertext, from the $24r$ linearly independent SOLEs we derived above, we will produce only $8r$ linearly independent linear equations in u_i. Write (12) in its matrix form:

$$\begin{pmatrix} X_5 & X_6 \\ X_7 & X_8 \end{pmatrix} \begin{pmatrix} Y_{15} & -Y_{14} \\ -Y_{13} & Y_{12} \end{pmatrix} \begin{pmatrix} Y_8 & Y_{10} \\ Y_9 & Y_{11} \end{pmatrix} = (Y_{12}Y_{15} - Y_{13}Y_{14}) \begin{pmatrix} X_1 & X_3 \\ X_2 & X_4 \end{pmatrix}, \quad (16)$$

which results in $4r$ SOLEs. Given the values of Y_i of a nonsingular ciphertext, the eight linear equations in X_i derived from (16) and (7) are linearly independent, because the coefficient matrix corresponding to the set of eight linear equations, with the four equations from (16) as the first four ones, is in the form $\begin{pmatrix} I & * & 0 \\ 0 & I & * \end{pmatrix}$, where each row is scaled by a factor $Y_8Y_{11} - Y_9Y_{10}$ or $Y_{12}Y_{15} - Y_{13}Y_{14}$ correspondingly, and I and 0 are respectively the identity matrix and the zero matrix of order 4. This matrix is clearly of rank 8. This shows that the s' introduced in the next subsection is at least $8r$. The reason that the other SOLEs will not produce any new linear equations on u_i for any given values of v_i of a nonsingular ciphertext is that when the Y_i are assigned a nonsingular value, (14) can be easily deduced from (6) and (12).

3.2   Ciphertext-Only Attack

Now assume we have found a basis of the linear space of all SOLEs.

Given a ciphertext $(v'_1, \cdots, v'_{15r})$, our aim is to recover its plaintext $(u'_1, \cdots, u'_{12r})$. We plug the values of ciphertext $(v'_1, \cdots, v'_{15r})$ into the basis SOLEs:

$$\begin{cases} \sum_i u_i \left(\sum_{j \le k} a^{(l)}_{ijk} v'_j v'_k + \sum_j b^{(l)}_{ij} v'_j + c^{(l)}_i \right) + \sum_{j \le k} d^{(l)}_{jk} v'_j v'_k + \sum_j e^{(l)}_j v'_j + f^{(l)} = 0 \\ 1 \le l \le s \end{cases}$$
$$(17)$$

giving us a linear system on $u_1, \cdots, u_{12r}$. Assume it has s' linearly independent solutions. From the previous subsection, we know $8r \le s' \le 12r$. We can represent s' of the variables $u_1, \cdots, u_{12r}$ by linear affine expressions of the remaining $t := 12r - s'$. Let $w_1, \cdots, w_t$ be these t variables.

Substitute these s' linear expressions into the original public key polynomials to get $15r$ new quadratic polynomials $\widetilde{h}_1(w_1, ..., w_t), \widetilde{h}_2(w_1, ..., w_t), \cdots$, and $\widetilde{h}_{15r}(w_1, ..., w_t)$.

Let S be the solution space of (17). Let Y_i' and Z_i' be components and matrices corresponding to the given $(v_1', \cdots, v_{15r}')$, namely

$$(Y_1', \cdots, Y_{15}') = \pi_2^{-1} \circ \phi_3^{-1}(v_1', \cdots, v_{15r}'),$$

$$Z_3' = \begin{pmatrix} Y_4' & Y_5' \\ Y_6' & Y_7' \end{pmatrix}, Z_2' = \begin{pmatrix} Y_8' & Y_9' \\ Y_{10}' & Y_{11}' \end{pmatrix}, Z_1' = \begin{pmatrix} Y_{12}' & Y_{13}' \\ Y_{14}' & Y_{15}' \end{pmatrix}.$$

We have found a basis of all SOLEs and each SOLE is a linear combination of this basis. This fact holds when the variables v_i in the equations are substituted by v_i'. Applying this fact to (7), we know the four resulting equations in u_i from

$$M_3(Z_2')^* \cdot Z_3' = \det(Z_2')M_2 \tag{18}$$

are all linear combinations of the equations in (17). In other words, (18) holds on S. Let $P_{23} = \det(Z_2')\left((Z_2')^* \cdot Z_3'\right)^{-1}$; then $M_3 = M_2 P_{23}$. P_{23} is a constant matrix dependent only on the ciphertext.

Now we have that $M_2^T M_3 = Z_1$ always holds on $\mathbb{K}^{12r}$; therefore, we have that $M_3^T M_3 = M_3^T M_2 P_{23} = Z_1 P_{23}$ holds on S. That is,

$$\begin{pmatrix} X_9^2 + X_{11}^2 & X_9 X_{10} + X_{11} X_{12} \\ X_9 X_{10} + X_{11} X_{12} & X_{10}^2 + X_{12}^2 \end{pmatrix} = \begin{pmatrix} Y_{12} & Y_{13} \\ Y_{14} & Y_{15} \end{pmatrix} P_{23} \tag{19}$$

holds on S. Comparing the diagonal entries of the matrices in both sides of (19), we find $X_9^2 + X_{11}^2$ and $X_{10}^2 + X_{12}^2$ are linear combinations of the Y_i. Applying ϕ_1 and ϕ_3 to these combinations and utilizing the fact that squaring is a linear operation on a field of characteristic 2, we have, on S, the $2r$ expressions corresponding to $X_9^2 + X_{11}^2$ and $X_{10}^2 + X_{12}^2$ are of the form $\sum a_i' u_i^2 + b'$ and $\mathbb{K}$-linear combinations of $h_1(u_1, ..., u_{12r}), h_2(u_1, ..., u_{12r}), \cdots, h_{15r}(u_1, ..., u_{12r})$ and 1 (constant).

Thus, of linear combinations of $\widetilde{h}_1(w_1, ..., w_t), \cdots, \widetilde{h}_{15r}(w_1, ..., w_t)$ and 1, there must exist $2r$ which contain only squaring terms and a constant term and correspond to $X_9^2 + X_{11}^2$ and $X_{10}^2 + X_{12}^2$.

It is easy to solve the following linear system on the $\widetilde{a}_i$ and $\widetilde{b}_j$:

$$\begin{cases} \sum_{i=1}^{15r} \widetilde{a}_i \widetilde{h}_i(w_1, ..., w_t) + \sum_{j=1}^{t} \widetilde{b}_j w_j^2 + \widetilde{c} = 0 \\ \forall w_1, ..., w_t \in \mathbb{K} \end{cases} \tag{20}$$

Essentially, this is to solve a linear equation system whose coefficients are the coefficients of the cross-terms and linear terms of the $\widetilde{h}_i(w_1, ..., w_t)$.

Let $(\widetilde{a}_1^{(l)}, \cdots, \widetilde{a}_{15r}^{(l)}, \widetilde{b}_1^{(l)}, \cdots, \widetilde{b}_t^{(l)})$, $1 \le l \le p$, be a basis of the solutions of (20). Set

$$\begin{cases} \sum_{j=1}^{t} \left(\widetilde{b}_j^{(l)}\right)^{1/2} w_j + \left(\sum_{i=1}^{15r} \widetilde{a}_i^{(l)} v_i' + \widetilde{c}^{(l)}\right)^{1/2} = 0. \\ 1 \le l \le p \end{cases} \tag{21}$$

For each $(u_1, ..., u_{12r}) \in S$, its corresponding $(w_1, ..., w_t)$ satisfies (21). From (21) we can represent p of the variables $w_1, ..., w_t$ by the remaining $t - p$ linearly. Totally, $s' + p$ components of the plaintext vector $(u'_1, ..., u'_{12r})$ are represented linearly by the remaining $12r - s' - p$.

Note that we surely have $s' + p \geq 10r$, since the matrix of the coefficients on $X_1, X_2, \cdots, X_{12}$ of ten expansions in (16), (7), and $(X_9^2 + X_{11}^2)^{1/2}$, and $(X_{10}^2 + X_{12}^2)^{1/2}$

is $\begin{pmatrix} I * 0 \\ 0 \, I \, * \\ 0 \, 0 \, A \end{pmatrix}$, where $A = \begin{pmatrix} 1 \, 0 \, 1 \, 0 \\ 0 \, 1 \, 0 \, 1 \end{pmatrix}$, and the matrix is obviously of rank 10. In

other words, solving two systems (17) and (21) eliminates at least $10r$ variables of the plaintext components. If $p = 0$, i.e., there is no nonzero linear combination of the $\widetilde{h}_i(w_1, ..., w_t)$ being of the form $\sum a'_i w_i^2 + b'$, then we must have $s' \geq 10r$ and after the first elimination (i.e., via (17)), the expressions corresponding to $X_9^2 + X_{11}^2$ and $X_{10}^2 + X_{12}^2$ are constants.

3.3   Finding the Plaintext

We substitute these linear expressions that result from solving (21), into $\widetilde{h}_1(w_1, ..., w_t), \cdots, \widetilde{h}_{15r}(w_1, ..., w_t)$ to get $15r$ new quadratic polynomials on $12r - s' - p$ ($\leq 2r$) variables. Denote them by $\widehat{h}_1, \cdots, \widehat{h}_{15r}$. Since $12r - s' - p$ is very small (at most 8 and 10 for MFE-1 and MFE-1', respectively), in principle, we can use the Gröbner basis method to solve the system

$$\widehat{h}_i = v'_i, \quad \forall \, i = 1, \cdots, 15r \tag{22}$$

very easily to find the plaintext finally.

However, we know here that we start from $15r$ equations; therefore we expect to get many more than $2r$ (the number of variables) equations. This means we can solve it easily, for example, using the XL method [CKPS00]. In our experiments, this set of equations does turn out to be very easy to solve.

3.4   A Practical Attack Procedure, Its Complexity and Experimental Verification

Our attack can be divided into the following four steps:

Step 1 of the attack: *Find a basis of the linear space of the coefficient vectors $(a_{ijk}, b_{ij}, \cdots, f)$ of all SOLEs.*

As mentioned in §3.1, this is solving a system of linear equations obtained by evaluating sufficiently many plain/cipher-texts in (9). There are $\binom{12r+1}{1}\binom{15r+2}{2}$ monomials of the form $u_i^\alpha v_j^\beta v_k^\gamma$ on u_i and v_j ($\alpha, \beta, \gamma = 0$ or 1). This number is 92659 and 178486 for $r = 4$ and 5, respectively, and is somewhat large. Choosing a number of plain/cipher-text pairs slightly more than the number of unknowns, say 1000, we can completely find the solution space in general. The complexity is respectively $\frac{1}{2} \cdot 92659^3 \approx 2^{48.5} < 2^{49}$ and $\frac{1}{2} \cdot 178486^3 \approx 2^{51.34} < 2^{52}$ $\mathbb{F}_{2^{16}}$-multiplications using a naive Gaussian elimination.

This step is an one-time computation for any given public key. Let $(a_{ijk}^{(l)}, b_{ij}^{(l)},$ $\cdots, f^{(l)})$, $1 \le l \le s$, be a basis of the equation system.

Our computer experiments confirm that the dimension of SOLE is exactly $24r$, which is performed on the level of the Medium field $\mathbb{L}$ not on the small field K.

Step 2 of the attack: *Given a valid ciphertext $(v_1', \cdots, v_{15r}')$, we plug it into (17) and solve the system of linear equations to obtain linear expressions of the remaining $12r - s'$ in terms of the other s' variables of the plaintext components.* The complexity of this step is $15rs^2 < (15r)^3$, and is less than 2^{19}.

Substitute these linear expressions into the original public key polynomials to get new quadratic polynomials $\widetilde{h}_1(w_1, ..., w_t), \cdots$, and $\widetilde{h}_{15r}(w_1, ..., w_t)$.

Step 3 of the attack: *Solve the system (20) and obtain its solution basis $(\widetilde{a_1}^{(l)}, \cdots, \widetilde{a_{15r}}^{(l)}, \widetilde{b_1}^{(l)}, \cdots, \widetilde{b_t}^{(l)})$, $1 \le l \le p$. Then solve the system (21) to find expression of the p components of the plaintext by the remaining $12r - s' - p$ linearly.*

The complexity of solving (20) is $(15r + t)^3 < (30r)^3 < 2^{22}$, and that for (21) is $pt^2 < (15r)^3 < 2^{19}$.

Our computer experiments show that s' is indeed $8r$ and p is $2r$.

Step 4 of the attack: *Derive new public key polynomials $(\widehat{h}_1, \cdots, \widehat{h}_{15r})$ from the solutions of (21), solve the system (22) and finally obtain the value of p components of the plaintext by using a Gröbner base or a linearization method. Then we use the linear expressions on the remaining plaintext components derived in steps 2 and 3 to find the eliminated components.*

In 1000 experimental samples we have done, we find that after Step 3, the number of linearly independent quadratic equations are actually 20 for MFE-1. We solve them by finding a set of $2r$ linearly independent linear equations inside the space spanned by these equations. It takes almost no time.

Therefore the total attack complexity is less than 2^{52}. The complexity of the attack recovering the plaintext (steps 2, 3 and 4) is less than 2^{23}.

3.5   Experimental Results

We chose 10 different pairs of ϕ_1 and ϕ_3, for each of which we chose 100 different valid ciphertext for experiments. For all chosen ciphertexts, the attack successively found their corresponding plaintexts.

The time-consuming step of our attack is the first step. In our experiments, we randomly selected 92800 plain/cipher-text pairs and substituted them into the public key. Then the main work we will do is a Gaussian elimination on a 92800 × 92659 matrix on $\mathbb{F}_{2^{16}}$. The complexity of this process is less than 2^{52}. We estimate the time to do this Gaussian elimination will be about two years on a standard PC.

So, we performed our experiment on a DELL PowerEdge 7250, a mincom with 4 Itanium2 CPU and 32GB ECC fully buffered DIMM memory. The operating system we used was 64-bit Windows Server2003. We programmed the attack using VC++. Multiple threads can improve the efficiency of programs on a computer with multiple CPU. In our experiments, we used four threads to deal with Gaussian elimination. And we designed a method which will be patented to speed up the multiplication on $\mathbb{F}_{2^{16}}$.

Our experiments showed that 282 hours and 6 minutes (11 days and 18 hours and 6 minutes) were required for the first step, which is an one time computation for any given public key. Only about 2 seconds were needed to execute the remaining steps.

For MFE-1, our experiments confirm that we can find 96 linearly independent SOLEs for a given valid public key in step 1. And we can eliminate 32 plaintext variables in step 2 and 8 plaintext variables in step 3, namely, $s' = 32$ and $p = 8$.

One more important point of our experiments is the fact that we actually used parallel computation (4 Itanium2 CPU) to speed up and accomplish the computation in a reasonable time, which, we thought, was impossible at the very beginning. This demonstrated that parallel computation, in particular, large scale parallel computation, could extend much further the limit of our computation capacity. We believe this is a direction that deserves serious consideration especially in practical attacks.

3.6 Extension of MFE and High Order Linearization Attack

The construction of MFE relies on the multiplicative structure of 2×2 matrices and it is not difficult to see that one can extend this construction in a straightforward way by using matrices of larger sizes $m \times m$, for example, 3×3 or 4×4, to build new MFE cryptosystems. For any such an construction using matrix of $m \times m$, it is not difficult to see that the m-th order LE can be applied to attack the cryptosystem. The fundamental reason behind is the formula that for any matrix Q of size $m \times m$, we know that

$$Q^{-1} = \frac{1}{det(Q)} Q^*,$$

where Q^* is the associated matrix of Q. In terms of algebraic formulas for $det(Q)$ and Q^*, we know that $det(Q)$ can be expressed as a degree m polynomial of the components Q_{ij} of Q and each component of Q^* can be expressed in terms of a degree $(m-1)$ polynomial of the components Q_{ij} of Q. With this and the formulas (6) and (10) and other similar formulas, we can see that, for such a case, the order m linearization equations exists and they can be used to attack such a system. Therefore the current design of MFE needs to increase m substantially to avoid such an attack.

4   The Connection of HOLE with XL

One important point we want to make is that the HOLE method is closely related to the XL method [CKPS00]. In particular one may also explore the possibility of combining these two algebraic methods together to develop additional techniques.

Assume we are given a system of equations $f_i(u_1, \cdots, u_n) = v_i'$, $1 \le i \le m$. Let $U = (u_1, \cdots, u_n)$ and $g_i(U) = f_i(U) - v_i'$. For any nonnegative integral vector

$\alpha = (\alpha_1, \cdots, \alpha_n)$, denote $u_1^{\alpha_1} \cdots u_n^{\alpha_n}$ by U^α. Similarly, for $\beta = (\beta_1, \cdots, \beta_m)$, denote $f_1^{\beta_1} \cdots f_m^{\beta_m}$ by F^β and $g_1^{\beta_1} \cdots g_m^{\beta_m}$ by G^β.

A variant of the XL method first translates the equation system above into another system of equations of the form: $\sum a_{\alpha,i} U^\alpha g_i(U) = 0$, where $1 \le i \le m$ and α are nonnegative integral vectors with small component sum (upper-bounded by some small integer D). Then define all terms $U^\alpha U^\gamma$ as new unknowns and solve the resulting linear equation system.

On the other hand, the HOLE method attempts to solve a system of equations of the form: $\sum_{i,\beta} a_{i,\beta} u_i G^\beta = 0$, where $1 \le i \le n$ and β are chosen small vectors. Since the $f_i(U)$ are equivalent to the $g_i(U)$ under affine transformations, the above system is equivalent to the form: $\sum_{i,\beta} b_{i,\beta} u_i F^\beta = 0$. Our attack presented in the previous section actually finds **identical** equations with the form above, and hence we can substitute F^β by $v_1'^{\beta_1} \cdots v_m'^{\beta_m}$ and get a linear system that the plaintext satisfies.

As a comparison, we find that if a HOLE with order D could be used to successfully attack a system by finding linear equations, then one should expect that the XL method should work as well. But the order of XL should be of degree $2D - 1$ (the total degree is $2D + 1$), because the v_i in general are of degree 2. From this consideration, we conclude that though HOLE definitely cannot be a replacement for the XL method. Yet there could be cases that the HOLE method would be much more efficient than XL. In one case we consider polynomials of degree $D+1$ (HOLE), while in the other case, we consider polynomials of degree $2D + 1$ (XL). Another critical point is that when we use the HOLE method, the computation of HOLEs is performed only once for a given public key, then the HOLEs are used for any ciphertext; while the general XL algorithm needs to run its main part each time for different values of ciphertext. Thus one should think HOLE as a possibly more efficient alternative to XL, if it can work; and there would be cases that HOLE can work practically while the XL cannot.

More importantly, one may consider unifying the XL and HOLE methods. We may expect to efficiently solve the system of equations of the form:

$$\sum_{\alpha,\beta} a_{\alpha,\beta} U^\alpha G^\beta = 0. \tag{23}$$

From the point view of algebraic geometry, this definitely makes sense. But at this moment, we have not yet found any example where such a method could indeed be more efficient in an attack. Furthermore, one can expect that this method may be useful to attack other cryptosystems, such as symmetric ciphers.

5 Conclusion

In this paper, we use an extension of the linearization equation attack method of Patarin, which we call the high order linearization equation method, to break the

MFE multivariate public key cryptosystem in CT-RSA 2006. This shows that the high order linearization equation method is indeed an important algebraic attack method. For any multivariate public key cryptosystem, one should take into account this new method.

References

[ACDG03] Mehdi-Laurent Akkar, Nicolas T. Courtois, Romain Duteuil, and Louis Goubin. A fast and secure implementation of Sflash. In *PKC-2003, LNCS*, volume 2567, pages 267–278. Springer, 2003.

[AFIKS04] Gwénolé Ars and Jean-Charles Faugère and Hideki Imai and Mitsuru Kawazoe and Makoto Sugita Comparison between XL and Gröbner Basis Algorithms, *Asiacrypt 2004*, LNCS, V. 3329.

[MFSY05] M. Bardet, J-C. Fauge, B. Salvy and B-Y. Yang Asymptotic Behaviour of the Degree of Regularity of Semi-Regular Polynomial Systems MEGA 2005, Eighth International Symposium on Effective Methods in Algebraic Geometry, Porto Conte, Alghero, Sardinia (Italy), May 27th - June 1st, 2005, 15 pages.

[C00] Nicolas T. Courtois The security of hidden field equations (HFE) In C. Naccache, editor, Progress in cryptology, CT-RSA, LNCS, volume 2020, pages 266–281. Springer, 2001

[CKPS00] Nicolas Courtois, Alexander Klimov, Jacques Patarin, and Adi Shamir. Efficient algorithms for solving overdefined systems of multivariate polynomial equations. In B. Preenel, editor, *Advances in cryptology, Eurocrypt 2000, LNCS*, volume 1807, pages 392–407. Springer, 2000.

[CPi02] Nicolas Courtois, Josef Pieprzyk: Cryptanalysis of Block Ciphers with Overdefined Systems of Equations. ASIACRYPT 2002, LNCS 2501, 267-287, Springer 2002.

[CM01] J. Chen and T. Moh. On the Goubin-Courtois attack on TTM. *Cryptology ePrint Archive*, 72, 2001. http://eprint.iacr.org/2001/072.

[DH76] Whitfield Diffie and Martin Hellman. New directions in cryptography. *IEEE Transactions on Information Theory*, 22(6):644–654, 1976.

[Din04a] Jintai Ding. A new variant of the Matsumoto-Imai cryptosystem through perturbation. In F. Bao, R. Deng, and J. Zhou, editors, *the 7th International Workshop on Practice and Theory in Public key Cryptography, Singapore, (PKC'04), LNCS*, volume 2947, pages 305–318. Springer, 2004.

[DG05] Jintai Ding and Jason Gower Inoculating Multivariate Schemes Against Differential Attacks. Accepted for PKC-2006, IACR eprint 2005/255.

[DS03a] J. Ding and D. S. Schmidt. A common defect of the TTM cryptosystem. In *Proceedings of the technical track of the ACNS'03, ICISA Press*, pages 68–78, 2003. http://eprint.iacr.org.

[DS03b] J. Ding and D. S. Schmidt. The new TTM implementation is not secure. In H. Niederreiter K.Q. Feng and C.P. Xing, editors, *Proceedings of International Workshop on Coding, Cryptography and Combinatorics (CCC 2003)*, pages 106–121, 2003.

[DS04a]   Jintai Ding, and D. S. Schmidt Cryptanalysis of HFEV and the internal perturbation of HFE. The 8th International Workshop on Practice and Theory in Public key Cryptography, Jan. 2005, Switzerland (PKC'05), Lecture Notes in Computer Sciences, volume 3386, pages 288-301 Springer, 2005.

[DS05]   Jintai Ding, and D. S. Schmidt Rainbow, a new multivariate public key signature scheme. The Third International Conference of Applied Cryptography and Network Security (ACNS 2005), New York, June 7-10, 2005, Lecture Notes in Computer Science 3531, Page 164-175, Springer, 2005.

[Fau99]   Jean-Charles Faugère A new efficient algorithm for computing Gröbner bases (F_4), Journal of Pure and Applied Algebra, V. 139, P. 61-88, June 199.

[FGS05]   P.-A. Fouque, L. Granboulan, and J. Stern. Differential Cryptanalysis for Multivariate Schemes Advances in Cryptology - EUROCRYPT 2005, Lecture Notes in Computer Science 3494 Springer 2005, Page 341-353.

[GC00]   L. Goubin and N. Courtois. Cryptanalysis of the TTM cryptosystem. *LNCS, Springer Verlag*, 1976:44–57, 2000.

[KS99]   Aviad Kipnis and Adi Shamir. Cryptanalysis of the HFE public key cryptosystem by relinearization. In M. Wiener, editor, *Advances in crytology – Crypto '99, LNCS*, volume 1666, pages 19–30. Springer, 1999.

[MI88]   T. Matsumoto and H. Imai. Public quadratic polynomial-tuples for efficient signature verification and message encryption. In C. G. Guenther, editor, *Advances in cryptology – EUROCRYPT'88, LNCS*, volume 330, pages 419–453. Springer, 1988.

[Moh99]   T. T. Moh. A fast public key system with signature and master key functions. *Lecture Notes at EE department of Stanford University.*, May 1999. http://www.usdsi.com/ttm.html.

[MCY04]   T.Moh and J.M.Chen and Boyin Yang Building Instances of TTM Immune to the Goubin-Courtois Attack and the Ding-Schmidt Attack. IACR eprint 2004/168, http://eprint.iacr.org.

[NES]   NESSIE. European project IST-1999-12324 on New European Schemes for Signature, Integrity and Encryption. http://www.cryptonessie.org.

[Pat95]   J. Patarin. Cryptanalysis of the Matsumoto and Imai public key scheme of Eurocrypt'88. In D. Coppersmith, editor, *Advances in Cryptology – Crypto '95, LNCS*, volume 963, pages 248–261, 1995.

[Pat96]   J. Patarin. Hidden field equations (HFE) and isomorphism of polynomials (IP): Two new families of asymmetric algorithms. In U. Maurer, editor, *Eurocrypt'96, LNCS*, volume 1070, pages 33–48. Springer, 1996.

[Pat97]   J. Patarin. The oil and vinegar signature scheme. *Dagstuhl Workshop on Cryptography, September 1997*, 1997.

[PCG01a]   Jacques Patarin, Nicolas Courtois, and Louis Goubin. Flash, a fast multivariate signature algorithm. In *LNCS*, volume 2020, pages 298–307. Springer, 2001.

[PGC98]   Jacques Patarin, Louis Goubin, and Nicolas Courtois. C_{-+}^* and HM: variations around two schemes of T. Matsumoto and H. Imai. In K. Ohta and D. Pei, editors, *ASIACRYPT'98, LNCS*, volume 1514, pages 35–50. Springer, 1998.

[PQ]   PQCrypto 2006: International Workshop on Post-Quantum Cryptography http://postquantum.cr.yp.to/

[RSA78]   Ronald Rivest, Adi Shamir, and Leonard M. Adleman. A method
             for obtaining digital signatures and public key cryptosystems. *ACM*,
             21(2):120–126, 1978.
[Sho99]   Peter Shor. Polynomial-time algorithms for prime factorization and
             discrete logarithms on a quantum computer. *SIAM Rev.*, 41(2):303–
             332, 1999.
[WHLCY05]   Lih-Chung Wang and Yuh-Hua Hu and Feipei Lai and Chun-Yen Chou
             and Bo-Yin Yang, Tractable Rational Map Signature, Public Key Cryp-
             tosystems 2005, LNCS 3386, Springer, P. 244-257.
[WYH06]   Lih-Chung Wang, Bo-yin Yang, Yuh-Hua Hu and Feipei Lai, A Medium-
             Field Multivariate Public key Encryption Scheme, CT-RSA 2006: The
             Cryptographers' Track at the RSA Conference 2006, LNCS 3860, 132-
             149, Springer, 2006.
[YC05]   B. Yang and J. Chen. Building Secure Tame-like Multivariate Public
             key Cryptosystems–The New TTS. Information Security and Privacy:
             10th Australasian Conference–ACISP 2005, LNCS 3574, 2005, Springer,
             P. 518-531.

Cryptanalysis of HFE with Internal Perturbation

Vivien Dubois, Louis Granboulan, and Jacques Stern[*]

École normale supérieure
DI, 45 rue d'Ulm, 75230 Paris cedex 05, France
{vivien.dubois,louis.granboulan,jacques.stern}@ens.fr

Abstract. Multivariate Cryptography has been an active line of research for almost twenty years. While most multivariate cryptosystems have been under attack, variations of the basic schemes came up as potential repairs. In this paper, we study the Internal Perturbation variation of HFE recently proposed by Ding and Schmidt. Although several results indicate that HFE is vulnerable against algebraic attacks for moderate size parameters, Ding and Schmidt claim that the cryptosystem with internal perturbation should be immune against them. However in this paper, we apply the recently discovered method of differential analysis to the Internal Perturbation of HFE and we find a subtle property which allows to disclose the kernel of the perturbation. Once this has been achieved, the public key can be inverted by attacking the underlying HFE provided the parameters were taken low enough to make the perturbed scheme of competitive performance.

Keywords: multivariate cryptography, HFE, internal perturbation, differential cryptanalysis, binary vector spaces.

1 Introduction

Multivariate Cryptography has been an active line of research for almost twenty years. Initiated independently in the early 80's by Matsumoto-Imai and Fell-Diffie [11,7], the field was revived by the work of Patarin and Shamir [14,17,15]. The interest for multivariate primitives can be explained in several ways. First, these schemes are not related to factorization or discrete logarithm problems. They rely on the intractability of solving systems of multivariate quadratic equations over a finite field. This problem is proved NP-hard [12] and moreover no quantum polynomial algorithm has been found to solve it. Next, these schemes benefit from several nice properties such as providing very short or very fast signatures, as well as a very particular flexibility: from all basic trapdoors can be derived a number of generic variations. These variations are often considered to thwart structural attacks against the original cryptosystems.

Today most basic trapdoors have been under attack. Among the most promising, HFE was introduced by Patarin as a repair of the Matsumoto-Imai

---

[*] This work is supported in part by the French government through X-Crypt, in part by the European Commission through ECRYPT.

cryptosystem [15]. The scheme was quickly subject to a cryptanalytic attack by Kipnis and Shamir [9], and further attacked by Courtois [1], but the first successful cryptanalysis of HFE was only provided by Faugère and Joux, eight years after its invention [6]. The latter attack made use of a general Gröbner bases algorithm and its success can only be explained by some inherent algebraic properties allowing a peculiarly fast computation of the algorithm. These algebraic properties were recently mathematically explained by Granboulan-Joux-Stern [10] and a rather clear picture of how to choose parameters to withstand attacks is emerging.

On the other hand, very few studies are dedicated to the security of variations, and the respective effects of the many variations remain unclear in terms of security. However variations are powerful and can have a crucial impact on security: as an example, the SFlash signature algorithm chosen by the NESSIE European consortium is a variation of the broken Matsumoto-Imai cryptosystem [13]. Also, most attacks against the basic cryptosystems do not extend to variations. The gain on security brought by variations has to be understood to determine whether they result in secure schemes.

Our results. In this paper, we consider a variation of HFE called the Internally Perturbed HFE. This variation was recently proposed by Ding and Schmidt [4]. It was designed to counter Kipnis-Shamir's attack, and is expected to withstand Gröbner bases attack as well. A simpler internal variation had been previously proposed based on the Matsumoto-Imai cryptosystem [2] and had already been asserted to provide immunity against algebraic attacks [3]. Unfortunately, the Matsumoto-Imai cryptosystem has a very specific structure and the internal perturbation could actually be removed using the recently introduced differential technique [8]. In this work, we consider the enhanced internal perturbation variation as applied to HFE and defined in [4]. We show that the original internal perturbation variation applied to HFE still suffers from the drawback exhibited in [8], while the enhanced version has indeed a much subtler differential visibility. However, a differential bias can still be captured and exploited to disclose the kernel of the perturbation. Once this has been achieved, the public key can be inverted by attacking the underlying HFE provided the parameters were taken low enough to make the perturbed scheme of competitive performance. Precise complexity estimates for the attack are provided.

Organization of the paper. In section 2, we recall the construction of HFE and its Internal Perturbation variation. Next, in section 3, we recall the basics of differential analysis for multivariate schemes and its application to the internally Perturbed Matsumoto-Imai. In section 4, we analyze the differential of the Internally Perturbed HFE and we exhibit a provable distinguisher of elements cancelling the perturbation. In section 5, we turn this distinguisher into an algorithm to find the kernel of the perturbation. In section 6, we show that the public key can be easily inverted once this kernel is known. The method being quite technical in character, all proofs could not be included; the full paper is available from the authors.

2   The Internally Perturbed HFE Cryptosystem

2.1   Notations

We denote by $\mathbb{F}_2$ the finite field with two elements and by $\mathbb{F}_{2^n}$ the degree n extension field of $\mathbb{F}_2$. $\mathbb{F}_{2^n}$ is an $\mathbb{F}_2$-vector space of dimension n isomorphic to $\mathbb{F}_2^n$. The squaring operation $x \mapsto x^2$ is $\mathbb{F}_2$-linear (or additive) in $\mathbb{F}_{2^n}$. As a consequence, sums of monomials of the form ax^{2^i} where a is an element of $\mathbb{F}_{2^n}$ and i is an integer in $[0, n-1]$, are the $\mathbb{F}_2$-linear maps over $\mathbb{F}_{2^n}$. Polynomials of this type will be therefore called $\mathbb{F}_2$-*linear polynomials*. Given an $\mathbb{F}_2$-linear polynomial, the set of its cancelling elements is a linear subspace of $\mathbb{F}_{2^n}$ that will be referred to as its *kernel*. $\mathbb{F}_2$-linear polynomials are isomorphic to (multivariate) linear maps of $\mathbb{F}_2^n$ by an extension of the isomorphism between $\mathbb{F}_{2^n}$ and $\mathbb{F}_2^n$. Similarly, sums of monomials of the form $ax^{2^i+2^j}$ where a is an element of $\mathbb{F}_{2^n}$ and i, j are integers in $[0, n-1]$, will be called $\mathbb{F}_2$-*quadratic polynomials*. $\mathbb{F}_2$-quadratic polynomials translate through the isomorphism between $\mathbb{F}_{2^n}$ and $\mathbb{F}_2^n$ into quadratic maps of $\mathbb{F}_2^n$, defined by n polynomials of degree 2 in n variables.

2.2   The Original HFE Setting

Informally speaking, the generic construction of multivariate schemes consists in disguising an easily solvable system of multivariate quadratic equations as random, by a secret transformation. In most schemes, the secret transformation is the composition by two randomly chosen invertible affine maps S, T; one is applied on the variables and the other one on the equations. The way to generate an easily solvable quadratic system P defines each scheme. The public key $\boldsymbol{P}$ is given by:

$$\boldsymbol{P} = T \circ P \circ S$$

An encrypted message $\boldsymbol{P}(a)$ is decrypted by solving the quadratic system $\boldsymbol{P}(x) = \boldsymbol{P}(a)$. Solving this system is intractable except for the legitimate user which can invert T and S and solve the easy internal system. In Matsumoto-Imai and HFE, the easily solvable system P exploits the isomorphism between $\mathbb{F}_{2^n}$ and $\mathbb{F}_2^n$. In Matsumoto-Imai, the internal function P is the multivariate expression of an $\mathbb{F}_2$-quadratic monomial $x^{2^i+2^j}$, where i, j are suitably chosen so that it is invertible. In HFE, the internal polynomial is the multivariate expression of an $\mathbb{F}_2$-quadratic polynomial which has low degree to allow decryption by a root-finding algorithm.

Different cryptanalytic approaches [9,6,1] made clear that the low degree of the internal polynomial in HFE makes the system vulnerable to algebraic attacks. In particular, Faugère and Joux demonstrated that systems of quadratic equations coming from HFE public keys allow much easier Gröbner basis computations than random systems of the same size [6] - the first challenge of HFE of parameters $n = 80$ and degree 96 was broken in a hundred hours. Now the question is : how to enhance the security of HFE?

2.3   The Internally Perturbed HFE

To withstand low degree attacks, the internal polynomial should be modified so
that it no more has low degree while still allowing decryption. An interesting
idea to realize this, was presented by Ding and Schmidt [4] and is known as the
Internally Perturbed HFE. The suggested modification consists in "noising" the
low degree internal polynomial by a few terms of high degree which can only be
removed by the legitimate user. We next recall this scheme in detail.

For a given degree parameter D, the user chooses a bivariate polynomial
$\ddot{P}(x, y)$ as the sum of three basic components:

- a univariate $\mathbb{F}_2$-quadratic polynomial $P(x)$ in variable x of low degree under
  2^{D+1}, that will be called the HFE-part of $\ddot{P}$.
- a bivariate $\mathbb{F}_2$-bilinear polynomial $M(x, y)$ in variables x, y of low degree 2^D
  in x, that will be called the the mixing part of $\ddot{P}$.
- a univariate $\mathbb{F}_2$-quadratic polynomial $\bar{P}(y)$ in variable y, that will called the
  pure perturbation part of $\ddot{P}$.

In addition, the user randomly selects an $\mathbb{F}_2$-linear polynomial $Z(x)$ of low rank
r. The $\mathbb{F}_2$-quadratic polynomial $\tilde{P}(x) = \ddot{P}(x, Z(x))$ has very high degree in
general, nevertheless its roots can be found indirectly: the image of Z, that we
note $\text{Im}(Z)$, has only 2^r elements and for any b of them, one can find the roots of
$\ddot{P}(x, b)$ since it has small degree. $\tilde{P}(x)$ consists in the internal polynomial in the
Internally Perturbed HFE, and the public key is $\boldsymbol{P} = T \circ \tilde{P} \circ S$, as in HFE. One
can observe that the decryption process is 2^r times slower than for an HFE of the
same degree parameter. The prescribed parameters are $n = 89, D = 3, r = 2$ [4].
It can be noticed that in our definition of the internal polynomial $\tilde{P}$, all linear
and constant terms of the definition of [4] were omitted. Indeed in the sequel,
we will only be interested in the differential of $\tilde{P}$, and as we will see, linear and
constant terms disappear when taking the differential.

3   Internal Perturbation and Differential Analysis

We let $\boldsymbol{Z}$ to be the composition of Z with the linear part of S. As a basic
observation, an Internally Perturbed HFE public key is just an HFE public
key on any affine subspace parallel to the kernel of $\boldsymbol{Z}$. Indeed, this is required
by the decryption process: for any element b, $\tilde{P}(x)$ coincides with the small
degree polynomial $\ddot{P}(x, b)$ over the affine subspace $b + \ker Z$. Therefore, if we
could discover the kernel of $\boldsymbol{Z}$, we could invert the public key by attacking the
underlying HFEs with Gröbner bases, as shown by Faugère and Joux [6]. Hence,
the Internally Perturbed scheme would be broken by the ability to recover the
kernel of the perturbation.

Differential Analysis is a generic tool of analysis of multivariate schemes which
can allow learning information about the hidden structure. It was in particular
used to discover the kernel of the perturbation of a former internally perturbed
scheme, the Perturbed Matsumoto-Imai cryptosystem. We next recall the basics of differential analysis for multivariate schemes and its application to the
Perturbed Matsumoto-Imai.

3.1 Basic Properties of the Differential of a Quadratic Function

For any quadratic function P and any element a, the difference $P(x+a) - P(x)$ is an affine function in x of constant term $P(a) - P(0)$. Its linear part is called the differential of P at a and will be denoted DP_a in the sequel.

$$DP_a(x) = P(a+x) - P(x) - P(a) + P(0)$$

In multivariate schemes, we have two quadratic functions $\boldsymbol{P}$ and P which are related by two bijective affine transforms S and T following $\boldsymbol{P} = T \circ P \circ S$. Denoting $\underline{S}$ and $\underline{T}$ the linear parts of S and T, the differential of $\boldsymbol{P}$ and P are related the following way:

$$D\boldsymbol{P}_a = \underline{T} \circ DP_{\underline{S}(a)} \circ \underline{S}$$

Therefore, $\underline{S}$ and $\underline{T}$ being invertible, the distribution of the kernel-dimension of the differential for a random a is the same for the public key as for the internal function. This was first noticed in [8] to attack the Perturbed Matsumoto-Imai.

3.2 Application to the Perturbed Matsumoto-Imai

The Matsumoto-Imai scheme uses an internal polynomial P of the form $x^{2^i+2^j}$. Ding proposed an internal perturbation with *no mixing part* (i.e. $M(x,y) = 0$) [2]. Considering the differential of $\tilde{P}$ at a,

$$D\tilde{P}_a(x) = DP_a(x) + D\bar{P}_{Z(a)}(Z(x)) \tag{1}$$

it was observed in [8] that the differential at points in the kernel of Z is exactly the differential of the original Matsumoto-Imai function at these points. Besides, the differential of the Matsumoto-Imai internal function $x^{2^i+2^j}$ has kernel-dimension $gcd(n, i - j)$ at any non-zero point. On the other side, when taken at a point which is not in the kernel of Z, the perturbation part interferes and may cause the differential to have a larger of smaller kernel. This provides an easy criteria to detect elements which are not in the kernel of Z, and with sufficiently many such points, the kernel can be recovered.

As a remark, observe that the internal perturbation without mixing terms applied on HFE yields the same drawback. Again the differential of $\tilde{P}$ at a point of the kernel of Z is the differential of the HFE internal polynomial. The differential of an HFE internal polynomial of degree under 2^{D+1} has degree at most 2^D, and therefore, as a linear map, its kernel has dimension at most D [5]. On the other side, when the perturbation interferes, the differential may have a larger kernel.

4   A Differential Bias of the Internally Perturbed HFE

In this section, we prove the spinal cord of our attack: whether the perturbation vanishes or not yields a differential bias. First, we characterize the form of the differential in both cases, in terms of sums of linear maps of two kinds. Second, we compute the distribution of the kernel-dimensions in both cases, using combinatorics in binary vector spaces. Third, we define a distinguisher of kernel elements whose advantage can be exactly computed for a random secret key.

4.1 Differential Structure of the Perturbed Internal Polynomial

From now on, the kernel of Z will be denoted $\mathcal{K}$. Depending on the membership of a to $\mathcal{K}$, the differential at a is:

$$
\begin{aligned}
a \notin \mathcal{K}, \quad & D\tilde{P}_a(x) = DP_a(x) + M(x, Z(a)) + M(a, Z(x)) + D\bar{P}_{Z(a)}(Z(x)) \\
a \in \mathcal{K}, \quad & D\tilde{P}_a(x) = DP_a(x) \qquad\qquad\qquad + M(a, Z(x))
\end{aligned}
$$

As we can see, the *differential of the perturbed internal at points where the perturbation vanishes is not the differential of the non-perturbed internal* as it was for PMI. In particular, the kernel-dimension of the differential will be more than D for some elements in $\mathcal{K}$ while this could never happen with a PMI-like perturbation. In fact, we will next show that the differential reaches the same kernel dimensions in both cases. Therefore, it will not be possible to use the "cut-off" based strategy as for PMI to detect the effectiveness of the perturbation. A more elaborate analysis of the differential is therefore required.

As a first step, we can observe that the structure of the differential is very similar in both cases. In both cases, this is the sum of an $\mathbb{F}_2$-linear polynomial of degree 2^D and a linear map of rank r which take the same value at a. What differs is: the common value is 0 when a is in $\mathcal{K}$ and non-zero when it is not. This actually captures the structure of this differential, as stated by the following theorem.

Theorem 1. *Let a be a non-zero element of $\mathbb{F}_2^n$. A random instance $(P, M, \bar{P}, Z)$ of Internally Perturbed HFE with parameters (D, r) has an internal polynomial denoted $\tilde{P}$. We denote by L_D a random $\mathbb{F}_2$-linear polynomial of degree 2^D and by l_r a random linear map of rank r. Then, for a proportion $1 - \epsilon_{n,r}$ of all instances $(P, M, \bar{P}, Z)$ of the cryptosystem, we have:*

$$
Pr\left[\dim \ker D\tilde{P}_a = t \,\middle|\, a \in \mathcal{K}\right] = Pr\left[\dim \ker(L_D + l_r) = t \,\middle|\, L_D(a) = l_r(a) = 0\right]
$$

and

$$
Pr\left[\dim \ker D\tilde{P}_a = t \,\middle|\, a \notin \mathcal{K}\right] = Pr\left[\dim \ker(L_D + l_r) = t \,\middle|\, L_D(a) = l_r(a) \neq 0\right]
$$

where $\epsilon_{n,r} = 2^{-(n-r)} + \mathcal{O}(2^{-2n})$.

A proof of the theorem can be found in the full paper available from the authors. It will be clear from the sequel that, for the suggested parameters, $\epsilon_{n,r}$ is negligible compared to the probabilities of interest. Accordingly, the kernel dimensions of the differential at points inside and outside $\mathcal{K}$ respectively follow the distributions of probability denoted π^+ and π^- defined by:

$$\pi^+(t) = \Pr{}_{(L_D,l_r)} [\dim \ker(L_D + l_r) = t \mid L_D(a) = l_r(a) = 0]$$
$$\pi^-(t) = \Pr{}_{(L_D,l_r)} [\dim \ker(L_D + l_r) = t \mid L_D(a) = l_r(a) \neq 0]$$

We next study both distributions in detail.

4.2 Distribution of the Kernel-Dimension of the Differential Depending on the Position of the Point

Distributions π^+ and π^- can be exactly computed using combinatorics in binary vector spaces, which are of independent interest. We will not recall these combinatorics here since they are not the subject of this paper, however all details are provided in Appendix A. We nevertheless describe the three steps that we follow to determine the distribution of the kernel-dimension of the sum of a random $\mathbb{F}_2$-linear polynomial of degree 2^D and a random linear map of rank r:

- first, we compute the distribution of the kernel-dimension of $\mathbb{F}_2$-linear polynomials of degree 2^D. The kernel-dimension of such polynomials is at most D, and the vanishing of one such polynomial over a subspace of dimension d with $d \leq D$ can be expressed in d independent linear constraints over the $D + 1$ coefficients defining this $\mathbb{F}_2$-linear polynomial.
- fixing an $\mathbb{F}_2$-linear polynomial L of kernel-dimension d, we can compute the probability that a random subspace of dimension $n - r$ has intersection of dimension i with the kernel of L.
- fixing a subspace G of dimension $n - r$ which intersects the kernel of L with dimension i, we can enumerate the number of linear maps l of kernel G such that $\ker(L + l)$ has dimension t. Observe that in characteristic 2, $\ker(L + l)$ is the subspace where L and l are equal.

The overall probability for the dimension t requires to sum over all possible values of d and i; unfortunately, we could not find a closed formula (if any) for this probability. Nevertheless the sum itself is enough for all practical purposes.

Finding the laws π^+ and π^- consists in redoing the previous enumeration while taking into account the constraint at a. For any d and i, we can extract the correction factors coming from the constraint at a in either case. This leads to the following proposition.

Proposition 1. Let $\pi_{d,r,i}(t)$ be the probability that the sum $L_D + l_r$ of a random $\mathbb{F}_2$-linear polynomial L_D of degree 2^D and kernel-dimension d and a random linear map l_r of rank r with kernels intersecting with dimension i, has kernel dimension t. Formally,

$$\pi_{d,r,i}(t) = \Pr{}_{(L_D,l_r)} \left[\dim \ker(L_D + l_r) = t \, ; \, \begin{cases} \dim \ker L_D = d \\ \dim(\ker L_D \cap \ker l_r) = i \end{cases} \right]$$

For a prescribed non-zero element a, we denote

- $\pi^+_{d,r,i}(t)$ *for the probability of the same event knowing* $L_D(a) = l_r(a) = 0$
- $\pi^-_{d,r,i}(t)$ *for the probability of the same event knowing* $L_D(a) = l_r(a) \neq 0$

We have:

$$\pi^+_{d,r,i}(t) = 2^r \ (2^i - 1) \ \pi_{d,r,i}(t) \ (1 + 2^{-(n-r)} + \mathcal{O}(2^{-2(n-r)}))$$
$$\pi^-_{d,r,i}(t) = \tfrac{2^r}{2^r-1} \ (2^t - 2^i) \ \pi_{d,r,i}(t)$$

on average over a.

Again, a proof can be found in the full paper. Neglecting terms of order $2^{-(n-r)}$, we obtain for π^+ and π^-:

$$\pi^+(t) = 2^r \ \sum_{d=0}^{D} \sum_{i=0}^{d} (2^i - 1) \ \pi_{d,r,i}(t)$$

$$\pi^-(t) = \tfrac{2^r}{2^r-1} \sum_{d=0}^{D} \sum_{i=0}^{d} (2^t - 2^i) \ \pi_{d,r,i}(t)$$

Though these probabilities are not provided under a closed form, they can be computed for any choice of the parameters. For example, for the suggested parameters $(n, D, r) = (89, 3, 2)$ their values are given in the table below:

dimension t	π^+	$\pi^-(t)$	$\mathrm{sign}(\pi^+ - \pi^-)$
1	$\simeq 0.57764$	$\simeq 0.57756$	$+$
2	$\simeq 0.38495$	$\simeq 0.38507$	$-$
3	$\simeq 0.036718$	$\simeq 0.036662$	$+$
4	$\simeq 0.00069427$	$\simeq 0.00070045$	$-$
5	$\simeq 0.0000025431$	$\simeq 0.0000029064$	$-$

The kernel-dimension of the differential at some point a is now fully understood: it can follow two well determined distributions depending on the membership to $\mathcal{K}$ of a. We next compare these two distributions and show that the kernel-dimension of the differential at a yields some information about its membership or non-membership to $\mathcal{K}$.

4.3   Distinguishing Kernel Elements

Definition of our Distinguisher. Let $\tilde{P}$ be a public key associated to a given instance $(P, M, \bar{P}, Z)$ of the cryptosystem, and let $\mathcal{K}$ be the subspace isomorphic to K through the linear masking. Our distinguisher is built on the differential bias exhibited in the preceding section. For a random non-zero element a, we compute the kernel dimension of the differential of $\tilde{P}$ at a and obtain the dimension t. If for this dimension t we have $\pi^+(t) \geq \pi^-(t)$ then the hypothesis that a is in $\mathcal{K}$ is more favorable and our decision will therefore follow this way. Put in a formal way, we define the function

$$T : \begin{cases} T(a) = 1 \text{ when } \dim \ker D\tilde{P}_a = t \text{ with } \pi^+(t) \geq \pi^-(t) \\ T(a) = 0 \text{ when } \dim \ker D\tilde{P}_a = t \text{ with } \pi^+(t) \leq \pi^-(t) \end{cases}$$

T is our distinguisher of kernel elements. We next compute its advantage.

Advantage of the Distinguisher. The advantage of T for a random instance of the cryptosystem and a random a is by definition

$$|\Pr\left[T(a) = 1 \,|\, a \in \mathcal{K}\right] - \Pr\left[T(a) = 1 \,|\, a \notin \mathcal{K}\right]|$$

The inner difference values to

$$\sum_{t:\pi^+(t) \geq \pi^-(t)} \Pr\left[\dim \ker D\tilde{P}_a = t \,|\, a \in \mathcal{K}\right] - \Pr\left[\dim \ker D\tilde{P}_a = t \,|\, a \notin \mathcal{K}\right]$$

The summand of the above is $\pi^+(t) - \pi^-(t)$ and is therefore positive for the prescribed values of t. Hence, the expected advantage of the distinguisher for a random instance of the cryptosystem, denoted Adv, is

$$Adv = \sum_{t:\pi^+(t) \geq \pi^-(t)} \pi^+(t) - \pi^-(t)$$

We summarize in the table below the values of Adv for some parameters.

(n, D, r)	Adv
$(89, 2, 2)$	$2^{-7.49}$
$(89, 3, 2)$	$2^{-12.95}$
$(89, 3, 3)$	$2^{-16.17}$
$(89, 4, 4)$	$2^{-27.97}$

In the above table, the second line corresponds to the preferred parameters in [4].

5 Recovering the Kernel of the Internal Perturbation

In the previous section, we designed a distinguisher T which can be seen as a two-sided error test of membership to $\mathcal{K}$. In this section, we aim at turning the test T into an algorithm for finding elements of $\mathcal{K}$.

5.1 Behaviour of the Test with Respect to Linearity

The set $\mathcal{K}$ benefits from a property that its complement does not share: it is closed under addition. Accordingly, when x is a member of $\mathcal{K}$ then any y and $x + y$ must be both members of both non-members of $\mathcal{K}$, while it can happen differently when x is not in $\mathcal{K}$. Analogously, the probability for a random y that both y and $x + y$ are detected inside or outside $\mathcal{K}$ by the test should be higher on average over the elements x of $\mathcal{K}$ than over those not in $\mathcal{K}$. We next show that this intuition is correct and compute the distance between these two probabilities.

Given an element y, we denote by μ_y^+ the probability that $T(x + y) = T(y)$ when x is in $\mathcal{K}$, and by μ_y^- the same probability when x is outside $\mathcal{K}$.

$$\mu_y^+ = \Pr_x[T(x + y) = T(y) \,|\, x \in \mathcal{K}]$$
$$\mu_y^- = \Pr_x[T(x + y) = T(y) \,|\, x \notin \mathcal{K}]$$

The mean values of μ_y^+ and μ_y^- over the y are denoted μ^+ and μ^-.

$$\mu^+ = \Pr_{x,y}[\, T(x+y) = T(y) \,|\, x \in \mathcal{K}\,]$$
$$\mu^- = \Pr_{x,y}[\, T(x+y) = T(y) \,|\, x \notin \mathcal{K}\,]$$

Probabilities μ^+ and μ^- can be computed for a random instance of the cryptosystem; their distance denoted $\Delta\mu$ is

$$\Delta\mu = \mu^+ - \mu^- = 2.\frac{Adv^2}{2^r} \tag{2}$$

The details of these computations can be found in the full paper.

Given an element y, we define the random variable δ_y which values 1 at x whenever $T(x+y) = T(y)$ and 0 otherwise. The mean value of δ_y over $\mathcal{K}$ is μ_y^+, and is μ_y^- over the complement of $\mathcal{K}$. In the sequel, we will consider a large assembly of random variables δ_{y_i} for some fixed y_i. The idea is that, whenever $\delta_{y_i}(x)$ is 1 for many i, x should belong to $\mathcal{K}$ with high probability.

5.2   Building a Reliable Test of Membership

Definition of the Test. For any N non-zero distinct elements $y_1, \ldots, y_N$, we define the random variable

$$S_N(x) = \sum_{i=1}^{N} \delta_{y_i}(x)$$

For any such random variable S_N, a test of membership can be defined as follows. Given an element x, we compute $S_N(x)$; whenever $S_N(x) \geq N\mu^+$, the test answers **yes**, and **no** otherwise.

The intention behind the test is the following. Since $\delta_{y_i}(x)$ is more likely to be 1 when x is in $\mathcal{K}$ than when x is not in $\mathcal{K}$, we expect $S_N(x)$ to be higher when x is in $\mathcal{K}$ than when x is not in $\mathcal{K}$. When N increases, we expect the intersection between the values of S_N over $\mathcal{K}$ and the values of S_N outside $\mathcal{K}$ to become smaller. Finally, for N large enough, we expect the probability that $S_N(x) \geq N\mu^+$ to be large when x is in $\mathcal{K}$ and very small when x is not in $\mathcal{K}$.

Analysis of the Test. Let us first consider S_N over $\mathcal{K}$. For any y_i, the mean value of δ_{y_i} over $\mathcal{K}$ is $\mu_{y_i}^+$. This latter value is not known, however we know that it follows a distribution of mean value μ^+. Likewise, the mean value of S_N over $\mathcal{K}$, denoted A_N^+, follows a distribution over the N-tuples $(y_1, \ldots, y_N)$ of mean value $N\mu^+$. Hence, for half the choices of a N-tuple $(y_1, \ldots, y_N)$, we have $A_N^+ \geq N\mu^+$. When this is the case, we have :

$$\Pr_x\left[S_N(x) \geq N\mu^+ \,|\, x \in \mathcal{K}\right] \geq \Pr_x\left[S_N(x) \geq A_N^+ \,|\, x \in \mathcal{K}\right] = \frac{1}{2}$$

Therefore, in at least half the cases, more than the half of the elements of $\mathcal{K}$ will pass our test of membership, whatever is the value of N.

Now we consider S_N over the complement of $\mathcal{K}$. We want to find some N so that the probability for the elements of the complement of $\mathcal{K}$ to pass the test is very small. We can notice as before, that the mean value of S_N over the complement of $\mathcal{K}$, denoted A_N^-, follows a distribution of mean value $N\mu^-$. Hence, for half the choices of a N-tuple $(y_1, \ldots, y_N)$, we have $A_N^- \leq N\mu^-$. When this is the case, we have :

$$\Pr_x\left[S_N(x) \geq N\mu^+ \mid x \notin \mathcal{K}\right] \leq \Pr_x\left[S_N(x) - A_N^- \geq N\Delta\mu \mid x \notin \mathcal{K}\right] \quad (3)$$

and our task is now to find an upper-bound of the right-hand probability.

We observe that, when the y_i are independently chosen, the random variables δ_{y_i} are independent. Sequences of independent non-identically distributed binary random variables are known as Poisson trials in the litterature. Applying the Chernoff bound [16]:

$$\Pr_x\left[S_N(x) - A_N^- \geq N\Delta\mu \mid x \notin \mathcal{K}\right] \leq \exp(-\frac{1}{4}\frac{N^2\Delta\mu^2}{A_N^-})$$

Besides, we have $A_N^- \leq N\mu^-$ and $\mu^- \leq \mu$ where μ is the probability to have $T(x+y) = T(y)$ for random x and y. Therefore, using (3), we finally obtain:

$$\Pr_x\left[S_N(x) \geq N\mu^+ \mid x \notin \mathcal{K}\right] \leq \exp(-\frac{N}{4}\frac{\Delta\mu^2}{\mu})$$

We now estimate the value of μ. When x and y are random, $x + y$ and y are independent and therefore $\mu = \alpha^2 + (1 - \alpha)^2$ where $\alpha = \Pr[T = 1]$. Probability α can be computed for a random instance of the cryptosystem from

$$\alpha = \sum_{t:\pi^+(t)\geq\pi^-(t)} (2^{-r})\pi^+(t) + (1 - 2^{-r})\pi^-(t) \simeq \sum_{t:\pi^+(t)\geq\pi^-(t)} \pi^-(t)$$

Using the table 1, we see that $\alpha \simeq 0.6$ and $\mu \simeq 0.5$.

Finally, to make the probability to have a false-positive under ϵ, we can take

$$N = \frac{2}{\Delta\mu^2} \ln\left(\frac{1}{\epsilon}\right) = \frac{2^{2r-1}}{Adv^4} \ln\left(\frac{1}{\epsilon}\right) \quad (4)$$

Complexity for Recovering $\mathcal{K}$. A random element x is in $\mathcal{K}$ with probability $\frac{1}{2^r}$ and is detected in $\mathcal{K}$ by the test with probability $\frac{1}{2}$. Computing all the $\delta_{y_i}(x)$ values is achieved by computing the differentials at $x + y_i$ and at y_i, and then computing their ranks. The complexity for computing a differential or a rank is n^3, the same as for evaluating the public key. Recovering $\mathcal{K}$ requires to discover about n of its elements. Therefore, the complexity for recovering $\mathcal{K}$ is $2^{r+1}Nn$ evaluations of the public key. When taking N as given by Formula 4, recovering $\mathcal{K}$ amounts to

$$\frac{n2^{3r}}{Adv^4} \ln\left(\frac{1}{\epsilon}\right)$$

evaluations of the public key. This is given by the table below for practical parameters and $\epsilon = 0.001$. It should be remarked that Formula 4 gives us an upper-bound on the value of N to be chosen. In practice, taking a smaller N might allow the attack as well.

(n, D, r)	Recovering $\mathcal{K}$
$(89, 2, 1)$	$2^{32.26}$
$(89, 2, 2)$	$2^{45.20}$
$(89, 3, 2)$	$2^{67.03}$
$(89, 3, 3)$	$2^{82.92}$

In the above table, the third line corresponds to the preferred parameters in [4].

6   Invertion of the Public Key

At this point, we assume that $\mathcal{K}$ has been retrieved using the preceding techniques. We next show how the public key of the Internally Perturbed HFE can be inverted using the attack of Faugère-Joux against HFE.

Let $l_1, \ldots, l_r$ to be r independent linear forms orthogonal to $\mathcal{K}$; an element $(x_1, \ldots, x_n)$ lies in $\mathcal{K}$ if and only if $l_k(x_1, \ldots, x_n) = 0$ for all k in $[1, r]$. As already pointed, the public key of an Internally Perturbed HFE is just an HFE public key on any affine subspace parallel to $\mathcal{K}$. Fixing one such subspace, we call $p_1, \ldots, p_n$ the multivariate quadratic forms of the perturbed public key, and $p'_1, \ldots, p'_n$ the multivariate quadratic forms of its equivalent HFE public key on this affine subspace. All linear forms l_k are constant on this subspace; for instance they all value to 0 (the affine subspace considered is $\mathcal{K}$). For any point $(b_1, \ldots, b_n)$, the multivariate quadratic systems $\{p_i = b_i, i \in [1, n]\} \cap \{l_k = 0, k \in [1, r]\}$ and $\{p'_i = b_i, i \in [1, n]\} \cap \{l_k = 0, k \in [1, r]\}$ have the same solutions. Equivalently, the ideal generated by $p_1 - b_1, \ldots, p_n - b_n$ together with $l_1, \ldots, l_r$ is the same as the ideal generated by $p'_1 - b_1, \ldots, p'_n - b_n$ together with $l_1, \ldots, l_r$ in the ring $R = \mathbb{F}_2[x_1, \ldots, x_n]/\{x_1^2 - x_1, \ldots, x_n^2 - x_n\}$. We call I this ideal, and J the ideal generated by $p'_1 - b_1, \ldots, p'_n - b_n$ without the kernel linear forms.

The ideal J is generated by quadratic equations coming from an HFE cryptosystem; computing a Gröbner basis for such ideals was shown much easier than in the general case by Faugère and Joux [6]. In particular, Faugère could break an HFE with parameters $n = 80$ and $D = 6$ in a hundred hours, while HFE arising in practical realizations of the perturbed HFE scheme have suggested parameters $n = 89$ and $D = 3$ only [4]. Now the key point is: computing a Gröbner basis of I cannot be harder than computing a Gröbner basis of J. Indeed I and J only differ by generators of degree 1, and computing a Gröbner basis of these generators is achieved by simple Gaussian elimination. Rather, they will help in the reduction of higher degree polynomials occurring in the computation. This is experimentally checked, as it could be done in about 2h10 when feeding with public and kernel equations and about 2h45 for the corresponding HFE, for any tested instance of the cryptosystem with $(n, D, r) = (60, 3, 2)$, using Magma's implementation of the $F4$ algorithm [18] on a standard machine.

Of course, in practice, $b_1, \ldots, b_n$ are made variables and the Gröbner basis computation is made only once. It outputs a set of polynomials $g_1, \ldots, g_L$ with the shape, $g_l = f_l(x_1, \ldots, x_{i_l}) - h_l(b_1, \ldots, b_n)$ where f_l is only in the i_l first x_i. This Gröbner basis allows to solve the system $\{p_1 = b_1, \ldots, p_n = b_n\}$ for any values $b_1, \ldots, b_n$ by sequentially solving the equations $f_l(x_1, \ldots, x_{i_l}) = h_l(b_1, \ldots, b_n)$ in increasing order of i_l.

7 Conclusion

The Internally Perturbed HFE cryptosystem is a variation of HFE, designed to fix the potential vulnerability of HFE against algebraic attacks. It is one of the rare candidates liable to enhance HFE as a cryptosystem. A major security element of the cryptosystem is the kernel of the perturbation, since the knowledge of this subspace allows to view the public key as a small set of HFE public keys, which can be inverted for the suggested parameters. However, in this work, we show that some correlation exists between the membership to the kernel of the perturbation and the kernel-dimension of the differential of the public key. This correlation can be accurately measured for any parameters, using sophisticated methods based on combinatorics in binary vector spaces. It yields a distinguisher which can be turned into an algorithm for finding elements of the kernel of the perturbation. For the preferred parameters in [4], recovering the kernel of the perturbation amounts to at most 2^{67} evaluations of the public key, which is well below the usual 2^{80} barrier. Although the designers of the scheme believed that the best attack might be exhaustive search in the space of messages [4], our attack is at least 2^{22} times faster and recovers an equivalent secret key. Accordingly, the elements presented in this work shed a new light on the security of the scheme presented by Ding and Schmidt. It should be emphasized that these elements could not be perceived without the advanced combinatorial methods provided in this paper, which are of independent interest.

References

1. Nicolas Courtois. The Security of Hidden Field Equations (HFE). In David Naccache, editor, *CT-RSA*, volume 2020 of *Lecture Notes in Computer Science*, pages 266–281. Springer, 2001.
2. Jintai Ding. A New Variant of the Matsumoto-Imai Cryptosystem through Perturbation. In Feng Bao, Robert H. Deng, and Jianying Zhou, editors, *Public Key Cryptography*, volume 2947 of *Lecture Notes in Computer Science*, pages 305–318. Springer, 2004.
3. Jintai Ding, Jason E. Gower, Dieter Schmidt, Christopher Wolf, and Z. Yin. Complexity Estimates for the F_4 Attack on the Perturbed Matsumoto-Imai Cryptosystem. In Nigel P. Smart, editor, *IMA Int. Conf.*, volume 3796 of *Lecture Notes in Computer Science*, pages 262–277. Springer, 2005.
4. Jintai Ding and Dieter Schmidt. Cryptanalysis of HFEv and Internal Perturbation of HFE. In Serge Vaudenay, editor, *Public Key Cryptography*, volume 3386 of *Lecture Notes in Computer Science*, pages 288–301. Springer, 2005.

5. Vivien Dubois, Louis Granboulan, and Jacques Stern. An Efficient Provable Distinguisher for HFE. In Michele Bugliesi, Bart Preneel, Vladimiro Sassone, and Ingo Wegener, editors, *ICALP (2)*, volume 4052 of *Lecture Notes in Computer Science*, pages 156–167. Springer, 2006.
6. Jean-Charles Faugère and Antoine Joux. Algebraic Cryptanalysis of Hidden Field Equation (HFE) Cryptosystems Using Gröbner Bases. In Dan Boneh, editor, *CRYPTO*, volume 2729 of *Lecture Notes in Computer Science*, pages 44–60. Springer, 2003.
7. Harriet J. Fell and Whitfield Diffie. Analysis of a Public Key Approach Based on Polynomial Substitution. In Hugh C. Williams, editor, *CRYPTO*, volume 218 of *Lecture Notes in Computer Science*, pages 340–349. Springer, 1985.
8. Pierre-Alain Fouque, Louis Granboulan, and Jacques Stern. Differential Cryptanalysis for Multivariate Schemes. In Ronald Cramer, editor, *EUROCRYPT*, volume 3494 of *Lecture Notes in Computer Science*, pages 341–353. Springer, 2005.
9. Aviad Kipnis and Adi Shamir. Cryptanalysis of the HFE Public Key Cryptosystem by Relinearization. In Michael J. Wiener, editor, *CRYPTO*, volume 1666 of *Lecture Notes in Computer Science*, pages 19–30. Springer, 1999.
10. Louis Granboulan and Antoine Joux and Jacques Stern. Inverting HFE Is Quasipolynomial. In Cynthia Dwork, editor, *CRYPTO*, volume 4117 of *Lecture Notes in Computer Science*, pages 345–356. Springer, 2006.
11. Tsutomu Matsumoto and Hideki Imai. Public Quadratic Polynominal-Tuples for Efficient Signature-Verification and Message-Encryption. In *EUROCRYPT*, pages 419–453, 1988.
12. M.Garey and D.Johnson. *Computer and Intractability: A guide to the theory of NP-completeness*. Freeman, 1979.
13. NESSIE. European project IST-1999-12324 on New European Schemes for Signature, Integrity and Encryption.
14. Jacques Patarin. Cryptanalysis of the Matsumoto and Imai Public Key Scheme of Eurocrypt'88. In Don Coppersmith, editor, *CRYPTO*, volume 963 of *Lecture Notes in Computer Science*, pages 248–261. Springer, 1995.
15. Jacques Patarin. Hidden Fields Equations (HFE) and Isomorphisms of Polynomials (IP): Two New Families of Asymmetric Algorithms. In *EUROCRYPT*, pages 33–48, 1996.
16. R.Motwani and P.Raghavan. *Randomized Algorithms*, chapter 4, pages 67–74. Cambridge University Press, 1995.
17. Adi Shamir. Efficient Signature Schemes Based on Birational Permutations. In Douglas R. Stinson, editor, *CRYPTO*, volume 773 of *Lecture Notes in Computer Science*, pages 1–12. Springer, 1993.
18. University of Sydney Computational Algebra Group. The MAGMA Computational Algebra System.

A   The Kernel-Dimension of the Sum of a Random $\mathbb{F}_2$-Linear Polynomial and a Random Linear Map of Rank r

In characteristic 2, the kernel of the sum of two linear maps is the subspace where they coincide. We denote $\mathcal{L}^D$ the set of $\mathbb{F}_2$-linear polynomials of degree 2^D and $\mathcal{L}_r$ the set of linear maps of rank r. We aim at determining the distribution of probability of the dimension of the subspace where L and l coincide, denoted $\{L = l\}$, when L is a random element of $\mathcal{L}^D$ and l is a random element of $\mathcal{L}_r$.

We recall that the number $S(n, s)$ of linearly independent sequences of length s in a space of dimension n is

$$S(n, s) = \prod_{i=0}^{s-1}(2^n - 2^i)$$

Each such sequence generates a subspace of dimension s which is also generated by $S(s, s)$ other linearly independent sequences of length s. Therefore the number $E(n, s)$ of subspaces of dimension s in a space of dimension n is $S(n, s)/S(s, s)$.

An $\mathbb{F}_2$-linear polynomial of degree 2^D has at most 2^D roots as a polynomial. Its roots are the elements of its kernel as a linear map. Therefore the dimension of this kernel cannot exceed D and the probability that it has kernel dimension d is given by the following lemma:

Lemma 1. *The probabilities* $(p_D(0), \ldots, p_D(D))$ *that a random element of* $\mathcal{L}^D$ *has kernel dimension respectively* $0, \ldots, D$ *satisfy the following invertible triangular system:*

$$d \in [0, D], \quad E(n, d)2^{-nd} = \sum_{m=d}^{D} E(m, d)p_D(m)$$

Proof. The number of $\mathbb{F}_2$-linear polynomials of degree 2^D is $(2^n - 1)2^{nD}$ and those which vanish at a are 2^n times less numerous. Given a subspace of dimension d with d in $[0, D]$, the vanishing of an $\mathbb{F}_2$-linear polynomial of degree 2^D results in d linear constraints over its $D + 1$ coefficients. It implies that for each subspace of dimension d, there are exactly $(2^n - 1)2^{n(D-d)}$ $\mathbb{F}_2$-linear polynomials which vanish on it. In the product $E(n, d)(2^n - 1)2^{n(D-d)}$, the $\mathbb{F}_2$-linear polynomials whose kernel has dimension m with $m \geq d$ are counted $E(m, d)$ times. Therefore, the proportions $p_D(d)$ of $\mathbb{F}_2$-linear polynomials of degree 2^D which have kernel dimension d satisfy the above invertible triangular system. □

We now suppose given an $\mathbb{F}_2$-linear polynomial L of degree 2^D and kernel-dimension d. The subspace on which L and a randomly chosen linear map of rank r coincide at least contains the intersection of the two kernels. We therefore should fix this dimension of intersection as a new parameter.

Lemma 2. *Given a subspace of dimension d, the probability $p_{d,r}(i)$ that a random subspace of dimension $n - r$ intersects this subspace with dimension i is*

$$\frac{S(d, i)S(n, d + n - r - i)S(n - r, i)}{S(n, d)S(i, i)S(n, n - r)}$$

Proof. Let call F the prescribed subspace of dimension d. The number of possible intersection subspaces is $E(d, i)$. For each of them I, the number of linearly independent sequences of length $n - r$ whose generating subspace has intersection with F exactly I is the number of linearly independent sequences outside F:

$$(2^n - 2^d) \ldots (2^n - 2^{d+n-r-i-1}) = S(n, d+n-r-i)/S(n, d)$$

This generating subspace G is also generated by as many linearly independent sequences of length $n - r$ as the number of linearly independent sequences of length $n - r - i$ of G outside I; this is likewise $S(n-r, n-r)/S(n-r, i)$.

The number of subspaces of dimension $n - r$ which intersect F with dimension i is therefore

$$E(d, i) \frac{S(n, d+n-r-i)}{S(n, d)} \frac{S(n-r, i)}{S(n-r, n-r)}$$

and the expected proportion is obtained by dividing by $E(n, n - r)$.   □

We now suppose given both an $\mathbb{F}_2$-linear polynomial L of degree 2^D and kernel F of dimension d and a subspace G of dimension $n - r$ which has intersection of dimension i with F. A map of kernel G coincides with L on a subspace H such that $H \cap F = H \cap G = F \cap G$. We now enumerate the number of subspaces of dimension t satisfying this condition.

Lemma 3. *Given a subspace F of dimension d and a subspace G of dimension $n - r$ whose intersection has dimension i, the number of subspaces of dimension t such that $H \cap F = H \cap G = F \cap G$ is*

$$\sum_{j=i}^{t} \frac{S(d-i, j-i)S(n-r-i, j-i)}{S(j-i, j-i)} \frac{S(n, d+n-r-i+t-j)}{S(n, d+n-r-i)} \frac{S(t, j)}{S(t, t)}$$

Proof. This enumeration comes in two steps: first we count the number of subspaces J of $F + G$ which have dimension j and satisfy the condition, second we count for each such J the number of subspaces H of dimension t whose intersection with $F + G$ is J.

The subspaces of $F + G$ of dimension j containing $F \cap G$ are in bijection with the subspaces of dimension $j - i$ in the quotient space $(F + G)/(F \cap G)$. Let $\bar{x}$ denote the class modulo $F \cap G$ of the element x. The number of subspaces J such that $F \cap J = G \cap J = F \cap G$ is the number of subspaces $\bar{J}$ such that $\bar{F} \cap \bar{J} = \bar{G} \cap \bar{J} = \{\bar{0}\}$ in the quotient space. Now notice that the set of linearly independent sequences of length $j - i$ in $\bar{F} + \bar{G}$ generating a subspace of zero intersection with both $\bar{F}$ and $\bar{G}$ is in bijection with the Cartesian product of lin. indep. sequences of length $j - i$ in $\bar{F}$ and lin. indep. sequences of length $j - i$ in $\bar{G}$. Besides each such sequence generates a subspace which is also generated by $S(j - i, j - i)$ others. The number of subspaces J of $F + G$ of dimension j such that $J \cap F = J \cap G = F \cap G$ is therefore $S(d-i, j-i)S(n-r-i, j-i)/S(j-i, j-i)$.

The number of subspaces of dimension t whose intersection with $F + G$ has dimension j is enumerated as given by Lemma 2.   □

It now only remains to determine the proportion of linear maps of kernel G which coincide with L on a subspace of dimension t.

Lemma 4. *Let L a linear map of kernel F of dimension d, G a subspace of dimension $n - r$ which has intersection of dimension i with F and $E_{d,r,i}(t)$ the number of subspaces H of dimension t such that $H \cap F = H \cap G = F \cap G$. The proportions $p_{d,r,i}(t)$ of linear maps of kernel G which coincide with L on a subspace of dimension t for t in $[i, r+i]$ satisfy the following invertible triangular system:*

$$t \in [i, r + i], \quad \frac{E_{d,r,i}(t)}{S(n, t-i)} = \sum_{m=t}^{r+i} E(m, t) \frac{S(t, i)}{S(m, i)} p_{d,r,i}(m)$$

Proof. For each subspace H of dimension t such that $H \cap F = H \cap G = F \cap G$, we construct a linear map of kernel G which equal L on H by choosing for its image on the remaining dimension $r - t + i$ a linearly independent sequence outside the image of H by L which has dimension $t - i$. The number of such maps is thus $S(n, r)/S(n, t - i)$, and their proportion over all maps of kernel G is $1/S(n, t - i)$. Now, making the product of the number of subspaces H of dimension t and satisfying $H \cap F = H \cap G = F \cap G$ by the number of linear maps l of kernel G which coincide with L on H, we see that the linear maps of kernel G which coincide with L on a subspace of dimension $m \geq t$ are counted as many as the number of subspaces of dimension t containing $F \cap G$ in this subspace. This number is $E(m, t)S(t, i)/S(m, i)$ as it can be easily checked. □

Putting all this together, we obtain that the probability that a random $\mathbb{F}_2$-linear polynomial L of degree 2^D and kernel F of dimension d coincides on a subspace of dimension t with a linear map l of rank r whose kernel has intersection of dimension i with F is

$$\pi_{d,r,i}(t) = p_D(d) p_{d,r}(i) p_{d,r,i}(t)$$

Of course the probability in term of the sole parameter t comes by summing over all possible values for d and i.

ℓ-Invertible Cycles for Multivariate Quadratic (MQ) Public Key Cryptography

Jintai Ding[1,*], Christopher Wolf[2], and Bo-Yin Yang[3,**]

[1] University of Cincinnati and Technische Universität Darmstadt
ding@math.uc.edu
[2] Ecole Normale Superieur
chris@christopher-wolf.de
[3] Institute of Information Science, Academia Sinica and TWISC
by@moscito.org

Abstract. We propose a new basic trapdoor ℓIC (ℓ-Invertible Cycles) of the mixed field type for Multivariate Quadratic public key cryptosystems. This is the first new basic trapdoor since the invention of Unbalanced Oil and Vinegar in 1997. ℓIC can be considered an extended form of the well-known Matsumoto-Imai Scheme A (also MIA or C^*), and share some features of stagewise triangular systems. However ℓIC has very distinctive properties of its own. In practice, ℓIC is much faster than MIA, and can even match the speed of single-field MQ schemes.

Keywords: Public Key, MQ, Trapdoor, Encryption, Signing.

1 Introducing MQ Public Key Cryptosystems

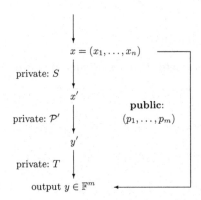

We work over a finite field $\mathbb{F}$ of q elements (the *base field*). $\mathcal{P}' \in MQ(\mathbb{F}^n, \mathbb{F}^m)$ is a system of m quadratic polynomials in n variables in $\mathbb{F}$, called the *central map* and its components *central polynomials*. Composition with the affine maps S, T masks the structure of $\mathcal{P}'$ and gives the public map:

$$\mathcal{P} = (p_1, \ldots, p_m) := T \circ \mathcal{P}' \circ S \qquad (1)$$

We usually write, for $1 \le i \le m, 1 \le j \le k \le n$,

$$p_i(x_1, \ldots, x_n) := \sum_{1 \le j \le k \le n} \gamma_{i,j,k} x_j x_k + \sum_{j=1}^{n} \beta_{i,j} x_j + \alpha_i$$

where α_i is usually normalized to zero. The Public key comprise the $mn(n+3)/2$ coefficients $\gamma_{ijk}, \beta_{ij} \in \mathbb{F}$.

Fig. 1. Illustration of Terminology and Notation for a modern MQ-trapdoor

Multivariate Quadratic (MQ) public-key cryptography first appeared in the English literature in the mid '80s [FD85, IM85] as alternatives to traditional

* Also partially sponsored by grants from the Charles Phelps Taft Research Center and the Alexander von Humboldt Foundation.
** Also sponsored by Taiwan's National Science Council project 95-2115-M-001-021 and indirectly via TWISC (Taiwan Information Security Center) @ NTUST.

T. Okamoto and X. Wang (Eds.): PKC 2007, LNCS 4450, pp. 266–281, 2007.
© International Association for Cryptologic Research 2007

PKCs. A common excuse given to study them is "for ecological diversity", inevitably mentioning Quantum Computers that will easily break factoring and discrete-log-based PKCs (Shor's algorithm [Sho97]). However, we hope to show that there is independent interest in studying $\mathcal{MQ}$ PKCs below.

To construct a PKC, we need to be able to invert $\mathcal{P}'$ efficiently. A simple method to build $\mathcal{P}'$ for consequent inversion is a *basic trapdoor*, which can be combined or modified slightly to create variants. Using the terminology of [WP05b], we have a handful of systemic ways to create new central maps, which we call "Modifiers", from the following four previously known basic trapdoors:

Mixed-Field (or "Big Field"): Operates over an extension field $\mathbb{E} = \mathbb{F}^k$.
  MIA: Matsumoto-Imai Scheme A or C^* ([IM85], Imai-Matsumoto).
  HFE: Hidden Field Equations ([Pat96], Patarin), a generalization of MIA.
Single-Field (or "True"): Works on the individual components of x' and y'.
  UOV: Unbalanced Oil and Vinegar ([Pat97, KPG99], Patarin *et al*).
  STS: Stepwise Triangular System (lectures in Japanese from '85 – [TKI$^+$86], Tsujii; in English, [Sha93]). Generalized later to its present form [GC00, WBP04].

Some primitives are composite, e.g., Medium Field Encryption (triangular stages [WYHL06]) or enTTS/TRMS/Rainbow [DS05b, WHL$^+$05, YC05] (UOV stages).

Outline. In the next section, we introduce our new trapdoor and discuss its basic properties. In particular, we show that certain instances can be inverted very quickly. Section 3 give cryptanalytic properties of this basic trapdoor and enumerates possible attacks. Section 4 discusses counter-measures to these attacks, *i.e.*, *modifiers*. We give the practical instances in Section 5. These we verify to withstand known attacks. The main text of the paper concludes with Section 6.

2   ℓ-Invertible Cycles (ℓIC)

In this section, we will introduce a new basic way to construct central maps for $\mathcal{MQ}$ public key cryptography that does not fit into the above taxonomy and hence can be considered a new basic trapdoor with properties in between that of MIA and STS. It runs much faster than MIA, and hence has practical value especially in resource-limited environments (e.g. smart cards). Due to its structure, we call it "ℓ-Invertible Cycles" (ℓIC). We will motivate this name later.

2.1   Basic Trapdoor

A *Cremona Transformation* is a map on the projective plane that is quadratic in the homogeneous coordinates [Ful89]. A standard example is the map (A_1, A_2, A_3) $\rightarrow$ $(A_2 A_3, A_3 A_1, A_1 A_2)$ which easily checks to be well-defined. The map is uniquely and efficiently invertible when $A_1 A_2 A_3 \neq 0$.

We extend this idea below to any integral cycle length $\ell \geq 2$; we illustrate with the case $\ell = 3$ since (unfortunately) the case $\ell = 2$ is a bit more technical.

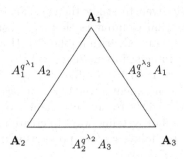

Fig. 2. Graphical Representation of 3-Invertible Cycles

Note that we write $\mathbb{N}$ for the non-negative integers, *i.e.*, we have $\mathbb{N} := \mathbb{Z}^+ \cup \{0\}$. To express properly the successor in $\{1, \ldots, \ell\}$ we define

$$\mu : \{1, \ldots, \ell\} \to \{1, \ldots, \ell\} : \mu(i) := \begin{cases} 1 & \text{for } i = \ell \\ i+1 & \text{otherwise} \end{cases} \tag{2}$$

Definition 1. *Fix an integer $\ell \geq 2$ as the length of the cycle. Let $\mathbb{F}$ be the base field with $q := |\mathbb{F}|$ elements and $\mathbb{E} := GF(q^k)$ its kth-degree extension for some $k \in \mathbb{Z}^+$. Computations in $\mathbb{E}$ are modulo the irreducible polynomial $\pi(t) \in \mathbb{F}[t]$. We denote $Q := |\mathbb{E}| = q^k$ and have $m = n = \ell k$ for the number of variables and equations over the ground field $\mathbb{F}$, respectively. In addition, let $S, T \in \text{Aff}^{-1}(\mathbb{F}^n)$ be two invertible affine mappings and the vector $\Lambda := (\lambda_1, \ldots, \lambda_\ell) \in \{0, \ldots, k-1\}^\ell$. We now have the following mapping:*

$$P : \mathbb{E}^\ell \to \mathbb{E}^\ell : (A_1, \ldots, A_\ell) \to (A_1^{q^{\lambda_1}} A_2, \ldots, A_{\ell-1}^{q^{\lambda_{\ell-1}}} A_\ell, A_\ell^{q^{\lambda_\ell}} A_1) \tag{3}$$

Identifying the corresponding coefficients in the vector spaces $\mathbb{F}^n$ and $\mathbb{E}^\ell$, we get a canonical bijection

$$\phi : \mathbb{F}^n \to \mathbb{E}^\ell : (x_1, \ldots, x_n) \to (x_1' + x_2't + \ldots x_k't^{k-1}, \ldots, x_{n-k+1}' + x_{n-k+2}'t + x_n't^{k-1}) \tag{4}$$

and its inverse ϕ^{-1}. The public key is computed as the composition

$$\mathcal{P} : \mathbb{F}^n \to \mathbb{F}^m : \mathcal{P} := T \circ \phi^{-1} \circ P \circ \phi \circ S. \tag{5}$$

We then call such a Multivariate Quadratic public key system of the ℓIC-type.

The name "invertible cycle" is due to that the variables $A_1, \ldots, A_\ell$ can be drawn in the form of a cycle (cf. Fig. 2 for $\ell = 3$). The variables $\mathbf{A}_1, \mathbf{A}_2, \mathbf{A}_3$ are the nodes while each edge stands for a product $A_i^{q^{\lambda_i}} A_{\mu(i)}$ with $i = 1, 2, 3$.

Note that the use of the canonical bijection ϕ is similar for the Matsumoto-Imai Scheme A (MIA) and Hidden Field Equations (HFE). However, we have $\ell = 1$ here, and also a different form of the central mapping $P \in \mathbb{E}[X]$. In the sequel, we denote the output of P by $B_1, \ldots, B_\ell$, where

$$B_1 := A_1^{q^{\lambda_1}} A_2, \ldots, B_{\ell-1} := A_{\ell-1}^{q^{\lambda_{\ell-1}}} A_\ell, B_\ell := A_\ell^{q^{\lambda_\ell}} A_1$$

Remark 1. The mapping $A_i^{q^{\lambda_i}}$ is linear over the ground field $\mathbb{F}$. Hence, the central equation P can be expressed as quadratic polynomials over $\mathbb{F}$.

Remark 2. Replacing $A_i^{q^{\lambda_i}} A_{\mu(i)}$ by $A_i^{q^{\lambda_i}} A_{\mu(i)}^{q^{\kappa_i}}$ for $1 \leq i \leq \ell$ and some $\kappa_i \in \mathbb{N}$ does not increase the security of ℓIC: we can always reduce the second expression to $A_i^{q^{\lambda_i - \kappa_i} \pmod{k}} A_{\mu(i)}$ by using Frobenius transformations. In a nutshell, we exploit that Frobenius transformations are invertible linear mappings over the vector spaces $\mathbb{F}^n$ and $\mathbb{F}^k$, respectively, and can hence be "absorbed" into the mappings $S, T \in \mathrm{Aff}^{-1}(\mathbb{F}^n)$. For $\mathcal{M}$ultivariate $\mathcal{Q}$uadratic systems, this idea has been introduced under the name *Frobenius sustainers* [WP05a].

2.2   Singularities

To use ℓIC in as an encryption or as a signature scheme, we need to invert the central map P, *i.e.*, we need to find a solution $(A_1, \dots, A_\ell) \in \mathbb{E}^\ell$ for given input $(B_1, \dots, B_\ell) \in \mathbb{E}^\ell$. Unfortunately, this is not possible in all cases; due to its form ℓIC has the following singularities:

$$\{ (A_1, \dots, A_\ell) \in \mathbb{E}^\ell \mid A_1 = 0 \vee \dots \vee A_\ell = 0 \}$$

Having $Q := |\mathbb{E}|$ and exploiting that Q in comparison with ℓ is usually "big" for practical and secure schemes we can approximate the probability that a singularity occurs by

$$\left(\sum_{i=1}^{\ell} (Q-1)^{\ell-1} \right) / Q^\ell \approx \frac{\ell}{Q}$$

In the Matsumoto-Imai Scheme A, we do not have this problem as MIA forms a bijection. In comparison, Hidden Field Equations does not allow to compute an inverse in about 40% of all cases for a practical choice of parameters [Pat96, CGP01, WP04]. Our new trapdoor ℓIC is hence between these two extreme cases. Practical values for Q will be discussed in Sec. 5.

2.3   Inversion

As we have as many free variables A_i as conditions B_i for $1 \leq i \leq \ell$, we may expect one solution on average when inverting P. Alas, this is not always true, as shown by the obvious counterexample:

$$(B_1, B_2) := P(A_1, A_2) := (A_1 A_2, A_2 A_1) \in \mathbb{E}^2.$$

So some instances of ℓIC that cannot be inverted usefully. For practical use, we construct below a sequence of specific ℓIC instances which allows easy inversion.

Lemma 1. *For a fixed $\ell \geq 2$, let our ℓIC central map $P : (A_1, \dots, A_\ell) \mapsto (B_1, \dots, B_\ell)$ be*

$$B_1 := \begin{cases} A_1 A_2 & \text{for } \ell \text{ odd and} \\ A_1^q A_2 & \text{for } \ell \text{ even} \end{cases}, \qquad B_i := A_i A_{\mu(i)} \text{ for } 2 \leq i \leq \ell.$$

Then the inverse image of $(B_1 \ldots B_\ell)$, *where* $B_i \in \mathbb{E}^* := \mathbb{E}\backslash\{0\}$, $\forall i$ *is given by*

$$
A_1 := \begin{cases} \sqrt{\dfrac{\prod_{i=0}^{(\ell-1)/2} B_{2i+1}}{\prod_{i=1}^{(\ell-1)/2} B_{2i}}} & \text{for } \ell \text{ odd and} \\[2ex] \sqrt[q-1]{\dfrac{\prod_{i=0}^{\ell/2-1} B_{2i+1}}{\prod_{i=1}^{\ell/2} B_{2i}}} & \text{for } \ell \text{ even} \end{cases} \qquad A_i := \frac{B_i}{A_{\mu(i)}} \text{ for } i = 2, \ldots, \ell.
$$

Proof. **Case** $\ell = 3$: We have $B_1 := A_1 A_2, B_2 := A_2 A_3, B_3 := A_3 A_1$. Simple computations yield $A_1 := \sqrt{B_1 B_3 / B_2}, A_3 := B_3 / A_1, A_2 := B_2 / A_3$.

Case ℓ **odd,** $\ell > 3$: We use induction to extend the result from $\ell = 3$ to all odd $\ell > 3$. Therefore we observe that the structure of the central mapping P allows us to write equations of the form $A_i = A_{\mu(\mu(i))} \frac{B_i}{B_{i+1}}$ for $1 < i < \ell$ by eliminating the variable $A_{\mu(i)}$. Hence, the fraction $\frac{B_i}{B_{i+1}}$ can be inserted in the inversion formula for A_1 in the case $(\ell - 2)$.

Case ℓ **even:** The proof for this case is analogous. We start our induction with $\ell = 2$ and have $B_1 := A_1^q A_2, B_2 := A_2 A_1$ and its inverse $A_1 := \sqrt[q-1]{B_1 / B_2}, A_2 := B_2 / A_1$.

Bijectivity. For ℓ odd or $\mathbb{F}$ of characteristic 2, the above mapping is a bijection in $(\mathbb{E}^*)^\ell$. For ℓ even, the situation is more difficult as $(q-1) \mid (q^a - 1)$ for any $a \in \mathbb{Z}^+$, and we loose bijectivity for any $q > 2$. However, for $q = 2$, we obtain a bijection. Moreover, inversion now only costs two divisions in the extension field $\mathbb{E}$ and we need not solve any nontrivial equations.

Special instances. When $\ell = 2$ we say it is a *Binary Invertible Cycle* (2IC) and when $\ell = 3$ a *Delta Invertible Cycle* (3IC) (see Fig. 2).

3   Cryptanalytic Properties of ℓIC

We herein discuss some basic cryptanalytic properties of the new trapdoor. This serves a dual purpose: We find an easy cryptanalysis for ℓIC in its basic form. Simultaneously, we effectively put ℓIC through the same screening process as other $\mathcal{MQ}$ trapdoors, particularly Matsumoto Imai Scheme A. This points us toward ways to build practical, more resilient ℓIC-based schemes.

One attack is left to a later section because we only heard of it succeeding, and do not even have any details.

3.1   Patarin Relations

We start with an extension of the Patarin relations used to cryptanalyse MIA [Pat95]. This was used by Fouque, Granboulan, and Stern to cryptanalyse the internally perturbed MIA encryption scheme (PMI/MIAi) [FGS05]. As is more customarily employed against symmetric cryptosystems, we examine this multivariate differential :

$$
P(A_1, \ldots, A_\ell) - P(A_1 - \delta_1, \ldots, A_\ell - \delta_\ell) + P(\delta_1, \ldots, \delta_\ell)
$$
$$
= (A_1^{q^{\lambda_1}} \delta_2 + A_2 \delta_1^{q^{\lambda_1}}, \ldots, A_\ell^{q^{\lambda_\ell}} \delta_1 + A_1 \delta_\ell^{q^{\lambda_\ell}})
$$

We observe that the above equations are linear in the unknowns $A_i \in \mathbb{E}$ for any given values $\delta_i \in \mathbb{E}$ and $1 \leq i \leq \ell$. Now we simply pick δ_i at random and compute many differentials of the public key. Soon we recover enough linear relations to invert the public map. This effectively finds an equivalent private key. It may be estimated that the number of linearization equations for $\mathbb{F} = \mathrm{GF}(2)$ is 4ℓ, which we do not have space to describe here.

This resembles MIA and HFE in that the Patarin attack is very efficient against the former, and an extended version of the attack defeats the latter if bijective central maps are used [Pat95, Pat96].

3.2   Rank Attacks

In a *rank attack*, the quadratic parts central and public polynomials of a given $\mathcal{M}$ultivariate $\mathcal{Q}$uadratic public key system are written as symmetric matrices. We try to recover the private key by finding linear combinations of the public matrices with certain specific ranks. Their initial cryptographical use was by Coppersmith-Stern-Vaudenay to break Birational Permutations [CSV93]. Goubin and Courtois [GC00] have the most straightforward exposition of rank attacks. Later extensions and analysis can be seen in [WBP04, YC05].

There are two distinct types: In one the cryptanalyst randomly tries to hit kernel vectors of a linear combination of the public matrices with the lowest rank R. The running time is proportional to $q^{R\lfloor m/n \rfloor}$. In the other random linear combinations are taken, hoping to locate a precipitous fall in rank. This takes time $\propto q^u$, where u counts the central equations whose coefficients must vanish.

For ℓIC, we want to write matrices in blocks corresponding to pairs of variables in the larger field $\mathbb{E}$. Express central matrices as $H_1, \ldots, H_\ell \in \mathbb{E}^{\ell \times \ell}$ and their $\mathbb{E}$-blocks as $\eta_{i,j,k} \in \mathbb{E}$ for $1 \leq i, j, k \leq \ell$.

$$\eta_{i,j,k} := \begin{cases} M_{\lambda_i} & \text{if } i = j, k = \mu(i), \\ M_{\lambda_i}^T & \text{if } i = k, j = \mu(i), \\ 0 & \text{otherwise}, \end{cases}$$

where M_r is the matrix in $\mathbb{F}^{k \times k}$ that correspond to the Frobenius map $A \mapsto A^{q^r}$. Note that these matrices are symmetric. In the case of 3IC, *i.e.*, $\ell = 3$, they effectively specialize to

$$H_1 := \begin{pmatrix} 0 & 1 & 0 \\ 1 & 0 & 0 \\ 0 & 0 & 0 \end{pmatrix}, \ H_2 := \begin{pmatrix} 0 & 0 & 0 \\ 0 & 0 & 1 \\ 0 & 1 & 0 \end{pmatrix}, \ H_3 := \begin{pmatrix} 0 & 0 & 1 \\ 0 & 0 & 0 \\ 1 & 0 & 0 \end{pmatrix}.$$

All these matrices have essentially rank 2 over the extension field $\mathbb{E}$. For the actual attack, we would need to transfer $M \in \mathbb{E}^{\ell \times \ell}$ to $\mathbb{F}^{n \times n}$. However the overall attack complexity is not affected by this change of vector space. Just as in other schemes using extension fields (e.g. cf. Medium Field Encryption [WYHL06]), when performed in $\mathbb{F}$ we have a rank of $2k$ for all these matrices. We may see that the running time of the both the above algorithms are $Q^2 = q^{2k}$ times some polynomial factor in n and m, which is cubic in the practical range.

Note that there are instances in which one or the other rank attack simply fails to work. One example is the case of 2IC, *i.e.*, for $\ell = 2$. Here rank attacks will not apply as any nontrivial linear combination of the private polynomials (matrices) has the maximum rank $n = 2k$. The above discussion of rank attacks are in line with results of tests on ℓIC and modified ℓIC schemes with blocks of 24 and 32 bits (which are admittedly very small).

3.3 Gröbner Basis Computations

Another important type of attack are Gröbner attacks as in the cryptanalysis of HFE [FJ03]. The most powerful algorithms known are of the Faugère-Lazard type. These essentially run eliminations on an extended Macaulay matrix, and include $\mathbf{F_4}/\mathbf{F_5}$ and what is known as XL [CKPS00, Fau99, Fau02] plus variations.

We know from the cryptanalysis of MIA and HFE that their easy algebraic structure leads to a low running time of the corresponding Gröbner bases algorithm. Due to the very easy structure of ℓIC, we expect a similar behaviour here. This is in line small scale experiments using Magma [MAG], so we must disrupt the regular structure. In general, when the structure of the system is sufficiently perturbed, the behavior is as in generic systems studied by Bardet, Faugère *et al* [BFS04, BFSY05, YC04b, YC04a]. E.g., we tested 3IC– systems with MAGMA v2.12-8 on a 2GB machine using $\mathbb{E} = (\mathrm{GF}(256))^4$ or $(\mathrm{GF}(256))^5$. If we removed at least least two components, the resulting system resolved in exactly the amount of time as a generic one (including segfaulting on 13-variable systems). With only one component removed, it resolved nearly instantly.

3.4 Separation of Oil and Vinegar

In the original 3IC, we see that variables corresponding to the components of A_1 are only multiplied with those of A_2 and A_3. This makes for a UOV type of attack [KPG99] which has a complexity roughly proportional to $n^4 q^d$, where d is the difference between the size of the oil and vinegar sets. We can proceed similarly for other choices of ℓ. We see that the UOV attack has time complexity $\sim Q$ for odd ℓ and very small complexity for even ℓ. Since the minus modifier does not change the complexity of the UOV attack, 3IC– as a signature scheme is ok if we use large enough Q. The plus modifier disrupts the UOV attack so the 2ICi+ that we will investigate later is not susceptible.

3.5 Further Attacks

There is a special attack from Felke [Fel04] to defeat the technique called "branching" as used in the original C^*. We have investigated this matter and concluded that the attacks against branching do not apply against ℓIC.

A different class from XL are algorithms from [CGMT02] which deal with the case $n \gg m$. As we usually have $m = n$, or $n \approx m$ for the embedding modification (cf Sec. 4.3), these algorithms are not applicable to our setting.

4   Modified Versions

Due to the effectiveness of the attacks considered above, we need to apply modifiers [WP05b, Sec. 4] to the basic trapdoor to obtain secure schemes. This is the same situation as for MIA and HFE. To the best of our knowledge every published attack against a system of this type is covered by this paper.

4.1 ℓ-Invertible Cycles Minus (ℓIC-)

The first modification is the so-called "minus" modification. Here, Let R be the projection from $\mathbb{F}^n \mapsto \mathbb{F}^m$ that simply discards the final parameters. $r := n - m$ as "reduction parameter". The public key is now $\mathcal{P} := R \circ T \circ \phi^{-1} \circ P \circ \phi \circ S$. In contrast to (5), we have inserted the reduction R after the affine transformation T. When inverting ℓIC, we assign random values to these missing r coordinates over $\mathbb{F}$. Hence, we have q^r possible inputs for each message $y \in \mathbb{F}^m$.

As for MIA and HFE, the minus modifier increases the complexity of the Patarin attack (Sec. 3.1) by a factor of q^r, since instead of one possible solution, the attacker is now faced with an r-dimensional vector space over $\mathbb{F}$ of possible solutions. To our current knowledge, picking the right one requires brute force and hence at least q^r operations. In addition, the attack complexity of the Faugère-Joux attack [FJ03] also increases by at least q^r.

Like with MIA, we cannot use ℓIC- for encryption, only for signature schemes: as there are r equations missing, the legitimate user must work equally hard to recover the correct solution $x \in \mathbb{F}^n$. As our security assumption is that q^r computations are not possible, we reached a contradiction if we assume that the legitimate user can obtain the message x while the attacker cannot. As for Stepwise-Triangular, rank attacks are unaffected by the minus modification.

4.2 ℓ-Invertible Cycles Internally Perturbed Plus (ℓICi+)

The generic plus modifier adds $a \in \mathbb{Z}^+$ random equations in n input variables each to the private key. This is applicable to encryption only, as the extra equations (without trapdoor) slow down signature generation by q^a — it takes that many tries to find one output of the ℓIC mapping P to meet those conditions.

Patarin relations and Gröbner attacks are not affected by the plus modification. However, it is still useful to build an encryption scheme. In the case of MIA because the "plus" helps to overcome some attacks against the internally perturbated modification. Here, it also prevents a UOV attack.

Internal perturbation has been introduced for MIA and HFE as PMI ("Perturbated Matsumoto-Imai") and ipHFE respectively [Din04, DS05a]. We can also call them MIAi and HFEi. As PMI/MIAi has been broken in [FGS05], a new variant PMI+/MIAi+ has been proposed [DG06]. Due to space limitations we do not go into details, but we believe PMI+ unaffected by the attack from [FGS05]. Hence, combining the two modifications *internal perturbation* and *plus* allows the construction of an efficient encryption scheme. However, the central mapping $\mathcal{P}'$ and all its components need to have full rank. In our setting, this means that we cannot use any other cycle length but $\ell = 2$, *i.e.*, 2IC.

After talking about the impact of the internal perturbation modification, we now properly introduce it: Let $w \in \mathbb{Z}^+$ for $w < n$ be the perturbation dimension, $\mathcal{P}^i \in_R \mathcal{MQ}(\mathbb{F}^w, \mathbb{F}^n)$ a uniformly randomly chosen system in w input variables and n equations, and $S^i \in \text{Aff}^{-1}(\mathbb{F}^n, \mathbb{F}^w)$ the so-called "perturbation space". Note that the perturbation space has the same input variables $x_1, \ldots, x_n$ as the affine transformation $S \in \text{Aff}^{-1}(\mathbb{F}^n)$. However, it has only dimension w. Hence we can write $(z_1', \ldots, z_w') := S^i(x_1, \ldots, x_n)$ for the perturbation variables $z_1', \ldots, z_w'$. As for the plus modification, we denote with $\mathcal{P}^* := \phi^{-1} \circ P \circ \phi$ the ℓIC mapping over the ground field $\mathbb{F}$.

The public key for ℓICi is now composed as

$$\mathcal{P} := T \circ [(\mathcal{P}^* \circ S) + (\mathcal{P}^i \circ S^i)],$$

i.e., we add the perturbation polynomials to the original ℓIC-polynomials. To invert this modified trapdoor, *i.e.*, to compute $x \in \mathbb{F}^n$ for given $y \in \mathbb{F}^m$, we need to guess correctly the values of the perturbation variables $(z_1', \ldots, z_w') \in \mathbb{F}^w$ — which translates to a workload proportional to q^w. As the number of equations and the number of variables matches, we expect one solution on average for any given input $y \in \mathbb{F}^m$. However, when used as an encryption scheme, there is at least one valid output $x \in \mathbb{F}^n$. We know that the i modifier by itself is not secure, and it must be combined with the $+$ modifier as shown by the Fouque-Granboulan-Stern differential attack [FGS05].

4.3 ℓ-Invertible Cycles Embedded (ℓIC $\nearrow$) Without Singularities

Here we introduce the new modifier embedding ($\nearrow$), motivated by the practical need to avoid singularities in trapdoors of the ℓIC-type.

With the minus modification, singularities are of no concern: they are too few and we can always change the input in the missing equations to obtain a possible signature. However, when ℓIC is used in the context of an encryption scheme, its singularities pose a problem as they lead to decryption failures. The modification described in this section can also be used in other schemes which suffer from a decryption failure such as [WYHL06]. In fact, it is a new generic modifier and can be used in any $\mathcal{M}$ultivariate $\mathcal{Q}$uadratic construction.

For our new embedding modifier we embedding the following translation from $\mathbb{F}^{k-1} \rightarrow \mathbb{F}^k$ that takes $(x_1, \ldots, x_{k-1})$ to $(x_1, \ldots, x_{k-1}, 1)$. In effect, we have eliminated the zero-point from the vector space $\mathbb{F}^k$. As we used the canonical bijection ϕ between the vector space $\mathbb{F}^k$ and the extension field $\mathbb{E}$, the zero of $\mathbb{E}$ cannot be reached anymore for any given input $(x_1, \ldots, x_{k-1}) \in \mathbb{F}$. The price we pay are fewer input variables, *i.e.*, we now obtain an overdetermined system of polynomials. We can do the same to all ℓ variables $A_1, \ldots, A_\ell \in \mathbb{E}$. Calling the corresponding transformation $\nu : \mathbb{F}^n \rightarrow \mathbb{F}^{n-\ell}$ and setting $k := (n - \ell)/\ell$ for $k \in \mathbb{N}$ we obtain the following construction for the public key

$$\mathcal{P} = T \circ \phi^{-1} \circ P \circ \nu \circ S. \tag{6}$$

To do signing, the "inverse" transformation $\nu^{-1} : (y_1, \ldots, y_{k-1}, 1) \to (y_1, \ldots, y_{k-1})$ needs to be inserted between the affine transformation T and the ℓIC mapping P. To the same effect, we could have used the construction of (6). However, this would have slowed down signature generation by a factor of q^ℓ as we have ℓ additional equations over $\mathbb{F}$ to satisfy for any given input $B_1, \ldots, B_\ell \in \mathbb{E}$.

5   Practical Instances

We use the previous section to develop practical instances of ℓIC. Main purpose is to see how variations on ℓIC scales up for different security levels.

5.1   Signature

To obtain a secure signature scheme, we use ℓIC$-$, in particular 3IC$-$, as this seems the most suitable modification for our purpose. In particular, the security of the minus modification is well understood; we are therefore able to give instances of ℓIC$-$ for several security levels. Different choice of parameters are possible, 3IC$-$ with $q = 256$ seems most suitable(cf. Sec. 3), and still allows efficient implementation on 8-bit microprocessors which are still dominant in low-end smart cards. We summarize optimal choices in Table 1. Preliminary tests show that ℓIC- is orders of magnitude faster than MIA-; further data will be posted if we can avoid the differential attack on ℓIC-.

Table 1. ℓIC- over GF(256) with Different Security Levels for Signing

Claimed Security	Input [bits]	Output [bits]	n	m	ℓ	k	Parameters r	Attack Complexity Gröbner	Rank/UOV	Key Size [kBytes] Public	Private
2^{80}	160	240	30	20	3	10	20	2^{80}	2^{85}	9.92	1.86
2^{96}	192	288	36	24	3	12	24	2^{96}	2^{104}	16.8	2.59
2^{128}	256	384	48	32	3	16	32	2^{130}	2^{137}	39.20	4.70

5.2   More on Differential Attacks

[FGS05] was a differential attack in the classical sense – take differentials and try to find a distinguisher. It was announced at the rump session of Asiacrypt 2006 that SFLASH (MIA-) was finally broken on the extension of such an attack. This is so far an unpublished attack, because the details are very sketchy. However, due to the extreme similarity between MIA and ℓIC, if SFLASH (MIA-) cannot be patched, ℓIC- will likely suffer the same fate, so now we do not recommend ℓIC- unless this can be circumvented.

5.3   Encryption

We base our proposed encryption scheme on 2ICi+$\nearrow$, i.e., 2-Invertible Cycles with internal perturbation, added equations, and embedding (to avoid decryption errors). With this choice of scheme, we suggest the following parameters: $q = 2, n = 132, m = 146, \ell = 2, k = 67, w = 6, a = 12$. This leads to a public key of 160.2 kBytes and a private key of 5.7 kBytes, respectively. The claimed security level is 2^{80}. Our choice of parameters is based on [DG06]. Due to space limitations in this paper we do not repeat their arguments but point to [DG06]. However, we want to stress that at present, our understanding of the security of the internal perturbation modification is limited although there some results on Gröbner bases in [DGS+05]. This means in particular that we do not have precise security estimations for higher security levels.

5.4   Implementation and Speed

A good overview on implementing finite field operations can be found in [LD00]. Computing direct division in finite fields is given in [FW02]. Counting operations for the inversion formula in Lemma 1 over $\mathbb{E} = \mathrm{GF}(q^k)$, we see that we need ℓ divisions, $(\ell - 2)$ multiplications, and one root. Note that the operations do not take place in a big field $\mathrm{GF}(q^n)$ but in a much smaller extension field $\mathrm{GF}(q^k)$. It is difficult to give a closed formula for the speed of basic arithmetic operations as they largely depend on the model used, *e.g.*, hardware vs. software, operations on bits vs. operations on processor words. Nevertheless, when counting our costs in operations in the ground field $\mathbb{F}$, we can roughly say that we have $O(a^2)$ for squaring/multiplying and $O(a^3)$ for division/exponentiation. Here we have $l \in \mathbb{Z}^+$ the extension degree of the corresponding field $\mathbb{E} = \mathrm{GF}(q^a)$ over the ground field $\mathbb{F} = \mathrm{GF}(q)$. We have to keep this in mind when comparing ℓIC with the other two mixed field schemes MIA and HFE.

Comparison with MIA and HFE. Inverting the mixed field scheme MIA costs one exponentiation with large exponent [CGP02]. In a nutshell, this translates to n squaring operations and $1/2n$ multiplications in $\mathrm{GF}(q^n)$. Therefore, we obtain an overall workload of $O(n^3)$. Tricks to speed this operation up can be found in [ACDG03]. In the case of HFE, the situation is even worse as we need to execute a complete root finding algorithm to invert the central mapping [CGP01]. Its running time is estimated to be in $O(n^3d^2 + n^2d^3)$ for d the total degree of the central mapping [Pat96]. In practice, we have $d = 129, \ldots, 257$.

We can summarize our results for the three maps MIA, HFE, and ℓIC as follows: the first needs $O(n^3)$ operations in the ground field $\mathbb{F}$ for n the extension degree as it needs to compute Y^h for given $Y \in \mathrm{GF}(q^n)$ and $h \in \mathbb{Z}^+$, *i.e.*, an exponentiation. The second needs to solve a univariate polynomial equation $P(X) = Y$ for P being a polynomial of fixed degree $d \in \mathbb{Z}^+$. The corresponding running time is about $O(n^3d^2 + n^2d^3)$ operations in the ground field $\mathbb{F}$. Finally, ℓIC needs $O(\ell k^3 + \ell k^2)$ operations over the ground field $\mathbb{F}$.

A choice for MIA is SFLASH$^{\mathrm{v}2}$ with $q = 128$, $n = 37$ [CGP02]. For HFE, we have $q = 2$, $n = 103$ in Quartz [CGP01]. Choices for ℓIC are given in Sec. 5.3 and Table 1, respectively. Both trapdoors have a claimed security level of 2^{80} 3DES computations as required in NESSIE [NES]. Note that Quartz uses the underlying trapdoor four times to achieve very short signatures of 128 bit. This special construction is called a "Chained Patarin Construction" (CPC). We summarize our comparison in Table 2. Preliminary runs to sign with $m = 24, n = 36$ matches the speed enTTS [YC05] which means it is much faster than SFLASH.

Further Speed up. ℓIC is amenable to parallelizing on multiple arithmetic units.

ℓIC i+ implementations. We compare simple runs of ℓIC i+ on a 10MHz 8052 simulator with $q = 2, n = 134, m = 146, \ell = 2, k = 67, w = 6, a = 12$ (public key 160.2 kBytes, private key 5.7 kBytes), and per transmission time 1.4 seconds. Our PMI+ program has $n = 84$, $m = 96$, $q = 2$, and a transmission time of 2.5 seconds per block. ℓIC i+ is clearly quite a bit faster.

6 Conclusions

In this article, we have constructed a new basic $\mathcal{M}$ultivariate $\mathcal{Q}$uadratic trapdoor called ℓ-invertible cycles (ℓIC). It is the first time since nearly a decade that a basic trapdoor has been found. The main motivation for this new trapdoor is speed: instead of computing operations in the big finite field $\mathbb{E} = \mathrm{GF}(q^n)$ for $q := |\mathbb{F}|$ and n the number of variables, we compute in the much smaller extension field $\mathbb{E} = \mathrm{GF}(q^k)$ for $n = \ell k$ for some cycle length ℓ. Typical choices of ℓ are 2 and 3. Depending on the architecture, finite field arithmetic costs up to $O(n^3)$. Hence, decreasing the size of the extension field $\mathbb{E}$ results in a significant speedup in practice. In particular, our implementation is expected to outperform the previously fastest trapdoor Matsumoto-Imai Scheme A (MIA). In addition, we have formally introduced the new embedding modifier ($\nearrow$). It is motivated by the practical need to achieve ℓIC-type schemes without decryption failure. Apart from ℓIC, constructions like [WYHL06] suffer from this problem.

Table 2 shows the different complexities, parameters and public key sizes for trapdoors of the mixed field types with a claimed security level of 2^{80}. Unfortunately, we do not have exact estimations on their inherent complexity but asymptotic ones. Nevertheless, we see that ℓIC for a similar security level is expected to perform significantly better than the two other basic trapdoors HFE (using parameters from Quartz) and MIA (parameters from SFLASH$^{\mathrm{v2}}$). Apart from this, we have shown that ℓIC can be used both in signature schemes of various security levels as well as in an encryption scheme. We want to stress

Table 2. Mixed Field Trapdoors with Claimed Security Level 2^{80}

Trapdoor	Complexity to Invert Trapdoor	Parameters	Key Size [kBytes] Public	Private
HFE (Quartz)	$O(n^3 d^2 + n^2 d^3)$	$q = 2,\, n = 103,\, d = 129$	71	3
MIA (Sflash)	$O(n^3)$	$q = 128\ n = 37$	15.4	2.45
ℓIC, $\ell = 3$	$O(\ell k^3 + \ell k^2)$	$q = 256,\, k = 10$	9.92	1.86

here that trapdoors from the single field class, *i.e.*, Unbalanced Oil and Vinegar (UOV) and Stepwise-Triangular Schemes (STS) do *not* allow constructions leading to encryption schemes.

So as an overall conclusion, we have presented a new trapdoor which is both interesting from a theoretical point of view and also has advantages over previously known schemes. At present we have to leave it as an open question exactly which forms of ℓIC than these given in Lemma 1 allow efficient inversion.

We stress that it is still an original sin that no list of possible attacks can be exhaustive. Multivariate Quadratic schemes are still in need of some provable security results. But we hope to have shown that the variety available in the genre keeps it in play and interesting.

Acknowledgements

The authors would like to thank TWISC (Taiwan Information Security Center) for sponsoring a series of lectures on $\mathcal{MQ}$ cryptosystems at Nat'l Taiwan U. of Sci. and Tech. in January 2006, the discussions following which led to this work.

Note: An updated version will be made available online either at the authors' website or at ePrint archive after more details are known about the new attacks.

References

[ACDG03] Mehdi-Laurent Akkar, Nicolas T. Courtois, Romain Duteuil, and Louis Goubin. A fast and secure implementation of SFlash. In *Public Key Cryptography — PKC 2003*, volume 2567 of *Lecture Notes in Computer Science*, pages 267–278. Y. Desmedt, editor, Springer, 2002.

[ACN05]   *Conference on Applied Cryptography and Network Security — ACNS 2005*, volume 3531 of *Lecture Notes in Computer Science*. Springer, 2005. ISBN 3-540-26223-7.

[BFS04]   M. Bardet, J.-C. Faugère, and B. Salvy. On the complexity of Gröbner basis computation of semi-regular overdetermined algebraic equations. In *Proceedings of the International Conference on Polynomial System Solving*, pages 71–74, 2004. Previously appeared as INRIA report RR-5049.

[BFSY05] M. Bardet, J.-C. Faugère, B. Salvy, and B.-Y. Yang. Asymptotic expansion of the degree of regularity for semi-regular systems of equations. In P. Gianni, editor, *MEGA 2005 Sardinia (Italy)*, 2005.

[CGMT02] Nicolas Courtois, Louis Goubin, Willi Meier, and Jean-Daniel Tacier. Solving underdefined systems of multivariate quadratic equations. In *Public Key Cryptography — PKC 2002*, volume 2274 of *Lecture Notes in Computer Science*, pages 211–227. David Naccache and Pascal Paillier, editors, Springer, 2002.

[CGP01]   Nicolas Courtois, Louis Goubin, and Jacques Patarin. *Quartz: Primitive specification (second revised version)*, October 2001. https://www.cosic.esat.kuleuven.be/nessie Submissions, Quartz, 18 pages.

[CGP02]   Nicolas Courtois, Louis Goubin, and Jacques Patarin. *Sflash: Primitive specification (second revised version)*, 2002. https:// www.cosic.esat.kuleuven.be/nessie, Submissions, Sflash, 11 pages.

[CKPS00]   Nicolas T. Courtois, Alexander Klimov, Jacques Patarin, and Adi Shamir. Efficient algorithms for solving overdefined systems of multivariate polynomial equations. In *Advances in Cryptology — EUROCRYPT 2000*, volume 1807 of *Lecture Notes in Computer Science*, pages 392–407. Bart Preneel, editor, Springer, 2000. Extended Version: http://www.minrank.org/xlfull.pdf.

[Cry93]   Douglas R. Stinson, editor. *Advances in Cryptology — CRYPTO 1993*, volume 773 of *Lecture Notes in Computer Science*. Springer, 1993. ISBN 3-540-57766-1.

[CSV93]   Don Coppersmith, Jacques Stern, and Serge Vaudenay. Attacks on the birational permutation signature schemes. In Crypto [Cry93], pages 435–443.

[DG06]   Jintai Ding and Jason Gower. Inoculating multivariate schemes against differential attacks. In *PKC*, volume 3958 of *LNCS*. Springer, April 2006. Also available at http://eprint.iacr.org/2005/255.

[DGS+05]   Jintai Ding, Jason E. Gower, Dieter Schmidt, Christopher Wolf, and Z. Yin. Complexity estimates for the F_4 attack on the perturbed Matsumoto-Imai cryptosystem. In *CCC*, volume 3796 of *LNCS*, pages 262–277. Springer, 2005.

[Din04]   Jintai Ding. A new variant of the Matsumoto-Imai cryptosystem through perturbation. In *Public Key Cryptography — PKC 2004*, volume 2947 of *Lecture Notes in Computer Science*, pages 305–318. Feng Bao, Robert H. Deng, and Jianying Zhou (editors), Springer, 2004.

[DS05a]   Jintai Ding and Dieter Schmidt. Cryptanalysis of HFEv and internal perturbation of HFE. In PKC [PKC05], pages 288–301.

[DS05b]   Jintai Ding and Dieter Schmidt. Rainbow, a new multivariable polynomial signature scheme. In ACNS [ACN05], pages 164–175.

[Fau99]   Jean-Charles Faugère. A new efficient algorithm for computing Gröbner bases (F_4). *Journal of Pure and Applied Algebra*, 139:61–88, June 1999.

[Fau02]   Jean-Charles Faugère. A new efficient algorithm for computing Gröbner bases without reduction to zero (F_5). In *International Symposium on Symbolic and Algebraic Computation — ISSAC 2002*, pages 75–83. ACM Press, July 2002.

[FD85]   Harriet Fell and Whitfield Diffie. Analysis of public key approach based on polynomial substitution. In *Advances in Cryptology — CRYPTO 1985*, volume 218 of *Lecture Notes in Computer Science*, pages 340–349. Hugh C. Williams, editor, Springer, 1985.

[Fel04]   Patrick Felke. On the affine transformations of HFE-cryptosystems and systems with branches. Cryptology ePrint Archive, Report 2004/367, 2004. http://eprint.iacr.org/2004/367, version from 2004-12-17, 10 pages.

[FGS05]   Pierre-Alain Fouque, Louis Granboulan, and Jacques Stern. Differential cryptanalysis for multivariate schemes. In *Advances in Cryptology — EUROCRYPT 2005*, Lecture Notes in Computer Science. Ronald Cramer, editor, Springer, 2005. 341–353.

[FJ03]   Jean-Charles Faugère and Antoine Joux. Algebraic cryptanalysis of Hidden Field Equations (HFE) using Gröbner bases. In *Advances in Cryptology — CRYPTO 2003*, volume 2729 of *Lecture Notes in Computer Science*, pages 44–60. Dan Boneh, editor, Springer, 2003.

[Ful89]   William Fulton. *Algebraic curves. An introduction to algebraic geometry, a Reprint of 1969 original in Advanced Book Classics*. Addison-Wesley Publishing Company, Redwood City, CA, 1989. ISBN: 0-201-51010-3.

[FW02]   Patrick Fitzpatrick and Christopher Wolf. Direct division in factor rings. *Electronic Letters*, 38(21):1253–1254, October 2002. Extended version: http://eprint.iacr.org/2004/353, 7 pages.

[GC00]   Louis Goubin and Nicolas T. Courtois. Cryptanalysis of the TTM cryptosystem. In *Advances in Cryptology — ASIACRYPT 2000*, volume 1976 of *Lecture Notes in Computer Science*, pages 44–57. Tatsuaki Okamoto, editor, Springer, 2000.

[IM85]   Hideki Imai and Tsutomu Matsumoto. Algebraic methods for constructing asymmetric cryptosystems. In *Algebraic Algorithms and Error-Correcting Codes, 3rd International Conference, AAECC-3, Grenoble, France, July 15-19, 1985, Proceedings*, volume 229 of *Lecture Notes in Computer Science*, pages 108–119. Jacques Calmet, editor, Springer, 1985.

[KPG99]   Aviad Kipnis, Jacques Patarin, and Louis Goubin. Unbalanced Oil and Vinegar signature schemes. In *Advances in Cryptology — EUROCRYPT 1999*, volume 1592 of *Lecture Notes in Computer Science*, pages 206–222. Jacques Stern, editor, Springer, 1999.

[LD00]   Julio Lopéz and Ricardo Dahab. An overview of elliptic curve cryptography. Technical report, Institute of Computing, State University of Campinas, Brazil, 22nd of May 2000. http://citeseer.nj.nec.com/333066.html or http://www.dcc.unicamp.br/ic-tr-ftp/2000/00-14.ps.gz.

[MAG]   Computational Algebra Group, University of Sydney. *The MAGMA Computational Algebra System for Algebra, Number Theory and Geometry*. http://magma.maths.usyd.edu.au/magma/.

[NES]   NESSIE: New European Schemes for Signatures, Integrity, and Encryption. Information Society Technologies programme of the European commission (IST-1999-12324). http://www.cryptonessie.org/.

[Pat95]   Jacques Patarin. Cryptanalysis of the Matsumoto and Imai public key scheme of Eurocrypt'88. In *Advances in Cryptology — CRYPTO 1995*, volume 963 of *Lecture Notes in Computer Science*, pages 248–261. Don Coppersmith, editor, Springer, 1995.

[Pat96]   Jacques Patarin. Hidden Field Equations (HFE) and Isomorphisms of Polynomials (IP): two new families of asymmetric algorithms. In *Advances in Cryptology — EUROCRYPT 1996*, volume 1070 of *Lecture Notes in Computer Science*, pages 33–48. Ueli Maurer, editor, Springer, 1996. Extended Version: http://www.minrank.org/hfe.pdf.

[Pat97]   Jacques Patarin. The oil and vinegar signature scheme. presented at the Dagstuhl Workshop on Cryptography, September 1997. transparencies.

[PKC05]   Serge Vaudenay, editor. *Public Key Cryptography — PKC 2005*, volume 3386 of *Lecture Notes in Computer Science*. Springer, 2005. ISBN 3-540-24454-9.

[RSA05]   David Pointcheval, editor. *The Cryptographer's Track at RSA Conference 2005*, volume 3860 of *Lecture Notes in Computer Science*. Springer, 2005. ISBN 3-540-31033-9.

[Sha93]   Adi Shamir. Efficient signature schemes based on birational permutations. In Crypto [Cry93], pages 1–12.

[Sho97]   Peter W. Shor. Polynomial-time algorithms for prime factorization and discrete logarithms on a quantum computer. *SIAM Journal on Computing*, 26(5):1484–1509, October 1997.

[TKI$^+$86]   S. Tsujii, K. Kurosawa, T. Itoh, A. Fujioka, and T. Matsumoto. A public key cryptosystem based on the difficulty of solving a system of nonlinear equations. *ICICE Transactions (D) J69-D*, 12:1963–1970, 1986.

[WBP04]   Christopher Wolf, An Braeken, and Bart Preneel. Efficient cryptanalysis of RSE(2)PKC and RSSE(2)PKC. In *Conference on Security in Communication Networks — SCN 2004*, volume 3352 of *Lecture Notes in Computer Science*, pages 294–309. Springer, September 8–10 2004. Extended version: http://eprint.iacr.org/2004/237.

[WHL$^+$05]   Lih-Chung Wang, Yuh-Hua Hu, Feipei Lai, Chun yen Chou, and Bo-Yin Yang. Tractable rational map signature. In PKC [PKC05], pages 244–257. ISBN 3-540-24454-9.

[WP04]   Christopher Wolf and Bart Preneel. Asymmetric cryptography: Hidden Field Equations. In *European Congress on Computational Methods in Applied Sciences and Engineering 2004*. P. Neittaanmäki, T. Rossi, S. Korotov, E. Oñate, J. Périaux, and D. Knörzer, editors, Jyväskylä University, 2004. 20 pages, extended version: http://eprint.iacr.org/2004/072/.

[WP05a]   Christopher Wolf and Bart Preneel. Equivalent keys in HFE, C*, and variations. In *Proceedings of Mycrypt 2005*, volume 3715 of *Lecture Notes in Computer Science*, pages 33–49. Serge Vaudenay, editor, Springer, 2005. Extended version http://eprint.iacr.org/2004/360/, 15 pages.

[WP05b]   Christopher Wolf and Bart Preneel. Taxonomy of public key schemes based on the problem of multivariate quadratic equations. Cryptology ePrint Archive, Report 2005/077, 12th of May 2005. http://eprint.iacr.org/2005/077/, 64 pages.

[WYHL06]   Lih-Chung Wang, Bo-Yin Yang, Yuh-Hua Hu, and Feipei Lai. A "medium-field" multivariate public-key encryption scheme. In RSA [RSA05], pages 132–149. ISBN 3-540-31033-9.

[YC04a]   Bo-Yin Yang and Jiun-Ming Chen. All in the XL family: Theory and practice. In *ICISC 2004*, volume 3506 of *Lecture Notes in Computer Science*, pages 67–86. Springer, 2004.

[YC04b]   Bo-Yin Yang and Jiun-Ming Chen. Theoretical analysis of XL over small fields. In *ACISP 2004*, volume 3108 of *Lecture Notes in Computer Science*, pages 277–288. Springer, 2004.

[YC05]   Bo-Yin Yang and Jiun-Ming Chen. Building secure tame-like multivariate public-key cryptosystems: The new TTS. In *ACISP 2005*, volume 3574 of *Lecture Notes in Computer Science*, pages 518–531. Springer, July 2005.

Chosen-Ciphertext Secure Key-Encapsulation Based on Gap Hashed Diffie-Hellman

Eike Kiltz

CWI Amsterdam
The Netherlands
kiltz@cwi.nl
http://kiltz.net

Abstract. We propose a practical key encapsulation mechanism with a simple and intuitive design concept. Security against chosen-ciphertext attacks can be proved in the standard model under a new assumption, the Gap Hashed Diffie-Hellman (GHDH) assumption. The security reduction is tight and simple.

Secure key encapsulation, combined with an appropriately secure symmetric encryption scheme, yields a hybrid public-key encryption scheme which is secure against chosen-ciphertext attacks. The implied encryption scheme is very efficient: compared to the previously most efficient scheme by Kurosawa and Desmedt [Crypto 2004] it has 128 bits shorter ciphertexts, between 25-50% shorter public/secret keys, and it is slightly more efficient in terms of encryption/decryption speed. Furthermore, our scheme enjoys (the option of) public verifiability of the ciphertexts and it inherits all practical advantages of secure hybrid encryption.

1   Introduction

One of the main fields of interest in cryptography is the design and the analysis of the security of encryption schemes in the public-key setting (PKE schemes). In this work our goal is to provide schemes for which we can provide theoretical proofs of security (without relying on heuristics such as the random oracle), but which are also efficient and practical.

KEY ENCAPSULATION. Instead of providing the full functionality of a public-key encryption scheme, in many applications it is sufficient to let sender and receiver agree on a common random session key. This can be accomplished with a *key encapsulation mechanism* (KEM) as formalized by Cramer and Shoup [11]. In this protocol a sender (knowing the receivers public key) runs an encapsulation algorithm to produce a random session key together with a corresponding ciphertext. This ciphertext is sent (over a potentially insecure channel) to the receiver, who (using his secret key) can uniquely reconstruct the session key using a decapsulation algorithm. In the end both parties share a common random session key. A strong notion of security (security against *chosen-ciphertext attacks* [23]) requires that, roughly, not even an active eavesdropper (interacting with a decapsulation oracle that allows him to obtain session keys corresponding

T. Okamoto and X. Wang (Eds.): PKC 2007, LNCS 4450, pp. 282–297, 2007.

to ciphertexts of his choosing) can learn any information about the random session key corresponding to a given ciphertext. After the execution of the protocol the random session key may now be used for arbitrary symmetric-key operations such as a symmetric encryption scheme. If both, the KEM and the symmetric primitive, are secure against chosen-ciphertext attacks then composition theorems are used to obtain the same security guarantees for the hybrid encryption protocol.

In this work we are interested in designing key encapsulation mechanisms that are both efficient and provably secure with respect to a reasonable intractability assumption. To motivate our approach we start with some history on key encapsulation.

DIFFIE-HELLMAN KEY ENCAPSULATION. In the Diffie-Hellman key encapsulation mechanism [12] the receiver's public key consists of the group element g^x (we assume a commutative cyclic group of prime order and generator g to be given), the secret key of the random index x. Key encapsulation is done by computing the ciphertext as g^y for random y; the corresponding session key is the group element $g^{xy} = (g^x)^y$ (and therefore called *Diffie-Hellman Key*). This key is recovered from the ciphertext by the possessor of the secret key x by computing g^{xy} as $(g^y)^x$. In practice one mostly requires the session key to be a binary string rather of fixed length than a group element. This is overcome by feeding the Diffie-Hellman key g^{xy} to a hash function H with binary image to obtain a session key $\mathsf{H}(g^{xy})$. This simple key encapsulation scheme can be proved secure against chosen-plaintext attacks under the *Hashed Diffie-Hellman* (HDH) assumption, as formalized in [1]. The HDH assumption (relative to a hash function H) states, roughly, that the two distributions $(g^x, g^y, \mathsf{H}(g^{xy}))$ and (g^x, g^y, R) for random indices x, y and a random bit-string R (of appropriate length) are computational indistinguishable. Under the HDH assumption, Hashed Diffie-Hellman can be proven secure against chosen-plaintext attacks (IND-CPA).

For various reasons, the stronger notion of chosen-ciphertext (IND-CCA) security [23] has emerged as the "right" notion of security for key encapsulation and encryption. Hashed Diffie-Hellman will be our starting point and the goal will be to modify the scheme in order to obtain security against chosen-ciphertext attacks under a reasonable intractability assumption.

OUR CONSTRUCTION. We modify the Hashed Diffie-Hellman key encapsulation in order to obtain a KEM that is provably secure against chosen-ciphertext attacks under the *Gap Hashed Diffie-Hellman assumption* (to be introduced later). Our main idea is to add some redundant information to the ciphertext of the Hashed Diffie-Hellman key encapsulation. This information is used to check if a given ciphertext was properly generated by the encapsulation algorithm (and hence is "consistent"); if the ciphertext is consistent then decapsulation returns the session key, otherwise it simply rejects. Our scheme's security relies on the Gap Hashed Diffie-Hellman (GHDH) assumption which states that, roughly, the two distributions $(g^x, g^y, \mathsf{H}(g^{xy}))$ and (g^x, g^y, R) are hard to distinguish even relative to a "Diffie-Hellman oracle" that efficiently distinguishes (g^x, g^y, g^{xy}) from (g^x, g^y, g^z). Here the term "gap" stems from the fact that there is a gap between the Decisional and the Computational version of the Diffie-Hellman problem: the computational problem is hard to solve even though the corresponding decisional problem is easy.

MAIN RESULTS. Our main result shows that our key encapsulation mechanism is secure against chosen-ciphertext attacks assuming the GHDH assumption holds. The scheme has very short ciphertexts (2 groups elements or approximately 512 bits for 128 bits security) and its security reduction is *tight*. When our scheme gets instantiated in gap-groups [20] a given ciphertext can get checked for consistency solely based on the knowledge of the public key. This feature (sometimes called "public verifiability of the ciphertext") has proved very useful, e.g. for building a chosen-ciphertext secure threshold encapsulation scheme [9]. Furthermore, we show that our framework extends to building KEMs based on the Gap Hashed Multi Diffie-Hellman (GHMDH) assumption, a natural generalization of GHDH with potentially stronger security properties. The GHMDH assumption states that given many independent Diffie-Hellman instances $(g_i, h_i, g_i^{r_i})_{1 \le i \le \ell}$, evaluating the ℓ^2 possible (hidden) Diffie-Hellman keys $(h_i)^{r_j}$ $(1 \le i, j \le \ell)$ on a fixed public predicate $\mathsf{H} : \mathbb{G}^{\ell \times \ell} \to \mathbb{G}$ yields an element that is indistinguishable from a random one, even relative to a DDH oracle. The GHMDH assumption in particular includes (a paring-free variant of) the Gap Linear Diffie-Hellman (GLDH) assumption [6].

RELATED WORK. Cramer and Shoup [10,11] proposed the first practical public-key encryption scheme in the standard model. More recently, Kurosawa and Desmedt came up with a direct hybrid encryption scheme [19] improving the performance of the original CS scheme both in computational efficiency and in ciphertext length. In their hybrid construction the symmetric scheme has to be secure in the sense of *authenticated encryption* [2] which is a strictly stronger security requirement than in the standard KEM/DEM hybrid paradigm [11], and in particular it necessarily adds 128 bits of redundancy to the symmetric ciphertext. The KD-KEM (i.e. the KEM part of the Kurosawa Desmedt hybrid encryption scheme) is similar to our KEM construction. In fact, the KD-KEM can be obtained from our KEM by (roughly) switching the symmetric key with one element from the ciphertext. Our scheme can be proved chosen-ciphertext secure whereas there exists a simple chosen-ciphertext attack against the KD-KEM [14]. We think that this is really a surprising fact since a small difference in the constellation of the ciphertexts seems to turn the scale when it comes to security of the two schemes.

An alternative group of schemes ("IBE-based schemes") is based on recent results [7,16] observing that identity-based encryption (IBE) implies chosen-ciphertext secure encryption. The recent approach taken by Boyen, Mei, and Waters [9] was to improve efficiency of one particular instantiation [5] (based on the BDH assumption) obtained by the above IBE transformation. Similar results were also obtained independently by Kiltz [16]. All the encryption schemes constructed this way, however, so far remained less efficient than the reference scheme from Kurosawa-Desmedt. Our KEM constructions based on GHDH and GHMDH are related (and generalize) the KEMs obtained in [9,16] and therefore fits best into the latter class of IBE-based [7,16] schemes (even though they are not derived from any IBE scheme).

DISCUSSION AND COMPARISON. Our porposed hybrid PKE scheme based on GHDH is more efficient than the "reference scheme" by Kurosawa and Desmedt [19]: it has "one MAC" shorter ciphertexts (by combining it with redundancy-free symmetric encryption [21]), between 25-50% shorter public/ secret keys, and it is slightly more efficient in terms of encryption/decryption. However, an arguable disadvantage of our scheme is that security can only be proven on the new GHDH assumption, whereas security of the KD scheme provably relies on the well-established and purely algebraic DDH assumption. An extensive comparison with all known KEM/PKE schemes in the standard model is done in Table 1 (Section 5).

RECENT RESULTS. Recently, building on this work, Hofheinz and Kiltz [15] combined a variation of our scheme with symmetric authenticated encryption (and hence adding 128 bits redundancy to the ciphertexts) to obtain public-key encryption secure under the DDH assumption. Their technique also extends to the more general class of (Hashed) Multi Diffie-Hellman assumptions which can be seen as the "DDH-oracle free" variant of HGMDH.

FULL VERSION. A full version of this extended abstract is available on the Cryptology ePrint archive [18].

2   Public Key Encapsulation Mechanisms

A *public-key encapsulation* (KEM) scheme $\mathcal{KEM} = (\mathsf{Kg}, \mathsf{Enc}, \mathsf{Dec})$ with keyspace $\mathsf{KeySp}(k)$ consists of three polynomial-time algorithms. Via $(pk, sk) \xleftarrow{\$} \mathsf{Kg}(1^k)$ the randomized key-generation algorithm produces keys for security parameter $k \in \mathbb{N}$; via $(K, C) \xleftarrow{\$} \mathsf{Enc}(1^k, pk)$ a key $K \in \mathsf{KeySp}(k)$ together with a ciphertext C is created; via $K \leftarrow \mathsf{Dec}(sk, C)$ the possessor of secret key sk decrypts ciphertext C to get back a key. For consistency, we require that for all $k \in \mathbb{N}$, and all $(K, C) \xleftarrow{\$} \mathsf{Enc}(1^k, pk)$ we have $\Pr[\mathsf{Dec}(C) = K] = 1$, where the probability is taken over the choice of $(pk, sk) \xleftarrow{\$} \mathsf{Kg}(1^k)$, and the coins of all the algorithms in the expression above.

We require the KEM to be secure against chosen-ciphertext attacks. Formally, we associate to an adversary $\mathcal{A}$ the following experiment:

> **Experiment $\mathbf{Exp}_{\mathcal{KEM}, \mathcal{A}}^{kem\text{-}cca}(k)$**
>
> $(pk, sk) \xleftarrow{\$} \mathsf{Kg}(1^k)$; $K_0^* \xleftarrow{\$} \mathsf{KeySp}(k)$; $(K_1^*, C^*) \xleftarrow{\$} \mathsf{Enc}(pk)$
> $\delta \xleftarrow{\$} \{0, 1\}$; $\delta' \xleftarrow{\$} \mathcal{A}^{\mathsf{DecO}(sk, \cdot)}(pk, K_\delta^*, C^*)$
> If $\delta \neq \delta'$ then return 0 else return 1

where the oracle $\mathsf{DecO}(sk, \cdot)$ queried on C returns $K \leftarrow \mathsf{Dec}(sk, C)$ with the restriction that $\mathcal{A}$ is not allowed to query $\mathsf{DecO}(sk, \cdot)$ on the target ciphertext C^*. We define the advantage of $\mathcal{A}$ in the left experiment as

$$\mathbf{Adv}_{\mathcal{KEM},\mathcal{A}}^{kem\text{-}cca}(k) \;=\; \left| \Pr\left[\,\mathbf{Exp}_{\mathcal{KEM},\mathcal{A}}^{kem\text{-}cca}(k) = 1\right] - \frac{1}{2}\right|.$$

A key encapsulation mechanism $\mathcal{KEM}$ is said to be *indistinguishable against chosen-ciphertext attacks* (IND-CCA) if the advantage function $\mathbf{Adv}_{\mathcal{KEM},\mathcal{A}}^{kem\text{-}cca}(k)$ is a negligible function in k for all polynomial-time adversaries $\mathcal{A}$.

Note that in contrast to the original definition given by Cramer and Shoup [11] we consider a simplified (but equivalent) security experiment without a "find-stage".

3   Complexity Assumptions

3.1   Standard Diffie-Hellman Assumptions

We first start with the following well known standard assumptions which we review for completeness. The *Computational Diffie-Hellman assumption* (CDH) states, that given the input (g, g^x, g^y) where x, y are drawn at random from $\mathbb{Z}_p$ (g is a generator of a group $\mathbb{G}$ of prime order p), it should be computationally infeasible to compute g^{xy}. However, under the CDH assumption it might be as well possible to efficiently compute some information about g^{xy}, say a single bit of the binary representation or even all but super-logarithmically many bits. A stronger assumption that has been gaining popularity is the *Decisional Diffie-Hellman assumption* (DDH). It states, roughly, that the distributions (g, g^x, g^y, g^{xy}) and (g, g^x, g^y, g^z) are computationally indistinguishable when x, y, z are drawn at random from $\mathbb{Z}_p$. Another variant of the Diffie-Hellman assumption is the *Gap Diffie-Hellman assumption* (GDH). It states that the CDH assumption is still hard even though an adversary has additional access to an oracle that solves the DDH problem.

3.2   The Gap Hashed Diffie-Hellman Assumption

As indicated above, semantic security requires that we will be able to get some number of hard-core bits from the Diffie-Hellman key (i.e. bits that cannot be distinguished from random bits). We will be using a gap-assumption relative to a DDH oracle, so clearly we are not allowed to take the whole Diffie-Hellman key. Our assumption is that applying a suitable hash function H (for example, a cryptographic hash function like SHA-1) to g^{xy} will yield such bits. The assumption we make, called the Gap Hashed Diffie-Hellman assumption (GHDH) is a "composite one"; it concerns the interaction between a hash function H and the group $\mathbb{G}$. The GHDH is an extension of the HDH assumption formalized by Abdalla, Bellare, Rogaway [1].

Our schemes will be parameterized by a *parameter generator*. This is a polynomial-time algorithm Gen that on input 1^k returns the description of a multiplicative cyclic group $\mathbb{G}$ of prime order p, where $2^k < p < 2^{k+1}$, and a random generator g of $\mathbb{G}$. Gen furthermore outputs the description of a random hash function $H : \mathbb{G} \to \{0,1\}^{l(k)}$ that outputs $l(k)$ bits for a fixed polynomial $l(\cdot)$.

Throughout the paper we use $\mathcal{HG} = (\mathbb{G}, g, p, \mathsf{H})$ as shorthand for the description of the hash group obtained by running Gen.

The GHDH assumption relative to Gen states that the two distributions $(g^x, g^y, \mathsf{H}(g^{xy}))$ and (g^x, g^y, R) are computationally indistinguishable when x, y are drawn at random from $\mathbb{Z}_p$ and R is drawn at random from $\{0,1\}^{l(k)}$. This assumption should hold relative to an oracle that efficiently solves the DDH problem. More formally, to an adversary $\mathcal{B}$ we associate the following experiment.

> **Experiment $\mathbf{Exp}_{\mathsf{Gen},\mathsf{H},\mathcal{B}}^{\mathrm{ghdh}}(1^k)$**
> $\mathcal{HG} \xleftarrow{\$} \mathsf{Gen}(1^k)$; $x, y \xleftarrow{\$} \mathbb{Z}_p^*$; $W_0 \xleftarrow{\$} \{0,1\}^{l(k)}$; $W_1 \leftarrow \mathsf{H}(g^{xy})$
> $\gamma \xleftarrow{\$} \{0,1\}$; $\gamma' \xleftarrow{\$} \mathcal{B}^{\mathsf{DDHsolve}_{\mathbb{G}}(\cdot,\cdot,\cdot,\cdot)}(1^k, \mathcal{HG}, g^x, g^y, W_\gamma)$
> If $\gamma \neq \gamma'$ then return 0 else return 1

Here the oracle $\mathsf{DDHsolve}_{\mathbb{G}}(g, g^a, g^b, g^c)$ returns 1 iff $ab = c \bmod p$. We define the advantage of $\mathcal{B}$ in the above experiment as

$$\mathbf{Adv}_{\mathsf{Gen},\mathcal{B}}^{\mathrm{ghdh}}(k) \;=\; \left| \Pr\left[\mathbf{Exp}_{\mathsf{Gen},\mathcal{B}}^{\mathrm{ghdh}}(1^k) = 1 \right] - \frac{1}{2} \right|.$$

We say that the *Gap Hashed Diffie-Hellman (GHDH) assumption relative to group generator* Gen holds if $\mathbf{Adv}_{\mathsf{Gen},\mathcal{B}}^{\mathrm{ghdh}}$ is a negligible function in k for all polynomial-time adversaries $\mathcal{B}$.

We remark that in so called gap-groups, i.e. in groups where the Decisional Diffie-Hellman (DDH) problem is easy on every input while the computational Diffie-Hellman (CDH) problem CDH problem is hard [20], the GHDH assumption is equivalent to the HDH assumption. A possible implementation of gap-groups is given by the Weil/Tate bilinear pairing allowing to efficiently compute a bilinear pairing which can be used to solve DDH [8].

At first glance one may argue that assuming the hashed key $\mathsf{H}(g^{xy})$ to be indistinguishable from a random string even though we can efficiently distinguish g^{xy} from a random group element sounds quite unreasonable and that, in a sense, hardness falls back on "random-oracle-like" properties of the hash function. However, this intuition is not true. We can show that in generic groups [24] GHDH holds (unconditionally) assuming the hash function H is "weakly one-way". The latter result basically means that the GHDH assumption depends on the hardness of computing the Diffie-Hellman key plus the fact that given only $\mathsf{H}(g^{xy})$ it is hard to recover sufficient information on the Diffie-Hellman key g^{xy}. This should in particular hold for cryptographic hash functions like SHA-1. Also, the well known and often employed Bilinear Diffie-Hellman (BDH) assumption [8] can in fact be seen as a special (algebraic) instantiation of the GHDH assumption. More precisely, using the specific algebraic hash function $\mathsf{H}(X) := \hat{e}_Z(X)$, where $\hat{e}_Z(X) := \hat{e}(X, Z)$ is a bilinear mapping for fixed $Z = g^z$ (but chosen uniformly at setup), we get $\mathsf{H}(g^{xy}) = \hat{e}(g^{xy}, g^z) = \hat{e}(g,g)^{xyz}$ and GHDH actually gets BDH (here the output of H is a group element, not a binary string). In this context, GHDH instantiated with a cryptographic hash function appears not to be a less reasonable assumption than the "standard" BDH assumption.

More details are given in the full version [18]. There we also propose various candidates for Gen (i.e., for the prime-order group $\mathbb{G}$ and the hash function H) and provide a detailed security analysis of the GHDH assumption. In practice however, we recommend using a cryptographic hash function like MD5 or SHA-1.

4   Key Encapsulation Based on GHDH

4.1   The Key Encapsulation Mechanism

Let $\mathcal{HG} = (\mathbb{G}, g, p, \mathsf{H})$ be random parameters obtained by running the parameter algorithm $\mathsf{Gen}(1^k)$, where $\mathsf{H} : \mathbb{G} \to \{0,1\}^{l(k)}$ is a random instance of a hash function such that the GHDH assumptions holds relative to Gen. Let $\mathsf{INJ} : \mathbb{G} \to \mathbb{Z}_p$ be an efficiently computable injective encoding.[1] We build a key encapsulation mechanism $\mathcal{KEM} = (\mathsf{Kg}, \mathsf{Enc}, \mathsf{Dec})$ as follows.

$\mathsf{Kg}(1^k)$	$\mathsf{Enc}(pk)$	$\mathsf{Dec}(sk, C)$
$x, y \xleftarrow{\$} \mathbb{Z}_p^*$	$r \xleftarrow{\$} \mathbb{Z}_p^* \; ; \; c \leftarrow g^r$	Parse C as (c, π)
$u \leftarrow g^x \; ; \; v \leftarrow g^y$	$t \leftarrow \mathsf{INJ}(c) \; ; \; \pi \leftarrow (u^t v)^r$	$t \leftarrow \mathsf{INJ}(c)$
$pk \leftarrow (u, v)$	$K \leftarrow \mathsf{H}(u^r) \in \{0,1\}^{l(k)}$	If $c^{xt+y} \neq \pi$ then $\bot$
$sk \leftarrow (x, y)$	$C \leftarrow (c, \pi) \in \mathbb{G}^2$	Else $K \leftarrow \mathsf{H}(c^x)$
Return (pk, sk)	Return (C, K)	Return K

Decapsulation also has to perform one subgroup-membership test, i.e. it checks if $c \in \mathbb{G}$, and returns $\bot$ (reject) otherwise. Note that $c^{xt+y} = \pi$ then automatically also implies $\pi \in \mathbb{G}$.

EFFICIENCY. The public key contains two group elements, the secret key of two elements from $\mathbb{Z}_p$. A ciphertext C consists of two group elements, the key K is a binary string of length $l(k)$. Ignoring all "symmetric operations", encapsulation needs three regular exponentiations, whereas decapsulation can be carried out in two exponentiation. Using the concept sequential/multi-exponentiations[2] (see, e.g., [22,4]) a considerable (and practical) speed-up can be obtained: encapsulation needs two regular exponentiations (to compute c and K) plus one multi-exponentiation (to compute $\pi = u^{tr} v^r$), whereas decapsulation can be carried out in one single sequential exponentiation (to compute c^{xt+y} and c^x).

CORRECTNESS. Fix a pair of keys (pk, sk). We call a ciphertext $C = (c, \pi) \in \mathbb{G}^2$ *consistent* if $c^{xt+y} = \pi$ for $t = \mathsf{INJ}(c)$. For a correctly generated ciphertext

---

[1] Actually, an "almost injective" encoding is sufficient for our purpose, see [9]. Most interesting groups allow for such an encoding [11,9,13]. If such an encoding is not available one can also use a target collission resistant hash function $\mathsf{TCR} : \mathbb{G} \to \mathbb{Z}_p$, see [18] for more details.

[2] One multi-exponentiaion computes the group element $g^a h^b$ and one sequential exponentiation computes the two group elements g^a and g^b in one single step (for the same fixed base g). Both concepts are related and (using Pippenger's algorithm [22]) can be carried out in about $(1 + 2/\log\log p)\log p$ multiplications over $\mathbb{G}$ [4] which we will count as ≈ 1.2 exponentiations.

$C = (c, \pi) = (g^r, u^{tr}v^r)$ we have $c^{xt+y} = (g^{xt+y})^r = (u^t v)^r = \pi$ and hence C is consistent. In that case decapsulation reconstructs the session key as $K = H(c^x) = H((g^r)^x) = H(u^r)$, as the key in encapsulation.

PUBLIC VERIFIABILITY IN GAP-GROUPS. Let $C = (c, \pi) \in \mathbb{G}^2$ be a ciphertext with $c = g^r$ for some value $r \in \mathbb{Z}_p$. Then $(g, u^t v = g^{xt+y}, c = g^r, \pi)$ is a Diffie-Hellman-tuple if and only if $g^{(xt+y)\cdot r} = \pi$ what is equivalent to $c^{xt+y} = \pi$. Therefore in gap-groups consistency of a ciphertext can be publicly checked using one call to the Diffie-Hellman oracle, i.e. by verifying if $\mathsf{DDHsolve}_{\mathbb{G}}(g, u^t v = g^{xt+y}, c = g^r, \pi)$ returns true. This property is denoted as *public verifiability of the ciphertext* and it give rise to a public-key threshold KEM [9].

4.2   Security

Our main theorem can be stated as follows:

Theorem 1. *Under the Gap Hashed Diffie-Hellman assumption relative to generator* Gen, *the key encapsulation mechanism from Section 4.1 is secure against chosen-ciphertext attacks. In particular, for any adversary $\mathcal{A}$ against the KEM running for time $\mathbf{Time}_{\mathcal{A}}(k)$, there exist an adversary $\mathcal{B}$ with $\mathbf{Adv}_{\mathsf{Gen},\mathcal{B}}^{\mathrm{ghdh}}(k) \geq \mathbf{Adv}_{\mathcal{KEM},\mathcal{A}}^{\mathrm{kem\text{-}cca}}(k)$ and $\mathbf{Time}_{\mathcal{B}}(k) = \mathbf{Time}_{\mathcal{A}}(k) + \mathcal{O}(q \cdot \mathbf{Time}_{\mathbb{G}}(k))$, where q is an upper bound on the number of decapsulation queries made by adversary $\mathcal{A}$ and $\mathbf{Time}_{\mathbb{G}}(k)$ is the time for a standard operation in $\mathbb{G}$.*

We want to stress that the key encapsulation mechanism does not make use of the Decision Diffie-Hellman oracle DDHsolve. Its existence is part of the assumption and solely needed for the proof of security.

The proof is quite simple. An intuitive way to understand it is as follows: first consider a modified KEM that is obtained by abandoning the hash function H from the construction in Section 4.1, i.e. the symmetric key is now computed as $K = u^r$. What we can prove is that this modified KEM is *one-way chosen-ciphertext secure* under the gap Diffie-Hellman (GDH) assumption. In the security reduction the DDH oracle provided by the GDH assumption is used to reject (as in the original scheme) every invalid ciphertext submitted by the adversary to the decryption oracle. The key idea of the reduction is based on an algebraic technique from [5] that was also used in [9,16] in the context of KEMs. An attacker $\mathcal{B}$ against the GDH problem can setup the public-key for the adversary attacking the security of the KEM in a way that (i) adversary $\mathcal{B}$ (without knowing the secret key) can decapsulate every ciphertexts except the challenge ciphertext; (ii) decapsulating the challenge ciphertext is equivalent to solving GDH. If the adversary against the KEM is successfull (i.e. it decapsulates the challenge ciphertext) so this adversary can be used to break the GDH problem using the above simulation.

More details. Adversary $\mathcal{B}$ inputs a GDH instance (g, u, g^a) and it's goal is to compute $T = u^a$ (recall that we are attacking one-way chosen-ciphertext security). He picks a random value d and defines the (thereby correctly distributed) public key as $pk = (u, v = u^{-t^*} g^d)$, where $t^* = \mathsf{INJ}(g^a)$. Note that this way a consistent ciphertext (c, π) properly created by the encapsulation algorithm has the form

$$c = g^r, \quad \pi = (u^t v)^r = (u^r)^{t-t^*} c^d , \tag{1}$$

for some $t \in \mathbb{Z}_p$. Hence, in order to decapsulate the challenge ciphertext $C^* = (c^*, \pi^*)$ defined as $c^* := g^a$, $\pi^* := (g^a)^d = (u^a)^{t^* - t^*} c^d$ (i.e., a ciphertext computed with unknown randomness a from the GDH instance, where $t^* = \mathsf{INJ}(c^*)$), adversary $\mathcal{A}$ (which is run on pk and C^*) has to compute the target key $K^* = u^a$ what is equivalent to breaking GDH. On the other hand, for a decapsulation query for ciphertext (c, π), $\mathcal{B}$ first checks for consistency using the DDH oracle $\mathsf{DDHsolve}$ provided by the GDH assumption. If the ciphertext is inconsistent it gets rejected. Otherwise, by injectivity of INJ, we have $t = \mathsf{INJ}(c) \neq \mathsf{INJ}(c^*) = t^*$ and the correct key $K = u^r$ can be reconstructed by Eqn. (1) as $K = (\pi/c^d)^{1/(t-t^*)}$.

The step to full security (i.e., indistinguishability compared to one-wayness) now can be intuitively understood by the fact that (in terms of the assumption) we move from GDH to GHDH, i.e. under GHDH the hash function H hides all information about the Diffie-Hellman key u^r. A more formal proof is given in Appendix A.

4.3   KEM/DEM: From KEM to Full Encryption

A KEM and a symmetric encryption scheme (aka DEM) can be used to obtain a hybrid public-key encryption scheme. It is well known that if both the KEM and the DEM are chosen-ciphertext secure, then the resulting hybrid encryption is also chosen-ciphertext secure [11, Sec. 7]. The security reduction is tight. A DEM secure against chosen-ciphertext attacks can be built from relatively weak primitives, i.e. from any one-time symmetric encryption scheme by essentially adding a MAC. Phan and Pointcheval [21] showed that strong pseudorandomn permutations directly imply redundancy-free chosen-ciphertext secure DEMs that avoid the usual overhead due to the MAC. It seems reasonable to believe that known block-ciphers (auch as AES) are strong PRPs.

In the full version [18] we also sketch how to obtain a direct PKE scheme that may be usefull to non-interactive chosen-ciphertext secure threshold encryption scheme [9].

4.4   Relation to Other Encryption Schemes

The KEMs based on "identity-based techniques" [9,16,17] are very similar to our construction. In fact, (a slight variation of) the KEM from [9] (which itself is based on the first IBE scheme Boneh and Boyen [5]) can be obtained from our KEM by instantiating the hash function H with a bilinear map, i.e. by defining $\mathsf{H}(X) = \hat{e}(g^z, X)$ (further simplifications in the decapsulation algorithm must be applied). As we already sketched in Section 3.2, security of the KEM then can be proved relative to the BDH assumption (just as in [9]). However, since it involves computing bilinear maps, the BWM-KEM is considerably less efficient than our proposal when H is a cryptographic hash function.

Surprisingly, the KEM part (KD-KEM) of the Kurosawa-Desmedt public-key encryption scheme [19] looks quite similar to our construction. Indeed, the KD-KEM encapsulates by computing the ciphertext as $(c_1, c_2) = (g^r, \hat{g}^r)$ and the corresponding symmetric key is defined as $K = (u^t v)^r$, where $g, \hat{g}, u = g^x \hat{g}^{\hat{x}}, v = g^y \hat{g}^{\hat{y}}$ are elements from the public key and t is computed as $t = \mathsf{TCR}(c_1, c_2)$. In comparison (and ignoring the hash function) our scheme basically *swaps* the elements c_2 and K, i.e. the ciphertexts of our scheme are given by $(g^r, (u^t v)^r)$ (t now only depends on g^r), where the corresponding key is $\mathsf{H}(u^r)$.

In contrast our KEM is provably secure under a well-defined number-theoretic assumption whereas the KD-KEM was recently shown to be not even one-way chosen-ciphertext secure [14]. One could possible remark that the stronger security properties of our KEM inherently rely on the stronger assumption, i.e., the hash function H and the DDH oracle in the GHDH assumption (the gap-property). However, this is not true as we will explain now; security rather seems to depend on the particular constellation of the ciphertexts of our KEM. First, the attack from [14] aganst the KD-KEM is still valid if the two elements in the KD-KEM ciphertext get checked for consistency before decapsulating the key, i.e. the attack does not rely on "inconsistent ciphertext queries". In other words it is not the "gap"-property of the GHDH assumptions that makes the difference in the (in-)security of the two KEMs. Second, chosen-ciphertext security of our KEM does also not depend on the hash function H since without H our KEM is still *one-way* chosen-ciphertext secure under the gap computational Diffie-Hellman assumption. As pointed out earlier the hash function H is only responsible to provide indistinguishability (rather than one-wayness).

4.5   Key-Encapsulation Based on GHMDH

In this section we sketch a usefull generalization of our KEM construction to build schemes based on the general class of GHMDH assumptions which we now introduce.

For an integer $\ell \geq 1$ let $\mathbf{D} \in \mathbb{G}^{\ell \times \ell}$ be a matrix with entries $D_{i,j} \in \mathbb{G}$ ($1 \leq i, j \leq \ell$). Let $\mathsf{H} : \mathbb{G}^{\ell \times \ell} \to \mathcal{K}$ be a hash-function that maps ℓ^2 group elements into a key-space $\mathcal{K}$. Informally, the Gap Hashed Multi Diffie-Hellman (GHMDH) assumption (reative to hash function H and group $\mathbb{G}$) states that, given $g_1, \ldots, g_\ell, h_1, \ldots, h_\ell, g_1^{r_1}, \ldots, g_\ell^{r_\ell}$ and access to a DDH oracle, it is computationally infeasible to distinguish $\mathsf{H}(\mathbf{D})$ from a random element in $\mathcal{K}$, where the (hidden) entries of matrix $\mathbf{D}$ contain all ℓ^2 possible combinations of Diffie-Hellman keys, i.e. $D_{i,j} = h_i^{r_j}$. Intuitively, the hash function H can be viewed as a hard predicate of the ℓ^2 different Diffie-Hellman keys. Clearly, for $\ell = 1$ and $\mathcal{K} = \{0,1\}^{l(k)}$ this simplifies to the GHDH assumption but in this section we focus mostly on algebraic candidates of the form $\mathsf{H} : \mathbb{G}^{\ell \times \ell} \to \mathbb{G}$, for $\ell \geq 2$.

As one illustrating example of the much general class of GHMDH assumptions, the Gap Decision Linear Diffie-Hellman (GLDH) assumption [6] is obtained by setting $\ell = 2$ and defining $\mathsf{H} : \mathbb{G}^{2 \times 2} \to \mathbb{G}$ as $\mathsf{H}(\mathbf{D}) = D_{1,1} \cdot D_{1,2}$. More precisely, the GLDH assumption states that, given $g_1, g_2, g_1^{r_1}, g_2^{r_2}, h_1, W$, destinguishing $W = h_1^{r_1 + r_2}$ from a uniform $W \in \mathbb{G}$ is computational infeasible, even relative to a DDH oracle. Originally, the GLDH assumption was defined over bilinear maps [6] (called Decision Linear Diffie-Hellman assumption), whereas here we only require the assumption to hold relative to a DDH oracle. This, in particilar, makes it possible to define (and apply) it relative to any cyclic group [16].

More generally, for any polynomial $\ell = \ell(k) \geq 2$, one can also define the class of ℓ-GLDH assumptions for arbitrary $\ell = \ell(k) = \mathrm{poly}(k)$ by defining $H : \mathbb{G}^{\ell \times \ell} \to \mathbb{G}$ as $H(\mathbf{D}) = \prod_{i=1}^{\ell} D_{1,i}$. (Note that the 1-GLDH assumption states that DDH is hard relative to a DDH oracle which is clearly insecure without applying any further hash function to the Diffie-Hellman key.) The ℓ-GLDH assumptions form a strict hierarchy of security assumptions with 2-GLDH = GLDH and, the larger the ℓ, the weaker the ℓ-GLDH assumption. More precisely, for any $\ell \geq 2$ we have that ℓ-GLDH implies $\ell+1$-GLDH. On the other hand (extending [6]) we can show that in the generic group model [24], the $\ell+1$-GLDH assumption holds, even relative to an ℓ-GLDH oracle.

We now (extending Section 4.1) build a key encapsulation mechanism $\mathcal{KEM} = (\mathsf{Kg}, \mathsf{Enc}, \mathsf{Dec})$ based on the HGMDH assumption. We define S_H as the subset of indices $(i,j) \in \{1, \ldots, \ell\}^2$ such that the hash function $H(\mathbf{D})$ depends on entry $D_{i,j}$. (For example, for ℓ-GLDH we have $S_H = \{(1,1), \ldots, (1,\ell)\}$.) Let $\mathsf{TCR} : \mathbb{G}^{\ell} \to \mathbb{Z}_p$ be a target collision-resistant hash function.

Key generation $\mathsf{Kg}(1^k)$ generates random group elements $g_1, \ldots, g_\ell, h_1, \ldots, h_\ell$ and indices $x_{i,j}$ $((i,j) \in S_H)$ such that $h_i = g_j^{x_{i,j}}$. Furthermore it defines $u_{i,j} = g_j^{y_{i,j}}$, for random $y_{i,j}$ $((i,j) \in S_H)$. The public key contains the elements $(g_i)_{1 \leq i \leq \ell}$, $(h_i)_{1 \leq i \leq \ell}$, and $(u_{i,j})_{(i,j) \in S_H}$, and the secret key contains all corresponding indices.

$\mathsf{Enc}(pk)$	$\mathsf{Dec}(sk, C)$
For $j \in \{1, \ldots, \ell\}$: $r_j \xleftarrow{\$} \mathbb{Z}_p^*$; $c_j \leftarrow g_j^{r_j}$	$t \leftarrow \mathsf{TCR}(c_1, \ldots, c_\ell)$
$t \leftarrow \mathsf{TCR}(c_1, \ldots, c_\ell)$	For each $(i,j) \in S_H$:
For $(i,j) \in S_H$:	if $c_j^{x_{i,j}t+y_{i,j}} \neq \pi_{i,j} \perp$
$\pi_{i,j} \leftarrow (h_i^t u_{i,j})^{r_j}$; $K_{i,j} \leftarrow h_i^{r_j}$	$K_{i,j} \leftarrow c_j^{x_{i,j}}$
$K \leftarrow H(\mathbf{K})$; $C \leftarrow (c_1, \ldots, c_\ell, (\pi_{i,j})_{(i,j) \in S_H})$	Return $K \leftarrow H(\mathbf{K})$
Return (C, K)	

The ciphertexts of this KEM contain $\ell + |S_H|$ group elements, public/secret keys $2\ell + |S_H|$ elements. The above scheme instantiated with the 2-GLDH assumption reproduces the KEM from [16] which, for any polynomial $\ell \geq 2$, generalizes to the class of ℓ-GLDH schemes. Using simiar techniques as for the proof of Theorem 1, the above scheme can be proved secure under the GHMDH assumption, see [18] for details.

5   Comparison

The usual efficiency comparison with all previously known chosen-ciphertext secure KEMs/encryption schemes in the standard model is assembled in Table 1. Here KD is the hybrid encryption scheme from Kurosawa and Desmedt [19] and CS refers to the Cramer-Shoup encryption scheme [10] which we compare in its

Table 1. Efficiency comparison for chosen-ciphertext secure hybrid encryption schemes. Some figures are borrowed from [9,16]. For efficiency we count the number of pairings + [multi exponentiations, regular exponentiations] used for encryption and decryption. All "symmetric" operations are ignored. Ciphertext overhead represents the difference (in bits) between ciphertext and plaintext length. For concreteness the expected ciphertext overhead for an 128-bit implementation is also given. The keysize is measured in two parameters: the size of the system parameters (which are fixed for every public-key) plus the size of the public key pk, and the size of the secret key sk. Here we only take into account the number of group elements for params plus pk, and the number of elements in $\mathbb{Z}_p^*$ for sk. A "$\sqrt{}$" in the "Publ. Vfy" column means that the scheme supports public verifiability. A "$\sqrt{}$" in the "Any group?" column means that the scheme can be implemented in any prime-order group, whereas a "—" means that the scheme has to be implemented in pairing groups. For comparison we mention that relative timings for the various operations are as follows: bilinear pairing $\approx 3 - 5$, multi(=sequential)-exponentiation ≈ 1.2 [4], and regular exponentiation $= 1$.

Scheme	Security Assmptn	Cipher Overhead	Enc #pair+#[mult,reg]-exp	Dec	Keysize (pk/sk)	Publ Vfy?	Any group?
KD	DDH	$2|p|$ 640	$0 + [1, 2]$	$0 + [1, 0]$	4/4	—	$\sqrt{}$
CS	DDH	$3|p|$ 768	$0 + [1, 3]$	$0 + [1, 1]$	5/5	—	$\sqrt{}$
BMW	BDH	$2|p|$ 512	$0 + [1, 2]$	$1 + [0, 1]$	4/3	$\sqrt{}$	—
Ours §4.1	GHDH	$2|p|$ 512	$0 + [1, 2]$	$0 + [1, 0]$	3/2	$\sqrt{}^*$	$\sqrt{}$
Ours §4.5	ℓ-GLDH	$2\ell|p|$ 512ℓ	$0 + [\ell, 2\ell]$	$0 + [\ell, 0]$	$2\ell + 1/2\ell$	$\sqrt{}^*$	$\sqrt{}$

*In gap and pairing groups only.

hybrid variant from [11]. BMW is the KEM from Boyen, Mei, and Waters [9]. Our first scheme is the GHDH-based KEM from Section 4.1 instantiated with an efficient cryptographic hash function $\mathsf{H} : \mathbb{G} \to \{0, 1\}^{l(k)}$. Our second scheme refers to the ℓ-GLDH-based scheme from Section 4.5 which, for the case $\ell = 2$, simplifies to the GLDH-based KEM from [16]. All KEMs are assumed to be instatiated using a redundancy-free chosen-ciphertext secure symmetric scheme to obtain a full hybrid PKE scheme. The KD encryption scheme can only be proved secure in combination with an authenticated symmetric encryption scheme [2] which inherently adds "one MAC" overhead to the ciphertext size.

Even though our scheme shares the same number of exponentiations for encryption/decryption with the KD scheme, it has some practical advantages which makes a more efficient implementation possible. First, it is possible to use a bijective encoding $\mathsf{INJ} : \mathbb{G} \to \mathbb{Z}_p$ and does not have to rely on expensive number-theoretic constructions of provably secure TCR functions. Second, one only needs one subgroup membership test for decryption, whereas the KD-scheme needs two. Depending on the underlying group such subgroup membership tests may be as expensive as one exponentiation. Third, the class of symmetric encryption schemes our KEM can be securely instantiated with is larger since we do not require authenticated encryption. This in particular makes it possible to rely on free redundancy-free "one-pass" symmetric techniques (which process the message to be encrypted only once). For authenticated encryption there are only less efficient two-pass schemes freely available since all one-pass techniques are covered by patents [3].

Acknowledgments. We thank Michel Abdalla, Mihir Bellare, Yevgeniy Dodis, Martijn Stam, and Moti Yung for comments and suggestions. This research was partially supported by the research program Sentinels (`http://www.sentinels.nl`). Sentinels is being financed by Technology Foundation STW, the Netherlands Organization for Scientific Research (NWO), and the Dutch Ministry of Economic Affairs. Parts of this paper were written while the author was a visitor at University of California San Diego supported by a DAAD postdoc fellowship.

References

1. M. Abdalla, M. Bellare, and P. Rogaway. The oracle Diffie-Hellman assumptions and an analysis of DHIES. In D. Naccache, editor, *CT-RSA 2001*, volume 2020 of *LNCS*, pages 143–158. Springer-Verlag, Berlin, Germany, Apr. 2001.
2. M. Bellare, T. Kohno, and V. Shoup. Stateful public-key cryptosystems: How to encrypt with one 160-bit exponentiation. In A. Juels, R. N. Wright, and S. Vimercati, editors, *ACM CCS 06*, pages 380–389. ACM Press, Oct. / Nov. 2006.
3. M. Bellare, P. Rogaway, and D. Wagner. The EAX mode of operation. In B. K. Roy and W. Meier, editors, *FSE 2004*, volume 3017 of *LNCS*, pages 389–407. Springer-Verlag, Berlin, Germany, Feb. 2004.
4. D. J. Bernstein. Pippenger's exponentiation algorithm. Available from `http://cr.yp.to/papers.html`, 2001.
5. D. Boneh and X. Boyen. Efficient selective-ID secure identity based encryption without random oracles. In C. Cachin and J. Camenisch, editors, *EUROCRYPT 2004*, volume 3027 of *LNCS*, pages 223–238. Springer-Verlag, Berlin, Germany, May 2004.
6. D. Boneh, X. Boyen, and H. Shacham. Short group signatures. In M. Franklin, editor, *CRYPTO 2004*, volume 3152 of *LNCS*, pages 41–55. Springer-Verlag, Berlin, Germany, Aug. 2004.
7. D. Boneh, R. Canetti, S. Halevi, and J. Katz. Chosen-ciphertext security from identity-based encryption. *SIAM Journal on Computing*, 5(36):915–942, 2006.
8. D. Boneh and M. K. Franklin. Identity based encryption from the Weil pairing. *SIAM Journal on Computing*, 32(3):586–615, 2003.
9. X. Boyen, Q. Mei, and B. Waters. Direct chosen ciphertext security from identity-based techniques. In V. Atluri, C. Meadows, and A. Juels, editors, *ACM CCS 05*, pages 320–329. ACM Press, Nov. 2005.
10. R. Cramer and V. Shoup. A practical public key cryptosystem provably secure against adaptive chosen ciphertext attack. In H. Krawczyk, editor, *CRYPTO'98*, volume 1462 of *LNCS*, pages 13–25. Springer-Verlag, Berlin, Germany, Aug. 1998.
11. R. Cramer and V. Shoup. Design and analysis of practical public-key encryption schemes secure against adaptive chosen ciphertext attack. *SIAM Journal on Computing*, 33(1):167–226, 2003.
12. W. Diffie and M. E. Hellman. New directions in cryptography. *IEEE Transactions on Information Theory*, 22(6):644–654, 1976.
13. R. R. Farashahi, B. Schoenmakers, and A. Sidorenko. Efficient pseudorandom generators based on the DDH assumption. In *PKC 2007*, volume 4450 of *LNCS*, pages 426–441. Springer-Verlag, 2007.

14. D. Hofheinz, J. Herranz, and E. Kiltz. The Kurosawa-Desmedt key encapsulation is not chosen-ciphertext secure. Cryptology ePrint Archive, Report 2006/207, 2006. http://eprint.iacr.org/.
15. D. Hofheinz and E. Kiltz. Concise Hybrid Encryption. Manuscript, 2006.
16. E. Kiltz. Chosen-ciphertext security from tag-based encryption. In S. Halevi and T. Rabin, editors, *TCC 2006*, volume 3876 of *LNCS*, pages 581–600. Springer-Verlag, Berlin, Germany, Mar. 2006.
17. E. Kiltz. On the limitations of the spread of an IBE-to-PKE transformation. In M. Yung, Y. Dodis, A. Kiayias, and T. Malkin, editors, *PKC 2006*, volume 3958 of *LNCS*, pages 274–289. Springer-Verlag, Berlin, Germany, Apr. 2006.
18. E. Kiltz. Chosen-ciphertext secure key-encapsulation based on Gap Hashed Diffie-Hellman (full version). Cryptology ePrint Archive, 2007. http://eprint.iacr.org/.
19. K. Kurosawa and Y. Desmedt. A new paradigm of hybrid encryption scheme. In M. Franklin, editor, *CRYPTO 2004*, volume 3152 of *LNCS*, pages 426–442. Springer-Verlag, Berlin, Germany, Aug. 2004.
20. T. Okamoto and D. Pointcheval. The gap-problems: A new class of problems for the security of cryptographic schemes. In K. Kim, editor, *PKC 2001*, volume 1992 of *LNCS*, pages 104–118. Springer-Verlag, Berlin, Germany, Feb. 2001.
21. D. H. Phan and D. Pointcheval. About the security of ciphers (semantic security and pseudo-random permutations). In H. Handschuh and A. Hasan, editors, *SAC 2004*, volume 3357 of *LNCS*, pages 182–197. Springer-Verlag, Berlin, Germany, Aug. 2004.
22. N. Pippenger. On the evaluation of powers and related problems. In *Proceedings of FOCS 1976*, pages 258–263, 1976.
23. C. Rackoff and D. R. Simon. Non-interactive zero-knowledge proof of knowledge and chosen ciphertext attack. In J. Feigenbaum, editor, *CRYPTO'91*, volume 576 of *LNCS*, pages 433–444. Springer-Verlag, Berlin, Germany, Aug. 1992.
24. V. Shoup. Lower bounds for discrete logarithms and related problems. In W. Fumy, editor, *EUROCRYPT'97*, volume 1233 of *LNCS*, pages 256–266. Springer-Verlag, Berlin, Germany, May 1997.

A   Proof of Theorem 1

Suppose there exists a polynomial time adversary $\mathcal{A}$ that breaks the chosen-ciphertext security of the encapsulation scheme with (non-negligible) advantage $\mathbf{Adv}_{\mathcal{KEM},\mathcal{A}}^{kem\text{-}cca}(k)$ and makes at most q decapsulation queries.

We show that there exists an adversary $\mathcal{B}$ that runs in time $\mathbf{Time}_{\mathcal{B}}(k) = \mathbf{Time}_{\mathcal{A}}(k) + O(q \cdot \mathbf{Time}_{\mathbb{G}}(k))$, (where $\mathbf{Time}_{\mathbb{G}}(k)$ is the time to perform a basic operation in $\mathbb{G}$) and runs adversary $\mathcal{A}$ as a subroutine to solve a random instance of the GHDH problem with advantage

$$\mathbf{Adv}_{\mathsf{Gen},\mathcal{B}}^{ghdh}(k) \geq \mathbf{Adv}_{\mathcal{KEM},\mathcal{A}}^{kem\text{-}cca}(k) . \tag{2}$$

Now Eqn. (2) proves the Theorem.

We now give the description of adversary $\mathcal{B}$. Adversary $\mathcal{B}$ inputs an instance of the GHDH problem, i.e. $\mathcal{B}$ inputs the values $(1^k, \mathcal{HG}, \mathsf{H}, g, u = g^a, g^b, W)$. $\mathcal{B}$'s goal is to determine whether $W = \mathsf{H}(u^b)$ or $W \in \{0,1\}^l$ is a random bit string.

Adversary $\mathcal{B}$ runs adversary $\mathcal{A}$ simulating its view as in the original KEM security experiment as follows:

Key Generation & Challenge. Initially adversary $\mathcal{B}$ picks a random value $d \in \mathbb{Z}_p^*$ and defines the target ciphertext

$$C^* = (c^*, \pi^*) \leftarrow (g^b, (g^b)^d) . \tag{3}$$

and the challenge key as $K^* = W$. We denote $t^* = \mathsf{INJ}(c^*)$ as the target tag (associated with the target ciphertext). The value v from the public key $pk = (u, v)$ is defined as

$$v \leftarrow u^{-t^*} \cdot g^d . \tag{4}$$

Note that the public key is identically distributed as in the original KEM.

With each ciphertext $C = (c, \pi)$ we associate a tag $t = \mathsf{INJ}(c)$. Recall that we call a ciphertext consistent if $\pi = (u^t v)^r$, where $r = \log_g c$. Note that the way the keys are setup for a consistent ciphertext we have

$$\pi = (u^t v)^r = (u^t u^{-t^*} g^d)^r = (u^r)^{t - t^*} \cdot c^d . \tag{5}$$

Given a consistent ciphertext $C = (c, \pi)$ with associated tag $t \neq t^*$ the session key $K = \mathsf{H}(c^x)$ can alternatively be computed by Eqn. (5) as

$$K = \mathsf{H}((\pi/c^d)^{(t - t^*)^{-1}}) . \tag{6}$$

By Eqn. (5) and since $t^* = \mathsf{INJ}(c^*)$ the challenge ciphertext $C^* = (c^*, \pi^*) = (g^b, (g^b)^d) = (c^*, (c^*)^d)$ is a correctly generated ciphertext for randomness b. If $W = \mathsf{H}(u^b)$ then it follows by Eqn. (4) that $C^* = (g^b, (g^b)^d)$ is a correct ciphertext of key $K^* = W = \mathsf{H}(u^b)$, distributed as in the original experiment. On the other hand, when W is uniform and independent in $\{0,1\}^l$ then C^* is independent of $K^* = W$ in the adversary's view.

Adversary $\mathcal{B}$ runs $\mathcal{A}$ on input (pk, K^*, C^*) answering to its queries as follows:

Decryption queries. The KEM decapsulation queries are simulated by $\mathcal{B}$ as follows: Let $C = (c, \pi)$ be an arbitrary ciphertext submitted to the decapsulation oracle $\mathsf{DecO}(sk, \cdot)$. First $\mathcal{B}$ performs a consistency check of the ciphertext, i.e. it checks (using the Diffie-Hellman oracle $\mathsf{DDHsolve}_\mathbb{G}(\cdot, \cdot, \cdot, \cdot)$) if $(g, u^t v, c, \pi)$ is a valid Diffie-Hellman tuple.[3]

We remark that this is the only case where the simulation depends on the existence of the DDH oracle $\mathsf{DDHsolve}$. If C is not consistent then $\mathcal{B}$ returns $\perp$. Otherwise, if the ciphertext is consistent $\mathcal{B}$ computes $t = \mathsf{INJ}(c)$ and distinguishes the following three cases:

Case 1: $t = t^*$ and $c = c^*$: adversary $\mathcal{B}$ rejects the query. In this case consistency (Eqn. (5)) implies $\pi = c^d = (c^*)^d = \pi^*$ and hence $C = C^*$ and the query made by $\mathcal{A}$ is illegal. Therefore it may be rejected by $\mathcal{B}$.

---

[3] At this point the existence of a weak DDH oracle $\mathsf{DDHsolve}_{g,u}(\cdot, \cdot)$ for fixed u is sufficient. This is since $(g, u^t v, c, \pi)$ is a valid Diffie-Hellman tuple iff $(g, u, c, (\pi/c^d)^{(t - t^*)^{-1}})$ is a valid Diffie-Hellman tuple. So to verify consistency of the KEM ciphertext, $\mathcal{B}$ equivalently queries $\mathsf{DDHsolve}_{g,u}(c, (\pi/c^d)^{(t - t^*)^{-1}})$.

Case 2: $t = t^*$ and $c \neq c^*$: this is not possible since $\mathsf{INJ} : \mathbb{G} \to \mathbb{Z}_p$ is an injection. (If more generally we use a TCR function then at this point adversary $\mathcal{B}$ found a collision $c \neq c^*$ in TCR with $\mathsf{TCR}(c) = \mathsf{TCR}(c^*)$.)

Case 3: $t \neq t^*$: adversary $\mathcal{B}$ computes the correct session key by Eqn. (6) as $K \leftarrow \mathsf{H}((\pi/c^d)^{(t-t^*)^{-1}})$.

This completes the description of the decapsulation oracle.

We have shown that the simulation of the decapsulation oracle is always perfect, i.e. the output of the simulated decapsulation oracle is identically distributed as the output of $\mathsf{Dec}(sk, C)$.

Guess. Eventually, $\mathcal{A}$ outputs a guess $\delta' \in \{0, 1\}$ where $\delta' = 1$ means that K^* is the correct key. Algorithm $\mathcal{B}$ concludes its own game by outputting $\gamma' := \delta'$ where $\gamma' = 1$ means that $W = \mathsf{H}(g^{ab})$ (i.e. $\gamma = 1$) and $\gamma' = 0$ means that W is random ($\gamma = 0$).

This completes the description of adversary $\mathcal{B}$.

ANALYSIS. Define "F" to be the event that $\mathcal{B}$ wins its GHDH game, i.e. it outputs $\delta' = 1$ if $W = \mathsf{H}(g^{ab})$ and $\delta' = 0$ if W is random. On the one hand, if W is uniform and independent in $\{0, 1\}^l$ then the challenge ciphertext C^* is independent of $K^* = W$ in the adversary's view. In that case we have $\Pr[\mathrm{F}] = \Pr[\delta' = 0] = \frac{1}{2}$. On the other hand, when $W = \mathsf{H}(g^{ab})$ then C^* is a correct ciphertext of the challenge key K^*, distributed as in the original experiment. Then, by our assumption, $\mathcal{A}$ must make a correct guess $\delta' = 1$ with advantage at least $\mathbf{Adv}^{kem\text{-}cca}_{\mathcal{KEM}, \mathcal{A}}(k)$ and we have $|\Pr[\mathrm{F}] - \frac{1}{2}| = |\Pr[\delta' = 1] - \frac{1}{2}| \geq \mathbf{Adv}^{kem\text{-}cca}_{\mathcal{KEM}, \mathcal{A}}(k)$.

Therefore, adversary $\mathcal{B}$'s advantage in the GHDH game is $\mathbf{Adv}^{ghdh}_{\mathsf{Gen}, \mathcal{B}}(k) \geq \mathbf{Adv}^{kem\text{-}cca}_{\mathcal{KEM}, \mathcal{A}}(k)$ which proves Eqn. (2) and completes the proof of the theorem.

Parallel Key-Insulated Public Key Encryption Without Random Oracles

Benoît Libert[1,*], Jean-Jacques Quisquater[1], and Moti Yung[2]

[1] UCL, Microelectronics Laboratory, Crypto Group, Belgium
[2] RSA Labs and Columbia University, USA

Abstract. Key-insulated cryptography is a crucial technique for protecting private keys. To strengthen the security of key-insulated protocols, Hanaoka, Hanaoka and Imai recently introduced the idea of parallel key-insulated encryption (PKIE) where distinct physically-secure devices (called helpers) are independently used in key updates. Their motivation was to reduce the risk of exposure for helpers by decreasing the frequency of their connections to insecure environments. Hanaoka *et al.* showed that it was non-trivial to achieve a PKIE scheme fitting their model and proposed a construction based on the Boneh-Franklin identity-based encryption (IBE) scheme. The security of their system was only analyzed in the idealized random oracle model. In this paper, we provide a fairly efficient scheme which is secure in the standard model (i.e. without random oracles). To do so, we first show the existence of a relation between PKIE and the notion of aggregate signatures (AS) suggested by Boneh *et al.* We then describe our random oracle-free construction using bilinear maps. Thus, our contributions are both on the concrete side, namely the first realization of parallel key-insulated encryption without the random oracle idealization, and on the conceptual side revealing the relationships between two seemingly unrelated primitives.

Keywords: parallel key-insulated encryption, standard model, pairings.

1   Introduction

Nowadays, protecting cryptographic keys is an issue of huge importance. Hazards of key exposure are indeed ever-increasing due the growing use of mobile devices allowing remote unprotected access. This problem has been major concern to the research community for a decade. It is certainly a more serious threat for security customers than algorithms attempting to solve number theoretic problems by brute force.

To mitigate its potential damages, key-evolving protocols were studied in various flavors: forward-security [1,3,14], intrusion-resilience [27,19] and key-insulation [20,21]. The latter paradigm was introduced in 2002 by Dodis, Katz,

---

* Work done during a visit at the CS Dept. of the Columbia University. This author also acknowledges the DGTRE's First Europe Program of the Walloon Region in Belgium for his financial support.

T. Okamoto and X. Wang (Eds.): PKC 2007, LNCS 4450, pp. 298–314, 2007.

Xu and Yung [20]. It was motivated by the upcoming setting of "Ubiquitous Computing" where each user will possess more than one computer (e.g. a computer at the office and a mobile phone which is also a computer) where not all computers have the same availability and/or security. The general idea of key-insulated security was to store long-term keys in a physically-secure but computationally-limited device called *base* or *helper*. Short-term secret keys are kept by users on a powerful but insecure device where cryptographic computations take place. Short term secrets are then refreshed at discrete time periods via interaction between the user and the base while the public key remains unchanged throughout the lifetime of the system. For a total of N time periods, such a mechanism is said to be (t, N)-key-insulated if a compromise of up to t periods leaves the remaining $N - t$ time periods unharmed. A scheme is additionally said *strongly* key-insulated when adversaries corrupting the base remain unable to perform private key operations on behalf of the user.

An increased tolerance against key exposures is thus allowed by frequent updates of private keys. This unfortunately implies frequent connections between the helper device and the network and thereby an increased risk of helper key exposure. A theft of the helper's base key is quite damaging as it typically requires to restart the system with a new public key. It even jeopardizes strongly keyinsulated protocols where the additional exposure of a single time period at the user definitely crashes the system. This recently motivated Hanaoka, Hanaoka and Imai [26] to make a significant step forward and introduce the concept of parallel key-insulated encryption (PKIE for short) where distinct independent helpers are alternatively used in key update operations. As argued in [26], the involvement of two helpers may simultaneously increase the security of helpers and users by allowing for frequent updates without incurring a higher risk of helper exposure. In [26], Hanaoka *et al.* provided a PKIE constuction which will be referred to as the HHI scheme in this paper. It was obtained from the BonehFranklin identity-based encryption (IBE) scheme [8] and provably fits properly defined security requirements in the random oracle model [4]. However, a proof in the random oracle model can only serve as a heuristic argument as it is known (see e.g. [13]) not to imply the security in the real world.

It is natural to wonder if secure PKIE schemes exist in the standard model and if they can be generically built from IBE. Indeed, equivalence relations are known [5,20] between $(N - 1, N)$-key-insulated systems and identity-based schemes [36], hierarchical extensions of which [24,6,7] also allowed for the design of other key-evolving protocols [29,14,19,16,38,7].

To answer those questions, we first point out an intuitive relation between PKIE and IBE systems that involve a signature scheme supporting aggregation as in the aggregate signing (AS) protocol put forth by Boneh *et al.* [9]. We then describe a PKIE scheme which, although non-generic, is demonstrably secure in the sense of [26] without resorting to the random oracle methodology. Our construction uses a selective-ID secure IBE due to Boneh and Boyen [6] as a building block. It is fairly efficient and enjoys a security resting on the (by now well-studied) Decisional Bilinear Diffie-Hellman assumption.

In the upcoming sections, we first recall functional definitions and security notions for PKIE schemes. Section 3 discusses necessary conditions for building such a primitive from identity-based protocols. Our system and its security are respectively analyzed in sections 4 and 5. Section 6 then explains how to further secure our protocol against chosen-ciphertext attacks.

2   Preliminaries

2.1   Model and Security Notions

A PKIE scheme over N stages consists of the following five algorithms.

Key generation: takes a security parameter λ and returns helpers' private keys mst_1, mst_2, a user's private key usk_0 and a public key pk.

Helper-Update: takes as input helper j's private key mst_j and a period number i to return an update key hsk_i if $i = j \bmod 2$ and $\perp$ otherwise.

User-Update: is given user's private key usk_{i-1} for period $i-1$, an update key hsk_i and computes the private key usk_i for period i.

Encrypt: is given a message m, a public key pk and a period number $i \in \{1, \ldots, N\}$ and returns a ciphertext σ.

Decrypt: given a ciphertext σ, a period number i and the matching private key usk_i, returns either a plaintext m or $\perp$.

The usual completeness requirement imposes **Decrypt**$(\mathsf{pk}, \mathsf{usk}_i, \sigma) = m$ whenever $\sigma = $ **Encrypt**(m, i, pk) for any $i \in \{1, \ldots, N\}$.

In the basic (i.e. non-strong) key-insulation security, if no helper is compromised, the exposure of any short-term secret leaves other periods safe as in [20,21]. Besides, if a single helper is broken into while some stage i is exposed, only one other stage adjacent to i is also exposed (recall that even strongly key-insulated traditional schemes collapse in this scenario).

Definition 1. *A PKIE scheme is (t, ϵ)-secure against chosen-ciphertext attacks if no adversary has better advantage than ϵ in the following game within running time t.*

1. *The challenger $\mathcal{C}$ runs the key generation algorithm, hands pk to the adversary $\mathcal{A}$ and keeps mst_0, mst_1 and uks_0 to itself.*
2. *$\mathcal{A}$ adaptively issues queries which are either:*
   - *Exposure queries $\langle j, \textit{class} \rangle$: if $\textit{class} = $ "user", $\mathcal{C}$ runs helper and user update algorithms to generate usk_j and send it to $\mathcal{A}$. If $\textit{class} = $ "helper", $\mathcal{A}$ obtains mst_j.*
   - *Decryption queries $\langle j, \sigma \rangle$: $\mathcal{C}$ responds by generating usk_j (via calls to update algorithms) to decrypt σ and pass the result to $\mathcal{A}$.*
3. *At some point, $\mathcal{A}$ comes up with messages M_0, M_1 and a period number $j^\star \in \{1, \ldots, N\}$. She obtains a challenge $\sigma^\star = $ **Encrypt**$(M_{b^\star}, j^\star, \mathsf{pk})$ for a random bit $b^\star \xleftarrow{R} \{0, 1\}$ selected by $\mathcal{C}$.*

4. $\mathcal{A}$ *issues new queries as in stage 2. She finally outputs* $b \in \{0,1\}$ *and wins if* $b = b^\star$ *provided*
   - $\langle j^\star, \sigma^\star \rangle$ *does not appear in the list of decryption queries,*
   - $\langle j^\star, \text{``user''} \rangle$ *is not in the list of exposure queries,*
   - $\langle j^\star - 1, \text{``user''} \rangle$ *and* $\langle 2 - (j^\star \bmod 2), \text{``helper''} \rangle$ *do not simultaneously appear in the list of exposure queries and neither does the pair* $\langle j^\star + 1, \text{``user''} \rangle$, $\langle (j^\star \bmod 2) + 1, \text{``helper''} \rangle$,
   - $\langle 1, \text{``helper''} \rangle$ *and* $\langle 2, \text{``helper''} \rangle$ *were not both queried.*

As usual, $\mathcal{A}$'s advantage is measured by $Adv^{PKIE}(\mathcal{A}) = |\Pr[b = b^\star] - 1/2|$.

This definition considers two kinds of adversaries: Type I attackers do not corrupt helpers during the game. In contrast, Type II adversaries corrupt exactly one helper without requesting a private key that would trivially expose the target period $j^\star$. For example, if $j^\star$ is odd, $\mathcal{A}$ may not obtain $\mathsf{usk}_{j^\star - 1}$ if she ever learns mst_1 as the latter is involved in all updates from even to odd time periods. Besides, she is disallowed to query $\mathsf{usk}_{j^\star + 1}$ if she also receives mst_2 since $\mathsf{usk}_{j^\star}$ could be trivially retrieved from $\mathsf{usk}_{j^\star + 1}$ and the helper's key that allowed the update from period $j^\star$ to $j^\star + 1$.

According to [20,21], a parallel key-insulated scheme is said *strongly* key-insulated if breaking into all helpers does not help the adversary as long as she does not also obtain any user secret for any period. Unlike [26], we follow [20,21] and address this problem in a separate game where $\mathcal{A}$ is provided with *both* base keys and may not request usk_i for any i.

2.2   Bilinear Maps and Related Problems

Groups $(\mathbb{G}, \mathbb{G}_T)$ of prime order p are called *bilinear map groups* if there is a mapping $e : \mathbb{G} \times \mathbb{G} \to \mathbb{G}_T$ with the following properties:

1. bilinearity: $e(g^a, h^b) = e(g, h)^{ab}$ for any $(g, h) \in \mathbb{G} \times \mathbb{G}$ and $a, b \in \mathbb{Z}$;
2. efficient computability for any input pair;
3. non-degeneracy: $e(g, h) \neq 1_{\mathbb{G}_T}$ whenever $g, h \neq 1_{\mathbb{G}}$.

We require the intractability of these problems in bilinear map groups.

Definition 2. *Let* $(\mathbb{G}, \mathbb{G}_T)$ *be bilinear map groups of order* p *and* $g \in \mathbb{G}$.

1. *the* **Bilinear Diffie-Hellman Problem** *(BDH) [28,8] is to compute* $e(g, g)^{abc} \in \mathbb{G}_T$ *given* (g^a, g^b, g^c);
2. *the* **Decision Bilinear Diffie-Hellman Problem** *(DBDH) is to distinguish the distributions* $(g^a, g^b, g^c, e(g, g)^{abc})$ *and* $(g^a, g^b, g^c, e(g, g)^z)$. *A distinguisher* $\mathcal{B}$ (t, ε)-*solves it if it runs in time at most* t *and*

$$\left| Pr[\mathcal{B}(g^a, g^b, g^c, e(g,g)^{abc}) = 1 | a, b, c \xleftarrow{R} \mathbb{Z}_p^*] \right.$$
$$\left. - Pr[\mathcal{B}(g^a, g^b, g^c, e(g,g)^z) = 1 | a, b, c, z \xleftarrow{R} \mathbb{Z}_p^*] \right| \geq \varepsilon.$$

3   On Obtaining PKIE from IBE

The HHI scheme [26] (recalled in appendix A) uses the Boneh-Franklin IBE [8] as a building block. It is pointed out in [26] that constructing parallel key-insulated schemes from identity-based ones is non-trivial. For instance, one cannot settle for simply combining two IBE schemes by letting two Private Key Generators (PKGs) alternatively act as helpers for even and odd time periods. This naive approach indeed leaves half of the stages exposed after the compromise of only one helper. Another idea that falls short is to doubly encrypt (using the techniques of [22]) messages for period i under identities i and $i-1$ and let private key usk_i consist of IBE private keys for identities i and $i-1$. Unfortunately, the key $\mathsf{usk}_{i^\star}$ may be exposed by merely corrupting periods $i^\star - 1$ and $i^\star + 1$.

Nevertheless, the HHI construction stems from a careful double application of the Boneh-Franklin IBE. Although it was not explicitly mentioned in [26], the key idea is to let a private key for period i be an aggregation of identity-based private keys for periods i and $i-1$. We recall that identity-based cryptosystems traditionally involve private keys that are authorities' signatures on identities. As noted in [9], the signature algorithm [11] that derives private keys from identifiers in [8] is compatible with a signature aggregation. This means that n signatures generated by distinct signers on possibly distinct messages may be merged into a single signature in such a way that verifiers can still ensure that all signers each signed their original message. In [26], a private key for period i is the aggregation of both helpers' signatures on messages i and $i-1$. The security in the sense of definition 1 relies on the intractability of extracting individual signatures from an aggregate of even only two signatures. In Boneh $et\ al.$'s scheme [9], this problem was shown equivalent to the Diffie-Hellman problem in [17].

An intuitive connection thus turns out to exist between parallel key-insulated cryptosystems and identity-based encryption schemes extracting private keys using a signature scheme supporting aggregation. The infeasibility of extracting individual signatures from a 2-aggregate appears as a necessary condition for the underlying AS to provide a secure PKIE system. In the next section, we take advantage of this connection to devise a PKIE in the standard model. Our construction uses the selective-ID secure[1] [14] scheme of Boneh-Boyen [6] as a starting point. As previously mentioned by Canetti, Halevi and Katz [14], selective-ID secure schemes are sufficient as building blocks for key-evolving protocols. Indeed, in security proofs, simulators have to guess in advance which time period will be the prey of attacks. This degrades security bounds by a factor that remains acceptable for any realistic number of time periods (such as $N \leq 2^{30}$). We emphasize that constructing a PKIE scheme using Waters's fully secure IBE [37] would be overkill and would not yield a tighter reduction here[2].

In the selective-ID secure IBE of [6], private keys are computed using a signature scheme which bears similarities with Waters's signature [37] but is only

---

[1] i.e. Secure in a model where attackers are required to announce the identity they intend to attack ahead of time, even before seeing the system parameters.

[2] Indeed, the condition for the simulator of [37] not to abort in the challenge phase would have to be satisfied for both "identities" i and $i-1$.

selective-message secure against chosen-message attacks. Unlike a recent variant [33] where signatures are sequentially computed, it only supports a limited aggregation as the size of an aggregate remains linear in the number of signers (as in a similar method suggested in [34]). However, this scheme is sufficient for the pursued goal here as, in our construction, private keys are aggregates of only 2 individual signatures.

4   A Scheme with Chosen-Plaintext Security

As in [26], private keys stored by users at period i are 2-aggregate signatures computed by helpers on "messages" i and $i - 1$.

Key generation: given a security parameter $\lambda \in \mathbb{N}$, this algorithm

1. chooses bilinear map groups $(\mathbb{G}, \mathbb{G}_T)$ of order $p > 2^\lambda$, a generator $g \in \mathbb{G}$, a collision-resistant hash function $H : \mathbb{N} \to \mathbb{Z}_p^*$ and a pseudorandom function $f : \{0,1\}^{1+\log_2 p} \times \mathbb{N} \to \mathbb{Z}_p^*$,
2. picks $\alpha_1, \alpha_2 \xleftarrow{R} \mathbb{Z}_p^*$ and computes $g_1 = g^{\alpha_1}$, $g_2 = g^{\alpha_2}$,
3. selects elements $h, g_1', g_2' \xleftarrow{R} \mathbb{G}$ and defines functions $F_1, F_2 : \mathbb{N} \to \mathbb{G}$ as $F_1(i) = g_1^{I_i} g_1'$ and $F_2(i) = g_2^{I_i} g_2'$ where $I_i = H(i) \in \mathbb{Z}_p^*$,
4. initializes the user's private key to

$$\mathsf{usk}_0 = \left(h^{\alpha_1 + \alpha_2} F_1(-1)^{r_{-1}} F_2(0)^{r_0}, g^{r_0}, g^{r_{-1}} \right)$$

where $r_{-1} = f(\mathsf{sd}_1, -1)$ and $r_0 = f(\mathsf{sd}_2, 0)$ are respectively derived from randomly chosen seeds $\mathsf{sd}_1, \mathsf{sd}_2 \in \{0,1\}^{1+\log_2 p}$,
6. Helpers' private keys are set to $\mathsf{mst}_1 = \mathsf{sd}_1$ and $\mathsf{mst}_2 = \mathsf{sd}_2$ and the public key is
$$\mathsf{pk} := \{p, \mathbb{G}, \mathbb{G}_T, e, g, g_1, g_2, h, g_1', g_2', H, f\}.$$

Elements α_1, α_2 are *erased*.

Helper-Update: given $\mathsf{mst}_j = \mathsf{sd}_j$ and a period number $i \in \{1, 2, \ldots, N\}$, helper $j \in \{1, 2\}$
1. returns $\perp$ if $i \neq j \bmod 2$,
2. computes $r_{i-2} = f(\mathsf{sd}_j, i-2)$, $r_i = f(\mathsf{sd}_j, i)$
3. outputs an update key $\mathsf{hsk}_i = \left(F_j(i)^{r_i} / F_j(i-2)^{r_{i-2}}, g^{r_i - r_{i-2}} \right)$

User-Update: given $\mathsf{usk}_{i-1}, \mathsf{hsk}_i$ and i,
1. parse hsk_i into (h_i, h_i') and usk_{i-1} into $(u_{i-1,0}, u_{i-1,1}, u_{i-1,2})$.
2. set $\mathsf{usk}_i = (u_{i-1,0} \cdot h_i, u_{i-1,2} \cdot h_i', u_{i-1,1})$,
3. return usk_i, discard usk_{i-1} and hsk_i.

At time period i, user's private key is always set to

$$\mathsf{usk}_i = \left(h^{\alpha_1 + \alpha_2} F_j(i)^{r_i} F_{j-1}(i-1)^{r_{i-1}}, g^{r_i}, g^{r_{i-1}} \right),$$

with $j = 2 - (i \bmod 2)$ and for uniformly distributed exponents $r_i = f(\mathsf{sd}_j, i)$, $r_{i-1} = f(\mathsf{sd}_{j-1}, i-1) \in \mathbb{Z}_p^*$ determined by helpers.

Encrypt: given pk, $i \in \mathbb{N}$, a message $m \in \mathbb{G}_T$ is encrypted into

$$\sigma = (m \cdot e(h, g_1 g_2)^s, g^s, F_j(i)^s, F_{j-1}(i-1)^s)$$

where $s \stackrel{R}{\leftarrow} \mathbb{Z}_p^*$ is randomly chosen and $j = 2 - (i \bmod 2)$.

Decrypt: given $\sigma = (A, B, C, D)$ and $\mathsf{usk}_i = (u_{i,0}, u_{i,1}, u_{i,2})$, compute

$$m = A \cdot \frac{e(C, u_{i,1}) \cdot e(D, u_{i,2})}{e(B, u_{i,0})}$$

The completeness is checked by noting that $\mathsf{usk}_i = (u_{i,0}, u_{i,1}, u_{i,2})$ satisfies

$$e(u_{i,0}, g) = e(h, g_1 g_2) \cdot e\left(F_j(i), u_{i,1}\right) \cdot e\left(F_{j-1}(i-1), u_{i,2}\right)$$

and raising both members of this equality to the power s.

The function f plays the crucial role of a "memory function" seeded by sd_j for $j = 2 - (i \bmod 2)$ and allowing helpers to remember the exponent r_{i-2} of their latest update. Those exponents must be unpredictable without the seed sd_j as an adversary obtaining usk_{i-1} could trivially compute a private key for period i without knowing hsk_i if she could find out r_{i-2}.

5   Security

Theorem 1. *If no algorithm (t, ε)-breaks the Decision Bilinear Diffie-Hellman assumption, the scheme is $(t', 4N\varepsilon)$-secure against chosen-plaintext attacks for $t' < t - O(N\tau_{exp})$ where N is the number of time periods and τ_{exp} stands for the cost of an exponentiation in $\mathbb{G}$.*

Proof. We construct an algorithm $\mathcal{B}$ that solves the DBDH problem in $(\mathbb{G}, \mathbb{G}_T)$ using an adversary $\mathcal{A}$ against the IND-CPA security of our scheme. The input of $\mathcal{B}$ is a tuple $(g^a, g^b, g^c, T) \in \mathbb{G}^3 \times \mathbb{G}_T$ and it aims at deciding whether $T = e(g, g)^{abc}$ thanks to its interaction with $\mathcal{A}$. As explained in section 2.1, two kinds of adversaries are distinguished:

Type I adversaries: do not corrupt helpers during the game.
Type II adversaries: corrupt exactly one helper without exposing a private key that would trivially compromise the attacked period i^*.

At the outset of the simulation, $\mathcal{B}$ tosses a coin $\mathcal{COIN} \stackrel{R}{\leftarrow} \{0,1\}$ to guess which kind of attack $\mathcal{A}$ will produce. If $\mathcal{COIN} = 0$, it expects to face a Type I adversary. If $\mathcal{COIN} = 1$, it forecasts a Type II behaviour from $\mathcal{A}$. Our simulator $\mathcal{B}$ also chooses an index $\ell \stackrel{R}{\leftarrow} \{1, \ldots, N\}$ as a guess for the time period to be attacked by $\mathcal{A}$. W.l.o.g., we shall assume that ℓ is odd as the case of an even ℓ can be handled in a completely similar manner. In all cases, $\mathcal{B}$ generates the public key as follows. It selects $\gamma \stackrel{R}{\leftarrow} \mathbb{Z}_p^*$, and defines $g_1 = g^a$, $g_2 = g_1^\gamma = (g^a)^\gamma$ and $h = g^b$. It also computes $I_\ell = H(\ell)$ and $I_{\ell-1} = H(\ell-1)$ and sets $g_1' = g_1^{-I_\ell} g^{t_1}$, $g_2' = g_2^{-I_{\ell-1}} g^{t_2}$ for randomly chosen $t_1, t_2 \stackrel{R}{\leftarrow} \mathbb{Z}_p^*$ and thereby implicitly defines functions

$$F_1(i) = g_1^{I_i - I_\ell} g^{t_1}, \quad F_2(i) = g_2^{I_i - I_{\ell-1}} g^{t_2}.$$

$\mathcal{A}$ is initialized on input of $(g, g_1, g_2, h, g_1', g_2')$ and issues exposure queries that are handled differently when $\mathcal{COIN} = 0$ and $\mathcal{COIN} = 1$. Informally, $\mathcal{B}$ uses the fact that $\mathcal{A}$ has no information on exponents r_i ($i \in \{1, \dots, N\}$) unless she breaks into helper $j = 2 - (i \bmod 2)$. When dealing with exposure queries, these exponents may be freely chosen for both even and odd stages when facing Type I attacks. In Type II attacks, they are constrained for either odd or even stages and $\mathcal{B}$ has to guess in advance the parity of constrained indexes.

- $\mathcal{COIN} = 0$: $\mathcal{B}$ aborts if $\mathcal{A}$ issues a query $\langle i, \texttt{class} \rangle$ with $\texttt{class} = $ "helper" or with $i = \ell$. Otherwise, it can answer the query as private keys usk_i are computable for $i \neq \ell$. To do so, $\mathcal{B}$ selects $r_0 \xleftarrow{R} \mathbb{Z}_p^*$. For $i = 1, 2, \dots, (\ell - 1)/2$, it picks $r_{2i-1}, r_{2i} \xleftarrow{R} \mathbb{Z}_p^*$ and computes

$$\mathsf{usk}_{2i} = \left(h^{-\frac{(1+\gamma)t_1}{I_{2i-1} - I_\ell}} F_1(2i-1)^{r_{2i-1}} F_2(2i)^{r_{2i}}, h^{-\frac{1+\gamma}{I_{2i-1} - I_\ell}} g^{r_{2i-1}}, g^{r_{2i}} \right), \tag{1}$$

$$\mathsf{usk}_{2i-1} = \left(h^{-\frac{(1+\gamma)t_1}{I_{2i-1} - I_\ell}} F_1(2i-1)^{r_{2i-1}} F_2(2i-2)^{r_{2i-2}}, g^{r_{2i-2}}, h^{-\frac{1+\gamma}{I_{2i-1} - I_\ell}} g^{r_{2i}} \right) \tag{2}$$

where $I_{2i-1} = H(2i-1)$. We observe that $\mathsf{usk}_1, \dots, \mathsf{usk}_{\ell-1}$ have the correct shape. If we define $\tilde{r}_{2i-1} = r_{2i-1} - b(1+\gamma)/(I_{2i-1} - I_\ell)$, we have

$$h^{-\frac{(1+\gamma)t_1}{I_{2i-1} - I_\ell}} F_1(2i-1)^{r_{2i-1}} = h^{-\frac{(1+\gamma)t_1}{I_{2i-1} - I_\ell}} \left(g_1^{I_{2i-1} - I_\ell} g^{t_1} \right)^{\tilde{r}_{2i-1} + \frac{b(1+\gamma)}{I_{2i-1} - I_\ell}} \tag{3}$$

$$= g_1^{b(1+\gamma)} (g_1^{I_{2i-1} - I_\ell} g^{t_1})^{\tilde{r}_{2i-1}} \tag{4}$$

$$= g^{(a\gamma + a)b} F_1(2i-1)^{\tilde{r}_{2i-1}} \tag{5}$$

$$= h^{\alpha_1 + \alpha_2} F_1(2i-1)^{\tilde{r}_{2i-1}} \tag{6}$$

and $h^{-\frac{1+\gamma}{I_{2i-1} - I_\ell}} g^{r_{2i-1}} = g^{-\frac{b(1+\gamma)}{I_{2i-1} - I_\ell}} g^{r_{2i-1}} = g^{\tilde{r}_{2i-1}}$ for $i = 1, \dots, (\ell - 1)/2$.

Next, $\mathcal{B}$ repeats a similar procedure to generate $\mathsf{usk}_{\ell+1}, \dots, \mathsf{usk}_N$. It picks $r_\ell \xleftarrow{R} \mathbb{Z}_p^*$. For $i = (\ell - 1)/2 + 1, \dots, N/2$ (we assume that N is even), it chooses $r_{2i}, r_{2i+1} \xleftarrow{R} \mathbb{Z}_p^*$ and computes

$$\mathsf{usk}_{2i} = \left(h^{-\frac{(1+\gamma^{-1})t_2}{I_{2i} - I_{\ell-1}}} F_2(2i)^{r_{2i}} F_1(2i-1)^{r_{2i-1}}, h^{-\frac{1+\gamma^{-1}}{I_{2i} - I_{\ell-1}}} g^{r_{2i}}, g^{r_{2i-1}} \right), \tag{7}$$

$$\mathsf{usk}_{2i+1} = \left(h^{-\frac{(1+\gamma^{-1})t_2}{I_{2i} - I_{\ell-1}}} F_2(2i)^{r_{2i}} F_1(2i+1)^{r_{2i+1}}, g^{r_{2i+1}}, h^{-\frac{1+\gamma^{-1}}{I_{2i} - I_{\ell-1}}} g^{r_{2i}} \right) \tag{8}$$

where $I_{2i} = H(2i)$. We check that $\mathsf{usk}_{\ell+1}, \dots, \mathsf{usk}_N$ are correct keys as, if we define $\tilde{r}_{2i} = r_{2i} - b(1+\gamma^{-1})/(I_{2i} - I_{\ell-1})$ for $i = (\ell - 1)/2 + 1, \dots, N/2$,

$$h^{-\frac{(1+\gamma^{-1})t_2}{I_{2i} - I_{\ell-1}}} F_2(2i)^{r_{2i}} = h^{-\frac{(1+\gamma^{-1})t_2}{I_{2i} - I_{\ell-1}}} \left(g_2^{I_{2i} - I_{\ell-1}} g^{t_2} \right)^{\tilde{r}_{2i} + \frac{b(1+\gamma^{-1})}{I_{2i} - I_{\ell-1}}} \tag{9}$$

$$= g_2^{b(1+\gamma^{-1})} (g_2^{I_{2i} - I_{\ell-1}} g^{t_2})^{\tilde{r}_{2i}} \tag{10}$$

$$= g^{(a\gamma + a)b} F_2(2i)^{\tilde{r}_{2i}} = h^{\alpha_1 + \alpha_2} F_2(2i)^{\tilde{r}_{2i}} \tag{11}$$

and $h^{-\frac{1+\gamma^{-1}}{I_{2i} - I_{\ell-1}}} g^{r_{2i}} = g^{-\frac{b(1+\gamma^{-1})}{I_{2i} - I_{\ell-1}}} g^{r_{2i}} = g^{\tilde{r}_{2i}}$.

- $\mathcal{COIN} = 1$: $\mathcal{B}$ expects $\mathcal{A}$ to corrupt either $\mathsf{mst}_1 = \mathsf{sd}_1$ or $\mathsf{mst}_2 = \mathsf{sd}_2$. It picks random values $\mathsf{b} \xleftarrow{R} \{1, 2\}$ and $\mathsf{sd}_\mathsf{b} \xleftarrow{R} \{0, 1\}^{1 + \log_2 p}$ and bets on an exposure query involving $\mathsf{mst}_\mathsf{b} = \mathsf{sd}_\mathsf{b}$. As ℓ is odd, if $\mathcal{A}$ indeed attacks stage ℓ, she is restricted not to request $\mathsf{usk}_{\ell-1}$ (resp. $\mathsf{usk}_{\ell+1}$) if $\mathsf{b} = 1$ (resp. $\mathsf{b} = 2$). When $\mathcal{A}$ issues a query $\langle i, \mathsf{class} \rangle$, $\mathcal{B}$ returns sd_b if $\mathsf{class} = $ "helper" and $i = \mathsf{b}$. It aborts if $\mathsf{class} = $ "helper" with $i = \bar{\mathsf{b}}$ (where $\bar{\mathsf{b}} = 2$ if $\mathsf{b} = 1$ and vice versa). When $\mathsf{class} = $ "user", it also aborts if $i = \ell$, if $i = \ell - 1$ while $\mathsf{b} = 1$ and if $i = \ell + 1$ while $\mathsf{b} = 2$. Otherwise, two cases are distinguished:

  $\mathsf{b} = 1$: we have $i \neq \ell - 1, \ell$. For all $i = 1, \ldots, N/2$, exponents r_{2i-1} are imposed by the relation $r_{2i-1} = f(\mathsf{sd}_1, 2i - 1)$ but exponents r_{2i} can be freely chosen. For $i = 0, \ldots, (\ell + 1)/2 - 2, (\ell + 1)/2, \ldots, N/2$, $\mathcal{B}$ chooses $r_{2i} \xleftarrow{R} \mathbb{Z}_p^*$ and generates $\mathsf{usk}_{2i}, \mathsf{usk}_{2i+1}$ following equations (7)-(11). Therefore, it obtains all private keys but $\mathsf{usk}_{\ell-1}, \mathsf{usk}_\ell$ (though usk_0 and usk_{N+1} are never requested by the adversary, they are computable). Those private keys have the correct shape for uniformly distributed (unknown) elements $\tilde{r}_{2i} \in \mathbb{Z}_p^*$.

  $\mathsf{b} = 2$: $\mathcal{B}$ has to compute private keys usk_i with $i \neq \ell, \ell + 1$ as $\mathcal{A}$ is assumed not to request $\mathsf{usk}_{\ell+1}$. This time, exponents of even time periods have to comply with the constraint $r_{2i} = f(\mathsf{sd}_2, 2i)$ for all i but exponents r_{2i-1} are free. For $i = 1, \ldots, (\ell - 1)/2, (\ell - 1)/2 + 2, \ldots, N/2$, $\mathcal{B}$ chooses $r_{2i-1} \xleftarrow{R} \mathbb{Z}_p^*$ and computes $\mathsf{usk}_{2i}, \mathsf{usk}_{2i-1}$ according to equations (1)-(6) and thereby obtains well-formed $\mathsf{usk}_1, \ldots, \mathsf{usk}_{\ell-1}, \mathsf{usk}_{\ell+2}, \ldots, \mathsf{usk}_N$ for random (unknown) implicitly defined $\tilde{r}_{2i-1}$.

Challenge: when $\mathcal{A}$ decides that phase 1 is over, she comes up with messages M_0, M_1 and a target time period i^*, $\mathcal{B}$ halts and reports "failure" if $i^* \neq \ell$. Otherwise, it flips a fair coin $b^* \xleftarrow{R} \{0, 1\}$ a returns the challenge

$$\sigma^* = \left(M_{b^*} \cdot T^{1+\gamma}, g^c, (g^c)^{t_1}, (g^c)^{t_2} \right).$$

Since $F_1(\ell) = g^{t_1}$ and $F_2(\ell - 1) = g^{t_2}$, σ^* has the same distribution as the output of the encryption algorithm if $T = e(g, g)^{abc}$. In contrast, if T is random in $\mathbb{G}_T$, σ^* is independent of b^* and $\mathcal{A}$ cannot guess b^* with a higher probability than $1/2$. Hence, $\mathcal{B}$ deduces that $T = e(g, g)^{abc}$ if $\mathcal{A}$'s final output equals b^*. Otherwise, it bets that $T \in_R \mathbb{G}_T$.

When assessing $\mathcal{B}$'s success probability, we note that it may fail to provide $\mathcal{A}$ with a consistent view because of the following events:

  E_1 : a key exposure is made for period ℓ
  E_2 : a helper key exposure occurs and $\mathcal{COIN} = 0$
  E_3 : helper $\bar{\mathsf{b}}$'s private key is exposed while $\mathcal{COIN} = 1$
  E_4 : a key exposure on $\mathsf{usk}_{\ell-1}$ occurs while $\mathsf{b} = 1$ and $\mathcal{COIN} = 1$
  E_5 : a key exposure on $\mathsf{usk}_{\ell+1}$ occurs while $\mathsf{b} = 2$ and $\mathcal{COIN} = 1$

We also consider the following events:

  H_0 : $\mathcal{B}$ correctly guesses $i^* = \ell$
  H_1 : $\mathcal{B}$ successfully foresees the kind of attack produced by $\mathcal{A}$
  H_2 : $\mathcal{B}$ luckily predicts which helper's key is exposed when $\mathcal{COIN} = 1$

Clearly $\Pr[H_0] = 1/N$ and $\Pr[H_1] = 1/2$. Also, we have $H_0 \Rightarrow \neg E_1$, $H_1 \Rightarrow \neg E_2$, $H_2 \Rightarrow \neg E_3$ and $H_2 \wedge H_0 \Rightarrow \neg E_4 \wedge \neg E_5$. The conjunction of events H_0, H_1 and H_2 is readily seen to occur with probability greater than $1/4N$ and it suffices to prevent a failure of the simulation.   □

6   Chosen-Ciphertext Security

Chosen-ciphertext security in the standard model can be achieved using ideas from [15,10] but it is more directly obtained following the techniques of Boyen, Mei and Waters [12] which require to turn our scheme into a key-encapsulation mechanism (KEM) [35].

A KEM [35] is a public key algorithm that, instead of encrypting messages as a regular public key cryptosystem, takes only a public key as input and returns pairs (K, σ) made of a randomly distributed key K and an encapsulation σ of it. The reverse operation is achieved by a decapsulation algorithm which, on input of a private key and an encapsulation σ, either outputs a key K or a rejection message $\perp$. It is well-known [35] that a KEM immediately provides a public key encryption scheme when combined with a suitable symmetric cryptosystem.

The methods of [12] involve a piece of ciphertext acting as a checksum treated as part of an identity-based system by the simulator handling decryption queries.

In order to optimize the decapsulation algorithm, we use a trick suggested in [30,32] to minimize the number of pairing calculations and render the consistency checking implicit in the computation of the key.

Key generation: is unchanged except that it additionally chooses a function $H' : \mathbb{G} \to \mathbb{Z}_p$ which is either a collision-resistant hash function or a suitable injective encoding (see [12] for details on how to define such an encoding). The algorithm also picks another element $g' \xleftarrow{R} \mathbb{G}$ to define the "checksum function" $F_3 : \mathbb{Z}_p \to \mathbb{G} : x \to F_3(x) = (g_1 g_2)^x g'$.

$$\mathsf{pk} := \{p, \mathbb{G}, \mathbb{G}_T, e, g, g_1, g_2, h, g_1', g_2', g', H, H', f\}.$$

Helper-Update and **User-Update** do not change. At period i, user's private key is still

$$\mathsf{usk}_i = \left(h^{\alpha_1 + \alpha_2} F_j(i)^{r_i} F_{j-1}(i-1)^{r_{i-1}}, g^{r_i}, g^{r_{i-1}} \right),$$

with $j = 2 - (i \bmod 2)$ and $r_i = f(\mathsf{sd}_j, i)$, $r_{i-1} = f(\mathsf{sd}_{j-1}, i-1) \in \mathbb{Z}_p^*$.

Encapsulate: given i and pk, let $j = 2 - (i \bmod 2)$, pick $s \xleftarrow{R} \mathbb{Z}_p^*$ and compute $A = g^s$, $\omega = H'(g^s) \in \mathbb{Z}_p$. Set $B = F_j(i)^s$, $C = F_{j-1}(i-1)^s$ and $D = F_3(\omega)^s$ to get

$$\sigma = (A, B, C, D) = \left(g^s, F_j(i)^s, F_{j-1}(i-1)^s, F_3(\omega)^s \right)$$

which encapsulates the key $K = e(h, g_1 g_2)^s$.

Decapsulate: given $\sigma = (A, B, C, D)$ and $\mathsf{usk}_i = (u_{i,0}, u_{i,1}, u_{i,2})$, the receiver sets $\omega = H'(A) \in \mathbb{Z}_p$, picks $z_1, z_2, z_3 \xleftarrow{R} \mathbb{Z}_p^*$ and computes

$$K = \frac{e(A, u_{i,0}\, F_j(i)^{z_1} F_{j-1}(i-1)^{z_2} F_3(\omega)^{z_3})}{e(B, u_{i,1}\, g^{z_1}) \cdot e(C, u_{i,2}\, g^{z_2}) \cdot e(D, g^{z_3})} \qquad (12)$$

To explain the decapsulation mechanism, we note that any properly formed encapsulation satisfies the (publicly verifiable) conditions

$$\tau_1 = \frac{e(A, F_j(i))}{e(B, g)} = 1, \ \tau_2 = \frac{e(A, F_{j-1}(i-1))}{e(C, g)} = 1, \ \tau_3 = \frac{e(A, F_3(\omega))}{e(D, g)} = 1_{\mathbb{G}_T}.$$

The naive approach is to return $K = e(A, u_{i,0})/(e(B, u_{i,1}) \cdot e(C, u_{i,2}))$ if they hold and $\perp$ (or a random $K \xleftarrow{R} \mathbb{G}_T$ from the key space) otherwise. This approach is perfectly equivalent to choose $z_1, z_2, z_3 \xleftarrow{R} \mathbb{Z}_p^*$ and return

$$K = \tau_1^{z_1} \cdot \tau_2^{z_2} \cdot \tau_3^{z_3} \cdot \frac{e(A, u_{i,0})}{e(B, u_{i,1}) \cdot e(C, u_{i,2})}$$

which is the actual decapsulated key if the encapsulation was correct and a random key otherwise. This alternative decapsulation mechanism is easily seen to be exactly the one suggested by relation (12).

Overall, the cost of the decapsulation operation amounts to a product of four pairings (which is much faster to compute than a naive evaluation of four pairings as discussed in [25]) plus a few exponentiations in $\mathbb{G}$.

In appendix B, we formally define the KEM counterpart of parallel key-insulated security. We then prove theorem 2 which claims the chosen-ciphertext security of our key-insulated KEM under the Decision BDH assumption.

Borrowing ideas from [31], we can construct a CCA-secure KEM with as short ciphertexts and almost as efficient decryption as in section 4. As in [31], this is obtained at the expense of longer private keys and a security resting on a slightly stronger assumption.

We also mention that a regular CCA-secure PKIE scheme can be directly achieved (without using the KEM-DEM framework) by implementing the check-sum function F_3 using Waters's "hashing" technique [37], much in the fashion of the cryptosystem described in section 3 of [12]. It unfortunately entails a much longer public key and a looser reduction.

7   Strong Key-Insulation

The scheme inherently provides strong key-insulation thanks to the erasure of discrete logarithms α_1, α_2 of g_1, g_2 after generation of the initial key usk_0. Indeed, base keys $\mathsf{sd}_1, \mathsf{sd}_2$ (that uniquely determine $r_1, \ldots, r_N$) are useless to adversaries as long as they do not additionally obtain any local secret usk_i for any period.

To formally prove this fact (in a distinct game from the one of definition 1), we proceed as in the proof of theorem 1 with the sole difference that no key exposure query has to be tackled with. Hence, it does not matter if $\mathcal{A}$ knows exponents r_i.

8   Key-Insulated Encryption with Auxiliary Helper

In [2], Anh *et al.* generalized the notion of PKIE into a new primitive called key-insulated public key encryption *with auxiliary helper*. Such a scheme also involves two independent helpers but one of them is auxiliary and used in updates much less frequently (say every ℓ time periods) than the main helper. In practice, the latter can be a laptop performing updates every day while the auxiliary helper (e.g. a smart card) can be kept in a much safer location most of the time in order to decrease the chance of compromise of both helpers.

This results in noticeable enhancements since, when the main helper is compromised, another exposure at the user only harms ℓ time periods: the next update carried out by the auxiliary helper restores the security. Furthermore, simultaneous break-ins at the user and the auxiliary helper compromise at most two adjacent periods as long as the main helper is not also exposed.

In [2], the HHI system [26] was extended into a key-insulated scheme with auxiliary helper (implicitly using aggregate signatures). Our constructions can be similarly extended to fit security definitions of [2] without using random oracles.

9   Conclusion

We pinpointed connections between the concept of parallel key-insulated encryption and certain identity-based cryptosystems using signatures supporting aggregation. This observation allowed for the design of a secure system in the standard model.

This motivates the open problem (with or without random oracles) of increasing the number of helpers without paying an important loss of efficiency. Our scheme and the one of [26] can both be extended to involve more than two helpers but this entails a significant computational penalty.

References

1. R. Anderson. Two Remarks on Public Key Cryptology. Invited lecture, *ACM Conference on Computer and Communications Security*, 1997.
2. P.T.L. Anh, Y. Hanaoka, G. Hanaoka, K. Matsuura, H. Imai. Reducing the Spread of Damage of Key Exposures in Key-Insulated Encryption. In *Vietcrypt'06*, to appear in *LNCS series*.
3. M. Bellare, S. Miner. A Forward-Secure Digital Signature Scheme. In *Crypto'99*, *LNCS* 1666, pp. 431–448. Springer, 1999.
4. M. Bellare, P. Rogaway. Random oracles are practical: A paradigm for designing efficient protocols. In *1st ACM Conference on Computer and Communications Security*, pages 62–73, ACM Press, 1993.
5. M. Bellare, A. Palacio. Protecting against Key Exposure: Strongly Key-Insulated Encryption with Optimal Threshold. Cryptology ePrint Archive: Report 2002/064, 2002.
6. D. Boneh, X. Boyen. Efficient selective-ID secure identity based encryption without random oracles. In *Eurocrypt'04*, *LNCS* 3027, pp. 223–238. Springer, 2004.

7. D. Boneh, X. Boyen, E.-J. Goh. Hierarchical Identity Based Encryption with Constant Size Ciphertext. In *Eurocrypt'05*, *LNCS* 3494, pp. 440–456. Springer, 2005.
8. D. Boneh, M. Franklin. Identity-based encryption from the Weil pairing. In *Crypto'01*, *LNCS* 2139, pp. 213–229. Springer, 2001.
9. D. Boneh, C. Gentry, B. Lynn, H. Shacham. Aggregate and verifiably encrypted signatures from bilinear maps. In *Eurocrypt'03*, volume 2656 of *LNCS*, pages 416–432. Springer, 2003.
10. D. Boneh, J. Katz. Improved Efficiency for CCA-Secure Cryptosystems Built Using Identity-Based Encryption. In *CT-RSA'05*, volume 3376 of *LNCS*, pages 87–103. Springer, 2005.
11. D. Boneh, B. Lynn, H. Shacham. Short signatures from the Weil pairing. In *Asiacrypt'01*, volume 2248 of *LNCS*, pages 514–532. Springer, 2002.
12. X. Boyen, Q. Mei, B. Waters. Direct Chosen Ciphertext Security from Identity-Based Techniques. in *ACM CCS'05*, ACM Press, pages 320–329, 2005.
13. R. Canetti, O. Goldreich, S. Halevi. The random oracle methodology, revisited. Journal of the ACM 51(4), 557–594 (2004)
14. R. Canetti, S. Halevi, J. Katz. A forward secure public key encryption scheme. In *Eurocrypt'03*, volume 2656 of *LNCS*, pages 254–271. Springer, 2003.
15. R. Canetti, S. Halevi, J. Katz. Chosen-Ciphertext Security from Identity-Based Encryption. In *Eurocrypt'04*, volume 3027 of *LNCS*, pages 207–222. Springer, 2004.
16. S. S. Chow, L. C. Kwong Hui, S. M. Yiu, K. P. Chow. Secure Hierarchical Identity Based Signature and Its Application. In *ICICS'04*, volume 3269 of *LNCS*, pages 480–494, Springer, 2004.
17. J. S. Coron, D. Naccache. Boneh *et al.*'s k-Element Aggregate Extraction Assumption Is Equivalent to the Diffie-Hellman Assumption. In *Asiacrypt'03*, volume 2894 of *LNCS*, pages 392–397. Springer, 2003.
18. R. Cramer, V. Shoup, *Design and analysis of practical public-key encryption schemes secure against adaptive chosen ciphertext attack*, in *SIAM* Journal of Computing 33, pages 167–226, 2003.
19. Y. Dodis, M. Franklin, J. Katz, A. Miyaji, M. Yung. Intrusion-Resilient Public-Key Encryption. In *CT-RSA'03*, volume 2612 of *LNCS*, pages 19–32. Springer, 2003.
20. Y. Dodis, J. Katz, S. Xu, M. Yung. Key-Insulated Public Key Cryptosystems. In *Eurocrypt'02*, volume 2332 of *LNCS*, pages 65–82. Springer, 2002.
21. Y. Dodis, J. Katz, S. Xu, M. Yung. Strong key-insulated signature schemes. In *PKC'03*, volume 2567 of *LNCS*, pages 130–144. Springer, 2003.
22. Y. Dodis, J. Katz. Chosen-Ciphertext Security of Multiple Encryption. In *TCC'05*, volume 3378 of *LNCS*, pages 188–209, Springer, 2005.
23. E. Fujisaki, T. Okamoto. How to enhance the security of public-key encryption at minimum cost. In *PKC'99*, *LNCS* 1560, pp. 53–68. Springer, 1999.
24. C. Gentry, A. Silverberg. Hierarchical ID-based cryptography. In *Asiacrypt'02*, volume 2501 of *LNCS*, pages 548–566. Springer, 2002.
25. R. Granger, N. P. Smart. On Computing Products of Pairings. Cryptology ePrint Archive: Report 2006/172, 2006.
26. G. Hanaoka, Y. Hanaoka, H. Imai. Parallel Key-Insulated Public Key Encryption. In *PKC'06*, volume 3958 of *LNCS*, pages 105–122, Springer, 2006.
27. G. Itkis, L. Reyzin. SiBIR: Signer-Base Intrusion-Resilient Signatures. In *Crypto'02*, volume 2442 of *LNCS*, pages 499–514, Springer, 2002.
28. A. Joux. A One Round Protocol for Tripartite Diffie-Hellman. In *ANTS'00*, volume 1838 of *LNCS*, pages 385–394, Springer, 2000.

29. J. Katz. A Forward-Secure Public-Key Encryption Scheme. Cryptology ePrint Archive: Report 2002/060, 2002.
30. E. Kiltz. On the Limitations of the Spread of an IBE-to-PKE Transformation. In *PKC'06*, LNCS 3958, pp. 274–289, Springer, 2006.
31. E. Kiltz. Chosen-Ciphertext Secure Identity-Based Encryption in the Standard Model with short Ciphertexts. Cryptology ePrint Archive: Report 2006/122, 2006.
32. E. Kiltz, D. Galindo. Direct Chosen-Ciphertext Secure Identity-Based Key Encapsulation without Random Oracles. In *ACISP'06*, volume 4058 of *LNCS*, pages 336–347 Springer, 2006.
33. S. Lu, R. Ostrovsky, A. Sahai, H. Shacham, B. Waters. Sequential Aggregate Signatures and Multisignatures Without Random Oracles. In *Eurocrypt'06*, volume 4004 of *LNCS*, pages 465–485, Springer, 2006.
34. K. G. Paterson, J. C. N. Schuldt. Efficient Identity-based Signatures Secure in the Standard Model. In *ACISP'06*, volume 4058 of *LNCS*, pages 207–222, Springer, 2006.
35. V. Shoup. Using Hash Functions as a Hedge against Chosen Ciphertext Attack. In *Eurocrypt'00*, volume 1807 of *LNCS*, pages 275–288, Springer, 2000.
36. A. Shamir. Identity based cryptosystems and signature schemes. In *Crypto'84*, volume 196 of *LNCS*, pages 47–53. Springer, 1984.
37. B. Waters. Efficient Identity-Based Encryption Without Random Oracles. In *Eurocrypt'05*, volume 3494 of *LNCS*, pages 114–127. Springer 2005.
38. D. Yao, N. Fazio, Y. Dodis, A. Lysyanskaya. ID-based encryption for complex hierarchies with applications to forward security and broadcast encryption. In *ACM CCS'04*, ACM Press, pages 354–363, 2004.

A   The HHI Construction

The original PKIE system proposed by Hanaoka, Hanaoka and Imai [26] is recalled below. In some sense, it can be thought of as a double application of a key-insulated scheme obtained from the Boneh-Franklin IBE [8] using two distinct Private Key Generators (PKGs) as helpers. To ensure the security in the sense of definition 1, a private key for period i consists of an aggregation of private keys for identities i and $i - 1$.

Key generation: given a security paramter $\lambda \in \mathbb{N}$, this algorithm
1. chooses bilinear map groups $(\mathbb{G}, \mathbb{G}_T)$ of order $p > 2^\lambda$, a generator $g \in \mathbb{G}$, hash functions $H : \{0,1\}^* \to \mathbb{G}$, $G : \mathbb{G}_T \to \{0,1\}^n$ (modeled as random oracles in the security analysis),
2. picks $\alpha_1, \alpha_2 \xleftarrow{R} \mathbb{Z}_p^*$ and computes $g_1 = g^{\alpha_1}$, $g_2 = g^{\alpha_2}$,
3. computes $u_{-1} = H(-1)$, $u_0 = H(0)$,
4. computes $d_{-1} = u_{-1}^{\alpha_1}$, $d_0 = u_0^{\alpha_2}$,
5. initializes the user's private key to $\mathsf{usk}_0 = d_{-1}d_0 \in \mathbb{G}$,
6. Helpers' private keys are set to $\mathsf{mst}_1 = \alpha_1$ and $\mathsf{mst}_2 = \alpha_2$ while the public key is $\mathsf{pk} := \{p, \mathbb{G}, \mathbb{G}_T, e, g, g_1, g_2, H, G\}$.

Helper-Update: given $\mathsf{mst}_j = \alpha_j$ and a period number $i \in \{1, 2, \ldots, N\}$, helper $j \in \{1, 2\}$

1. returns $\perp$ if $i \neq j \bmod 2$,
2. computes $d_{i-2} = H(i-2)^{\alpha_j}$, $d_i = H(i)^{\alpha_j}$,
3. outputs an update key $\mathsf{hsk}_i = d_i/d_{i-2} \in \mathbb{G}$

User-Update: given usk_{i-1}, hsk_i and i,

1. set $\mathsf{usk}_i = \mathsf{usk}_{i-1} \cdot \mathsf{hsk}_i \in \mathbb{G}$,
3. return usk_i and discard usk_{i-1}, hsk_i.

At time period i, user's private key is always set to

$$\mathsf{usk}_i = d_i d_{i-1} = H(i)^{\alpha_j} H(i-1)^{\alpha_{j-1}} \in \mathbb{G}$$

with $j = 2 - (i \bmod 2)$.

Encrypt: given pk, $i \in \mathbb{N}$, a message $m \in \{0,1\}^n$ is encrypted into

$$\sigma = \left(g^s, m \oplus G(W)\right)$$

for a random $s \xleftarrow{R} \mathbb{Z}_p^*$ and $W = \left(e(g_j, H(i)) \cdot e(g_{j-1}, H(i-1))\right)^s$ with $j = 2 - (i \bmod 2)$.

Decrypt: given $\sigma = (A, B)$ and usk_i, compute

$$m = B \oplus G(e(A, \mathsf{usk}_i))$$

The above version of the scheme is only secure against chosen-plaintext attacks. The authors of [26] obtain the CCA-security in the random oracle model through the Fujisaki-Okamoto conversion [23].

B   Security Proof for the Parallel Key-Insulated KEM

Chosen-ciphertext security is defined as follows for parallel key-insulated KEMs.

Definition 3. *A parallel key-insulated KEM is secure against chosen-ciphertext attacks if no PPT adversary has non-negligible advantage in the following game:*

1. *The challenger $\mathcal{C}$ runs the key generation algorithm, gives pk to the adversary $\mathcal{A}$ and keeps mst_0, mst_1 and uks_0 to itself.*
2. *$\mathcal{A}$ adaptively issues a series of queries which are either:*
   - *Key Exposure queries as in definition 1*
   - *Decapsulation queries $\langle j, \sigma \rangle$: $\mathcal{C}$ responds by generating usk_j to run the decapsulation algorithm on σ and pass the result to $\mathcal{A}$.*
3. *When $\mathcal{A}$ is ready to be challenged, she chooses period number $j^\star \in \{1, \ldots, N\}$. The challenger $\mathcal{C}$ runs algorithm **Encapsulate**$(j^\star, \mathsf{pk})$ to produce a random key $K^\dagger$ along with its encapsulation $\sigma^\star$. At this point, $\mathcal{C}$ tosses a coin $b^\star \xleftarrow{R} \{0,1\}$. If $b^\star = 1$, $\mathcal{C}$ defines $K^\star = K^\dagger$. Otherwise, it sets $K^\star \xleftarrow{R} \mathcal{K}$ as a randomly chosen element from the key space $\mathcal{K}$. The pair $(K^\star, \sigma^\star)$ is sent as a challenge to $\mathcal{A}$.*
4. *$\mathcal{A}$ issues new queries as in stage 2.*
5. *She eventually outputs $b \in \{0,1\}$ and wins if $b = b^\star$ provided similar restrictions to those of definition 1 are respected.*

As shown in [18], a chosen-ciphertext secure KEM immediately gives rise to an IND-CCA2 public key cryptosystem when combined with a suitable symmetric encryption scheme. Although the present setting slightly differs from the traditional public key setting, it is straightforward to extend the proof of theorem 5 in [18] to our context.

The next theorem now states the security of our parallel key-insulated KEM in the sense of definition 3 and under the DBDH assumption.

Theorem 2. *If no algorithm (t, ε)-breaks the DBDH assumption, our parallel key-insulated KEM is $(t', 4N(1-q_d/p)\varepsilon)$-secure against chosen-ciphertext attacks for $t' < t - O(N\tau_{exp} + q_d\tau_p)$ where N is the number of time periods, q_d denotes the number of decapsulation queries and τ_{exp}, τ_p respectively stand for the time complexity of an exponentiation in $\mathbb{G}$ and a pairing evaluation.*

Proof. We outline an algorithm $\mathcal{B}$ receiving as input a tuple (g^a, g^b, g^c, T) randomly sampled from either $D_{bdh} = \{(g^a, g^b, g^c, e(g, g)^{abc}) | a, b, c \xleftarrow{R} \mathbb{Z}_p^*\}$ or $D_{rand} = \{(g^a, g^b, g^c, e(g, g)^z) | a, b, c, z \xleftarrow{R} \mathbb{Z}_p^*\}$ and uses the adversary $\mathcal{A}$ to tell which distribution it was taken from.

The simulator $\mathcal{B}$ generates public key components h, g_1, g_2, g_1', g_2' as in the proof of theorem 1. Namely, it sets $h = g^b$, $g_1 = g^a$, $g_2 = g_1^\gamma$ for some randomly chosen $\gamma \xleftarrow{R} \mathbb{Z}_p^*$ while g_1' and g_2' are chosen to properly handle key exposure queries as in the proof of theorem 1. In addition, $\mathcal{B}$ publishes the description of a collision-resistant hash function $H : \mathbb{N} \to \mathbb{Z}_p^*$ and some injective encoding function $H' : \mathbb{G} \to \mathbb{Z}_p$ (we refer to [12] for details on how to obtain such an encoding). Next, $\mathcal{B}$ computes $\omega^* = H'(g^c) \in \mathbb{Z}_p$ and defines the group element $g' = (g_1 g_2)^{-\omega^*} g^{t_3}$ for a random $t_3 \xleftarrow{R} \mathbb{Z}_p^*$. The function F_3 is implicitly defined as $F_3(x) = (g_1 g_2)^{x-\omega^*} g^{t_3}$. The adversary is started with $\{p, \mathbb{G}, \mathbb{G}_T, g, g_1, g_2, h, g_1', g_2', g', H, H'\}$ as input. She then issues a series of key exposure queries which are handled exactly as in the proof of theorem 1. Other queries are treated as follows.

Decapsulation queries: When $\mathcal{A}$ issues a pair $\langle i, \sigma \rangle$ containing a ciphertext $\sigma = (A, B, C, D)$ and a period i, $\mathcal{B}$ computes $\omega = H'(A) \in \mathbb{Z}_p$. If $\omega = \omega^*$, it aborts. Assuming that H' is injective, this implies that $A = g^c$. Since the DBDH instance was randomly distributed, such a situation only happens with probability q_d/p throughout all queries. If $\omega \neq \omega^*$, $\mathcal{B}$ determines whether σ is valid by checking if

$$\frac{e(A, F_j(i))}{e(B, g)} = \frac{e(A, F_{j-1}(i-1))}{e(C, g)} = \frac{e(A, F_3(\omega))}{e(D, g)} = 1_{\mathbb{G}_T}.$$

If the above checking fails, $\mathcal{B}$ returns a random element $K \xleftarrow{R} \mathbb{G}_T$ from the key space. Otherwise, it knows that

$$\sigma = (A, B, C, D) = (g^s, F_j(i)^s, F_{j-1}(i-1)^s, F_3(\omega)^s),$$

where $D = (g_1 g_2)^{s(\omega-\omega^*)} g^{st_3}$, for some unknown $s \in \mathbb{Z}_p^*$. Algorithm $\mathcal{B}$ then computes $g_1^s g_2^s = (D/A^{t_3})^{1/\omega-\omega^*}$ which yields the key $K = e(h, g_1 g_2)^s$.

Challenge: when $\mathcal{A}$ produces her challenge request, the returned ciphertext is

$$\sigma^\star = \left(g^c, (g^c)^{t_1}, (g^c)^{t_2}, (g^c)^{t_3}\right)$$

while the challenge key is $K^\star = T^{1+\gamma}$. As $F_1(\ell) = g^{t_1}$, $F_2(\ell - 1) = g^{t_2}$ (we still assume that ℓ is odd) and $F_3(\omega^\star) = g^{t_3}$, $\sigma^\star$ is a valid encapsulation of $K^\star$ if $T = e(g, g)^{abc}$. If T is random in $\mathbb{G}_T$, so is $K^\star$ and the result follows.

$\square$

Multi-bit Cryptosystems Based on Lattice Problems

Akinori Kawachi, Keisuke Tanaka, and Keita Xagawa

Department of Mathematical and Computing Sciences, Tokyo Institute of Technology,
W8-55, 2-12-1 Ookayama Meguro-ku, Tokyo 152-8552, Japan
{kawachi,keisuke,xagawa5}@is.titech.ac.jp

Abstract. We propose multi-bit versions of several single-bit cryptosystems based on lattice problems, the error-free version of the Ajtai-Dwork cryptosystem by Goldreich, Goldwasser, and Halevi [CRYPTO '97], the Regev cryptosystems [JACM 2004 and STOC 2005], and the Ajtai cryptosystem [STOC 2005]. We develop a universal technique derived from a general structure behind them for constructing their multi-bit versions without increase in the size of ciphertexts. By evaluating the trade-off between the decryption errors and the hardness of underlying lattice problems, it is shown that our multi-bit versions encrypt $O(\log n)$-bit plaintexts into ciphertexts of the same length as the original ones with reasonable sacrifices of the hardness of the underlying lattice problems. Our technique also reveals an algebraic property, named *pseudohomomorphism*, of the lattice-based cryptosystems.

1 Introduction

Lattice-Based Cryptosystems. The lattice-based cryptosystems have been well-studied since Ajtai's seminal result [1] on a one-way function based on the worst-case hardness of lattice problems, which initiated the cryptographic use of lattice problems. Ajtai and Dwork first succeeded to construct public-key cryptosystems [2] based on the unique shortest vector problem (uSVP). After their results, a number of lattice-based cryptosystems have been proposed in the last decade by using cryptographic advantages of lattice problems [3,4,5,6].

We can roughly classify the lattice-based cryptosystems into two types: (A) those who are efficient on the size of their keys and ciphertexts and the speed of encryption/decryption procedures, but have no security proofs based on the hardness of well-known lattice problems, and (B) those who have security proofs based on the lattice problems but are inefficient.

For example, the GGH cryptosystem [7], NTRU [8] and their improvements [9,10,11] belong to the type A. These are efficient multi-bit cryptosystems related to lattices, but it is unknown whether their security is based on the hardness of well-known lattice problems. Actually, a few papers reported security issues of cryptosystems in this type [12,13].

On the other hand, those in the type B have security proofs based on well-known lattice problems such as uSVP, the shortest vector problem (SVP) and

T. Okamoto and X. Wang (Eds.): PKC 2007, LNCS 4450, pp. 315–329, 2007.

the shortest linearly independent vectors problem (SIVP) [2,4,6]. In particular, the security of these cryptosystems can be guaranteed by the worst-case hardness of the lattice problems, i.e., breaking the cryptosystems on average is at least as hard as solving the lattice problems in the worst case. This attractive property of the average-case/worst-case connection has been also studied from a theoretical point of view [1,14,15,16].

Aside from the interesting property, such cryptosystems generally have longer keys and ciphertexts than those of the cryptosystems in the type A. To set their size practically reasonable, their security parameters must be small, which possibly makes the cryptosystems insecure in a practical sense [17]. Therefore, it is important to improve their efficiency for secure lattice-based cryptosystems in the type B.

In recent years, several researchers actually considered more efficient lattice-based cryptosystems with security proofs. For example, Regev constructed an efficient lattice-based cryptosystem with shorter keys [6]. The security is based on the worst-case quantum hardness of certain approximation versions of SVP and SIVP, that is, his cryptosystem is secure if we have no polynomial-time quantum algorithm that solves the lattice problems in the worst case. Ajtai also constructed an efficient lattice-based cryptosystem with shorter keys by using a compact representation of special instances of uSVP [5], whose security is based on a certain Diophantine approximation problem.

Our Contributions. We continue to study efficient lattice-based cryptosystems with security proofs based on well-known lattice problems or other secure cryptosystems. In particular, we focus on the size of plaintexts encrypted by the cryptosystems in the type B. To the best of the authors' knowledge, all those in this type are single-bit cryptosystems. We therefore obtain more efficient lattice-based cryptosystems with security proofs if we succeed to construct their multi-bit versions without increase in the size of ciphertexts.

In this paper, we consider multi-bit versions of the improved Ajtai-Dwork cryptosystem proposed by Goldreich, Goldwasser, and Halevi [3], the Regev cryptosystems given in [4] and in [6], and the Ajtai cryptosystem [5]. We develop a universal technique derived from a general structure behind them for constructing their multi-bit versions without increase in the size of ciphertexts.

Our technique requires precise evaluation of trade-offs between decryption errors and hardness of underlying lattice problems in the original lattice-based cryptosystems. We firstly give precise evaluation for the trade-offs to apply our technique to constructions of the multi-bit versions. This precise evaluation also clarifies a quantitative relationship between the security levels and the decryption errors in the lattice-based cryptosystems, which may be useful to improve the cryptosystems beyond our results.

Due to this evaluation of the cryptosystems, it is shown that our multi-bit versions encrypt $O(\log n)$-bit plaintexts into ciphertexts of the same length as the original ones with reasonable sacrifices of the hardness of the underlying lattice problems.

Table 1. summary.(ε is any positive constant and $\tilde{O}(f(n))$ means $O(f(n)\,\mathrm{poly}(\log n))$.)

	Ajtai-Dwork		Regev'04	
cryptosystem	$\mathrm{AD_{GGH}}$ [3]	$\mathrm{mAD_{GGH}}$	R04 [4]	mR04
security	$O(n^{11})$-uSVP	$O(n^{11+\varepsilon})$-uSVP	$\tilde{O}(n^{1.5})$-uSVP	$\tilde{O}(n^{1.5+\varepsilon})$-uSVP
size of public key	$O(n^5 \log n)$	$O(n^5 \log n)$	$O(n^4)$	$O(n^4)$
size of private key	$O(n^2)$	$O(n^2)$	$O(n^2)$	$O(n^2)$
size of plaintext	1	$O(\log n)$	1	$O(\log n)$
size of ciphertext	$O(n^2 \log n)$	$O(n^2 \log n)$	$O(n^2)$	$O(n^2)$
rounding precision	2^{-n}	2^{-n}	2^{-8n^2}	2^{-8n^2}
	Regev'05		Ajtai	
cryptosystem	R05 [6]	mR05	A05 [5]	mA05
security	$\mathrm{SVP}_{\tilde{O}(n^{1.5})}$	$\mathrm{SVP}_{\tilde{O}(n^{1.5+\varepsilon})}$	DA'	A05
size of public key	$O(n^2 \log^2 n)$	$O(n^2 \log^2 n)$	$O(n^2 \log n)$	$O(n^2 \log n)$
size of private key	$O(n \log n)$	$O(n \log n)$	$O(n \log n)$	$O(n \log n)$
size of plaintext	1	$O(\log n)$	1	$O(\log n)$
size of ciphertext	$O(n \log n)$	$O(n \log n)$	$O(n \log n)$	$O(n \log n)$
rounding precision	2^{-n}	2^{-n}	$1/n$	$1/n$

The ciphertexts of our multi-bit version are distributed in the same ciphertext space, theoretically represented with real numbers, as the original cryptosystem. To represent the real numbers in their ciphertexts, we have to round their fractional parts with certain precision. The size of ciphertexts then increases if we process the numbers with high precision. We stress that our technique does not need higher precision than that of the original cryptosystems, i.e., we take the same precision in our multi-bit versions as that of the original ones.

See Table 1 for the cryptosystems studied in this paper. We call the cryptosystems proposed in [3,4,6,5] $\mathrm{AD_{GGH}}$, R04, R05, and A05, respectively. We also call the corresponding multi-bit versions $\mathrm{mAD_{GGH}}$, mR04, mR05, and mA05.

The problems in the security fields are deeply related to lattice problems. The shortest vector problem within approximation factor γ (SVP_γ) is generally considered as a hard problem for polynomial factor of γ, which is defined as follows. Given a lattice L, the problem is to find a shortest non-zero vector $u \in L$ within approximation factor γ.

The unique shortest vector problem (uSVP) is also well known as a hard lattice problem applicable to cryptographic constructions. We say the shortest vector u of a lattice L is f-unique if for any non-zero vector $v \in L$ which is not parallel to u, $f\|u\| \le \|v\|$. Given a lattice L whose shortest vector is f-unique, the problem is to find a non-zero vector $u \in L$ such that for any non-zero vector $v \in L$ which is not parallel to u, $f\|u\| \le \|v\|$.

While the security of $\mathrm{AD_{GGH}}$, R04, and R05 is based on the above two lattice problems, that of A05 is on a variant of Diophantine approximation problem (DA'). See [5] for the definition of this problem.

We also focus on the algebraic property we call *pseudohomomorphism* of the lattice-based cryptosystems. The homomorphism of ciphertexts is quite useful for many cryptographic applications. (See, e.g., [18].) In fact, the single-bit cryptosystems AD_{GGH}, R04, R05 and A05 implicitly have a similar property to the homomorphism. Let $E(x_1)$ and $E(x_2)$ be ciphertexts of x_1 and $x_2 \in \{0, 1\}$, respectively. Then, $E(x_1) + E(x_2)$ becomes a variant of $E(x_1 \oplus x_2)$. More precisely, $E(x_1) + E(x_2)$ does not obey the distribution of the ciphertexts, but we can guarantee the same security level as that of the original cryptosystem and decrypt $E(x_1) + E(x_2)$ to $x_1 \oplus x_2$ by the original private key with a small decryption error. We refer to this property as the pseudohomomorphism. Goldwasser and Kharchenko actually made use of a similar property to construct the plaintext knowledge proof system for the Ajtai-Dwork cryptosystem [19].

Unfortunately, it is only over $\mathbb{Z}_2$ (and direct product groups of $\mathbb{Z}_2$ by concatenating the ciphertexts) that we can operate the addition of the plaintexts in the single-bit cryptosystems. It is unlikely that we can naively simulate the addition over large cyclic groups by concatenating ciphertexts in such single-bit cryptosystems.

In this paper, we present the pseudohomomorphic property of mAD_{GGH} over larger cyclic groups. The property of mR04, mR05, and (a slightly modified version of) mA05 can be shown similarly, whose proof will be given in the full paper. We believe that this property extends the possibility of the cryptographic applications of the lattice-based cryptosystems.

Main Idea for Multi-Bit Constructions and Their Security. We can actually find the following general structure behind the single-bit cryptosystems AD_{GGH}, R04, R05, and A05: Their ciphertexts of 0 are basically distributed according to a periodic Gaussian distribution and those of 1 are also distributed according to another periodic Gaussian distribution whose peaks are shifted to the middle of the period. We thus embed two periodic Gaussian distributions into the ciphertext space such that their peaks appear alternatively and regularly. (See the left side of Figure 1.)

Our technique is based on a generalization of this structure. More precisely, we regularly embed *multiple* periodic Gaussian distributions into the ciphertext space rather than only two ones. (See the right side of Figure 1.) Embedding p periodic Gaussian distributions as shown in this figure, the ciphertexts for a plaintext $i \in \{0, \ldots, p-1\}$ are distributed according the i-th periodic Gaussian distribution. This cyclic structure enables us not only to improve the efficiency of the cryptosystems but also to guarantee their security.

If we embed too many periodic Gaussian distributions, the decryption errors increase due to the overlaps of the distributions. We can then decrease the decryption errors by reducing their variance. However, it is known that smaller variance generally makes such cryptosystems less secure, as commented in [3]. We therefore have to evaluate the trade-offs in our multi-bit versions between the decryption errors and their security, which depend on their own structures of the cryptosystems.

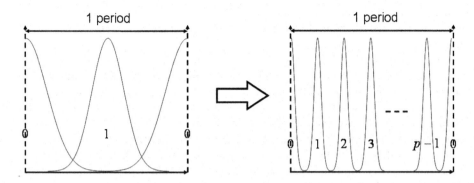

Fig. 1. the embedding of periodic Gaussian distributions

Once we evaluate their trade-offs, we can apply a general strategy based on the cyclic structure to the security proofs. The security of the original cryptosystems basically depends on the indistinguishability between a certain periodic Gaussian distribution Φ and a uniform distribution U since it is shown in their security proofs that we can construct an efficient algorithm for a certain hard lattice problem by employing an efficient distinguisher between Φ and U. The goal is thus to construct the distinguisher from an adversary against the multi-bit version.

We first assume that there exists an efficient adversary for distinguishing between two Gaussian distributions corresponding two kinds of ciphertexts in our multi-bit version with its public key. By the hybrid argument, the adversary can distinguish either between Φ_i and U or between Φ_j and U. We now suppose that it can distinguish between Φ_i and U. Note that we can slide Φ_i to Φ_0 corresponding to ciphertexts of 0 even if we do not know the private key by the cyclic property of the ciphertexts. Thus, we obtain an efficient distinguisher between Φ_0 and U. Φ_0 is in fact a variance-reduced version of the periodic Gaussian distribution Φ used in the original cryptosystem. We can guarantee the indistinguishability between such a version Φ_0 and U is based on the hardness of another lattice problem slightly easier than the original one. We can therefore guarantee the security of our multi-bit versions similarly to the original ones.

Encryption and Decryption in Multi-Bit Versions. We also exploit this cyclic structure for the correctness of encryption and decryption procedures. In the original cryptosystems except for R05, the private key is the period d of the periodic Gaussian distribution, and the public key consists of the information for generating the periodic Gaussian distribution corresponding to 0 and the information for shifting the distribution to the other distribution corresponding to 1. The latter information for the shift essentially is $k(d/2)$ for a random odd number k. Then, if we want to encrypt a plaintext 0, we generate the periodic

Gaussian distribution corresponding to 0. Also, if we want to encrypt 1, we generate the distribution corresponding to 0 and then shift it using the latter information.

The private and public keys in our multi-bit versions are slightly different from those of the original ones. The major difference is the information for shifting the distribution. If the size of the plaintext space is p, the information for the shift is essentially $k(d/p)$, where the number k must be a coprime to p for unique decryption. We then interpret the number k as a generator of the *group* of periodic Gaussian distributions. We adopt a prime as the size of the plaintext space p for efficient public key generation in our constructions. The private key also contains this number k other than the period d. Therefore, we can construct correct encryption and decryption procedures using this information k.

In the cases of R05 and mR05, it is not necessary for keys to contain the information for the shift. We can actually obtain such information due to their own structures even if it is not given from the public key. Thus, p is not necessarily a prime in mR05.

Pseudohomomorphism in Multi-Bit Versions. The regular embedding of the periodic Gaussian distributions also gives our multi-bit cryptosystems the algebraic property named *pseudohomomorphism*. Recall that a Gaussian distribution has the following reproducing property: For two random variables X_1 and X_2 according to $N(m_1, s_1^2)$ and $N(m_2, s_2^2)$, where $N(m, s^2)$ is a Gaussian distribution with mean m and standard deviation s, the distribution of $X_1 + X_2$ is equal to $N(m_1 + m_2, s_1^2 + s_2^2)$. This property implies that the sum of two ciphertexts (i.e., the sum of two periodic Gaussian distributions) becomes a variant of a ciphertext (i.e., a periodic Gaussian distribution with larger variance). This sum can be moreover decrypted into the sum of two plaintexts with the private key of the multi-bit version, and has the indistinguishability based on the security of the multi-bit version. By precise analysis of our multi-bit versions, we estimate the upper bound of the number of the ciphertexts which can be summed without the change of the security and the decryption errors.

Organization. The rest of this paper is organized as follows. We describe basic notions and notations for lattice-based cryptosystems in Section 2. In Section 3, we first review the improved Ajtai-Dwork cryptosystem AD_{GGH} and then describe the corresponding multi-bit version mAD_{GGH} in detail. We omit the description of the other multi-bit versions mR04, mR05, and mA05 since the main idea of their constructions are based on the same universal technique and the difference among them is mainly the evaluation of the trade-offs in each of cryptosystems. They will appear in the full paper. We also give concluding remarks in Section 4.

2   Basic Notions and Notations

The length of a vector $\boldsymbol{x} = {}^t(x_1, \ldots, x_n) \in \mathbb{R}^n$, denoted by $\|\boldsymbol{x}\|$, is $(\sum_{i=1}^n x_i^2)^{1/2}$, where ${}^t\boldsymbol{x}$ is the transpose of $\boldsymbol{x}$. The inner product of two vectors $\boldsymbol{x} = {}^t(x_1, \ldots, x_n) \in \mathbb{R}^n$ and $\boldsymbol{y} = {}^t(y_1, \ldots, y_n) \in \mathbb{R}^n$, denoted by $\langle \boldsymbol{x}, \boldsymbol{y} \rangle$, is $\sum_{i=1}^n x_i y_i$.

The security parameter n of lattice-based cryptosystems is given by dimension of a lattice in the lattice problems on which security of the cryptosystems are based. Let $\lfloor x \rceil$ be the closest integer to $x \in \mathbb{R}$ (if there are two such integers, we choose the smaller.) and $\text{frc}\,(x) = |x - \lfloor x \rceil|$ for $x \in \mathbb{R}$, i.e., $\text{frc}\,(x)$ is the distance from x to the closest integer.

A function $f(n)$ is called negligible for sufficiently large n if $\lim_{n \to \infty} n^c f(n) = 0$ for any constant $c > 0$. We similarly call $f(n)$ a non-negligible function if there exists a constant $c > 0$ such that $f(n) > n^{-c}$ for sufficiently large n. We call probability p exponentially close to 1 if $p = 1 - 2^{-\Omega(n)}$. We represent a real number by rounding its fractional part. If the fractional part of $x \in \mathbb{R}$ is represented in m bits, the rounded number $\bar{x}$ has the precision of $1/2^m$, i.e., we have $|x - \bar{x}| \le 1/2^m$.

We say that an algorithm distinguishes between two distributions if the gap between the acceptance probability for their samples is non-negligible.

Lattices. An n-dimensional lattice in $\mathbb{R}^n$ is the set $L(\boldsymbol{b}_1, \ldots, \boldsymbol{b}_n) = \{\sum_{i=1}^n \alpha_i \boldsymbol{b}_i : \alpha_i \in \mathbb{Z}\}$ of all integral combinations of n linearly independent vectors $\boldsymbol{b}_1, \ldots, \boldsymbol{b}_n$. The sequence of vectors $\boldsymbol{b}_1, \ldots, \boldsymbol{b}_n$ is called a *basis* of the lattice L. For clarity of notations, we represent a basis by the matrix $\mathbf{B} = (\boldsymbol{b}_1, \ldots, \boldsymbol{b}_n) \in \mathbb{R}^{n \times n}$. For any basis $\mathbf{B}$, we define the *fundamental parallelepiped* $\mathcal{P}(\mathbf{B}) = \{\sum_{i=1}^n \alpha_i \boldsymbol{b}_i : 0 \le \alpha_i < 1\}$. The vector $\boldsymbol{x} \in \mathbb{R}^n$ reduced modulo the parallelepiped $\mathcal{P}(\mathbf{B})$, denoted by $\boldsymbol{x} \bmod \mathcal{P}(\mathbf{B})$, is the unique vector $\boldsymbol{y} \in \mathcal{P}(\mathbf{B})$ such that $\boldsymbol{y} - \boldsymbol{x} \in L(\mathbf{B})$. The dual lattice L^* of a lattice L is the set $L^* = \{\boldsymbol{x} \in \mathbb{R}^n : \langle \boldsymbol{x}, \boldsymbol{y} \rangle \in \mathbb{Z} \text{ for all } \boldsymbol{y} \in L\}$. If L is generated by basis $\mathbf{B}$, then $({}^t\mathbf{B})^{-1}$ is a basis for the dual lattice, where ${}^t\mathbf{B}$ is the transpose of $\mathbf{B}$.

For more details on lattices, see the textbook by Micciancio and Goldwasser [20].

3   A Multi-bit Version of the Improved Ajtai-Dwork Cryptosystem

On behalf of four cryptosystems AD_{GGH}, R04, R05, and A05, we discuss the improved Ajtai-Dwork cryptosystem AD_{GGH} given by Goldreich, Goldwasser, and Halevi [3] in detail and apply our technique to construction of its multi-bit version mAD_{GGH} in this section.

3.1   The Improved Ajtai-Dwork Cryptosystem and Its Multi-bit Version

For understanding our construction intuitively, we first overview the protocol of AD_{GGH}. Let $N = n^n = 2^{n \log n}$. We define an n-dimensional hypercube C and an n-dimensional ball B_r as $C = \{\boldsymbol{x} \in \mathbb{R}^n : 0 \le x_i < N, i = 1, \ldots, n\}$ and $B_r = \{\boldsymbol{x} \in \mathbb{R}^n : \|\boldsymbol{x}\| \le n^{-r}/4\}$ for any constant $r \ge 7$, respectively. For $\boldsymbol{u} \in \mathbb{R}^n$ and an integer i we define a hyperplane H_i as $H_i = \{\boldsymbol{x} \in \mathbb{R}^n : \langle \boldsymbol{x}, \boldsymbol{u} \rangle = i\}$.

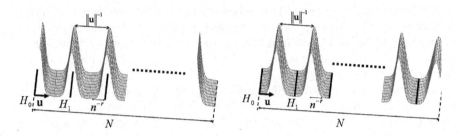

Fig. 2. ciphertexts of 0 in AD_{GGH} **Fig. 3.** ciphertexts of 1 in AD_{GGH}

Roughly speaking, AD_{GGH} encrypts 0 into a vector distributed closely around hidden $(n-1)$-dimensional parallel hyperplanes $H_0, H_1, H_2, \ldots$ for a normal vector u of H_0, and encrypts 1 into a vector distributed closely around their intermediate parallel hyperplanes $H_0 + u/(2\|u\|^2), H_1 + u/(2\|u\|^2), \ldots$. (See Figure 2 and Figure 3.) Then, the private key is the normal vector u. These distributions of ciphertexts can be obtained from its public key, which consists of vectors on the hidden hyperplanes and information i_1 for shifting a vector on the hyperplanes to another vector on the intermediate hyperplanes. If we know the normal vector, we can reduce the n-dimensional distribution to on the 1-dimensional one along the normal vector. Then, we can easily find whether a ciphertext distributed around the hidden hyperplanes or the intermediate ones.

We now describe the protocol of AD_{GGH} as follows. Our description slightly generalizes the original one by introducing a parameter r, which controls the variance of the distributions since we need to estimate a trade-off between the security and the size of plaintexts in our multi-bit version.

Preparation: All the participants agree with the security parameter n, the variance-controlling parameter r, and the precision 2^{-n} for rounding real numbers.

Key Generation: We choose u uniformly at random from the n-dimensional unit ball. Let $m = n^3$. Repeating the following procedure m times, we sample m vectors $v_1, \ldots, v_m$: (1) We choose a_i from $\{x \in C : \langle x, u \rangle \in \mathbb{Z}\}$ uniformly at random, (2) choose $b_1, \ldots, b_n$ from B_r uniformly at random, (3) and output $v_i = a_i + \sum_{j=1}^{n} b_j$ as a sample. We then take the minimum index i_0 satisfying that the width of $\mathcal{P}(v_{i_0+1}, \ldots, v_{i_0+n})$ is at least $n^{-2}N$, where width of a parallelepiped $\mathcal{P}(x_1, \ldots x_n)$ is defined as $\min_{i=1,\ldots,n} \text{Dist}(x_i, \text{span}(x_1, \ldots, x_{i-1}, x_{i+1}, \ldots, x_n))$ for a distance function $\text{Dist}(\cdot, \cdot)$ between a vector and an $(n-1)$-dimensional hyperplane.

Now let $w_j = v_{i_0+j}$ for every $j \in \{1, \ldots, n\}$, $V = (v_1, \ldots, v_m)$, and $W = (w_1, \ldots, w_n)$. We also choose an index i_1 uniformly at random from $\{i : \langle a_i, u \rangle$ is odd$\}$, where a_i is the vector appeared in the sampling procedure for v_i. Note that there are such indices i_0 and i_1 with probability $1 - o(1)$. If such indices do not exist, we perform this procedure again. To guarantee the security, $\|u\|$ should be in $[1/2, 1)$. The probability of this event is exponentially close to 1. If the condition is not satisfied, we sample the vector $\boldsymbol{u}$ again. Then, the private key is $\boldsymbol{u}$ and the public key is (V, W, i_1).

Encryption: Let S be a uniformly random subset of $\{1, 2, \ldots, m\}$. We encrypt a plaintext $\sigma \in \{0, 1\}$ to $\boldsymbol{x} = \frac{\sigma}{2}\boldsymbol{v}_{i_1} + \sum_{i \in S} \boldsymbol{v}_i \bmod \mathcal{P}(W)$.

Decryption: Let $\boldsymbol{x} \in \mathcal{P}(W)$ be a received ciphertext. We decrypt $\boldsymbol{x}$ to 0 if $\mathrm{frc}\,(\langle \boldsymbol{x}, \boldsymbol{u}\rangle) \leq 1/4$ and to 1 otherwise.

Carefully reading the results in [2,3], we obtain the following theorem on the cryptosystem $\mathrm{AD}_{\mathrm{GGH}}$.

Theorem 1 ([3]). *The cryptosystem $\mathrm{AD}_{\mathrm{GGH}}$ encrypts a 1-bit plaintext into an $n\lceil n(\log n + 1)\rceil$-bit ciphertext with no decryption errors. The security of $\mathrm{AD}_{\mathrm{GGH}}$ is based on the worst case of $O(n^{r+5})$-uSVP for $r \geq 7$. The size of the public key is $O(n^5 \log n)$ and the size of the private key is $O(n^2)$.*

As commented in [21], we can actually improve the security of $\mathrm{AD}_{\mathrm{GGH}}$ by a result in [21]. We will give the proof in the full paper.

Theorem 2. *The security of $\mathrm{AD}_{\mathrm{GGH}}$ is based on the worst case of $O(n^{r+4})$-uSVP for $r \geq 7$.*

We next describe the multi-bit version $\mathrm{mAD}_{\mathrm{GGH}}$ of $\mathrm{AD}_{\mathrm{GGH}}$. Let p be a prime such that $2 \leq p \leq n^{r-7}$, where the parameter r controls a trade-off between the size of the plaintext space and the hardness of underlying lattice problems. In $\mathrm{mAD}_{\mathrm{GGH}}$, we can encrypt a plaintext of $\log p$ bits into a ciphertext of the same size as $\mathrm{AD}_{\mathrm{GGH}}$. The strategy of our construction basically follows the argument in Section 1. Note that the parameter r is chosen to keep our version error-free.

Preparation: All the participants agree with the parameters n, r and the precision 2^{-n} similarly to $\mathrm{AD}_{\mathrm{GGH}}$, and additionally the size p of the plaintext space.

Key Generation: The key generation procedure is almost the same as that of $\mathrm{AD}_{\mathrm{GGH}}$. We choose an index i_1' uniformly at random from $\{i : \langle \boldsymbol{a}_i, \boldsymbol{u}\rangle \not\equiv 0 \bmod p\}$ instead of i_1 in the original key generation procedure. We set decryption information $k \equiv \langle \boldsymbol{a}_{i_1'}, \boldsymbol{u}\rangle \bmod p$. Note that there is such a k with probability $1 - (1/p)^m = 1 - o(1)$. Then, the private key is $(\boldsymbol{u}, k)$ and the public key is (V, W, i_1').

Encryption: Let S be a uniformly random subset of $\{0, 1\}^m$. We encrypt $\sigma \in \{0, \ldots, p-1\}$ to $\boldsymbol{x} = \frac{\sigma}{p}\boldsymbol{v}_{i_1'} + \sum_{i \in S} \boldsymbol{v}_i \bmod \mathcal{P}(W)$.

Decryption: We decrypt a received ciphertext $\boldsymbol{x} \in \mathcal{P}(W)$ to $\lfloor p\langle \boldsymbol{x}, \boldsymbol{u}\rangle\rceil k^{-1} \bmod p$, where k^{-1} is the inverse of k in $\mathbb{Z}_p$.

Before evaluating the performance of $\mathrm{mAD}_{\mathrm{GGH}}$ precisely, we give the summary of the results as follows.

Theorem 3 (security and decryption errors). *Let $r \geq 7$ be any constant and let $p(n)$ be a prime such that $2 \leq p(n) \leq n^{r-7}$. The cryptosystem $\mathrm{mAD}_{\mathrm{GGH}}$ encrypts a $\lfloor \log p(n)\rfloor$-bit plaintext into an $n\lceil n(\log n + 1)\rceil$-bit ciphertext without* *the decryption errors. The security of* mAD$_{\mathrm{GGH}}$ *is based on the worst case of* $O(n^{r+4})$*-uSVP. The size of the public key is the same as that of the original one. The size of the private key is* $\lceil \log p(n) \rceil$ *plus that of the original one.*

Theorem 4 (pseudohomomorphism). *Let* $r \geq 7$ *be any constant. Also, let* p *be a prime and let* κ *be an integer such that* $\kappa p \leq n^{r-7}$. *Let* E_{m} *be the encryption function of* mAD$_{\mathrm{GGH}}$. *For any* κ *plaintexts* $\sigma_1, \ldots, \sigma_\kappa$ $(0 \leq \sigma_i \leq p - 1)$, *we can decrypt the sum of* κ *ciphertexts* $\sum_{i=1}^{\kappa} E_{\mathrm{m}}(\sigma_i) \bmod \mathcal{P}(W)$ *into* $\sum_{i=1}^{\kappa} \sigma_i \bmod p$ *without decryption error. Moreover, if there exist two sequences of plaintexts* $(\sigma_1, \ldots, \sigma_\kappa)$ *and* $(\sigma'_1, \ldots, \sigma'_\kappa)$, *and a polynomial-time algorithm that distinguishes between* $\sum_{i=1}^{\kappa} E_{\mathrm{m}}(\sigma_i) \bmod \mathcal{P}(W)$ *and* $\sum_{i=1}^{\kappa} E_{\mathrm{m}}(\sigma'_i) \bmod \mathcal{P}(W)$ *with its public key, then there exists a polynomial-time algorithm that solves* $O(n^{r+4})$*-uSVP in the worst case with non-negligible probability.*

In what follows, we demonstrate the performance of mAD$_{\mathrm{GGH}}$ stated in the above theorems.

3.2   Decryption Errors of mAD$_{\mathrm{GGH}}$

We first evaluate the decryption error probability in mAD$_{\mathrm{GGH}}$. The following theorem can be proven by a similar argument to the analysis of [2,3]. Since we generalize this theorem for analysis of the pseudohomomorphism in mAD$_{\mathrm{GGH}}$ (Theorem 7), we here give a precise proof.

Theorem 5. *The cryptosystem* mAD$_{\mathrm{GGH}}$ *makes no decryption errors.*

Proof. Since the decryption error probability for any ciphertext can be estimated by sliding the distribution to that of the ciphertext of 0, we first estimate the decryption error probability for the ciphertext of 0.

Let $H := \{\boldsymbol{x} \in \mathbb{R}^n : \langle \boldsymbol{x}, \boldsymbol{u} \rangle \in \mathbb{Z}\}$. From the definition, $\mathrm{Dist}(\boldsymbol{v}_i, H) \leq n \cdot n^{-r}/4$ for $1 \leq i \leq m$. Thus, we can obtain $\mathrm{frc}\left(\langle \boldsymbol{v}_i, \boldsymbol{u} \rangle\right) \leq n^{1-r}/4$ and $\mathrm{frc}\left(\langle \sum_{i \in S} \boldsymbol{v}_i, \boldsymbol{u} \rangle\right) \leq n^{4-r}/4$. Next, we estimate an inner product between $\sum_{i \in S} \boldsymbol{v}_i \bmod \mathcal{P}(W)$ and $\boldsymbol{u}$. Let $\sum_{i \in S} \boldsymbol{v}_i = \boldsymbol{r} + \sum_{j=1}^{n} q_j \boldsymbol{w}_j$, where $\boldsymbol{r} \in \mathcal{P}(W)$. Since $\|\boldsymbol{w}_j\| \geq n^{-2}N$ and $p \leq n^{r-7}$, we have $|q_j| \leq n^5$ and

$$\mathrm{frc}\left(\langle \boldsymbol{r}, \boldsymbol{u} \rangle\right) \leq n \cdot n^5 \cdot \frac{1}{4} n^{1-r} + \frac{1}{4} n^{4-r} \leq \frac{5}{16} n^{7-r} \leq \frac{1}{2p}.$$

Therefore, we decrypt a ciphertext of 0 into 0 without decryption errors.

Now let $\boldsymbol{\rho}$ be a ciphertext of σ. Let $\mathbb{Z} \pm a := \{x \in \mathbb{R} : \mathrm{frc}\,(x) \leq a\}$ for $a \geq 0$ and $\mathbb{Z} + a \pm b := \{x \in \mathbb{R} : \mathrm{frc}\,(x - a) \leq b\}$ for $a, b \geq 0$. By a property of the key generation, we have $\langle \boldsymbol{v}_{i'_1}/p, \boldsymbol{u} \rangle \in \mathbb{Z} + k/p \pm n^{1-r}/4p$ and

$$\langle \boldsymbol{\rho}, \boldsymbol{u} \rangle \in \mathbb{Z} + \frac{k}{p} \sigma \pm \frac{5}{16} n^{7-r} \pm \frac{1}{4p} n^{1-r} \sigma \pm \frac{1}{4} n^{4-r} \subset \mathbb{Z} + \frac{k}{p} \sigma \pm \frac{3}{8} n^{7-r}.$$

Therefore, we obtain $\langle \boldsymbol{\rho}, \boldsymbol{u} \rangle \in \mathbb{Z} + k\sigma/p \pm 1/(2p)$ and decrypt $\boldsymbol{\rho}$ into σ without decryption errors. $\square$

3.3 Security of mAD_GGH

We next prove the security of mAD_{GGH}. Let $U_{\mathcal{P}(W)}$ be a uniform distribution on $\mathcal{P}(W)$. We denote the encryption function of AD_{GGH} by E defined as a random variable $E(\sigma, (V, W, i_1))$ for a plaintext σ and a public key (V, W, i_1). If the public key is obvious, we abbreviate $E(\sigma, (V, W, i_1))$ to $E(\sigma)$. Similarly, the encryption function E_m is defined for mAD_{GGH}.

First, we show that the indistinguishability between two certain distributions is based on the worst-case hardness of uSVP. The following lemma can be obtained by combining Theorem 2 and the results in [2] and [3] with our generalization.

Lemma 1 ([2,3]). *If there exists a polynomial-time distinguisher between* $(E(0), (V, W, i_1))$ *and* $(U_{\mathcal{P}(W)}, (V, W, i_1))$, *there exists a polynomial-time algorithm for the worst case of* $O(n^{r+4})$-uSVP *for* $r \geq 7$.

We next present the indistinguishability between the ciphertexts of 0 in mAD_{GGH} and $U_{\mathcal{P}(W)}$.

Lemma 2. *If there exists a polynomial-time algorithm* $\mathcal{D}_1$ *that distinguishes between* $(E_m(0), (V, W, i_1'))$ *and* $(U_{\mathcal{P}(W)}, (V, W, i_1'))$, *there exists a polynomial-time algorithm* $\mathcal{D}_2$ *that distinguishes between* $(E(0), (V, W, i_1))$ *and* $(U_{\mathcal{P}(W)}, (V, W, i_1))$.

Proof. We denote by $\varepsilon(n)$ the non-negligible gap of the acceptance probability of $\mathcal{D}_1$ between $E_m(0)$ and $U_{\mathcal{P}(W)}$ with its public key. We will construct the distinguisher $\mathcal{D}_2$ from the given algorithm $\mathcal{D}_1$. To run $\mathcal{D}_1$ correctly, we first find the index i_1' by estimating the gap of acceptance probability between $E_m(0)$ and $U_{\mathcal{P}(W)}$ with the public key. If we can find i_1', we output the result of $\mathcal{D}_1$ using i_1' with the public key. Otherwise, we output a uniformly random bit. For random inputs of ciphertexts and public keys, the above procedure can distinguish between them.

We now describe the details of $\mathcal{D}_2$ as follows. We denote by x and (V, W, i_1) a ciphertext and a public key of AD_{GGH} given as an input for $\mathcal{D}_2$, respectively. Also, let $p_0 = \Pr[\mathcal{D}_1(E_m(0), (V, W, j)) = 1]$ and $p_U = \Pr[\mathcal{D}_1(U_{\mathcal{P}(W)}, (V, W, j)) = 1]$, where the probability p_0 is taken over the inner random bits of the encryption procedure and p_U is taken over $U_{\mathcal{P}(W)}$.

(D1) For every $j \in \{1, \ldots, m\}$, we run $\mathcal{D}_1(E_m(0), (V, W, j))$ and $\mathcal{D}_1(U_{\mathcal{P}(W)}, (V, W, j))$ $T = n/\varepsilon^2$ times. Let $x_0(j)$ and $x_U(j)$ be the number of 1 in the outputs of $\mathcal{D}_1$ for the ciphertexts of 0 and the uniform distribution with the index j, respectively.

(D2) If there exists the index j' such that $|x_0(j') - x_U(j')|/T > \varepsilon/2$, we take j' as the component of the public key.

(D3) We output $\mathcal{D}_1(x, (V, W, j'))$ if we find j'. Otherwise, we output a uniformly random bit.

Note that we have $|p_0 - x_0(j')/T| \leq \varepsilon/4$ and $|p_U - x_U(j')/T| \leq \varepsilon/4$ with probability exponentially close to 1 by the Hoeffding bound [22]. Therefore, we succeed to choose the index j' with which $\mathcal{D}_1$ can distinguish between the target distributions with probability exponentially close to 1 if j' exists. By the above argument, $\mathcal{D}_1$ works correctly for a non-negligible fraction of all the inputs. $\quad\square$

The next lemma can be proven by the hybrid argument.

Lemma 3. *If there exist $\sigma_1, \sigma_2 \in \{0, \ldots, p-1\}$ and a polynomial-time algorithm $\mathcal{D}_3$ that distinguishes between $(E_m(\sigma_1), (V, W, i_1'))$ and $(E_m(\sigma_2), (V, W, i_1'))$, there exists a polynomial-time algorithm $\mathcal{D}_4$ that distinguishes between $(E_m(0), (V, W, i_1'))$ and $(U_{\mathcal{P}(W)}, (V, W, i_1'))$.*

Proof. By the hybrid argument, the distinguisher $\mathcal{D}_3$ can distinguish between $E_m(\sigma_1)$ and $U_{\mathcal{P}(W)}$ or between $E_m(\sigma_2)$ and $U_{\mathcal{P}(W)}$ with its public key. Without loss of generality, we can assume that $\mathcal{D}_3$ can distinguish between $E_m(\sigma_1)$ and $U_{\mathcal{P}(W)}$ with its public key. Note that we have $E_m(\sigma_1, (V, W, i_1')) = E_m(0, (V, W, i_1')) + \frac{\sigma_1}{p} v_{i_1'} \bmod \mathcal{P}(W)$ by the definition of E_m. Then, we can transform a given $\boldsymbol{x}$ from $E_m(0, (V, W, i_1'))$ to another sample $\boldsymbol{y}$ from $E_m(\sigma_1, (V, W, i_1'))$. We can therefore obtain the polynomial-time algorithm $\mathcal{D}_4$ that distinguishes between $(E_m(0), (V, W, i_1'))$ and $(U_{\mathcal{P}(W)}, (V, W, i_1'))$. $\quad\square$

By the above three lemmas, we obtain the security proof for our multi-bit version $\mathrm{mAD_{GGH}}$.

Theorem 6. *If there exist plaintexts $\sigma_1, \sigma_2 \in \{0, \ldots, p-1\}$ and a polynomial-time algorithm that distinguishes between the ciphertexts of σ_1 and σ_2 of $\mathrm{mAD_{GGH}}$ with its public key, there exists a polynomial-time algorithm for the worst-case of $O(n^{r+4})$-uSVP for $r \geq 7$.*

3.4   Pseudohomomorphism of mAD$_{GGH}$

As stated in Theorem 4, $\mathrm{mAD_{GGH}}$ has the pseudohomomorphic property. To demonstrate this property, we have to evaluate the decryption errors for sum of ciphertexts and prove its security.

Decryption Errors for Sum of Ciphertexts. First, we evaluate the decryption errors when we apply the decryption procedure to the sum of ciphertexts in $\mathrm{mAD_{GGH}}$. Recall that $\mathbb{Z} \pm a := \{x \in \mathbb{R} : \mathrm{frc}\,(x) \leq a\}$ for $a \geq 0$ and $\mathbb{Z} + a \pm b := \{x \in \mathbb{R} : \mathrm{frc}\,(x - a) \leq b\}$ for $a, b \geq 0$.

Theorem 7. *Let $r \geq 7$ be any constant. Also let p be a prime and κ be an integer such that $\kappa p \leq n^{r-7}$. For any κ plaintexts $\sigma_1, \ldots, \sigma_\kappa$ $(0 \leq \sigma_i \leq p - 1)$, we can decrypt the sum of κ ciphertexts $\sum_{i=1}^{\kappa} E_m(\sigma_i) \bmod \mathcal{P}(W)$ into $\sum_{i=1}^{\kappa} \sigma_i \bmod p$ without the decryption errors.*

Proof. We define $\boldsymbol{\rho}_1, \ldots, \boldsymbol{\rho}_\kappa$ as ciphertexts of $\sigma_1, \ldots, \sigma_\kappa$, respectively. We will show that we can decrypt $\boldsymbol{\rho} := \sum_{i=1}^{\kappa} \boldsymbol{\rho}_i \bmod \mathcal{P}(W)$ into $\sum_{i=1}^{\kappa} \sigma_i \bmod p$. From the proof of Theorem 5, we have

$$\langle \boldsymbol{\rho}_i, \boldsymbol{u} \rangle \in \mathbb{Z} + \frac{k}{p}\sigma_i \pm \frac{3}{8}n^{7-r}.$$

Hence, we obtain

$$\left\langle \sum_{i=1}^{\kappa} \boldsymbol{\rho}_i, \boldsymbol{u} \right\rangle \in \mathbb{Z} + \frac{k}{p}\sum_{i=1}^{\kappa}\sigma_i \pm \frac{3}{8}\kappa n^{7-r}.$$

Combining with the fact $\boldsymbol{\rho}_i \in \mathcal{P}(W)$ and $\kappa p \leq n^{r-7}$, we have

$$\langle \boldsymbol{\rho}, \boldsymbol{u} \rangle \in \mathbb{Z} + \frac{k}{p}\sum_{i=1}^{\kappa}\sigma_i \pm \frac{3}{8}\kappa n^{7-r} \pm \frac{1}{4}\kappa n^{2-r}$$

$$\subset \mathbb{Z} + \frac{k}{p}\sum_{i=1}^{\kappa}\sigma_i \pm \frac{1}{2}\kappa n^{7-r}$$

$$\subset \mathbb{Z} + \frac{k}{p}\sum_{i=1}^{\kappa}\sigma_i \pm \frac{1}{2p}.$$

Therefore, we correctly decrypt $\boldsymbol{\rho}$ into $\sum_{i=1}^{\kappa} \sigma_i \bmod p$.   □

Security for Sum of Ciphertexts. We can also give the security proof for the sum of ciphertexts in mAD$_{\mathrm{GGH}}$. The security proof obeys so general framework that we can apply the same argument to the security of sum of ciphertexts in the other multi-bit versions mR04, mR05, and mA05′. For convenience of the other multi-bit versions, we here present an abstract security proof for sum of ciphertexts. We denote the encryption function of our multi-bit cryptosystems by E_{m}, also regarded as a random variable $E_{\mathrm{m}}(\sigma, pk)$ for a plaintext σ and a public key pk. If the public key is obvious, we abbreviate $E_{\mathrm{m}}(\sigma, pk)$ to $E_{\mathrm{m}}(\sigma)$. Let $\mathcal{C}$ be the ciphertext space and $U_{\mathcal{C}}$ be the uniform distribution on $\mathcal{C}$.

We first show that it is hard to distinguish between the sum of ciphertexts and the uniform distribution if it is hard to distinguish between κ samples from $E_{\mathrm{m}}(0)$ and those from $U_{\mathcal{C}}$.

Lemma 4. *If there exist two sequences of plaintexts $(\sigma_1, \ldots, \sigma_\kappa)$ and $(\sigma_1', \ldots, \sigma_\kappa')$ and a polynomial-time algorithm $\mathcal{D}_1$ that distinguishes between $(\sum_{i=1}^{\kappa} E_{\mathrm{m}}(\sigma_i), pk)$ and $(\sum_{i=1}^{\kappa} E_{\mathrm{m}}(\sigma_i'), pk)$, then there exists a polynomial-time algorithm $\mathcal{D}_2$ that distinguishes between κ ciphertexts and its public key $(E_{\mathrm{m}}(0, pk), \ldots, E_{\mathrm{m}}(0, pk), pk)$ and uniformly random κ ciphertexts and the public key $(U_{\mathcal{C}}, \ldots, U_{\mathcal{C}}, pk)$.*

Proof. By the hybrid argument, the distinguisher $\mathcal{D}_1$ can distinguish between $\sum_{i=1}^{\kappa} E_{\mathrm{m}}(\sigma_i)$ and $U_{\mathcal{C}}$ or between $\sum_{i=1}^{\kappa} E_{\mathrm{m}}(\sigma_i')$ and $U_{\mathcal{C}}$ with its public key. Without loss of generality, we can assume that $\mathcal{D}_1$ can distinguish between $(\sum_{i=1}^{\kappa} E_m(\sigma_i), pk)$ and (U_C, pk). By $(\sigma_1, \ldots, \sigma_\kappa)$, we can transform $(E_m(\sigma_1), \ldots, E_m(\sigma_\kappa), pk)$ into $(\sum_{i=1}^{\kappa} E_m(\sigma_i), pk)$. This shows the polynomial-time distinguisher $\mathcal{D}_2$. □

As already stated in Section 1 (and Lemma 2 in the case of AD_{GGH}), the original security proofs of AD_{GGH}, R04, R05 and A05 show that we have efficient algorithms for certain lattice problems if there is an efficient distinguisher between $E_m(0)$ and U_C with its public key. By the similar argument to that in original proofs, we also have such algorithms from efficient distinguisher $\mathcal{D}_2$ between $(E_m(0), \ldots, E_m(0), pk)$ and $(U_C, \ldots, U_C, pk)$. Thus, we obtain from $\mathcal{D}_2$ in Lemma 4 a probabilistic polynomial-time algorithm $\mathcal{A}$ that solve the worst case of $O(n^{r+4})$-uSVP in the case of mAD_{GGH}.

By combining the above discussion with Lemma 4, we guarantee the security of the sum of ciphertexts in mAD_{GGH}.

Theorem 8. *If there exist two sequences of plaintext $(\sigma_1, \ldots, \sigma_\kappa)$ and $(\sigma'_1, \ldots, \sigma'_\kappa)$ and a polynomial-time algorithm $\mathcal{D}_1$ that distinguishes between $(\sum_{i=1}^{\kappa} E_m(\sigma_i), pk)$ and $(\sum_{i=1}^{\kappa} E_m(\sigma'_i), pk)$, then there exists a probabilistic polynomial-time algorithm $\mathcal{A}$ that solves the worst case of $O(n^{r+4})$-uSVP in the case of mAD_{GGH}.*

4   Concluding Remarks

We have developed a universal technique for constructing multi-bit versions of lattice-based cryptosystems using periodic Gaussian distributions and revealed their pseudohomomorphism. In particular, we have showed the details of the multi-bit version of the improved Ajtai-Dwork cryptosystem in Section 3.

Although our technique achieved only logarithmic improvements on the length of plaintexts, we also obtained precise evaluation of the trade-offs between decryption errors and the hardness of underlying lattice problems in the single-bit cryptosystems. We believe that our evaluation is useful for further improvements of such single-bit cryptosystems.

Another direction of research on lattice-based cryptosystems is to find interesting cryptographic applications by their algebraic properties such as the pseudohomomorphism. Number-theoretic cryptosystems can provide a number of applications due to their algebraic structures, whereas lattice-based ones have few applications currently. For demonstration of the cryptographic advantages of lattice problems, it is important to develop the algebraic properties and their applications such as [19].

References

1. Ajtai, M.: Generating hard instances of lattice problems. Electronic Colloquium on Computational Complexity (ECCC) **3**(007) (1996).
2. Ajtai, M., Dwork, C.: A public-key cryptosystem with worst-case/average-case equivalence. In STOC '97 (1997) 284–293. See also ECCC TR96-065.

3. Goldreich, O., Goldwasser, S., Halevi, S.: Eliminating decryption errors in the Ajtai-Dwork cryptosystem. In CRYPTO '97 (1997) 105–111. See also ECCC TR097-018.
4. Regev, O.: New lattice based cryptographic constructions. In STOC 2003 (2003) 407–416.
5. Ajtai, M.: Representing hard lattices with $O(n \log n)$ bits. In STOC 2005 (2005) 94–103.
6. Regev, O.: On lattices, learning with errors, random linear codes, and cryptography. In STOC 2005 (2005) 84–93.
7. Goldreich, O., Goldwasser, S., Halevi, S.: Public-key cryptosystems from lattice reduction problems. In CRYPTO '97 (1997) 112–131.
8. Hoffstein, J., Pipher, J., Silverman, J.H.: NTRU: A ring-based public key cryptosystem. In ANTS-III (1998) 267–288.
9. Micciancio, D.: Improving lattice based cryptosystems using the Hermite normal form. In CaLC 2001 (2001) 126–145.
10. Nguyen, P.Q.: Analysis and improvements of NTRU encryption paddings. In CRYPTO 2002 (2002) 210–225.
11. Howgrave-Graham, N., Nguyen, P.Q., Pointcheval, D., Proos, J., Silverman, J.H., Singer, A., Whyte, W.: The impact of decryption failures on the security of NTRU encryption. In CRYPTO 2003 (2003) 226–246.
12. Nguyen, P.Q.: Cryptanalysis of the Goldreich-Goldwasser-Halevi cryptosystem from Crypto '97. In CRYPTO '99 (1999) 288–304.
13. Gentry, C.: Key recovery and message attacks on NTRU-composite. In EUROCRYPT 2001 (2001) 182–194.
14. Micciancio, D., Regev, O.: Worst-case to average-case reductions based on Gaussian measures. In FOCS 2004 (2004) 372–181.
15. Micciancio, D.: Generalized compact knapsacks, cyclic lattices, and efficient one-way functions from worst-case complexity assumptions. Electronic Colloquium on Computational Complexity (ECCC) 11(095) (2004).
16. Peikert, C., Rosen, A.: Efficient collision-resistant hashing from worst-case assumptions on cyclic lattices. In TCC 2006 (2006) 145–166.
17. Nguyen, P.Q., Stern, J.: Cryptanalysis of the Ajtai-Dwork cryptosystem. In CRYPTO '98 (1998) 223–242.
18. Rappe, D.: Homomorphic Cryptosystems and Their Applications. PhD thesis, University of Dortmund (2004). Also available at http://eprint.iacr.org/2006/001.
19. Goldwasser, S., Kharchenko, D.: Proof of plaintext knowledge for the Ajtai-Dwork cryptosystem. In TCC 2005 (2005) 529–555.
20. Micciancio, D., Goldwasser, S.: Complexity of Lattice Problems: a cryptographic perspective. Kluwer Academic Publishers, Boston, Massachusetts (2002).
21. Cai, J.Y.: A new transference theorem in the geometry of numbers and new bounds for Ajtai's connection factor. Discrete Applied Mathematics 126(1) (2003) 9–31.
22. Hoeffding, W.: Probability inequalities for sums of bounded random variables. Journal of the American Statistical Association 58(301) (1963) 13–30.

Practical and Secure Solutions
for Integer Comparison

Juan Garay[1], Berry Schoenmakers[2], and José Villegas[2]

[1] Bell Labs – Alcatel-Lucent, 600 Mountain Ave., Murray Hill, NJ 07974
garay@research.bell-labs.com
[2] Dept. of Mathematics and Computing Science, TU Eindhoven,
P.O. Box 513, 5600 MB Eindhoven, The Netherlands
berry@win.tue.nl, j.a.villegas@tue.nl

Abstract. Yao's classical *millionaires' problem* is about securely determining whether $x > y$, given two input values x, y, which are held as private inputs by two parties, respectively. The output $x > y$ becomes known to both parties.

In this paper, we consider a variant of Yao's problem in which the inputs x, y as well as the output bit $x > y$ are encrypted. Referring to the framework of secure n-party computation based on threshold homomorphic cryptosystems as put forth by Cramer, Damgård, and Nielsen at Eurocrypt 2001, we develop solutions for integer comparison, which take as input two lists of encrypted bits representing x and y, respectively, and produce an encrypted bit indicating whether $x > y$ as output. Secure integer comparison is an important building block for applications such as secure auctions.

In this paper, our focus is on the two-party case, although most of our results extend to the multi-party case. We propose new logarithmic-round and constant-round protocols for this setting, which achieve simultaneously very low communication and computational complexities. We analyze the protocols in detail and show that our solutions compare favorably to other known solutions.

Keywords: Millionaires' problem; secure multi-party computation; homomorphic encryption.

1 Introduction

The *millionaires' problem,* introduced by Yao [Yao82], involves two parties who want to compare their riches: they wish to know who is richer but do not want to disclose any other information about their riches to each other. More formally, the problem is to find a two-party protocol for the secure evaluation of the function $f(x, y) = [x > y]$ where the bracket notation $[B]$, for a condition B, is defined by $[B] = 1$ if B holds and $[B] = 0$ otherwise (this is called Iverson's convention; see [Knu97]).

T. Okamoto and X. Wang (Eds.): PKC 2007, LNCS 4450, pp. 330–342, 2007.

Rather than requiring that the inputs x and y are actually known as private inputs to the parties, we will work in the more general setting where the inputs are not necessarily known to the parties running the protocol. Instead, the inputs to the protocol may be given as encrypted values only, and the output will also be made available in encrypted form. Note that the inputs to our protocols will actually be encryptions of the individual bits, representing the integers to be compared. For these encryptions we will use a threshold homomorphic cryptosystem, as in the framework of secure n-party computation based on threshold homomorphic cryptosystems put forth by Cramer, Damgård, and Nielsen [CDN01]. In line with this, we consider the case of an *active*, static adversary[1], i.e., we consider the malicious case.

Requiring (i) that the inputs are given in encrypted form (without anyone knowing these inputs) and (ii) that the output bit $[x > y]$ also be encrypted (without anyone learning its value) sets our problem setting apart from the setting of Yao's paper [Yao82] and much of the follow-up literature. Indeed, consider computing $[x = y]$ in the case of encrypted inputs but *public* output, where the following well-known solution works. Let $[\![M]\!]$ denote a (probabilistic) encryption of a message M in a threshold homomorphic cryptosystem. Given encryptions $[\![x]\!]$ and $[\![y]\!]$, the encryption $[\![x - y]\!]$ is publicly computed. Furthermore, the parties jointly compute an encryption $[\![r]\!]$ for a (jointly) random r. Using one invocation of a secure multiplication protocol, the parties then produce encryption $[\![(x - y)r]\!]$, which is jointly decrypted. If the result is 0, then $x = y$; otherwise, $x \neq y$, and the result is a random number. In contrast, when the output is required in encrypted form, such simple solutions are not known and typically protocols (including ours) work over the encrypted values of the binary representation of the inputs x and y.

Furthermore, unlike many publications on the millionaires' problem, we consider the malicious case rather than the semi-honest (or honest-but-curious) case.

1.1 Our Contributions

The contributions of this paper are as follows:

- A logarithmic-round protocol for secure integer comparison, which is based on an elegant Boolean circuit for integer comparison of depth $\log_2 m$ for m-bit integers. In addition, the size of the circuit is only $3m$ (counting the number of secure multiplication gates). The circuit can be readily used as a drop-in replacement for the $O(1)$-depth circuit for integer comparison in [DFK$^+$06], which is only of theoretical interest as it uses 19 rounds and $22m$ secure multiplications. Note that the depth of our log-depth circuit exceeds their constant-depth circuit for integer comparison only if the inputs consist of integers of *bit length* $m = 2^{20}$ *or longer*.)

---

[1] In principle, the case of adaptive adversaries could be handled at the expense of additional tools (e.g., [DN00, DN03, GMY03]); in this paper we focus on the static (and stand-alone) case.

- A constant-round protocol for secure integer comparison for which the number of rounds is a small constant and the number of secure multiplications is a small multiple of m. Our constant-round solution is restricted to the case of two parties (or, rather, any constant number of parties). Our protocol builds on a protocol by Blake and Kolesnikov [BK04] for integer comparison for a different setting. In particular, we provide an efficient technique for securely returning the output bit in an encrypted form.

We like to stress that application of our log-depth circuit is not restricted to the framework of [CDN01]: the circuit can be used in any framework for secure n-party computation that assumes that the function to be computed is given as a circuit. In particular, the log-depth circuit can be used for secure computation based on verifiable secret sharing, thus yielding solutions which are unconditionally secure—rather than computationally secure, as described in this paper.

Furthermore, the proof of security of our constant-round protocol is interesting in its own right. Theorem 1, as explained below, essentially captures the security of the protocol in a modular way. Here, we have adopted the approach suggested recently in [ST06], and we show how the required simulator can be built even though our protocol is of a much different nature than the ones in [ST06].

1.2   Related Work

There appear to be only a few publications in the literature which consider encrypted inputs *and* outputs for integer comparison. Above we have already mentioned the work of Damgård *et al.* [DFK+06]. The main difference is that they work in an unconditional setting, reflected by the use of sharings for an underlying linear secret sharing scheme, while we work in the *cryptographic* model where we use encryptions for an underlying threshold homomorphic cryptosystem.

Together with a secure multiplication protocol for a homomorphic threshold ElGamal scheme, Schoenmakers and Tuyls [ST04] also present a solution for secure integer comparison for encrypted inputs and outputs. Their solution, however, requires a linear ($O(m)$) number of rounds and secure multiplication gates. With more relaxed requirements than ours, Brandt [Bra06] presents a solution where the inputs are encrypted but the output is in the clear for both participants, and furthermore, it is not 0 or 1 but instead 0 or 'random,' which limits its applicability.

A different approach to solve the integer comparison problem is when one of the parties acts as a server. In this setting, say, Alice knows the private keys to open encryptions and Bob works over his input bits and Alice's encrypted input bits to produce some information that allows Alice to know the output of the function being evaluated. Examples of these approaches to integer comparison are presented in [DiC00, Fis01, BK04, LT05]. In contrast to our solutions, these solutions do not provide encrypted output and the actual encrypted inputs are known to the parties running the protocols.

1.3   Organization of the Paper

The rest of the paper is organized as follows. In Section 2 we introduce the main building blocks used by our protocols and we give some background on threshold homomorphic cryptosystems. In Section 3 we present our two new protocols for integer comparison, together with their proof of security (specifically, of the second protocol, as the proof of the first protocol follows directly from the security guarantees provided by the [CDN01] setting). We conclude in Section 4 with a brief performance analysis and comparison to existing results.

2   Preliminaries

Our results apply to any threshold homomorphic cryptosystem, such as those based on ElGamal or Paillier. It is assumed that a secure multiplication protocol is available, as in [CDN01, ST04]. Since we only need secure multiplication of binary values, we use the *conditional gate* of [ST04], which allows for an efficient implementation based on threshold homomorphic ElGamal—which in turn allows for the use of elliptic curves, hence yielding compact and efficient implementations.

We write $[\![x]\!]$ for a (probabilistic) encryption of the value x, using the public key of the underlying threshold homomorphic ElGamal cryptosystem. Further, let $\mathbb{Z}_q$ denote the message space, for a large prime q (of, say, size 160 bits). The cyclic group G used for ElGamal is also of order q, and we assume that elements of G are represented using $|q|$ bits only (which is the case for elliptic curves). Thus, an ElGamal encryption consisting of two group elements is of size $2|q|$.

In order to withstand active attacks, we use Σ-protocols [CDS94], a standard type of zero-knowledge proofs/arguments. Assuming the random oracle model, all proofs can be converted into non-interactive ones and can be simulated easily.

As mentioned above, we make use of *secure multiplication gates* which on input $[\![x]\!]$ and $[\![y]\!]$ allows two or more parties (who share the private key of the underlying threshold homomorphic cryptosystem) to jointly compute an encryption $[\![xy]\!]$. Secure multiplication gates can be implemented in a constant number of rounds [CDN01], using the Paillier cryptosystem. Using a number of rounds linear in the number of parties (which is constant in case of two-party computation), the *conditional gate* [ST04] can be used instead, in case one of the multiplicands is from a two-valued domain (e.g., if $x \in \{0, 1\}$).

Furthermore, in case one of inputs, say, x is private to one of the parties, a simplified multiplication protocol can be used with no interaction between the parties. The protocol consists in letting the party knowing the private value x broadcast a re-encryption of $[\![xy]\!] = [\![y]\!]^x$ using the homomorphic properties of the scheme, and generate a Σ-proof showing that $[\![xy]\!]$ was correctly computed with respect to $[\![x]\!]$ and $[\![y]\!]$. Following [ST04], we will refer to this protocol as the *private-multiplier* gate.

For the performance comparisons presented at the end of this paper, we will assume a setup using a (2,2)-threshold homomorphic ElGamal cryptosystem. We note that in this case a conditional gate requires about 50 exponentiations and $34|q|$ bits of communication, per invocation. Similarly, a private-multiplier gate requires about 10 exponentiations and $6|q|$ bits of communication, per invocation. In the same setting, a threshold decryption requires 6 exponentiations and $6|q|$ bits of communication.

A final tool that we will use are *verifiable mixes* [SK95], a tool for verifiably mixing lists of ciphertexts. More formally, a verifiable mix takes as input a list of encryptions $[\![x_1]\!], \ldots, [\![x_m]\!]$, and produces another list of encryptions $[\![x'_1]\!], \ldots, [\![x'_m]\!]$ as output such that $[\![x'_{\pi(1)}]\!] = [\![x_1]\!] * [\![0]\!], \ldots, [\![x'_{\pi(m)}]\!] = [\![x_m]\!] * [\![0]\!]$ for some random permutation π of $\{1, \ldots, m\}$. Here, each occurrence of $[\![0]\!]$ denotes a probabilistic encryption of 0.

A verifiable mix also outputs a non-interactive zero-knowledge proof (for which we assume the random-oracle model throughout). For concreteness, we assume Groth's efficient proof [Gro03], which for our setting requires about $14m$ exponentiations and is of size $6m|q|$ bits.

We are now ready to describe our protocols for integer comparison.

3 New Solutions to the Integer Comparison Problem

In this section we present two new protocols for integer comparison following different approaches. In both cases, the inputs x and y are given as sequences of encrypted bits, $[\![x_{m-1}]\!], \ldots, [\![x_0]\!]$ and $[\![y_{m-1}]\!], \ldots, [\![y_0]\!]$, with $x = \sum_{i=0}^{m-1} x_i 2^i$, $y = \sum_{i=0}^{m-1} y_i 2^i$. The output is $[\![[x > y]]\!]$. Hence, both inputs and output are available in encrypted form only.

As a starting point and for later comparison, we first the linear-depth circuit of [ST04] for computing $x > y$, using simple arithmetic gates only (addition, subtraction, conditional gates). The circuit (or, oblivious program) is fully described by the following recurrence:

$$t_0 = 0, \qquad t_{i+1} = (1 - (x_i - y_i)^2)t_i + x_i(1 - y_i),$$

where t_m is the output bit (hence $t_m = [x > y]$). Rather than starting from the most significant bit, this circuit computes $[x > y]$ starting from the least significant bit. Although somewhat counterintuitive, the advantage of this approach is that the circuit contains $2m - 1$ conditional gates only (compared to about $3m$ conditional gates when starting from the most significant bit, see [ST04]).

A disadvantage is that the depth of the circuit is m, hence inducing a critical path of m sequential secure multiplications (the terms $[\![x_1 y_1]\!], \ldots, [\![x_m y_m]\!]$ can be computed in parallel, but the computation of $t_1, \ldots, t_m$ must be done sequential). The computational complexity and communication complexity of a protocol for integer comparison based on this circuit is thus determined by the work required for the conditional gates. For later comparison, in the two-party case, we have about $100m$ exponentiations and $68m|q|$ bits of communication—and a linear number of rounds.

3.1   Logarithmic Round Complexity with Low Computational Complexity

The result in this section shows how to reduce the depth of the circuit to $O(\log m)$ without increasing its size beyond $O(m)$. The idea relies on the following simple but crucial property of integer comparison. Write $x = X_1 X_0$ and $y = Y_1 Y_0$ as bit strings, where $0 \leq |X_1| = |Y_1| \leq m$ and $0 \leq |X_0| = |Y_0| \leq m$. Then,

$$[x > y] = \begin{cases} [X_1 > Y_1], & X_1 \neq Y_1; \\ [X_0 > Y_0], & X_1 = Y_1, \end{cases}$$

which may be "arithmetized" as

$$[x > y] = [X_1 > Y_1] + [X_1 = Y_1][X_0 > Y_0].$$

This property suggests a protocol that would first split the bit strings x and y in about equally long parts, compare these parts recursively, and then combine these to produce the final output. To evaluate the expression for $[x > y]$ using simple arithmetic gates, we introduce the following auxiliary function:

$$z(x, y) = [x = y] = 1 - (x - y)^2$$

Let $t_{i,j}$ stand for the value of $>$ when applied to the substrings $x_{i+j-1}, \ldots,$ x_{i+1}, x_i and $y_{i+j-1}, \ldots, y_{i+1}, y_i$. Expressed explicitly in terms of the bits of x and y, a full solution for $[x > y]$ is obtained by evaluating $t_{0,m}$ from (using $l = \lfloor j/2 \rfloor)^2$:

$$t_{i,j} = \begin{cases} x_i - x_i y_i, & j = 1; \\ t_{i+l,j-l} + z_{i+l,j-l} t_{i,l}, & j > 1. \end{cases}$$

$$z_{i,j} = \begin{cases} 1 - x_i + 2 x_i y_i - y_i, & j = 1; \\ z_{i+l,j-l} z_{i,l}, & j > 1. \end{cases}$$

Correctness of the computation should be   immediate, and its security follows from the security guarantees provided by the framework we are considering [CDN01], assuming secure arithmetic gates.

Regarding overhead, the number of conditional gates required for $z_{i,j}$ is $2j - 1$. The number of conditional gates for $t_{i,j}$ is $j - 1$, not counting the conditional gates for z. Thus, the total number of conditional gates for $t_{0,m}$ is bounded above by $3m - 2$. About $\log_2 m$ conditional gates can be saved by observing that some z-values are not needed for the evaluation of t.

The computational and communication complexities are dominated by the number of conditional gates. In the worst case, $3m - 2$ conditional gates are required, resulting in about $150m$ exponentiations and $102m|q|$ broadcast bits.

---

[2] Any value l, $0 < l < j$, actually works, but only $l \approx j/2$ gives logarithmic depth. The msb-to-lsb and lsb-to-msb circuits in [ST04] are special cases, obtained respectively by setting $l = 1$ and $l = j - 1$.

The depth of the circuit is exactly $\lceil \log_2 m \rceil$, hence $O(\log m)$ with hidden constant equal to 1 for the base-2 logarithm.

As a further remark we note that this log-depth circuit allows for the computation of $\mathrm{sgn}(x - y)$ at virtually no extra cost. Here, $\mathrm{sgn}(z)$ is the signum function, which is equal to the sign of z (which is equal to -1 if $z < 0$, 0 if $z = 0$, and 1 if $z > 0$). This follows form the fact that the circuit also computes $[x = y]$, next to $[x > y]$, hence one obtains $\mathrm{sgn}(x - y) = 2[x > y] - 1 + [x = y]$ as well.

3.2   Constant Round Complexity with Low Computational Complexity

In this section we seek to reduce the round complexity to $O(1)$, adopting an approach quite different from the one above. We consider the problem of computing $[[x > y]]$ in the two-party case, and we wish to achieve a low, constant-round complexity while keeping the size of the circuit small as well.

First, we note that the $O(1)$-depth and $O(m)$-size circuit for integer comparison of [DFK+06] is only of theoretical interest to us: the depth of the circuit is actually 19, and its size is $22m$ (only counting secure multiplication gates). For a result that possibly competes with our logarithmic solution we take the protocol for *conditional oblivious transfer* of Blake and Kolesnikov [BK04] (where the condition is also an integer comparison) as a starting point. The main idea in that protocol is to calculate the first position where the bits of x and y differ, starting from the most-significant bit. Let i^* be that position; then $x_{i^*} - y_{i^*} \in \{-1, 1\}$ indicates whether $x > y$ or not. Jumping ahead a little, the position i^* will be determined as the unique index satisfying $\gamma_{i^*} = 1$ (which is guaranteed to exist if we assume $x \neq y$; see below). Of course, the value of i^* must remain hidden, which is achieved by the parties randomly permuting (i.e., mixing) the relevant sequences.

The protocol is described in detail below. As said above, our starting point is the protocol in [BK04] for the passive adversary setting. New ingredients include the fact that we allow for encrypted inputs $[x]$ and $[y]$, rather than private inputs x and y. Accordingly, we use a (2,2)-threshold homomorphic cryptosystem instead of just a homomorphic cryptosystem, and we use secure multiplication (conditional gates). Furthermore, we use a specific kind of blinding at the end of the protocol in order to extract the outcome of the integer comparison in encrypted form. Finally, as an important difference, we can actually use other homomorphic cryptosystems, such as ElGamal, whereas [BK04] makes essential use of Paillier.

Constant-round protocol. The protocol consists of the following steps:

1. Using m conditional gates, parties A and B jointly compute $[f_i] = [[x_i \neq y_i]]$. Then they publicly compute the γ-sequence: $[\gamma_m] = [0]$; $[\gamma_i] = [2\gamma_{i+1} + f_i]$, for $i = m - 1, \ldots, 0$.
2. For $i = m - 1, \ldots, 0$, party A broadcasts $[r_i^A]$ for random $r_i^A \in_R \mathbb{Z}_q$ and produces sequence $[u_i^A] = [r_i^A(\gamma_i - 1)]$ using a private-multiplier gate.

3. Party B does the same with $[\![r_i^B]\!]$ producing sequence $[\![u_i^B]\!] = [\![r_i^B(\gamma_i - 1)]\!]$, where $r_i^B \in_R \mathbb{Z}_q$. Now they publicly produce sequence $[\![u_i]\!] = [\![u_i^A]\!][\![u_i^B]\!]$ $[\![x_i - y_i]\!] = [\![(r_i^A + r_i^B)(\gamma_i - 1) + (x_i - y_i)]\!]$.

4. Party A verifiably mixes sequence $[\![u_i]\!]$ producing sequence $[\![u_i']\!]$.

5. Party B verifiably mixes sequence $[\![u_i']\!]$ producing sequence $[\![v_i]\!]$.

   Now, parties A and B take turns to multiply this last sequence by a randomly selected number in $\{-1, 1\}$:

6. Party A broadcasts $[\![s_A]\!]$, $s_A \in_R \{-1, 1\}$, and uses a private-multiplier gate to produce sequence $[\![v_i']\!] = [\![s_A v_i]\!]$. A proof that $[\![s_A]\!]$ is an encryption of either -1 or 1 is also given.

7. Party B does the same, broadcasting $[\![s_B]\!]$, $s_B \in_R \{-1, 1\}$, and producing sequence $[\![w_i]\!] = [\![s_B v_i']\!]$ along with the required proofs.

8. Finally, parties A and B proceed to decrypt the sequence $[\![w_i]\!]$ until they find the unique index i^* satisfying $w_{i^*} \in \{-1, 1\}$. The output is defined as $[\![(v_{i^*} + 1)/2]\!]$.

The value v_{i^*} is either -1 or 1, hence $(v_{i^*} + 1)/2$ is either 0 or 1. This linear transformation can be done for free because of homomorphic properties.

The above protocol assumes that $x \neq y$, in order that index i^* is well defined. If $x = y$, then no entry in the w-sequence will be equal to -1 or 1. One can put "sentinels" to resolve possible equality, by setting $f_{-1} = 1$ and $u_{-1} = (r_{-1}^A + r_{-1}^B)(\gamma - 1) + 1$. The rest of the protocol is adapted accordingly.

In case the output need not be encrypted, steps 6 and 7 are omitted, and the participants directly open the sequence v to find the position i^* where v_{i^*} is in $\{-1, 1\}$, where -1 means that x is less than or equal to y, and 1 means x is greater than y.

For the complexities, the number of rounds for the protocol is small: at most 9 rounds (two rounds for the conditional gates in step 1, and one round for each of the subsequent steps). For the number of exponentiations, we have $50m$ for the conditional gates (step 1), $40m$ for the multiplication gates (steps 2, 3, 6, and 7), $28m$ for the verifiable mixes, and $3m$ for the decryption ($m/2$ expected decryptions), which amounts to $124m$ exponentiations in total. Similarly, $77m|q|$ is the number of bits of communication. We have omitted further optimizations for clarity of exposition.

The protocol easily extends to the multiparty case, but since the mixing is done sequentially, constant round complexity is not achieved (note that secure multiplication gates can be constant-round even in the multi-party case if Paillier encryption is used, as in [CDN01]).

Proof of security. For the proof of security, we want to be able to simulate this protocol assuming that one of the participants is corrupted. The idea is to give the simulator the inputs $[\![x_i]\!]$ and $[\![y_i]\!]$ in such a way that a consistent view of the protocol can be constructed without making use of the private information of the honest participant.

We first review the simulation requirements for the building blocks. In order to simulate a conditional gate, encryptions $[\![x]\!]$ and $[\![y]\!]$ are required, as well as one encryption of $[\![xy]\!]$ with the requirement that $x \in \{-1, 1\}$ (or, any other two-value domain) and the contents of the encryptions are consistent. The actual values x, y and xy need not be known. The same holds for the private multiplier gate, where in this case the proof of knowledge of, say, x is simulated. For a threshold decryption, we need to provide both $[\![x]\!]$ and x to the corresponding simulator.

We now turn to the overall simulation strategy. We note that one problem already arises at the first step of the protocol: in order to simulate the conditional gate invocations in Step 1, the simulator has to produce $[\![x_i y_i]\!]$ only given $[\![x_i]\!]$ and $[\![y_i]\!]$, which is impossible! We circumvent such problems by adopting the approach recently introduced in [ST06], in which it is explained that simulation for input/output pairs of a special form (see Theorem 1 below) suffice to ensure integration with the framework of [CDN01]. This is a consequence of the fact that the security proof in [CDN01] centers around the construction of a so-called YAD^b *distribution*, which is defined as a function of an encrypted bit $[\![b]\!]$.

The structure of the security proof [CDN01] follows an ideal-model/real-model approach. The YAD^0 distribution is identical to the distribution of the ideal case, whereas the YAD^1 distribution is statistically indistinguishable from the distribution in the real case. Therefore, if an adversary can distinguish between the ideal/real cases, it implies that the adversary can distinguish the YAD^0 distribution from the YAD^1 distribution. But as the choice between these two distributions is determined by the value of the encrypted bit b, it follows that the distinguisher for the ideal/real cases is a distinguisher for the underlying encryption scheme. And this is done in tight way, i.e., without loss in the success probability for the distinguisher. (See [CDN01, ST06] for more details.)

Thus, it is sufficient to show a simulation for inputs of a special form, namely, $[\![\tilde{x}]\!] = [\![(1 - b)x^{(0)} + bx^{(1)}]\!]$, where $x^{(0)}$ and $x^{(1)}$ are given in the clear to the simulator, but b is only given in encrypted form $[\![b]\!]$. The values $x^{(0)}$ and $x^{(1)}$ correspond to the values arising in the YAD^0 and YAD^1 cases, respectively.

Theorem 1. *Given input values $x_i^{(0)}$, $y_i^{(0)}$, $x_i^{(1)}$ and $y_i^{(1)}$ and an encryption $[\![b]\!]$ with $b \in \{0, 1\}$ the above protocol can be simulated statistically indistinguishably for inputs $[\![\tilde{x}_i]\!] = [\![(1 - b)x_i^{(0)} + bx_i^{(1)}]\!]$ and $[\![\tilde{y}_i]\!] = [\![(1 - b)y_i^{(0)} + by_i^{(1)}]\!]$.*

Proof. Let $x_i^{(0)}$, $y_i^{(0)}$, $x_i^{(1)}$ and $y_i^{(1)}$ and encryption $[\![b]\!]$ with $b \in \{0, 1\}$ be given. Assuming that party A is corrupted, the simulation works as follows:

1. For Step 1, we rely on the simulator for the conditional gates, which we need to provide with the inputs $[\![\tilde{x}_i]\!]$ and $[\![\tilde{y}_i]\!]$ and the corresponding output $[\![\tilde{f}_i]\!] = [\![\tilde{x}_i \tilde{y}_i]\!]$. The latter values are computed as $[\![(1 - b)x_i^{(0)} y_i^{(0)} + bx_i^{(1)} y_i^{(1)}]\!]$, using $[\![b]\!]$ and the homomorphic properties of the cryptosystem.

   Similarly, the simulator also computes $[\![\tilde{\gamma}_i]\!] = [\![(1 - b)\gamma_i^{(0)} + b\gamma_i^{(1)}]\!]$. Let i_0 and i_1 denote the indices such that $\gamma_{i_0}^{(0)} = \gamma_{i_1}^{(1)} = 1$ as these values are known to the simulator.

2. Next, we let party A do her work. She will broadcast $[\![\tilde{r}_i^A]\!]$ and $[\![\tilde{u}_i^A]\!]$, for all i. The values $\tilde{r}_i^A$ can be extracted by rewinding the proof of knowledge of the private-multiplier invocation.

3. The idea of this step is to generate values $r_i^{B(j)}$ such that the simulator may put equal values (up to sign) in the u-sequences, which will later decrypt to the same value independently of b. For this the simulator does the following. First, he selects $s_B^{(0)} \in_R \{-1, 1\}$. The value of $s_B^{(1)}$ depends on the result of the comparison of $x^{(0)}$ against $y^{(0)}$, and $x^{(1)}$ against $y^{(1)}$. If both comparisons have the same result, then $s_B^{(1)} = s_B^{(0)}$, otherwise $s_B^{(1)} = -s_B^{(0)}$.

Now the simulator selects $r_i^{B(0)}, r_i^{B(1)}$ in such a way that $u_i^{(0)}$ and $u_i^{(1)}$ satisfy the following:

(a) $u_i^{(0)} s_B^{(0)} = u_i^{(1)} s_B^{(1)}$, for $i \notin \{i_0, i_1\}$;

(b) $u_{i_0}^{(1)} s_B^{(1)} = u_{i_1}^{(0)} s_B^{(0)}$;

(c) $u_{i_0}^{(0)} s_B^{(0)} = u_{i_1}^{(1)} s_B^{(1)}$.

First, we note that, for $j = 0, 1$:

$$u_i^{(j)} = (\tilde{r}_i^A + r_i^{B(j)})(\gamma_i^{(j)} - 1) + (x_i^{(j)} - y_i^{(j)}).$$

For case (a) we essentially need that $s_B^{(0)} s_B^{(1)} u_i^{(0)} = u_i^{(1)}$, which means that

$$s_B^{(0)} s_B^{(1)} ((\tilde{r}_i^A + r_i^{B(0)})(\gamma_i^{(0)} - 1) + (x_i^{(0)} - y_i^{(0)})) = (\tilde{r}_i^A + r_i^{B(1)})(\gamma_i^{(1)} - 1) + (x_i^{(1)} - y_i^{(1)}),$$

where $i \notin \{i_0, i_1\}$.

This can be achieved by first selecting $r_i^{B(0)}$ at random, and then isolating and obtaining $r_i^{B(1)}$ (which in turn is random in each selection of b). Similarly, in case (b), we require that $s_B^{(1)} s_B^{(0)} u_{i_0}^{(1)} = u_{i_1}^{(0)}$, which is equivalent to

$$s_B^{(1)} s_B^{(0)} ((\tilde{r}_{i_0}^A + r_{i_0}^{B(1)})(\gamma_{i_0}^{(1)} - 1) + (x_{i_0}^{(1)} - y_{i_0}^{(1)})) = (\tilde{r}_{i_1}^A + r_{i_1}^{B(0)})(\gamma_{i_1}^{(0)} - 1) + (x_{i_1}^{(0)} - y_{i_1}^{(0)}),$$

and it is solved as in case (a).

For case (c), just taking $r_{i_0}^{B(0)}$ and $r_{i_1}^{B(1)}$ at random is enough: in those positions the γ-sequences take the value 1 and the randomization is "lost" when considering u-sequences.

The simulator now prepares $[\![\tilde{r}_i^B]\!]$ as $[\![(1 - b)r_i^{B(0)} + br_i^{B(1)}]\!]$ and $[\![\tilde{u}_i^B]\!]$ as $[\![\tilde{r}_i^B(\tilde{\gamma}_i - 1)]\!]$, for all i. These encrypted values are broadcast, and the simulator for the private-multiplier gate is invoked, with multiplicands $[\![\tilde{r}_i^B]\!]$ and $[\![\tilde{\gamma}_i]\!]$, and result $[\![(1 - b)r_i^{B(0)}\gamma_i^{(0)} + br_i^{B(1)}\gamma_i^{(1)}]\!]$.

The sequence $[\![\tilde{u}_i]\!]$ is constructed as in the protocol:

$$[\![\tilde{u}_i]\!] = [\![\tilde{u}_i^A]\!][\![\tilde{u}_i^B]\!][\![\tilde{x}_i - \tilde{y}_i]\!].$$

By construction, it follows that $[\![\tilde{u}_i]\!] = [\![(1 - b)u_i^{(0)} + bu_i^{(1)}]\!]$, for all i.

4. The simulator lets party A mix the sequence $[\![\tilde{u}_i]\!]$, producing a new sequence $[\![\tilde{u}_i']\!]$. The simulator can also extract the permutation π_A that links both sequences.

5. Now the simulator randomly selects two indices, call them $\tilde{i}^*$ and $\tilde{i}^{**}$, and constructs two permutations $\pi_B^{(0)}$ and $\pi_B^{(1)}$ as follows:

- $\pi_B^{(0)}(\pi_A(i_0)) = \pi_B^{(1)}(\pi_A(i_1)) = \tilde{i}^*$;
- $\pi_B^{(0)}(\pi_A(i_1)) = \pi_B^{(1)}(\pi_A(i_0)) = \tilde{i}^{**}$;
- for the remaining positions the permutations are randomly defined under the condition that $\pi_B^{(0)}(\pi_A(i)) = \pi_B^{(1)}(\pi_A(i))$, $i \notin \{i_0, i_1\}$.

The next step is to call the simulator of the mix proof depending on $[\![b]\!]$, because the simulator will never know which permutation, $\pi_B^{(0)}$ or $\pi_B^{(1)}$, is actually used. For this, he constructs the sequences $v_i^{(j)} = u_{\pi_A^{-1}(\pi_B^{(j)-1}(i))}^{(j)}$, for $j = 0, 1$, and then defines the sequence $[\![\tilde{v}_i]\!] = [\![(1 - b)v_i^{(0)} + bv_i^{(1)}]\!]$, for all i. With the mixed sequence broadcast by party A in the previous step and this last sequence, the simulator now calls the simulator for the mix proof.

6. Party A multiplies the entire sequence $[\![\tilde{v}_i]\!]$ by a number $\tilde{s}_A$ (which is extracted from the corresponding private-multiplier proof for $[\![\tilde{s}_A]\!]$), resulting in sequence $[\![\tilde{v}_i']\!]$.

7. Now the simulator has almost all the work already done. At this stage he constructs $[\![\tilde{s}_B]\!] = [\![(1 - b)s_B^{(0)} + bs_B^{(1)}]\!]$, and broadcasts it. Then he constructs the sequence $[\![\tilde{w}_i]\!] = [\![(1 - b)v_i^{(0)}\tilde{s}_A s_B^{(0)} + bv_i^{(1)}\tilde{s}_A s_B^{(1)}]\!]$. Note that $\tilde{v}_i' = \tilde{v}_i\tilde{s}_A$. The private-multiplier simulator is now invoked on inputs $[\![\tilde{s}_B]\!]$ and $[\![\tilde{v}_i']\!]$, and output $[\![\tilde{w}_i]\!]$.

8. To simulate the last step, the simulator can link back the plaintext of encryptions $[\![\tilde{w}_i]\!]$ by using permutation $\pi_A \circ \pi_B^{(j)}$, for $j = 0, 1$; note that the sign of these values is affected by the factor $\tilde{s}_A$. Thus,

$$w_i^{(j)} = \tilde{s}_A s_B^{(j)} u_{\pi_A^{-1}(\pi_B^{(j)-1}(i))}^{(j)},$$

for all i, due to the construction at step 5.

Moreover, the plaintexts in $[\![w_i^{(0)}]\!]$ and $[\![w_i^{(1)}]\!]$ are equal, as a result of the work of the simulator at step 3. It also follows that $w_i^{(0)} = w_i^{(1)} = \tilde{w}_i$, independently of $[\![b]\!]$. Hence, the simulator for the threshold decryption is called, for instance, over inputs $[\![\tilde{w}_i]\!]$ and $\tilde{s}_A s_B^{(0)} u_{\pi_A^{-1}(\pi_B^{(0)-1}(i))}^{(0)}$.

The values generated in this way by the simulator are consistent, and therefore an adversary cannot statistically distinguish them from the ones resulting in a real execution. The case when party B is corrupted is similar with some minor differences, due to the order in which tasks are executed. This completes the proof. $\square$

4   Conclusions

In this paper we have presented two new solutions to the integer comparison problem. Our first solution achieves a logarithmic round complexity of exactly $\lceil \log_2 m \rceil$ rounds for m-bit integers, whereas the second solution achieves a

Table 1. Comparison of different secure solutions for $[x > y]$

Integer Comparison Solution	No. Exponentiations	Broadcast Bits
Linear-depth circuit [ST04]	$100m$	$68m|q|$
Logarithmic-depth circuit	$150m$	$102m|q|$
Constant-round protocol (two-party)	$124m$	$77m|q|$

constant number of rounds (in the two-party case). In Table 1 we show a comparison between the different solutions presented in this paper and the linear-depth circuit of [ST04].

Evidently, going below $O(m)$ rounds comes at the cost of an increase in computational and communication complexity. For the constant round solution, the additional costs are smaller than for the logarithmic round solution; however, the logarithmic round solution also applies to the multi-party case.

From a practical point of view, our multi-party logarithmic-depth solution is very good compared to the known results so far: communication and computation are are only 50% worse than for a linear-depth solution. Even though $O(1)$-round is not achieved this way, the number of rounds is *very low* when considering integers x and y of practical size, e.g., $m = 32$ or $m = 64$, in which cases the depth is only 5 and 6, respectively.

References

[BK04]   I. Blake and V. Kolesnikov. Strong conditional oblivious transfer and computing on intervals. In *Advances in Cryptology—ASIACRYPT '04*, volume 3329 of *Lecture Notes in Computer Science*, pages 515–529, Berlin, 2004. Springer-Verlag.

[Bra06]   F. Brandt. Efficient cryptographic protocol design based on distributed El Gamal encryption. In *Information Security and Cryptology - ICISC 2005*, volume 3935 of *Lecture Notes in Computer Science*, pages 32–47. Springer-Verlag, 2006.

[CDN01]   R. Cramer, I. Damgård, and J.B. Nielsen. Multiparty computation from threshold homomorphic encryption. In *Advances in Cryptology— EUROCRYPT '01*, volume 2045 of *Lecture Notes in Computer Science*, pages 280–300, Berlin, 2001. Springer-Verlag. Full version eprint.iacr.org/2000/055, October 27, 2000.

[CDS94]   R. Cramer, I. Damgård, and B. Schoenmakers. Proofs of partial knowledge and simplified design of witness hiding protocols. In *Advances in Cryptology—CRYPTO '94*, volume 839 of *Lecture Notes in Computer Science*, pages 174–187, Berlin, 1994. Springer-Verlag.

[DFK+06] I. Damgård, M. Fitzi, E. Kiltz, J.B. Nielsen, and T. Toft. Unconditionally secure constant-rounds multi-party computation for equality, comparison, bits and exponentiation. In *Proc. 3rd Theory of Cryptography Conference, TCC 2006*, volume 3876 of *Lecture Notes in Computer Science*, pages 285–304, Berlin, 2006. Springer-Verlag.

[DN00]   I. Damgård and J. Nielsen. Improved non-committing encryption schemes based on a general complexity assumption. In *Advances in Cryptology— Crypto 2000*, volume 1880 of *Lecture Notes in Computer Science*, pages 433–451. Springer, 2000.

[DN03]   I. Damgård and J.B. Nielsen. Universally composable efficient multiparty computation from threshold homomorphic encryption. In *Advances in Cryptology—CRYPTO '03*, volume 2729 of *Lecture Notes in Computer Science*, pages 247–264, Berlin, 2003. Springer-Verlag.

[DiC00]   G. Di Crescenzo. Private Selective Payment Protocols. In *FC '00: Proc. 4th International Conference on Financial Cryptography, Lecture Notes in Computer Science*, pages 72–89, London, 2001, Springer-Verlag.

[Fis01]   M. Fischlin. A cost-effective pay-per-multiplication comparison method for millionaires. In *Progress in Cryptology – CT-RSA 2001*, volume 2020 of *Lecture Notes in Computer Science*, pages 457–471, Berlin, 2001. Springer-Verlag.

[GMY03]   J. Garay, P. MacKenzie, and K. Yang. Strengthening zero-knowledge protocols using signatures. In *Advances in Cryptology—Eurocrypt 2003*, volume 2656, pages 177–194. Springer, 2003.

[Gro03]   J. Groth. A verifiable secret shuffle of homomorphic encryptions. In *Public Key Cryptography—PKC '03*, volume 2567 of *Lecture Notes in Computer Science*, pages 145–160, Berlin, 2003. Springer-Verlag.

[Knu97]   D. E. Knuth. *The Art of Computer Programming (Vol. 1: Fundamental Algorithms)*. Addison Wesley, Reading (MA), 3rd edition, 1997.

[LT05]   H. Lin and W. Tzeng. An efficient solution to the millionaires' problem based on homomorphic encryption. In *ACNS 2005*, volume 3531 of *Lecture Notes in Computer Science*, pages 456–466. Springer-Verlag, 2005.

[SK95]   K. Sako and J. Kilian. Receipt-free mix-type voting scheme—a practical solution to the implementation of a voting booth. In *Advances in Cryptology—EUROCRYPT '95*, volume 921 of *Lecture Notes in Computer Science*, pages 393–403, Berlin, 1995. Springer-Verlag.

[ST04]   B. Schoenmakers and P. Tuyls. Practical two-party computation based on the conditional gate. In *Advances in Cryptology—ASIACRYPT '04*, volume 3329 of *Lecture Notes in Computer Science*, pages 119–136, Berlin, 2004. Springer-Verlag.

[ST06]   B. Schoenmakers and P. Tuyls. Efficient binary conversion for Paillier encryptions. In *Advances in Cryptology—EUROCRYPT '06*, volume 4004 of *Lecture Notes in Computer Science*, pages 522–537, Berlin, 2006. Springer-Verlag.

[Yao82]   A. Yao. Protocols for secure computations. In *Proc. 23rd IEEE Symposium on Foundations of Computer Science (FOCS '82)*, pages 160–164. IEEE Computer Society, 1982.

Multiparty Computation
for Interval, Equality, and Comparison
Without Bit-Decomposition Protocol

Takashi Nishide[1,2] and Kazuo Ohta[1]

[1] Department of Information and Communication Engineering, The University of
Electro-Communications, 1-5-1 Chofugaoka Chofu-shi, Tokyo 182-8585 Japan
{t-nishide,ota}@ice.uec.ac.jp
[2] Hitachi Software Engineering Co., Ltd.; 4-12-7 Higashi-Shinagawa Shinagawa-ku,
Tokyo, 140-0002 Japan

Abstract. Damgård *et al.* [11] showed a novel technique to convert
a polynomial sharing of secret a into the sharings of the bits of a in
constant rounds, which is called the bit-decomposition protocol. The
bit-decomposition protocol is a very powerful tool because it enables bit-
oriented operations even if shared secrets are given as elements in the
field. However, the bit-decomposition protocol is relatively expensive.

In this paper, we present a simplified bit-decomposition protocol by
analyzing the original protocol. Moreover, we construct more efficient
protocols for a comparison, interval test and equality test of shared secrets without relying on the bit-decomposition protocol though it seems
essential to such bit-oriented operations. The key idea is that we do computation on secret a with c and r where $c = a + r$, c is a revealed value,
and r is a random bitwise-shared secret. The outputs of these protocols
are also shared without being revealed.

The realized protocols as well as the original protocol are constant-
round and run with less communication rounds and less data communication than those of [11]. For example, the round complexities are reduced
by a factor of approximately 3 to 10.

Keywords: Multiparty Computation, Secret Sharing, Bitwise Sharing.

1 Introduction

Secure *multiparty computation* (MPC) allows a set of mutually distrustful parties
to jointly compute an agreed function of their inputs in such a way that the
correctness of the output and the privacy of the parties' inputs are guaranteed.
That is, when a function is represented as $(y_1, \ldots, y_n) = f(x_1, \ldots, x_n)$, each
party with its private input x_i obtains only the output y_i but nothing else.

A great deal of work (e.g., [3,17,7,25]) has been done in this research field.
By using generic circuit based protocols, it is shown that any function can be
computed securely [3,17]. However, the general protocols tend to be inefficient;
hence the main aim of our research is to construct efficient protocols for specific
functions.

When we are interested in integer arithmetic, there are two choices to represent a function: an arithmetic circuit over a prime field $\mathbb{Z}_p$ and a Boolean circuit.

T. Okamoto and X. Wang (Eds.): PKC 2007, LNCS 4450, pp. 343–360, 2007.

Inputs (and outputs) in the arithmetic circuit are represented as elements in $\mathbb{Z}_p$ (or a ring), while inputs in the Boolean circuit are represented as bits. The input encoding has an influence on the efficiency of computation. Addition and multiplication of shared secrets can be performed efficiently in the arithmetic circuit, whereas not in the Boolean circuit. On the other hand, bit-oriented operations like interval tests, equality tests, and comparisons of shared secrets are easy in the Boolean circuit, whereas they are non-trivial tasks in the arithmetic circuit.

To bridge the gap between arithmetic circuits and Boolean circuits, Damgård et al. [11] have proposed the MPC protocol called bit-decomposition in the secret sharing setting (e.g., [3,16]). Also, Schoenmakers and Tuyls [21] have proposed a similar protocol for MPC [10,13] based on threshold homomorphic cryptosystems (THC) [12,14]. In the bit-decomposition protocol, a sharing of an element in the field (or an encryption of an element in the ring in the threshold homomorphic setting) is converted into sharings (encryptions) of bits.

The bit-decomposition protocol is very useful and has many applications because it enables bit-oriented operations to be performed in the arithmetic circuit without performing the entire computation bitwise. For example, when computing a^b by using the techniques in [1,11], or the Hamming distance between a and b where shared secrets a and b are elements in $\mathbb{Z}_p$, the bit-decomposition protocol is essential because we need the bitwise sharings of the shared secrets. Other important applications are comparisons, interval tests and equality tests of shared secrets. For example, in the comparison protocol, a single shared bit is computed such that it indicates the result of a comparison between two shared secrets. In the Boolean circuit, it is relatively easy to compare two shared secrets because the bits of the secrets are shared. That is, in the comparison protocol based on the Boolean circuit (which we call the bitwise less-than protocol in Section 3.3 as in [11]), we can check the secrets *bit by bit* privately and compare the two shared secrets even without revealing the bit position that determines the comparison result. Therefore, even if inputs are given as sharings of elements in the field, the comparison can be performed easily with the bit-decomposition protocol.

Thus the bit-decomposition protocol is a very powerful tool because changing the representations of shared secrets enables us to gain the benefits of both Boolean circuits and arithmetic circuits. However, the bit-decomposition protocol involves expensive computation in terms of round and communication complexities.

In this paper, we present a simplified bit-decomposition protocol by analyzing the original protocol. Moreover, we construct more efficient protocols for the main applications of the bit-decomposition protocol, which are interval tests, equality tests, and comparisons, without relying on the bit-decomposition protocol though it seemed essential. For example, the equality test protocol is an important subprotocol in [8,20], so it will be meaningful to construct efficient protocols for these applications without relying on the bit-decomposition protocol if possible. For the equality test, we present deterministic and probabilistic protocols.

In our constructions, the outputs of the protocols are also shared without being revealed, so they can be secret inputs for the subsequent computation. Therefore, our protocols can be used as building blocks in the more complex computation.

Our Results. We construct constant-round protocols for bit-decomposition, interval test, comparison, and equality test, building on the subprotocols in [11]. The proposed bit-decomposition protocol runs with less communication rounds and less data communication than the original protocol [11]. Therefore, the interval test, comparison and equality test protocols are also improved inevitably by using the proposed bit-decomposition protocol. However, we present new protocols dedicated to them without relying on the bit-decomposition protocol. By using our protocols, given shared secrets as elements in $\mathbb{Z}_p$, we can perform the interval tests, equality tests, and comparisons of the shared secrets more efficiently than the bit-decomposition based protocols. For the equality test, we propose two kinds of protocols. One (Proposed1) is a deterministic protocol and the other (Proposed2) is a probabilistic protocol with a negligible error probability and a much smaller round complexity. The key idea is that we do computation on secret a with c and r where $c = a + r$, c is a revealed value, and r is a random bitwise-shared secret.

In Table 1, we summarize the results of the round and communication (comm.) complexities of each protocol where ℓ is the bit length of prime p of the underlying field for linear secret sharing schemes and k must be chosen such that the error probability $\left(\frac{1}{2}\right)^k$ is negligible. Here "BD-based" means that the protocol is based on the proposed bit-decomposition protocol. As shown in Table 1, we can see that these bit-oritented operations can be realized with smaller complexities than those of the bit-decomposition based protocols by constructing them without the bit-decomposition protocol. For example, the round complexities are reduced by a factor of approximately 3 to 10.

Our protocols (except the probabilistic equality test protocol which is only applicable to the secret sharing setting) are applicable to both the secret sharing setting [11] and the threshold homomorphic setting [21] though we describe our constructions based on the secret sharing setting.

Related Work. Damgård *et al.* [11] have shown a novel technique to convert a polynomial sharing of an element in $\mathbb{Z}_p$ into sharings of bits in constant rounds. Also Shoenmakers and Tuyls [21] have shown a similar conversion technique for multiparty computation based on threshold homomorphic cryptosystems [10,13]. These protocols are the first to bridge the gap between arithmetic circuits and Boolean circuits.

Toft [24] has proposed another version of a probabilistic equality test protocol independently of and concurrently with our probabilistic equality test protocol. Both the protocols use the property of quadratic residues in a probabilistic way.

Recently, as a practical approach (rather than theoretical constant-round protocols), in [4,15,23], the implementation for multiparty integer computation, including the bit-decomposition and comparison, is described with non-constant-round protocols where shared secrets are assumed to be sufficiently small

Table 1. Comparison of Round / Communication Complexities

Protocol		Round	Comm.
Bit-Decomposition	[11]	38	$93\ell + 94\ell \log_2 \ell$
	Proposed	25	$93\ell + 47\ell \log_2 \ell$
Interval Test	[11]	44	$127\ell + 94\ell \log_2 \ell + 1$
	BD-based	31	$127\ell + 47\ell \log_2 \ell + 1$
	Proposed	13	$110\ell + 1$
Comparison	[11]	44	$205\ell + 188\ell \log_2 \ell$
	BD-based	31	$205\ell + 94\ell \log_2 \ell$
	Proposed	15	$279\ell + 5$
Equality Test	[11]	39	$98\ell + 94\ell \log_2 \ell$
	BD-based	26	$98\ell + 47\ell \log_2 \ell$
	Proposed1	8	81ℓ
	Proposed2	4	$12k$

compared with prime p of the underlying secret sharing scheme, whereas we do not assume that shared secrets are upper bounded by a certain value as in [11]. We mention this aspect in Section 7.

2   Preliminaries

We assume that n parties $P_1, \ldots, P_n$ are mutually connected by secure and authenticated channels in a synchronous network and the index i for each P_i is public among the parties. Let p be an odd prime and ℓ be the bit length of p. $\mathbb{Z}_p$ is a prime field. When we write $a \in \mathbb{Z}_p$, it means that $a \in \{0, 1, \ldots, p-1\}$. We use $[a]_p$ to denote a polynomial sharing [22] of secret $a \in \mathbb{Z}_p$. That is, $[a]_p$ means that a is shared among the parties where f_a is a random polynomial $f_a(x) = a + a_1 x + a_2 x^2 + \cdots + a_t x^t \mod p$ with randomly chosen $a_i \in \mathbb{Z}_p$ for $1 \le i \le t$, $t < \frac{n}{2}$, and $f_a(i)$ is the P_i's share of a. An adversary can corrupt up to t parties. We describe our protocols in the so-called "honest-but-curious" model, but standard techniques will be applicable to make our protocols robust.

Let C be a Boolean test. When we write $[C]_p$, it means that $C \in \{0, 1\}$ and $C = 1$ iff C is true. For example, we use $[a < b]_p$ to denote the output of the comparison protocol.

Because the multiplication protocol is a dominant factor of the complexity, as in [11], we measure the round complexity of a protocol by the number of rounds of parallel invocations of the multiplication protocol [16] and we also measure the communication complexity by the number of invocations of the multiplication protocol. The round complexity relates to the time required for a protocol to be completed and the communication complexity relates to the amount of data communicated among the parties during a protocol run. Though our measurement of complexities basically follows that of [11], the complexity analysis in [11] is rough. In this paper, we reevaluate the round and communication complexities of the protocols in [11] to compare our protocols with those of [11] based on the same measurement.

3   Building Blocks

3.1   Distributed Computation with Shared Secrets for Addition and Multiplication

Let's assume now that n parties have two shared secrets a and b as $[a]_p = \{f_a(1), \ldots, f_a(n)\}$ and $[b]_p = \{f_b(1), \ldots, f_b(n)\}$. Then the parties can obtain $[c+a \bmod p]_p$, $[ca \bmod p]_p$, and $[a+b \bmod p]_p$ easily where c is a public constant as follows: To compute $[c+a \bmod p]_p$, $[ca \bmod p]_p$, and $[a+b \bmod p]_p$, each P_i has only to locally compute $c + f_a(i) \bmod p$, $cf_a(i) \bmod p$, and $f_a(i) + f_b(i) \bmod p$ respectively. Therefore, these can be done efficiently without communication among n parties. When we write $[c+a]_p = c + [a]_p$, $[ca]_p = c[a]_p$, and $[a+b]_p = [a]_p + [b]_p$, these mean that the parties perform these operations. We also use $\sum$, for example, like $\sum_{i=1}^{3}[a_i]_p$ to denote $[a_1]_p + [a_2]_p + [a_3]_p$.

Multiplication to obtain $[ab \bmod p]_p$ is a bit more complex and it requires the parties to communicate with each other. We assume that the parties perform the multiplication protocol in [16]. When we write $[ab]_p = [a]_p \times [b]_p$, it means that the parties perform the multiplication protocol to compute $[ab \bmod p]_p$.

We will evaluate the round complexity of a protocol by performing the multiplication protocol in parallel as much as possible.

3.2   Bitwise Sharing

The concept of bitwise sharing is to share $a \in \mathbb{Z}_p (= \{0, 1, \ldots, p-1\})$ in the form of $\{[a_{\ell-1}]_p, \ldots, [a_0]_p\}$ such that $a = \sum_{i=0}^{\ell-1} 2^i a_i$ where $a_i \in \{0, 1\}$. We use $[a]_B$ to denote $\{[a_{\ell-1}]_p, \ldots, [a_1]_p, [a_0]_p\}$.

3.3   Subprotocols

We describe several subprotocols in [2,11] necessary for our constructions. All these subprotocols run in a constant number of rounds. By combining these subprotocols, we will construct our interval test, equality test, comparison, and bit-decomposition protocols that also run in a constant number of rounds.

Joint Random Number Sharing. The parties can share a uniformly random, unknown number r [2] as follows: Each P_i picks up $r_{-i} \in \mathbb{Z}_p$ at random and shares it by a sharing $[r_{-i}]_p = \{f_i(1), \ldots, f_i(n)\}$ where $f_i(0) = r_{-i}$ and f_i is a random polynomial. That is, P_i distributes $f_i(j)$'s to other P_j's. From each $[r_{-i}]_p$, the parties compute $[r]_p = \sum_{i=1}^{n}[r_{-i}]_p$. We assume that the complexity for this is almost the same as the complexity of 1 invocation of the multiplication protocol. We denote this subprotocol as $[r \in_R \mathbb{Z}_p]_p$.

Joint Random Bit Sharing. The parties can share a uniformly random $a \in \{0, 1\}$ as follows: The parties compute $[r \in_R \mathbb{Z}_p]_p$, perform the multiplication protocol to obtain $[r^2]_p$ and reveal r^2. If $r^2 = 0$, the parties retry. If $r^2 \neq 0$, the parties compute $r' = \sqrt{r^2}$ such that $0 < r' < \frac{p}{2}$. This can be done in polynomial time because p is an odd prime. Then the parties set $[a]_p = 2^{-1}(r'^{-1}[r]_p + 1)$. It is clear that $r'^{-1}r \in \{-1, 1\}$; hence $a \in \{0, 1\}$. The total complexity is 2 rounds and 2 invocations. We denote this subprotocol as $[a \in_R \{0,1\}]_p$. In the setting [10,13], this can be computed as $a = \oplus_{i=1}^n b_i$ where $b_i \in_R \{0,1\}$ is generated by P_i (see [21] for the details).

Unbounded Fan-In Or. Given $[a_{\ell-1}]_p, \ldots, [a_0]_p$ where $a_i \in \{0,1\}$, the parties can compute $[\vee_{i=0}^{\ell-1} a_i]_p$ in a constant number of rounds. For this, as in [11], we can use the same technique to evaluate symmetric Boolean functions as follows:

The parties compute $[A]_p = 1 + \sum_{i=0}^{\ell-1}[a_i]_p$. Note that $1 \leq A \leq \ell + 1$. Next, the parties define a ℓ-degree polynomial $f_\ell(x)$ such that $f_\ell(1) = 0$ and $f_\ell(2) = f_\ell(3) = \cdots = f_\ell(\ell + 1) = 1$. $f_\ell(x)$ can be determined by using Lagrange interpolation. Note that $f_\ell(A) = \vee_{i=0}^{\ell-1} a_i$. Then the parties try to obtain $[\vee_{i=0}^{\ell-1} a_i]_p$ by computing $[f_\ell(A)]_p$ from $[A]_p$ and $f_\ell(x)$. This can be done in a constant number of rounds by using an unbounded fan-in multiplication and the inversion protocol [2] as follows:

Let's assume that $f_\ell(x)$ is represented as $f_\ell(x) = \alpha_0 + \alpha_1 x + \cdots + \alpha_\ell x^\ell \bmod p$. To obtain $[f_\ell(A)]_p$, the parties compute $[A]_p, [A^2]_p, \ldots, [A^\ell]_p$ because $[f_\ell(A)]_p = \alpha_0 + \sum_{i=1}^{\ell} \alpha_i [A^i]_p$.

For $1 \leq i \leq \ell$, the parties generate $[b_i \in_R \mathbb{Z}_p]_p$ and $[b_i' \in_R \mathbb{Z}_p]_p$ in parallel, compute $[B_i]_p = [b_i]_p \times [b_i']_p$, and reveal B_i. Note that $[b_i^{-1}]_p$ can be computed as $[b_i^{-1}]_p = B_i^{-1}[b_i']_p$ at the same time (inversion protocol).

Next, the parties compute in parallel

$$[c_1]_p = [A]_p \times [b_1^{-1}]_p$$
$$[c_2]_p = [A]_p \times [b_1]_p \times [b_2^{-1}]_p$$
$$\vdots$$
$$[c_{\ell-1}]_p = [A]_p \times [b_{\ell-2}]_p \times [b_{\ell-1}^{-1}]_p$$
$$[c_\ell]_p = [A]_p \times [b_{\ell-1}]_p \times [b_\ell^{-1}]_p$$

and reveal all c_i's.

Then the parties can compute $[A^i]_p = (\prod_{k=1}^i c_k)[b_i]_p$.

If $A = 0$, information about A is leaked. That is why we used $[A]_p = 1 + \sum_{i=0}^{\ell-1}[a_i]_p$ to guarantee that A is not zero.

The complexity of computing each component is as follows: 2 rounds and 3ℓ invocations for $[b_i]_p$'s, $[b_i']_p$'s, and B_i's and 2 rounds and 2ℓ invocations for c_i's. $[b_i]_p \times [b_{i+1}^{-1}]_p$ for $1 \leq i \leq \ell-1$ can be precomputed as $[b_i]_p \times [b_{i+1}']_p$ in the second round in parallel with $[b_i]_p \times [b_i']_p$. Therefore, the total complexity is 3 rounds (including 2 rounds for random value generation) and 5ℓ invocations.

Note that we can compute unbounded fan-in And and Xor similarly because a symmetric Boolean function depends only on the number of 1's in its inputs. Also note that the random values necessary for this protocol can be generated in advance rather than on demand when this subprotocol is used as a building block in the larger protocol, thus reducing the round complexity. Actually all the random value generation (for bits and numbers) can be done in the first 2 rounds (3 rounds in the setting [21] by using an unbounded fan-in Xor).

Prefix-Or. Given $[a_1]_p, \ldots, [a_\ell]_p$ where $a_i \in \{0, 1\}$, the parties can compute the Prefix-Or $[b_1]_p, \ldots, [b_\ell]_p$ such that $b_i = \vee_{j=1}^i a_j$ in a constand number of rounds. As in [11], this can be done by using the technique from [5] as follows:

For notational convenience, let's assume that $\ell = \lambda^2$ for an integer λ and index the bits a_k as $a_{i,j} = a_{\lambda(i-1)+j}$ for $i, j = 1, \ldots, \lambda$. Other cases can be adapted quite straightforwardly.

First the parties compute $[x_i]_p = \vee_{j=1}^\lambda [a_{i,j}]_p$ for $i = 1, \ldots, \lambda$ in parallel by using unbounded fan-in Or where the size of problems is λ instead of ℓ. Then the parties compute similarly $[y_i]_p = \vee_{k=1}^i [x_k]_p$ for $i = 1, \ldots, \lambda$ in parallel. Now we can notice that $y_i = 1$ iff some block $\{a_{i',1}, \ldots, a_{i',\lambda}\}$ with $i' \leq i$ contains a $a_{i',j} = 1$.

Next, the parties set $[f_1]_p = [x_1]_p$, and for $i = 2, \ldots, \lambda$, set $[f_i]_p = [y_i]_p - [y_{i-1}]_p$. Now we can notice that $f_i = 1$ iff $\{a_{i,1}, \ldots, a_{i,\lambda}\}$ is the first block containing a $a_{i,j} = 1$. Let i_0 be such that $f_{i_0} = 1$. The parties can compute $\{[a_{i_0,1}]_p, \ldots, [a_{i_0,\lambda}]_p\}$ by $[a_{i_0,j}]_p = \sum_{i=1}^\lambda [f_i]_p \times [a_{i,j}]_p$ in parallel without revealing i_0.

Next, the parties compute $\{[b_{i_0,1}]_p, \ldots, [b_{i_0,\lambda}]_p\}$ where $b_{i_0,j} = \vee_{k=1}^j a_{i_0,k}$ by using unbounded fan-in Or in parallel.

Finally, the parties set $[s_i]_p = [y_i]_p - [f_i]_p$. Then $s_i = 1$ iff $i > i_0$. If we index the bits of Prefix-Or b_k as $b_{i,j} = b_{\lambda(i-1)+j}$ as we did for a_k, the Prefix-Or can be computed as $[b_k]_p = [b_{\lambda(i-1)+j}]_p = [b_{i,j}]_p = [f_i]_p \times [b_{i_0,j}]_p + [s_i]_p$ in the end.

When we use several invocations of unbounded fan-in Or all the necessary random values in unbounded fan-in Or can be generated in the first 2 rounds. Therefore, the total complexity is 7 rounds (including 2 rounds for random value generation) and 17ℓ invocations. [1] Similarly the Prefix-And can also be computed by using the same technique.

Bitwise Less-Than. Given two bitwise sharings $[a]_B$ and $[b]_B$, the parties can compute $[a < b]_p$ without revealing $(a < b)$ itself. The basic idea is the same as the circuit for the millionaire's problem. We will give an outline of this subprotocol based on the description in [11].

For $0 \leq i \leq \ell - 1$, the parties compute $[c_i]_p = [a_i \oplus b_i]_p = [a_i] + [b_i]_p - 2[a_ib_i]_p$ in parallel and then compute $[d_i]_p = \vee_{j=i}^{\ell-1}[c_j]_p$ by using Prefix-Or, and set $[e_i]_p = [d_i - d_{i+1}]_p$ where $[e_{\ell-1}]_p = [d_{\ell-1}]_p$. Finally, the parties compute $[a < b]_p = \sum_{i=0}^{\ell-1}([e_i]_p \times [b_i]_p)$ in parallel.

The complexity of computing each component is as follows: 1 round and ℓ invocations for c_i's, 7 rounds and 17ℓ invocations for the Prefix-Or, and 1 round and ℓ invocations for $\sum_{i=0}^{\ell-1}([e_i]_p \times [b_i]_p)$. Because c_i's can be computed in parallel with random value generation in the Prefix-Or, the total complexity is 8 rounds (including 2 rounds for random value generation) and 19ℓ invocations. We use

---

[1] The evaluation in [11] is 17 rounds and 20ℓ invocations by generating random values on demand.

$[a <_B b]_p$ in order to stress that a and b are bitwise-shared. Note that if b is known, the complexity is 7 rounds (including 2 rounds for random value generation) and 17ℓ invocations by saving the invocations for c_i's and $\sum_{i=0}^{\ell-1}([e_i]_p \times [b_i]_p)$.

Joint Random Number Bitwise-Sharing. The parties can bitwise-share a uniformly random, unknown number r such that $0 \leq r = \sum_{i=0}^{\ell-1} 2^i r_i < p$ as follows: The parties generate each bit, $[r_i \in_R \{0,1\}]_p$ for $0 \leq i \leq \ell - 1$ in parallel, compute $[r <_B p]_p$ by using the bitwise less-than protocol and reveal $(r < p)$. If $r \geq p$, the parties retry.

The complexity of computing each component is as follows: 2 rounds and 2ℓ invocations for r_i's and 7 rounds and 17ℓ invocations for the bitwise less-than protocol (note that p is known). Because r_i's can be generated in parallel with random value generation in the Prefix-Or of the bitwise less-than protocol, the complexity is 7 rounds and 19ℓ invocations. As in [11], we assume that at least one of four generated candidates is less than p and the amortized complexity is 7 rounds (including 2 rounds for random value generation) and 76ℓ invocations. We denote this subprotocol as $[r \in_R \mathbb{Z}_p]_B$.

Bitwise Sum. Given two bitwise sharings $[a]_B = \{[a_{\ell-1}]_p, \ldots, [a_0]_p\}$ and $[b]_B = \{[b_{\ell-1}]_p, \ldots, [b_0]_p\}$, the parties can compute the bitwise sharing $[d]_B = \{[d_\ell]_p, \ldots, [d_0]_p\}$ such that $d = a + b$ over the integers (not mod p). By using the method of [6], the bitwise sum protocol can be performed in constant rounds (see [11] for the details). The total complexity based on the complexity analysis in this paper is 15 rounds (including 2 rounds for random value generation) and $47\ell \log_2 \ell$ invocations. [2] See Appendix A for the details. We denote this subprotocol as $[d]_B = [a]_B + [b]_B$.

4   Existing Protocols [11,21]

Damgård *et al.* [11] have shown a novel technique to convert $[a]_p$ into $[a]_B$. This technique is called the bit-decomposition protocol (Fig. 1). Note that we can obtain $[a]_p$ from $[a]_B$ easily by computing $[a]_p = \sum_{i=0}^{\ell-1} 2^i [a_i]_p \mod p$. Also, Schoenmakers and Tuyls [21] have proposed a similar bit-decomposition protocol (called **BITREP** gate) in the context of multiparty computation [10,13] based on threshold additively-homomorphic cryptosystems.

The complexity of computing each component in [11] is as follows: 7 rounds (including 2 rounds for random value generation) and 76ℓ invocations for $[r \in_R \mathbb{Z}_p]_B$, 13 rounds and $47\ell \log_2 \ell$ invocations for $[d]_B$ (bitwise sum), 5 rounds and 17ℓ invocations for $[q]_p$, that is, $[d <_B p]_p$, and 13 rounds and $47\ell \log_2 \ell$ invocations for $[h]_B$ (bitwise sum). The total complexity is 38 rounds (including 2 rounds for random value generation) and $93\ell + 94\ell \log_2 \ell$ invocations.

By using the bit-decomposition protocol, any bit-oriented operation can be performed in arithmetic circuits where inputs are given as polynomial sharings (rather than bitwise sharings) of elements in $\mathbb{Z}_p$.

---

[2] The evaluation in [11] is 37 rounds and $55\ell \log_2 \ell$ invocations by generating random values on demand.

The parties convert $[a]_p$ into $[a]_B$.

1. The parties generate $[r]_B$ and obtain $[r]_p$ eventually.
2. The parties compute $[c]_p = [a]_p - [r]_p$ and reveal $c = a - r \bmod p \in \{0, 1, \ldots, p-1\}$.
3. The parties compute $[d]_B = [r]_B + [c]_B = \{[d_\ell]_p, \ldots, [d_0]_p\}$.
4. Note that d can be represented as $d = a + qp$ where $q \in \{0, 1\}$. The parties can compute the bit q as $[q]_p = [p \le d]_p = 1 - [d <_B p]_p$.
5. Consider $g = (2^\ell - qp) \bmod 2^\ell$ and its bitwise sharing $[g]_B = \{[g_{\ell-1}]_p, \ldots, [g_0]_p\}$. Let $(f_{\ell-1}, \ldots, f_0)_2$ be the bit representation of $2^\ell - p$ such that $2^\ell - p = \sum_{i=0}^{\ell-1} 2^i f_i$ and $f_i \in \{0, 1\}$. Then the parties can compute $[g]_B$ by $[g_i]_p = f_i [q]_p$ for $0 \le i \le \ell-1$ because $g = 0$ if $q = 0$ and $g = 2^\ell - p$ if $q = 1$.
6. The parties now have the two following bitwise sharings, $[d]_B = [a + qp]_B$ and $[g]_B = [(2^\ell - qp) \bmod 2^\ell]_B$. Therefore, the parties can compute $[h]_B = [d]_B + [g]_B$ where $h = a + q2^\ell$.
7. By discarding the sharing $[h_\ell]_p$ from $[h]_B$, they can obtain $[a]_B$.

Fig. 1. Bit-Decomposition [11]

However, the bit-decomposition protocol is not cheap, so we try to construct a simplified bit-decomposition protocol and construct more efficient protocols for interval tests, equality tests, and comparisons without relying on the bit-decomposition protocol.

5   Simplified Bit-Decomposition Protocol

In the original bit-decomposition protocol, we need 2 invocations of the bitwise sum protocol (in Steps 3 and 6 in Fig. 1). We can notice that the first invocation for $[d]_B$ can be eliminated by changing the way in which we compute $[q]_p$ based on the following observation.

In Step 4 of the original protocol, the parties compute $[q]_p = 1 - [d <_B p]_p$ where $d = r + c$, c is public, and r is bitwise-shared. Therefore, the condition, $(d < p)$ can be changed into $(r < p - c)$. The parties have $[r]_B$ and $p - c$ is public, so $(r < p - c)$ can be computed by using the bitwise less-than protocol without computing $[d]_B = [r]_B + [c]_B$, thus eliminating one invocation of the bitwise sum protocol.

Since we have eliminated $[d]_B$, we need to specify how to compute $[a]_B$ in the rest of the protocol. Fortunately, we can use $[r]_B$ itself to compute $[a]_B$ by using the bitwise sum protocol. The simplified bit-decomposition protocol is given in Fig. 2.

Complexity of Bit-Decomposition Protocol. The complexity of computing each component is as follows: 7 rounds (including 2 rounds for random value generation) and 76ℓ invocations for $[r \in_R \mathbb{Z}_p]_B$, 5 rounds and 17ℓ invocations for $[q]_p$, that is, $[r <_B p - c]_p$, and 13 rounds and $47\ell \log_2 \ell$ invocations for $[h]_B$. The total complexity is 25 rounds (including 2 rounds for random value generation) and $93\ell + 47\ell \log_2 \ell$ invocations.

The parties convert $[a]_p$ into $[a]_B$.

1. The parties generate $[r]_B$ and obtain $[r]_p$ eventually.
2. The parties compute $[c]_p = [a]_p - [r]_p$ and reveal $c = a - r \bmod p \in \{0, 1, \ldots, p-1\}$. If $c = 0$, the parties are successfully done because $[r]_B$ is equal to $[a]_B$ by a coincidence.
3. If $c \neq 0$, next, the parties compute the bit q, $[q]_p = [p \leq r + c]_p = 1 - [r <_B p - c]_p$ by using the bitwise less-than protocol.
4. Note that a can be represented as $a = c + r - qp$ over the integers where $q \in \{0, 1\}$. Therefore, we also have $2^\ell + a = 2^\ell + c - qp + r$ over the integers. Consider $\widetilde{g} = (2^\ell + c - qp) \bmod 2^\ell$ and its bitwise sharing $[\widetilde{g}]_B = \{[\widetilde{g}_{\ell-1}]_p, \ldots, [\widetilde{g}_0]_p\}$. Let $(\widetilde{f}_{\ell-1}, \ldots, \widetilde{f}_0)_2$ be the bit representation of $2^\ell + c - p$ such that $2^\ell + c - p = \sum_{i=0}^{\ell-1} 2^i \widetilde{f}_i$ and $\widetilde{f}_i \in \{0, 1\}$. Also, let $(\widetilde{f}'_{\ell-1}, \ldots, \widetilde{f}'_0)_2$ be the bit representation of c such that $c = \sum_{i=0}^{\ell-1} 2^i \widetilde{f}'_i$ and $\widetilde{f}'_i \in \{0, 1\}$. Then the parties can compute $[\widetilde{g}]_B$ by $[\widetilde{g}_i]_p = (\widetilde{f}_i - \widetilde{f}'_i)[q]_p + \widetilde{f}'_i$ for $0 \leq i \leq \ell - 1$ because $\widetilde{g} = c$ if $q = 0$ and $\widetilde{g} = 2^\ell + c - p$ if $q = 1$.
5. The parties now have the two following bitwise sharings, $[r]_B$ and $[\widetilde{g}]_B = [(2^\ell + c - qp) \bmod 2^\ell]_B$. Therefore, the parties can compute $[h]_B = [r]_B + [\widetilde{g}]_B$ where $h = a + q2^\ell$.
6. By discarding the sharing $[h_\ell]_p$ from $[h]_B$, they can obtain $[a]_B$.

Fig. 2. Simplified Bit-Decomposition

6   Proposed Protocols Without Bit-Decomposition

6.1   Interval Test Protocol

In the interval test protocol, given public constants $c_1, c_2 \in \mathbb{Z}_p$ (where $c_1 < c_2$) and shared secret $a \in \mathbb{Z}_p$, the parties compute $[c_1 < a < c_2]_p$ without revealing $(c_1 < a < c_2)$ itself.

If the parties use the bit-decomposition protocol, the parties compute $[a]_B$ from $[a]_p$ and compute $[c_1 < a < c_2]_p = [c_1 <_B a]_p \times [a <_B c_2]_p$.

The basic idea of our construction is as follows: We randomize a by $c = a + r$ and reveal c where r is a bitwise-shared random secret. We obtain an appropriate interval $[r_{\mathrm{low}}, r_{\mathrm{high}}]$ from c, c_1, and c_2. Then computing $[c_1 < a < c_2]_p$ is reduced to checking whether r exists in the appropriate interval $r_{\mathrm{low}} < r < r_{\mathrm{high}}$ (for example, see Fig. 3) by the bitwise less-than protocol.

Procedure. The parties generate $[r \in_R \mathbb{Z}_p]_B$ and obtain $[r]_p$ eventually. Next, the parties compute $[c]_p = [a]_p + [r]_p$ and reveal $c = a + r \bmod p \in \{0, 1, \ldots, p-1\}$. At this point, no information about a is leaked from c because r is uniformly random and unknown to the parties. Now we can think that $a \in \{-(p - c - 1), \ldots, -1, 0, 1, \ldots, c - 1, c\}$ because $r \in \{0, 1, \ldots, p-1\}$.

First, we consider the case where $c_1 < c < c_2$ does not hold. When $c_2 \leq c$ (see Fig. 3), obviously, we have $(c_1 < a < c_2) = 1$ if $(r_{\mathrm{low}} =)c - c_2 < r < c - c_1 (= r_{\mathrm{high}})$. Similarly, when $c \leq c_1$ (see Fig. 4), if $(r_{\mathrm{low}} =)c + p - c_2 < r < c + p - c_1 (= r_{\mathrm{high}})$, we have $-(p - c_1) < a < -(p - c_2)$. This means that $(c_1 < a < c_2) = 1$. Therefore, the parties compute, by using the bitwise less-than protocol,

$$[c_1 < a < c_2]_p = [r_{\mathrm{low}} <_B r]_p \times [r <_B r_{\mathrm{high}}]_p.$$

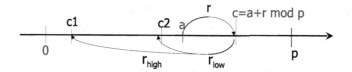

Fig. 3. Case of $c_2 \leq c$

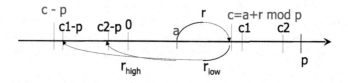

Fig. 4. Case of $c \leq c_1$

Next, we consider the case where $c_1 < c < c_2$ holds (see Fig. 5). In this case, if $(r_{\text{low}} =)c - c_1 - 1 < r < c + p - c_2 + 1(= r_{\text{high}})$, we have $-(p - c_2) \leq a \leq c_1$. This means that $(c_1 < a < c_2) = 0$. Therefore, the parties compute

$$[r_{\text{low}} < r < r_{\text{high}}]_p = [c - c_1 - 1 <_B r]_p \times [r <_B c + p - c_2 + 1]_p$$

by using the bitwise less-than protocol and set

$$[c_1 < a < c_2]_p = 1 - [r_{\text{low}} < r < r_{\text{high}}]_p.$$

Complexity of Interval Test Protocol. If we use the bit-decomposition protocol straightforwardly, the complexity of computing each component is as follows: 38 rounds (including 2 rounds for random value generation) and $93\ell + 94\ell \log_2 \ell$ invocations for $[a]_B$, 5 rounds and $(17\ell \times 2)$ invocations for $[c_1 <_B a]_p$ and $[a <_B c_2]_p$, and 1 round and 1 invocation for $[c_1 <_B a]_p \times [a <_B c_2]_p$. The total complexity is 44 rounds (including 2 rounds for random value generation) and $127\ell + 94\ell \log_2 \ell + 1$ invocations.

On the other hand, in our construction, the complexity of computing each component is as follows: 7 rounds (including 2 rounds for random value generation) and 76ℓ invocations for $[r \in_R \mathbb{Z}_p]_B$, 5 rounds and $(17\ell \times 2)$ invocations for $[r_{\text{low}} <_B r]_p$ and $[r <_B r_{\text{high}}]_p$, and 1 round and 1 invocation for $[r_{\text{low}} <_B r]_p \times [r <_B r_{\text{high}}]_p$. The total complexity is 13 rounds (including 2 rounds for random value generation) and $110\ell + 1$ invocations.

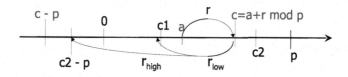

Fig. 5. Case of $c_1 < c < c_2$

6.2   LSB Protocol for Special Case of Interval Test Protocol

In order to construct our comparison protocol later, we consider computing $[a < \frac{p}{2}]_p$. Though it is possible for us to use the technique in Section 6.1, we compute $[a < \frac{p}{2}]_p$ more efficiently by using special properties of $\frac{p}{2}$ and apply this subprotocol (called the LSB protocol here) to our comparison protocol. By a simple observation, we can notice that $a \in \{0, 1, \ldots, \frac{p-1}{2}\} \Leftrightarrow (2a \bmod p)_0 = 0$, and that $a \in \{\frac{p-1}{2} + 1, \ldots, p - 1\} \Leftrightarrow (2a \bmod p)_0 = 1$ where $(x)_0$ is the least significant bit (LSB) of $x \in \{0, 1, \ldots, p - 1\}$. That is, if $a < \frac{p}{2}$, no wrap-around modulo p occurs when $2a \bmod p$ is computed and $2a \bmod p$ is even. On the other hand, if $a > \frac{p}{2}$, a wrap-around modulo p occurs when $2a \bmod p$ is computed and $2a \bmod p$ is odd. Therefore, if we can compute $[(x)_0]_p$ from $[x]_p$, we can use it to compute $[a < \frac{p}{2}]_p$.

To compute $[(x)_0]_p$ from $[x]_p$, we randomize x by $c = x + r$ and reveal c where r is a bitwise-shared random secret. Then we can obtain $[(x)_0]_p$ from $(c)_0$ and $[(r)_0]_p$.

Procedure. The parties want to compute $[(x)_0]_p$ from $[x]_p$. The parties generate $[r \in_R \mathbb{Z}_p]_B$ and obtain $[r]_p$ eventually. Next, the parties compute $[c]_p = [x]_p + [r]_p$ and reveal $c = x + r \bmod p \in \{0, 1, \ldots, p-1\}$. If *no* wrap-around modulo p occurs when c is computed, we have $(x)_0 = (c)_0 \oplus (r)_0$ and if a wrap-around modulo p occurs when c is computed, we have $(x)_0 = 1 - \{(c)_0 \oplus (r)_0\}$. Furthermore, we can use $(c < r)$ to know whether or not a wrap-around modulo p occurred when c was computed. That is, if $(c < r) = 0$, it means that no wrap-around modulo p occurred, and if $(c < r) = 1$, it means that a wrap-around modulo p occurred because $r \in \{0, 1, \ldots, p - 1\}$.

From these facts, the parties can compute $[(x)_0]_p$ as

$$[(x)_0]_p = [c <_B r]_p \times (1 - \{(c)_0 \oplus [(r)_0]_p\}) + (1 - [c <_B r]_p) \times \{(c)_0 \oplus [(r)_0]_p\}$$
$$= [c <_B r]_p + \{(c)_0 \oplus [(r)_0]_p\} - 2[c <_B r]_p \times \{(c)_0 \oplus [(r)_0]_p\}. \tag{1}$$

The interpretation of Eq. (1) is that if $(c <_B r) = 1$, we have $(1 - \{(c)_0 \oplus [(r)_0]_p\})$ and otherwise we have $\{(c)_0 \oplus [(r)_0]_p\}$. Because c is public, note that $(c)_0 \oplus [(r)_0]_p$ can be computed as

$$(c)_0 \oplus [(r)_0]_p = \begin{cases} [(r)_0]_p & \text{if } (c)_0 = 0 \\ 1 - [(r)_0]_p & \text{if } (c)_0 = 1. \end{cases}$$

Also note that the parties already have $[(r)_0]_p$ because r is generated by $[r \in_R \mathbb{Z}_p]_B$.

By using the LSB protocol, the parties can compute $[a < \frac{p}{2}]_p$ from $[a]_p$ as $[a < \frac{p}{2}]_p = 1 - [(2a)_0]_p$.

Complexity of LSB Protocol. The complexity of computing each component is as follows: 7 rounds (including 2 rounds for random value generation) and 76ℓ invocations for $[r \in_R \mathbb{Z}_p]_B$, 5 rounds and 17ℓ invocations for $[c <_B r]_p$, and

Table 2. Truth Table for $(a < b)$

$w = (a < p/2)$	$x = (b < p/2)$	$y = (a - b \bmod p < p/2)$	$z = (a < b)$
1	0	*	1
0	1	*	0
0	0	0	1
0	0	1	0
1	1	0	1
1	1	1	0

1 round and 1 invocation for $[c <_B r]_p \times [(r)_0]_p$. The total complexity is 13 rounds (including 2 rounds for random value generation) and $93\ell + 1$ invocations.

6.3 Comparison Protocol

In the comparison protocol, given two shared secrets $a, b \in \mathbb{Z}_p$, the parties compute $[a < b]_p$ without revealing $(a < b)$ itself. For example, we can compute $[\max(a, b)]_p = [a]_p + [a < b]_p \times [b - a]_p$ by using the comparison protocol.

If the parties use the bit-decomposition protocol, the parties compute $[a]_B$ and $[b]_B$ from $[a]_p$ and $[b]_p$ and compute $[a <_B b]_p$ as in [11].

It seems difficult for us to compare a and b directly without using the bit-decomposition protocol. Therefore, we compare a and b indirectly via the value of $\frac{p}{2}$ by computing $[a < \frac{p}{2}]_p$, $[b < \frac{p}{2}]_p$, and $[a - b \bmod p < \frac{p}{2}]_p$.

Procedure. By a simple observation, we can notice that $(a < b)$ is determined from $(a < \frac{p}{2})$, $(b < \frac{p}{2})$, and $(a - b \bmod p < \frac{p}{2})$. This observation can be confirmed by the truth table (Table 2).

When we denote $(a < \frac{p}{2})$, $(b < \frac{p}{2})$, $(a - b \bmod p < \frac{p}{2})$, and $(a < b)$ as w, x, y, and z respectively, then z is represented as

$$z = w\bar{x} \vee \bar{w}\bar{x}\bar{y} \vee wx\bar{y}$$
$$= w(1 - x) + (1 - w)(1 - x)(1 - y) + wx(1 - y)$$
$$= w(x + y - 2xy) + 1 - y - x + xy. \tag{2}$$

Therefore, if the parties can compute $[a < \frac{p}{2}]_p$, $[b < \frac{p}{2}]_p$, and $[a - b \bmod p < \frac{p}{2}]_p$, they can compute $[a < b]_p$ from Eq. (2) by using addition and the multiplication protocol. We can use the LSB protocol to compute all three of these values.

Complexity of Comparison Protocol. If we use the bit-decomposition protocol straightforwardly, the complexity of computing each component is as follows: 38 rounds (including 2 rounds for random value generation) and $2 \times (93\ell + 94\ell \log_2 \ell)$ invocations for $[a]_B$ and $[b]_B$ and 6 rounds and 19ℓ invocations for $[a <_B b]_p$. The total complexity is 44 rounds (including 2 rounds for random value generation) and $205\ell + 188\ell \log_2 \ell$ invocations.

On the other hand, in our construction, the complexity of computing each component is as follows: 13 rounds (including 2 rounds for random value generation) and $3 \times (93\ell + 1)$ invocations for $[a < \frac{p}{2}]_p$, $[b < \frac{p}{2}]_p$, and $[a - b \bmod p < \frac{p}{2}]_p$ and 2 rounds and 2 invocations for Eq. (2). The total complexity is 15 rounds (including 2 rounds for random value generation) and $279\ell + 5$ invocations.

6.4   Equality Test Protocol

In the equality test protocol, given two shared secrets $a, b \in \mathbb{Z}_p$, the parties compute $[a = b]_p$ without revealing $(a = b)$ itself.

Because $[a = b]_p$ can be computed by $[a - b = 0]_p$, we focus on computing $[a = 0]_p$.

If the parties use the bit-decomposition protocol, the parties compute $[d]_B$ from $[d]_p = [a - b]_p$ and compute $[\wedge_{i=0}^{\ell-1}(1 - d_i)]_p$ by using an unbounded fan-in And as in [11].

In our construction, we use a very simple observation that the randomization $c(= d + r)$ of d is equal to r if d is zero.

Procedure. First the parties generate $[r \in_R \mathbb{Z}_p]_B$ and obtain $[r]_p$ eventually. Next, the parties compute $[c]_p = [a]_p + [r]_p$ and reveal $c = a + r \bmod p \in \{0, 1, \ldots, p - 1\}$. We can note that $c = r$ iff $a = 0$. Therefore, the parties compute whether all bits of c are the same as $[r]_B$. Let $(c_{\ell-1}, \ldots, c_0)_2$ be the bit representation of c. Then the parties compute $[c_i']_p$ for $0 \leq i \leq \ell - 1$ as

$$[c_i']_p = \begin{cases} [r_i]_p & \text{if } c_i = 1 \\ 1 - [r_i]_p & \text{if } c_i = 0. \end{cases}$$

We can note that $c_i' \in \{0, 1\}$ and that $c_i' = 1$ iff $c_i = r_i$. Finally, the parties compute $[a = 0]_p$ as $[\wedge_{i=0}^{\ell-1} c_i']_p$ by using an unbounded fan-in And.

Complexity of Equality Test Protocol. If we use the bit-decomposition protocol straightforwardly, the complexity of computing each component is as follows: 38 rounds (including 2 rounds for random value generation) and $93\ell + 94\ell \log_2 \ell$ invocations for $[d]_B$ and 1 rounds and 5ℓ invocations for $[\wedge_{i=0}^{\ell-1}(1 - d_i)]_p$. The total complexity is 39 rounds (including 2 rounds for random value generation) and $98\ell + 94\ell \log_2 \ell$ invocations.

On the other hand, in our construction, the complexity of computing each component is as follows: 7 rounds (including 2 rounds for random value generation) and 76ℓ invocations for $[r]_B$ and 1 rounds and 5ℓ invocations for $[\wedge_{i=0}^{\ell-1} c_i']_p$. The total complexity is 8 rounds (including 2 rounds for random value generation) and 81ℓ invocations.

6.5   Probabilistic Equality Test Protocol

We consider another version of the equality test protocol with a very small round complexity. We focus on computing $[a = 0]_p$ again. In our construction, we assume that $p = 3 \bmod 4$ or $p = 5 \bmod 8$. These imply that Legendre symbol

$\left(\frac{-1}{p}\right) = -1$ if $p = 3 \bmod 4$ and that $\left(\frac{2}{p}\right) = -1$ if $p = 5 \bmod 8$. The basic idea is based on the property of quadratic residues as follows: If a is a zero, we always have $\left(\frac{c}{p}\right) = \left(\frac{r}{p}\right)$ where $c = a + r$, r is a random secret and c is a revealed value. If a is not a zero, we have $\left(\frac{c}{p}\right) \neq \left(\frac{r}{p}\right)$ with non-negligible probability. By checking whether $\left(\frac{c}{p}\right) = \left(\frac{r}{p}\right)$ secretly with sufficiently many trials, we can perform the equality test on a in a probabilistic way. Here note that we need to generate random secret r in a special way to compute $\left(\frac{r}{p}\right)$ secretly.

Procedure. First we describe the case of $p = 3 \bmod 4$. The case of $p = 5 \bmod 8$ can be obtained quite straightforwardly as we mention later.

The parties generate $[b_j \in_R \{-1, 1\}]_p$, $[r_j \in_R \mathbb{Z}_p]_p$, and $[r'_j \in_R \mathbb{Z}_p]_p$ for $1 \leq j \leq k$ in parallel where k is chosen such that the error probability $\left(\frac{1}{2}\right)^k$ is negligible. The value b_j can be generated by a joint random bit sharing. Next, the parties compute for $1 \leq j \leq k$ in parallel,

$$[c_j]_p = [a]_p \times [r_j]_p + [b_j]_p \times [r'_j]_p \times [r'_j]_p$$

and reveal all the c_j's. Note that $b_j r'^2_j$ is uniformly random and unknown to the parties, so no information about a is leaked from c_j. Actually we can confirm that $\Pr[b_j r'^2_j = 0] = \Pr[r'_j = 0] = \frac{1}{p}$, that $\Pr[b_j r'^2_j = y] = \Pr[b_j = 1] \times \Pr[r'_j = \pm\sqrt{y}] = \frac{1}{2} \times \frac{2}{p} = \frac{1}{p}$ if y is a quadratic residue , and that $\Pr[b_j r'^2_j = y] = \Pr[b_j = -1] \times \Pr[r'_j = \pm\sqrt{-y}] = \frac{1}{2} \times \frac{2}{p} = \frac{1}{p}$ if y is a quadratic nonresidue.

Also note that if $a = 0$, ar_j is always a zero and that if $a \neq 0$, ar_j is uniformly random.

If c_j is a zero, the parties discard the c_j and retry. The probability that c_j happens to be a zero is $\frac{1}{p}$ and negligible in the practical setting (e.g., $p > 2^{32}$).

Assuming that c_j is not a zero, we can notice that $a = 0 \Rightarrow \left(\frac{c_j}{p}\right) = \left(\frac{b_j r'^2_j}{p}\right) = b_j$ with prob. 1, and that $a \neq 0 \Rightarrow \left(\frac{c_j}{p}\right) = b_j$ with prob. $\frac{1}{2}$. The case of $a = 0$ is obvious. When $a \neq 0$, c_j is uniformly random whether b_j is -1 or 1 because ar_j is uniformly random, so the probability that $\left(\frac{c_j}{p}\right) = b_j$ is $\frac{1}{2}$.

Then the parties compute for $1 \leq j \leq k$,

$$[x_j]_p = \begin{cases} 2^{-1}([b_j]_p + 1) & \text{if } \left(\frac{c_j}{p}\right) = 1 \\ -2^{-1}([b_j]_p - 1) & \text{if } \left(\frac{c_j}{p}\right) = -1. \end{cases}$$

Note that $x_j \in \{0, 1\}$ and that $x_j = 1$ iff $\left(\frac{c_j}{p}\right) = b_j$. Finally, the parties compute $[a = 0]_p = [\wedge^k_{j=1} x_j]_p$ by using an unbounded fan-in And, assuming that at least one of x_j's is 0 if $a \neq 0$ with sufficiently large k.

The error probability that $(a = 0) = 1$ when $a \neq 0$ is $\left(\frac{1}{2}\right)^k$ and it can be negligible if we use sufficiently large k.

Similarly, when $p = 5 \bmod 8$, the parties compute and reveal for $1 \le j \le k$

$$c_j = ar_j + b'_j r'^2_j \bmod p$$

instead of $c_j = ar_j + b_j r'^2_j \bmod p$ where $b'_j = -2^{-1}(b_j - 3)$.

Note that $b'_j \in_R \{2,1\}$ because $b_j \in_R \{-1,1\}$. Therefore, noting that $\left(\frac{2}{p}\right) = -1$, we can notice that $a = 0 \Rightarrow \left(\frac{c_j}{p}\right) = \left(\frac{b'_j r'^2_j}{p}\right) = b_j$ with prob. 1, and that $a \ne 0 \Rightarrow \left(\frac{c_j}{p}\right) = b_j$ with prob. $\frac{1}{2}$. The rest of computation can be done as we did for $p = 3 \bmod 4$.

Though we assumed, for simplicity, that $p = 3 \bmod 4$ or that $p = 5 \bmod 8$, actually we can extend the idea to arbitrary primes if we generate $b_j \in_R \{y, 1\}$ such that $\left(\frac{y}{p}\right) = -1$.

Quadratic Residuosity Test Protocol. Incidentally, by using the random secret $b_j r^2_j$ in Section 6.5, we can also construct a quadratic residuosity test protocol where, given $[a \in \mathbb{Z}^*_p]_p$, the parties can compute $[\left(\frac{a}{p}\right)]_p$ as follows:

Here we assume that $p = 3 \bmod 4$ for simplicity. The parties generate $[br^2]_p$ in the same way as $b_j r^2_j$ is generated in Sect. 6.5, and reveal $c = br^2 a$. If c is a zero, the parties retry. The parties can compute $[\left(\frac{a}{p}\right)]_p$ as $\left(\frac{c}{p}\right)[b]_p$ since

$$\left(\frac{c}{p}\right) = \left(\frac{b}{p}\right)\left(\frac{a}{p}\right) = b\left(\frac{a}{p}\right).$$

Complexity of Probabilistic Equality Test Protocol. The complexity of computing each component is as follows: 3 rounds (including 2 rounds for random value generation) and $7k$ invocations for $[c_j]_p$'s and 1 rounds and $5k$ invocations for $[\wedge^k_{j=1} x_j]_p$. The total complexity is 4 rounds (including 2 rounds for random value generation) and $12k$ invocations.

7   Implementation

In the real implementation, we can use (odd-even) parallel prefix computation [19,18] based on carry propagation and generation for the bitwise less-than and bitwise sum protocols as in [4,15,23] where the complexity of bitwise less-than is roughly $2 + \log_2(\ell)$ rounds and $3\ell - 1$ invocations ($2\ell - 1$ invocations if one of the two operands is known) and the complexity of bitwise sum is roughly $2\log_2(\ell) - 1$ rounds and $5\ell - 2\log_2(\ell) - 4$ invocations ($4\ell - 2\log_2(\ell) - 4$ invocations if one of the two operands is known). Also, instead of joint random number sharing, we can use non-interactive pseudo-random secret sharing by Cramer, Damgård and Ishai [9] in the secret sharing setting in order to reduce the round and communication complexities. In Table 3, we summarize the number of invocations of main subprotocols in each protocol. Whether we use constant-round subprotocols or non-constant-round subprotocols as building blocks, our constructions are more efficient according to Table 3. Though, in the comparison protocol, we need 3 invocations of joint random number bitwise-sharing compared with 2 in [11], this can be done in advance and our protocol seems more advantageous.

Table 3. Number of Invocations of Subprotocols

Protocol		Random Bitwise-Sharing	Bitwise Less-Than	Bitwise Sum
Bit-Decomposition	[11]	1	1	2
	Proposed	1	1	1
Interval Test	[11]	1	3	2
	Proposed	1	2	0
Comparison	[11]	2	3	4
	Proposed	3	3	0
Equality Test	[11]	1	1	2
	Proposed1	1	0	0

Acknowledgements

We would like to thank Tomas Toft for giving us the idea in Section 6.2 that led to an efficient comparison protocol and the information on [24]. We also thank Prof. Ivan Damgård for suggesting the possibility of using quadratic residues to construct an efficient equality test protocol. We are also grateful to the anonymous reviewers and Prof. C.Pandu Rangan for their helpful comments.

References

1. J. Algesheimer, J. Camenisch, and V. Shoup, "Efficient computation modulo a shared secret with application to the generation of shared safe-prime products," CRYPTO'02, LNCS 2442, pp.417–432, Springer Verlag, 2002.
2. J. Bar-Ilan and D. Beaver, "Non-cryptographic fault-tolerant computing in a constant number of rounds of interaction," Proc. ACM Symposium on Principles of Distributed Computing, pp.201–209, 1989.
3. M. Ben-Or, S. Goldwasser, and A. Wigderson, "Completeness theorem for non-cryptographic fault-tolerant distributed computation," 20th Annual ACM Symposium on Theory of Computing, pp.1–10, 1988.
4. P. Bogetoft, I. Damgård, T. Jakobsen, K. Nielsen, J. Pagter, and T. Toft, "A practical implementation of secure auctions based on multiparty integer computation," Financial Cryptography 2006, LNCS 4107, pp.142–147, Springer Verlag, 2006.
5. A.K. Chandra, S. Fortune, and R.J. Lipton, "Lower bounds for constant depth circuits for prefix problems," ICALP, LNCS 154, pp.109–117, Springer Verlag, 1983.
6. A.K. Chandra, S. Fortune, and R.J. Lipton, "Unbounded fan-in circuits and associative functions," Proc. 15th ACM Symposium on Theory of Computing, pp.52–60, 1983.
7. D. Chaum, C. Crêpeau, and I. Damgård, "Multi-party unconditionally secure protocols," Proc. ACM STOC'88, pp.11–19, 1988.
8. R. Cramer and I. Damgård, "Secure distributed linear algebra in a constant number of rounds," CRYPTO'01, LNCS 2139, pp.119–136, Springer Verlag, 2001.
9. R. Cramer, I. Damgård, and Y. Ishai, "Share conversion, pseudorandom secret sharing and applications to secure computation," Proc. 2nd Theory of Cryptography Conference, LNCS 3378, pp.342–362, Springer Verlag, 2005.
10. R. Cramer, I. Damgård, and J.B. Nielsen, "Multiparty computation from threshold homomorphic encryption," EUROCRYPT'01, LNCS 2045, pp.280–300, Springer Verlag, 2001.

11. I. Damgård, M. Fitzi, E. Kiltz, J.B. Nielsen, and T. Toft, "Unconditionally secure constant-rounds multi-party computation for equality, comparison, bits and exponentiation," Proc. 3rd Theory of Cryptography Conference, LNCS 3876, pp.285–304, Springer Verlag, 2006.

12. I. Damgård and M. Jurik, "A generalisation, a simplification and some applications of Paillier's probabilistic public-key system," PKC 2001, LNCS 1992, pp.119–136, Springer Verlag, 2001.

13. I. Damgård and J.B. Nielsen, "Universally composable efficient multiparty computation from threshold homomorphic encryption," CRYPTO'03, LNCS 2729, pp.247–264, Springer Verlag, 2003.

14. P.-A. Fouque, G. Poupard, and J. Stern, "Sharing decryption in the context of voting or lotteries," Financial Cryptography 2000, LNCS 1962, pp.90–104, Springer Verlag, 2000.

15. S. L. From and T. Jakobsen, "Secure multi-party computation on integers," Master's Thesis, http://www.daimi.au.dk/~mas/thesis/index.html, 2006

16. R. Gennaro, M.O. Rabin, and T. Rabin, "Simplified VSS and fast-track multiparty computations with applications to threshold cryptography," Proc. 17th ACM Symposium on Principles of Distributed Computing, pp.101–110, 1998.

17. O. Goldreich, S. Micali, and A. Wigderson, "How to play any mental game or a complete theorem for protocols with honest majority," Proc. 19th STOC, pp.218–229, 1987.

18. H. Jordan and G. Alaghband "Fundamentals of parallel processing," Prentice Hall, 2003.

19. R. Ladner and M. Fischer, "Parallel prefix computation," Journal of the Association for Computing Machinery vol.27, pp.831–838, 1980.

20. E. Ong and J. Kubiatowicz, "Optimizing robustness while generating shared secret safe primes," PKC 2005, LNCS 3386, pp.120–137, Springer Verlag, 2005.

21. B. Schoenmakers and P. Tuyls, "Efficient binary conversion for Paillier encrypted values," EUROCRYPT'06, LNCS 4004, pp.522–537, Springer Verlag, 2006.

22. A. Shamir, "How to share a secret," Communications of ACM, vol.22, no.11, pp.612–613, 1979.

23. T. Toft, "Secure integer computation with applications in economy," http://www.aicis.alexandra.dk/uk/projects/scet_demo.htm#Tof05, Available from http://www.daimi.au.dk/~tomas/publications/progress.pdf

24. T. Toft, "An efficient, unconditionally secure equality test for secret shared values," Workshop on Models for Cryptographic Protocols (MCP 2006), Abstract available from http://www.daimi.au.dk/~buus/mcp2006/talks/T.pdf

25. A. Yao, "Protocols for secure computation," Proc. 23rd FOCS, pp.160–164, 1982.

A   Complexity of Bitwise Sum Protocol

Based on [11] (see unbounded fan-in carry propagation in Section 6.4), the complexity of the bitwise sum protocol is evaluated as follows:

If the Prefix-And is computed with x rounds and $y \times \ell$ invocations, the complexity of the bitwise sum protocol is upper bounded by $2(x+1)+1$ rounds and $(2(y+6)+1)\ell \log_2 \ell$ invocations. Assuming that all the random values are generated in the first 2 rounds and that the complexity of the Prefix-And is 5 rounds (not including 2 rounds for random value generation) and 17ℓ invocations, the total complexity is 15 rounds (including 2 rounds for random value generation) and $47\ell \log_2 \ell$ invocations.

Identity-Based Traitor Tracing

Michel Abdalla[1], Alexander W. Dent[2], John Malone-Lee[3],
Gregory Neven[1,4], Duong Hieu Phan[5], and Nigel P. Smart[3]

[1] Département d'Informatique, Ecole Normale Supérieure,
45 Rue d'Ulm, 75230 Paris Cedex 05, France
{Michel.Abdalla,Gregory.Neven}@ens.fr
[2] Information Security Group, Royal Holloway, University of London,
Egham, Surrey, TW20 0EX, United Kingdom
a.dent@rhul.ac.uk
[3] Department Computer Science, University of Bristol,
Woodland Road, Bristol, BS8 1UB, United Kingdom
{malone,nigel}@cs.bris.ac.uk
[4] Department of Electrical Engineering, Katholieke Universiteit Leuven,
Kasteelpark Arenberg 10, B-3001 Heverlee, Belgium
Gregory.Neven@esat.kuleuven.be
[5] France Télécom R&D, 38-40 rue du Général Leclerc,
92794 Issy les Moulineaux Cedex 9, France
duonghieu.phan@orange-ftgroup.com

Abstract. We present the first identity-based traitor tracing scheme. The scheme is shown to be secure in the standard model, assuming the bilinear decision Diffie-Hellman (DBDH) is hard in the asymmetric bilinear pairing setting, and that the DDH assumption holds in the group defining the first coordinate of the asymmetric pairing. Our traitor tracing system allows adaptive pirates to be traced. The scheme makes use of a two level identity-based encryption scheme with wildcards (WIBE) based on Waters' identity-based encryption scheme.[1]

1 Introduction

In 1984 Shamir proposed the concept of identity-based cryptography [15]. However, it took nearly twenty years for the problem of designing an efficient method to implement identity-based encryption (IBE) to be solved. In 2000 and 2001 respectively Sakai, Ohgishi and Kasahara [13] and Boneh and Franklin [6] proposed IBE schemes based on elliptic curve pairings. Also, in 2001 Cocks proposed a system based on the quadratic residuosity problem [10].

---

[1] The fourth author is a Postdoctoral Fellow of the Research Foundation – Flanders (FWO). The work described in this paper has been supported in part by the European Commission through the IST Programme under Contract IST-2002-507932 ECRYPT. The information in this document reflects only the author's views, is provided as is and no guarantee or warranty is given that the information is fit for any particular purpose. The user thereof uses the information at its sole risk and liability.

T. Okamoto and X. Wang (Eds.): PKC 2007, LNCS 4450, pp. 361–376, 2007.

Identity-based encryption is often justified as a useful technology by its possible use in an e-mail application. However, many people, whilst having a small set of e-mail identities, often belong to a larger set of e-mail groups. An e-mail group, or shared address, is an e-mail address which allows the sender to send a message to a large number of individual e-mail addresses without needing to know the actual individual addresses. Using existing identity-based encryption techniques one can easily implement such a scheme by giving each member of the e-mail group the same ID-private key. Thus all members of the group will share the same private key.

A common business model in PKI world is that the certificate authority charges for each certificate, or block of certificates, issued. In the ID-based world this model corresponds to the trust authority charging for each private key, or block of private keys. However, in our group e-mail example this would mean that the trust authority would only be able to charge for one private key for the whole group, since as soon as one person had the private key they could share it with the other members of the group. What is needed is a disincentive for the group members to collaborate in this manner.

A similar situation occurs in the traditional symmetric or public key setting in broadcast encryption. Here one solves the associated problem by using a traitor tracing scheme, which allows any person (or set of colluding people) who creates a new decryption device, or key, to be traced. Thus combining the above ideas together we see that there is a possible need for an identity-based traitor tracing scheme.

Surprisingly since the invention of identity-based cryptography by Shamir [15] in 1984, no one seems to have considered this issue. Thus in this paper we present the first identity-based traitor tracing scheme. Our scheme is based on the Waters' WIBE from [1], which is based on Waters' identity-based encryption scheme [17]. A WIBE is a variant of a hierarchical IBE (HIBE) scheme in that it encrypts to an identity string which is defined on various layers. However, unlike a HIBE, which allows only a single recipient, a WIBE allows one to encrypt to a string which is "wildcarded" on a given set of levels. A WIBE allows one to target a ciphertext at a given group of users by applying the appropriate wildcards.

Our construction is relatively simple: we use a two level WIBE in which the first level represents the name of the group and the second level represents the unique index of a user. This allows e-mails to be addressed to the entire group via the use of a wildcard in the second level. Group membership is 'policed' by the trust authority, which only releases a decryption key to a user if the user is entitled to decrypt messages sent to a particular group. The subtlety of our construction is in the construction of a traitor tracing algorithm.

We prove that our scheme protects the confidentiality of encrypted messages against passive attackers in the standard model, and show that it allows traitor tracing against an adaptive traitor.

Unfortunately, our scheme is not practical due to the combination of Waters' IBE and collusion secure codes [8], which results in infeasibly large public key and ciphertext sizes. Thus we leave the construction of a truly efficient identity-based traitor tracing scheme, even in the random oracle model [3], as an open problem. In addition we leave as open the problem of creating a scheme which allows a greater number of key extraction queries by the pirate than ours allows. Furthermore, our scheme does not protect against pirate decoder manufacturers mounting chosen-ciphertext attacks, however this later stronger pirate has not been considered in the public-key setting either.

2 Preliminaries

2.1 Notation

Let $\mathbb{N} = \{0, 1, 2, \ldots\}$ be the set of natural numbers and $\{0,1\}^*$ the set of all bit strings. If $k \in \mathbb{N}$ then $\{0,1\}^k$ is the set of bit strings of length k and 1^k is the string of k ones. If $\mathcal{A}$ is a randomized algorithm, then $y \xleftarrow{\$} \mathcal{A}^O(x)$ denotes the assignment to y of the output of $\mathcal{A}$ when run on input x with fresh random coins and with access to oracle O; we write $y \leftarrow \mathcal{A}^O(x)$ if $\mathcal{A}$ is deterministic. If S is a finite set, then $x \xleftarrow{\$} S$ denotes the random generation of an element $x \in S$ using the uniform distribution. A function $\nu : \mathbb{N} \to [0,1]$ is said to be *negligible* if for all $c \in \mathbb{N}$ there exists a $k_c \in \mathbb{N}$ such that $\nu(k) < k^{-c}$ for all $k > k_c$. It is said to be *non-negligible* if there exists a $c \in \mathbb{N}$ such that $\nu(k) > k^{-c}$ for all $k \in \mathbb{N}$.

2.2 Computational Assumptions

Our scheme employs asymmetric pairings, which we now recall. Let $\mathbb{G}_1$, $\mathbb{G}_2$ and $\mathbb{G}_T$ denote three finite multiplicative abelian groups of prime order $p > 2^k$. Let g and h be generators of $\mathbb{G}_1$ and $\mathbb{G}_2$, respectively, and let $\psi : \mathbb{G}_2 \to \mathbb{G}_1$ be an efficiently computable isomorphism such that $\psi(h) = g$. We assume that there exists an admissible bilinear map $\hat{e} : \mathbb{G}_1 \times \mathbb{G}_2 \to \mathbb{G}_T$, meaning that for all $a, b \in \mathbb{Z}_p$ (1) $\hat{e}(g^a, h^b) = \hat{e}(g, h)^{ab}$, (2) $\hat{e}(g^a, h^b) = 1$ iff $a = 0$ or $b = 0$, and (3) $\hat{e}(g^a, h^b)$ is efficiently computable.

The advantage of an algorithm $\mathcal{A}$ in solving the *computational bilinear Diffie–Hellman (CBDH)* problem in $\mathbb{G}_2$ is defined as

$$\mathbf{Adv}_{\mathcal{A}, \mathbb{G}_2}^{\mathrm{cbdh}}(k) = \Pr\left[Z = \hat{e}(g, h)^{xyz} \;:\; x, y, z \xleftarrow{\$} \mathbb{Z}_p \;;\; Z \xleftarrow{\$} \mathcal{A}(h^x, h^y, h^z)\right] .$$

The advantage of $\mathcal{A}$ in solving the decisional variant of this problem, called the *decisional bilinear Diffie–Hellman (DBDH)* problem in $\mathbb{G}_2$, is

$$\mathbf{Adv}_{\mathcal{A}, \mathbb{G}_2}^{\mathrm{dbdh}}(k) = \left| \Pr\left[\mathcal{A}(h^x, h^y, h^z, Z) = 1 \;:\; x, y, z \xleftarrow{\$} \mathbb{Z}_p \;;\; Z \leftarrow \hat{e}(g, h)^{xyz}\right] \right.$$
$$\left. - \Pr\left[\mathcal{A}(h^x, h^y, h^z, Z) = 1 \;:\; x, y, z \xleftarrow{\$} \mathbb{Z}_p \;;\; Z \xleftarrow{\$} \mathbb{G}_T\right] \right| .$$

We say that the CBDH and DBDH problems in $\mathbb{G}_2$ are *hard* if the respective advantages are negligible functions in k for all algorithms $\mathcal{A}$ with running time polynomial in k.

We also require that the DDH problem in $\mathbb{G}_1$ is hard, namely we require that for all algorithms $\mathcal{A}$, with running time polynomial in k, the following advantage is a negligible function in k,

$$\mathbf{Adv}_{\mathcal{A},\mathbb{G}_1}^{\mathrm{xddh}}(k) = \left| \Pr\left[\mathcal{A}(g^x, g^y, Z) = 1 \;:\; x, y \xleftarrow{\$} \mathbb{Z}_p \;;\; Z \leftarrow g^{xy}\right] \right.$$
$$\left. - \Pr\left[\mathcal{A}(g^x, g^y, Z) = 1 \;:\; x, y \xleftarrow{\$} \mathbb{Z}_p \;;\; Z \xleftarrow{\$} \mathbb{G}_1\right] \right|.$$

Note that if the DDH problem in $\mathbb{G}_1$ is hard, then there cannot exist a computable isomorphism from $\mathbb{G}_1$ to $\mathbb{G}_2$ and thus we must be working in the asymmetric pairing setting. The assumption that the DDH problem is hard in $\mathbb{G}_1$ is referred to as the external DDH problem (XDDH) and has been used before in [2,4,14].

3   Identity-Based Traitor Tracing

3.1   Syntax

In this section we will describe the general model for an identity-based traitor tracing scheme. Broadcast groups are referred to by an identity string $ID \in \{0,1\}^*$, individual users are referred to by an index $i \in \mathbb{N}$. To make user i member of the group ID, the trusted key distribution centre provides it with a personal decryption key $d_{ID,i}$. Anyone can encrypt a message to the general group ID such that all individual users belonging to the group can recover the message.

Formally, an identity-based traitor tracing scheme $\mathcal{IBTT}$ consists of five polynomial-time algorithms:

- A randomised key generation algorithm $\mathcal{G}(1^k)$ taking as input the security parameter k. This algorithm generates a set of domain parameters consisting of a master public key mpk and a master secret key msk.
- A key extraction algorithm $\mathcal{X}(msk, ID, i)$ which given the master secret key msk, a group identity $ID \in \{0,1\}^*$ and a user index i generates a user secret key $d_{ID,i}$. This algorithm could be probabilistic.
- A probabilistic encryption algorithm $\mathcal{E}(mpk, ID, \mathfrak{m})$ which on input of the master public key mpk, a group identity ID and a message $\mathfrak{m}$ outputs a ciphertext C.
- A decryption algorithm $\mathcal{D}(d_{ID,i}, C)$ which on input of a user secret key $d_{ID,i}$ and a ciphertext C outputs a plaintext message $\mathfrak{m}$, or $\bot$ to indicate a decryption error.
- A traitor tracing algorithm $\mathcal{T}^{\mathbb{D}}(msk, ID)$ which has oracle access to a "pirate" decryption box $\mathbb{D}$. The tracing algorithm takes as input the master secret key msk and a group identity ID, and outputs a set of user identifiers (called "traitors") $T \subset \mathbb{N}$.

An identity-based traitor tracing scheme whose tracing algorithm takes as input *mpk* instead of *msk* is said to be *publicly-traceable*, since then anyone can execute the tracing algorithm. We shall assume that all "pirate" decryption boxes are resettable [11], meaning that they retain no state between decryptions. In particular, pirate boxes cannot self-destruct.

For correctness we require that $\mathcal{D}(d, \mathcal{E}(mpk, ID, \mathfrak{m})) = \mathfrak{m}$ with probability one for all $k \in \mathbb{N}$, $ID, \mathfrak{m} \in \{0,1\}^*$, $i \in \mathbb{N}$, $(mpk, msk) \xleftarrow{\$} \mathcal{G}(1^k)$ and $d \xleftarrow{\$} \mathcal{X}(msk, ID, i)$.

3.2 Secrecy

We require that our ID-based traitor tracing scheme is semantically secure in the presence of adaptive adversaries who have access to a key extraction oracle and, in a chosen-ciphertext attack, a decryption oracle. These are standard notions in ID-based cryptography first introduced in [6]. The extension to the setting we have here is immediate, but for completeness we clarify it here.

Secrecy is defined by a two-stage game. The challenger first runs the key generation algorithm to generate a master key pair $(mpk, msk) \xleftarrow{\$} \mathcal{G}(1^k)$. The master public key *mpk* is passed to the adversary. In the first stage of the game the adversary has access to a key extraction oracle $\mathcal{X}(msk, \cdot, \cdot)$, which it can query on arbitrary pairs (ID, i) of group identities *ID* and user indices *i*. In a chosen-ciphertext attack, the adversary can also has access to a decryption oracle $\mathcal{D}(\mathcal{X}(msk, \cdot, \cdot), \cdot)$ from which it can obtain the decryption of any ciphertext *C* using the key to any pair (ID, i). The first stage ends when the adversary outputs two messages of equal length $\mathfrak{m}_0$ and $\mathfrak{m}_1$, plus a challenge group identity ID^*.

The challenger then selects a bit *b* and encrypts $\mathfrak{m}_b$ under the group identity ID^* to form the challenge ciphertext $C^* \leftarrow \mathcal{E}(mpk, ID^*, \mathfrak{m}_b)$. The challenge ciphertext is returned to the adversary for the second stage of the game. In this second stage the adversary can perform further queries to its oracles. At the end of the second stage the adversary outputs its guess b' as to the bit *b*. The adversary wins the game if $b = b'$, if ID^* never appeared in any of the key extraction oracle queries, and, in a chosen-ciphertext attack, if C^* was never submitted to the decryption oracle with group identity ID^*.

The advantage $\mathbf{Adv}^{\text{ind-id-cpa}}_{\mathcal{A}, \mathcal{IBTT}}(k)$, respectively $\mathbf{Adv}^{\text{ind-id-cca}}_{\mathcal{A}, \mathcal{IBTT}}(k)$, of an adversary $\mathcal{A}$ in breaking the indistinguishability of scheme $\mathcal{IBTT}$ is defined as the probability of $\mathcal{A}$ winning the corresponding game minus one-half. We say that the traitor tracing scheme is IND-ID-CPA, respectively IND-ID-CCA secure, if this advantage is a negligible function in *k* for any adversary $\mathcal{A}$ with running time polynomial in *k*.

3.3 Traceability

We extend the notion of traceability defined for the public key setting in [7] to the identity-based setting. We provide definitions for both chosen-plaintext and chosen-ciphertext attack; our scheme however is only proved secure in the chosen-plaintext setting. We note that to our knowledge there is no public-key traitor tracing system which has been considered in the presence of (the natural analogue of) chosen-ciphertext attacks against the traceability property.

Let $k, c \in \mathbb{N}$ be two security parameters associated to the experiment. The challenger first generates a master key pair $(mpk, msk) \xleftarrow{\$} \mathcal{G}(1^k)$ and gives mpk to the adversary. The adversary has access to a key extraction oracle $\mathcal{X}(msk, \cdot, \cdot)$ to which it can submit pairs (ID, i) of its choosing. In a chosen-ciphertext attack, it can also perform queries to a decryption oracle $\mathcal{D}(\mathcal{X}(msk, \cdot, \cdot), \cdot)$ specifying a group identity ID, a user index i and an arbitrary ciphertext C as in the above secrecy game. The adversary terminates by outputting a group identity ID^* and a pirate decoder $\mathbb{D}$, which is the description of a probabilistic circuit that takes as input ciphertexts and outputs messages. The challenger then runs the tracing algorithm with black-box access to $\mathbb{D}$ to obtain a set of user identifiers $S \xleftarrow{\$} \mathcal{T}^{\mathbb{D}}(msk, ID^*)$.

By modelling the pirate decoder as a probabilistic circuit, we assume that the decoder is *resettable* or *stateless* [11] in that it does not retain information from previous decryptions, and in particular that it cannot self-destruct. Thus, when being subjected to a series of tracing queries, the pirate decoder responds to each query as if it were the first.

If we let T denote the set of user indices i that the adversary submitted to the key extraction oracle in combination with the group identity ID^*, then we say that the adversary wins the game if the following conditions hold:

- The decryption box decrypts a non-negligible fraction of random ciphertexts encrypted under the group identity ID^*, i.e. for random messages $\mathfrak{m}$ we have that $\Pr[\mathbb{D}(\mathcal{E}(mpk, ID^*, \mathfrak{m})) = \mathfrak{m}] \geq \delta(k)$ where $\delta(k)$ is a non-negligible function and where the probability is taken over the random choice of $\mathfrak{m}$ and over the random coins of the encryption algorithm $\mathcal{E}$ and the pirate box $\mathbb{D}$.
- Either $S = \emptyset$ or $S \not\subseteq T$.
- $\mathcal{A}$ queried the key extraction oracle for at most c different user indices i. We do not restrict the number of different group identities ID for which $\mathcal{A}$ can obtain keys for each of these users (apart from being polynomial in k of course). This reflects that colluding users can use all their decryption keys to construct the pirate box, not just the key corresponding to ID^*. It also means that the number of different groups a single user subscribes to is *not* limited by c.
- In the chosen-ciphertext variant there are no restrictions on $\mathcal{A}$'s queries to the decryption oracle.

The advantage $\mathbf{Adv}_{\mathcal{A}, \mathcal{IBTT}}^{\text{tra-id-cpa}[c]}(k)$, respectively $\mathbf{Adv}_{\mathcal{A}, \mathcal{IBTT}}^{\text{tra-id-cca}[c]}(k)$, of $\mathcal{A}$ in breaking the traceability of the scheme $\mathcal{IBTT}$ is defined as its probability of winning the above game. We say that $\mathcal{IBTT}$ is c-TRA-ID-CPA, respectively c-TRA-ID-CCA secure, if this advantage is a negligible function in k for all adversaries $\mathcal{A}$ with running time polynomial in k.

The above definition is essentially a *full access* model. One can, following [5] and [7], define a *minimal access* model in which the oracle available to the tracing algorithm only outputs whether the decoder successfully decrypted the input ciphertext or not, but does not give it the resulting plaintext.

4   The Scheme

Our scheme makes use of the two-level WIBE scheme [1] based on Waters' HIBE scheme [17]. We assume that group identities ID are given by strings of length n_1. As user identifiers we associate to each user an element of a code. The mapping between individual users, their indices and their codewords is maintained by the trust authority. In practice the code will be a (c, N, ϵ)-collusion secure code [8], where N is the maximum number users in the system, c is the maximum number of colluders our tracing algorithm can tolerate, and ϵ is the probability of error that a colluder is not traced. A (c, N, ϵ) collusion secure code can be produced using codewords of size $\ell = O(c^2(\log(N) + \log(1/\epsilon)))$ over an alphabet of size $s = 2$ [16]. Our use of collusion secure codes will result in a scheme which is not publicly traceable, since the tracing algorithm for collusion secure codes requires secret randomness.

Before giving a more precise definition of collusion-secure codes, we need to introduce some additional notation. Let Σ be a symbol alphabet of size $|\Sigma| = s$. If $x = x_1 \ldots x_\ell \in \Sigma^\ell$ is a string of ℓ symbols and $I = \{1 \le i_1 < \ldots < i_n \le \ell\}$ is a set of indices, then $x|_I$ is the substring $x_{i_1} \ldots x_{i_n}$ containing only those symbols of x at positions in I. Let $W = \{w_1, \ldots, w_c \in \Sigma^\ell\}$ be a set of symbol strings, and let I be the set of all positions where all strings in W are equal, i.e. I is the maximal set such that $w_1|_I = w_2|_I = \ldots = w_c|_I$. Then the *feasible set* of W is defined as the set of all strings that are equal to $w_1, \ldots, w_c$ at positions in I, i.e.

$$\mathrm{FS}(W) = \{x \in \Sigma^\ell : x|_I = w_1|_I = \ldots = w_c|_I\} .$$

A (c, N, ϵ) collusion-secure code of length ℓ over alphabet Σ consists of a set $\mathbb{C}$, called the *codebook*, of indexed codewords $w_r^{(i)}$ for $1 \le i \le N$ and $r \in \{0,1\}^\rho$, and a *tracing algorithm* $\mathcal{T}_\mathbb{C}$. These are such that for all collusions $C \subseteq \{1, \ldots, N\}$ of size at most c, $W = \{w_r^{(i)} : i \in C\}$, and for all (unbounded) algorithms $\mathcal{A}$ it holds that

$$\Pr\left[\mathcal{T}_\mathbb{C}(x, r) \in C \mid x \in \mathrm{FS}(W); \; x \xleftarrow{\$} \mathcal{A}(W); \; r \xleftarrow{\$} \{0,1\}^\rho\right] > 1 - \epsilon ,$$

where the probability is taken over the choice of r and the random coins of $\mathcal{T}_\mathbb{C}$ and $\mathcal{A}$. Our scheme uses codewords as "identity strings". This presents a small problem: the definition insists that the set C is chosen *before* $\mathcal{A}$'s execution; whereas, we will allow the adversary to chose the set C adaptively via key extraction queries. We solve this problem by introducing a randomly chosen permutation on $\{1, 2, \ldots, N\}$, denoted $\pi \xleftarrow{\$} Perm(N)$ (or if it is desired for efficiency a pseudo-random permutation). We associate the codeword $w_r^{(\pi(i))}$ with the i-th user. It is therefore sufficient that

$$\Pr\left[\mathcal{T}_\mathbb{C}(x, r) \in C \;\middle|\; \begin{array}{c} x \in \mathrm{FS}(W); \; x \xleftarrow{\$} \mathcal{A}(W) \\ C \xleftarrow{\$} \mathcal{P}(\mathbb{C}, c, r); \; r \xleftarrow{\$} \{0,1\}^\rho \end{array}\right] > 1 - \epsilon ,$$

where $\mathcal{P}(\mathbb{C}, c, r)$ is the set of subsets of $\{w_r \in \mathbb{C}\}$ of size c.

For non-binary alphabets, we use the natural encoding of symbols as bit strings of length $\lceil \log_2 s \rceil$, so that codewords are represented by bit strings of length $n_2 = \lceil \log_2 s \rceil \cdot \ell$.

To set up the scheme we define two sets V_1 and V_2 of random elements in $\mathbb{G}_2$, denoted by $V_i = (v_{i,0}, v_{i,1}, \ldots, v_{i,n_i})$. We let $u_{i,j} \leftarrow \psi(v_{i,j})$ and let U_i denote the image of the set V_i under the isomorphism ψ, i.e. $U_i = (u_{i,0}, u_{i,1}, \ldots, u_{i,n_i})$. For a bit string B of length n_i we use these sets to define the so-called Waters' hash functions

$$H_i(B) \leftarrow v_{i,0} \prod_{j \in B} v_{i,j},$$

where the product is computed over all values of j for which the j-th bit of B is one. To simplify notation we define

$$G_i(B) \leftarrow u_{i,0} \prod_{j \in B} u_{i,j} = \psi(H_i(B)).$$

Note that $G_i(B)$ can be computed either from the set V_i using the isomorphism ψ, or from the set U_i directly. Also note that $v_{i,j} = h^{\kappa_{i,j}}$ and $u_{i,j} = g^{\kappa_{i,j}}$ for some, unknown, values $\kappa_{i,j} \in \mathbb{Z}_p$.

Our ID-based traitor tracing scheme can now be defined via the following algorithms:

Setup $\mathcal{G}(1^k)$: The key distribution centre generates a set of pairing groups $\mathbb{G}_1, \mathbb{G}_2$ as above at the security level k, along with the sets $V_i \xleftarrow{\$} (\mathbb{G}_2^*)^{n_i}$ for $i = 1, 2$. A random value $\alpha \xleftarrow{\$} \mathbb{Z}_p$ is selected, and one sets $g_1 \leftarrow g^\alpha \in \mathbb{G}_1$ and $h_1 \leftarrow h^\alpha \in \mathbb{G}_2$. We require a second random element $h_2 \xleftarrow{\$} \mathbb{G}_2^*$ and we let $g_2 \leftarrow \psi(h_2)$. Finally, the secret random permutation $\pi \xleftarrow{\$} Perm(N)$ and the secret randomness $r \xleftarrow{\$} \{0,1\}^\rho$ for the code $\mathbb{C}$ is chosen. The master public key is defined to be $mpk = (g, g_1, h_2, U_1, U_2)$ and the master secret key is $msk = (h, h_2^\alpha, V_1, V_2, \pi, r)$.

Key Extraction $\mathcal{X}(msk, ID, i)$: Let id be the codeword corresponding to index i, i.e. the bit string of length $n_2 = \lceil \log_2 s \rceil \cdot \ell$ that is the binary encoding of codeword $w_r^{(\pi(i))}$. The key distribution centre first select random values $r_1, r_2 \xleftarrow{\$} \mathbb{Z}_p$ and then define the private key as

$$d_{ID,i} = (id, a_0, a_1, a_2) \leftarrow (id, \ h_2^\alpha H_1(ID)^{r_1} H_2(id)^{r_2}, \ h^{r_1}, \ h^{r_2})$$

Encryption $\mathcal{E}(mpk, ID, \mathfrak{m})$: A message is defined as an element in $\mathbb{G}_T$. The sender first chooses a $t \xleftarrow{\$} \mathbb{Z}_p$ and then computes the ciphertext $C = (C_1, C_2, C_3, C_4) \in \mathbb{G}_1 \times \mathbb{G}_1 \times \mathbb{G}_T \times \mathbb{G}_1^{n_2+1}$ as

$$C_1 \leftarrow g^t, \quad C_2 \leftarrow G_1(ID)^t, \quad C_3 \leftarrow \mathfrak{m} \cdot \hat{e}(g_1, h_2)^t, \quad C_4 \leftarrow (u_{2,j}^t)_{j=0,\ldots,n_2}.$$

Decryption $\mathcal{D}(d_{ID,i}, C)$: Decryption works as follows, on input of C we first compute

$$C_2' \leftarrow C_4^{(0)} \cdot \prod_{j \in id} C_4^{(j)} = G_2(id)^t ,$$

where the last equality follows since $C_4^{(j)} = u_{2,j}^t$. Then we compute

$$
\begin{aligned}
C_3 \cdot \frac{\hat{e}(C_2, a_1) \cdot \hat{e}(C_2', a_2)}{\hat{e}(C_1, a_0)} &= \mathfrak{m} \cdot \hat{e}(g_1, h_2)^t \cdot \frac{\hat{e}(G_1(ID)^t, h^{r_1}) \cdot \hat{e}(G_2(id)^t, h^{r_2})}{\hat{e}(g^t, h_2^\alpha H_1(ID)^{r_1} H_2(id)^{r_2})} \\
&= \mathfrak{m} \cdot \hat{e}(g_1, h_2)^t \cdot \frac{\hat{e}(G_1(ID)^{r_1}, h^t) \cdot \hat{e}(G_2(id)^{r_2}, h^t)}{\hat{e}(g^t, h_2^\alpha) \cdot \hat{e}(g^t, H_1(ID)^{r_1} H_2(id)^{r_2})} \\
&= \mathfrak{m} \cdot \frac{\hat{e}(g^\alpha, h_2)^t}{\hat{e}(g^t, h_2^\alpha)} \cdot \frac{\hat{e}(g^\sigma, h^t)}{\hat{e}(g^t, h^\sigma)} \\
&\qquad \text{where } \sigma = r_1(\kappa_{1,0} + \sum_{j \in ID} \kappa_{1,j}) + r_2(\kappa_{2,0} + \sum_{j \in id} \kappa_{2,j}) \\
&= \mathfrak{m} \cdot \frac{\hat{e}(g^\alpha, h_2)^t}{\hat{e}(g^t, h_2^\alpha)} \\
&= \mathfrak{m}.
\end{aligned}
$$

Traitor Tracing Algorithm $\mathcal{T}^{\mathbb{D}}(msk, ID)$: Since we use a collusion-secure code, the tracing step requires the secret randomness r, so tracing can only be done by the key distribution centre. The tracing algorithm has access to a pirate box $\mathbb{D}$ that correctly decrypts ciphertexts for ID with probability $\delta(k)$. For convenience, we let $C_4^{(i,j)}$ denote the $(\lceil \log_2 s \rceil (i-1) + j)$-th element of C_4. For each $1 \le i \le \ell$ and $1 \le j \le \lceil \log_2 s \rceil$, initialise counter $ctr_{i,j} \leftarrow 0$ and run the following test $n = 16k/\delta(k)$ times:

1. Choose a random message $\mathfrak{m}$.
2. Encrypt $\mathfrak{m}$ under the group identity ID to form a ciphertext

$$C \leftarrow (C_1, C_2, C_3, C_4).$$

3. Replace $C_4^{(i,j)}$ with a random element from $\mathbb{G}_1$.
4. Query the pirate decoder $\mathbb{D}$ on the altered ciphertext C.
5. If the decoder outputs the message $\mathfrak{m}$ (or a valid ciphertext in the case of minimal access) then increase $ctr_{i,j}$.

After these iterations, reconstruct the bit string id' of length n_2 as follows. Let $id'_{i,j}$ denote the bit of id' at position $\lceil \log_2 s \rceil (i-1) + j$. Set $id'_{i,j} \leftarrow 1$ if $ctr_{i,j} < 4k$, or set $id'_{i,j} \leftarrow 0$ otherwise. Next, decode the bit string id' as a symbol string x of length ℓ, choosing any symbol if the corresponding bit string is not a valid encoding of a symbol in Σ. Finally, use the tracing algorithm of the code to compute $S \stackrel{\$}{\leftarrow} \mathcal{T}_{\mathbb{C}}(x, r)$ and return the set of traitors $\pi^{-1}(S)$.

5   Security Results

The IND-ID-CPA security of our scheme under the DBDH assumption follows from the security of the Waters' HIBE from [17] and an analogue of Theorem 6 of [1]. As one notices that the scheme is simply the Waters WIBE from [1] specialised to the 2-level case. In Appendix A we outline the asymmetric version of Waters' HIBE scheme that we are using.

The scheme as it stands is only secure against adversaries who do not make decryption oracle queries. However, extending to chosen-ciphertext security can be done using the techniques described in [1] based on the techniques of Canetti, Halevi and Katz [9]. This extension will not affect our traitor tracing algorithm given above.

We now turn to showing that our tracing algorithm works. Intuitively, for the $\mathcal{T}_{\mathbb{C}}$ algorithm to work (with error probability ϵ), we need the reconstructed symbol string x to fall within the feasible set of the codewords corresponding to the collusion. This means that on those positions where all the codewords in the collusion are the same, the symbols of x have to be the same as well. We prove that if the ciphertext component $C_4^{(i,j)}$ that is being "tampered" with corresponds to a bit position where all traitors' codewords have a zero, then the pirate box decrypts correctly, unless it can solve the DDH problem in $\mathbb{G}_1$. We also prove that if the tampered component corresponds to an all-one position, then the pirate box is unable to decrypt correctly, unless it can solve the CBDH problem. The $8k/\delta(k)$ iterations are needed because the pirate box only decrypts correctly with probability $\delta(k)$; we use a Chernoff bound to analyse the overall success probability of our tracing algorithm.

Theorem 1. *The $\mathcal{IBTT}$ scheme described above is c-TRA-ID-CPA secure under the assumptions that the underlying code is a (c, N, ϵ) collusion-secure code of length ℓ over an alphabet of size s, that the DDH problem in $\mathbb{G}_1$ is hard, and that the CBDH problem in $\mathbb{G}_2$ is hard. More specifically, the advantage of any polynomial-time adversary $\mathcal{A}$ in building an untraceable decoder that correctly decrypts a fraction $\delta(k)$ of ciphertexts using the keys of a collusion of at most c users is at most*

$$\mathbf{Adv}_{\mathcal{A},\mathcal{IBTT}}^{\text{tra-id-cpa}[c]}(k) \leq \epsilon + \ell\lceil\log_2 s\rceil \cdot \left(\mathbf{Adv}_{\mathcal{B}_2,\mathbb{G}_2}^{\text{cbdh}}(k) + e^{-k}\right)$$

whenever $\delta(k) \geq 2 \cdot \mathbf{Adv}_{\mathcal{B}_1,\mathbb{G}_1}^{\text{xddh}}(k)$ where $\mathcal{B}_1, \mathcal{B}_2$ are polynomial-time algorithms depending on $\mathcal{A}$ and e is the base of the natural logarithm.

Proof. Let $\mathcal{A}$ be an attacker against the tracing property of the encryption scheme; i.e. $\mathcal{A}$ takes as input mpk and outputs a pirate decryption box $\mathbb{D}$. We use $\mathcal{A}$ to define an attacker $\mathcal{A}'$ against the tracing property of the collusion-secure code; i.e. $\mathcal{A}'$ will take as input a collection of c random codewords $W = \{w_1, \ldots, w_c\}$ and output a value x. We will prove that if $\mathcal{A}$ successfully avoids being traced, then, with high probability, $\mathcal{A}'$ will successfully output a codeword x that cannot be traced. This will provide the required contradiction.

$\mathcal{A}'$ runs as follows. It chooses random unique indices $i_1, \ldots, i_c \in \{1, \ldots, N\}$ and mounts the following attack for the collusion $C = \{i_1, \ldots, i_c\}$. On input codewords $W = \{w_r^{(i_j)} : j = 1, \ldots, c\}$, it first generates a public key $mpk \leftarrow (g, g_1, h_2, U_1, U_2)$ as described in the setup algorithm $\mathcal{G}$ of the identity-based traitor tracing scheme. $\mathcal{A}'$ then runs $\mathcal{A}$. $\mathcal{A}$ may query a key extraction oracle for identities (ID, i) for at most c values of i. $\mathcal{A}'$ responds to the j-th such query as normal using the codeword $w_r^{(i_j)}$. Since W contains codewords corresponding to a random collusion C, and π is meant to be a random permutation, this response is identically distributed to the response of a correct key extraction algorithm. $\mathcal{A}$ terminates by outputting a pirate decryption box $\mathbb{D}$.

$\mathcal{A}'$ then applies the identity-based traitor tracing scheme's tracing algorithm $\mathcal{T}^{\mathbb{D}}$ to $\mathbb{D}$, halting after $\mathcal{T}^{\mathbb{D}}$ determines the value of the symbol string x. $\mathcal{A}'$ outputs the value x. We prove that the symbol string $x \in \Sigma^{\ell}$ reconstructed by our tracing algorithm falls outside the feasible set $\mathrm{FS}(W)$ with probability at most

$$\Pr\left[x \notin \mathrm{FS}(W)\right] \leq \ell \lceil \log_2 s \rceil \cdot \left(\mathbf{Adv}_{\mathcal{B}_2, \mathbb{G}_2}^{\mathrm{cbdh}}(k) + e^{-k}\right) .$$

The theorem statement then directly follows from the properties of the (c, N, ϵ) collusion-secure code's tracing algorithm $\mathcal{T}_C$.

Let $I \subseteq \{1, \ldots, \ell\}$ be the maximal set of symbol positions such that $w_r^{(i)}|_I = w_r^{(j)}|_I$ for all $i, j \in C$. For positions of x not in I there is nothing to prove, because they do not affect membership of $\mathrm{FS}(W)$. So we focus on the symbols x_i of x at positions $i \in I$. Let $id_{i,j}$ for $i \in I$ and $1 \leq j \leq \lceil \log_2 s \rceil$ be the bits in the binary representation of codewords corresponding to symbols at positions $i \in I$. Because of the way we defined I, these bits are the same for all users in the coalition. For a single iteration in the tracing algorithm at position (i, j), the following lemmas upper-bound the probability that the decryption box correctly decrypts $\mathfrak{m}$ in case $id_{i,j} = 0$ and that it does not correctly decrypt $\mathfrak{m}$ in case $id_{i,j} = 1$. Hence, we can distinguish between bit positions which are all zeros and all ones. This means we can recover the symbols which are the same in all the codewords for which the attacker has the keys. If the bits in a given bit position are different in the attacker's codewords, then the attacker can detect the tracing attempt and may output whatever they like. However, this does not matter as we only need to recover the symbols which are the same for all codewords in order to apply the code's tracing algorithm. We postpone the proofs of these lemmas until after the proof of the theorem.

Lemma 1. *If $id_{i,j} = 0$ in the codewords of all users in the collusion C, then $\mathbb{D}$ correctly decrypts a random ciphertext that has been tampered with at position (i, j) with probability*

$$p_0 \geq \delta(k) - \mathbf{Adv}_{\mathcal{B}_1, \mathbb{G}_1}^{\mathrm{xddh}}(k) .$$

Lemma 2. *If $id_{i,j} = 1$ in the codewords of all users in the collusion C, then $\mathbb{D}$ correctly decrypts a random ciphertext that has been tampered with at position (i, j) with probability*

$$p_1 \leq \mathbf{Adv}_{\mathcal{B}_2, \mathbb{G}_2}^{\mathrm{cbdh}}(k) .$$

We also use the following adaptation of the Chernoff bound from [12].

Lemma 3. *Let $X_1, \ldots, X_n$ be independent, 0/1 valued random variables with expected value p. Let $X = X_1 + \ldots + X_n$, let $\mu = \mathbf{E}[X] = np$ and let $0 \leq \alpha \leq 1$ be a real number. Then we have*

$$\Pr[X < (1 - \alpha)\mu] < e^{-\mu\alpha^2/2} .$$

We want to upper-bound the probability that $x_i \neq w_i$. For a position i, j where $id_{i,j} = 0$, we can see the final value of $ctr_{i,j}$ as the outcome of the sum of $n = 16k/\delta(k)$ independent 0/1 random variables with expected value $p = p_0$. The expected value of $ctr_{i,j}$ is $\mu = np_0$. From Lemma 1 and the assumption that $\mathbf{Adv}^{\text{xddh}}_{\mathcal{B}_1, \mathbb{G}_1}(k) \leq \delta(k)/2$, we know that

$$\mu = np_0 \geq n\big(\delta(k) - \mathbf{Adv}^{\text{xddh}}_{\mathcal{B}_1, \mathbb{G}_1}(k)\big) \geq \frac{n\delta(k)}{2} = 8k .$$

We can then apply the Chernoff bound of Lemma 3 with $\alpha = 1/2$ to upper-bound the probability that the tracing algorithm incorrectly decides that $id'_{i,j} = 1$ by

$$\begin{aligned} \Pr[ctr_{i,j} < 4k] &\leq \Pr[ctr_{i,j} < \mu/2] \\ &< e^{-\mu/8} \\ &\leq e^{-k} . \end{aligned}$$

On the other hand, for a position i, j where $id_{i,j} = 1$, the probability that the tracing algorithm incorrectly decides that $id'_{i,j} = 0$ can be upper-bounded by

$$\Pr[ctr_{i,j} \geq 4k] \leq \Pr[ctr_{i,j} \geq 1] = p_1 \leq \mathbf{Adv}^{\text{cbdh}}_{\mathcal{B}_2, \mathbb{G}_2}(k) .$$

The probability that $x_i \neq w_i$ is upper-bounded by the probability that the tracing algorithm makes an incorrect decision at any of the bit positions. Since there are $\lceil \log_2 s \rceil$ bits in the encoding of x_i, we have that

$$\Pr[x_i \neq w_i] \leq \lceil \log_2 s \rceil \cdot \big(\mathbf{Adv}^{\text{cbdh}}_{\mathcal{B}_2, \mathbb{G}_2}(k) + e^{-k}\big) ,$$

so that the overall probability that the symbol string x reconstructed by the tracing algorithm is not within the feasible set of W is

$$\Pr[x \notin \text{FS}(W)] \leq \ell \lceil \log_2 s \rceil \cdot \big(\mathbf{Adv}^{\text{cbdh}}_{\mathcal{B}_2, \mathbb{G}_2}(k) + e^{-k}\big) ,$$

from which the theorem follows.   □

We have left to prove the two lemmas that we used above.

Proof (Lemma 1). For the sake of contradiction, let $\mathcal{A}$ denote an adversary against the traitor tracing scheme that produces a decryption box that correctly decrypts random ciphertexts with probability $\delta(k)$, but that correctly decrypts ciphertexts that have been tampered with at position (i', j') with probability

$p_0 \leq \delta(k) - \gamma$ for some $\gamma > 0$. We will construct an algorithm $\mathcal{B}_1$ which uses $\mathcal{A}$ to gain an advantage γ in solving the DDH problem in $\mathbb{G}_1$.

Let (g^x, g^y, Z) denote the input to our DDH algorithm $\mathcal{B}_1$ and let $k' = s(i' - 1) + j' - 1$. It constructs the master public keys of the ID-based by choosing random exponents $\alpha, \kappa_{i,j} \xleftarrow{\$} \mathbb{Z}_p^*$ for $a = 1, 2$ and $b = 0, \ldots, n_a$ and a random element $h_2 \xleftarrow{\$} \mathbb{G}_2^*$. It sets $g_1 \leftarrow g^\alpha$, $h_1 \leftarrow h^\alpha$, $u_{i,j} \leftarrow g^{\kappa_{i,j}}$, $v_{i,j} \leftarrow h^{\kappa_{i,j}}$, except for $u_{2,k'}$ and $v_{2,k'}$ which it sets to $u_{2,k'} \leftarrow g^x$ and $v_{2,k'} \leftarrow \perp$, respectively. It also chooses secret randomness $r \xleftarrow{\$} \{0,1\}^\rho$ for the collusion-secure code.

$\mathcal{B}_1$ runs $\mathcal{A}$ on input $mpk = (g, g_1, h_2, U_1 = (u_{1,0}, \ldots, u_{1,n_1}), U_2 = (u_{2,0}, \ldots, u_{2,n_2}))$, responding to its key extraction queries (ID, i) as follows. Let id be the encoding of the codeword $w_r^{(i)}$. We know from the preconditions of the lemma that $id_{k'} = 0$. $\mathcal{B}_1$ chooses $r_1, r_2 \xleftarrow{\$} \mathbb{Z}_p$ and computes the secret key $d_{ID,i} = (id, a_0, a_1, a_2) = (id, h_2^\alpha H_1(ID)^{r_1} H_2(id)^{r_2}, h^{r_1}, h^{r_2})$. Note that because $id_{k'} = 0$, $\mathcal{B}_1$ can compute $H_2(id)$, even though it does not know $v_{2,k'}$.

At the end of this stage $\mathcal{A}$ will output a pirate decoder $\mathbb{D}$ with respect to a group identity ID of its choice.

All the identities used to create the box $\mathbb{D}$ will have the k'-th bit of their binary code word id set to zero. Algorithm $\mathcal{B}$ then generates a random message $\mathfrak{m}$ and forms the ciphertext

$$C_1 \leftarrow g^y, \qquad\qquad C_2 \leftarrow (g^y)^{\kappa_{1,0}} \cdot \prod_{i \in ID} (g^y)^{\kappa_{1,i}},$$

$$C_3 \leftarrow \mathfrak{m} \cdot \hat{e}(g^y, h_2)^\alpha, \qquad C_4^{(i)} \leftarrow \begin{cases} (g^y)^{\kappa_{2,i}} & \text{for } 0 \leq i \leq n_2, \, i \neq k', \\ Z & \text{for } i = k'. \end{cases}$$

This ciphertext is then passed to the decoder $\mathbb{D}$. Algorithm $\mathcal{B}_1$ outputs 1 if the decoder correctly decrypts $\mathfrak{m}$, or outputs 0 otherwise.

If $Z = g^{xy}$, then the ciphertext C is a correctly-formed random ciphertext, so $\mathbb{D}$ will correctly decrypt it with probability $\delta(k)$. If Z is random, then C looks exactly like a ciphertext that has been tampered with at position (i', j'), so $\mathbb{D}$ will correctly decrypt it with probability at most $\delta(k) - \gamma$. The advantage of an algorithm in solving the DDH problem is defined as the difference of the probability that it outputs 1 if $Z = g^{xy}$ and if Z is random, so for our algorithm $\mathcal{B}_1$ we have that

$$\mathbf{Adv}_{\mathcal{B}_1, \mathbb{G}_1}^{\mathrm{xddh}}(k) \geq \delta(k) - (\delta(k) - \gamma) = \gamma,$$

from which the lemma follows. $\qquad\qquad\qquad\qquad\qquad\qquad\qquad\qquad\qquad\qquad\square$

Proof (Lemma 2). For the sake of contradiction, let $\mathcal{A}$ denote an adversary against the traitor tracing scheme that will produce a decryption box $\mathbb{D}$ that correctly decrypts ciphertexts that have been tampered with at position (i', j') with probability p_1. We will construct an algorithm $\mathcal{B}_2$ which uses $\mathcal{A}$ as a subroutine to solve the bilinear computational Diffie–Hellman problem.

Let h^x, h^y, h^z, be $\mathcal{B}_2$'s input for the CBDH problem. Algorithm $\mathcal{B}_2$ chooses random integers $\kappa_{i,j} \xleftarrow{\$} \mathbb{Z}_p$ for $i = 1, 2$ and $0 \leq j \leq n_i$. Let $k' = s(i' - 1) + j' - 1$.

It sets
$$g_1 \leftarrow \psi(h^x) \qquad h_2 = h^z$$
$$v_{i,j} \leftarrow h^{\kappa_{i,j}} \text{ and } u_{i,j} \leftarrow g^{\kappa_{i,j}} \text{ for } i = 1, 2 \text{ and } 0 \le j \le n_i$$

except for $u_{2,k'}$ and $v_{2,k'}$ which it sets to

$$v_{2,k'} \leftarrow h^{\kappa_{2,k'}} / h^x = h^{\kappa_{2,k'} - x} \qquad u_{2,k'} \leftarrow \psi(v_{2,k'}) = g^{\kappa_{2,k'} - x} .$$

It also chooses secret randomness $r \xleftarrow{\$} \{0,1\}^\rho$ for the collusion-secure code. It then runs $\mathcal{A}$ on input $mpk = (g, g_1, h_2, (u_{1,0}, \ldots, u_{1,n_1}), (u_{2,0}, \ldots, u_{2,n_2}))$.

Algorithm $\mathcal{A}$ will make c key extraction queries (ID, i). Let id be the codeword corresponding to user i; we know from the preconditions of the lemma that $id_{k'} = 1$ for all users in the collusion. The decryption key $d_{ID,i} = (id, a_0, a_1, a_2)$ is generated by choosing $r_1, r_2 \xleftarrow{\$} \mathbb{Z}_p$ at random and computing

$$a_0 \leftarrow (h^z)^{\kappa_{2,k'}} \cdot (h^x)^{-r_2} \cdot h^{\kappa_{2,k'} r_2} \cdot H_1(ID)^{r_1} \cdot (h^z \cdot h^{r_2})^{\kappa_{2,0}} \cdot \prod_{i \in id, i \ne k'} (h^z \cdot h^{r_2})^{\kappa_{2,i}}$$

$$= h^{z\kappa_{2,k'} - xr_2 + \kappa_{2,k'} r_2} \cdot H_1(ID)^{r_1} \cdot \left(h^{\kappa_{2,0}} \prod_{i \in id, i \ne k'} h^{\kappa_{2,i}} \right)^{z+r_2}$$

$$= h^{xz - xz + z\kappa_{2,k'} - xr_2 + \kappa_{2,k'} r_2} \cdot H_1(ID)^{r_1} \cdot \left(v_{2,0} \prod_{i \in id, i \ne k'} v_{2,i} \right)^{z+r_2}$$

$$= h^{xz} \cdot H_1(ID)^{r_1} \cdot H_2(id)^{z+r_2}$$

$$a_1 \leftarrow h^{r_1},$$

$$a_2 \leftarrow h^z \cdot h^{r_2} = h^{z+r_2}$$

At the end of this stage $\mathcal{A}$ will output a pirate decoder $\mathbb{D}$ with respect to a group identity ID of its choice. Algorithm $\mathcal{B}_2$ then generates the challenge ciphertext with

$$C_1 \leftarrow \psi(h^y) , \qquad C_2 \leftarrow \psi(h^y)^{\kappa_{1,0}} \prod_{i \in ID} \psi(h^y)^{\kappa_{1,i}} ,$$

$$C_3 \xleftarrow{\$} \mathbb{G}_T , \qquad C_4^{(i)} \leftarrow \begin{cases} \psi(h^y)^{\kappa_{2,i}} & \text{for } 0 \le i \le n_2, \ i \ne k' , \\ Z & \text{where } Z \xleftarrow{\$} \mathbb{G}_1 \text{ for } i = k' . \end{cases}$$

By our assumption on the pirate decoder $\mathbb{D}$ with this ciphertext will output, with probability p_1, the corresponding plaintext $\mathfrak{m}$ as if $C_4^{(k')}$ were chosen correctly as $u_{2,k'}^y$. In this case $\mathcal{B}_2$ can recover $\hat{e}(g, h)^{xyz}$ by computing $C_3/\mathfrak{m}$. Algorithm $\mathcal{B}_2$ then returns this value as its solution to the bilinear computational Diffie–Hellman problem, giving it an advantage

$$\mathbf{Adv}_{\mathcal{B}_2, \mathbb{G}_2}^{\mathrm{cbdh}}(k) \ge p_1 ,$$

from which the lemma follows. $\square$

Acknowledgements. We would like to thank Yevgeniy Dodis and Aggelos Kiayias for suggesting that a simple method for the converting the q-ary alphabet into binary is sufficient for our purposes.

References

1. M. Abdalla, D. Catalano, A. Dent, J. Malone-Lee, G. Neven, and N. Smart. Identity-based encryption gone wild. In *ICALP 2006, Part II*, volume 4052 of *LNCS*, pages 300–311. Springer-Verlag, 2006.
2. L. Ballard, M. Green, B. de Medeiros, and F. Monrose. Correlation-resistant storage via keyword-searchable encryption. Cryptology ePrint Archive, Report 2005/417, 2005. http://eprint.iacr.org/.
3. M. Bellare and P. Rogaway. Random oracles are practical: A paradigm for designing efficient protocols. In *ACM CCS 93*, pages 62–73. ACM Press, 1993.
4. D. Boneh, X. Boyen, and H. Shacham. Short group signatures. In *CRYPTO 2004*, volume 3152 of *LNCS*, pages 41–55. Springer-Verlag, 2004.
5. D. Boneh and M. K. Franklin. An efficient public key traitor tracing scheme. In *CRYPTO'99*, volume 1666 of *LNCS*, pages 338–353. Springer-Verlag, 1999.
6. D. Boneh and M. K. Franklin. Identity-based encryption from the Weil pairing. In *CRYPTO 2001*, volume 2139 of *LNCS*, pages 213–229. Springer-Verlag, 2001.
7. D. Boneh, A. Sahai, and B. Waters. Fully collusion resistant traitor tracing with short ciphertexts and private keys. In *EUROCRYPT 2006*, volume 4004 of *LNCS*, pages 573–592. Springer-Verlag, 2006.
8. D. Boneh and J. Shaw. Collusion-secure fingerprinting for digital data (extended abstract). In *CRYPTO'95*, volume 963 of *LNCS*, pages 452–465. Springer-Verlag, 1995.
9. R. Canetti, S. Halevi, and J. Katz. Chosen-ciphertext security from identity-based encryption. In *EUROCRYPT 2004*, volume 3027 of *LNCS*, pages 207–222. Springer-Verlag, 2004.
10. C. Cocks. An identity based encryption scheme based on quadratic residues. In *Cryptography and Coding, 8th IMA International Conference*, volume 2260 of *LNCS*, pages 360–363. Springer-Verlag, 2001.
11. A. Kiayias and M. Yung. On crafty pirates and foxy tracers. In *ACM CCS Digital Rights Management Workshop 2001*, volume 2320 of *LNCS*, pages 22–39. Springer-Verlag, 2002.
12. R. Motwani and P. Raghavan. *Randomized Algorithms*. Cambridge University Press, 1995.
13. R. Sakai, K. Ohgishi, and M. Kasahara. Cryptosystems based on pairing. In *SCIS 2000*, 2000.
14. M. Scott. Authenticated id-based key exchange and remote log-in with simple token and pin number. Cryptology ePrint Archive, Report 2002/164, 2002. http://eprint.iacr.org/.
15. A. Shamir. Identity-based cryptosystems and signature schemes. In *CRYPTO'84*, volume 196 of *LNCS*, pages 47–53. Springer-Verlag, 1985.
16. G. Tardos. Optimal probabilistic fingerprint codes. In *35th ACM STOC*, pages 116–125. ACM Press, 2003.
17. B. R. Waters. Efficient identity-based encryption without random oracles. In *EUROCRYPT 2005*, volume 3494 of *LNCS*, pages 114–127. Springer-Verlag, 2005.

A Waters' HIBE with Asymmetric Pairings

Our scheme is built out of the HIBE suggested by Waters in [17], but in the asymmetric pairing setting and using a scheme of depth 2. In this section we describe the underlying HIBE in full generality.

A.1   Scheme Description

Suppose that we want a scheme of depth L. We define L sets $V_1, \ldots, V_L$ of random elements in $\mathbb{G}_2$, with elements denoted $V_i = (v_{i,0}, v_{i,1}, \ldots, v_{i,n_i})$. We let $u_{i,j} = \psi(v_{i,j})$ and let U_i denote the image of the set V_i under the isomorphism ψ, i.e. $U_i = (u_{i,0}, u_{i,1}, \ldots, u_{i,n_i})$.

Just as in our traitor tracing scheme for a bit string B of length n_i we use these sets to define the Waters' hash functions:

$$H_i(B) = v_{i,0} \prod_{j \in B} v_{i,j},$$

where the products are over all the set bits in B. To simplify notation we define

$$G_i(B) = u_{i,0} \prod_{j \in B} u_{i,j} = \psi(H_i(B)).$$

Note that $\psi(H_i(B)) = G_i(B)$ can be computed either from the set V_i using the isomorphism ψ, or from the set U_i directly. Also note that $v_{i,j} = h^{\kappa_{i,j}}$ and $u_{i,j} = g^{\kappa_{i,j}}$ for some, unknown, values $\kappa_{i,j} \in \mathbb{Z}_p$.

Using the entities above, the various algorithms that make up Waters' HIBE scheme are as follows. We assume that id is a tuple $(id_1, \ldots, id_l)$ where $l \leq L$ and id_i is a bit string of length n_i, applying a collision resistant hash function if necessary.

Setup $\mathcal{G}(1^k)$: We generate a set of pairing groups as above at the security level k, along with the sets $V_1, \ldots, V_L$ and $U_1, \ldots, U_L$. We require a random element $h \xleftarrow{\$} \mathbb{G}_2$ and let $g \leftarrow \psi(h) \in \mathbb{G}_1$. A random value $\alpha \xleftarrow{\$} \mathbb{Z}_p$ is selected, and we set $g_1 \leftarrow g^\alpha$ and $h_1 \leftarrow h^\alpha$. We require a second random element $h_2 \in \mathbb{G}_2$ and we let $g_2 \leftarrow \psi(h_2)$. The master public key is defined to be $mpk = \{g, g_1, h_2, U_1, \ldots, U_L\}$ and the master secret key is $msk = \{h, h_2^\alpha, V_1, \ldots, V_L\}$.

Key Extraction $\mathcal{X}(id, msk)$: We first select random values $r_1, \ldots, r_l \leftarrow \mathbb{Z}_p$ and then define the private key as

$$d_{id} = (a_0, a_1, \ldots, a_l) \leftarrow \left(h_2^\alpha \prod_{i=1}^{l} H_i(id_i)^{r_i}, h^{r_1}, \ldots, h^{r_l} \right) \in \mathbb{G}_2^{l+1}.$$

Encryption $\mathcal{E}(id, mpk, \mathfrak{m})$: A message is defined as an element in $\mathbb{G}_T$. The sender first choose a $t \leftarrow \mathbb{Z}_p$ and then computes the ciphertext

$$C = (C_1, C_2, C_3) \in \mathbb{G}_1 \times \mathbb{G}_1^l \times \mathbb{G}_T$$

as

$$C_1 \leftarrow g^t, \quad C_2 \leftarrow \left(C_{2,i} = G_i(id_i)^t \right)_{i=1}^{l}, \quad C_3 \leftarrow \mathfrak{m} \cdot \hat{e}(g_1, h_2)^t.$$

Decryption $\mathcal{D}(C, d_{id})$: Compute

$$C_3 \cdot \frac{\prod_{i=1}^{l} \hat{e}(C_{2,i}, a_i)}{\hat{e}(C_1, a_0)} = \mathfrak{m}.$$

Verifiable Shuffle of Large Size Ciphertexts

Jens Groth[1,*] and Steve Lu[2,**]

[1] UCLA, Computer Science Department
jg@cs.ucla.edu
[2] UCLA, Math Department
stevelu@math.ucla.edu

Abstract. A shuffle is a permutation and rerandomization of a set of ciphertexts. Among other things, it can be used to construct mix-nets that are used in anonymization protocols and voting schemes. While shuffling is easy, it is hard for an outsider to verify that a shuffle has been performed correctly. We suggest two efficient honest verifier zero-knowledge (HVZK) arguments for correctness of a shuffle. Our goal is to minimize round-complexity and at the same time have low communicational and computational complexity.

The two schemes we suggest are both 3-move HVZK arguments for correctness of a shuffle. We first suggest a HVZK argument based on homomorphic integer commitments, and improve both on round complexity, communication complexity and computational complexity in comparison with state of the art. The second HVZK argument is based on homomorphic commitments over finite fields. Here we improve on the computational complexity and communication complexity when shuffling large ciphertexts.

Keywords: Shuffle, homomorphic commitment, homomorphic encryption, mix-net, honest verifier zero-knowledge.

1 Introduction

The main motivating example for shuffling is mix-nets. Parties can encrypt messages and send them to the mix-net; the mix-net then permutes, decrypts and outputs the messages. This allows parties to submit messages anonymously, which for instance is very useful in voting.

One approach to construct a mix-net is the following. The authorities, one by one, permute and rerandomize the ciphertexts. When all authorities have done this, they run a threshold decryption protocol to get out the messages. The central operation here is the permutation and rerandomization of a set of ciphertexts, a *shuffle*.

Obviously, it may be problematic if a dishonest authority replaces some of the ciphertexts, or cheats in some other way. If the cryptosystem is semantically secure, we cannot detect the cheating directly. We therefore need to add verifiability to the shuffle.

---

* Supported by NSF grant No. 0456717, and NSF Cybertrust grant.
** Supported in part by NSF Cybertrust grant No. 0430254. This work was partially researched while the authors were at the Institute for Pure and Applied Mathematics, UCLA during the Securing Cyberspace program.

T. Okamoto and X. Wang (Eds.): PKC 2007, LNCS 4450, pp. 377–392, 2007.

One option is to request the shuffling authority to create a zero-knowledge argument for correctness of the shuffle. The goal of this paper is to present new honest verifier zero-knowledge arguments for correctness of a shuffle.

RELATED WORK. Due to the direct applicability of proofs for the correctness of a shuffle, several researchers have investigated the problem and suggested schemes. Proving the correctness of a shuffle is a complicated matter, and as a consequence the most efficient schemes are also very complex. We will mention the more recent and efficient schemes here.

Abe and Hoshino [Abe99, AH01] proposed a 3-move proof for correctness of a shuffle of size $\mathcal{O}(kn \log n)$ bits, where k is the security parameter and n is the number of ciphertexts. Neff [Nef01] suggested an honest verifier zero-knowledge proof for correctness of a n ElGamal ciphertext shuffle based on the invariance of polynomials under permutation of the roots. While giving an efficient proof of size $\mathcal{O}(kn)$ bits, the drawback of this scheme is that it is a 7-move proof. Groth [Gro03, Gro05b] generalized Neff's scheme to work with a large class of homomorphic cryptosystems.

Furukawa and Sako [FS01], later improved by Furukawa [Fur05], proposed a 3-move argument for correctness of a shuffle. This method is based on committing to a permutation matrix and proving that the ciphertexts have been shuffled according to this permutation. They focus on the verifiability of an ElGamal ciphertext shuffle. Subsequent work by Nguyen et al. [NSNK04, NSNK05] and Onodera and Tanaka [OT04] have used the permutation matrix approach to construct correctness arguments for shuffles of Paillier ciphertexts. Peng at al. [PBD05] also investigate shuffling of Paillier ciphertexts, but use different techniques.

Yet another method for proving the correctness of a shuffle has been suggested by Wikström [Wik05a] based on unique factorization of integers. Unlike the other schemes that use commitments over $\mathbb{Z}_q$ for a prime q, he uses a homomorphic integer commitment scheme as a central building block. In some instances, this is actually desirable, for instance in [WG06]. One drawback of this scheme is that it uses 5 rounds.

OUR CONTRIBUTION. We suggest honest verifier zero-knowledge arguments for correctness of a shuffle. Since shuffles are typically used for anonymization, and since anonymization works best when individuals or groups can hide among a large set of other people, it is possible that we need to shuffle a huge number of ciphertexts. As an example, a voting scheme may have thousands or even millions of voters casting ballots. This implies that communication complexity and computational complexity are both of high importance. Furthermore, in a mix-net the authorities shuffle the ciphertexts one at a time and cooperate to generate the challenges for the honest verifier zero-knowledge argument. In order to minimize this work, we want to have as low round complexity as possible.

Our first scheme uses homomorphic integer commitments as the central building block. By working with integers, instead of working over $\mathbb{Z}_q$ as [FS01, Fur05], we show a much simpler way to demonstrate that indeed we have committed to a permutation matrix. The relevant comparison for this scheme is Wikström's argument for correctness of a shuffle [Wik05b] that is also based on integer commitments. Our scheme is better on all performance parameters, a detailed comparison can be found in Section 5.

Our second scheme uses homomorphic commitments over a message space $\mathbb{Z}_q$ for a prime q, just like [FS01, Fur05]. We combine Furukawa's [Fur05] scheme with techniques from [Gro05b] to obtain a 3-move argument for correctness of a shuffle. This generalization of Furukawa's scheme permits shuffling of almost any homomorphic cryptosystem. If we look at the case of shuffling ElGamal ciphertexts, with the plaintexts belonging to a subgroup of relatively small order, our scheme is almost identical to Furukawa's scheme. However, a scenario with a large message space is perhaps more realistic. For instance, if we are looking at a voting scheme, we may want to permit write-in votes. If we are looking at a scheme for anonymous broadcast, senders may want to post large messages. For this setting, the most relevant comparison of our scheme is with the papers dealing with a shuffle of Paillier ciphertexts. Our scheme, has the same round complexity and is better on the other performance parameters. We refer to Section 5 for a detailed comparison with these schemes.

2 Preliminaries

We shuffle homomorphic ciphertexts and we use homomorphic commitments to shuffle them. For completeness, we will describe them here. We also recap the notion of an honest verifier zero-knowledge argument.

SPECIAL HONEST VERIFIER ZERO-KNOWLEDGE (SHVZK) ARGUMENT. We will describe 3-move public-coin arguments of knowledge with the special honest verifier zero-knowledge [CDS94] property. To explain this, consider a prover and a verifier. They both have access to a common reference string, in the paper it will consist of a public key for the commitment scheme and a public key for the cryptosystem. They also both have access to a statement x. In our case, this statement will consist of two sets of ciphertexts and a claim that one set is a shuffle of the other set. The prover sends an initial message a, the verifier selects a random challenge t, and the prover provides an answer z. The verifier can now evaluate (a, t, z) and decide whether to accept the truth of the statement.

That the protocol is public coin simply means that the challenge t is a random string. In the present paper the challenge will actually be n strings of bit-length ℓ_t. A possible choice is $\ell_t = 80$. If we wish to make the argument non-interactive, i.e., let the prover compute the challenges as a hash-value of x, a, then $\ell_t = 160$ would be suitable to account for the adversary being able to search many combinations of initial messages and hash-values offline.

The protocol must be complete, i.e., given a witness for the statement it should be easy for the prover to convince an honest verifier. It must be sound, i.e., it is infeasible to convince an honest verifier about a false statement. Moreover, the protocol will be an argument of knowledge in the following sense. If an adversary can produce a statement x and has non-negligible[1] probability ε of convincing the verifier, then with overwhelming probability it should be possible to extract a witness in expected polynomial time divided by ϵ. Finally, the protocols we present will have special honest verifier zero-knowledge (SHVZK). Given an arbitrary challenge t, we can simulate the argument (a, t, z).

---

[1] A non-negligible function is the inverse of some polynomial of the security parameter.

Well-known examples of 3-move public coin SHVZK arguments of knowledge are Schnorr's [Sch91] and Guillou-Quisquater's [GQ88] identification protocols.

HOMOMORPHIC ENCRYPTION. The public key of our cryptosystem specifies a message space, a randomizer space, and a ciphertext space that are abelian groups. The encryption algorithm E takes as input a message and a randomizer and outputs a ciphertext. The homomorphic property is

$$E(m \oplus m'; r \odot r') = E(m; r) \otimes E(m'; r'),$$

where $\oplus, \odot, \otimes$ are the binary operations for messages, randomizers and ciphertexts respectively. For notational convenience, we will in the rest of the paper use $+$ for the messages and randomizers, and $\cdot$ for the ciphertexts.

For the purpose of proving knowledge we assume the cryptosystem has the following root extraction property: Suppose an adversary produces a ciphertext E, an exponent e that is coprime with the order of the message space, and a message and randomizer so $E^e = E(M; R)$. Then we can efficiently extract m, r so $E = E(m; r)$. Examples of homomorphic cryptosystems with the root extraction property are ElGamal [ElG84], Okamoto-Uchiyama [OU98] and Paillier [Pai99].

We need an order of the message space that does not have any prime factors smaller than 2^{ℓ_t}. When specifying the protocols we will for simplicity assume that the randomizer space is $\mathbb{Z}$, and we encrypt M by choosing $R \leftarrow \{0,1\}^{\ell_R}$ and setting $E = E(M; R)$. This choice is purely out of notational convenience, the protocols work just as fine with other types of randomizer spaces.

HOMOMORPHIC COMMITMENT. The public key of the commitment scheme specifies a randomizer space and a commitment space that are abelian groups or abelian semi-groups. We allow commitment to multiple elements at once. The homomorphic property is

$$\text{com}(m_1 \oplus m'_1, \ldots, m_n \oplus m'_n; r \odot r') = \text{com}(m_1, \ldots, m_n; r) \otimes \text{com}(m'_1, \ldots, m'_n; r').$$

Again, for notational convenience we will in the rest of the paper use $+$ for the messages and randomizers, and $\cdot$ for the commitments.

In addition, the commitment scheme has a root extraction property which will be used for proving soundness. If an adversary produces a commitment c, and exponent $e \neq 0$ and a randomizer R and messages $M_1, \ldots, M_n$ so $c^e = \text{com}(M_1, \ldots, M_n; R)$, then we can find $m_1, \ldots, m_n, r$ so $c = \text{com}(m_1, \ldots, m_n; r)$.

The two shuffles we will propose make use of two different types of commitments: one will make use of integer commitments and the other will make use of commitments over a finite field $\mathbb{Z}_q$.

An example of a homomorphic commitment scheme over $\mathbb{Z}_q$ is the following variant of the Pedersen commitment [Ped91]. The public key consists of primes q, p with $q | p - 1$, and random generators $g_1, \ldots, g_n, h$ of the order-q subgroup of $\mathbb{Z}_p^*$. To commit to n messages $m_1, \ldots, m_n$ using randomness $(u, r) \in \mathbb{Z}_p^* \times \mathbb{Z}_q$ so $u^{\frac{p-1}{q}} = 1 \bmod p$, we compute the commitment $c = u g_1^{m_1} \cdots g_n^{m_n} h^r \bmod p$. Typically, we pick randomness $u = 1$ and $r \leftarrow \mathbb{Z}_q$ uniformly at random. Observe, any $0 < c < p$ is a valid commitment, so it is straightforward to check that a commitment is well-formed. Note also that the commitment scheme is perfectly hiding.

Examples of homomorphic integer commitment schemes can be found in [FO97], later revised in [DF02], and [Gro05a]. We present the latter homomorphic integer commitment scheme that is the most efficient one. The public key consists of an RSA modulus $N = pq$, where $p = 2p'r_p + 1, q = 2q'r_q + 1$ and p', q' are primes. We work in the unique subgroup G of order $p'q'$. Let $g_1, \ldots, g_n, h$ be randomly chosen generators of G. To commit to a set of integers $m_1, \ldots, m_k$ using randomness $(u, e > 0, r)$ so $u^e = 1 \bmod n$, we use

$$c = \mathrm{com}(m_1, \ldots, m_k; (u, e, r)) = u g_1^{m_1} \cdots g_k^{m_k} h^r \bmod N.$$

To open it we reveal $m_1, \ldots, m_k, (u, e, r)$. When selecting the randomness the usual choice is $u = 1, e = 1, r \leftarrow \{0,1\}^{\ell_r + \ell_s}$, where $\ell_r = |G|$ and ℓ_s is a small security parameter. It is of course straightforward to test whether c is a valid commitment, we simply test $c \in \mathbb{Z}_N^*$. This commitment scheme is statistically hiding.

3   Verifiable Secret Shuffle Based on Integer Commitment

A shuffle of input ciphertexts $e_1, \ldots, e_n$ consists of output ciphertexts $E_1, \ldots, E_n$ so there exists a permutation π and randomizers $R_1, \ldots, R_n$ so $E_k = e_{\pi(k)} E(0; R_k)$. E_i is then the encryption of message $M_i = m_{\pi(i)}$. In this section, we suggest a SHVZK argument of knowledge of correctness of a shuffle based on homomorphic integer commitments.

The permutation defines a permutation matrix in the following way. Let A have entries $a_{\pi(i)i} = 1$ and all other entries 0. We can visualize relating the messages $(m_1, \ldots, m_n)$ with the permuted ones $(M_1, \ldots, M_n) = (m_{\pi(1)}, \ldots, m_{\pi(n)})$ by a multiplication by the permutation matrix A:

$$\begin{pmatrix} m_1 \\ m_2 \\ \vdots \\ m_n \end{pmatrix} = \begin{pmatrix} a_{11} & a_{12} & \cdots & a_{1n} \\ a_{21} & a_{22} & \cdots & a_{2n} \\ \vdots & \vdots & \ddots & \vdots \\ a_{n1} & a_{n2} & \cdots & a_{nn} \end{pmatrix} \begin{pmatrix} m_{\pi(1)} \\ m_{\pi(2)} \\ \vdots \\ m_{\pi(n)} \end{pmatrix}$$

The idea in the shuffle argument is the following. We commit to the rows of A, $c_i \leftarrow \mathrm{com}(a_{i1}, \ldots, a_{in})$ for $i = 1, \ldots, n$. The verifier selects random challenges $t_1, \ldots, t_n \leftarrow \{0,1\}^{\ell_t}$ and we argue knowledge of the contents of $\prod_{i=1}^n c_i^{t_i}$. As we shall see this implies knowledge of the contents of each commitment c_i, i.e., knowledge of the matrix A.

The content of $\prod_{i=1}^n c_i^{t_i}$ is $(\sum_{i=1}^n a_{i1} t_i, \ldots, \sum_{i=1}^n a_{in} t_i)$. We will show that $\sum_{j=1}^n (\sum_{i=1}^n a_{ij} t_i) = \sum_{i=1}^n t_i$ for randomly chosen t_i's. Looking at each coefficient of the multi-variate polynomial, this means that with overwhelming probability we have $\sum_{j=1}^n a_{ij} = 1$ for $i = 1, \ldots, n$. In other words, each row of A sums to 1.

We also show that $\sum_{k=1}^n (\sum_{i=1}^n a_{ik} t_i)^2 = \sum_{i=1}^n t_i^2$ for randomly chosen t_i's. This gives us

$$0 = \sum_{k=1}^n \left(\sum_{i=1}^n a_{ik} t_i \right)^2 - \sum_{i=1}^n t_i^2 = \sum_{k=1}^n \sum_{i=1}^n \sum_{j=1}^n a_{ik} t_i a_{jk} t_j - \sum_{i=1}^n \sum_{j=1}^n \delta_{ik} t_i t_j$$

$$= \sum_{i=1}^{n} \sum_{j=1}^{n} \left[\left(\sum_{k=1}^{n} a_{ik} a_{jk} \right) - \delta_{ij} \right] t_i t_j.$$

Looking at coefficients of each pair $t_i t_j$ we see that $\sum_{k=1}^{n} a_{ik} a_{jk} = \delta_{ij}$, where $\delta_{ij} = 1$ if $i = j$ and 0 if $i \neq j$. I.e., the rows are orthogonal and have norm 1, so $AA^T = I$. Lemma 1 now shows that A is a permutation matrix defining some permutation π.

Finally, we have to connect the matrix A with the ciphertexts. We use the values $\sum_{i=1}^{n} a_{ij} t_i = t_{\pi(j)}$ that we have from the commitments. We show that

$$\prod_{i=1}^{n} E_i^{t_{\pi(i)}} = \prod_{i=1}^{n} e_i^{t_i} E\left(0; \sum_{i=1}^{n} t_{\pi(i)} R_i \right),$$

which implies

$$\prod_{i=1}^{n} (E_i e_{\pi(i)}^{-1})^{t_{\pi(i)}} = E\left(0; \sum_{i=1}^{n} t_{\pi(i)} R_i \right).$$

Since the t_i's are chosen at random this shows that with overwhelming probability E_i and $e_{\pi(i)}$ have the same message for any i. We shall see later that for cryptosystems with the root extraction property, we obtain a proof of knowledge, where we can extract randomizers R_i so $E_i = e_{\pi(i)} E(0; R_i)$.

These are the main ideas for obtaining soundness. What remains, is the problem of achieving zero-knowledge. We add some disguising values d_j to the sums we get out, i.e., we work with $d_j + \sum_{i=1}^{n} a_{ij} t_i$, where the d_j's are large random numbers. More precisely, $d_j \leftarrow \{0, 1\}^{\ell_t + \ell_s}$, where ℓ_s is a small security parameter, for instance $\ell_s = 80$. This way the actual value of $\sum_{i=1}^{n} a_{ij} t_i$ is hidden throughout the argument. This modification entails a few other modifications to the protocol. The resulting argument is described in Figure 1.

Lemma 1. *Consider an $n \times n$ integer matrix A with entries a_{ij}. If $AA^T = I$ and*
$$\sum_{j=1}^{n} a_{ij} = 1 \text{ for all } i \text{ then } A \text{ is a permutation matrix.}$$

Proof. The condition $AA^T = I$ shows us that all rows have norm 1. In other words, each row has $n - 1$ entries that are 0, and one single entry that is ± 1. Then $\sum_{j=1}^{n} a_{ij} = 1$ for all i shows us that these entries must be $+1$. Since A is invertible, the n 1-entries must be spread over all columns and all rows. In other words, A is a permutation matrix.   □

Theorem 1. *The protocol in Figure 1 is a 3-move public coin SHVZK argument of knowledge of a correct shuffle. If the commitment scheme is statistically hiding, then the argument is statistical SHVZK.*

Proof. Completeness follows from direct algebraic manipulations. Left is to argue SHVZK and soundness and knowledge.

SHVZK. Given arbitrary challenges $t_1, \ldots, t_n \in \{0, 1\}^{\ell_t}$ we have to simulate an argument. The simulation will mimic the real argument and we will highlight the main differences with a bar over the variable.

Shuffle Argument $\mathcal{SHUF}_{\mathbb{Z}}$

Common input: Ciphertexts $e_1, \ldots, e_n, E_1, \ldots, E_n$ and public keys.
Prover's input: Permutation $\pi \in \Sigma_n$ and randomizers $R_1, \ldots, R_n$ so $E_i = e_{\pi(i)} E(0; R_i)$.

Initial message $(\mathcal{P} \longrightarrow \mathcal{V})$: Choose randomness $r_i \leftarrow \{0,1\}^{\ell_r}, r_d \leftarrow \{0,1\}^{\ell_r + \log n + \ell_t + \ell_s}, d_j \leftarrow \{0,1\}^{\ell_t + \ell_s}, R_R \leftarrow \{0,1\}^{\ell_R + \log n + \ell_t + \ell_s}$ and set $d_n := -\sum_{j=1}^{n-1} d_j$. Set $E_R := E(0; -R_R) \prod_{i=1}^{n} E_i^{d_i}$. Generate commitments

$$
\begin{aligned}
c_1 &\leftarrow \mathrm{com}(\ 0\ \ 1_{\pi^{-1}(1)}\ \ 0 \quad \cdots \quad\quad 0, \quad 2d_{\pi^{-1}(1)}\ ; r_1) \\
c_2 &\leftarrow \mathrm{com}(\ 0 \quad\ \ 0 \quad\ \ 0 \quad \cdots \quad 1_{\pi^{-1}(2)},\ 2d_{\pi^{-1}(2)}\ ; r_2) \\
&\ \ \vdots \\
c_n &\leftarrow \mathrm{com}(\ 0 \quad \cdots \quad 0\ \ 1_{\pi^{-1}(n)} \quad 0, \quad 2d_{\pi^{-1}(n)}\ ; r_n)
\end{aligned}
$$
and
$$
c_d \leftarrow \mathrm{com}(\ d_1, \quad d_2, \quad \ldots, d_{n-1}, \quad d_n, \quad \textstyle\sum_{j=1}^{n} d_j^2\ ; r_d)
$$

Send $(c_1, \ldots, c_n, c_d, E_R)$ to the verifier.
Challenge $(\mathcal{P} \longleftarrow \mathcal{V})$: $t_1, \ldots, t_n \leftarrow \{0,1\}^{\ell_t}$.
Answer $(\mathcal{P} \longrightarrow \mathcal{V})$: Set $f_j := t_{\pi(j)} + d_j$, $z := \sum_{i=1}^{n} t_i r_i + r_d$ and
$Z := R_R + \sum_{i=1}^{n} t_{\pi(i)} R_i$.
Send $(f_1, \ldots, f_n, z, Z)$ to the verifier.
Verification: Check that $c_1, \ldots, c_n, c_d$ are valid commitments and E_R is a valid ciphertext.
Set $f_\Delta := \sum_{j=1}^{n} f_j^2 - \sum_{i=1}^{n} t_i^2$. Verify

$$
\sum_{j=1}^{n} f_j \overset{?}{=} \sum_{i=1}^{n} t_i
$$
$$
c_d \prod_{i=1}^{n} c_i^{t_i} \overset{?}{=} \mathrm{com}(f_1, \ldots, f_n, f_\Delta; z)
$$
$$
\prod_{i=1}^{n} E_i^{f_i} \overset{?}{=} E(0; Z) E_R \prod_{i=1}^{n} e_i^{t_i}
$$

Fig. 1. SHVZK Argument of Correct Shuffle Based on Integer Commitment

---

Initial message: Choose randomness r_i, r_d Choose random $\overline{f_j}$ so that $\sum_{j=1}^{n} \overline{f_j} = \sum_{i=1}^{n} t_i$ and set $f_\Delta := \sum_{j=1}^{n} \overline{f_j}^2 - \sum_{i=1}^{n} t_i^2$. Set $c_i \leftarrow \mathrm{com}(0, \ldots, 0)$. Choose random $\overline{z}$ and set $c_d \leftarrow \mathrm{com}(\overline{f_1}, \ldots, \overline{f_n}, f_\Delta; \overline{z}) \prod_{i=1}^{n} c_i^{-t_i}$. Choose random $\overline{Z}$ and set $E_R := E(0; -\overline{Z}) \prod_{i=1}^{n} E_i^{\overline{f_i}} e_i^{-t_i}$
Write $(c_1, \ldots, c_n, c_d, E_R)$ to the transcript.
Challenge: Write the $t_1, \ldots, t_n$ received as input to the transcript.
Answer: Send $(\overline{f_1}, \ldots, \overline{f_n}, \overline{z}, \overline{Z})$ to the verifier.

The simulated argument is $(c_1, \ldots, c_n, c_d, E_R, t_1, \ldots, t_n, \overline{f_1}, \ldots, \overline{f_n}, \overline{z}, \overline{Z})$.

To see that this is a good simulation, consider the following hybrid argument. We proceed exactly as in the simulation except when forming $c_1, \ldots, c_n$. Here we set $d_j := \overline{f_j} - t_{\pi(j)}$. We set $c_i \leftarrow \mathrm{com}(0, \ldots, 1_{\pi^{-1}(i)}, \ldots, 0, 2d_{\pi^{-1}(i)})$. Proceed with the rest of simulation as described above.

The hybrid argument is statistically indistinguishable from a real argument as the randomness chosen in the hybrid is linearly related to the randomness in the real argument, thus it retains the same distribution. On the other hand, the only thing that differs from the simulation is the way we form the c_i's. The hiding property of the commitment scheme therefore gives us indistinguishability between the hybrid argument and the simulated argument. If the commitment scheme is statistically hiding, then we have statistical indistinguishability between the hybrid argument and the simulated argument.

SOUNDNESS AND KNOWLEDGE. Consider an adversary that has already sent the initial message $(c_1, \ldots, c_n, c_d, E_R)$ to the verifier and has non-negligible probability ε of answering the challenge. We store the state of this prover and now wish to extract a witness for correctness of the shuffle.

We select at random challenges $t_1, \ldots, t_n$ and run the adversarial prover until we have $n + 1$ acceptable answers. We use an expected number of $(n + 1)/\varepsilon$ tries to do this. Call the challenges $t_1^{(j)}, \ldots, t_n^{(j)}$ for $j = 0, \ldots, n$ and the corresponding answers $f_1^{(j)}, \ldots, f_n^{(j)}, z^{(j)}, Z^{(j)}$. Since $c_d \prod_{i=1}^{n} c_i^{t_i^{(j)}} = \text{com}(f_1^{(j)}, \ldots, f_n^{(j)}, f_\Delta^{(j)}; z^{(j)})$ we have

$$\prod_{i=1}^{n} c_i^{t_i^{(0)} - t_i^{(j)}} = \text{com}(f_1^{(0)} - f_1^{(j)}, \ldots, f_n^{(0)} - f_n^{(j)}, f_\Delta^{(0)} - f_\Delta^{(j)}; z^{(0)} - z^{(j)}).$$

Consider the $n \times n$ matrix T with entries $t_{ij} = t_i^{(0)} - t_i^{(j)}$. With overwhelming probability over the choices of $t_i^{(j)}$ the columns are linearly independent. We can in polynomial time find the transpose of the cofactor matrix C^T so $TC^T = |T|I$, where $|T|$ is the determinant of T.

Call the entries of C^T as v_{jk}, then we have $|T| = \sum_{j=1}^{n} t_{kj} v_{jk}$ and $0 = \sum_{j=1}^{n} t_{ij} v_{jk}$ for $k \neq i$. So

$$c_k^{|T|} = c_k^{\sum_{j=1}^{n} t_{kj} v_{jk}} = \prod_{i=1}^{n} c_i^{\sum_{j=1}^{n} t_{ij} v_{jk}} = \prod_{i=1}^{n} \prod_{j=1}^{n} c_i^{t_{ij} v_{jk}} = \prod_{j=1}^{n} \left(\prod_{i=1}^{n} c_i^{t_i^{(0)} - t_i^{(j)}} \right)^{v_{jk}}.$$

This means

$$c_k^{|T|} = \text{com}\left(\sum_{j=1}^{n} v_{jk}(f_1^{(0)} - f_1^{(j)}), \ldots, \sum_{j=1}^{n} v_{jk}(f_n^{(0)} - f_n^{(j)}), \sum_{j=1}^{n} v_{jk}(f_\Delta^{(0)} - f_\Delta^{(j)}); \sum_{j=1}^{n} v_{jk}(z^{(0)} - z^{(j)}) \right).$$

By the root extraction property, we can open c_k. We call the opening $(a_{k1}, \ldots, a_{kn}, a_{k\Delta}, r_k)$. Since $c_d = \text{com}(f_1^{(0)}, \ldots, f_n^{(0)}, f_\Delta^{(0)}; z^{(0)}) \prod_{i=1}^{n} c_i^{-t_i^{(0)}}$, having openings of $c_1, \ldots, c_n$ means that we can find an opening $(d_1, \ldots, d_n, d_\Delta, r_d)$ of c_d.

The adversary, having noticeable probability of answering the challenge $t_1, \ldots, t_n$, is forced to use $f_j = d_j + \sum_{i=1}^{n} a_{ij} t_i$ and $f_\Delta = d_\Delta + \sum_{i=1}^{n} a_{i\Delta} t_i$. The equation $f_\Delta = \sum_{j=1}^{n} f_j^2 - \sum_{i=1}^{n} t_i^2$ implies

$$\sum_{i=1}^{n} a_{i\Delta} t_i + d_\Delta = \sum_{j=1}^{n} \left(\sum_{i=1}^{n} a_{ij} t_i + d_j \right)^2 - \sum_{i=1}^{n} t_i^2$$

$$= \sum_{j=1}^{n} \left(\sum_{i=1}^{n} \sum_{k=1}^{n} a_{ij} a_{kj} t_i t_k + 2 d_j \sum_{i=1}^{n} a_{ij} t_i + d_j^2 \right) - \sum_{i=1}^{n} \sum_{k=1}^{n} \delta_{ik} t_i t_k$$

$$= \sum_{i=1}^{n} \sum_{k=1}^{n} \left(\sum_{j=1}^{n} a_{ij} a_{kj} - \delta_{ik} \right) t_i t_k + \sum_{i=1}^{n} \left(2 \sum_{j=1}^{n} d_j a_{ij} \right) t_i + \sum_{j=1}^{n} d_j^2.$$

With overwhelming probability over $t_1, \ldots, t_n$ this can only happen if $\sum_{j=1}^{n} a_{ij} a_{kj} = \delta_{ik}$ for all i, k. Let A be the matrix with entries a_{ij}. Then the equation corresponds to saying $AA^T = I$.

We also have

$$0 = \sum_{j=1}^{n} f_j - \sum_{i=1}^{n} t_i = \sum_{j=1}^{n} \left(\sum_{i=1}^{n} a_{ij} t_i + d_j \right) - \sum_{i=1}^{n} t_i = \sum_{i=1}^{n} \left(\sum_{j=1}^{n} a_{ij} - 1 \right) t_i + \sum_{j=1}^{n} d_j.$$

With overwhelming probability over the t_i's this can only be the case if $\sum_{j=1}^{n} a_{ij} = 1$ for all i.

Lemma 1 tells us that A is a permutation matrix. This means, there exists a permutation π so $a_{\pi(i)i} = 1$ and all other entries are 0.

Look now at the ciphertext equations, $\prod_{i=1}^{n} E_i^{f_i^{(j)}} = E_R E(0; Z^{(j)}) \prod_{i=1}^{n} e_i^{t_i^{(j)}}$ giving us

$$\prod_{i=1}^{n} E_i^{t_{\pi(i)}^{(0)} - t_{\pi(i)}^{(j)}} = \prod_{i=1}^{n} E_i^{f_i^{(0)} - f_i^{(j)}} = E(0; Z^{(0)} - Z^{(j)}) \prod_{i=1}^{n} e_i^{t_i^{(0)} - t_i^{(j)}}.$$

Since $\sum_{j=1}^{n} t_{ij} v_{jk} = |T| \delta_{ik}$ we have

$$(E_k e_{\pi(k)}^{-1})^{|T|} = (E_k e_{\pi(k)}^{-1})^{\sum_{j=1}^{n} t_{\pi(k)j} v_{j\pi(k)}} = \prod_{i=1}^{n} (E_i e_{\pi(i)}^{-1})^{\sum_{j=1}^{n} t_{\pi(i)j} v_{j\pi(k)}}$$

$$= \prod_{j=1}^{n} \left(\prod_{i=1}^{n} (E_i e_{\pi(i)}^{-1})^{t_{\pi(i)}^{(0)} - t_{\pi(i)}^{(j)}} \right)^{v_{j\pi(k)}} = \prod_{j=1}^{n} \left(\prod_{i=1}^{n} E_i^{t_{\pi(i)}^{(0)} - t_{\pi(i)}^{(j)}} \prod_{i=1}^{n} e_i^{t_i^{(0)} - t_i^{(j)}} \right)^{v_{j\pi(k)}}$$

$$= E \left(0; \sum_{j=1}^{n} v_{j\pi(k)} (Z^{(0)} - Z^{(j)}) \right).$$

By the root extraction property we can find an opening $(0, R_k)$ of $E_k e_{\pi(k)}^{-1}$. Doing so for $k = 1, \ldots, n$ means we have found openings $R_1, \ldots, R_n$ so $E_1 = e_{\pi(1)} E(0; R_1)$, $\ldots, E_n = e_{\pi(n)} E(0; R_n)$.   □

4   Verifiable Secret Shuffle Based on Commitments over $\mathbb{Z}_q$

The ideas presented above also apply to the case of homomorphic commitment schemes over $\mathbb{Z}_q$. In this section, we suggest a SHVZK argument of knowledge of correctness of a shuffle based on homomorphic commitments in $\mathbb{Z}_q$ where $q \equiv 2 \bmod 3$. This shuffle will be a slight modification of the one in the previous section to accommodate the fact that Lemma 1 no longer applies in $\mathbb{Z}_q$. The scheme is more complicated, but the advantage is that it may be easier to set up a scheme with prime order groups instead of using composite order groups. In case of ElGamal encryption with the message space being a small subgroup, the scheme is almost identical to Furukawa's scheme [Fur05]. However, for large message spaces or large ciphertexts we gain much in comparison with the state of the art.

The idea in the shuffle argument is similar to the preceding section. Let A have entries $a_{\pi(i)i} = 1$ in $\mathbb{Z}_q$ and all other entries 0. We commit to the rows of A, $c_i \leftarrow \text{com}(a_{i1}, \ldots, a_{in})$ for $i = 1, \ldots, n$. The verifier selects random challenges $t_1, \ldots, t_n$ and we argue knowledge of the contents of $\prod_{i=1}^{n} c_i^{t_i}$. Just as before, we shall see this implies knowledge of the contents of each commitment c_i, i.e., knowledge of the matrix A.

In the case of commitments in $\mathbb{Z}_q$ we have a similar lemma (Theorem 2 [Fur05]) to identify when a matrix is a permutation matrix. We show that $\sum_{h=1}^{n}(\sum_{i=1}^{n} a_{ih}t_i)^3 = \sum_{i=1}^{n} t_i^3$. This gives us

$$0 = \sum_{h=1}^{n}(\sum_{i=1}^{n} a_{ih}t_i)^3 - \sum_{i=1}^{n} t_i^3 = \sum_{h=1}^{n}\sum_{i=1}^{n}\sum_{j=1}^{n}\sum_{k=1}^{n} a_{ih}t_i a_{jh}t_j a_{kh}t_k - \sum_{i=1}^{n}\sum_{j=1}^{n}\sum_{k=1}^{n} \delta_{ijk} t_i t_j t_k$$

$$= \sum_{i=1}^{n}\sum_{j=1}^{n}\sum_{k=1}^{n} \left[\left(\sum_{h=1}^{n} a_{ih}a_{jh}a_{kh}\right) - \delta_{ijk}\right] t_i t_j t_k.$$

Looking at coefficients of each triple $t_i t_j t_k$ we see that $\sum_{h=1}^{n} a_{ih}a_{jh}a_{kh} = \delta_{ijk}$, where $\delta_{ijk} = 1$ if $i = j = k$ and 0 otherwise. Lemma 2 now shows that A is a permutation matrix defining some permutation π.

Finally, we have to connect the matrix A with the ciphertexts. We use the values $\sum_{i=1}^{n} a_{ij}t_i = t_{\pi(j)}$ that we have from the commitments. We show that $\prod_{i=1}^{n} E_i^{t_{\pi(i)}} = \prod_{i=1}^{n} e_i^{t_i} E(0; \sum_{i=1}^{n} t_{\pi(i)}R_i)$, i.e., $\prod_{i=1}^{n}(E_i e_{\pi(i)}^{-1})^{t_{\pi(i)}} = E(0; \sum_{i=1}^{n} t_{\pi(i)}R_i)$. Since the t_i's are chosen at random this indicates that E_i and $e_{\pi(i)}$ have the same message for any i. Just as before, we add blinding factors to these values to ensure zero-knowledge. The resulting argument is described in Figure 2. If we let ℓ_s be an additional security parameter, we need to choose the d_i's from $\{0,1\}^{\ell_t + \ell_s}$. Because we are working with large ciphertexts, yet are performing all of the operations modulo q, to ensure the check on the ciphertexts still holds true we need to ensure that the equations $f_j = t_{\pi j} + d_j$ do not overflow. For this reason we require that $\ell_t + \ell_s < |q|$. The remaining random variables are only for verifying the commitments modulo q. Therefore, all of the prover's random variables may be reduced modulo q.

Lemma 2 (Theorem 2 [Fur05]). *Consider an $n \times n$ integer matrix A with entries a_{ij} in $\mathbb{Z}_q$ where $q \equiv 2 \mod 3$. We have that*

$$\sum_{h=1}^{n} a_{ih}a_{jh}a_{kh} = \delta_{ijk} \text{ for all } i, j, k \tag{1}$$

if and only if A is a permutation matrix.

Proof. ($\Leftarrow$) is trivial.

($\Rightarrow$): Let R_i denote the i-th row vector of A. First we show the matrix A has full rank, i.e. the rows form a basis for $\mathbb{Z}_q^n$. If there is a linear combination $\mathbf{0} = \sum_{i=1}^n b_i R_i$ we have that $0 = \sum_{i=1}^n b_i a_{ih}$ for all h. Observe now that for any choice of j, we may multiply $a_{jh} a_{jh}$ to each of these equations, so $0 = \sum_{i=1}^n b_i a_{ih} a_{jh} a_{jh}$. Summing over all h we obtain $0 = \sum_{h=1}^n \sum_{i=1}^n b_i a_{ih} a_{jh} a_{jh} = \sum_{i=1}^n b_i \sum_{h=1}^n a_{ih} a_{jh} a_{jh}$ which by assumption is equal to $\sum_{i=1}^n b_i \delta_{ijj} = b_j$ and hence $b_j = 0$. This shows that the rows are linearly independent in $\mathbb{Z}_q^n$ and hence form a basis for $\mathbb{Z}_q^n$. Next, we show that there is at most one non-zero entry in each column.

If $v = (v_1, \ldots, v_n)$ and $w = (w_1, \ldots, w_n)$ are vectors in $\mathbb{Z}_q^n$, define $\langle v, w \rangle = \sum_{i=1}^n v_i w_i$ to be the dot product of v and w and define $v \odot w = (v_1 w_1, \ldots, v_n w_n)$ to be a vector resulting in the component-wise multiplication of v and w. Notice that $\langle R_i \odot R_j, R_k \rangle = \sum_{h=1}^n a_{ih} a_{jh} a_{kh}$ which is equal to δ_{ijk} by assumption. Observe that if $i \neq j$ then $\langle R_i \odot R_j, R_k \rangle = 0$ for all k, and since the R_k's span all of $\mathbb{Z}_q^n$, we have that $R_i \odot R_j = \mathbf{0}$. Since the choice of i, j was arbitrary, this means between each pair of entries in a column, at most one of them is non-zero; therefore at most one entry is non-zero. The matrix is of full rank, so indeed there is exactly one non-zero entry in each column (and hence in each row). This entry must be a cube root of 1, and $q = 2 \mod 3$ implies there is a unique cube root, namely 1. Thus A is a permutation matrix over $\mathbb{Z}_q$. $\square$

Theorem 2. *The protocol in Figure 2 is a 3-move public coin SHVZK argument of knowledge of a correct shuffle. If the commitment scheme is statistically hiding, then the argument is statistical SHVZK.*

Proof. Completeness follows from direct algebraic manipulations. Left is to argue SHVZK and soundness.

SHVZK. Given challenges $t_1, \ldots, t_n \in \{0,1\}^{\ell_t}$ we have to simulate an argument. The simulation will mimic the real argument and we will highlight the main differences with a bar over the variable. Simulation input: Challenges $t_1, \ldots, t_n$. Ciphertexts $e_1, \ldots, e_n, E_1, \ldots, E_n$ and public keys.

Initial message: Pick $r_1, \ldots, r_n, \overline{f_1}, \ldots, \overline{f_n}, \overline{F_1}, \ldots, \overline{F_n}, r_d, r_D, \overline{y_d}, \overline{y_D}, \overline{Z}$ and $\overline{f_d}$
at random. Set $f_D := \sum_{j=1}^n \overline{f_j}^3 - \sum_{i=1}^n t_i^3 - \overline{f_d}$. Using the challenges, compute $z_d := \sum_{j=1}^n t_j r_j + r_d$ and $z_D := \sum_{j=1}^n t_j^2 r_j + r_D$. Generate commitments $c_i \leftarrow \text{com}(0, \ldots, 0; r_i)$ and $c_d \leftarrow \text{com}(\overline{f_1}, \ldots, \overline{f_n}, \overline{y_d}, \overline{f_d}; z_d) \prod_{i=1}^n c_i^{-t_i}$ and $c_D \leftarrow \text{com}(\overline{F_1}, \ldots, \overline{F_n}, f_D, \overline{y_D}; z_D) \prod_{i=1}^n c_i^{-t_i^2}$.
Set $E_R := E(0; -\overline{Z}) \prod_{i=1}^n E_i^{\overline{f_i}} e_i^{-t_i}$.
Write $(c_1, \ldots, c_n, c_d, c_D, E_R)$ to the transcript.

Challenge: Write the $t_1, \ldots, t_n$ received as input to the transcript.

Answer: Everything we need has already computed in an earlier phase. Thus we can immediately write $(\overline{f_1}, \ldots, \overline{f_n}, \overline{f_d}, \overline{y_d}, z_d, \overline{F_1}, \ldots, \overline{F_n}, \overline{y_D}, z_D, \overline{Z})$ to the transcript.

The simulated argument is

$$(c_1, \ldots, c_n, c_d, c_D, E_R, t_1, \ldots, t_n, \overline{f_1}, \ldots, \overline{f_n}, \overline{f_d}, \overline{y_d}, z_d, \overline{F_1}, \ldots, \overline{F_n}, \overline{y_D}, z_D, \overline{Z})$$

Shuffle Argument $\mathcal{SHUF}_{\mathbb{Z}_q}$

Common input: Ciphertexts $e_1, \ldots, e_n, E_1, \ldots, E_n$ and public keys.
Prover's input: Permutation $\pi \in \Sigma_n$ and randomizers $R_1, \ldots, R_n$ so $E_i = e_{\pi(i)} E(0; R_i)$.

Initial message $(\mathcal{P} \longrightarrow \mathcal{V})$: Choose randomness $d_1, \ldots, d_n \leftarrow \{0, 1\}^{\ell_t + \ell_s}$ and $r_1, \ldots, r_n$, $D_1, \ldots, D_n, r_d, r_D, s_d, s_D, \Delta \leftarrow \mathbb{Z}_q$. Choose randomness $R_R \leftarrow \{0, 1\}^{\ell_R + \log n + \ell_t + \ell_s}$. Set $E_R := E(0; -R_R) \prod_{i=1}^{n} E_i^{d_i}$. Generate commitments

$$
\begin{array}{llllllll}
c_1 \leftarrow \text{com}(& 0 & 1_{\pi^{-1}(1)} & 0 & \cdots & 0, & 3d_{\pi^{-1}(1)}, & 3d_{\pi^{-1}(1)}^2 & ; r_1) \\
c_2 \leftarrow \text{com}(& 0 & 0 & 0 & \cdots & 1_{\pi^{-1}(2)}, & 3d_{\pi^{-1}(2)}, & 3d_{\pi^{-1}(2)}^2 & ; r_2) \\
\vdots & & & & & & & & \\
c_n \leftarrow \text{com}(& 0 & \cdots & 0 & 1_{\pi^{-1}(n)} & 0, & 3d_{\pi^{-1}(n)}, & 3d_{\pi^{-1}(n)}^2 & ; r_n)
\end{array}
$$

and

$$
\begin{array}{llllllll}
c_d \leftarrow \text{com}(& d_1, & d_2, & \ldots, d_{n-1}, & d_n, & s_d, & \sum_{j=1}^{n} d_j^3 - \Delta & ; r_d) \\
c_D \leftarrow \text{com}(& D_1, & D_2, & \ldots, D_{n-1}, & D_n, & \Delta, & s_D & ; r_D)
\end{array}
$$

Send $(c_1, \ldots, c_n, c_d, c_D, E_R)$ to the verifier.

Challenge $(\mathcal{P} \longleftarrow \mathcal{V})$: $t_1, \ldots, t_n \leftarrow \{0, 1\}^{\ell_t}$.

Answer $(\mathcal{P} \longrightarrow \mathcal{V})$: Set $f_j := t_{\pi(j)} + d_j$ and $F_j := t_{\pi(j)}^2 + D_j$ for $j = 1, \ldots, n$. Also set

$f_d := 3 \sum_{j=1}^{n} t_j d_{\pi^{-1}(j)}^2 + \sum_{j=1}^{n} d_j^3 - \Delta$

$y_d := 3 \sum_{j=1}^{n} t_j d_{\pi^{-1}(j)} + s_d$ and $y_D := 3 \sum_{j=1}^{n} t_j^2 d_{\pi^{-1}(j)}^2 + s_D$

$z_d := \sum_{j=1}^{n} t_j r_j + r_d$ and $z_D := \sum_{j=1}^{n} t_j^2 r_j + r_D$

Set $Z := R_R + \sum_{i=1}^{n} t_{\pi(i)} R_i$.

Send $(f_1, \ldots, f_n, f_d, y_d, z_d, F_1, \ldots, F_n, y_D, z_D, Z)$ to the verifier.

Verification: Check that $c_1, \ldots, c_n, c_d, c_D$ are valid commitments and E_R is a valid ciphertext and $f_j > 2^{\ell_t}$ for $j = 1, \ldots, n$. Set $f_D := \sum_{j=1}^{n} f_j^3 - \sum_{i=1}^{n} t_i^3 - f_d$. Verify

$$
c_d \prod_{i=1}^{n} c_i^{t_i} \stackrel{?}{=} \text{com}(f_1, \ldots, f_n, y_d, f_d; z_d)
$$
$$
c_D \prod_{i=1}^{n} c_i^{t_i^2} \stackrel{?}{=} \text{com}(F_1, \ldots, F_n, f_D, y_D; z_D)
$$
$$
\prod_{i=1}^{n} E_i^{f_i} \stackrel{?}{=} E(0; Z) E_R \prod_{i=1}^{n} e_i^{t_i}
$$

Fig. 2. SHVZK Argument of Correct Shuffle Based on Commitment over $\mathbb{Z}_q$

To see that this is a good simulation, consider the following hybrid argument. We proceed exactly as in the simulation except when forming $c_1, \ldots, c_n$. Here we solve for the valid $d_1, \ldots, d_n$, i.e. set $d_j := \overline{f_j} - t_{\pi(j)}$. We similarly set the variables that differ between the simulation and the real argument, namely the appropriate $D_1, \ldots, D_n$, s_d, s_D, R_R and Δ. Observe that the relationship between the variables generated randomly in the simulation and the variables generated randomly in the real argument are governed by linear equations; hence this endows the hybrid argument with the same distribution of variables as a real argument. We generate $c_i \leftarrow \text{com}(0, \ldots, 0, 1_{\pi^{-1}(i)}, 0, \ldots, 0, 3d_{\pi^{-1}(i)}, 3d_{\pi^{-1}(i)}^2; r_i)$. Proceed with the rest of simulation as described above.

The hybrid argument is statistically indistinguishable from a real argument. On the other hand, the only thing that differs from the simulation is the way we form the c_i's. The hiding property of the commitment scheme therefore gives us indistinguishability between the hybrid argument and the simulated argument. If the commitment scheme is statistically hiding, then we have statistical indistinguishability between the hybrid argument and the simulated argument.

SOUNDNESS AND KNOWLEDGE. Consider an adversary that has already sent the initial message $(c_1, \ldots, c_n, c_d, c_D, E_R)$ to the verifier and has non-negligible probability ε of answering the challenge. We store the state of this prover and now wish to extract a witness for correctness of the shuffle.

We select at random challenges $t_1, \ldots, t_n$ and run the adversarial prover until we have $n + 1$ acceptable answers. We use an expected number of $(n + 1)/\varepsilon$ tries to do this. Call the challenges $t_1^{(j)}, \ldots, t_n^{(j)}$ for $j = 0, \ldots, n$ and the corresponding answers $f_1^{(j)}, \ldots, f_n^{(j)}, f_d^{(j)}, y_d^{(j)}, z_d^{(j)}, F_1^{(j)}, \ldots, F_n^{(j)}, y_D^{(j)}, z_D^{(j)}, Z^{(j)}$. Since $c_d \prod_{i=1}^n c_i^{t_i^{(j)}} = \mathrm{com}(f_1^{(j)}, \ldots, f_n^{(j)}, y_d^{(j)}, f_d^{(j)}; z_d^{(j)})$ we have

$$\prod_{i=1}^n c_i^{t_i^{(0)} - t_i^{(j)}} = \mathrm{com}(f_1^{(0)} - f_1^{(j)}, \ldots, f_n^{(0)} - f_n^{(j)}, y_d^{(0)} - y_d^{(j)}, f_d^{(0)} - f_d^{(j)}; z_d^{(0)} - z_d^{(j)}).$$

Consider the $n \times n$ matrix T with entries $t_{ij} = t_i^{(0)} - t_i^{(j)}$. With overwhelming probability over the choices of $t_i^{(j)}$ the columns are linearly independent. We can in polynomial time find the inverse matrix T^{-1} so $TT^{-1} = I$.

Call the entries of T^{-1} as v_{jk}, then we have $\sum_{j=1}^n t_{ij} v_{jk} = \delta_{ik}$. So

$$c_k = c_k^{\sum_{j=1}^n t_{kj} v_{jk}} = \prod_{i=1}^n c_i^{\sum_{j=1}^n t_{ij} v_{jk}} = \prod_{i=1}^n \prod_{j=1}^n c_i^{t_{ij} v_{jk}} = \prod_{j=1}^n \left(\prod_{i=1}^n c_i^{t_i^{(0)} - t_i^{(j)}} \right)^{v_{jk}}.$$

This means

$$c_k = \mathrm{com}(\sum_{j=1}^n v_{jk}(f_1^{(0)} - f_1^{(j)}), \ldots, \sum_{j=1}^n v_{jk}(f_n^{(0)} - f_n^{(j)}),$$

$$\sum_{j=1}^n v_{jk}(y_d^{(0)} - y_d^{(j)}), \sum_{j=1}^n v_{jk}(f_d^{(0)} - f_d^{(j)}); \sum_{j=1}^n v_{jk}(z_d^{(0)} - z_d^{(j)})).$$

By the root extraction property, we can open c_k. We call the opening $(a_{k1}, \ldots, a_{kn}, a_{kD}, a_{kd}, r_k)$. Since $c_d = \mathrm{com}(f_1^{(0)}, \ldots, f_n^{(0)}, y_d^{(0)}, f_d^{(0)}; z_d^{(0)}) \prod_{i=1}^n c_i^{-t_i^{(0)}}$, having openings of $c_1, \ldots, c_n$ means that we can find an opening $(d_1, \ldots, d_n, s_d, \Delta_d, r_d)$ of c_d. Similarly, we can find an opening $(D_1, \ldots, D_n, s_D, \Delta_D, r_D)$ of c_D.

The adversary, having noticeable probability of answering the challenge $t_1, \ldots, t_n$, is forced to use $f_j = d_j + \sum_{i=1}^n a_{ij} t_i$ and $f_d = \Delta_d + \sum_{i=1}^n a_{id} t_i$ and $f_D = \Delta_D + \sum_{i=1}^n a_{iD} t_i$. The equation $f_D = \sum_{j=1}^n f_j^3 - \sum_{i=1}^n t_i^3 - f_d$ implies

$$0 = \sum_{j=1}^n f_j^3 - \sum_{i=1}^n t_i^3 - f_d - f_D = \sum_{j=1}^n f_j^3 - \sum_{i=1}^n t_i^3 - \Delta_d - \sum_{i=1}^n a_{id} t_i - \Delta_D - \sum_{i=1}^n a_{iD} t_i$$

$$= \sum_{j=1}^n (d_j + \sum_{i=1}^n a_{ij} t_i)^3 - \sum_{i=1}^n t_i^3 - \Delta_d - \sum_{i=1}^n a_{id} t_i - \Delta_D - \sum_{i=1}^n a_{iD} t_i$$

With overwhelming probability over $t_1, \ldots, t_n$ this can only happen if every coefficient is zero (considering this as a multivariate polynomial in the t_i's). Indeed, the coefficient for $t_i t_j t_k$ is $\sum_{h=1}^{n} a_{ih} a_{jh} a_{kh} - \delta_{ijk}$ for all i, j, k. Then lemma 2 tells us that A is a permutation matrix. This means, there exists a permutation π so $a_{\pi(i)i} = 1$ and all other entries are 0.

For the ciphertext equations, we make use of a cofactor matrix as in the proof of the integer scheme. Because the f_j's are greater than 2^{ℓ_t}, we know an overflow did not occur $\bmod q$ and thus the equations $f_j = t_{\pi(j)} + d_j$ hold over $\mathbb{Z}$. Then the proof proceeds the same way as in the integer case, and then by the root extraction property we can find an opening $(0, R_k)$ of $E_k e_{\pi(k)}^{-1}$. Doing so for $k = 1, \ldots, n$ means we have found openings $R_1, \ldots, R_n$ so $E_1 = e_{\pi(1)} E(0; R_1), \ldots, E_n = e_{\pi(n)} E(0; R_n)$. $\square$

5   Comparison

As we mentioned in the introduction, there are many efficient shuffle arguments on different encryption schemes. While our shuffle argument can be used with many different homomorphic cryptosystems, its main advantage is when we look at cryptosystems with large message spaces or large ciphertexts. It is therefore natural to compare it to the shuffle arguments that have been proposed for Paillier encryption.

We compare the efficiency of our shuffle arguments with integer commitments ($\mathcal{SHUF}_{\mathbb{Z}}$) and with commitments over $\mathbb{Z}_q$ ($\mathcal{SHUF}_{\mathbb{Z}_q}$) to those of Nguyen et. al. [NSNK05], Peng et. al. [PBD05], and Wikström (Appendix G) [Wik05b]. We consider all schemes running on a 1024-bit Paillier modulus (giving ciphertexts of size $|N^2| = 2048$ bits) and 80-bit challenges. The reader may download a spreadsheet [GL07] to see compare the schemes for other parameter choices.

For the homomorphic integer commitment, we use a 1024-bit safe prime RSA-modulus as in [DF02], which corresponds to the choice in [Wik05a]. Both his and our scheme become faster if one uses the homomorphic integer commitment from [Gro05a]. Our choice of parameters for [Wik05b] (Appendix G) is $K_1 = 240, K_2 = 1024, K_3 = K_4 = K_5 = 80$, whereas for our scheme it is $\ell_t = 80, \ell_s = 80, \ell_r = 1024$.

For our shuffle over $\mathbb{Z}_q$, we use Pedersen commitments with $|q| = 240, |p| = 1024$, giving us parameters $\ell_t = 80, \ell_s = 80, \ell_r = 240$.

For [NSNK05] we chose $\ell_\eta = 1022, \ell_N = 1024, |N| = 1024, |M| = 592$ in their setup. This corresponds to working with a safe prime Paillier modulus. We do point out that their scheme can also be used for a variant of Paillier encryption that uses a smaller randomizer space. Both their scheme and our schemes are more efficient when used with this variant of Paillier encryption.

The argument in [PBD05] (Protocol 1) relies on a non-standard assumption, the linear ignorance assumption. They have a less efficient protocol 2 that does not rely on this assumption. Other than that their scheme just relies on the semantic security of Paillier encryption, and as in the other schemes we measure its performance on 80-bit challenges (L=80).

The table 1 list the number of exponentiations required for the prover and the verifier, the communication bits, the number of rounds, and the security assumptions. The exponentiations listed are the number of full-length (2048-bit modulus, 1024-bit exponent) exponentiations where we scale for a factor of 3 for doubling the length of the modulus and a factor of 2 for doubling the length of the exponent. We compare all schemes without using multi-exponentiation techniques, since it is situation dependent which techniques work best. Also, we compare all schemes for a deterministic verifier. Using batching techniques it is possible to speed up the verification process in all schemes. The table contains the cost of making the shuffle arguments, it does not include the cost of the shuffle itself.

Table 1. Comparison of shuffle arguments with Paillier encryption

	[NSNK05]	[PBD05][2]	$\mathcal{SHUF}_{\mathbb{Z}_q}$	[Wik05b]	$\mathcal{SHUF}_{\mathbb{Z}}$
Prover (expo.)	3.4n	5.5n	0.5n	2.3n	0.6n
Verifier (expo.)	5.4n	4.3n	0.4n	1.5n	0.3n
Communication (bits)	9376n	9376n	1504n	6080n	1264n
Rounds	3	4	3	5	3
Privacy	Perm. Hiding	Perm. Hiding	SHVZK	SHVZK	SHVZK

Acknowledgement

The first author would like to thank Douglas Wikström for helpful discussions.

References

[Abe99]   Masayuki Abe. Mix-networks on permutation networks. In *proceedings of ASI-ACRYPT '99*, pages 258–273, 1999.

[AH01]   Masayuki Abe and Fumitaka Hoshino. Remarks on mix-network based on permutation networks. In *proceedings of PKC '01, LNCS series, volume 1992*, pages 317–324, 2001.

[CDS94]   Ronald Cramer, Ivan Damgård, and Berry Schoenmakers. Proofs of partial knowledge and simplified design of witness hiding protocols. In *proceedings of CRYPTO '94, LNCS series, volume 893*, pages 174–187, 1994.

[DF02]   Ivan Damgård and Eiichiro Fujisaki. A statistically-hiding integer commitment scheme based on groups with hidden order. In *proceedings of ASIACRYPT '02, LNCS series, volume 2501*, pages 125–142, 2002.

[ElG84]   Taher ElGamal. A public key cryptosystem and a signature scheme based on discrete logarithms. In *proceedings of CRYPTO '84, LNCS series, volume 196*, pages 10–18, 1984.

[FO97]   Eiichiro Fujisaki and Tatsuaki Okamoto. Statistical zero knowledge protocols to prove modular polynomial relations. In *proceedings of CRYPTO '97, LNCS series, volume 1294*, pages 16–30, 1997.

---

[2] Our numbers deviate from their own estimates in [PBD05] since we compare all schemes without multi-exponentiation or randomization of the verifier and do not count the prize of shuffling itself. Also, we do not use hashing and the random oracle model and thus their protocol becomes a 4 round protocol. Finally, it has been pointed out to us that their protocol is not SHVZK [Wik06], but we guess that it is permutation hiding as defined in [NSNK05].

[FS01]   Jun Furukawa and Kazue Sako. An efficient scheme for proving a shuffle. In *proceedings of CRYPTO '01, LNCS series, volume 2139*, pages 368–387, 2001.

[Fur05]   Jun Furukawa. Efficient and verifiable shuffling and shuffle-decryption. *IEICE Transactions*, 88-A(1):172–188, 2005.

[GL07]   Jens Groth and Steve Lu. Comparison of shuffle arguments. http://www.brics.dk/~jg/ShuffleComparisons.xls, 2007.

[GQ88]   Louis C. Guillou and Jean-Jacques Quisquater. A practical zero-knowledge protocol fitted to security microprocessor minimizing both trasmission and memory. In *proceedings of EUROCRYPT '88, LNCS series, volume 330*, pages 123–128, 1988.

[Gro03]   Jens Groth. A verifiable secret shuffle of homomorphic encryptions. In *proceedings of PKC '03, LNCS series, volume 2567*, pages 145–160, 2003.

[Gro05a]   Jens Groth. Cryptography in subgroups of $\mathbb{Z}_n^*$. In *proceedings of TCC '05, LNCS series, volume 3378*, pages 50–65, 2005.

[Gro05b]   Jens Groth. A verifiable secret shuffle of homomorphic encryptions. Cryptology ePrint Archive, Report 2005/246, 2005. http://eprint.iacr.org/.

[Nef01]   Andrew C. Neff. A verifiable secret shuffle and its application to e-voting. In *CCS '01*, pages 116–125, 2001. Full paper available at http://www.votehere.net/vhti/documentation/egshuf.pdf.

[NSNK04]   Lan Nguyen, Reihaneh Safavi-Naini, and Kaoru Kurosawa. Verifiable shuffles: A formal model and a paillier-based efficient construction with provable security. In *proceedings of ACNS '04, LNCS series, volume 3089*, pages 61–75, 2004.

[NSNK05]   Lan Nguyen, Reihaneh Safavi-Naini, and Kaoru Kurosawa. A provably secure and effcient verifiable shuffle based on a variant of the paillier cryptosystem. *Journal of Universal Computer Science*, 11(6):986–1010, 2005.

[OT04]   Takao Onodera and Keisuke Tanaka. A verifiable secret shuffle of paillier's encryption scheme, 2004. Tokyo Institute of Technology, research report C-193.

[OU98]   Tatsuaki Okamoto and Shigenori Uchiyama. A new public-key cryptosystem as secure as factoring. In *proceedings of EUROCRYPT '98, LNCS series, volume 1403*, pages 308–318, 1998.

[Pai99]   Pascal Paillier. Public-key cryptosystems based on composite residuosity classes. In *proceedings of EUROCRYPT '99, LNCS series, volume 1592*, pages 223–239, 1999.

[PBD05]   Kun Peng, Colin Boyd, and Ed Dawson. Simple and efficient shuffling with provable correctness and zk privacy. In *proceedings of CRYPTO '05, LNCS series, volume 3621*, pages 188–204, 2005.

[Ped91]   Torben P. Pedersen. Non-interactive and information-theoretic secure verifiable secret sharing. In *proceedings of CRYPTO '91, LNCS series, volume 576*, pages 129–140, 1991.

[Sch91]   Claus-Peter Schnorr. Efficient signature generation by smart cards. *J. Cryptology*, 4(3):161–174, 1991.

[WG06]   Douglas Wikström and Jens Groth. An adaptively secure mix-net without erasures. In *proceedings of ICALP '06, LNCS series, volume 4052*, pages 276–287, 2006.

[Wik05a]   Douglas Wikström. A sender verifiable mix-net and a new proof of a shuffle. In *proceedings of ASIACRYPT '05, LNCS series, volume 3788*, pages 273–292, 2005.

[Wik05b]   Douglas Wikström. A sender verifiable mix-net and a new proof of a shuffle. Cryptology ePrint Archive, Report 2005/137, 2005. http://eprint.iacr.org/.

[Wik06]   Douglas Wikström. Private Communication, 2006.

A Survey of Single-Database Private Information Retrieval: Techniques and Applications

Rafail Ostrovsky* and William E. Skeith III**

[1] Computer Science Department and Department of Mathematics, UCLA, 90095
rafail@cs.ucla.edu
[2] Department of Mathematics, UCLA
wskeith@math.ucla.edu, wskeith@ucla.edu

Abstract. In this paper we survey the notion of Single-Database Private Information Retrieval (PIR). The first Single-Database PIR was constructed in 1997 by Kushilevitz and Ostrovsky and since then Single-Database PIR has emerged as an important cryptographic primitive. For example, Single-Database PIR turned out to be intimately connected to collision-resistant hash functions, oblivious transfer and public-key encryptions with additional properties. In this survey, we give an overview of many of the constructions for Single-Database PIR (including an abstract construction based upon homomorphic encryption) and describe some of the connections of PIR to other primitives.

1 Introduction

A Single-Database Private Information Retrieval (PIR) scheme is a game between two players: a user and a database. The database holds some public data (for concreteness, an n-bit string). The user wishes to retrieve some item from the database (such as the i-th bit) without revealing to the database which item was queried (i.e., i remains hidden). We stress that in this model the database data is public (such as stock quotes) but centrally located; the user, without a local copy, must send a request to retrieve some part of the central data[1]. A naive solution is to have the user download the entire database, which of course preserves privacy. However, the total communication complexity in this solution, measured as the number of bits transmitted between the user and the database is n. Private Information Retrieval protocols allow the user to retrieve data from a public database with communication strictly smaller than n, i.e., with smaller communication then just downloading the entire database.

* Supported in part by IBM Faculty Award, Xerox Innovation Group Award, NSF Cybertrust grant no. 0430254 and U.C. MICRO grant.
** Supported in part by NSF grant no. 0430254, and U.C. Presidential Fellowship.

[1] PIR should not be confused with a private-key *searching on encrypted data* problem, where user uploads his own encrypted data to a remote database and wants to privately search over that encrypted data without reveling any information to the database. For this model, see the discussion in [9,18] and references therein.

T. Okamoto and X. Wang (Eds.): PKC 2007, LNCS 4450, pp. 393–411, 2007.

1.1   Single-Database PIR

PIR was introduced by Chor, Goldreich, Kushilevitz and Sudan [8] in 1995 in the setting where there are many copies of the same database and none of the copies are
allowed to communicate with each other. In the same paper, Chor at. al. [8] showed that
single-database PIR does not exist (in the information-theoretic sense.) Nevertheless,
two years later, (assuming a certain secure public-key encryption) Kushilevitz and Ostrovsky [23] presented a method for constructing single-database PIR. The communica-
tion complexity of their solution is $O(2^{\sqrt{\log n \log \log N}})$ which for any $\epsilon > 0$ is less then
$O(n^\epsilon)$. Their result relies on the algebraic properties Goldwasser-Micali Public-Key
encryption scheme [17]. In 1999, Cachin, Micali and Stadler [7] demonstrated the first
single database PIR with polylogarithmic communication, under the so-called ϕ-hiding
number-theoretic assumption. Chang [6], and Lipmaa [25] showed $O(\log^2 n)$ communication complexity PIR protocol (with a multiplicative security parameter factor), using a construction similar to the original [23] but replacing the Goldwasser-Micali homomorphic encryption with the Damgård, M. Jurik variant of the Pailler homomorphic
encryption [10]. Gentry and Ramzan [15] also showed the current best bound for communication complexity of $O(\log^2 n)$ with an additional benefit that if one considers
retrieving more then one bit, and in particular many consecutive bits (which we call
blocks) then ratio of block size to communication is only a small constant. The scheme
of Lipmaa [25] has the property that when acting on blocks the ratio of block size to
communication actually approaches 1, yet the parameters must be quite large before
this scheme becomes an advantage over that of [15]. In general, the issue of *amortizing*
the cost of PIR protocol for many queries has received a lot of attention. We discuss it
separately in the next subsection.

All the works mentioned above exploit some sort of algebraic properties, often coming from homomorphic public-key encryptions. In [24] work, Kushilevitz and Ostrovsky have shown how to construct Single Database PIR without the use of any algebraic
assumptions, and instead relying on the existence of one-way trapdoor permutations.
However, the use of the more general assumption comes with a performance cost: they
show how to achieve $(n - O(\frac{n}{k} - k^2))$ communication complexity, and additionally,
the protocol requires more than one round of interaction.

In this survey, we give the main techniques and ideas behind all these constructions
(and in fact, show a generic construction from any homomorphic encryption scheme
with certain properties) and attempt to do so in a unified manner.

1.2   Amortizing Database Work in PIR

Instead of asking to retrieve blocks, one can ask what happens if one wants to retrieve k
out of n bits of the database (not necessarily consecutive). Indeed, this was considered
by Ishai, Kushilevitz, Ostrovsky and Sahai [20]. In this setting, in addition to communication complexity (of retrieving k out of n bits) there is another important consideration:
the total amount of *computation* needed to be performed by the database to compute all
k PIR answers. (Observe that for a single PIR query the amount of computation required
by the database must be linear: if this is not the case, the database will not touch at least
one bit, and hence the database can safely deduce that the "untouched" bits are not the

ones being retrieved, violating user's privacy.) Now, what is the total computation required to retrieve k different bits? A naive solution is to just run one of the PIR solutions k times. It is easy to see that using *hashing* one can do better: The user, with indices $i_1, \ldots, i_k$, picks at random a hash function h that sends all n entries of the database to k buckets and where the selection of h is made independently from $i_1, \ldots, i_k$. The user sends h to the database. Note that the expected size of each bucket is about n/k. The database partitions its database into buckets according to h (that is gets from the user), and treats every bucket as a new "tiny" database. For an appropriate choice of a hash family, this ensures that with probability $1 - 2^{-\Omega(\sigma)}$, the number of items hashed to any particular bucket is at most $\sigma \log k$. Now the user can apply the standard PIR protocol $\sigma \log k$ times to each bucket. Except for $2^{-\Omega(\sigma)}$ error probability, the user will be able get all k items. Note that the cost is much smaller then the naive solution. In particular, counting the length of all PIR invocations the total size of all databases on which we run standard PIR is $\sigma \log k \cdot n$, instead of naive kn. This idea is developed further, and in fact the error-probability is removed, and better performance is derived via explicit *batch codes* [20] instead of hashing.

Note however, that this approach requires that it is *the same* user that is interested in all k queries. What happens if the users are different? In this case, assuming the existence of *anonymous communication*, nearly-optimal PIR in all parameters can be achieved in the multi-user case [21].

1.3   Connections: Single Database PIR and OT

Single-database PIR has a close connection to the notion of Oblivious Transfer (OT), introduced by Rabin [35]. A different variant of Oblivious Transfer, called 1-out-of-2 OT, was introduced by Even, Goldreich and Lempel [14] and, more generally, 1-out-of-n OT was considered in Brassard, Crepeau and Robert [3]. Informally, 1-out-of-n OT is a protocol for two players: A *sender* who initially has n secrets $x_1, \ldots, x_n$ and a *receiver* who initially holds an index $1 \leq i \leq n$. At the end of the protocol the receiver knows x_i but has no information about the other secrets, while the sender has no information about the index i. Note that OT is different from PIR in that there is no communication complexity requirement (beyond being polynomially bounded) but, on the other hand, "secrecy" is required for *both* players, while for the PIR it is required only for the user. All Oblivious Transfer definitions are shown to be equivalent [5]. As mentioned, communication-efficient implementation of 1-out-of-n OT can be viewed as a single-server PIR protocol with an additional guarantee that only one (out of n) secrets is learned by the user and the remaining $n-1$ remain hidden. In [23], it is noted that their protocol can also be made into a 1-out-of-n OT protocol[2], showing the first 1-out-of-n OT with sublinear communication complexity. Naor and Pinkas [27] have subsequently shown how to turn any PIR protocol into 1-out-of-n protocol with one invocation of a Single-Database PIR protocol and logarithmic number of invocations of 1-out-of-2 OT.

---

[2] 1-out-of-n OT in the setting of *multiple copies of the database* where none of the copies are allowed to talk to each other was treated in [16] and renamed *Symmetric Private Information Retrieval* (SPIR), though for Single-dabatase PIR, the defitnion SPIR is identical to the more established notion of 1-out-of-n OT.

DiCresenzo, Malkin and Ostrovsky [12] showed that any single database PIR protocol implies OT. In fact, their result holds even if PIR protocol allows the communcation from database to the user to be as big as $n - 1$. Thus, [12] combined with [27] tells us that any Single-Database PIR implies 1-out-of-n OT. In [24], it is shown how to build 1-out-of-n OT based on any one-way trapdoor permutation with communication complexity strictly less than n.

1.4   Connections: PIR and Collision-Resistant Hashing

Ishai, Kushilevitz and Ostrovsky [19] showed that any one-round Single-Databe PIR protocol is also a collision-resistant hash function. Simply pick an index i for the PIR query at random, and generate a PIR query. Such a PIR query is the description of the hash function. The database contents serves as the input to the hash function and the evaluation of the PIR query on the database is the output of the hash function. It is easy to see that the PIR function is both length-decreasing and collision-resistant. It is length-decreasing by the non-triviality of PIR protocol, since it must return the answer with length which is less then the size of the database. Is it collision resistant since if the adversary can find two different databases that produce the same PIR answer, then these two databases must differ in at least one position, say j. Finding such a position tells us that $j \neq i$, hence it reveals information about i. This violates the PIR requirement that no information about i should be revealed.

1.5   Connections: PIR and Function-Hiding PKE

A classic view of a Public-Key Encryption/Decryption paradigm is that of an identity map: it takes a plaintext message m and creates a ciphertext which can be decrypted back to m. However, in many applications, instead of an identity map, there is a need for a Public-Key Encryption to perform some *secret computation* during encryption. That is, the key-generation algorithm takes as an additional input a function specification $f(\cdot) \in \mathcal{F}$ from some class $\mathcal{F}$ of functions and produces a Public Key. The resulting Public-Key is not much bigger then the description of a typical $f' \in \mathcal{F}$, yet the public-key should not reveal which f from $\mathcal{F}$ have been used during the key-generation phase. The encryption/decryption maps m to $f(m)$. The definition becomes nontrivial (in the sense that one can not push all the work of computing $f(\cdot)$ to the decryption phase) when for all $f \in \mathcal{F}$ it holds that $|f(m)| < |m|$, and we insist that the cyphertext size must be smaller than the size of m.

Any single-round PIR can be used to achieve this notion for the class of Encryption functions that encrypt a single bit out of the message, hiding *which* bit they encrypt: simply publish in your public key both the PIR query and an additional Public-Key Encryption (with small ciphertext expansion, compared to the plaintext, such as [34,10]). When encrypting the message, first compute PIR answer, and then encrypt the resulting answer with the Public-Key Encryption. (Some specific PIR constructions do not need this additional layer of encryption).

What makes the Function-Hiding PKE notion interesting, is that there are many examples of functions beyond PIR-based projection map. For example, as was shown by Ostrovsky and Skeith [31] that one can construct an encryption scheme which takes multiple documents, and encrypts only a subset of these documents – only those that contain a set of hidden keywords, where the public-key encryption function does not reveal which keywords are used as selectors of the subset.

1.6 Connections: PIR and Complexity Theory

Dziembowski and Maurer have shown the danger of mixing computational and information-theoretic assumptions in the bounded-storage model. The key tool to demonstrate an attack was a computationally-private PIR protocol [13]. The compressibility of NP languages was shown by Harnick and Naor to be intimately connected to computational PIR [22]. In particular, what they show that if certain NP language is compressible, then one can construct a single-database PIR protocol (and a collision-resistant hash function) that can be built (in a non-black-box way) based on any one-way function. Naor and Nissim [28] have shown how to use computational PIR (and Oblivious RAMs [18]) to construct communication-efficient secure function evaluation protocols.

There is an interesting connection between zero-knowledge arguments and Single-Database PIR. In particular, Tauman-Kalai and Raz have shown (for a certain restricted class) an extremely efficient zero-knowledge argument (with pre-processing) assuming Single-Database PIR protocols [36].

Another framework of constructing efficient PIR protocols is with the help of additional servers, such that even if some of the servers leak information to the database, the overall privacy is maintained [11]. The technique of [11] is also used to achieve PIR *combiners* [26], where given several PIR implementations, if some are faulty, they can still be combined into one non-faulty PIR.

1.7 Public-Key Encryption That Supports PIR Read and Write

Consider the following problem: Alice wishes to maintain her email using a storage-provider Bob (such as Yahoo! or hotmail e-mail account). She publishes a public key for a semantically-secure public-key Encryption scheme, and asks all people to send their e-mails encrypted under her Public Key to the intermediary Bob. Bob (i.e. the storage-provider) should allow Alice to collect, retrieve, search and delete emails at her leisure. In known implementations of such services, either the content of the emails is known to the storage-provider Bob (and then the privacy of both Alice and the senders is lost) or the senders can encrypt their messages to Alice, in which case privacy is maintained, but sophisticated services (such as search by keyword, and deletion) cannot be easily performed by Bob. Recently, Boneh, Kushilevitz, Ostrovsky and Skeith [2] (solving the open problem of [1]) have shown how to create a public key that allows arbitrary senders to send Bob encrypted e-mail messages that support PIR queries over these messages and the ability to modify (i.e. to do PIR writing) Bob's database, both with small communication complexity (approximately $O(\sqrt{n})$). It may be interesting to note, however, that manipulating the algebraic structures of currently available homomorphic encryption schemes cannot achieve PIR writing with communication better than $\Omega(\sqrt{n})$, as shown in the recent work of Ostrovsky and Skeith [32].

1.8 Organization of the Rest of the Paper

In the rest of the paper we give an overview of the basic techniques of single database PIR. It is by no means a complete account of all of the literature, but we hope that it rather serves as an introduction, and a clear exposition of the techniques that have proved themselves most useful. We begin with what we feel are the most natural and intuitive settings, which are based upon homomorphic encryption, and we attempt to give a fairly unified and clear account of this variety of PIR protocols. We then move to PIR based on the Φ-Hiding assumption, and to a construction based upon one-way trapdoor permutations. Throughout, our focus is primarily on the intuition behind these schemes; for complete technical details, one can of course follow the references.

1.9 Balancing the Communication Between Sender and Receiver

Virtually every computationally private information retrieval protocol is somewhat comparable to every other in that they all:

- Adhere to a strict definition of privacy
- Necessarily have $\Omega(n)$ computational complexity (where n is the size of the database).[3]

As such, it is the case that the primary metric of value or quality for a PIR protocol is the total amount of *communication* required for its execution. Therefore, it may be useful to examine a somewhat general technique for minimizing communication complexity in certain types of protocols, which we'll be able to apply to computational PIR. Suppose that a protocol $\mathcal{P}$ is executed between a user $\mathbf{U}$ and a database $\mathbf{DB}$, in which $\mathbf{U}$ should privately learn some function $f(X)$ where $X \in \{0,1\}^n$ is the collection of data held by $\mathbf{DB}$. By "privately", we mean that $\mathbf{DB}$ should not gain information regarding certain details of f. Let $g(n)$ represent the communication from $\mathbf{U}$ to $\mathbf{DB}$ and $h(n)$ be the communication from $\mathbf{DB}$ to $\mathbf{U}$ involved in the execution of $\mathcal{P}$. So, $g, h : \mathbb{Z}^+ \longrightarrow \mathbb{Z}^+$. As a simplifying assumption to illustrate the idea, suppose that:

1. The function of the database $f(X)$ that $\mathbf{U}$ wishes to compute via the protocol depends only on a single bit of X.
2. g, h can be represented, or at least estimated by polynomial (or rational) functions in n.

If all of these conditions are satisfied, then we'll often have a convenient way to take the protocol $\mathcal{P}$, and derive a protocol $\mathcal{P}'$ with lower communication which will just execute $\mathcal{P}$ as a subroutine. The idea is as follows: since the function of X we are computing is highly local (it depends only on a single bit of X) we can define $\mathcal{P}'$ to be a protocol that breaks down the database X into y smaller pieces (of size n/y) and executes $\mathcal{P}$ on each smaller piece. Then, the desired output will be obtained in one of the y executions of $\mathcal{P}$. Such a protocol will have total communication $T_n(y) = g(n/y) + yh(n/y)$. It may be the case that this will increase the communication of $\mathbf{U}$ or $\mathbf{DB}$, but will reduce the total communication involved. If indeed all functions

---

[3] In order to preserve privacy, the database's computation must involve every database element.

are differentiable as we've assumed, then we can use standard calculus techniques to minimize this function (for any positive n) with respect to y. For example, suppose that the user's communication is linear, and the database's communication is constant. For example, let $g(n) = rn + s$ and $h(n) = c$, so that $T_n(y) = yc + s + \frac{rn}{y}$. Solving the equation $\frac{d}{dy}T_n(y) = 0$ on $(0, \infty)$ gives

$$y = \frac{\sqrt{crn}}{c}$$

This value of y is easily verified to be a local minimum, and we see that by executing the protocol $\mathcal{O}(\sqrt{n})$ times on pieces of size $\mathcal{O}(\sqrt{n})$ we can minimize the total communication.

More generally, similar techniques can of course be applied when the function f depends on more than one bit of X, as long as there is a uniform way (independent of f) to break down the database X into pieces that contain the relevant bits. These techniques can be applied to more general situations still, in which the function depends on many database locations; however, in this case one will need a method of reconstructing the output from the multiple protocol returns (in our simple example, the method is just selecting the appropriate value from all the returns). Also, for this technique to be of value in such a situation, it will generally be necessary to have a uniform way to describe the problem on smaller database pieces.

2 PIR Based on Group-Homomorphic Encryption

The original work on computational PIR by Kushilevitz and Ostrovsky [23] presented a private information retrieval protocol based upon homomorphic encryption. Such techniques are often very natural ways to construct a variety of privacy-preserving protocols. It is often the case with such protocols based upon homomorphic encryption, that although the protocol is designed with a specific cryptosystem, there is a more fundamental, underlying design that could be instantiated with many different cryptosystems in place of the original, and furthermore this choice of cryptosystem can have a very non-trivial impact on performance. For example, the work of [23] used the homomorphic cryptosystem of Goldwasser and Micali [17] to create a PIR protocol, and in the following years, many other similar protocols were developed based upon other cryptosystems, e.g., the work of Chang [6] which is based upon the cryptosystem of Paillier [34], and also the work of Lipmaa [25]. However, the method of [23] was actually quite generic, although it was not originally stated in generality. In this section, we'll present an abstract construction based upon any group homomorphic encryption scheme which has [23] and [6] as special cases, as well as capturing the work of [25]. Hopefully, this section will provide the reader with general intuition regarding private information retrieval, as well as a pleasant way to understand the basics of a moderate amount of the literature in computational PIR.

2.1 Homomorphic Encryption Schemes

Let $(\mathcal{K}, \mathcal{E}, \mathcal{D})$ be a cryptosystem, the symbols representing the key generation, encryption, and decryption algorithms respectively. Generally, we say that such a cryptosystem is secure if it is secure against a chosen plaintext attack, i.e., if $\mathcal{E}$ produces distributions that are computationally indistinguishable, regardless of the input. Roughly speaking, this means that it is not feasible to extract any information from the output of $\mathcal{E}$. For example, even if a (computationally bounded) adversary knows that there are only two possible messages a and b, he still cannot tell $\mathcal{E}(a)$ apart from $\mathcal{E}(b)$, even if he repeatedly executes the (randomized) algorithm $\mathcal{E}$ on inputs of his choice.

To construct our PIR protocol, we only need a secure cryptosystem that is homomorphic over an abelian group, G. I.e., if the cryptosystem $(\mathcal{K}, \mathcal{E}, \mathcal{D})$ has plaintext set G, and ciphertext set G', where G, G' are groups, then we have that

$$\mathcal{D}(\mathcal{E}(a) \star \mathcal{E}(b)) = a * b$$

where $a, b \in G$, and $*, \star$ represent the group operations of G, G' respectively. So, the cryptosystem allows for oblivious distributed computation of the group operation of G. (Note that we reduce the equivalence to hold modulo decryption since the encryption algorithm $\mathcal{E}$ must be probabilistic in order to satisfy our requirements for security.)

For such a cryptosystem to be of any conceivable use, we of course have that $|G| > 1$. Hence, there is at least one element $g \in G$ of order greater than 1. Suppose that $\text{ord}(g) = m$. If the discrete log problem[4] in G is easy (as will often be the case e.g., when G is an additive group of integers) then we can represent our database as $X = \{x_i\}_{i=1}^{n}$ where each $x_i \in \{0, ..., m - 1\}$. Otherwise, we will just restrict the values of our database to be binary, which is the traditional setting for PIR. I.e., $x_i \in \{0, 1\}$ for all $i \in [n]$. As it turns out, a homomorphic encryption protocol alone is enough to create a PIR protocol.

2.2   Basic Protocols from Homomorphic Encryption

In what follows, we will provide a sequence of examples of PIR from homomorphic encryption, each becoming slightly more refined and efficient. Let us suppose that the i^* position of the database is desired by a user $\mathcal{U}$. Keeping the notation established above, let G, G' be groups which correspond to the plaintext and ciphertext of our homomorphic cryptosystem (resp.) and let $g \in G$ be a non-identity element. As a first attempt at a PIR protocol, a user $\mathcal{U}$ could send queries of the form $Q = \{q_i\}_{i=1}^{n}$ where each $q_i \in G'$ such that

$$\mathcal{D}(q_i) = \begin{cases} g & \text{if } i = i^* \\ \text{id}_G & \text{otherwise} \end{cases}$$

Then, the database can respond with

$$R = \sum_{i=1}^{n} x_i \cdot q_i$$

---

[4] We will refer to the problem of inverting the $\mathbb{Z}$-module action on an abelian group G as the "discrete log problem in G".

using additive notation for the operation of G' (and of G from this point forward) and using $\cdot$ to represent the $\mathbb{Z}$-module action. Now $\mathcal{U}$ can recover the desired database bit as follows, computing

$$\mathcal{D}(R) = \mathcal{D}\left(\sum_{i=1}^{n} x_i \cdot q_i\right) = \sum_{i=1}^{n} x_i \cdot \mathcal{D}(q_i) = x_{i^*} \cdot \mathcal{D}(q_{i^*}) = x_{i^*} \cdot g$$

and hence $\mathcal{U}$ determines $x_{i^*} = 1$ if and only if $\mathcal{D}(R) = g$. Or, in the case where the discrete log is easy in G, $\mathcal{U}$ would compute x_{i^*} as the log of $\mathcal{D}(R)$ to the base g (just by division, in the case of an additive group of integers). This protocol is clearly correct, but it is also easily seen to be private. The only information received by $\mathcal{DB}$ during the protocol was an array of ciphertexts, which by our assumptions on the cryptosystem, each come from (computationally) indistinguishable distributions, and hence contain no information that can be efficiently extracted. For a formal proof, one can apply a standard hybrid argument.

However, although our protocol is both correct and private, it unfortunately requires the communication of information proportional in size to the entire database in order to retrieve a single database element. This could have just as easily been done by sending the entire database to the user, which would also maintain the user's privacy. Setting $k = \log |G'|$ as a security parameter, the user must communicate $\mathcal{O}(nk)$ bits. Fortunately, this can be modified into a more communication-efficient protocol without much effort. To begin, one can organize the database as a square, $X = \{x_{ij}\}_{i,j=1}^{\sqrt{n}}$, and if the (i^*, j^*) position of the database is desired, the user can send a query of the form $Q = \{q_i\}_{i=1}^{\sqrt{n}}$ defined just as before (we will ignore the j^* index for reasons that will become clear shortly). Then, the database can compute $R_j = \sum_{i=1}^{\sqrt{n}} x_{ij} \cdot q_i$ for each j and send $\{R_j\}_{j=1}^{\sqrt{n}}$ back to the user as the query response. Now as we've seen, from $\mathcal{D}(R_j)$, $\mathcal{U}$ can recover $\{x_{i^*j}\}_{j=1}^{\sqrt{n}}$ just as before. In particular, $\mathcal{U}$ can compute $x_{i^*j^*}$ (even though much more information is actually received). Note that the total communication involved in the protocol has now become non-trivially small: it is now proportional to $\sqrt{n}$ for each party as opposed to the $\mathcal{O}(n)$ communication required by our original proposal and the trivial solution of communicating the entire database to $\mathcal{U}$.

However, we can make further improvements still. Let

$$\phi : G' \hookrightarrow \mathbb{Z}^l$$

be an injective map such that for all $y \in G'$, each component of $\phi(y)$ is less than $\mathrm{ord}(g)$. I.e., one can think of the map as $\phi : G' \hookrightarrow \mathbb{Z}_{\mathrm{ord}(g)}^l$. Any such map with do- we only require that both ϕ and ϕ^{-1} are efficiently, publicly computable. Note that in general, we will always have $l > 1$ since $\mathrm{ord}(g) \leq |G|$ and $|G| < |G'|$, the latter inequality following from the fact that the encryption scheme is always probabilistic ($\mathcal{D}$ is never injective, but of course is always surjective). Again, note that we do not ask for any algebraic conditions from the map ϕ; it can be any easily computed injective set map. (For example, we could just break down a binary representation of elements of G' into sufficiently small blocks of bits to obtain the map ϕ.) Now, we can refine our query, and send $Q = \left[\{q_i\}_{i=1}^{\sqrt{n}}, \{p_j\}_{j=1}^{\sqrt{n}} \right]$ where q_{i*} and p_{j*} are set to encryptions of g, but all others encrypt id_G. Then, the database will initially proceed as before, computing

$$R_j = \sum_{i=1}^{\sqrt{n}} x_{ij} \cdot q_i$$

but then further computing

$$\overline{R}_t = \sum_{j=1}^{n} \phi(R_j)_t \cdot p_j$$

where $\phi(R_j)_t$ represents the t-th component of $\phi(R_j)$. This is sent as the query response to $\mathcal{U}$. To recover the desired data, $\mathcal{U}$ computes for every $t \in [l]$

$$\mathcal{D}(\overline{R}_t) = \phi(R_{j*})_t \cdot g$$

from which $\phi(R_{j*})$ can be computed. Then since ϕ^{-1} is efficiently computable, $\mathcal{U}$ can recover $R_{j*} = \sum_{i=1}^{\sqrt{n}} x_{ij*} \cdot q_i$, and as we have seen x_{i*j*} is easily recovered from $\mathcal{D}(R_{j*})$.

So now what amount of communication is required by the parties? The database sends $\mathcal{O}(l \log(|G'|)) = \mathcal{O}(lk)$ bits of information, meanwhile the user $\mathcal{U}$ sends $\mathcal{O}(2k\sqrt{n})$ bits of information which will generally be a large improvement on the database side. We can naturally extend this idea to higher dimensional analogs. Representing the database as a d-dimensional cube (we have just seen the construction for $d = 1, 2$), we accomplish the following communication complexity: $\mathcal{O}(kd\sqrt[d]{n})$ for the user's query, and $\mathcal{O}(l^{d-1}k)$ communication for the database's response.

The preceding construction is essentially that of [23] and of [6]. Both are simply special cases of what has been described above:

The work of [23] is based upon the cryptosystem of [17], which is homomorphic over the group $\mathbb{Z}_2$, having ciphertext group $\mathbb{Z}_N$ for a large composite N. In this case, it is simply the binary representation of a group element that plays the role of the map $\phi : G \hookrightarrow \mathbb{Z}^l$. I.e., we have $l = k$, the security parameter, and $\phi : \mathbb{Z}_N \hookrightarrow \mathbb{Z}^k$ takes an element $h \in \mathbb{Z}_N$ and maps it to a sequence of k integers, each in $\{0, 1\}$ corresponding to a binary representation of h.

The work of [6] is also a special case of this construction. Here, the protocol is based upon the cryptosystem of [34], and we have $G = \mathbb{Z}_N$ and $G' = \mathbb{Z}_{N^2}^*$, hence we can greatly reduce the parameter l in comparison to the work of [23]. In this case, it is easy to see that we only need $l = 2$, which is in fact minimal, as we have discussed before. The author of [6] uses the map $\phi : \mathbb{Z}_{N^2}^* \hookrightarrow \mathbb{Z}_N$ defined by the division algorithm, dividing by N to obtain a quotient and remainder of appropriate size. Roughly speaking, (and using C-programming notation) he uses the map $x \mapsto (x/N, x\%N)$. However, as we have seen before, this is not necessary- any map could have been used (appropriately partitioning bits, etc.). Note also that since the discrete log in G is not hard (as we have defined it) we do not need to restrict our database to storing bits. Database elements could be any numbers in $\mathbb{Z}_N$.

These quite generic methods also capture the work of [25], as long as the appropriate cryptosystem is in place.

Consider a "length-flexible" cryptosystem, for example, that of Damgård and Jurik [10]. Such a cryptosystem has the property that given a message of arbitrary length, and given a *fixed* public key, one can choose a cryptosystem from a family of systems based on that key, so that the message *fits in one ciphertext block* regardless of the key and the message length. Using this, we can further reduce the database's communication in our PIR protocol, using essentially the very same generic technique described above. We'll demonstrate the following:

Theorem 1. *For all $d \in \mathbb{Z}^+$ there exists a PIR protocol based on the homomorphic cryptosystem of Damgård and Jurik with user communication of $\mathcal{O}(kd^2 \sqrt[d]{n})$ and database communication of $\mathcal{O}(kd)$ where k is a security parameter and n is the database size.*

What the Damgård and Jurik system affords us is the following: instead of having only one plaintext and ciphertext group G, G', we now have a countable family at our disposal:

$$\{G_i, G_i'\}_{i=1}^{\infty}$$

all of which correspond to a *single* public key. These groups are realized by $G_i \simeq \mathbb{Z}_{N^i}, G_i' \simeq \mathbb{Z}_{N^{i+1}}^*$, and hence we have natural inclusion maps of $G_i' \hookrightarrow G_{i+1}$. This, along with the observation that G_i is cyclic for all i, are essentially the only important facts regarding this system that we'll utilize. So, G_i is always cyclic, and we have a natural (although not algebraic) map

$$\psi_i : G_i' \hookrightarrow G_{i+1}$$

This is all we need to modify our generic method. We will just replace the map ϕ with the maps ψ_i, and accordingly, we will modify our query so that the vector for the i-th dimension encrypts id_{G_i} in all positions except for the index of interest, which will encrypt a generator of G_i. With only these minor substitutions to the abstract construction, the protocol will follow exactly as before. This will give us a protocol with communication complexity for the user $\mathcal{U}$ of

$$\sum_{i=1}^{d} ik \sqrt[d]{n} = \mathcal{O}(kd^2 \sqrt[d]{n})$$

and for the database, we require only

$$\mathcal{O}(kd)$$

as opposed to the previous exponential dependence on the dimension d of the cube used! Optimizing the parameters, setting $d = \frac{\log(n)}{2}$, we have $\mathcal{O}(k \log^2(n))$ communication for the user and $\mathcal{O}(k \log(n))$ for the database. So, as one can see, even a completely generic method can be quite useful, producing a near optimal, poly-logarithmic protocol.

3 PIR Based on the Φ-Hiding Assumption

Cachin, Micali, and Stadler recently developed a new cryptographic assumption called the Φ-Hiding Assumption, and successfully used this assumption to build a PIR protocol with logarithmic communication. Roughly, this assumption states that given two primes p_0, p_1 and a composite $m = pq$ such that either $p_0|\phi(m)$ or $p_1|\phi(m)$, it is hard to distinguish between the two primes. (Here, $\phi(m)$ is the Euler-ϕ function, so that $\phi(m) = (p-1)(q-1)$.) The assumption also of course states that given a small prime p, it is computationally feasible to find a composite m such that $p|\phi(m)$. Such an m is said to ϕ-*hide* p. A query for the i-th bit of the database essentially contains input to a prime sequence generator, a composite m that ϕ-hides p_i (the i-th prime in the sequence) and a random $r \in \mathbb{Z}_m^*$. The database algorithm returns a value $R \in \mathbb{Z}_m^*$ such that with very high probability, R has p_i-th roots if and only if the database bit at location i was 1.

3.1 Preliminaries

To understand the protocol, let us start with some very basic algebraic observations. Let G be a finite abelian group, and let $k \in \mathbb{Z}^+$. Consider the following map:

$$\varphi_k : G \to G \quad \text{defined by} \quad x \mapsto x^k$$

Since G is abelian, it is clear that φ_k is a homomorphism for all $k \in \mathbb{Z}^+$. What is $\varphi_k(G)$? Clearly it is precisely the set of all elements in G that posses a k-th root in G. I.e.,

$$\mathrm{Im}(\varphi_k) = \{x \in G \mid \exists y \in G \ni x = y^k\}$$

We will denote this set by $H_k = \mathrm{Im}(\varphi_k)$. Clearly it is a subgroup since it is the homomorphic image of a group. The size of this subgroup of course depends on k and G. If, for example, $(k, |G|) = 1$, then it is easy to see that $\varphi_k(G) = G$, since if $\mathrm{Ker}(\varphi_k) \neq \{e\}$ then there are non-identity elements of order dividing k, which is clearly impossible. In the case that $(k, |G|) > 1$, how big is $\mathrm{Ker}(\varphi_k)$? It is at least as big as the largest prime divisor of $(k, |G|) > 1$, by Cauchy's theorem if you like. For example, if k is a prime such that $k \mid |G|$, then the map φ_k is at least a k to 1 map.

Finally, let's take a look at the subgroups $H_k = \varphi_k(G) = \mathrm{Im}(\varphi_k)$. We will just need the following observation:

$$\forall k \in \mathbb{Z} \quad H_k \lhd\lhd G$$

Here the symbol $H_k \lhd\lhd G$ signifies that H_k is a *characteristic* subgroup of G, which is to say that the subgroups H_k are fixed by *every* automorphism of G. (Compare with *normal* subgroups which are those fixed by every *inner* automorphism of G.) Note that for any finite G, if $H \lhd\lhd G$ and $\varphi \in \mathrm{Aut}(G)$ then $\varphi(x) \in H \iff x \in H$ for all $x \in G$.

Let us summarize the few facts that will be of importance to us, and also narrow our view to correspond more directly to what we will need. Suppose that $p \in \mathbb{Z}$ is a prime, and define the maps φ_p as before. Then,

1. $\varphi_p \in \mathrm{Aut}(G) \iff p \nmid |G|$
2. φ_p is at least a p to 1 map if $p \mid |G|$.

3. $\forall p$, $H_p \lhd\lhd G$ (although this is trivial in the case that $p \nmid |G|$ and hence $H_p = G$). So for any $\varphi \in \text{Aut}(G)$ and $x \in G$ we have $\varphi(x) \in H_p \iff x \in H_p$.

3.2 A Brief Description of the Protocol

We now have enough information for a basic understanding of how and why the PIR protocol of [7] works. First, we will begin with the "how". Continuing with our preceding notation, suppose that $X = \{x_i\}_{i=1}^n$ is our database, with each $x_i \in \{0,1\}$, and again, suppose that the index of interest to $\mathcal{U}$ is i^*. The protocol executes the following steps, involving a database $\mathcal{DB}$ and a user $\mathcal{U}$.

1. $\mathcal{U}$ sends a random seed for a publicly known prime sequence generator to $\mathcal{DB}$, the primes being of intermediate size[5].
2. $\mathcal{U}$ computes p_{i^*}, the i^*-th prime in the sequence based on the random seed.
3. $\mathcal{U}$ finds a composite number m that ϕ-hides p_{i^*}, and sends m to $\mathcal{DB}$. In particular, we have that $p_{i^*} \mid \phi(m)$. Recall that $\phi(m) = |\mathbb{Z}_m^*|$.
4. $\mathcal{DB}$ selects $r \in \mathbb{Z}_m^*$ at random, and computes $R \in \mathbb{Z}_m^*$ as follows:

$$R = \varphi_{p_n^{x_n}} \circ \varphi_{p_{n-1}^{x_{n-1}}} \circ \cdots \circ \varphi_{p_1^{x_1}}(r)$$

$$= r^{\prod_{i=1}^n p_i^{x_i}} \bmod m$$

5. $\mathcal{U}$ receives R from $\mathcal{DB}$ as the response, and determines that $x_{i^*} = 1$ if and only if $R \in H_{p_{i^*}}$.

These steps are essentially the entire protocol at a high level. However, it may not be immediately obvious that the statement $R \in H_{p_{i^*}}$ has much to do with the statement $x_{i^*} = 1$. But using the 3 facts we established early on, it isn't too hard to see that these are in fact equivalent with very high probability.

From our first fact, we know that $\varphi_{p_i} \in \text{Aut}(G)$ whenever $i \neq i^*$ with overwhelming probability, since the only way for this to not be the case is if $p_i \mid \phi(m)$. However, due to the fact that there are at most only a logarithmic number of prime divisors of $\phi(m)$ out of many choices, this event will be extremely unlikely[6]. So, all of the φ_{p_i} are automorphisms, except for $\varphi_{p_{i^*}}$.

From our next fact, we know that with very high probability $r \notin H_{p_{i^*}}$, where $r \in \mathbb{Z}_m^*$ was the element randomly chosen by $\mathcal{DB}$. Since the map is at least p_{i^*} to 1, the entire group is at least p_{i^*} times the size of $H_{p_{i^*}}$. So, if we were to pick an element at random from $\mathbb{Z}_m^*$, there is at best a $\frac{1}{p_{i^*}}$ chance that it will be in $H_{p_{i^*}}$. So, in the length of our primes p_i, there is an exponentially small probability that a random r will be in $H_{p_{i^*}}$.

Finally, we noted that the subgroups H_{p_i} are characteristic subgroups, and hence our fixed by every automorphism of $\mathbb{Z}_m^*$. In particular, $H_{p_{i^*}} \lhd\lhd \mathbb{Z}_m^*$. So, all of the

---

[5] Revealing a large prime dividing $\phi(m)$, ($p > \sqrt[4]{m}$) enables one to factor m, so the primes must be chosen to be small.

[6] According to the prime number theorem, there are approximately $\frac{N}{2\log N}$ primes of bit length equal to that of N. Our chances of picking m such that another p_i inadvertently divides $\phi(m)$ are approximately $\frac{\text{polylog}(m)}{m}$ which is negligibly small as the length of m in bits (i.e., $\log m$, the security parameter) increases.

automorphisms $\{\varphi_{p_i}\}_{i \neq i^*}$ will preserve this group: things outside will stay outside, and things inside will stay inside, and of course $\varphi_{p_{i^*}}$ moves every element into $H_{p_{i^*}}$. I.e.,

$$\varphi_{p_{i^*}}(x) \in H_{p_{i^*}} \quad \forall x$$

and if $i \neq i^*$, then

$$\varphi_{p_i}(x) \in H_{p_{i^*}} \iff x \in H_{p_{i^*}}$$

We can trace the path that r takes to become R and see what happens: We have that the element r begins outside of the subgroup $H_{p_{i^*}}$ and then r is moved by many maps, all of which come from the set

$$\{\varphi_1, ... \varphi_{i^*-1}\} \cup \{\text{Id}\}$$

depending on whether or not $x_i = 1$. But what is important is that all of these maps are automorphisms, which therefore fix $H_{p_{i^*}}$. So, no matter what the configuration of the first $i^* - 1$ elements of the database, r will have not moved into $H_{p_{i^*}}$ at this point. Next, we conditionally apply the map $\varphi_{p_{i^*}}$ depending on whether or not $x_{i^*} = 1$, which conditionally moves our element into $H_{p_{i^*}}$. This is followed by the application of more automorphisms, which as we have seen have no effect on whether or not the response R will be in $H_{p_{i^*}}$. So, since $H_{p_{i^*}}$ is fixed by every automorphism, the only chance that r has to move from outside $H_{p_{i^*}}$ to inside $H_{p_{i^*}}$ is if the map $\varphi_{p_{i^*}}$ is applied, which happens if and only if $x_{i^*} = 1$. Hence, we have that (with overwhelming probability) $R \in H_{p_{i^*}}$ if and only if $x_{i^*} = 1$.

The privacy this protocol can be proved directly from the Φ-Hiding assumption, although it may be more pleasant to think of this in terms of the indistinguishability of the subgroup H_{p_i} to a party not knowing the factorization of m. Now, let us take a look back and examine the communication to see why this was useful. The challenge of creating PIR protocols is usually to minimize the amount of communication. A PIR protocol with linear communication is quite trivial to construct: just transfer the entire database. This is of course not very useful. The PIR protocol we have described above, however, has nearly optimal communication. The database's response is a single element $R \in \mathbb{Z}_m^*$ which has size proportional to the security parameter alone (which must be at least logarithmic in n), and the user's query has the size of the security parameter, and the random input to a prime sequence generator, which could also be as small as logarithmic in n. So, we have constructed a PIR protocol with only logarithmic communication, which is of course optimal: If $\mathcal{DB}$ wants to avoid sending information proportional to the size of the database, then $\mathcal{U}$ must somehow communicate information about what index is desired, which requires at least a logarithmic amount of communication. However, with the recommended parameters for security, the total communication is approximately $\mathcal{O}(\log^8 n)$.

3.3 Generalizations: Smooth Subgroups

More recently, Gentry and Ramzan [15] have generalized some of the fundamental ideas behind these methods, creating protocols based on *smooth subgroups*, which are those that have many small primes dividing their order. Somewhat similar to CMS [7], a list of primes is chosen corresponding to the positions of the database, and a query for position i essentially consists of a description of a group G such that $|G|$ is divisible by p_i. However, the work of [15] is designed to retrieve blocks of data at a single time (CMS [7] must be repeatedly executed to accomplish this functionality). Rather than repeatedly exponentiating by all of the primes, the database is represented as an integer e such that when reduced mod p_i, the value is the i-th block of the database (such an integer always exists of course by the Chinese Remainder Theorem). Now to recover the data (which is just $e \bmod p_i$), a discrete log computation can be made in the (small) subgroup of order p_i.

4 PIR from Any Trapdoor Permutation

In 2000, Kushilevitz and Ostrovsky [24] demonstrated that the existence of one-way trapdoor permutations suffices to create a non-trivial PIR, where non-trivial simply means that the total communication between the parties is strictly smaller than the size of the database. Although the protocol requires multiple rounds of interaction, the basic construction remains fairly simple in the case of an honest but curious server. In case of a malicious server the construction is more complicated and the reader is referred to the original paper for details. Here, we only illustrate the basic idea of the honest-but-curious case.

4.1 Preliminaries

For this construction, the existence of one way trapdoor permutations (f, f^{-1}) is assumed, as well as Goldreich-Levin hard core bits.

Another tool (used in the honest-but-curious case) is the universal one way hashing of Naor and Yung [29]. For the dishonest case, universal way-way hash functions are replaced with an *interactive hashing* protocol [33], and on top of that some additional machinery is needed. However, for the honest but curious case the proof is far more simple. Recall that universal one way hash functions satisfy a slightly weaker type of collision-resistance. Basically, if one first picks any input x from the domain, and a then independently a hash function h from a universal one way family, it is computationally infeasible to find $x' \neq x \in h^{-1}(h(x))$.

The PIR protocol we'll discuss here uses universal one way hash functions which are 2 to 1 (i.e., for all y in the codomain, $|h^{-1}(y)| = 2$) and each function will map $\{0,1\}^k \longrightarrow \{0,1\}^{k-1}$ for some integer k.

4.2 Outline of the Protocol

At a very high level, the protocol revolves around the following idea: The server takes an n bit database and partitions it into consecutive blocks of length k (k will be the input length to a trapdoor permutation f). It collapses every block of the database by one bit, and sends this (slightly) reduced-size database back to the user. The user then selects and sends to the server some information that will allow him to determine the one missing bit of information for the block in which he or she is interested. Now, using communication balancing techniques similar to what we've described in the introduction, we can hold on to the constant advantage (below n) given to us by the server collapsing the one bit of every database block. The trick, of course, is to avoid revealing information about which block the user is interested in when recovering this last bit. The solution is quite simple. As mentioned, the database collapses a bit of each database block before sending this information to the user. There are many obvious ways to do this, for example just sending all but one bit of each block. However, in these situations, the database knows exactly the two possibilities that arise from the collapsed data sent to the user, as well as knowing the actual value in the database. This would seemingly make it quite difficult for the user to determine which of the two possibilities exist in the database without the database gaining information. So instead, a method is devised in which the database collapses a bit of each block *without knowing the other possibility*. This will enable the user to determine which possibility exists for a given block without revealing what block he or she is interested in.

4.3 Sketch of Protocol Details

As we alluded to in the outline, we need to provide a way for the database to collapse a bit of each block, but without knowing the other possibility. This is accomplished precisely via a family $\mathcal{F}$ of universal one way hash functions, and in fact, the orginal construction of such a family by Naor and Yung [29] is used. The important point, is that the only assumption needed to build this family of universal one way hash functions was the existence of one-way permutations, and furthermore, because they were constructed via one-way permutations, a party holding the trapdoor *can find collisions*. To summarize, here are the important properties we need from the family $\mathcal{F}$:

1. Each function of $\mathcal{F}$ is efficiently computable.
2. Each function has the property of being 2 to 1.
3. Given only $x, f(x)$ for $f \in \mathcal{F}$, it is computationally infeasible to find $x' \neq x \in f^{-1}(f(x))$ without trapdoor information.
4. With trapdoor information, it is feasible to find collisions in every function $f \in \mathcal{F}$.

The protocol proceeds as follows:

The database is divided into blocks of size K, one of which the user is interested in. Furthermore, the database is organized into pairs of blocks, denote them by $z_{i,L}$ and $z_{i,R}$ (L, R standing for "left" and "right"). A query consists of two descriptions of universal one way hash functions, f_L, f_R, to which the user has the trapdoors. Upon receipt of the query, the database computes the values of $f_L(z_{i,L})$ and $f_R(z_{i,R})$ for each block of the database, and returns these values to the user. The user, who has trapdoors, can compute both possible pre-images (z, z') that may correspond to the block of the database of interest. It only remains to have the database communicate which one, while maintaining privacy. This is accomplished via hardcore predicates. Without loss of generality, suppose the user wishes to retrieve the left block, say $z_{s,L}$. Then, the user selects two hardcore predicates, r_L, r_R according to the conditions that $r_L(z_{s,L}) \neq r_L(z'_{s,L})$, yet $r_R(z_{s,R}) = r_R(z'_{s,R})$. These predicates are sent to the database, who responds with $r_L(z_{i,L}) \oplus r_R(z_{i,R})$ for every pair of blocks. Now, regardless of the possibilities of the right block, the hardcore predicates will be the same, hence the user can solve for the left hardcore predicate, and hence the left block, as we assumed the predicates evaluated on the two choices to be distinct. This completes a basic description of the protocol.

The descriptions of f_L, f_R, r_L, r_R are all $\mathcal{O}(K)$, which is the only communication from the user to the database. The communication from the database to the user is easily seen to be $n - \frac{n}{2K}$ bits in the initial round, and one more bit in the final response. Hence, the protocol does achieve smaller than n communication, for $n > O(k^2)$. Next we argue that the protocol is also secure. The only information sent to the database which contains any information about what block the user is interested in, is that of the hardcore predicates, r_L, r_R. The value of the hardcore predicates *on the two possible pre-images of a hash value* is exactly what gives us the information regarding the user's selection. We only need to show that given such predicates, they do not reveal information about the selected block. Informally, this is the right approach, as the definition of hardcore predicate states that the outcomes are hard to predict better than random when only given the output of a function. Indeed, as fairly straightforward hybrid argument shows, this is the case.

5 Conclusions

In this paper, we have given a general survey of Single-Database PIR and it's many connections to other cryptographic primitives. We also discussed several implementations of single-database PIR, including a very generic construction from homomorphic encryption. As well-studied as single database PIR seems to be, many open problems remain. For example, reducing the communication complexity of a PIR protocol based on general trapdoor permutations, as well as exploring the connections PIR has to other communication-efficient protocols both in cryptography and complexity theory.

References

1. D. Boneh, G. Crescenzo, R. Ostrovsky, G. Persiano. Public Key Encryption with Keyword Search. EUROCRYPT 2004: 506-522
2. D. Boneh E. Kushilevitzy R. Ostrovsky, W. Skeith Public Key Encryption that Allows PIR Queries IACR E-print archive, 2007.
3. G. Brassard, C. Crepeau and J.-M. Robert All-or-nothing disclosure of secrets In *Advances in Cryptology: Proceedings of Crypto '86* Springer-Verlag, 1987, pp. 234-238.
4. A. Beimel, Y. Ishai, E. Kushilevitz, and T. Malkin. One-way functions are essential for single-server private information retrieval. In *Proc. of the 31th Annu. ACM Symp. on the Theory of Computing*, 1999.
5. C. Crépeau. Equivalence between two flavors of oblivious transfers. In *Proc. of CRYPTO '87*, pages 350–354, 1988.
6. Y. C. Chang. Single Database Private Information Retrieval with Logarithmic Communication. ACISP 2004
7. C. Cachin, S. Micali, and M. Stadler. Computationally private information retrieval with polylogarithmic communication. In J. Stern, editor, *Advances in Cryptology – EUROCRYPT '99*, volume 1592 of *Lecture Notes in Computer Science*, pages 402–414. Springer, 1999.

8. B. Chor, O. Goldreich, E. Kushilevitz, and M. Sudan. Private information retrieval. In *Proc. of the 36th Annu. IEEE Symp. on Foundations of Computer Science*, pages 41–51, 1995. Journal version: *J. of the ACM*, 45:965–981, 1998.

9. R. Curtmola, J. Garay, S. Kamara, and R. Ostrovsky. Searchable symmetric encryption: improved definitions and efficient constructions. In *ACM Conference on Computer and Communications Security* CCS 2006, pages 79-88, 2006.

10. I. Damgård, M. Jurik. A Generalisation, a Simplification and some Applications of Paillier's Probabilistic Public-Key System. In Public Key Cryptography (PKC 2001)

11. G. DiCrescenzo, Y. Ishai, and R. Ostrovsky. Universal service-providers for database private information retrieval. In *Proc. of the 17th Annu. ACM Symp. on Principles of Distributed Computing*, pages 91–100, 1998. Full version in Journal of Cryptology 14(1): 37-74 (2001).

12. G. Di Crescenzo, T. Malkin, and R. Ostrovsky. Single-database private information retrieval implies oblivious transfer. In *Advances in Cryptology - EUROCRYPT 2000*, 122-138.

13. S. Dziembowski, U. Maurer On Generating the Initial Key in the Bounded-Storage Model. EUROCRYPT 2004: 126-137

14. S. Even, O. Goldreich and A. Lempel A Randomized Protocol for Signing Contracts Communications of the ACM, Vol 28, 1985, pp. 637-447.

15. C. Gentry and Z. Ramzan. Single Database Private Information Retrieval with Constant Communication Rate. ICALP 2005, LNCS 3580, pp. 803815, 2005.

16. Y. Gertner, Y. Ishai, E. Kushilevitz, and T. Malkin. Protecting data privacy in private information retrieval schemes. In *Proc. of the 30th Annu. ACM Symp. on the Theory of Computing*, pages 151–160, 1998.

17. S. Goldwasser and S. Micali. Probabilistic encryption. In J. Comp. Sys. Sci, 28(1):270–299, 1984.

18. O. Goldreich, R Ostrovsky. Software Protection and Simulation on Oblivious RAMs. J. ACM 43(3): 431-473 (1996)

19. Y. Ishai, E. Kushilevitz, R. Ostrovsky Sufficient Conditions for Collision-Resistant Hashing. TCC 2005: 445-456

20. Y. Ishai, E. Kushilevitz, R. Ostrovsky and A. Sahai. Batch codes and their applications. STOC 2004: 262-271

21. Y. Ishai, E. Kushilevitz, R. Ostrovsky and A. Sahai. Cryptography from Anonymity. FOCS 2006: 239-248

22. D. Harnik, M Naor On the Compressibility of NP Instances and Cryptographic Applications. FOCS 2006: 719-728

23. E. Kushilevitz and R. Ostrovsky. Replication is not needed: Single database, computationally-private information retrieval. In *Proc. of the 38th Annu. IEEE Symp. on Foundations of Computer Science*, pages 364–373, 1997.

24. E. Kushilevitz and R. Ostrovsky. One-Way Trapdoor Permutations Are Sufficient for Nontrivial Single-Server Private Information Retrieval. EUROCRYPT 2000: 104-121

25. H. Lipmaa. An Oblivious Transfer Protocol with Log-Squared Communication. ISC 2005: 314-328

26. R. Meier, B. Przydatek On Robust Combiners for Private Information Retrieval and Other Primitives. CRYPTO 2006: 555-569

27. M. Naor and B. Pinkas. Oblivious transfer and polynomial evaluation. In *Proc. of the 31th Annu. ACM Symp. on the Theory of Computing*, pages 245–254, 1999.

28. M. Naor, K. Nissim: Communication Complexity and Secure Function Evaluation Electronic Colloquium on Computational Complexity (ECCC) 8(062): (2001)

29. M. Naor, M. Yung. Universal One-Way Hash Functions and their Cryptographic Applications In *Proceedings of the Twenty First Annual ACM Symposium on Theory of Computing. (May 15–17 1989: Seattle, WA, USA)*

30. R. Ostrovsky and V. Shoup. Private information storage. In *Proc. of the 29th Annu. ACM Symp. on the Theory of Computing*, pages 294–303, 1997.
31. R. Ostrovsky and W. Skeith. Private Searching on Streaming Data. In *Advances in Cryptology – CRYPTO 2005*
32. R. Ostrovsky and W. Skeith. Algebraic Lower Bounds for Computing on Encrypted Data. In ECCC, Electronic Colloquium on Computational Complexity
33. R. Ostrovsky, R. Venkatesan, and M. Yung. Fair games against an all-powerful adversary. Presented at DIMACS Complexity and Cryptography workshop, October 1990, Princeton. Prelim. version in *Proc. of the Sequences II workshop* 1991, Springer-Verlag, pp. 418-429. Final version in *AMS DIMACS Series in Discrete Mathematics and Theoretical Computer Science*, Vol. 13 *Distributed Computing and Cryptography*, Jin-Yi Cai, editor, pp. 155-169. AMS, 1993.
34. P. Paillier. Public Key Cryptosystems based on CompositeDegree Residue Classes. Advances in Cryptology - EUROCRYPT 99, LNCS volume 1592, pp. 223-238. Springer Verlag, 1999.
35. M. O. Rabin How to exchange secrets by oblivious transfer Technical Memo TR-81, Aiken Computation Laboratory, Harvard University, 1981.
36. Y. Tauman Kalai, R. Raz: Succinct Non-Interactive Zero-Knowledge Proofs with Preprocessing for LOGSNP. FOCS 2006: 355-366

Deterministic Polynomial Time Equivalence Between Factoring and Key-Recovery Attack on Takagi's RSA

Noboru Kunihiro[1] and Kaoru Kurosawa[2]

[1] The University of Electro-Communications, Japan
kunihiro@ice.uec.ac.jp
[2] Ibaraki University, Japan
kurosawa@mx.ibaraki.ac.jp

Abstract. For RSA, May showed a deterministic polynomial time equivalence of computing d to factoring $N(= pq)$. On the other hand, Takagi showed a variant of RSA such that the decryption algorithm is faster than the standard RSA, where $N = p^r q$ while $ed = 1 \bmod (p-1)(q-1)$. In this paper, we show that a deterministic polynomial time equivalence also holds in this variant. The coefficient matrix T to which LLL algorithm is applied is no longer lower triangular, and hence we develop a new technique to overcome this problem.

Keywords: RSA, factoring, LLL algorithm.

1 Introduction

1.1 Background

Is the key-recovery attack on RSA equivalent to factoring? This is one of the fundamental questions on RSA. Remember that in RSA, a public-key is $N(= pq)$ and e, where p and q are large primes, and the secret-key is d, where $ed = 1 \bmod (p-1)(q-1)$. Given (N, e), it is not easy to factor N from d while computing d is easy if factoring N is easy. More specifically, our problem is to find a *deterministic* polynomial time algorithm which can factor N on input the RSA parameter (N, e, d).

For this problem, there exists a *probabilistic* polynomial time algorithm [12] based on the work by Miller [10]. Miller further proved that under the Extended Riemann's Hypothesis, there exists a *deterministic* polynomial time algorithm. However, it is a strong assumption.

At Crypto 2004, May showed the first deterministic polynomial time algorithm for this problem [9] for $ed \le N^2$ and $|p| = |q|$, where $|x|$ denotes the bit length of x. Coron and May extended this result to unbalanced p and q [4]. These results mean that the key-recovery attack on RSA is deterministically equivalent to factoring as far as $ed \le N^2$.

On the other hand, Takagi proposed a variant of RSA [13] such that $N = p^r q$ while $ed \equiv 1 \bmod (p-1)(q-1)$. He observed that the decryption can be

T. Okamoto and X. Wang (Eds.): PKC 2007, LNCS 4450, pp. 412–425, 2007.

significantly faster in this variant. Hence it is important to study if there exists a deterministic polynomial time equivalence even in this variant.

1.2 Our Contributions

In this paper, we show a deterministic polynomial time equivalence between the key-recovery attack on Takagi's variant of RSA and factoring. More precisely, we show a deterministic polynomial time algorithm which can factor $N(= p^r q)$ from (N, e, d) such that $ed \equiv 1 \bmod (p-1)(q-1)$ if $ed \leq N^{\frac{4}{r+1}}$, $|p| = |q|$ and $r = O(\log \log N)$. It is interesting to see that May's result is obtained as a special case for $r = 1$. Hence, our result is a natural generalization of May [9].

Lenstra et al. developed an efficient lattice reduction algorithm known as LLL algorithm [8]. Based on it, Coppersmith showed a method of finding small roots of univariate modular polynomials [3] which was simplified by Howgrave-Graham [7].

May [9] and Coron and May [4] used the simplified version of Howgrave-Graham [7] to show the deterministic polynomial time equivalence on RSA. These methods first find a set of polynomials, and then apply the lattice reduction algorithm to the coefficient matrix T. It works well because T is lower triangular and hence it is easy to compute $\det T$.

We use the same approach. One of main issues of using Coron-May's strategy in the case of Takagi's RSA is the fact that the matrix T is not triangular, which makes computing the determinant a problem. We overcome this problem by using another matrix M containing polynomials $g(x, y)$, whereas the matrix T contains the polynomials $t(x, y) = g(x + A, y + B)$. We prove that determinant of T is equal to that of M. We develop a new technique to prove it and believe that our new technique will be useful for many other lattice related problems.

1.3 Related Works

Boneh, Durfee and Howgrave-Graham studied how to factor $N = p^r q$ by using lattice reduction [2]. This type of composite N is very important since it is used in EPOC [11] and ESIGN [6][1] in addition to Takagi's variant of RSA. They showed a deterministic algorithm of finding p in time $O(p^{\frac{2}{r+1}})$. They also proved that p can be recovered in polynomial time if we can find an integer P such that $|P - p| < p^{\frac{r-1}{r+1}}$.

At Eurocrypt2005 [1], Blömer and May proposed a general method of finding small roots of bivariate polynomials over integers, and improved Boneh et al.'s result.

1.4 Organization

The rest of paper is organized as follows. The next section contains the preliminaries. First, we review LLL algorithm and Howgrave-Graham's Lemma. Then

---

[1] In EPOC and ESIGN, r is restricted in 2. And, our results give no influence to the security of EPOC and ESIGN.

we explain Takagi's variant of RSA and describe the motivation of this research. In section 3, we introduce and prove our main theorem. In particular, we show that the deterministic polynomial time equivalence holds for $ed \leq N^{\frac{4}{r+1}}$ and $r = O(\log \log N)$. Finally, Section 4 concludes the paper.

2   Preliminaries

This section describes LLL algorithm, Howgrave-Graham's lemma and Takagi's variant of RSA.

2.1   Notation

For a vector b, $||b||$ denotes the Euclidean norm of b. For a bivariate polynomial $h(x, y) = \sum h_{ij} x^i y^j$, define

$$||h(x, y)|| = \sqrt{\sum h_{ij}^2}.$$

That is, $||h(x, y)||$ denotes the Euclidean norm of the vector which consists of coefficients of $h(x, y)$.

2.2   LLL Algorithm and Howgrave-Graham's Lemma

Let $M = \{a_{ij}\}$ be a nonsingular $w \times w$ matrix of integers. The rows of M generate a lattice L, a collection of vectors closed under addition and subtraction; in fact the rows forms a basis of L. The lattice L is also represented as follows. Letting $a_i = (a_{i1}, a_{i2}, \ldots, a_{iw})$, the lattice L spanned by $\langle a_1, \ldots, a_w \rangle$ consists of all integral linear combinations of $a_1, \ldots, a_w$, that is :

$$L = \left\{ \sum_{i=1}^{w} n_i a_i | n_i \in \mathbb{Z} \right\}. \tag{1}$$

LLL algorithm outputs a short vector in the lattice L. This algorithm works in deterministic polynomial time.

Proposition 1 (LLL [8]). *Let $M = \{a_{ij}\}$ be a nonsingular $w \times w$ matrix of integers. The rows of M generate a lattice L. Given M, LLL algorithm finds a vector $b \in L$ such that*

$$||b|| \leq 2^{(w-1)/4} (\det M)^{1/w}$$

in polynomial time in (w, B), where $B = \max \log_2 |a_{ij}|$.

Lemma 1 (Howgrave-Graham [7]). *Let $h(x, y) \in \mathbb{Z}[x, y]$ be a polynomial, which is a sum of at most w monomials. Let m be an integer. Suppose that*

1. *$h(x_0, y_0) = 0 \bmod \phi^m$, where $|x_0| < X$ and $|y_0| < Y$.*
2. *$||h(xX, yY)|| < \phi^m / \sqrt{w}$.*

Then $h(x_0, y_0) = 0$ holds over integers.

2.3 Takagi's Variant of RSA

Takagi proposed a variant of RSA such that $N = p^r q$ and showed that a faster decryption algorithm can be obtained [13,14]. For example, for $r = 2$, it is 42% faster than the original RSA decryption algorithm.

Key Generation. Generate two distinct primes p and q. Let $N = p^r q$. Find e and d such that

$$ed \equiv 1 \bmod (p-1)(q-1). \tag{2}$$

Let $d_p = d \bmod p-1$ and $d_q = d \bmod q-1$. Then, e and N are the encryption keys and d_p, d_q, p, q are the decryption keys.

Encryption. For a plaintext $M \in \mathbb{Z}_N^*$, the ciphertext is computed as

$$C = M^e \bmod N. \tag{3}$$

Decryption. Given a ciphertext C, do:
1. Compute $M_q = C^{d_q} \bmod q$, where $M_q = M \bmod q$.
2. Compute $M_p = C^{d_p} \bmod p$, where $M_p = M \bmod p$.
3. Find $M_p^{(r)}$ such that $M_p^{(r)} = M \bmod p^r$ by using Hensel lifting.
4. Compute M by applying Chinese remainder theorem to M_q and $M_p^{(r)}$.

3 Deterministic Polynomial Time Equivalence in Takagi's RSA

In this section, we show a deterministic polynomial time equivalence between the key recovery attack on Takagi's variant of RSA and factoring.

3.1 Main Theorem

We say that (r, N, e, d) is a Takagi's RSA parameter[2] if

$$N = p^r q, ed = 1 \bmod (p-1)(q-1) \text{ and } |p| = |q|.$$

We then present a deterministic polynomial time algorithm which can factor $N = p^r q$ on input such a parameter.

Theorem 1. *Suppose that a Takagi's RSA parameter (r, N, e, d) is given such that $ed \leq N^{\frac{4}{r+1}}$. Then we can factor N in deterministic polynomial time in $(\log N, 2^r)$.*

Corollary 1. *Suppose that a Takagi's RSA parameter (r, N, e, d) is given such that $ed \leq N^{\frac{4}{r+1}}$ and $r = O(\log \log N)$. Then we can factor N in deterministic polynomial time in $\log N$.*

---

[2] We omit the discussion of unbalanced prime factors due to limitations of space. We can easily extend our analysis to unbalanced case as Coron-May's paper [4]. In the Takagi's original paper[13], e and d are set as $ed \equiv 1 (\bmod \ \mathrm{lcm}(p-1, q-1))$. In this case, we have the same result if $\gcd(p-1, q-1)$ is small or known.

Proof (of Corollary 1). Since $r = O(\log \log N)$, $2^r < (\log N)^c$ for some constant c. Then the running time of the factoring algorithm given by Theorem 1 is bounded by a polynomial time in $\log N$. $\qquad\square$

Remark 1. Let $r = 1$ in Theorem 1. Then we obtain the following corollary: Given (N, e, d), $N = pq$ can be factorized in deterministic polynomial time in $\log N$ if $ed \le N^2$. This corollary coincides with the result of May [9] and Coron and May [4] for balanced p and q. Hence, our result is a natural generalization of their result on RSA.

Remark 2. In Takagi's variant of RSA, since $ed = 1 \bmod (p-1)(q-1)$, e and d are usually chosen in such a way that $e < (p-1)(q-1)$ and $d < (p-1)(q-1)$. In this case, it holds that

$$ed < ((p-1)(q-1))^2 \le (pq)^2 \approx N^{\frac{4}{r+1}}.$$

Therefore, our bound is achieved for e and d that are chosen in the usual way.

Remark 3. The condition $r < c \log \log N$ leads to another equivalent condition: $r < c'(\log \log p + \log \log \log p)$ for some c'. On the other hand, Boneh et al. proved that if $r > c'' \log p$, N can be factorized in deterministic polynomial time of $\log N$ without the knowledge of d [2]. Consequently, the computational cost is not known when $c'(\log \log p + \log \log \log p) < r < c'' \log p$. But, this is a purely mathematical interest.

3.2   Affine Transform Lemma

We now prove an elemental lemma which plays an important role in the proof of Theorem 1. We believe that this lemma will be useful for many other lattice related problems.

Lemma 2. *Let* $g_1(x), \cdots g_r(x)$ *be* r *polynomials of degree* $r - 1$*. For each* $g_i(x)$*, define* $t_i(x)$ *as*

$$t_i(x) = g_i(x + \alpha),$$

where α *is an arbitrary constant. Let* $M = (g_{ij})$ *be the* $r \times r$ *coefficient matrix of* $g_1(x), \cdots g_r(x)$*, where*

$$g_i(x) = \sum_{j=1}^{r} g_{ij} x^{r-j},$$

and let $T = (t_{ij})$ *be the* $r \times r$ *coefficient matrix of* $t_1(x), \cdots t_r(x)$*, where*

$$t_i(x) = \sum_{j=1}^{r} t_{ij} x^{r-j}.$$

Then it holds that

$$\det T = \det M.$$

Proof. It holds that

$$t_i(x) = g_i(x + \alpha) = \sum_{u=1}^{r} g_{iu}(x + \alpha)^{r-u} = \sum_{u=1}^{r} \sum_{v=0}^{r-u} g_{iu} \times {}_{r-u}C_v \alpha^{r-u-v} x^v$$

$$= \sum_{u=1}^{r} \sum_{j=u}^{r} g_{iu} \times {}_{r-u}C_{j-u} \alpha^{j-u} x^{r-j}$$

Therefore, we obtain that

$$t_{ij} = \sum_{u=1}^{j} g_{iu} \times {}_{r-u}C_{j-u} \alpha^{j-u}. \tag{4}$$

Next, define an upper triangular $r \times r$ matrix $A = (a_{ij})$ as follows.

$$a_{ij} = \begin{cases} {}_{r-i}C_{j-i}\alpha^{j-i} & \text{if } i \le j \\ 0 & \text{if } i > j. \end{cases}$$

Then we can see that $T = MA$. Further, we have $\det A = 1$ because $a_{ii} = {}_{r-i}C_0 \times \alpha^0 = 1$. Consequently we obtain that $\det T = \det M \times \det A = \det M$. $\square$

3.3   Proof of Theorem 1

We will factor N by using the following strategy. Let X, Y, m, t be positive integers which will be determined later.

Step 0. Let $p = p_0 X + x_0$ and $q = q_0 Y + y_0$, where $x_0 < X$ and $y_0 < Y$.
　　Suppose that p_0 and q_0 are known, and we want to compute x_0 and y_0.
Step 1. Construct a set of polynomials $t_{ijk}(x, y)$ such that

$$t_{ijk}(x_0, y_0) \equiv 0 \bmod (((p-1)(q-1))^m).$$

Step 2. Apply LLL algorithm to the coefficient matrix of $\{t_{ijk}(x, y)\}$ to obtain $h(x, y)$, where $h(x, y)$ is a non-zero integer combination of $t_{ijk}(x, y)$ with small coefficients.
Step 3. Let

$$h'(x) = h\left(x, \frac{N}{(p_0 X + x)^r} - q_0 Y\right)$$

Then x_0 is a solution of $h'(x) = 0$.

　　We will find p_0 and q_0 by exhaustive search in Step 0. In what follows, we will show how to construct polynomials t_{ijk}, how to compute the determinant of the coefficient matrix of $\{t_{ijk}\}$ and how to determine X, Y, m, t. It will be seen that the above algorithm runs in polynomial time in $(\log N, 2^r)$ if $\max(p/X, q/Y)$ is polynomially bounded because Step 1 $\sim$ Step 3 are computed in polynomial time and p_0 and q_0 are bounded by $\max(p/X, q/Y)$.

Remark 4. $h'(x)$ is not identically zero since $h(x, y)$ is not identically zero.

How to construct t_{ijk}. Let

$$f(x, y) = (x - 1)(y - 1).$$

Note that $f(p, q) = (p - 1)(q - 1)$ is the modulus of Eq.(2). Let

$$U = ed - 1, \ S = (p - 1)(q - 1).$$

Define

$$g_{ijk}(x, y) = x^i y^j f(x, y)^k U^{m-k}.$$

Then it is easy to see that

$$g_{ijk}(p, q) = p^i q^j f(p, q)^k U^{m-k} = 0 \bmod S^m$$

for any (i, j, k). In $g_{ijk}(x, y)$, we will replace each occurrence of $x^r y$ by N because $N = p^r q$ (based on the Durfee-Nguyen technique [5]). Therefore, the resulting $g_{ijk}(x, y)$ contains monomials of the form x^a, y^b and $xy^{c_1}, x^2 y^{c_2}, \ldots, x^{r-1} y^{c_{r-1}}$ for some $a, b, c_1, \ldots$ and c_{r-1}.

Construct a list of polynomials $G = (g_{ijk})$ as follows, where s, t will be determined later.

> $G \leftarrow \emptyset$
> for $k = 0, \cdots, m - 1$, do;
>   append $g_{0,0,k}$ and $g_{1,0,k}$ into G in this order.
>   for $i = r - 1, \cdots, 1$, do; append $g_{i,1,k}$ to G.
> for $i = 0, \cdots, s$, do; append $g_{i,0,m}$ to G.
> for $j = 1, \cdots, t$, do;
>   for $i = r - 1, \cdots, 0$, do; append $g_{i,j,m}$ to G.
> return G.

Express each g_{ijk} as follows, where the leading monomial appears in the right most term of the right hand side. (For more details, see Appendix A.)

$$
\begin{aligned}
g_{0,0,0}(x, y) &= U^m \\
g_{1,0,0}(x, y) &= *** + xU^m \\
g_{r-1,1,0}(x, y) &= *** + x^{r-1} y U^m \\
&\vdots \\
g_{1,1,0}(x, y) &= *** + xy U^m
\end{aligned}
$$

- -

$$\vdots$$

- -

$$
\begin{aligned}
g_{0,0,m-1}(x, y) &= *** + y^{m-1} U \\
g_{1,0,m-1}(x, y) &= *** + x^m U X^m \\
g_{r-1,1,m-1}(x, y) &= *** + x^{r-1} y^m U
\end{aligned}
$$

$$\vdots$$

$$g_{1,1,m-1}(x,y) = *** + xy^m U$$

- -

$$g_{0,0,m}(x,y) = *** + y^m$$
$$g_{1,0,m}(x,y) = *** + x^{m+1}$$

$$\vdots$$

$$g_{s,0,m}(x,y) = *** + x^{m+s}$$

- -

$$g_{r-1,1,m}(x,y) = *** + x^{r-1}y^{m+1}$$

$$\vdots$$

$$g_{0,1,m}(x,y) = *** + y^{m+1}$$

- -

$$\vdots$$

- -

$$g_{r-1,t,m}(x,y) = *** + x^{r-1}y^{m+1}$$

$$\vdots$$

$$g_{0,t,m}(x,y) = *** + y^{m+t}$$

Next define

$$t_{ijk}(x,y) = g_{ijk}(p_0 X + x, q_0 Y + y). \tag{5}$$

It is easy to see that

$$t_{ijk}(x_0, y_0) = g_{ijk}(p_0 X + x_0, q_0 Y + y_0) \equiv g_{ijk}(p, q) \equiv 0 (\mathrm{mod}\, S^m).$$

We have now finished Step 1.

How to compute $\det T$. Let M be the coefficient matrix of $\{g_{ijk}(xX, yY)\}$ and T be the coefficient matrix of $\{t_{ijk}(xX, yY)\}$. Tables 1 and 2 show small examples.

We want to apply Proposition 1 to T, where we need to know $\det T$. However, computing $\det T$ is not easy because T is not lower triangular. (See from Table 1.) This is the big difference from the previous works [4,9]. We prove the following lemma based on Lemma 2.

Lemma 3. *It holds that*

$$\det T = \det M. \tag{6}$$

Proof. For $1 \le j \le m+t$, define r polynomials $f_{1,j}, \cdots, f_{r,j}$ of degree $r-1$ as follows.

- For $1 \le j \le m$,
  - $f_{a,j}(x)$ is the coefficient of y^j in $g_{r-a,1,j-1}(xX, yY)$ for $1 \le a \le r-1$.

Table 1. Example of T for $r = 2, m = 3, s = 2, t = 2$

	1	x	xy	y	x^2	xy^2	y^2	x^3	xy^3	y^3
$t_{000}(xX,yY)$	U^3									
$t_{100}(xX,yY)$	$*$	U^3X								
$t_{110}(xX,yY)$	$*$	$*$	U^3XY	U^3XYp_0						
$t_{001}(xX,yY)$	$*$	$*$	U^2XY	$U^2(p_0X-1)Y$						
$t_{101}(xX,yY)$	$*$	$*$	$*$	$*$	$-U^2X^2$					
$t_{111}(xX,yY)$	$*$	$*$	$*$	$*$	$*$	$-U^2XY^2$	$-U^2XY^2p_0$			
$t_{002}(xX,yY)$	$*$	$*$	$*$	$*$	$*$	$-2UXY^2$	$UY^2(1-2p_0X)$			
$t_{102}(xX,yY)$	$*$	$*$	$*$	$*$	$*$	$*$	$*$	UX^3		
$t_{112}(xX,yY)$	$*$	$*$	$*$	$*$	$*$	$*$	$*$	$*$	UXY^3	UXY^3p_0
$t_{003}(xX,yY)$	$*$	$*$	$*$	$*$	$*$	$*$	$*$	$*$	$3XY^3$	$Y^3(3p_0X-1)$

	$1\cdots y^3$	x^4	x^5	xy^4	y^4	xy^5	y^5
$t_{103}(xX,yY)$	$*$	$-X^4$					
$t_{203}(xX,yY)$	$*$	$*$	$-X^5$				
$t_{113}(xX,yY)$	$*$	$*$	$*$	$-XY^4$	$-p_0XY^4$		
$t_{013}(xX,yY)$	$*$	$*$	$*$	$3XY^4$	$(3p_0X-1)Y^4$		
$t_{123}(xX,yY)$	$*$	$*$	$*$	$*$	$*$	$-XY^5$	$-p_0XY^5$
$t_{023}(xX,yY)$	$*$	$*$	$*$	$*$	$*$	$-4XY^5$	$(1-4p_0X)Y^5$

Table 2. Example of M for $r = 2, m = 3, s = 2, t = 2$

	1	x	xy	y	x^2	xy^2	y^2	x^3	xy^3	y^3	x^4	x^5	xy^4	y^4	xy^5	y^5
$g_{000}(xX,yY)$	U^3															
$g_{100}(xX,yY)$	$*$	U^3X														
$g_{110}(xX,yY)$	$*$	$*$	U^3XY													
$g_{001}(xX,yY)$	$*$	$*$	$*$	$-U^2Y$												
$g_{101}(xX,yY)$	$*$	$*$	$*$	$*$	$-U^2X^2$											
$g_{111}(xX,yY)$	$*$	$*$	$*$	$*$	$*$	$-U^2XY^2$										
$g_{002}(xX,yY)$	$*$	$*$	$*$	$*$	$*$	$*$	UY^2									
$g_{102}(xX,yY)$	$*$	$*$	$*$	$*$	$*$	$*$	$*$	UX^3								
$g_{112}(xX,yY)$	$*$	$*$	$*$	$*$	$*$	$*$	$*$	$*$	UXY^3							
$g_{003}(xX,yY)$	$*$	$*$	$*$	$*$	$*$	$*$	$*$	$*$	$*$	$-Y^3$						
$g_{103}(xX,yY)$	$*$	$*$	$*$	$*$	$*$	$*$	$*$	$*$	$*$	$*$	$-X^4$					
$g_{203}(xX,yY)$	$*$	$*$	$*$	$*$	$*$	$*$	$*$	$*$	$*$	$*$	$*$	$-X^5$				
$g_{113}(xX,yY)$	$*$	$*$	$*$	$*$	$*$	$*$	$*$	$*$	$*$	$*$	$*$	$*$	$-XY^4$			
$g_{013}(xX,yY)$	$*$	$*$	$*$	$*$	$*$	$*$	$*$	$*$	$*$	$*$	$*$	$*$	$*$	$-Y^4$		
$g_{123}(xX,yY)$	$*$	$*$	$*$	$*$	$*$	$*$	$*$	$*$	$*$	$*$	$*$	$*$	$*$	$*$	$-XY^5$	
$g_{023}(xX,yY)$	$*$	$*$	$*$	$*$	$*$	$*$	$*$	$*$	$*$	$*$	$*$	$*$	$*$	$*$	$*$	$-Y^5$

- • $f_{r,j}(x)$ is the coefficient of y^j in $g_{0,0,j}(xX,yY)$.
- For $m+1 \le j \le m+t$,
  - • $f_{a,j}(x)$ is the coefficient of y^j in $g_{r-a,j-m,m}(xX,yY)$ for $1 \le a \le r$.

Similarly, define r polynomials $e_{1,j}, \cdots, e_{r,j}$ of degree $r-1$ as follows.

- For $1 \le j \le m$,
  - • $e_{a,j}(x)$ is the coefficient of y^j in $t_{r-a,1,j-1}(xX,yY)$ for $1 \le a \le r-1$.
  - • $e_{r,j}(x)$ is the coefficient of y^j in $t_{0,0,j}(xX,yY)$.
- For $m+1 \le j \le m+t$,
  - • $e_{a,j}(x)$ is the coefficient of y^j in $t_{r-a,j-m,m}(xX,yY)$ for $1 \le a \le r$.

Let M_j be the $r \times r$ coefficient matrix of $f_{1,j}, \cdots, f_{r,j}$, and T_j be the $r \times r$ coefficient matrix of $e_{1,j}, \cdots, e_{r,j}$.

For example, T_1, M_1, T_2 and M_2 of Table 1 and 2 are as follows.

$$T_1 = \begin{pmatrix} U^3XY, & U^3XYp_0 \\ U^2XY, & U^2Y(p_0X - 1) \end{pmatrix}, M_1 = \begin{pmatrix} U^3XY, & 0 \\ U^2XY, & -U^2Y \end{pmatrix}.$$

$$T_2 = \begin{pmatrix} -U^2XY^2, & -U^2XY^2p_0 \\ -2UXY^2, & UY^2(1 - 2p_0X) \end{pmatrix}, M_2 = \begin{pmatrix} -U^2XY, & 0 \\ -2UXY^2, & UY^2 \end{pmatrix}.$$

From Eq.(5), we obtain that

$$t_{ijk}(xX, yY) = g_{ijk}(p_0X + xX, q_0Y + yY) = g_{ijk}(X(x + p_0), Y(y + q_0)).$$

Hence, it is easy to see that $e_{i,j}(x) = f_{i,j}(x + p_0)$ because y^j is the highest term in $g_{r-a,1,j-1}(xX, yY)$, $g_{0,0,j}(xX, yY)$ and $g_{r-a,j-m,m}(xX, yY)$. Therefore, from Lemma 2, we obtain that $\det T_j = \det M_j$ for $1 \leq j \leq m + t$. Consequently, we can see that $\det T = \det M$.   □

Since M is a triangular matrix, we can compute $\det M$ easily as follows[3].

$$\det M = U^{(r+1)m(m+1)/2} \cdot X^{(m+s)(m+s+1)/2+r(r-1)(m+t)/2} \cdot Y^{r(m+t)(m+t+1)/2}$$

Applying LLL. Note that T and M are $w \times w$ matrices, where

$$w = (r + 1)m + (s + 1) + rt = (r + 1)m + s + rt + 1.$$

Now by applying LLL algorithm to T, we can obtain

$$h(x, y) = \sum a_{ijk} t_{ijk}(x, y)$$

such that

$$\|h(xX, yY)\| \leq 2^{(w-1)/4}(\det M)^{1/w}$$

for some integers a_{ijk}. From the definition of $t_{ijk}(x, y)$, it holds that

$$h(x_0, y_0) = \sum a_{ijk} t_{ijk}(x_0, y_0) = 0 \bmod S^m.$$

Therefore, if $\|h(xX, yY)\| < S^m/\sqrt{w}$, then from Howgrave-Graham's lemma, we have $h(x_0, y_0) = 0$ over integers. Therefore, it is sufficient to show that

$$2^{(w-1)/4}(\det M)^{1/w} < \frac{S^m}{\sqrt{w}}. \tag{7}$$

Since p and q are the same bit length, it satisfies that $S = (p - 1)(q - 1) > pq/2 > \max(p^2, q^2)/4 > N^{2/(r+1)}/4$. Using the inequality $\sqrt{w} \leq 2^{(w-1)/2}$, we obtain the following sufficient condition:

$$\det M < N^{\frac{2mw}{r+1}} 2^{-(2mw + \frac{3}{4}w(w-1))}. \tag{8}$$

---

[3] In what follows, we omit the sign of $\det M$.

How to determine X and Y. By setting $X = Y$ and $s = t$, $\det M$ can be simplified as

$$\det M = U^{(r+1)m(m+1)/2} \cdot X^{(r+1)(m+s)(m+s+1)/2+r(r-1)(m+s)/2}. \tag{9}$$

The dimension of the lattice is given as $w = (r+1)(m+s)+1$.

Since it holds that $U \le N^{\frac{4}{r+1}}$ from our assumption, we obtain

$$\det M \le N^{\frac{(r+1)m(m+1)}{2} \cdot \frac{4}{r+1}} \cdot X^{(r+1)(m+s)(m+s+1)/2+r(r-1)(m+s)/2}$$
$$= N^{2m(m+1)} \cdot X^{(r+1)(m+s)(m+s+1)/2+r(r-1)(m+s)/2}. \tag{10}$$

From inequalities (8) and (10) we obtain

$$N^{2m(m+1)} \cdot X^{(r+1)(m+s)(m+s+1)/2+r(r-1)(m+s)/2} \le N^{2mw/(r+1)} \cdot 2^{-(2mw+\frac{3}{4}w(w-1))}$$
$$X^{(r+1)(m+s)(m+s+1)/2+r(r-1)(m+s)/2} \le N^{2m(s+\frac{1}{r+1}-1)} 2^{-(2mw+\frac{3}{4}w(w-1))}.$$

The above inequality can be transformed into

$$X \le N^{2m\frac{s+1/(r+1)-1}{(r+1)(m+s)(m+s+1)/2+r(r-1)(m+s)/2}} \cdot 2^{-\frac{2mw+3w(w-1)/4}{(r+1)(m+s)(m+s+1)/2+r(r-1)(m+s)/2}}. \tag{11}$$

Letting

$$\gamma(m, s; r) = 2m\frac{s+1/(r+1)-1}{(r+1)(m+s)(m+s+1)/2+r(r-1)(m+s)/2}$$

and

$$\delta(m, s; r) = \frac{2mw+3w(w-1)/4}{(r+1)(m+s)(m+s+1)/2+r(r-1)(m+s)/2},$$

we can express inequality (11) as

$$X \le N^{\gamma(m,s;r)} 2^{-\delta(m,s;r)}. \tag{12}$$

The next thing to do is to find s which maximize $\gamma(m, s; r)$ for a fixed m to maximize the bound X on x_0. Such s is given by $s = m$. In this setting, $\gamma(m, m; r)$ is calculated as follows.

$$\gamma(m, m; r) = 2\frac{m+1/(r+1)-1}{2(r+1)m+r^2+1} = \frac{1}{r+1} - \frac{r+1}{2(r+1)m+r^2+1}$$

$\delta(m, m; r)$ is calculated as

$$\delta(m, m; r) = \frac{2mw+3w(w-1)/4}{(r+1)(m+m)(m+m+1)/2+r(r-1)(m+m)/2}$$
$$= \frac{(2(r+1)m+1)(\frac{3}{2}(r+1)+2)}{2(r+1)m+1+r^2} < \frac{1}{2}(3r+5).$$

From the above discussion, we obtain

$$X < 2^{-\frac{(3r+5)}{2}} N^{\frac{1}{r+1} - \frac{r+1}{2(r+1)m+r^2+1}}. \tag{13}$$

Total Computational time. Taking the largest integer X of inequality (13), we obtain

$$\frac{p}{X} < \frac{2N^{1/(r+1)}}{X} \leq N^{\frac{r+1}{2(r+1)m+r^2+1}} \cdot 2^{\frac{3r+7}{2}}. \tag{14}$$

By setting $m = \lfloor \log N \rfloor$, we obtain

$$\frac{p}{X} < O(1) \cdot 2^{\frac{3r+7}{2}}. \tag{15}$$

Hence, the number of repetition for selection of p_0 is upper bounded by a polynomial of 2^r.

The dimension of the lattice is given by $w = (r+1)m + s + rt + 1 = 2(r+1)m+1 = O(\log N)$. The maximum entry of the lattice is given by $N^{\frac{4m}{r+1}+1}$. This implies that the logarithm of the maximum entry is given by $O(\log N^{\frac{4m}{r+1}}) = O(m \log N) = O((\log N)^2)$. Hence, the total computation cost for the bivariate polynomial $h(x, y)$ is given by the polynomial of $(\log N, 2^r)$. Note that LLL algorithm works deterministically.

The rest of our algorithm works in deterministic polynomial time of $\log N$. From the above discussion, N can be factorized in deterministic polynomial time of $\log N$ and 2^r. □

4   Concluding Remarks

We used the same approach as Coron-May[4]. But, Theorem 1 cannot be obtained trivially from[4]. We had to overcome the following two difficulties in order to prove our theorem.

1. How should we arrange the order of polynomials g_{ijk} and monomials so that M is triangular?
2. How should we calculate $\det T$? Since T is not triangular, calculation of determinant seems difficult.

First, we explain how to overcome the first difficulty. In the analysis of standard RSA [4], each occurrence of xy is replaced by N because $N = pq$. Hence only x^a or y^b appears in the resulting $g_{i,j,k}$ which makes it easy to form a triangular matrix.

On the other hand, we replace each occurrence of $x^r y$ by N because $N = p^r q$ in Takagi's RSA. Then the resulting $g_{ijk}(x, y)$ contains monomials of the form x^a, y^b and $xy^{c_1}, x^2 y^{c_2}, \ldots, x^{r-1} y^{c_{r-1}}$ for some $a, b, c_1, \ldots$ and c_{r-1}. A technical difficulty is how to make a triangular matrix M from these $g_{i,j,k}$. We have given an efficient solution for this problem.

Remark 5. We can apply Blömer-May's method [1] to our problem. In this method, however, the lattice is uniquely determined by the Newton polygon of the target polynomial $f(x, y)$, and hence there is no room for replacing $x^r y$ with N. Consequently we would get a smaller range of ed.

Next, we explain how to overcome the second difficulty. Since the only monomials x^a and y^b appear in Coron-May's g_{ijk}, the matrix generated from t_{ijk} is naturally triangular. Hence, in Coron-May's case, the determinant of T can be easily obtained. However, in our polynomials g_{ijk}, the monomial $x^i y^j$ appears. Hence, our matrix T cannot be triangular (for example, see Table 1). By showing Lemma 3 (that is $\det T = \det M$), we overcome this problem. In the proof of Lemma 3, Lemma 2 plays an important role. Note that in proof of lemma 3, we did not use the property that M is triangular. We enjoy this property in calculating $\det M$. We believe that our new technique will be useful for many other lattice related problems.

Acknowledgment

This research was supported in part by the Grants-in-Aid No. 16500009 for Scientific Research, JSPS. We thank the anonymous reviewers for their helpful comments.

References

1. J. Blömer and A. May, "A Tool Kit for Finding Small Roots of Bivariate Polynomials over the Integers," Proc. of Eurocrypt2005, LNCS 3494, pp. 251–267, 2005.
2. D.Boneh, G.Durfee and N.Howgrave-Graham, "Factoring $N = p^r q$ for Large r," in Proc. of Crypto'99, LNCS 1666, pp. 326–337, 1999.
3. D. Coppersmith, "Small Solutions to Polynomial Equations, and Low Exponent RSA Vulnerabilities," J. Cryptology 10(4): 233-260, 1997.
4. J.S. Coron and A.May, "Deterministic Polynomial Time Equivalence of Computing the RSA Secret Key and Factoring," IACR ePrint Archive: Report 2004/208, 2004, to appear in Journal of Cryptology.
5. G. Durfee and P. Nguyen, "Cryptanalysis of the RSA Schemes with Short Secret Exponent from Asiacrypt'99," Proc. of Asiacrypt2000, LNCS 1976, pp. 14–29, 2000.
6. A. Fujioka, T. Okamoto and S. Miyaguchi, "ESIGN: An Efficient Digital Signature Implementation for Smart Cards," In Proc. of Eurocrypt'91, LNCS 547, pp.446-457, 1992.
7. N.Howgrave-Graham, "Finding Small Roots of Univariate Modular Equations Revisited," IMA Int. Conf., pp.131–142 (1997)
8. A.K. Lenstra, H.W. Lenstra, L. Lovász, "Factoring polynomials with rational coefficients," Mathematische Annalen 261, pp.515–534, 1982.
9. A. May, "Computing the RSA Secret Key Is Deterministic Polynomial Time Equivalent to Factoring," in Proc. of Crypto2004, LNCS 3152, pp. 213–219, 2004.
10. G. L. Miller, "Riemann's Hypothesis and Tests for Primality," Seventh Annual ACM Symposium on the Theory of Computing, pp. 234–239, 1975.
11. T. Okamoto and S. Uchiyama, "A New Public Key Cryptosystem as secure as factoring," in Proc. of Eurocrypt'98, LNCS 1403, pp. 310–318, 1998.
12. R. Rivest, A. Shamir and L. Adleman, "A Method for Obtaining Digital Signatures and Public-Key Cryptosystems," Communications of the ACM, vol. 21(2), pp. 120–126, 1978.

13. T. Takagi, "Fast RSA-Type Cryptosystem Modulo $p^k q$, " in Proc. of Crypto'98, LNCS 1462, pp.318–326, 1998.
14. T. Takagi, "A Fast RSA-Type Public-Key Primitive Modulo $p^k q$ Using Hensel Lifting," IEICE Trans. Fundamentals, Vol. 87-A, no. 1, pp. 94–101, 2004.

A   Our Matrix M Is Triangular

In this section, we describe the matrix M of Sec.3.2 more formally, and show that it is a lower triangular matrix.

We say that $g_{i,j,k}$ is the ℓth polynomial of G if it is the ℓth polynomial that is appended to G by the algorithm of Sec.3.2. For a monomial $x^a y^b$ which is included in the ℓth $g_{i,j,k}$, we say that $x^a y^b$ appears here first if it does not appear in the first $(\ell - 1)$ polynomials of G. Let $d_k = (k-1)(r+1)$. (Note that each occurrence of $x^r y$ is replaced by N.)

Lemma 4. $g_{0,0,k}$ is the $(d_k + 1)$th polynomial of G, and y^k appears here first for $1 \leq k \leq m$.

Lemma 5. $g_{1,0,k}$ is the $(d_k + 2)$th polynomial of G, and x^{k+1} appears here first for $0 \leq k \leq m$.

Lemma 6. $g_{r-i,1,k}$ is the $(d_k + i + 2)$th polynomial of G, and $x^{r-i} y^{k+1}$ appears here first for $1 \leq i \leq r - 1$ and $0 \leq k \leq m - 1$.

Lemma 7. $g_{i,0,m}$ is the $(d_m + i + 1)$th polynomial of G, and x^{i+m} appears here first for $1 \leq i \leq s$.

Lemma 8. $g_{0,j,m}$ is the $(d_m + s + j)$th polynomial of G, and x^{j+m} appears here first for $1 \leq j \leq t$.

Consider an expression of $g_{i,j,k}$ as follows.

- The leading monomial of $g_{0,0,k}$ is y^k for $1 \leq k \leq m$.
- The leading monomial of $g_{1,0,k}$ is x^{k+1} for $0 \leq k \leq m$.
- The leading monomial of $g_{r-i,1,k}$ is $x^{r-i} y^{k+1}$ for $1 \leq i \leq r - 1$ and $0 \leq k \leq m - 1$.
- The leading monomial of $g_{i,0,m}$ is x^{i+m} for $1 \leq i \leq s$.
- The leading monomial of $g_{0,j,m}$ is x^{j+m} for $1 \leq j \leq t$.

Lemma 9. In the ℓth $g_{i,j,k}$, all the monomials other than the leading one appears in some polynomial of $G_{\ell-1}$.

Let M be a $w \times w$ matrix such that ℓth row consists of the coefficients of the ℓth $g_{i,j,k}$ of G, where the leading monomial of each $g_{i,j,k}$ is given as above. Then it is easy to see that M is a lower triangular matrix from the above lemmas.

The proofs of the lemmas will be given in the full version.

Efficient Pseudorandom Generators Based on the DDH Assumption

Reza Rezaeian Farashahi[1,2], Berry Schoenmakers[1], and Andrey Sidorenko[1]

[1] Dept. of Mathematics and Computer Science, TU Eindhoven,
P.O. Box 513, 5600 MB Eindhoven, The Netherlands
[2] Dept. of Mathematical Sciences, Isfahan University of Technology,
P.O. Box 85145 Isfahan, Iran

Abstract. A family of pseudorandom generators based on the decisional Diffie-Hellman assumption is proposed. The new construction is a modified and generalized version of the Dual Elliptic Curve generator proposed by Barker and Kelsey. Although the original Dual Elliptic Curve generator is shown to be insecure, the modified version is provably secure and very efficient in comparison with the other pseudorandom generators based on discrete log assumptions.

Our generator can be based on any group of prime order provided that an additional requirement is met (i.e., there exists an efficiently computable function that in some sense enumerates the elements of the group). Two specific instances are presented. The techniques used to design the instances, for example, the new probabilistic randomness extractor are of independent interest for other applications.

1   Introduction

A pseudorandom generator is a deterministic algorithm that converts a short sequence of uniformly distributed random bits into a longer sequence of bits that cannot be distinguished from uniformly random by a computationally bounded algorithm. It is known that a pseudorandom generator can be constructed from any one-way function [13]. Thus, intractability of the discrete logarithm problem suffices to construct a pseudorandom generator. Such a construction was first proposed by Blum and Micali [2]. However, the Blum-Micali pseudorandom generator and similar ones are inefficient in the sense that only a single bit is output per modular exponentiation. In this paper, we show that the stronger assumption that the decisional Diffie-Hellman problem is hard to solve (DDH assumption) gives rise to much more efficient pseudorandom generators.

Using strong assumptions in order to improve performance of cryptographic schemes is a common practice nowadays. In particular, several pseudorandom generators based on strong number theoretic assumptions have been proposed during the last decade. For instance, Patel and Sundaram [25], Gennaro [8] show that efficient pseudorandom generators can be built if one assumes that computing discrete logarithms with short exponents is a hard problem. Steinfeld et al. [29] propose an improved version of the well-known RSA generator assuming the

T. Okamoto and X. Wang (Eds.): PKC 2007, LNCS 4450, pp. 426–441, 2007.

intractability of a strong variant of the RSA problem. In comparison with many other assumptions, the DDH assumption is thoroughly studied (for more details about intractability of the DDH problem, refer e.g. to [24]) and has become a basis for a wide variety of cryptographic schemes.

Security of our construction is tightly related to the intractability of the DDH problem.

1.1 Related Work

Our work is inspired by the publication of Barker and Kelsey [1], in which the so-called Dual Elliptic Curve generator is proposed. Let P and Q be points on a prime order elliptic curve over a prime field $\mathbb{F}_p$ such that p is close to 2^{256}. Let q denote the order of the curve. On input s_0 chosen uniformly at random from $\mathbb{Z}_q$ the Dual Elliptic Curve generator produces two sequences of points $s_i P$ and $s_i Q$ such that s_i is set to be the x-coordinate of $s_{i-1}P$, $i = 1, 2, \ldots, k$. The generator outputs k binary strings each string consisting of the 240 least significant bits of the x-coordinate of $s_i Q$. The sequence of points $s_i Q$ is shown to be indistinguishable from the sequence of uniformly random points of the elliptic curve under the assumption that the DDH problem and the non-standard x-logarithm problem are intractable in $\mathrm{E}(\mathbb{F}_p)$ [3]. However, the binary sequence produced by the generator turns out to be distinguishable from uniform. The reason is that points of the elliptic curve are transformed into random bits in an improper way [10,27].

Some ideas of the Dual Elliptic Curve generator are present in the earlier work by Naor and Reingold [24]. Let p be a prime and let g be a generator of a subgroup of $\mathbb{Z}_p^*$ of prime order q. Let $a \in \mathbb{Z}_q$ be a fixed number. Naor and Reingold [24] propose a simple function G that on input $b \in \mathbb{Z}_q$ outputs (g^b, g^{ab}). If b is chosen uniformly at random, the output of the function is computationally indistinguishable from uniform under the DDH assumption in the subgroup. Note, however, that function G produces random elements of the subgroup rather than random bits and therefore it is not a pseudorandom generator in the sense of Definition 1 (converting random elements of the subgroup into random bits is a nontrivial problem). Moreover, although function G doubles the input it cannot be iterated to produce as much pseudorandomness as required by the application. Namely, it is not clear how to produce a new value of b given two group elements g^b and g^{ab}. Accordingly, the goal of Naor and Reingold [24] is to construct not a pseudorandom generator but a pseudorandom function, for which function G turns out to be a suitable building block.

1.2 Our Contributions

We modify and generalize the Dual Elliptic Curve generator such that the modified version is provably secure under the DDH assumption. In comparison with the original Dual Elliptic Curve generator, our generator can be based on any group of prime order meeting an additional requirement (i.e., there exists an efficiently computable function that in some sense enumerates the elements of the group). The new generator is more efficient than all known pseudorandom generators based on discrete log assumptions.

We present two specific instances of the new pseudorandom generator.

The first instance is based on the group of quadratic residues modulo a safe prime $p = 2q+1$. This instance uses an elegant idea of Cramer and Shoup [5] who show that there exists a simple bijective function that maps quadratic residues modulo p to $\mathbb{Z}_q$.

The second instance is based on an arbitrary prime order subgroup of $\mathbb{Z}_p^*$, where p is prime but not necessarily a safe prime. To construct this instance, we first propose a surprisingly simple probabilistic randomness extractor that provided with some extra randomness converts a uniformly random element of the subgroup of order q into a uniformly random number in $\mathbb{Z}_q$, which in turn can be easily converted into a string of *uniformly random bits* using, for instance, algorithm Q_2 from [15] (for an overview of probabilistic randomness extractors, refer to [28]). Note that all (probabilistic and deterministic) extractors known so far can only convert random elements of the subgroup into *bits that are statistically close to uniform*.

We derive the security parameters of the new pseudorandom generators from the corresponding security reductions. For this purpose, we make practical assumptions about intractability of the discrete logarithm problems in the corresponding groups.

2   Preliminaries

In this section, we introduce some conventions and recall basic definitions.

2.1   Notation

Let x and y be random variables taking on values in a finite set S. The statistical distance between x and y is defined as

$$\Delta(x,y) = \frac{1}{2} \sum_{\alpha \in S} |\Pr[x = \alpha] - \Pr[y = \alpha]|.$$

We say that algorithm $\mathcal{D}$ distinguishes x and y with advantage ϵ if and only if

$$|\Pr[\mathcal{D}(x) = 1] - \Pr[\mathcal{D}(y) = 1]| \geq \epsilon.$$

If the statistical distance between x and y is less than ϵ then no algorithm distinguishes x and y with advantage ϵ (see, e.g., [20, Exercise 22]).

Throughout, we let U_m denote a random variable uniformly distributed on $\mathbb{Z}_m$. And, we say that an algorithm is T-time if it halts in time at most T.

2.2   Pseudorandom Generators

Consider a deterministic algorithm PRG $: \{0,1\}^n \mapsto \{0,1\}^M$, where $M > n$. Loosely speaking, PRG is called a pseudorandom generator if it maps uniformly distributed input into an output which is computationally indistinguishable from uniform. The input is called the seed and the output is called the pseudorandom sequence. The precise definition is given below.

A T-time algorithm $\mathcal{D} : \{0,1\}^M \mapsto \{0,1\}$ is said to be a (T, ϵ)-distinguisher for PRG if

$$| \Pr[\mathcal{D}(\mathsf{PRG}(U_{2^n})) = 1] - \Pr[\mathcal{D}(U_{2^M}) = 1] | \geq \epsilon. \qquad (1)$$

Definition 1 (Pseudorandom generator). *Algorithm* PRG *is called a* (T, ϵ)-*secure pseudorandom generator if no* (T, ϵ)-*distinguisher exists for* PRG.

An important question is what level of security (T, ϵ) suffices for practical applications of pseudorandom generators. Unfortunately, the level of security is often chosen arbitrarily. Knuth ([17], p. 176) sets $\epsilon = 0.01$ and consider several values for T up to $53.5 \cdot 10^{12}$ Mips-Years[1]. In [6], the security level is set to $T = 1$ Mips-Year and $\epsilon = 0.01$. In [8], $T = 3.5 \cdot 10^{10}$ Mips-Years, $\epsilon = 0.01$.

The fact that a pseudorandom generator is (T, ϵ)-secure does not automatically mean that the generator is (T', ϵ')-secure for all T' and ϵ' such that $T'/\epsilon' \leq T/\epsilon$. For instance, if a pseudorandom generator is $(T, 0.01)$-secure it does not necessarily mean that the generator is $(T', 0.009)$-secure even if $T \gg T'$. The reason is that a $(T', 0.009)$-distinguisher cannot always be transformed into a $(T, 0.01)$-distinguisher. Indeed, the only way to improve the success probability of the distinguisher is to run it several times on the same input. However, the latter does not always help since there might be "bad" inputs, that is, inputs for which the success probability of the distinguisher is very low or equals 0.

It is reasonable to require that a pseudorandom generator is secure for *all* pairs (T, ϵ) such that the *time-success ratio* T/ϵ is below a certain bound that is set to be 2^{80} time units throughout this paper (the time unit is defined in Section 2.4). Time-success ratio is a standard way to define security of cryptographic schemes [20,13].

2.3   Decisional Diffie-Hellman Problem

Let $\mathbb{G}$ be a multiplicative group of prime order q. For $x, y \in \mathbb{G}$ and $s \in \mathbb{Z}_q$ such that $y = x^s$, s is called the discrete logarithm of y to the base x. We write $s = \log_x y$. The discrete logarithm (DL) problem is to find s given x and y.

Definition 2 (DDH problem). *Let* $X_{DDH} \in \mathbb{G}^4$ *be a random variable uniformly distributed on the set consisting of all 4-tuples* $(x, y, v, w) \in \mathbb{G}^4$ *such that* $\log_x v = \log_y w$ *and let* $Y_{DDH} \in_R \mathbb{G}^4$. *Algorithm* $\mathcal{D}$ *is said to solve the decisional Diffie-Hellman (DDH) problem in* $\mathbb{G}$ *with advantage* ϵ *if it distinguishes the random variables* X_{DDH} *and* Y_{DDH} *with advantage* ϵ, *that is,*

$$| \Pr[\mathcal{D}(X_{DDH}) = 1] - \Pr[\mathcal{D}(Y_{DDH}) = 1] | \geq \epsilon.$$

---

[1] A Mips-Year is defined as the amount of computation that can be performed in one year by a single DEC VAX 11/780 (see also [19]).

Related to the decisional Diffie-Hellman problem is the computational Diffie-Hellman (CDH) problem (given x, y and x^s, compute y^s).

Clearly, the DL problem is at least as hard to solve as the CDH problem. The CDH problem is proved to be equivalent to the DL problem under certain conditions [21,22]. Moreover, no groups are known such that the CDH problem is strictly easier to solve than the DL problem. The common practice is to assume that these two problems are equally hard.

On the other hand, there exist groups (e.g., $\mathbb{Z}_p^*$) in which a random instance of the CDH problem is believed to be hard while the DDH problem is easy. The latter groups are referred to as the non-DDH groups [9]. Furthermore, Wolf [30] shows that for *all* groups $\mathbb{G}$ an algorithm that solves the DDH problem in $\mathbb{G}$ is of no help for solving the CDH problem in $\mathbb{G}$. However, the computational gap between the DDH problem and the CDH problem is difficult to estimate. It is believed that except for the non-DDH groups, there is no way to solve the DDH problem rather than to solve the CDH problem.

We do not use non-DDH groups in this paper. To compute security parameters for the pseudorandom generators, we assume that the DDH problem and the DL problem are equally hard, in agreement with common practice. We formalize this as follows.

Let T_{DL} be the running time of the best known algorithm for solving a random instance of the DL problem in a group $\mathbb{G}$. Of course, T_{DL} depends on the group $\mathbb{G}$, that is, $T_{DL} = T_{DL}(\mathbb{G})$. For instance, in the case of finite fields, T_{DL} corresponds to the running time of the discrete logarithm variant of the Number Field Sieve, while for most of the ordinary elliptic curves the best known algorithms are the exponential square root attacks.

Assumption 1. *Unless $\mathbb{G}$ is a non-DDH group, no T-time algorithm solves the DDH problem in $\mathbb{G}$ with probability ϵ if $T/\epsilon \leq T_{DL}(\mathbb{G})$.*

2.4   Conventions

Time Units. A unit of time has to be set to measure the running time of the algorithms. Throughout this paper, the unit of time is one DES encryption. According to the data from [19], a software implementation of DES is estimated to take about 360 Pentium clock cycles. Therefore, we assign

$$1 \text{ time unit} = 360 \text{ Pentium clock cycles.}$$

Security level. The table by Lenstra and Verheul [19] implies that 2^{80} DES encryptions will be infeasible for classical computers until the year 2013. Therefore, we set 2^{80} time units as the security level to be reached.

Modular multiplication cost. In [19], it is reported that multiplication modulo p takes about $(\log_2 p)^2/24$ Pentium clock cycles, that is,

$$(\log_2 p)^2/(24 \cdot 360) \text{ time units.}$$

Complexity of discrete logarithm variant of the NFS. The discrete logarithm variant of the Number Field Sieve (NFS) algorithm solves the discrete logarithm problem in a n-bit prime field in expected time $L(n) =$

$A \exp((1.9229 + o(1))(n \ln 2)^{1/3}(\ln(n \ln 2))^{2/3})$, where A is a constant. Following [19], we assume that the $o(1)$-term is zero and estimate the constant A from experimental data. Unfortunately, practical experience with the discrete logarithm variant of the NFS is limited. On the other hand, there are several data points for the Number Field Sieve factoring algorithm. For instance, factoring a 512-bit integer is reported to take about $3 \cdot 10^{17}$ Pentium clock cycles [19]. Since computing discrete logarithms in n-bit fields takes about the same amount of time as factoring n-bit integers for any n in the current range of interest (cf. [19]), this suggests that $A \approx 4.7 \cdot 10^{-5}$ and thus

$$L(n) = 4.7 \cdot 10^{-5} \exp(1.9229(n \ln 2)^{1/3}(\ln(n \ln 2))^{2/3}) \text{ time units.}$$

It is believed that the discrete logarithm problem in the extension field is as hard as the discrete logarithm problem in the prime field of similar size (cf. [18]).

3   DDH Generator

In this section, our main result is presented. We propose a new provably secure pseudorandom generator. We call it the *DDH generator*, since the security of this generator relies on the intractability of the DDH problem in the corresponding group. In contrast with the Dual Elliptic Curve generator [1], the DDH generator can be based on *any* group of prime order provided that an additional requirement is met (i.e., there exists an efficiently computable function enum that "enumerates" the elements of the group).

3.1   Construction of the Generator

Let $\mathbb{G}$ be a multiplicative group of prime order q and let enum $: \mathbb{G} \times \mathbb{Z}_l \mapsto \mathbb{Z}_q \times \mathbb{Z}_l$, $l > 0$, be a bijection. Thus, on uniformly distributed input, function enum produces uniformly distributed output. Typically, but not necessarily, l is chosen to be small. The advantage of a smaller l is that the seed of the generator is shorter.

Let $x, y \in_R \mathbb{G}$. The seed of the DDH generator (Algorithm 1) is $s_0 \in_R \mathbb{Z}_q$ and $\mathsf{randp}_0, \mathsf{randq}_0 \in_R \mathbb{Z}_l$. The DDH generator transforms the seed into the sequence of k pseudorandom numbers from $\mathbb{Z}_q$.

Note that the random elements x and y are not part of the seed. These two elements are system parameters that are not necessarily kept secret. In the security analysis of the generator we assume that x and y are known to the distinguisher.

3.2   Security Analysis

The following theorem implies that under the DDH assumption for group $\mathbb{G}$ an output sequence of the DDH generator is indistinguishable from a sequence of uniformly random numbers in $\mathbb{Z}_q$.

Algorithm 1. DDH generator

Input: $s_0 \in \mathbb{Z}_q$, $\mathrm{randp}_0 \in \mathbb{Z}_l$, $\mathrm{randq}_0 \in \mathbb{Z}_l$, $k > 0$
Output: k pseudorandom integers from $\mathbb{Z}_q$
    for $i = 1$ to k **do**
        Set $(s_i, \mathrm{randp}_i) \leftarrow \mathrm{enum}_2(x^{s_{i-1}}, \mathrm{randp}_{i-1})$
        Set $(\mathrm{output}_i, \mathrm{randq}_i) \leftarrow \mathrm{enum}_2(y^{s_{i-1}}, \mathrm{randq}_{i-1})$
    end for
    Return $\mathrm{output}_1, \ldots, \mathrm{output}_k$

Theorem 2. *Suppose there exists a T-time algorithm that distinguishes the output of the DDH generator from the sequence of independent uniformly distributed random numbers in $\mathbb{Z}_q$ with advantage ϵ. Then the DDH problem in $\mathbb{G}$ can be solved in time T with advantage ϵ/k.*

Proof. Suppose there exists a T-time algorithm $\mathcal{D}$ that distinguishes the output of the DDH generator from a sequence of independent uniformly distributed random numbers in $\mathbb{Z}_q$ with advantage ϵ, that is,

$$| \Pr[\mathcal{D}(\mathrm{output}_1, \ldots, \mathrm{output}_k) = 1] - \Pr[\mathcal{D}(U) = 1] | \geq \epsilon,$$

where $U = (u_1, \ldots, u_k)$, $u_i \in_R \mathbb{Z}_q$, $i = 1, \ldots, k$. Let $j \in_R \{1, 2, \ldots, k\}$. Due to the classical hybrid argument (see, e.g., [11, Section 3.2.3]),

$$| \Pr[\mathcal{D}(Z_j) = 1] - \Pr[\mathcal{D}(Z_{j+1}) = 1] | \geq \epsilon/k,$$

where

$$Z_j = (u_1, \ldots, u_{j-1}, \mathrm{output}_1, \ldots, \mathrm{output}_{k-j+1}),$$
$$Z_{j+1} = (u_1, \ldots, u_{j-1}, u_j, \mathrm{output}_1, \ldots, \mathrm{output}_{k-j}),$$

the probability is taken not only over internal coin flips of $\mathcal{D}$ but also over the choice of j. Now, we show how to solve the DDH problem in $\mathbb{G}$ using the distinguisher $\mathcal{D}$ as a building block. Let $(x, y, v, w) \in \mathbb{G}^4$. A solver for the DDH problem decides if $\log_x v = \log_y w$ or v and w are independent uniformly distributed random elements of $\mathbb{G}$ as follows.

    Select $j \leftarrow_R \{1, 2, \ldots, k\}$
    Select $r_1, \ldots, r_{j-1} \leftarrow_R \mathbb{Z}_q$, $\mathrm{randp}_0 \leftarrow_R \mathbb{Z}_l$, $\mathrm{randq}_0 \leftarrow_R \mathbb{Z}_l$
    Set $(s_1, \mathrm{randp}_1) \leftarrow \mathrm{enum}(v, \mathrm{randp}_0)$
    Set $(r_j, \mathrm{randq}_1) \leftarrow \mathrm{enum}(w, \mathrm{randq}_0)$
    for $i = 2$ to $k - j$ **do**
        Set $(s_i, \mathrm{randp}_i) \leftarrow \mathrm{enum}(x^{s_{i-1}}, \mathrm{randp}_{i-1})$
        Set $(r_{i+j-1}, \mathrm{randq}_i) \leftarrow \mathrm{enum}(y^{s_{i-1}}, \mathrm{randq}_{i-1})$
    end for
    Set $Z \leftarrow (r_1, \ldots, r_k)$
    Return $\mathcal{D}(Z)$

If there exists $s_0 \in \mathbb{Z}_q$ such that $v = x^{s_0}$ and $w = y^{s_0}$ then r_j and r_{j+1} are distributed as the first and the second outputs of the DDH generator respectively, so Z is distributed as Z_j.

Otherwise, if v and w are independent uniformly distributed random elements of $\mathbb{G}$ then r_{j+1} is distributed as the first output of the DDH generator while r_j is uniformly distributed over $\mathbb{Z}_q$ and independent of r_{j+1}, so Z is distributed as Z_{j+1}.

Therefore, the above algorithm solves the DDH problem in $\mathbb{G}$ in time at most T with advantage ϵ/k.

The DDH generator is not a pseudorandom generator in terms of Definition 1. It outputs numbers in $\mathbb{Z}_q$ rather than bits. However, converting random numbers into random bits is a relatively easy problem. For instance, one can use Algorithm Q_2 from [15], which was presented without analysis. It can actually be shown, however, that Algorithm Q_2 produces on average $n - 2$ bits given a uniformly distributed random number U_q, where n denotes the bit length of q. In the latter case, the average number of bits produced by the generator is $k(n - 2)$.

For the sake of simplicity, throughout this paper, we assume that q is close to a power of 2, that is, $0 \leq (2^n - q)/2^n \leq \delta$ for a small δ. So, the uniform element U_q is statistically close to n uniformly random bits.

The following simple lemma is a well-known result (the proof can be found, for instance, in [4]).

Lemma 1. *Under the condition that $0 \leq (2^n - q)/2^n \leq \delta$, the statistical distance between U_q and U_{2^n} is bounded above by δ.*

The next statement implies that if q is close to a power of 2, the DDH generator is a cryptographically secure pseudorandom generator under the DDH assumption in $\mathbb{G}$.

Corollary 1. *Let $0 \leq (2^n - q)/2^n \leq \delta$. Suppose the DDH generator is not (T, ϵ)-secure. Then there exists an algorithm that solves the DDH problem in $\mathbb{G}$ in time at most T with advantage $\epsilon/k - \delta$.*

Proof. Suppose there exists a distinguisher $\mathcal{D} : \{0, 1\}^{kn} \mapsto \{0, 1\}$ that runs in time at most T and

$$| \Pr[\mathcal{D}(\text{output}_1, \ldots, \text{output}_k) = 1] - \Pr[\mathcal{D}(U_{2^{kn}}) = 1] | \geq \epsilon.$$

Let $u_i \in_R \mathbb{Z}_q$, $i = 1, \ldots, k$, and $U = (u_1, \ldots, u_k)$. Lemma 1 implies that the statistical distance $\Delta(U, U_{2^{kn}}) \leq k\delta$. Thus,

$$| \Pr[\mathcal{D}(\text{output}_1, \ldots, \text{output}_k) = 1] - \Pr[\mathcal{D}(U) = 1] | \geq \epsilon - k\delta.$$

Now, the statement follows from Theorem 2.

4   Specific Instances of the DDH Generator

To implement the DDH generator, one has to choose the group $\mathbb{G}$ of prime order q and function enum that enumerates the group elements. In this section, we propose two specific instances of the DDH generator.

Throughout this section we assume that q is close to a power of 2, that is, $0 \leq (2^n - q)/2^n \leq \delta$ for a small δ and some integer n. We like to emphasize that this assumption is made for the sake of simplicity only. M denotes the total number of pseudorandom bits produced by the generator.

4.1   Group of Quadratic Residues Modulo Safe Prime

To construct the first instance of the DDH generator, we use an elegant idea of Cramer and Shoup [5] who show that there exists a simple deterministic function that enumerates elements of the group of quadratic residues modulo safe prime p.

Let p be a safe prime, $p = 2q + 1$, where q is prime. Let $\mathbb{G}_1$ be a group of nonzero quadratic residues modulo p. The order of $\mathbb{G}_1$ equals q. Consider the following function $\mathsf{enum}_1 : \mathbb{G}_1 \mapsto \mathbb{Z}_q$,

$$\mathsf{enum}_1(x) = \begin{cases} x, & \text{if } 1 \leq x \leq q; \\ p - x, & \text{if } q + 2 \leq x < p; \\ 0, & \text{otherwise.} \end{cases}$$

It is shown in [5] that function enum_1 is a bijection. Moreover, enum_1 does not require any additional input, so in terms of Section 3.1 $l = 1$.

Let $x, y \in \mathbb{G}_1$. Let $s_0 \in_R \mathbb{Z}_q$ be the seed. Generator PRG_1 (Algorithm 4.1) is a deterministic algorithm that transforms the seed into the sequence of kn pseudorandom bits.

Algorithm 2. Generator PRG_1

Input: $s_0 \in \mathbb{Z}_q, k > 0$
Output: kn pseudorandom bits
   for $i = 1$ to k **do**
      Set $s_i \leftarrow \mathsf{enum}_1(x^{s_{i-1}})$
      Set $\mathsf{output}_i = \mathsf{enum}_1(y^{s_{i-1}})$
   end for
   Return $\mathsf{output}_1, \ldots, \mathsf{output}_k$

The next statement follows from Corollary 1.

Proposition 1. *Suppose pseudorandom generator* PRG_1 *is not* (T, ϵ)*-secure. Then there exists an algorithm that solves the DDH problem in* $\mathbb{G}_1$ *in time at most* T *with advantage* $\epsilon/k - \delta$.

The seed length n plays the role of security parameter of the generator. Clearly, smaller n gives rise to a faster generator. On the other hand, for larger n the generator is more secure. Our goal is to select n as small as possible such that the generator is (T, ϵ)-secure for all T, ϵ such that $T/\epsilon < 2^{80}$ time units.

For $\delta = \epsilon/(2k)$, the generator is (T, ϵ)-secure if

$$2kT/\epsilon < T_{DL}(\mathbb{G}_1), \tag{2}$$

where $T_{DL}(\mathbb{G}_1)$ is the running time of the fastest known method for solving the discrete logarithm problem in $\mathbb{G}_1$. According to the current state of the art, we set $T_{DL}(\mathbb{G}_1)$ to be the running time of the discrete logarithm variant of the Number Field Sieve $L(n)$ (see Section 2.4). Note that $k = M/n$. Then, (2) holds if $2MT/(n\epsilon) < L(n)$. For $M = 2^{20}$ and $T/\epsilon = 2^{80}$, the smallest parameter n that satisfies the above inequality is $n \approx 1600$.

Recall that q satisfies $0 \leq (2^n - q)/2^n \leq \delta$. We have assumed that $\delta = \epsilon/(2k)$. For $M = 2^{20}$, $n = 1600$, and $\epsilon = 2^{-80}$, this condition implies that $0 < 2^n - q < 2^{1500}$. There are plenty of safe primes $p = 2q+1$ such that $0 < 2^{1600} - q < 2^{1500}$.

4.2 Arbitrary Prime Order Subgroup of $\mathbb{Z}_p^*$

In this section, we show that the DDH generator can be based not only on the group of quadratic residues modulo a safe prime but on any prime order subgroup of $\mathbb{Z}_p^*$, where p is a prime but not necessarily a safe prime.

Let q be a prime factor of $p-1$, $p-1 = lq$, $l \geq 2$, such that $\gcd(l, q) = 1$. If p is a safe prime then $l = 2$. Denote by $\mathbb{G}_2$ a subgroup of $\mathbb{Z}_p^*$ of order q. Throughout this section, multiplication of integers is done modulo p.

Let $\text{split}_2 : \mathbb{Z}_p^* \mapsto \mathbb{Z}_q \times \mathbb{Z}_l$ denote a bijection that splits an element of $\mathbb{Z}_p^*$ into two smaller numbers. An example of split_2 is a function that on input $z \in \mathbb{Z}_p^*$ returns $(z - 1) \bmod q$ and $\lfloor (z - 1)/q \rfloor$. Let $t \in \mathbb{Z}_p^*$ be an element of order l. Let $\text{enum}_2 : \mathbb{G}_2 \times \mathbb{Z}_l \mapsto \mathbb{Z}_q \times \mathbb{Z}_l$ be the following function:

$$\text{enum}_2(x, \text{rand}) = \text{split}_2(xt^{\text{rand}}),$$

where $x \in \mathbb{G}_2$, $\text{rand} \in \mathbb{Z}_l$. The following lemma shows that enum_2 is a bijection and thus it is suitable for building the DDH generator.

Lemma 2. *Function* enum_2 *defined above is a bijection.*

Proof. Let $f : \mathbb{G}_2 \times \mathbb{Z}_l \mapsto \mathbb{Z}_p^*$ be defined as $f(x, \text{rand}) = xt^{\text{rand}} \bmod p$ for $x \in \mathbb{G}_2$ and $\text{rand} \in \mathbb{Z}_l$. To prove the statement of the lemma, we first show that f is a bijection.

Suppose that $x_1 t^{\text{rand}_1} = x_2 t^{\text{rand}_2}$ for $x_i \in \mathbb{G}_2$, $\text{rand}_i \in \mathbb{Z}_l$, $i = 1, 2$. Since $x_2 \in \mathbb{G}_2$, $x_2 \neq 0$. Then, $x_1/x_2 = t^{\text{rand}_1 - \text{rand}_2} \in \mathbb{G}_2$, so $t^{q(\text{rand}_1 - \text{rand}_2)} = 1$. Therefore, l divides $q(\text{rand}_1 - \text{rand}_2)$. Since $\gcd(q, l) = 1$, it implies that l divides $\text{rand}_1 - \text{rand}_2$. The latter implies that $\text{rand}_1 = \text{rand}_2$ and thus $x_1 = x_2$.

Therefore, f is indeed a bijection and thus enum_2 is also a bijection as a composition of two bijective functions.

Let PRG_2 denote the instance of the DDH generator that uses the group $\mathbb{G}_2$ and the function enum_2 defined above. The next statement follows from Corollary 1.

Proposition 2. *Suppose pseudorandom generator* PRG_2 *is not* (T, ϵ)*-secure. Then there exists an algorithm that solves the DDH problem in* $\mathbb{G}_2$ *in time at most* T *with advantage* $\epsilon/k - \delta$.

Let m denote the bit length of p. At each step $i = 1, \ldots, n$, pseudorandom generator PRG_2 computes $x^{s_{i-1}}$ and $y^{s_{i-1}}$ and then uses these elements to evaluate the corresponding outcomes of function enum_2. Therefore, each step implies two modular exponentiations with n-bit exponents and two modular exponentiations with $(m - n)$-bit exponents. Since PRG_2 outputs n bits per step the computational effort per output bit is proportional to m^3/n. Our goal is now to determine parameters m and n that minimize the computational effort under the condition that the generator is (T, ϵ)-secure for all T, ϵ satisfying $T/\epsilon < 2^{80}$.

For $\delta = \epsilon/(2k)$, generator PRG_2 is (T, ϵ)-secure if

$$2kT/\epsilon < T_{DL}(\mathbb{G}_2), \tag{3}$$

where $T_{DL}(\mathbb{G}_2)$ is the running time of the fastest known method for solving the discrete logarithm problem in $\mathbb{G}_2$. The best algorithms for solving the discrete logarithm problem in $\mathbb{G}_2$ are Pollard's rho method in $\mathbb{G}_2$ and the discrete logarithm variant of the Number Field Sieve in the full multiplicative group $\mathbb{Z}_p^*$. The running time of Pollard's rho method is estimated to be $0.88\sqrt{q}$ group operations (cf. [19]). Since $k = M/n$, condition (3) implies that

$$2MT/(n\epsilon) < \min[L(m),\ 0.88 \cdot 2^{n/2} m^2/(24 \cdot 360)].$$

For $M = 2^{20}$, $T/\epsilon = 2^{80}$, the above condition is satisfied for $m \gtrsim 1600$, $n \gtrsim 160$. The computational effort is minimized if $n \approx m$.

In comparison with PRG_1, the seed of PRG_2 is somewhat longer, although if $n \approx m$ it is roughly of the same size. Moreover, PRG_2 is less efficient than PRG_1 in terms of computational effort since computation of enum_2 implies a modular exponentiation while enum_1 implies at most 1 integer subtraction. A significant advantage of PRG_2 versus PRG_1 is that the former can be based on any prime order subgroup of $\mathbb{Z}_p^*$ for any prime p provided that the size of the subgroup is sufficiently large to resist Pollard's rho attack.

4.3   Discussion

Function enum_2 used as a building block of generator PRG_2 is of independent interest. The reason is that this function can be viewed as a *probabilistic randomness extractor* (for an overview of probabilistic randomness extractors, refer to [28]). Provided with some extra randomness, it converts a uniformly random element of a subgroup of $\mathbb{Z}_p^*$ of order q into a uniformly random number in $\mathbb{Z}_q$, which in turn can be easily converted into a string of *uniformly random bits* using, for instance, algorithm Q_2 from [15]. Note that all (probabilistic and deterministic) extractors known so far can only convert random elements of the subgroup into *bits that are statistically close to uniform*.

The new extractor can be used not only for designing pseudorandom generators but also for key exchange protocols to convert the random group element shared by the parties involved into the random binary string.

If the size of the subgroup q is sufficiently large, our extractor is more efficient than the general purpose probabilistic randomness extractors (e.g., the universal hash functions [13]) in terms of the number of extra random bits required. For instance, if the statistical distance to be reached is 2^{-80} our extractor requires less extra randomness than universal hash functions if the size of the subgroup is at least $p/2^{160}$. If the size of the subgroup is close to the size of the group p, our extractor requires just few extra random bits.

The recently proposed deterministic extractor by Fouque et al. [7] does not require any extra randomness to produce the output. However, it extracts substantially less than half of the bits of a uniformly distributed random element of the subgroup. Our extractor does require extra randomness rand $\in \mathbb{Z}_l$, $l \geq 1$, but one gets this randomness back in the sense that the extractor outputs not only the integer from $\mathbb{Z}_q$ but also an element of $\mathbb{Z}_l$. The crucial advantage of our extractor is that it *extracts all the bits of the subgroup element.*

5   Generator PRG_1 Versus Gennaro's Generator

In this section, we compare PRG_1 with the well-known Gennaro's generator [8] in the setting of concrete security. For both generators, we determine parameters (e.g., the size of the seed) such that a desired level of provable security is reached, while minimizing the computational effort per output bit.

Security of Gennaro's generator is based on a variant of the discrete logarithm problem, that is, the discrete logarithm with short exponent (DLSE) problem. Let x, y be elements of a multiplicative group $\mathbb{G}$. The c-DLSE problem is to find s, $0 \leq s < 2^c$, such that $y = x^s$ given x, y and the parameter c. Clearly, the DLSE problem is not harder to solve than the original discrete logarithm problem.

Now, we recall the basic results of [8].

Let g be a generator of $\mathbb{Z}_p^*$, where p is an n-bit safe prime. For a nonnegative integer x let $\ell_j(x) \in \{0, 1\}$ denote the j-th least significant bit of x:

$$x = \sum_j \ell_j(x) 2^{j-1}.$$

Let $x_1 \in_R \mathbb{Z}_{p-1}$ be the seed. Gennaro's generator (Algorithm 3) transforms the seed into the pseudorandom sequence of length $k(n - c - 1)$.

The following statement is the concrete version of Theorem 2 of [8].

Theorem 3 (Gennaro). *Suppose Gennaro's pseudorandom generator is not (T, ϵ)-secure. Then there exists an algorithm that solves the c-DLSE in $\mathbb{Z}_p^*$ in time $8c(\ln c)(k/\epsilon)^3 T$ with probability $1/2$.*

Gennaro's generator outputs $(n - c - 1)$ bits per modular exponentiation with c-bit exponent. The standard right-to-left exponentiation costs on average $c/2$ multiplications and c squarings. Assume that a squaring modulo p takes about 80% of the time of a multiplication modulo p (cf. [18]). Then, the average computational effort is $1.3cn^2/(24 \cdot 360(n - c - 1))$ time units per output bit. Our goal is now to determine n and c that minimize the computational effort under

---

Algorithm 3. Gennaro's pseudorandom generator
***
Input: $x_1 \in \mathbb{Z}_{p-1}$, $k > 0$
Output: $k(n - c - 1)$ pseudorandom bits
  for $i = 1$ to k **do**
    Set $\text{output}_i \leftarrow \ell_2(x_i), \ell_3(x_i), \ldots, \ell_{n-c}(x_i)$
    Set $x_{i+1} \leftarrow g^{\sum_{j=n-c+1}^{n} \ell_j(x_i)2^{j-1} + \ell_1(x_i)}$
  end for
  Return $\text{output}_1, \ldots, \text{output}_k$

---

the condition that the generator is (T, ϵ)-secure for all T, ϵ satisfying $T/\epsilon < 2^{80}$ with a natural limitation $T \geq 1$ time unit.

Theorem 3 implies that Gennaro's generator is (T, ϵ)-secure if

$$16c(\ln c)(k/\epsilon)^3 T < T_{DLSE}(\mathbb{Z}_p^*),$$

where $T_{DLSE}(\mathbb{Z}_p^*)$ is the running time of the fastest algorithm for solving the c-DLSE problem in $\mathbb{Z}_p^*$. The fastest algorithms for solving the DLSE problem are the discrete logarithm variant of the NFS and the Pollard's lambda method. The complexity of the latter is close to $2 \cdot 2^{c/2}$ multiplications in $\mathbb{Z}_p^*$, that is, $2^{c/2+1}n^2/(24 \cdot 360)$ time units (cf. [26]). Note that $k = M/(n - c - 1)$, where M is the total number of pseudorandom bits produced by the generator. Thus, Gennaro's generator is (T, ϵ)-secure if

$$\frac{16c(\ln c)M^3 T}{\epsilon^3(n - c - 1)^3} < \min[L(n),\ 2^{c/2+1}n^2/(24 \cdot 360)].$$

For $M = 2^{20}$, $T/\epsilon < 2^{80}$ with a natural limitation $T \geq 1$ the optimal parameters are $n \approx 18000$, $c \approx 520$.

The secure length of the modulus turns out to be quite large. Recall that generator PRG_1 is provably secure for much smaller parameter n, namely, $n \approx 1600$. The reason is that the reduction in Theorem 3 is *not tight* in the sense that a distinguisher for Gennaro's generator is transformed into the far less efficient solver for the DLSE problem (note that ϵ is raised to the power of 3 in the statement of Theorem 3). On the contrary, the reduction in Theorem 2 is much tighter.

To compare Gennaro's generator with generator PRG_1, we determine the computational effort for both generators.

1. The average computational effort of Gennaro's generator is $1.3cn^2/(24 \cdot 360(n - c - 1))$ time units per output bit. For $n = 18000$, $c = 520$, we get about 1500 time units per output bit.
2. The generator PRG_1 outputs n bits at the cost of 2 modular exponentiations with n-bit exponent. The average computational effort for $n = 1600$ is $2.6n^2/(24 \cdot 360) \approx 770$ time units per output bit.

Thus, for $M = 2^{20}$ bits to be produced and for the level of security of 2^{80} time units, generator PRG_1 is about 2 times faster than Gennaro's generator.

Furthermore, the seed length of generator PRG_1 is more than 10 times shorter (1600 bits versus 18000 bits).

We draw the attention of the reader to the way the comparison is done. At first sight, it seems that Gennaro's generator is more efficient than generator PRG_1 since Gennaro's generator outputs almost n bits per modular exponentiation with a short c-bit exponent, while generator PRG_1 outputs n bits per 2 exponentiations with a full-size exponent. However, *it should not be neglected* that the n's in these two cases are different. Due to the tighter reduction, generator PRG_1 is provably secure for much smaller n. This is the main reason why generator PRG_1 turns out to be more efficient for the same level of security.

6 Concluding Remarks and Open Problems

Independent of our work, Jiang recently proposed a pseudorandom generator which is also provably secure under the DDH assumption [14]. The security properties of Jiang's generator are similar to ours (hence his generator compares similarly to Gennaro's generator). On the other hand, in comparison with our construction Jiang's generator has two major disadvantages. Firstly, Jiang's generator can be based only on the group of quadratic residues modulo a safe prime while our construction extends to many other groups of prime order. Secondly, the seed of our generator PRG_1 is twice as short as the seed of Jiang's generator.

The seed length is a critical issue for pseudorandom generators. For instance, if a pseudorandom generator is used as a keystream generator for a stream cipher the seed length corresponds to the length of the secret key. Also, from a theoretical point of view, the seed length is perhaps the most important parameter of a pseudorandom generator, as discussed in detail in the recent paper by Haitner et al. [12].

In this respect, we make the following observation. The seed of Jiang's generator can be reduced in length by a factor of two, making it as short as the seed of our generator PRG_1, provided one assumes the intractability of the so-called square decisional Diffie-Hellman problem (see, e.g., [31]). The modification to Jiang's generator is to update the state A_t as follows: set $A_t = g^{|A_{t-1}|_p^2}$, using the notation of [14], rather than setting $A_t = g^{|A_{t-2}|_p|A_{t-1}|_p}$. Note, however, that the square decisional Diffie-Hellman problem has not been studied as extensively as the standard DDH problem.

Finally, we note that constructing an efficient provably secure pseudorandom generator based on the intractability of the DDH problem on an ordinary elliptic curve is an interesting open problem. For most ordinary elliptic curves, the best known methods for solving the elliptic curve discrete logarithm problem are the exponential square root attacks, so to reach a security level of 2^{80} time units it suffices to let the size of the group be about 160 bits. Hence, such an elliptic curve based generator would allow for a considerable reduction of the seed length, potentially to a seed of 160 bits only.

To implement the DDH generator based on an elliptic curve, one has to construct an efficiently computable function that bijectively maps the points of the curve to $\mathbb{Z}_q$, where q is the order of the group. This function seems to be difficult to construct for ordinary elliptic curves. For some supersingular elliptic curves, the function can be constructed (see, e.g., [16]). However, the latter curves cannot be used for the DDH generator since the DDH problem in these curves can be easily solved by computing Weil pairings [23].

Acknowledgements

We thank David Galindo for fruitful discussions. We also thank the anonymous referee for pointing us to the paper of Jiang [14].

References

1. E. Barker and J. Kelsey, *Recommendation for random number generation using deterministic random bit generators*, December 2005, NIST Special Publication (SP) 800-90.
2. M. Blum and S. Micali, *How to generate cryptographically strong sequences of pseudo-random bits*, SIAM Journal on Computing **13** (1984), no. 4, 850–864.
3. D. Brown, *Conjectured security of the ANSI-NIST Elliptic Curve RNG*, Cryptology ePrint Archive, Report 2006/117, 2006, http://eprint.iacr.org/.
4. O. Chevassut, P. Fouque, P. Gaudry, and D. Pointcheval, *The Twist-AUgmented Technique for Key Exchange*, Public Key Cryptography—PKC 2006, Lecture Notes in Computer Science, vol. 3958, Springer-Verlag, 2006, pp. 410–426.
5. R. Cramer and V. Shoup, *Design and analysis of practical public-key encryption schemes secure against adaptive chosen ciphertext attack*, SIAM Journal on Computing (2003), 167–226.
6. R. Fischlin and C. P. Schnorr, *Stronger security proofs for RSA and Rabin bits*, Journal of Cryptology **13** (2000), no. 2, 221–244.
7. P. Fouque, D. Pointcheval, J. Stern, and S. Zimmer, *Hardness of distinguishing the MSB or LSB of secret keys in Diffie-Hellman schemes*, ICALP (2), 2006, pp. 240–251.
8. R. Gennaro, *An improved pseudo-random generator based on the discrete logarithm problem*, Journal of Cryptology **18** (2005), no. 2, 91–110.
9. R. Gennaro, H. Krawczyk, and T. Rabin, *Secure hashed Diffie-Hellman over non-DDH groups*, Cryptology ePrint Archive, Report 2004/099, 2004, http://eprint.iacr.org/.
10. K. Gjøsteen, *Comments on Dual-EC-DRBG/NIST SP 800-90, Draft December 2005*, March 2006, http://www.math.ntnu.no/~kristiag/drafts/dual-ec-drbg-comments.pdf.
11. O. Goldreich, *Foundations of cryptography*, Cambridge University Press, Cambridge, UK, 2001.
12. I. Haitner, D. Harnik, and O. Reingold, *On the power of the randomized iterate*, Advances in Cryptology—Crypto 2006, Lecture Notes in Computer Science, vol. 4117, Springer-Verlag, 2006, pp. 22–40.
13. J. Håstad, R. Impagliazzo, L. A. Levin, and M. Luby, *Construction of a pseudorandom generator from any one-way function*, SIAM Journal on Computing **28** (1999), 1364–1396.

14. S. Jiang, *Efficient primitives from exponentiation in* $\mathbb{Z}_p$, ACISP, Lecture Notes in Computer Science, vol. 4058, Springer-Verlag, 2006, pp. 259–270.
15. A. Juels, M. Jakobsson, E. Shriver, and B. K. Hillyer, *How to turn loaded dice into fair coins*, IEEE Transactions on Information Theory **46** (2000), no. 3, 911–921.
16. B. S. Kaliski, *Elliptic curves and cryptography: A pseudorandom bit generator and other tools*, Ph.D. thesis, MIT, Cambridge, MA, USA, 1988.
17. D. E. Knuth, *Seminumerical algorithms*, third ed., vol. 3, Addison-Wesley, Reading, MA, USA, 1997.
18. A. K. Lenstra and E. R. Verheul, *The XTR public key system*, Advances in Cryptology—Crypto 2000, Lecture Notes in Computer Science, vol. 1880, Springer-Verlag, 2000, pp. 1–19.
19. _____, *Selecting cryptographic key sizes*, Journal of Cryptology **14** (2001), no. 4, 255–293.
20. M. Luby, *Pseudorandomness and cryptographic applications*, Princeton University Press, Princeton, NJ, USA, 1994.
21. U. M. Maurer, *Towards the equivalence of breaking the Diffie-Hellman protocol and computing discrete algorithms*, CRYPTO, 1994, pp. 271–281.
22. U. M. Maurer and S. Wolf, *Diffie-Hellman oracles*, CRYPTO, 1996, pp. 268–282.
23. A. Menezes, T. Okamoto, and S. A. Vanstone, *Reducing elliptic curve logarithms to logarithms in a finite field*, IEEE Transactions on Information Theory **39** (1993), no. 5, 1639–1646.
24. M. Naor and O. Reingold, *Number-theoretic constructions of efficient pseudorandom functions*, Journal of the ACM **51** (2004), no. 2, 231–262.
25. S. Patel and G. S. Sundaram, *An efficient discrete log pseudo random generator*, CRYPTO, 1998, pp. 304–317.
26. J. M. Pollard, *Kangaroos, monopoly and discrete logarithms*, Journal of Cryptology **13** (2000), no. 4, 437–447.
27. B. Schoenmakers and A. Sidorenko, *Cryptanalysis of the Dual Elliptic Curve pseudorandom generator*, Cryptology ePrint Archive, Report 2006/190, 2006, http://eprint.iacr.org/.
28. R. Shaltiel, *Recent developments in explicit constructions of extractors.*, Bulletin of the EATCS **77** (2002), 67–95.
29. R. Steinfeld, J. Pieprzyk, and H. Wang, *On the provable security of an efficient RSA-based pseudorandom generator*, Cryptology ePrint Archive, Report 2006/206, 2006, http://eprint.iacr.org/.
30. S. Wolf, *Information-theoretically and computationally secure key agreement in cryptography*, Ph.D. thesis, ETH Zurich, 1999.
31. F. Zhang, R. Safavi-Naini, and W. Susilo, *An efficient signature scheme from bilinear pairings and its applications*, Public Key Cryptography 2004, Lecture Notes in Computer Science, vol. 2947, Springer-Verlag, 2004, pp. 277–290.

Fast Batch Verification of Multiple Signatures

Jung Hee Cheon[1] and Jeong Hyun Yi[2]

[1] ISaC and Dept. of Mathematics
Seoul National University, Republic of Korea
jhcheon@snu.ac.kr
[2] Communication and Networking Lab
Samsung Advanced Institute of Technology, Republic of Korea
jeong.yi@samsung.com

Abstract. We propose an efficient batch verification of multiple signatures generated by *different signers* as well as a single signer. We first introduce a method to generate width-w Non-Adjacent Forms (w-NAFs) uniformly. We then propose a batch verification algorithm of exponentiations using w-NAF exponents, and apply this to batch verification for the modified DSA and ECDSA signatures. The performance analysis shows that our proposed method is asymptotically seven and four times as fast as individual verification in case of a single signer and multiple signers, respectively. Further, the proposed algorithm can be generalized into τ-adic w-NAFs over Koblitz curves and requires asymptotically only six elliptic curve additions per each signature for batch verification of the modified ECDSA signatures by a single singer. Our result is the first one to efficiently verify multiple signatures by multiple signers that can introduce much wider applications.

Keywords: Batch verification, exponentiation, sparse exponent, non-adjacent form, elliptic curve, Koblitz curve, Frobenius map.

1 Introduction

Batch verification was introduced by Naccache *et al.* to verify multiple signatures more efficiently [NMVR94]. Their method is to use a set of small exponents to verify multiple exponentiations simultaneously: Let G be an abelian group with a generator g. Given a batch instance of n pairs $\{(x_1, y_1), (x_2, y_2), \ldots, (x_n, y_n)\}$ with $x_i \in \mathbb{Z}$ and $y_i \in G$, the algorithm checks if $g^{\sum_{i=1}^{n} x_i s_i} = \prod_{i=1}^{n} y_i^{s_i}$ for randomly chosen $s_i \in S$, where the exponent set S is taken to be the set of e-bit prime integers for small e. This test was improved by adopting small exponent set $\{0, 1\}^{\ell}$ by Yen and Laih [YL95] and Bellare *et al.* [BGR98]. Another improvement [CL06] was obtained by taking longer integers of small weights, so called *sparse exponents*, as elements of S rather than small integers.

In this paper, we improve the previous results by employing generalized sparse exponents, so called *width-w non-adjacent forms* (w-NAFs for short). A w-NAF of weight t is a radix 2 representation satisfying: (1) each nonzero digit is an odd integer less than 2^w, (2) at most one of any w consecutive digits is nonzero,

T. Okamoto and X. Wang (Eds.): PKC 2007, LNCS 4450, pp. 442–457, 2007.

and (3) the number of nonzero digits is t. We first introduce a method to generate w-NAFs uniformly and then propose a batch verification algorithm of exponentiations using w-NAF exponents. The performance analysis shows that N exponentiations can be verified with $16N + 241$ multiplications over a finite field. In the previous method, it was $40N + 241$ and $19N + 241$ using small exponent test [BGR98] and sparse exponent test [CL06], respectively. Our verification cost becomes $14N + 235$ elliptic curve additions over elliptic curves in which a subtraction is as efficient as an addition.

To apply batch verification technique to DSA [DSA], one needs to slightly modify the signature scheme as in [NMVR94]. We apply the proposed algorithm for batch verification of the modified DSA and ECDSA signatures. The verification can be asymptotically 7.1 and 8.3 times as fast as individual verifications in a finite field and an elliptic curve with 160 bit security, respectively. Furthermore, for digital signatures by the multiple signers with the same system parameters the proposed verification performs asymptotically 4.3 and 4.8 times faster than the individual verifications in a finite field and an elliptic curve, respectively. Our result is the first one about the batch verification of signatures by different signers.

We further generalize our method to τ-adic w-NAFs over Koblitz curves. In [CL06], the authors proposed a batch verification algorithm for the modified ECDSA signatures by one signer, in which only 9 elliptic curve additions are required for one additional signature. Using τ-adic w-NAFs, we reduce it to 6 elliptic curve additions. It is very surprising that only 6 elliptic curve additions are required asymptotically to verify one signature.

Applications. Batch verification will be useful in any settings where multiple signatures need to be verified at once. We have a variety of applications in which our proposed method can be employed. In some cases, we may need to adjust our techniques. For example, in e-cash applications, merchants and/or consumers need to verify the validity of lots of electronic coins signed by the bank. E-voting systems need to verify huge number of signed ballots as fast as possible. In the outsourced database applications [MNT04], numbers of clients' query request messages need to be authenticated by servers. Another example is authenticated routing based on public key cryptography, in which network packets are signed and verified in each node and each router has to verify many signatures. We also are able to apply to Mixnet [Abe99] for making systems or protocols privacy-preserving, and VSS (Verifiable Secret Sharing) [Fel87] scheme which is a fundamental technique for fault-tolerant and secure distributed computations such as reliable broadcast, peer group membership management, and Byzantine agreement.

Organization. The rest of paper is organized as follows: we first define batch verification and introduce fast exponentiation methods in Section 2. An efficient batch verification algorithm is proposed in Section 3, and its applications to signature schemes are described in Section 4. We then present more efficient algorithm over Koblitz curves in Section 5 and conclude in Section 6.

2   Preliminary

2.1   Batch Verification

Let G be a cyclic group of prime order p with a generator g. Given a subset S of $\mathbb{Z}_p$, we define a *batch verifier* $\mathcal{V}_S$ following [BGR98, CL06]:

1. Input a batch instance $\{(x_i, y_i) \in \mathbb{Z}_p \times G | i = 1, 2, \dots, N\}$
2. $\mathcal{V}_S$ takes N elements $c_1, c_2, \dots, c_N$ uniformly from the exponent set S
3. $\mathcal{V}_S$ computes $x = \sum_{i=1}^N c_i x_i$ and $y = \prod_{i=1}^N y_i^{c_i}$
4. If $g^x = y$ output 1 and otherwise output 0

We say a batch instance $\{(x_i, y_i) \in \mathbb{Z}_p \times G | i = 1, 2, \dots, N\}$ is correct if $g^{x_i} = y_i$ for all i and incorrect otherwise. Note that the verifier $\mathcal{V}_S$ outputs 1 for a correct instance regardless of S. We define the $Fail(\mathcal{V}_S)$ to be the maximum probability that an incorrect batch instance passes the test. That is,

$$Fail(\mathcal{V}_S) = \max_{\text{A batch instance } X} \{Prob[\mathcal{V}_S(X) = 0]\}, \qquad (1)$$

where probability is over the random choice of $c_1, \dots, c_N$ uniformly from S. Then, if $c_1, c_2, \dots, c_N$ are uniformly chosen from S, we have

$$Fail(\mathcal{V}_S) = \max_{\alpha \in \mathbb{Z}_p^N \setminus \{(0,\dots,0)\}} \frac{|\{(c_1, \dots, c_n) | c_1, \dots, c_n \in S, g^{c_1 \alpha_1 + \dots + c_n \alpha_n} = 1\}|}{|\{(c_1, \dots, c_n) | c_1, \dots, c_n \in S\}|}.$$
$$(2)$$

Theorem 1 in [CL06] shows that it is upper-bounded by $1/|S|$; that is, we have $g^{x_i} = y_i$ for all i with probability at least $1 - 1/|S|$.

2.2   Fast Exponentiations

To evaluate the performance of the proposed algorithm, we apply the most up-to-date fast exponentiation methods to our batch verification and individual ones. Following [HHM00], Lim-Lee method (fixed based comb) and the window method appeared to be most efficient methods for a fixed base and a non-fixed base, respectively. We consider an exponentiation on a group of m-bit prime order. Lim-Lee method with window size w requires at average $(m/w - 1)$ doublings and $(m/w - 1)(1 - 2^{-w})$ additions. Window method with window size w requires at average $(m/(w + 1) + 2^{w-1} - s)$ multiplications and $(m + 1)$ squarings over a finite field, and $(m/(w + 1) + 2^{w-1} - s)$ additions and $(m + 1)$ doublings over an elliptic curve. Refer to [LL94, HHM00] for more details.

In this paper, we will consider a finite field of 160 bit order, an elliptic curve of 160 bit order and Koblitz curve $K163$ as a base group G. $K163$ is given by $E : y^2 + xy = x^3 + x^2 + 1$ over $\mathbb{F}_{2^{163}}$ and has 162 bit order (cofactor=2). Notation

Table 1. Notation

w	window size
m	bit length of exponents
t	Hamming weight
Mem	number of finite field elements or elliptic curve points to be stored
$\mathcal{E}_f$	finite field exponentiation
$\mathcal{M}_f$	finite field multiplication
$\mathcal{S}_f$	finite field squaring
$\mathcal{M}_e$	scalar multiplication in elliptic curves
$\mathcal{A}_e$	elliptic curve addition
$\mathcal{D}_e$	elliptic curve doubling

Table 2. Performance of Fast Exponentiation Algorithms

Group	Method	w	Mem	$\mathcal{M}_f$ or $\mathcal{A}_e$	$\mathcal{S}_f$ or $\mathcal{D}_e$
Finite	Window NAF	4	7	39	161
Field	Lim-Lee	4	14	38	40
Elliptic	w-NAF	4	3	36	161
Curve	Lim-Lee	4	14	38	40
Koblitz	τ-adic w-NAF	5	7	34	0
Curve	Fixed-based τ-adic w-NAF	6	15	23	0

used in the rest of paper is summarized in Table 1. We present the number of group operations for fast exponentiations in Table 2.

3   Batch Verification of Exponentiations on Abelian Groups

Let $w \geq 2$ be an integer. A radix 2 representation is called a *width-w nonadjacent Form* (w-NAF, for short) if it satisfies: (1) each nonzero digit is an odd integer with absolute value less than 2^{w-1}, and (2) for any w consecutive digits, at most one is nonzero [MS06].

Although w-NAF gives an efficient exponentiation on a group admitting fast inversion, it is not useful for a group such as a multiplicative subgroup of a finite field in which an inversion is much slower than a multiplication. We here introduce a generalized version of w-NAF with a digit set D.

Definition 1. *Let w be an integer ≥ 2 and $D = \{\alpha_1, \alpha_2, \ldots, \alpha_{2^{w-1}}\}$ where α_i's are nonzero odd integers and distinct modulo 2^w. A w-NAF with the digit set D is a sequence of digits satisfying the following conditions:*

1. *Each digit is zero or an element in D.*
2. *Among any w consecutive digits, at most one is nonzero.*

A w-NAF with the digit set D is denoted by $a = (a_{m-1} \cdots a_1 a_0)_2$ or $a = \sum_{i=0}^{m-1} a_i 2^i$ where $a_i \in D \cup \{0\}$.

Definition 2. *Let* $a = (a_{m-1}a_{m-2}\ldots a_0)_2$ *be a w-NAF with the digit set* D. *Then the* length *of* a, *denoted by* $\text{len}(a)$, *is defined to be the smallest* i *such that* $a_{i-1} \neq 0$. *By notation, we let* $\text{len}(0) = 0$. *The number of nonzero digits in its representation is called the* weight *of* a *and denoted by* $\text{wt}(a)$.

The uniqueness of the representation can be easily shown as follows. The argument is a simple generalization of Proposition 2.1 in [MS06].

Theorem 1. *Let* q *be a positive integer. All w-NAFs of length* $\leq m$ *with the digit set* D *are distinct modulo* q *if* $m \leq \log_2(q/C)$ *where* $C = \max\{|x - y| : x, y \in D \cup \{0\}\}$.

Proof. Suppose there are two different w-NAFs which represent the same integer. Let $(a_{\ell-1}a_{\ell-2}\cdots a_0)_2$ and $(b_{\ell'-1}b_{\ell'-2}\cdots b_0)_2$ are different representation such that

$$a = \sum_{i=0}^{\ell-1} a_i 2^i = \sum_{i=0}^{\ell'-1} b_i 2^i. \tag{3}$$

Assume ℓ is the smallest integer satisfying the above property.

If $a_0 = b_0$, we have two different and shorter w-NAFs which stand for the same integer. Thus it should be $a_0 \neq b_0$. If a is even, both of a_0 and b_0 should be zero and $a_0 = b_0$. It therefore should be odd and both of a_0 and b_0 should be nonzero. Since the representations are w-NAFs, $a_0 \neq 0$ and $b_0 \neq 0$ implies $a_1 = \cdots = a_w = 0$ and $b_1 = \cdots = b_w = 0$. From the equation (3), we have $a_0 \equiv b_0 \mod 2^w$. Since all elements in D are distinct modulo 2^w, we must have $a_0 = b_0$, which contradicts with the minimality of ℓ. Thus each integer has only one w-NAF with the digit set D.

Moreover, let C_1 and C_2 be the maximal and minimal element in $D \cup \{0\}$. Then $C = C_1 - C_2$. The largest w-NAF of length $\leq m$ is less than $C_1 2^m$. The smallest w-NAF of length $\leq m$ is greater than $C_2 2^m$. Thus the difference of any two w-NAFs is less than $(C_1 - C_2)2^m = C2^m \leq q$ for $m \leq \log(q/C)$. Therefore any two w-NAF of length $\leq m$ must be distinct modulo q or identical.

Theorem 2. *The number of w-NAFs of length* $\leq m$ *and weight* t *with the digit set* D *is*

$$\binom{m - (w - 1)(t - 1)}{t} 2^{(w-1)t}.$$

Proof. Consider an algorithm to choose t positions out of $m - (w - 1)(t - 1)$ positions and fill each of them by $w - 1$ consecutive zeros followed by an element in D. This algorithm gives a w-NAF of length $m + (w - 1)$. Then its first $(w - 1)$ positions should be always zero since each nonzero digit is preceded by $(w - 1)$ consecutive nonzeros. By discarding the first $(w - 1)$ zeros, we get a w-NAF of length $\leq m$. Since the algorithm covers all w-NAFs of length $\leq m$ and the algorithm outputs one of $\binom{m-(w-1)(t-1)}{t} 2^{(w-1)t}$ strings, we have the theorem.

From the proof of Theorem 2, we introduce Algorithm 1 to produce a random secret exponent in a finite field of 2^n elements.

Algorithm 1. (Generation of w-NAF exponents of weight t)

Input: m, w, t and the digit set D
Output: w-NAF of length $\leq m$

1: Choose t positions out of $n - (w - 1)(t - 1)$ positions.
2: Fill each position by $(w - 1)$ consecutive zeros followed by an element in D.
3: Discard the first $(w - 1)$ positions of the string.
4: Print the string which is a w-NAF of length $\leq m$

Algorithm 2. (Batch Verification of Exponentiations using w-NAF Exponent)

Input: m, w, t, D, and N exponentiation pairs $(x_i, y_i) \in \mathbb{Z}_q \times G$ for an abelian group G of order q with a generator g
Output: True or false

1: Take N random exponents $c_1, c_2, \ldots, c_N$ from the set of w-NAFs of length $\leq m$ and weight t, where $c_i = \sum_{j=0}^{m} c_{ij} 2^j$ and $c_{ij} \in D \cup \{0\}$.
2: **for** $\alpha \in D$ **do**
3:    $y_{i,\alpha} \leftarrow y_i^{\alpha}$ /* precomputation */
4: **end for**
5: $y \leftarrow 1$
6: **for** $j = m - 1$ downto 0 **do**
7:    $y \leftarrow y^2$
8:    **for** $i = 1$ upto N **do**
9:       **if** $c_{ij} = \alpha \in D$ **then**
10:          $y \leftarrow y \cdot y_{i,\alpha}$
11:       **end if**
12:    **end for**
13: **end for**
14: Compute g^x for $x = \sum_{i=1}^{N} c_i x_i \mod q$.
15: **if** $y = g^x$ **then**
16:    Accept all of N instances
17: **else**
18:    Reject
19: **end if**

Using the set of w-NAFs, we can perform efficient batch verification of exponentiations on a group as in Algorithm 2. Here we use simultaneous multiplication methods and online precomputation method.

We need to take an appropriate digit set for each of specific groups. For a multiplicative subgroup of a finite field in which an inversion is much slower than a multiplication, we take $D = \{1, 3, \ldots, 2^w - 1\}$. It then requires the precomputation that takes one squaring and 2^{w-1} multiplications. Steps 6-13 take $m - 1$ squarings and $tN - 1$ multiplications since each exponent has t nonzero digit. Hence the total complexity is m squarings and $N(t+2^{w-1})$ multiplications plus one exponentiation using memory for $2^{w-1} - 1$ group elements.

For an elliptic curve group in which a subtraction is as efficient as an addition, we take $D = \{\pm 1, \pm 3, \ldots, \pm(2^{w-2} - 1)\}$. In this case, the precomputation cost reduces to one elliptic doubling and 2^{w-2} elliptic additions. Hence the total complexity is m elliptic doublings and $N(t + 2^{w-2})$ elliptic additions plus one scalar multiplication using memory for $2^{w-2} - 1$ elliptic curve points.

Table 3. Number of Multiplications for Batch Verification on Abelian Groups

Common				Finite Field		Elliptic Curve	
w	m	t	Security	Mem	Complexity	Mem	Complexity
1	159	19	$2^{80.6}$	0	$19N\mathcal{M}_f+159\mathcal{S}_f+1\mathcal{E}_f$	0	$19N\mathcal{A}_e+159\mathcal{D}_e+1\mathcal{M}_e$
2	158	15	$2^{81.2}$	1	$17N\mathcal{M}_f+158\mathcal{S}_f+1\mathcal{E}_f$	0	$15N\mathcal{A}_e+158\mathcal{D}_e+1\mathcal{M}_e$
3	157	12	$2^{79.4}$	3	$16N\mathcal{M}_f+157\mathcal{S}_f+1\mathcal{E}_f$	1	$14N\mathcal{A}_e+157\mathcal{D}_e+1\mathcal{M}_e$
4	156	11	$2^{83.9}$	7	$19N\mathcal{M}_f+156\mathcal{S}_f+1\mathcal{E}_f$	3	$15N\mathcal{A}_e+156\mathcal{D}_e+1\mathcal{M}_e$
5	155	9	$2^{79.6}$	15	$25N\mathcal{M}_f+155\mathcal{S}_f+1\mathcal{E}_f$	7	$17N\mathcal{A}_e+155\mathcal{D}_e+1\mathcal{M}_e$

Table 4. Comparison of Batch Verification of Exponentiations

Method	Finite Field	Elliptic Curve
Individual	$N(39\mathcal{M}_f+161\mathcal{S}_f)$	$N(36\mathcal{A}_e+161\mathcal{D}_e)$
[YL95, BGR98]	$N(40\mathcal{M}_f)+80\mathcal{M}_f+161\mathcal{S}_f$	$N(40\mathcal{A}_e)+74\mathcal{A}_e+161\mathcal{D}_e$
[CL06]	$N(19\mathcal{M}_f)+80\mathcal{M}_f+161\mathcal{S}_f$	$N(15\mathcal{A}_e)+74\mathcal{A}_e+161\mathcal{D}_e$
Proposed	$N(16\mathcal{M}_f)+80\mathcal{M}_f+161\mathcal{S}_f$	$N(14\mathcal{A}_e)+74\mathcal{A}_e+161\mathcal{D}_e$

Table 3 presents the performance of batch verification over a finite field and an elliptic curve and shows appropriate weight t on a group of 160-bit prime order q for various w. We take $m = 160 - w$ to guarantee the uniqueness of exponents by Theorem 1. For example, we can use 3-NAF for a finite field, which requires only $16N$ multiplications, 157 squarings and one exponentiation. For an elliptic curve, we can use 2-NAF requiring only $15N$ multiplications, 158 squarings and one exponentiation. Note that *security* in Table 3 implies the security of the batch verification with the given parameters, which is computed as $\binom{m-(w-1)(t-1)}{t}2^{(w-1)t}$ by Theorem 2.

4   Batch Verification of Multiple Signatures

To apply the batch verification of exponentiations to verification of signatures, one need to modify signature schemes. Naccache *et al.* presented a modified DSA for batch verification [NMVR94]. Our batch verification is also applicable to this modified DSA. But, considering the attack by Boyd and Pavlovski [BP00], we made a little change to the verification procedure. The performance of the batch verification algorithm is evaluated based on the screening parameter $\ell = 80$.

4.1 Modified DSA

Let p be a 1024 bit prime and q a 160 bit prime dividing $p - 1$. We assume that $(p - 1)/(2q)$ has no divisor less than q to resist the attack in [BP00]. Let g be a generator of a subgroup G of order q in $\mathbb{F}_p$. Take a random $x \in \mathbb{Z}_p$. The private key is x and the corresponding public key is $y = g^x$. A signature for a message $m \in \mathbb{Z}_p$ is given by

$$(r = g^k \bmod p, \quad \sigma = k^{-1}(m + xr) \bmod q)$$

for a random $k \in \mathbb{Z}_p$. It is verified by checking if $r = \pm g^a y^b \bmod p$ for $a = m\sigma^{-1} \bmod q$ and $b = r\sigma^{-1} \bmod q$. Note that $r = ((g^k \bmod p) \bmod q)$ is used in the original DSA. The verification admits only $r = g^a y^b \bmod q$, but here we relax the verification to admit $r = \pm g^a y^b \bmod q$ due to Boyd and Pavlovski attack, in which the security loss is only one bit.

Signatures by Multiple Signers. Given N signatures (m_i, r_i, σ_i), each of which is signed by a signer with the public key y_i, we apply the batch verification by 3-NAFs with the digit set $D = \{1, 3, 5, 7\}$, which gives best performance as in Table 3. First, take random w-NAFs $c_1, \ldots, c_N$. Next, compute $a = -\sum_{i=1}^{N} a_i c_i \bmod q$ and $b_i = -r_i \sigma_i^{-1} c_i \bmod q$ for each i. Finally compute

$$g^a \prod_{i=1}^{N} y_i^{b_i'} \prod_{i=1}^{N} r_i^{c_i} \bmod p, \tag{4}$$

and if it is 1 or $p - 1$, accept all N signatures.

We now evaluate the verification cost. For simplicity, we only count F_p operations. Since g is fixed, we apply Lim-Lee method of window size $w = 4$ to compute g^a, and each of g^b or $g_i^{b_i'}$ is computed by 4-NAF. Thus an individual signature verification consists of one Lim-Lee, one 4-NAF method and one multiplication. On the other hand, the batch verification consists of one Lim-Lee, N 4-NAF, $16N$ multiplications and N multiplications. Table 5 shows the achieved gains as ratio of the proposed method and individual one. Note that the measurement is conducted only in case of $S_f = M_f$ and $S_f = 0.8 M_f$. Following [BHLM01], it is between 0.8 and 0.86.

Signatures by A Single Signer. We consider N signatures (m_i, r_i, σ_i) by a single signer. We apply the batch verification by 3-NAFs with the digit set $D = \{1, 3, 5, 7\}$. First, take random w-NAFs $c_1, \ldots, c_N$. Next, compute $a = -\sum_{i=1}^{N} a_i c_i \bmod q$ and $b = -\sum_{i=1}^{N} r_i \sigma_i^{-1} c_i \bmod q$. Finally compute

$$g^a \prod_{i=1}^{N} y^b \prod_{i=1}^{N} r_i^{c_i} \bmod p, \tag{5}$$

and if it is 1 or $p - 1$, accept all n signatures.

Now we evaluate the verification cost. Since both of g and y are fixed, we may apply Lim-Lee method to compute g^a and y^b. The individual verification consists of two Lim-Lee and one multiplication. On the other hand, the batch verification consists of two Lim-Lee and $14N$ additions. The performance is given in Table 5.

Table 5. Performance of Batch Verifications of Signatures over a Finite Field

Signers	Individual	Proposed	Ratio($\mathcal{S}_f = \mathcal{M}_f$)	Ratio($\mathcal{S}_f = 0.8\mathcal{M}_f$)
Multi.	$N(78\mathcal{M}_f + 161\mathcal{S}_f)$	$N(55\mathcal{M}_f) + 40\mathcal{M}_f + 161\mathcal{S}_f$	$0.23 + 0.84/N$	$0.27 + 0.82/N$
Single	$N(76\mathcal{M}_f + 40\mathcal{S}_f)$	$N(16\mathcal{M}_f) + 76\mathcal{M}_f + 40\mathcal{S}_f$	$0.14 + 2.04/N$	$0.15 + 1.90/N$

4.2 Modified ECDSA

ECDSA is an elliptic curve analogue of DSA [ECDSA]. Our batch verification algorithm is applied to the modified ECDSA [ABGLSV05] as in DSA case. The security of the modified ECDSA is equivalent to the standard ECDSA [ABGLSV05].

Let E be an elliptic curve. Assume that the order q of E is prime and $G \in E$ a generator (If E has a cofactor $\neq 1$, the signature scheme should be modified due to [BP00]). The private key is x and the corresponding public key is $Q = xG$. A signature for given message $m \in \mathbb{Z}_p$ is

$$(R = kG, \quad \sigma = k^{-1}(m + xr) \mod q)$$

where $R = (x_1, y_1)$ and $r = x_1 \mod q$ for a random $k \in \mathbb{Z}_p$. The verification is done by checking if $R = aG + bQ$ for $a = m\sigma^{-1} \mod q$ and $b = r\sigma^{-1} \mod q$.

Given N signatures (m_i, R_i, σ_i), we compute $t_i = \sigma_i^{-1} \mod q$ first, and then $a_i = m_i t_i \mod q$ and $b_i = r_i t_i \mod q$ for each i. Next, take random $s_i \in S$ and compute $a = -\sum_{i=1}^{n} a_i s_i \mod q$ and $b = -\sum_{i=1}^{n} b_i s_i \mod q$. Finally compute

$$aG + bQ + \sum_{i=1}^{n} s_i R_i,$$

and if it is a point at infinity O, accept all n signatures.

Signatures by Multiple Signers. Given N signatures (m_i, R_i, σ_i), each of which is signed by a signer with the public key Q_i, we apply the batch verification by 3-NAFs with the digit set $D = \{\pm 1, \pm 3\}$. First, take random w-NAFs $c_1, \ldots, c_N$. Next, compute $a = -\sum_{i=1}^{N} a_i c_i \mod q$ and $b_i' = -r_i \sigma_i^{-1} c_i \mod q$ for each i. Finally compute

$$aG + \sum_{i=1}^{N} b_i' Q_i + \sum_{i=1}^{N} c_i R_i, \tag{6}$$

and if it is the point at infinity O, accept all N signatures. Remark that if we take an elliptic curve whose order is prime as above, the Boyd and Pavlovski attack [BP00] can not be applied.

Signatures by A Single Signer. We consider N signatures (m_i, R_i, σ_i) by a single signer. We apply the batch verification by 3-NAFs with the digit set $D = \{\pm 1, \pm 3\}$. First, take random w-NAFs $c_1, \ldots, c_N$. Next, compute $a = -\sum_{i=1}^{N} a_i c_i \bmod q$ and $b = -\sum_{i=1}^{N} r_i \sigma_i^{-1} c_i \bmod q$ for each i. Finally compute

$$aG + bQ + \sum_{i=1}^{N} c_i R_i, \qquad (7)$$

and if it is the point at infinity O, accept all N signatures.

Performance comparison of individual and batch verifications of ECDSA is given in Table 6. The performance of individual verifications is evaluated based on the standard verification equation. Note that the cost can be reduced by 40 % using some special method in [ABGLSV05].

Table 6. Performance of Batch Verification of Signatures over an Elliptic Curve

Signers	Individual	Proposed	Ratio($\mathcal{S}_f = \mathcal{M}_f$)	Ratio($\mathcal{S}_f = 0.8\mathcal{M}_f$)
Multi.	$N(78\mathcal{M}_f + 161\mathcal{S}_f)$	$N(55\mathcal{M}_f) + 40\mathcal{M}_f + 161\mathcal{S}_f$	$0.23 + 0.84/N$	$0.27 + 0.82/N$
Single	$N(76\mathcal{M}_f + 40\mathcal{S}_f)$	$N(16\mathcal{M}_f) + 76\mathcal{M}_f + 40\mathcal{S}_f$	$0.14 + 2.04/N$	$0.15 + 1.90/N$

5   Batch Verification on Koblitz Elliptic Curves

Consider an ordinary elliptic curve E defined over $\mathbb{F}_q$ with $\#E(\mathbb{F}_q) = q + 1 - t$ and $\gcd(q, t) = 1$. The Frobenius map τ is defined as follows:

$$\tau : E(\overline{\mathbb{F}}_q) \rightarrow E(\overline{\mathbb{F}}_q); (x, y) \mapsto (x^q, y^q),$$

where $\overline{\mathbb{F}}_q$ is the algebraic closure of $\mathbb{F}_q$. The Frobenius map τ is a root of the characteristic equation $\chi_E(T) = T^2 - tT + q$ in the ring of endomorphisms $\mathrm{End}(E)$. We denote $E(\mathbb{F}_{q^n})$ by the subgroup of $E(\overline{\mathbb{F}}_q)$ consisting of $\mathbb{F}_{q^n}$-rational points. Let G be the subgroup of $E(\mathbb{F}_{q^n})$ generated by P with a prime order ℓ satisfying $\ell^2 \nmid \#E(\mathbb{F}_{q^n})$ and $\ell \nmid \#E(\mathbb{F}_q)$.

We now introduce a generalization of τ-adic NAF into τ-adic w-NAF, which was introduced in [Sol00] on Koblitz curves.

Definition 3. *Let w be an integer ≥ 2. A τ-adic w-NAF is a sequence of digits satisfying the following two conditions:*

1. *Each non-zero digit is an integer which is not divisible by q and whose absolute value is less than $q^w/2$.*
2. *Among any w consecutive digits, at most one is non-zero.*

A τ-adic w-NAF is denoted by $a = (a_{m-1} \cdots a_1 a_0)_\tau$ or $a = \sum_{i=0}^{m-1} a_i \tau^i$.

The length and the weight of a τ-adic w-NAF are defined similarly to w-NAFs. Note that given a τ-adic w-NAF $a = (a_{m-1} \cdots a_1 a_0)_\tau$ and a point $Q \in E$, aQ is computed as $aQ = \sum_{i=0}^{m-1} a_i \tau^i(Q)$.

Theorem 3. *Let $a = (a_{m-1}, \ldots, a_0)_\tau$ and $b = (b_{m'-1}, \ldots, b_0)_\tau$ be two τ-adic w-NAFs. Then $aQ = bQ$ for some nonzero $Q \in G$ implies that $m = m'$ and $a_i = b_i$ for all i if*

$$\max\{m, m'\} \le M_{q,\ell,w} = \log_q \left(\frac{\ell}{(q^{w/2} + 1)^2} \right) - (w - 1). \tag{8}$$

Proof. Assume there is a nonzero point $Q \in G$ such that $aQ = bQ$ for two distinct τ-adic w-NAFs $a = (a_{m-1}, \ldots, a_0)_\tau$ and $b = (b_{m'-1}, \ldots, b_0)_\tau$. By adding zero digits to the front of the strings, we may assume $m = m'$. Then we have $O = aQ - bQ = \sum_{i=0}^{m-1} d_i \tau^i(Q)$ for $d_i = a_i - b_i$.

Let $F(T) = \sum_{i=0}^{m-1} d_i T^i$. Since $End(E)$ is an order of the imaginary quadratic field, $F(\tau)$ can be considered as an element of $\mathbb{Z}[i]$ divisible by ℓ. Since $\chi_E(\tau) = 0$, $F(T)$ and $\chi_E(T)$ must have a common root in the algebraic closure of $\mathbb{F}_\ell$. Thus the resultant $R = Res(T^2 - tT + q, F(T))$ satisfies $R \equiv 0 \mod \ell$.

Let τ_1 and τ_2 be the roots of χ_E. Then $R = F(\tau_1)F(\tau_2)$ and $|\tau_1| = |\tau_2| = \sqrt{q}$. For each $\tau \in \{\tau_1, \tau_2\}$, we have

$$\begin{aligned}
|F(\tau)| &\le \sum_{i=0}^{m-1} |d_i||\tau|^i \le \sum_{i=0}^{m-1} |a_i||\tau|^i + \sum_{i=0}^{m-1} |b_i||\tau|^i \\
&\le 2 \left(\left\lceil \frac{q^w}{2} \right\rceil - 1 \right) \left(\sqrt{q}^{m-1} + \sqrt{q}^{m-1-w} + \cdots + \sqrt{q}^{m-1 \bmod w} \right) \\
&= 2 \left(\left\lceil \frac{q^w}{2} \right\rceil - 1 \right) \frac{(q^{(m+w-1)/2} - 1)}{q^{w/2} - 1} < q^{(m+w-1)/2}(q^{w/2} + 1).
\end{aligned}$$

Thus, $|R| < q^{m+w-1}(q^{w/2} + 1)^2 \le \ell$. Hence $R = 0$. Because χ_E is irreducible over $\mathbb{Z}$, this implies $\chi_E | F(T)$ over $\mathbb{Z}$.

Assume that d_{i_0} is the lowest nonzero coefficient of F. Then we can write

$$T^{-i_0} F(T) = (g_0 + g_1 T + \cdots + g_{m-3-i_0} T^{m-3-i_0}) \chi_E(T)$$

for some $g_i \in \mathbb{Z}$. By equating the coefficients, we know $d_{i_0} = qg_0$ and $d_{i_0+j} = qg_j - tg_{j-1} + g_{j-2}$ for $1 \le j \le w - 1$, where we set $g_{-1} := 0$ by convention. Since each of a_{i_0} and b_{i_0} is not divisible by q, both a_{i_0+1} and b_{i_0+1} is nonzero. Hence $d_{i_0+1} = \cdots = d_{i_0+w-1} = 0$. That is,

$$Eqn(j) = qg_j - tg_{j-1} + g_{j-2} = 0 \quad \text{for } 1 \le j \le w - 1. \tag{9}$$

From $d_{i_0+1} = 0$ and $g_{-1} = 0$, we have $q|g_0$ since $\gcd(q,t) = 1$. By repeating this procedure, we have $g_0, g_1, \ldots, g_{w-2}$ are divisible by q.

After replacing g_i by g_i/q in the $Eqn(1), \ldots, Eqn(c-1)$, we repeat the above procedure to obtain $q^2|g_0, g_1, \ldots, g_{w-3}$. At the end, we have $q^c|g_0$. Therefore, we have $q^w|d_{i_0}$. However, this is impossible since $|d_{i_0}| < q^w$.

The above theorem tells us that distinct τ-adic w-NAFs of length $m < M_{q,\ell,w}$ play an role of distinct group homomorphisms of G. Moreover, if $a = b$ in $\mathrm{End}(E)$, we have $R = Res(T^2 - tT + q, \sum_{i=0}^{m-1}(a_i - b_i)T^i)$ satisfies $R = 0$. By the same argument with Theorem 3, we have $a_i = b_i$ for all i regardless of k, which implies that every endomorphism of E has at most one τ-adic w-NAF.

Theorem 4. *The number of τ-adic w-NAFs of length $\leq m$ and weight t is*

$$\binom{m - (w-1)(t-1)}{t} 2^t \left(\left\lfloor \frac{q^w}{2} \right\rfloor - \left\lfloor \frac{q^{w-1}}{2} \right\rfloor\right)^t.$$

Proof. As in Theorem 2, we consider an algorithm to choose t positions out of $m + (w-1) - wt$ positions and fill each of them by $w - 1$ consecutive zeros followed by an integer not divisible by q whose absolute value is less than $q^w/2$. By discarding the first $(w-1)$ zeros, we get a τ-adic w-NAF of length $\leq m$ with weight t. Conversely, any string with the property can be produced by the algorithm.

Now we count the number of cases. First we have $\binom{m-(w-1)(t-1)}{t}$ choices for t positions. Next, each position is filled by an integer x such that x is not divisible by q and $|x| < q^w/2$. The number of such integers is

$$2^t \left(\left\lfloor \frac{q^w}{2} \right\rfloor - \left\lfloor \frac{q^{w-1}}{2} \right\rfloor\right)^t,$$

which completes the proof.

We introduce an algorithm to output a random secret exponent in a subgroup G of order ℓ in an elliptic curve $E(\mathbb{F}_{q^n})$. Algorithm 3 produces uniformly distributed w-NAFs of length $\leq m$ with weight t if $m \leq M_{q,\ell,w}$

Algorithm 3. (τ-adic w-NAF Exponent of weight t)

Input: q, m, w, and t
Output: τ-adic w-NAF of length $\leq m$

1: Choose t positions out of $m - (w-1)(t-1)$ positions
2: Fill each position by $(w-1)$ consecutive zeros followed by an integer not divisible by q whose absolute value is less than $q^w/2$
3: Discard the first $(w-1)$ positions of the string
4: Print the string which is a τ-adic w-NAF of length $\leq m$

Algorithm 4. (Batch Verification using τ-adic NAF on Koblitz Curves)

Input: (x_i, Q_i) for $1 \le i \le N$
Output: True or false

1: Choose N random elements $c_i = \sum_{j=0}^{e} c_{ij}\tau^j$ $(1 \le i \le N)$ from the set of τ-adic w-NAF of length $\le m$ and weight t, where c_{ij} is an integer not divisible by q whose absolute value is less than $q^w/2$ and $\epsilon_{ij} = c_{ij}/|c_{ij}|$ for nonzero c_{ij} for each i, j.
2: **for** $1 \le k \le 2^{w-2}$ **do**
3:    $R[2k - 1] \leftarrow O$
4: **end for**
5: **for** $j = 0$ to e **do**
6:    **for** $i = 1$ to N **do**
7:       **if** $c_{ij} \ne 0$ **then**
8:          $R[|c_{ij}|] \leftarrow R[|c_{ij}|] + \epsilon_{ij}\tau^j(Q_i)$
9:       **end if**
10:    **end for**
11: **end for**
12: $Q \leftarrow R[2^{w-1} - 1]$
13: $T \leftarrow R[2^{w-1} - 1]$
14: **for** $k = 2^{w-2} - 1$ to 2 **do**
15:    $T \leftarrow T + R[2k - 1]$
16:    $Q \leftarrow Q + T$
17: **end for**
18: $Q \leftarrow 2Q + T + R[1]$
19: **if** $Q = cP$ **then**
20:    Accept all of N instances
21: **else**
22:    Reject
23: **end if**

Algorithm 4 describes batch verification using τ-adic NAF on Koblitz Curves, given (x_i, Q_i) for $1 \le i \le N$. For ease of notation, we describe the algorithm in case of $q = 2$, but it can be easily extended into the general case. For more details, Steps 2-11 compute

$$R_k = \sum_{i=1}^{N} \sum_{j=0, c_j=k}^{m-1} sign(c_j)\tau^j(Q_i)$$

for each odd integer $1 \le k \le 2^{w-1} - 1$. Steps 12-18 compute

$$Q = \sum_{k=1, 2 \nmid k}^{2z-1} kQ_k = (R_{2z-1} + \cdots + R_1) + 2((z-1)R_{2z-1} + (z-2)R_{2z-3} + 2R_5 + R_3)$$

for $z = 2^{w-2}$ where the last term is computed using BGMW method [BGMW93]. From complexity point of view, Step 1 requires $tN - 2^{w-2}$ additions at average and Steps 5-11 require at most $3 + 2(z - 1) = 2z + 1 = 2^{w-1} + 1$ additions. Hence the total complexity is at average $tN + 2^{w-2} + 1$ additions with $2^{w-2} - 1$ memory.

Table 7 presents an appropriate weight t and the corresponding attack complexity for each w over Koblitz curve. The length m is taken to be the largest integer to preserve the uniqueness as in Theorem 3. *Additions* is the number of additions to be required for batch verification, where $\#A_{M_e}$ is the number of additions for one scalar multiplication. For example, $\#A_{M_e}$ can be 34 using τ-adic 5-NAF. Note that when enumerating the number of elliptic curve additions, we ignore the τ operations since their cost is negligible; they are implemented merely by a circular shift and very efficient even in polynomial basis.

Table 7. Number of Additions for Batch Verification over a Koblitz Curve

w	m	t	Mem	Additions	Complexity
2	159	15	0	$15N + 2 + \#A_{M_e}$	$2^{81.4}$
3	156	13	1	$13N + 3 + \#A_{M_e}$	$2^{84.5}$
4	154	11	3	$11N + 5 + \#A_{M_e}$	$2^{83.6}$
5	152	10	7	$10N + 9 + \#A_{M_e}$	$2^{86.2}$
6	150	9	15	$9N + 17 + \#A_{M_e}$	$2^{87.1}$
7	148	8	31	$8N + 33 + \#A_{M_e}$	$2^{86.1}$
8	146	7	63	$7N + 65 + \#A_{M_e}$	$2^{83.3}$
9	144	6	127	$6N + 129 + \#A_{M_e}$	$2^{78.5}$
10	142	6	255	$6N + 257 + \#A_{M_e}$	$2^{83.9}$

Table 8 gives a comparison with other methods. We apply the fixed-based τ-adic w-NAF method for fixed base computation with the precomputation. In a single signer case, the proposed method is asymptotically 9 times faster than the individual one.

Table 8. Comparison of Batch Verifications over Koblitz Curve

Method	Exponentiation	Single Signer	Multiple Signers
Individual	$23N$	$57N$	$57N$
[CL06]	$9N + 84$	$9N + 118$	-
Proposed	$6N + 163$	$6N + 186$	$30N + 152$
Proposed/Ind	$0.26 + 7.09/N$	$0.11 + 3.26/N$	$0.53 + 2.67/N$

6 Conclusion

We propose an efficient batch verification method of exponentiation. By applying the proposed algorithm, we can improve the efficiency of batch verification of digital signatures. To the best of our knowledge, we firstly propose a batch verification of signatures by multiple signers so that we can speed up verification of digital signatures about four times faster than individual verification thereof. In particular, our method can be applied to *any* servers or devices that need to verify multiple signatures at once. It would be an interesting problem to apply our algorithm to various applications involving many exponentiations including Mix-Net [Abe99], proof of knowledge, anonymous authentications, and authenticated routing.

Acknowledgements. The authors thank the anonymous reviewers for their valuable comments.

References

[Abe99]   M. Abe, *Mix-Networks on Permutation Networks*, Advances in Cryptology - Asiacrypt'99, LNCS Vol. 1716, Springer-Verlag, pp. 258-273, 1999.

[ABGLSV05] A. Antipa, D. Brown, R. Gallant, R. Lambert, R. Struik, and S. Vanstone, *Accelerated Verification of ECDSA Signatures*, SAC 2005, LNCS Vol. 3897, pp.307-318, 2006.

[BGMW93]   E. Brickell, D. Gordon, K. McCurley, and D. Wilson, *Fast Exponentiation with Precomputation*, Eurocrypt'92, LNCS Vol. 658, Springer-Verlag, pp. 200-207, 1993.

[BGR98]   M. Bellare, J. Garay, and T. Rabin, *Fast Batch Verification for Modular Exponentiation and Digital Signatures*, Proc. of Eurocrypt '98, LNCS Vol. 1403, Springer-Verlag, pp. 236–250, 1998. Full version is available via http://www-cse.ucsd.edu/users/mihir.

[BP00]   C. Boyd and C. Pavlovski, *Attacking and Repairing Batch Verification Schemes*, Proc. of Asiacrypt 2000, LNCS Vol. 1976, pp. 58-71, Springer-Verlag, 2000.

[BHLM01]   M. Brown, D. Hankerson, J. López, and A. Menezes, *Software Implementation of the NIST Elliptic Curves over Primes Fields*, Proc. of CT-RSA 2001, LNCS, Vol. 2020, pp. 250-265, Springer-Verlag, 2001.

[CL06]   J. Cheon and D. Lee, "Use of Sparse and/or Complex Exponents in Batch Verification of Exponentiations," IEEE. T. on Computers, Vol. 55, No. 12, 2006.(December 2006)

[DSA]   *Digital Signature Standard (DSS) (DSA, RSA, and ECDSA algorithms)*, Available at http://csrc.nist.gov/cryptval/dss.htm.

[ECDSA]   *Public Key Cryptography for the Financial Services Industry: The Elliptic Curve Digital Signature Algorithm (ECDSA)*, ANSI X9.62, approved January 7, 1999.

[Fel87]   P. Feldman, *A Practical Scheme for Non-interactive Verifiable Secret Sharing*, IEEE Symposium on Foundations of Computer Science, pp. 427-437, 1987.

[Fiat89]   A. Fiat, *Batch RSA*, J. Cryptology, Vol. 10, No. 2, pp. 75-88, Springer-Verlag, 1997. A preliminary version appeared in *Proc. of Crypto'89*, LNCS Vol. 435, pp. 175-185, Springer-Verlag, 1989.

[HHM00]   D. Hankerson, J. Hernandez, and A. Menezes, *Software Implementation of Elliptic Curve Cryptography Over Binary Fields*, Proc. of CHES 2000, LNCS, Vol. 1965, pp. 1-24, Springer-Verlag, 2000.

[Harn98]   L. Harn, *Batch Verifying Multiple DSA-Type Digital Signatures*, Electronic Letters, Vol. 34, No. 9, pp. 870-871, 1995.

[LL94]   C.H. Lim and P.J. Lee, *More Flexible Exponentiation with Precomputation*, Proc. of Crypto '94, LNCS Vol. 839, pp. 95-107, Springer-Verlag, 1994.

[MN96]   D. M'Raithi and D. Naccache, *Batch Exponentiation - A Fast DLP based Signature Generation Strategy*, ACM Conference on Computer and Communications Security, pp. 58-61, ACM, 1996.

[MNT04]   E. Mykletun, M. Narasimha and G. Tsudik, *Authentication and Integrity in Outsourced Databases*, Proc. of ISOC Symposium on Network and Distributed Systems Security (NDSS04), 2004.

[MS06]   J. Muir and D. Stinson, *Minimality and Other Properties of the Width-w Non-Adjacent Form*, Mathematics of Computation, Vol. 75, pp. 369-384, 2006.

[NMVR94]   D. Naccache, D. M'Raithi, S. Vaudenay, and D. Raphaeli, *Can D.S.A be Improved? Complexity trade-offs with the Digital Signature Standard*, Proc. of Eurocrypt '94, LNCS Vol. 950, pp. 77-85, Springer-Verlag, 1994.

[Sol97]   J. Solinas, *An Improved Algorithm for Arithmetic on a Family of Elliptic Curves*, Proc. of Crypto 97, pp. 357-371, Springer-Verlag, 1997. Full version is avaiable at http://www.cacr.math.uwaterloo.ca/techreports/

[Sol00]   J. Solinas, *Efficient Arithmetic on Elliptic Curves*, Design, Codes and Cryptography, Vol. 19, No. 3, pp. 195-249, 2000.

[YL95]   S. Yen and C. Laih, *Improved Digital Signature suitable for Batch Verification*, IEEE Trans. on Computers, Vol. 44, No. 7, pp. 957-959, 1995.

A Closer Look at PKI: Security and Efficiency

Alexandra Boldyreva[1], Marc Fischlin[2], Adriana Palacio[3],
and Bogdan Warinschi[4]

[1] Georgia Institute of Technology, USA
sasha@gatech.edu
[2] Darmstadt University of Technology, Germany
marc.fischlin@gmail.com
[3] Bowdoin College, USA
apalacio@bowdoin.edu
[4] University of Bristol, UK
bogdan@cs.bris.ac.uk

Abstract. In this paper we take a closer look at the security and efficiency of public-key encryption and signature schemes in public-key infrastructures (PKI). Unlike traditional analyses which assume an "ideal" implementation of the PKI, we focus on the security of joint constructions that consider the certification authority (CA) and the users, and include a key-registration protocol and the algorithms of an encryption or a signature scheme. We therefore consider significantly broader adversarial capabilities. Our analysis clarifies and validates several crucial aspects such as the amount of trust put in the CA, the necessity and specifics of proofs of possession of secret keys, and the security of the basic primitives in this more complex setting. We also provide constructions for encryption and signature schemes that provably satisfy our strong security definitions and are more efficient than the corresponding traditional constructions that assume a digital certificate issued by the CA must be verified whenever a public key is used. Our results address some important aspects for the design and standardization of PKIs, as targeted for example in the standards project ANSI X9.109.

1 Introduction

Public key cryptography implicitly relies on the existence of a *public-key infrastructure* (PKI), where each user has a pair of public and secret keys for the cryptosystem, and that this association is publicly available. The designers of public-key cryptosystems always define how the public and the secret keys are generated and used, but almost never carefully specify how the binding between keys and user identities takes place. The tacit assumption is that this binding is established *a priori* through PKI management operations.

T. Okamoto and X. Wang (Eds.): PKC 2007, LNCS 4450, pp. 458–475, 2007.

1.1   Motivation

The policies and the procedures regarding PKIs are continuously changing and detailed descriptions are invariably long and tedious.[1] Unfortunately, existing literature still does not answer several important questions. What exactly is the certification authority (CA), the entity that links public keys to identities, trusted not to do? Can and should some degree of security be ensured even when the CA is malicious or becomes compromised? Proofs of possession (POP) —in which a user proves possession of the secret key when registering a public key with the CA— are a defense mechanism for protecting against rogue-key and key-substitution attacks, but what exactly should they be and, more importantly, are they really necessary?

A question that is perhaps even more important is whether provably-secure encryption and signature schemes are indeed secure when used in a particular PKI. Although it is largely believed to be the case, the question is far from moot since most existing schemes are analyzed in settings where compositional aspects are neglected. In particular, the security of the combination of a key-registration protocol with existing encryption or signature schemes does not immediately follow from the security of the individual components. In principle, by cleverly combining its ability to attack the key-registration protocol and its ability to attack the primitive (encryption or signatures), an adversary could mount a successful attack against the joint construction.

Limitations of security analyses that do not explicitly include the behavior of the CA or the key-registration protocol have been previously pointed out in other contexts. In the case of key exchange, Shoup [41] suggests that registration of public keys should be considered explicitly as part of the key agreement protocol to be analyzed. Kaliski [27] exemplifies the importance of such measures by presenting unknown key-share attacks on the MQV key exchange protocol [34]. These attacks could have been discovered with a thorough analysis that considers the CA as an active party participating in the protocol. We review further related work at the end in Section 5.

1.2   Contributions

In this paper we initiate a study of PKIs with respect to security of the two most important public-key primitives: encryption and digital signature schemes. Our main motivation is to answer the questions raised above and other related issues.

MODELS. Security arguments in the absence of rigorous models do not provide strong security guarantees, and such models are conspicuously absent in the case of PKIs. Our first contribution are rigorous definitions for primitives when used in this setting together with appropriate security notions. The inherent complexity of the PKI settings, the non-typical adversarial powers, and the difficulty of

---

[1] See for example the document that describe the current state-of-the-art: "Internet X.509 Public Key Infrastructure – Certificate Management Protocol (CMP)" [1].

precisely identifying the situations that constitute a security breach make the design of such models an entirely non-trivial task.

Since security goals depend on the primitive used, we treat the cases in which keys are used for encryption and for signing separately. Specifically, we define two primitives, called *certified encryption* and *certified signature* schemes, and for each primitive we define a notion of security. Besides the standard algorithms for encryption and signing, we model explicitly interactive protocols for registering the public keys with a CA. Consequently, our security notions are against an adversary with broad capabilities that take into account threats arising from the key-registration protocol, possibly run concurrently, the presence of several parties, including the users and the (possibly corrupt) CA. The details are in Sections 2, 3 and 4.

Our security definitions are general and powerful. The models we propose directly capture settings where users have multiple public keys, and where keys have additional attributes, such as an expiration date. They easily extend to handle hierarchical certification and certificate revocation. Moreover, while we capture the original goal for which PKI was invented we make flexible assumptions on how certification is achieved. In particular, schemes that aim at achieving certification but avoid the original mechanism of explicit certificates specific to the traditional PKIs (e.g. schemes similar to those in [21,2]) can still be analyzed in our models. We provide a detailed discussion in Sections 3 and 4.

The design of our models in general and that of the security goals in particular are motivated by the "core" properties of the primitives, namely, confidentiality for encryption and integrity and authenticity for signatures. For protocols in which encryption schemes or signatures are used beyond these basic properties, e.g., encryption schemes used as commitments, additional analysis in light of the new goals is required. Yet, our attack model should be easily transferable to those scenarios, and only the security definitions would need to be adapted.

ANALYSIS OF TRADITIONAL SCHEMES. Next we focus on constructions that satisfy the proposed notions of security. We start with an analysis of "traditional" certified encryption and certified signature schemes. In these constructions, the CA uses a signature scheme to issue digital certificates, and then parties produce ciphertexts (resp., signatures) using a standard encryption (resp., signature) scheme. These schemes are defined in detail in Sections 3 and 4, respectively.

Although it seems folklore that the traditional approach is "secure", to the best of our knowledge no formal validation in a sound model with respect to clearly expressed security goals has been devised prior to our work. We offer a rigorous analysis that shows that these schemes are indeed secure in the appropriate security model we design. Our proof gives concrete security bounds that support recommendations for practical parameter choices. While expected, these results are important to increase confidence in the use of the schemes and allow to make security statements based on solid foundations. Our concrete security results are in Sections 3 and 4.

The results that we obtain regarding the design of proofs of possession are less expected, if not surprising. Our investigation shows that formal proofs of knowledge are not necessary for basic security of the certified encryption and signature schemes, and that simpler challenge-response protocols suffice. For signatures, the user simply signs a distinct message[2] provided by the CA. Perhaps surprisingly, we show that for basic encryption no proof of possession is required. Intuitively, in the case of encryption, this means that data privacy is not compromised if a user does not have the secret key associated to the public key it registers. We note that these results do not eliminate the proof-of-knowledge requirements imposed on these primitives in other settings (e.g., [4,11,9,24,32,36]) and only concern the security of certified encryption and signatures.

MORE EFFICIENT CONSTRUCTIONS. Since our models do not require that solutions use explicit certificates as in the traditional constructions, it is natural to ask if it is possible to obtain improvements over the traditional solutions, e.g., in terms of efficiency. We answer this question affirmatively. We present more efficient constructions for certified encryption and certified signature schemes that use implicit certificates therefore avoiding the explicit verification of the binding between public keys and identities.

Our certified encryption scheme uses a variant of ElGamal encryption [19] combined with implicit certificates realized through Schnorr signatures, and is proven secure according to our definition in the random oracle model [6] under the Computational Diffie-Hellman assumption. This scheme is more efficient than the traditional certified encryption scheme where the CA uses Schnorr signatures to issue explicit certificates and users employ ElGamal encryption[3]. For security parameter k the latter requires $4.75k$ modular multiplications to encrypt (using the square-and-multiply exponentiation method combined with well-known speed-up techniques for multi-exponentiations) while our scheme only requires $3.25k$ multiplications, coming thus quite close to the performance of regular ElGamal encryption without certification.

For signatures, we propose a construction based on Schnorr signatures [38], provably secure according to our definition in the random oracle model under the Discrete Logarithm assumption. Compared to the traditional approach of using such signatures as explicit certificates, our solution reduces the average number of modular multiplications for verification from $3.5k$ to $1.875k$, and thus achieves almost the same efficiency as regular Schnorr signatures without certification. Notice that the increase in efficiency comes at the expense of a loss in provable security due to looser reductions. It is an open problem to find tighter reductions.

We define the schemes and provide concrete security results in [10]. We note that in the stateful settings where valid certificates of the other parties are stored permanently, traditional schemes are the expedient choice. For the stateless case, however, our constructions offer computational savings over the traditional approach.

---

[2] It is necessary to ensure that this message will not be signed by this user later. One way to achieve this, which is also our approach, is to prepend the "challenge" messages chosen by the CA with 0, and the messages the user signs with 1.

[3] Or a version of ElGamal that is IND-CCA secure in the random oracle model.

2   Modeling Public-Key Infrastructures

To model public-key infrastructures we assume that there is a designated party, the certification authority (CA), and a set of users. Each user has a unique identity ID ∈ {0, 1}* in form of an X.509 entry, an e-mail address or a similar distinguished name. The identity may also contain auxiliary information like an expiration date which refers for example to the contract period of an employee or to the validity period of the certificate.

CERTIFICATION AUTHORITY. The CA holds a public key pk_{CA} and a corresponding secret key sk_{CA}. We presume that the public key is authenticated and known to all parties, i.e., once it is published it cannot be changed by the adversary. This is usually accomplished by a hierarchical arrangement of CAs, each intermediate CA certifying the validity of the public key of its successor. Only the key of the root CA has to be authenticated by other means. Here we focus on the the simpler one-tier approach of having only one CA, i.e., our model can be viewed as a condensed hierarchy with our single CA as the root CA. We discuss the more general case of hierarchical CAs in [10].

REGISTRATION OF KEYS. Each user can register keys with the CA by running the registration protocol. The required validation of the user's identity ID is usually done before by the so-called registration authority (RA), which sometimes coincides with the CA. Checking the identity of the user wishing to register its public key is typically performed by the RA through personal identification and physical validation (e.g., with help of a passport or a driver license). Hence, this part is beyond our computational model and we simply assume that bindings between user identities and their public keys are authentic.

We do not assume the existence of private channels. We do, however, presume authenticated channels between the CA and the users, even though the user most likely does not have a certified signature key when the registration starts. Without this minimal assumption about authenticated communication achieving any reasonable security guarantee seems to be impossible. The assumption can be enforced by a variety of means that include for example having the certification authority confirm the registration of a key through regular mail, signed electronic mail (with the signature verification key included in pk_{CA}), legally binding documents, or simply meeting in person.

The registration protocol itself is defined very generically. In this process the user derives a public key pk which may be used for encryption or signature verification and a secret key sk for decrypting or signing. We do not specify how the keys are generated (i.e., picked by the user alone or generated jointly between the user and the CA), yet we postulate that the CA should not be able to learn the corresponding secret key of the user. This inevitably requires interaction between both parties. The user also obtains a certificate cert which, classically, is an *explicit certificate* of type X.509, including the CA's signature. But since we also use other approaches like *implicit certificates* cert should be rather thought of as an arbitrary, possibly empty string. We assume, however, that each pair

(ID, pk), where pk is registered, is unique; this can be achieved as is done for X.509 certificates by issuing serial numbers or other auxiliary information.

REVOCATION. For simplicity, we do not introduce revocation techniques in our basic model. Due to the lack of space the discussion on how to augment our definitions and schemes to address revocations is delegated to the full version of the paper [10].

3   Secure Encryption in Public-Key Infrastructures

SYNTAX OF CERTIFIED ENCRYPTION SCHEMES. A *certified encryption scheme* is a tuple $\mathsf{CS} = (\mathcal{EG}, \mathcal{K}, (\mathcal{C}, \mathcal{U}), \mathcal{E}, \mathcal{D})$ of probabilistic polynomial-time algorithms:

- $\mathcal{EG}$ is a randomized *parameter-generation* algorithm. It takes input 1^k, where k is the security parameter, and outputs some global parameters I, available to all parties. For sake of readability we omit I from the input of the parties.
- $\mathcal{K}$ is a randomized *key-generation* algorithm. It takes input I, and outputs a pair $(pk_{\mathsf{CA}}, sk_{\mathsf{CA}})$ consisting of a public key and a matching secret key.
- $(\mathcal{C}, \mathcal{U})$ is a pair of interactive randomized algorithms forming the (two-party) *public-key registration protocol*. $\mathcal{C}$ takes input a secret key sk_{CA}. $\mathcal{U}$ takes input the identity ID of a user and the public key pk_{CA} corresponding to sk_{CA}. As result of the interaction, the output of $\mathcal{C}$ is (ID, pk, cert), where pk is a public key and cert is an issued certificate. The local output of $\mathcal{U}$ is (ID, pk, sk, cert), where sk is a secret key that user ID uses to decrypt ciphertexts. We write $((\mathsf{ID}, pk, \mathsf{cert}), (\mathsf{ID}, pk, sk, \mathsf{cert})) \xleftarrow{\$} (\mathcal{C}(sk_{\mathsf{CA}}), \mathcal{U}(\mathsf{ID}, pk_{\mathsf{CA}}))$ for the result of this interaction. Either party can quit the execution prematurely, in which case the output of the party is set to $\perp$.
- $\mathcal{E}$ is a randomized *encryption* algorithm that takes input a user's identity ID, a public encryption key pk, a certificate cert, the authority's public key pk_{CA}, and a message $M \in \mathrm{MsgSp}(I)$, and outputs a ciphertext $C \in \{0,1\}^* \cup \{\perp\}$.
- $\mathcal{D}$ is a deterministic *decryption* algorithm which takes input a user's identity ID, a secret decryption key sk, a certificate cert, the authority's public key pk_{CA}, and a ciphertext C, and outputs $M \in \mathrm{MsgSp}(I) \cup \{\perp\}$. If $M = \perp$ we say that the ciphertext C is invalid (relative to ID, sk, cert, pk_{CA}).

The scheme is *correct* iff for any parameters I, any pk_{CA}, any message $M \in \mathrm{MsgSp}(I)$, any user ID, and any $((\mathsf{ID}, pk, \mathsf{cert}), (\mathsf{ID}, pk, sk, \mathsf{cert})) \xleftarrow{\$} (\mathsf{CA}(sk_{\mathsf{CA}}), \mathcal{U}(\mathsf{ID}, pk_{\mathsf{CA}}))$, and any $C \xleftarrow{\$} \mathcal{E}(\mathsf{ID}, pk, \mathsf{cert}, pk_{\mathsf{CA}}, M)]$, it holds that $\mathcal{D}(\mathsf{ID}, sk, pk_{\mathsf{CA}}, \mathsf{cert}, C) = M$.

REMARK 1. Our syntax does not explicitly deal with verifying the certificates, even though this may be necessary for security of the scheme. We assume that the constructions include such checks as part of their encryption algorithms.

REMARK 2. The certificateless encryption schemes of [21,2] are special cases of certified encryption schemes where the certificate cert is empty.

SECURITY OF CERTIFIED ENCRYPTION SCHEMES. We start with an informal discussion of the more interesting aspects of our model for secure certified encryption, and motivate some of the design choices that we made.

We envision a powerful adversary that is allowed to even corrupt the CA (i.e. learn its secret key and act on its behalf). At a superficial glance it may seem that no security requirements would make sense in this case since under these circumstances the adversary could create new keys with valid certificates on behalf of honest users, and then decrypt any ciphertext created with these keys. We wish however to ensure that even if the CA is corrupt, the communication encrypted with keys truly registered by honest users is still protected. At least that requires the CA not to have users' secret keys. This requirement is somewhat akin to forward security. Without loss of generality, we treat the case when the corruption of the CA is static, i.e., the adversary decides at the beginning of its execution whether to control the CA or not. Indeed, we are able to show that our definition is equivalent (up to a constant factor in the security statement) to the analogous definition where the adversary can corrupt the CA at any point (see [10]).

Naturally the fundamental security requirement for certified encryption is privacy of encrypted data. However, as discussed in the introduction, we take into account potential threats arising from the use of the registration protocol. In particular, we require that an adversary cannot pass as genuine (registered) an unregistered key upon an honest user, in a way that allows the adversary to recover messages encrypted with this key. In other words, encryptions with unregistered keys can not be decrypted by the adversary.

Our model uses the standard definitional idea of indistinguishabiliy [22] captured via left-right encryption oracles [5]. The left-right encryption oracle is initialized with a secret bit b and encrypts either the left message M_0 or the right message M_1 of the two messages submitted by the adversary. The oracle is universal in the sense that the adversary can query it about any party ID and for any (not necessarily valid) key/certificate pair pk, cert. We restrict the kind of queries that are allowed in order to exclude trivial attacks. We demand that either (1) user ID is honest and (ID, pk, cert) has been registered before with the CA, or (2) (ID, pk, cert) is not registered but the CA is still honest.

The first condition covers the case of "standard" queries for proper keys of honest users, and encompasses the case when the CA might be corrupt. The second restriction prevents the adversary to register a key for some honest user (after corrupting the CA) and to determine the bit b easily. Also, if the CA is corrupt then the adversary can generate a certificate for any user locally, without invoking the registration protocol. This would also allow the adversary to create unregistered keys for which the oracle produces a valid ciphertext and which the adversary can still decrypt. Hence, we only permit queries where the key of the user has not been registered with the honest CA.

Finally, we emphasize that in our model we do not assume that the communication between the users and the CA is encrypted, i.e., we assume public channels. We therefore avoid the "chicken-and-egg"-like problem: how to assume secret transmissions if one is still trying to establish a public encryption key through this communication?

Definition 1. *[Security of Certified Encryption Schemes] Let* $\mathsf{CE} = (\mathcal{G}, \mathcal{K}, (\mathcal{C}, \mathcal{U}), \mathcal{E}, \mathcal{D})$ *be a certified encryption scheme. We associate to scheme* CE*, an adversary* $\mathcal{A}$*, and a bit* b *the experiments* $\mathbf{Exp}_{\mathsf{CE},\mathcal{A},b}^{\mathrm{cenc\text{-}ind\text{-}atk}}(k)$ *for* $\mathrm{atk} \in \{\mathrm{cpa}, \mathrm{cca}\}$*. In both experiments* $\mathcal{A}$ *is given as input* $I \xleftarrow{\$} \mathcal{G}(1^k)$*. The experiment maintains two virtual arrays RegListPub, RegListSec used to store public and secret information pertaining to users (respectively). We note that* $\mathcal{A}$ *knows the elements of RegListPub but not those of RegListSec. Also the adversary has access to all transcripts of the protocols executed during the experiment.*

- Corruption of certification authority: *First,* $\mathcal{A}$ *decides if to corrupt the* CA*. If so,* $\mathcal{A}$ *chooses the key* $\mathrm{pk}_{\mathsf{CA}}$ *of the* CA*, else* $\mathrm{pk}_{\mathsf{CA}}$ *is generated via* $(\mathrm{pk}_{\mathsf{CA}}, \mathrm{sk}_{\mathsf{CA}}) \xleftarrow{\$} \mathcal{K}(I)$ *and given to* $\mathcal{A}$*.*

- Registering keys of users: *During the experiment,* $\mathcal{A}$ *can specify a user* ID *from the set of identities, to initiate a run of the public-key registration protocol with the honest or corrupt certification authority. If this is the first time the user* ID *is activated then* $\mathcal{A}$ *first decides whether to corrupt this user or not. In the execution with the CA we assume wlog. that at least one party is honest. At the end of the execution, when* $\mathcal{C}$ *outputs values* $(\mathsf{ID}, \mathrm{pk}, \mathrm{cert})$ *and* $\mathcal{U}$ *outputs (possibly different) values* $(\mathsf{ID}', \mathrm{pk}', \mathrm{sk}', \mathrm{cert}')$*, we store* $(\mathsf{ID}', \mathrm{pk}', \mathrm{cert}')$ *in RegListPub and* $(\mathsf{ID}', \mathrm{pk}', \mathrm{sk}', \mathrm{cert}')$ *in RegListSec if* $\mathcal{U}$ *is honest, or merely* $(\mathsf{ID}, \mathrm{pk}, \mathrm{cert})$ *in RegListPub if only* $\mathcal{C}$ *is honest. If one of the parties is dishonest or stops prematurely then* $\perp$ *is stored in the corresponding array. Notice that all steps in the experiment, including steps of this interactive protocol may be arbitrarily interleaved.*

- Encryption queries: $\mathcal{A}$ *can query* $\mathcal{UE}_{\mathsf{CE}}(b, \mathrm{pk}_{\mathsf{CA}}, \cdot, \cdot, \cdot)$*, a universal left-right encryption oracle. It takes as input a tuple* $(\mathsf{ID}, \mathrm{pk}, \mathrm{cert})$ *and two messages* $M_0, M_1 \in \mathrm{MsgSp}(I)$ *of equal length and returns a ciphertext* $C \xleftarrow{\$} \mathcal{E}(\mathsf{ID}, \mathrm{pk}, \mathrm{cert}, \mathrm{pk}_{\mathsf{CA}}, M_b)$*. We impose the restriction that user* ID *is honest and at this point* $(\mathsf{ID}, \mathrm{pk}, \mathrm{cert})$ *is listed in RegListPub, or that the certification authority is still honest but* $(\mathsf{ID}, \mathrm{pk}, \mathrm{cert})$ *does not appear in RegListPub at this point.*

- Decryption queries: *In experiment* $\mathbf{Exp}_{\mathsf{CE},\mathcal{A},b}^{\mathrm{cenc\text{-}ind\text{-}cca}}(k)$ *the adversary is also given access to a universal decryption oracle* $\mathcal{UD}_{\mathsf{CE}}(\mathrm{pk}_{\mathsf{CA}}, \cdots)$ *which has access to the array RegListSec. The queries to the oracle are tuples* $(\mathsf{ID}, \mathrm{pk}, \mathrm{cert}, C)$ *where we require that* C *has not been previously returned by oracle* $\mathcal{UE}_{\mathsf{CE}}(b, \mathrm{pk}_{\mathsf{CA}}, \cdots)$ *as answer to some query* $((\mathsf{ID}, \mathrm{pk}, \mathrm{cert}), M_0, M_1)$*. If* $(\mathsf{ID}, \mathrm{pk}, \mathrm{sk}, \mathrm{cert})$ *occurs in RegListSec the oracle returns* $\mathcal{D}(\mathsf{ID}, \mathrm{sk}, \mathrm{cert}, \mathrm{pk}_{\mathsf{CA}}, C)$*; otherwise, it returns* ?$\perp$*.*

The adversary eventually stops and outputs a guess bit d *which is also considered to be the output of the experiment. For* $\mathrm{atk} \in \{\mathrm{cpa}, \mathrm{cca}\}$ *the adversary's advantages in attacking the scheme are defined as follows.*

$$\mathbf{Adv}_{\mathsf{CE},\mathcal{A}}^{\mathrm{cenc\text{-}ind\text{-}atk}}(k) = \Pr[\mathbf{Exp}_{\mathsf{CE},\mathcal{A},1}^{\mathrm{cenc\text{-}ind\text{-}atk}}(k) = 1] - \Pr[\mathbf{Exp}_{\mathsf{CE},\mathcal{A},0}^{\mathrm{cenc\text{-}ind\text{-}atk}}(k) = 1] .$$

CE *is said to be IND-CPA (resp. IND-CCA) secure if the corresponding advantage of any* poly(k)-*time adversary* $\mathcal{A}$ *is negligible.* ∎

"TRADITIONAL" CERTIFIED ENCRYPTION SCHEMES. We confirm that the classical approach of using signature-based certificates for the encryption scheme yields a secure certified encryption scheme. We show this to be the case even when during a public key registration a user does not prove that it knows the corresponding secret key. The schemes that we use in our construction satisfy standard security notions (see the full version [10] for precise definitions of syntax and security). We now give the scheme (Construction 1) and state our security result (Theorem 1). The proof is in the full version [10].

Construction 1. [Traditional Certified Encryption Scheme] Let DS = $(\mathcal{SG}_s, \mathcal{SK}_s, \mathcal{S}_s, \mathcal{V}_s)$ be a digital signature scheme, and AE = $(\mathcal{EG}_e, \mathcal{EK}_e, \mathcal{E}_e, \mathcal{D}_e)$ be an asymmetric encryption scheme. Define TCE = $(\mathcal{EG}, \mathcal{K}, (\mathcal{C}, \mathcal{U}), \mathcal{E}, \mathcal{D})$:

- *Parameter generation:* Algorithm $\mathcal{EG}(1^k)$ executes $I_s \xleftarrow{\$} \mathcal{SG}_s(1^k)$, $I_e \xleftarrow{\$} \mathcal{EG}_e(1^k)$ and outputs $I = (I_s, I_e)$.
- *Key generation:* Algorithm $\mathcal{K}$ generates a key pair $(pk_{\mathsf{CA}}, sk_{\mathsf{CA}}) \xleftarrow{\$} \mathcal{SK}_s(I_s)$.
- *Registration:* In order to register a key user, ID first generates a key pair $(pk, sk) \xleftarrow{\$} \mathcal{EK}_e(I_e)$ and sends (ID, pk) to $\mathcal{C}$ who computes $s \xleftarrow{\$} \mathcal{S}_s(sk_{\mathsf{CA}}, \mathsf{ID}\|$ pk) and outputs (ID, pk, s). The user sets cert = s and outputs (ID, pk, sk, cert).
- *Encryption:* To encrypt a message M under identity ID, public key pk, certificate cert and key pk_{CA} the encryption algorithm $\mathcal{E}$ first verifies with $\mathcal{V}_s$ that cert is a valid signature for ID$\|pk$ under key pk_{CA}. If not then return $\perp$. Else compute $C \xleftarrow{\$} \mathcal{E}_e(pk, M)$ and return C.
- *Decryption:* To decrypt a ciphertext C with (ID, sk, cert) and pk_{CA} run algorithm $\mathcal{D}_e(sk, C)$ and return the answer. ∎

Theorem 1. *Let* DS *be a secure signature scheme and let* AE *be an IND-CPA secure (resp. IND-CCA secure) encryption scheme. Then the certified encryption scheme in Construction 1 is IND-CPA secure (resp. IND-CCA secure).* ∎

The proof idea is as follows. We turn a successful adversary $\mathcal{A}$ on the certified encryption scheme into an adversary $\mathcal{B}_{\mathsf{AE}}$ on the underlying encryption scheme. This algorithm $\mathcal{B}_{\mathsf{AE}}$ tries to guess in advance which of the registered keys adversary $\mathcal{A}$ will use to break the security of the certified scheme. This simulation works as long as adversary $\mathcal{A}$ does not use an unregistered but valid key, in which case we derive a successful attack on the signature scheme used in the certification procedure.

EFFICIENT CERTIFIED ENCRYPTION SCHEME. In the sequel we present our ElGamal-based encryption scheme with implicit certificates. We show that if the computational Diffie-Hellman problem is hard (see [10] for a precise statement of this assumption), our scheme guarantees IND-CCA security. At the same time, the efficiency of our scheme is close to that of the basic ElGamal encryption *without* certificate verifications. The security of the following construction is captured by Theorem 2. Its security is also provided in [10].

The idea of our scheme is to let the CA issue certificates in forms of Schnorr signatures for identity ID and to use these values for a CCA2-version of the ElGamal encryption. That is, for the CA's public key $pk_{CA} = Z = g^z$ the CA hands the user the values $R = g^r$ and $\log_g RZ^c$ for $c = H(R, \text{ID})$. To send the user encrypted messages one uses the value RZ^c as the public ElGamal key, and the user can decrypt with his decryption key $sk = \log_g RZ^c$. Below we use a slightly different variant in which the user contributes to the Schnorr signature via a random value $S = g^s$, in order to deny the CA knowledge of the decryption key.

Construction 2. [Certified ElGamal Encryption] We construct the certified ElGamal encryption scheme $\mathsf{CE} = (\mathcal{EG}, \mathcal{EK}, (\mathcal{C}, \mathcal{U}), \mathcal{E}, \mathcal{D})$ as follows:

- *Parameter generation:* Algorithm $\mathcal{EG}$ on input 1^k generates a (description of a) group $\mathcal{G}$ of prime order $q = q(k)$, as well as a generator g of this group. Let $2^k \leq q < 2^{k+1}$. Algorithm $\mathcal{EG}$ also picks (descriptions of) hash functions $F = \{0,1\}^* \to \mathbf{Z}_q$, $G : \{0,1\}^* \to \{0,1\}^{t+k}$, $H : \{0,1\}^* \to \mathbf{Z}_q$. It returns $I = (\mathcal{G}, q, g, F, G, H)$. The associated message space is $\{0,1\}^t$. These parameters are given to all parties and algorithms as additional input.

- *Key generation:* Algorithm $\mathcal{EK}$ on input I selects $z \xleftarrow{\$} \mathbf{Z}_q$ and computes $Z = g^z$. It returns $(pk_{CA}, sk_{CA}) = (Z, (Z, z))$.

- *Key registration:* The pair $(\mathcal{C}, \mathcal{U})$ of interactive algorithms is defined by the following steps. $\mathcal{C}$ gets as input $sk_{CA} = (Z, z)$, while $\mathcal{U}$ gets some identity ID and $pk_{CA} = Z$. The authority $\mathcal{C}$ first picks $r \xleftarrow{\$} \mathbf{Z}_q$, computes $R = g^r$ and and sends R to $\mathcal{U}$. User $\mathcal{U}$ chooses $s \xleftarrow{\$} \mathbf{Z}_q$, computes $S = g^s$ and sends (S, ID) back to $\mathcal{C}$. Upon receiving (S, ID) algorithm $\mathcal{C}$ sets $c = H(R, S, \text{ID})$ and $y = r + cz \bmod q$. Let $pk = (R, S)$ and $\mathsf{cert} = \varepsilon$ be empty. $\mathcal{C}$ returns (R, y) to $\mathcal{U}$ and outputs $(\text{ID}, pk, \mathsf{cert})$. $\mathcal{U}$ verifies that $g^y = RZ^c$ for $c = H(R, S, \text{ID})$, computes $sk = s + y \bmod q$ and outputs $(\text{ID}, pk, sk, \mathsf{cert})$. Note that $sk = \log_g RSZ^c$.

- *Encryption:* For input $\text{ID}, pk = (R, S), \mathsf{cert} = \varepsilon, pk_{CA} = Z$ and message $M \in \{0,1\}^t$ the encryption algorithm picks $\alpha \xleftarrow{\$} \{0,1\}^k$, computes $a = F(\text{ID}, pk, \mathsf{cert}, \alpha\|M)$, $A = g^a$ and $B = G(\text{ID}, pk, \mathsf{cert}, (RSZ^c)^a) \oplus \alpha\|M$ where $c = H(R, S, \text{ID})$. It outputs $C = (A, B)$.

- *Decryption:* For input $\text{ID}, sk, \mathsf{cert} = \varepsilon, pk_{CA} = Z$ and $C = (A, B)$ the decryption algorithm computes $\alpha\|M = B \oplus G(\text{ID}, pk, \mathsf{cert}, A^{sk})$ and verifies that $A = g^{F(\text{ID}, pk, \mathsf{cert}, \alpha\|M)}$. In this case it returns M, else it returns $\perp$. ∎

Theorem 2. *Suppose that the parameter generator $\mathcal{EG}$ in the encryption scheme in Construction 2 generates CDH-secure groups, and that F, G, H are modeled as random oracles. Then the scheme CE in Construction 2 is IND-CCA secure in the random oracle model.* ∎

The efficiency of our scheme is comparable to the one of regular ElGamal encryption *without* certificate verification. With the square-and-multiply exponentiation method, basic ElGamal encryption without certification needs $3k$ expected multiplications, our scheme based on implicit certificates requires $3.25k$ multiplications on the average, whereas regular ElGamal encryption with explicit Schnorr signature certificates would require $4.75k$ expected modular multiplications.

4   Secure Signatures in Public-Key Infrastructures

SYNTAX OF CERTIFIED-SIGNATURE SCHEMES. A *certified-signature scheme* is a tuple $\mathsf{CS} = (\mathcal{SG}, \mathcal{K}, (\mathcal{C}, \mathcal{U}), \mathcal{S}, \mathcal{V})$, where the constituent algorithms run in polynomial time and are defined as follows.

- Algorithms $\mathcal{SG}, \mathcal{K}$ and registration protocol $(\mathcal{C}, \mathcal{U})$ are as in the definition of certified encryption schemes (here, $\mathcal{SG}$ replaces $\mathcal{EG}$).
- $\mathcal{S}$ is a (possibly) randomized *signing* algorithm. It takes input an identity ID, a secret key sk, a certificate cert, the authority's public key pk_{CA} and a message $M \in \{0, 1\}^*$, and outputs a signature σ.
- $\mathcal{V}$ is a deterministic *verification* algorithm. It takes input an identity ID, a public key pk, a certificate cert, a public key pk_{CA}, a message M and a signature σ, and outputs 0 or 1. In the latter case, we say that σ is a *valid* signature for M relative to $(\mathsf{ID}, pk, \mathsf{cert}, pk_{\mathsf{CA}})$.

We require that for all $M \in \{0, 1\}^*$ and all users ID, if (pk, sk) is a key pair for user ID with cert, i.e., $((\mathsf{ID}, pk, \mathsf{cert}), (\mathsf{ID}, pk, sk, \mathsf{cert})) \overset{\$}{\leftarrow} (\mathcal{C}(sk_{\mathsf{CA}}), \mathcal{U}(\mathsf{ID}, pk_{\mathsf{CA}}))$ for $(pk_{\mathsf{CA}}, sk_{\mathsf{CA}})$ generated by $\mathcal{K}(I)$ and I output by $\mathcal{G}(1^k)$, then, for verification, $\mathcal{V}(\mathsf{ID}, pk, \mathsf{cert}, pk_{\mathsf{CA}}, M, \mathcal{S}(\mathsf{ID}, sk, \mathsf{cert}, pk_{\mathsf{CA}}, M)) = 1$.

SECURITY OF CERTIFIED-SIGNATURE SCHEMES. Our model is for the basic setting outlined in Section 2. Users register public-keys by interacting with a certification authority on public, authenticated channels. After registration, parties can sign messages using the secret keys associated to the public key the have registered. Signatures can then be verified, and we emphasize that the verification process involves both the public key of the CA and that of the user.

We consider again a powerful adversary whose capabilities combine the more standard chosen-message attacks with additional capabilities specific to our setting. The adversary attempts a forgery by outputting a user identity, a public key, a message and a signature. Roughly, the adversary wins if the signature is valid with respect to the chosen public key, and either (1) the honest user has registered the public key and has not priorly signed the message, (2) the public key has not been registered, or (3) the same public key has been registered by a different (honest) user. Condition (1) corresponds to the notion of existential unforgeability [23] for standard digital signature schemes, and we require that it holds even if the CA is corrupt. Condition (2) guarantees that signatures for keys that are not bound to identities of the users (i.e., "outside of the PKI") are not valid. Condition (3) prevents attacks where for example a malicious user claims authorship of a message signed by another user.

Definition 2. [Security of Certified-Signature Schemes] *Let* CS = $(\mathcal{SG}, \mathcal{K},$ $(\mathcal{C}, \mathcal{U}), \mathcal{S}, \mathcal{V})$ *be a certified-signature scheme. We associate to scheme* CS, *an adversary* $\mathcal{A}$, *and security parameter* k *an experiment* $\mathbf{Exp}_{\mathsf{CS},\mathcal{A}}^{\mathrm{cs\text{-}uf}}(k)$. *The experiment maintains arrays RegListPub, RegListSec which are as in the experiments defining security for certified encryption schemes. In the beginning of the experiment, public parameters are generated via* $I \xleftarrow{\$} \mathcal{G}(1^k)$ *and are given as input to the adversary, and then,* $\mathcal{A}$ *can make the following requests or queries:*

- Corruption of certification authority: *This stage is as in the experiment defining the security of certified encryption.*

- Registering keys of users: *This is handled as in the model for defining security of certified encryption.*

- Signature queries: $\mathcal{A}$ *can make signature requests to a universal signing oracle* $\mathcal{US}_{\mathsf{CS}}^{\mathrm{pk_{CA}}}$: *on a query* (ID, pk, cert, M) *the oracle verifies that user* ID *is honest, and if so it looks up the corresponding entry* (ID, pk, sk, cert) *in RegListSec and returns to* $\mathcal{A}$ *a signature* $\mathcal{S}(\mathsf{ID}, \mathrm{sk}, \mathrm{cert}, \mathrm{pk_{CA}}, M)$. *Otherwise, the answer of the oracle is* $\perp$.

Eventually, $\mathcal{A}$ *stops and outputs an attempted forgery* (ID, pk, cert, M, σ). *The experiment returns* 1 *if* $\mathcal{V}(\mathrm{pk_{CA}}, \mathsf{ID}, \mathrm{pk}, \mathrm{cert}, M, \sigma) = 1$ *and the following conditions are satisfied (otherwise it returns* 0):

1. ID *is honest, and no valid signing query* (ID, pk, cert$'$, M) *was made for any* cert$'$, *or*

2. CA *is honest and* (ID, pk, cert$'$) $\notin$ *RegListPub, for any* cert$'$ *(i.e. the user* ID *never registered the key* pk), *or*

3. CA *is honest and* (ID$'$, pk, cert$'$) $\in$ *RegListPub for some honest user* ID$'$ $\neq$ ID *(i.e. some honest user registered* pk),

We define the advantage of adversary $\mathcal{A}$ *as*

$$\mathbf{Adv}_{\mathsf{CS},\mathcal{A}}^{\mathrm{cs\text{-}uf}}(k) = \Pr\left[\mathbf{Exp}_{\mathsf{CS},\mathcal{A}}^{\mathrm{cs\text{-}uf}}(k) = 1\right].$$

We say that CS *is a secure certified-signature scheme if the function* $\mathbf{Adv}_{\mathsf{CS},\mathcal{A}}^{\mathrm{cs\text{-}uf}}(\cdot)$ *is negligible for all poly(k)-time adversaries* $\mathcal{A}$. ∎

"TRADITIONAL" CERTIFIED SIGNATURE SCHEMES. Here we analyze the traditional approach to certified signatures, where the public-keys of users are certified by the certification authority using a a digital signature scheme. In turn, users produce signatures by using the secret keys associated with their certificated public-keys. Signature verification consist in verifying the signature of the user and the validity of the certificates for the users' public-keys. An interesting aspect that we clarify is that proofs of knowledge of the secret key associated to the public key of the user are not necessary to ensure security of the scheme. We show that simply signing a designated message in a proof of possession is sufficient for security. We now give the scheme (Construction 3) and state our security result (Theorem 3). The proof is in [10], along with the concrete security result.

Construction 3. [**Traditional Certified Signature Scheme**] Let DS = $(\mathcal{SG}, \mathcal{SK}, \mathcal{S}_1, \mathcal{V}_1)$ be a digital signature scheme[4]. The first two algorithms of a certified-signature scheme TCS = $(\mathcal{G}, \mathcal{K}, (\mathcal{C}, \mathcal{U}), \mathcal{S}, \mathcal{V})$ are those of DS, and the rest of polynomial time algorithms are defined as follows.

- *Parameter and key generation:* $\mathcal{G} \equiv \mathcal{SG}, \mathcal{K} \equiv \mathcal{SK}$.
- *Registration:* To register pk, a user ID sends pk to the CA. CA sends to the user a random "challenge" message[5] $M' \xleftarrow{\$} \{0,1\}^k$. The user computes $\sigma' \xleftarrow{\$} \mathcal{S}(sk, 0||M')$ and sends it to CA. If $\mathcal{V}(pk, 0||M', \sigma') = 1$ then CA computes cert $\xleftarrow{\$} \mathcal{S}(sk_{\mathsf{CA}}, (\mathsf{ID}, pk))$, sends cert to the user and outputs $(\mathsf{ID}, pk, \mathsf{cert})$. The user outputs $(\mathsf{ID}, pk, sk, \mathsf{cert})$.
- *Signing:* $\mathcal{S}$ on input $(\mathsf{ID}, sk, \mathsf{cert}, pk_{\mathsf{CA}}, M)$ outputs $\sigma \xleftarrow{\$} \mathcal{S}_1(sk, 1||M)$.
- *Verification:* $\mathcal{V}$ takes $(\mathsf{ID}, pk, \mathsf{cert}, pk_{\mathsf{CA}}, M, \sigma)$. It outputs 1 iff $\mathcal{V}_1(pk_{\mathsf{CA}}, (\mathsf{ID}, pk), \mathsf{cert}) = 1$ and $\mathcal{V}_1(pk, 1||M, \sigma) = 1$. ∎

Theorem 3. *Let* DS = $(\mathcal{SG}, \mathcal{SK}, \mathcal{S}, \mathcal{V})$ *be a digital signature scheme. Then if* DS *is secure (existentially unforgeable under chosen-message attack), then* TCS *is a secure certified signature scheme.* ∎

The proof idea is to transform an attacker against the certified signature scheme into one against the underlying signature scheme (by guessing the right target key in advance). It is not hard to see that each successful attack on the certified scheme (new signatures under keys of honest users, generating an unregistered but valid key, and registering keys of honest users under different names) immediately yields a forgery for the signature scheme.

EFFICIENT CERTIFIED SIGNATURE SCHEMES. Here we give a construction of an efficient, provably secure certified signature scheme based on Schnorr signatures. Its security, captured by Theorem 4, is based on the discrete logarithm assumption (a precise definition is given in [10]). The idea is similar to the encryption case, where the CA issued Schnorr signatures to be used as the secret and public ElGamal keys by users, only this time we let the users deploy the key pairs for Schnorr signatures themselves.

Construction 4. [**Schnorr-based Certified Signature Scheme**] We define scheme CS = $(\mathcal{SG}, \mathcal{K}, (\mathcal{C}, \mathcal{U}), \mathcal{S}, \mathcal{V})$ by the algorithms:

- *Parameter generation:* Algorithm $\mathcal{SG}$ on input 1^k generates a (description of a) group $\mathcal{G}$ of prime order $q = q(k)$, as well as a generator g of this group. Let $2^k \leq q < 2^{k+1}$. Algorithm $\mathcal{SG}$ also picks (descriptions of) hash functions $G : \{0,1\}^* \to \mathbf{Z}_q$, $H : \{0,1\}^* \to \mathbf{Z}_q$. It returns $I = (\mathcal{G}, q, g, G, H)$. These parameters are given to all parties and algorithms as additional input.

---

[4] For simplicity we consider a case when the certification authority and a user use a single signature scheme. The definition and other results can be easily modified to accommodate a case when different signatures are used by the parties.

[5] We need that all challenge messages be different with overwhelming probability. An alternative approach would be to include a current date and time in the challenge message.

- *Key generation:* Algorithm $\mathcal{EK}$ on input I selects $z \xleftarrow{\$} \mathbf{Z}_q$ and computes $Z = g^z$. It returns $(pk_{\mathsf{CA}}, sk_{\mathsf{CA}}) = (Z, (Z, z))$.
- *Key registration:* The pair $(\mathcal{C}, \mathcal{U})$ of interactive algorithms is defined by the following steps. $\mathcal{C}$ gets as input $sk_{\mathsf{CA}} = (Z, z)$, while $\mathcal{U}$ gets some identity ID and $pk_{\mathsf{CA}} = Z$. The authority $\mathcal{C}$ first picks $r \xleftarrow{\$} \mathbf{Z}_q$, computes $R = g^r$ and sends R to $\mathcal{U}$. User $\mathcal{U}$ chooses $s \xleftarrow{\$} \mathbf{Z}_q$, computes $S = g^s$ and sends (S, ID) back to $\mathcal{C}$. Upon receiving (S, ID) algorithm $\mathcal{C}$ sets $c = H(R, S, \mathsf{ID})$ and $y = r + cz \bmod q$. Let $pk = (R, S)$ and $\mathsf{cert} = \varepsilon$. $\mathcal{C}$ returns (R, y) to $\mathcal{U}$ and outputs $(\mathsf{ID}, pk, \mathsf{cert})$. $\mathcal{U}$ verifies that $g^y = RZ^c$ for $c = H(R, S, \mathsf{ID})$, computes $sk = s + y \bmod q$ and outputs $(\mathsf{ID}, pk, sk, \mathsf{cert})$. Note that $sk = \log_g RSZ^c$.
- *Signing:* For input ID, sk, $\mathsf{cert} = \varepsilon$, (R, S), certificate ε and Z the signing algorithm picks $a \xleftarrow{\$} \mathbf{Z}_q$ and computes $A = g^a$ and $B = a + sk \cdot G(\mathsf{ID}, A, M)$. The signature is $\sigma = (A, B)$.
- *Verification:* For input ID, $pk = (R, S)$, ε, $pk_{\mathsf{CA}} = Z$, a message M and a signature $\sigma = (A, B)$ the verification algorithm outputs 1 if the equation $g^B = A(RSZ^c)^d$ holds, where $c = H(R, S, \mathsf{ID})$ and $d = G(\mathsf{ID}, A, M)$. Otherwise it outputs 0. ∎

Theorem 4. *The certified-signature scheme of Construction 4 is secure in the random oracle model if the parameter generation algorithm generates DL-secure groups.* ∎

For the above scheme, signing is exactly as in standard Schnorr signature schemes and thus as efficient. Verification of a signature, however, now requires on the average only $1.875k$ modular multiplications with the square-and-multiply method, as opposed to $3.5k$ modular multiplications as required to verify two separate Schnorr signatures.

5 Related Work

Here we review several PKI-related works in the literature and put our results in the context [21, 2, 15, 16, 28, 29, 41, 27, 34, 30, 40, 17, 7, 18, 42, 43, 25, 31].

Gentry [21], Al-Riyami and Paterson [2] and subsequent works [30, 40, 17, 7, 18, 3, 42, 43, 25, 31] recently proposed public-key encryption schemes that do not assume a standard PKI. Similarly to our efficient scheme, certificates are implicit, that is, a sender does not have to verify the certificate before sending an encrypted message, yet only the user who properly registered its public key is able to decrypt. The goals of their schemes and ours, however, differ. The motivation for the works of [21, 2, 30, 40, 17, 7, 18, 42, 43, 25, 31] is to overcome the main weakness of identity-based encryption (IBE) [39, 12], namely, the requirement that the trusted party called a private key generator (PKG) knows the secret keys of the users, while preserving the advantage of IBE of simplified management of expired and revoked public keys. Gentry also eliminates the requirement of a secure channel between a user and the PKG. On the other hand, the goal of our scheme is to achieve an efficiency improvement over "traditional" discrete-logarithm-based certified encryption schemes and, similar, for certified signature schemes. While our schemes require the key management support of a traditional PKI, they come with computational savings.

Security of implicit certificates in the context of digital signatures had been priorly investigated by Brown, Gallant, and Vanstone [13]. Their security model is only concerned with the certification process and does not consider the usage of the resulting keys. However, for the particular application analyzed in the paper, the resulting security model (which is strictly weaker and less general than the one we introduce here) appears to suffice.

Canetti [15] recently presented a universally composable certification protocol, that uses traditional signature-based certificates. And while universal composition provides very strong security guarantees, his approach falls again short of investigating the combined certification and encryption or signature process, neither does his model take CA corruptions and the broader adversarial capabilities into account. In contrast to our more efficient solutions based on implicit certificates, alternatives to the traditional approach are not discussed in [15].

Stronger security requirements on signatures are imposed by the model suggested by Menezes and Smart [35] for the use of signatures in the "multi-user setting". Condition (3) of our definition of security for signature schemes is reminiscent of their security requirement. However, the framework proposed in [35] does not explicitly consider the registration protocol.

Since our basic model is concerned with security under one-level of certification, some of the issues specific to hierarchical PKIs do not show up explicitly. When tackling such settings (which naturally arise in practice, e.g. when using PGP [44]), special attention needs to be payed to the trust that parties put in certificate chains, given that one or several of the CAs could have been corrupted. Prior research that could prove useful in extending our framework to these settings include various models for trust in key authenticity [33, 14, 26], quantitative trust evaluation [8], as well as various defenses against multiple CA corruption (e.g. multi-certificate chains [37]).

Our efficient certified encryption scheme resembles the PKI-enabled CA-Oblivious encryption scheme independently proposed by Castelluccia et al. in their recent work [16] as a building block for a secret handshake protocol. The authors analyze their schemes with respect to a significantly weaker security notion, namely one-wayness. Moreover, in their scheme the CA knows the secret keys of the users and is trusted to behave honestly. In their model, it is also assumed that the CA is trusted not to use the knowledge of the secret keys. Moreover, no standard outsider attacks are considered, that is a scheme where an adversary can decrypt messages addressed to the registered users can be proven secure! The authors prove that their scheme satisfies their security notion in the RO model. The authors suggest how to modify the scheme to allow the CA to be less trusted, but the security of the resulting scheme is unclear. It is also suggested in [16] that the scheme can be made IND-CCA secure using the Fujisaki-Okamoto transform [20]. We note, however, that it is not immediate without a new proof that this would work, since the Fujisaki-Okamoto transform can be provably applied to basic encryption schemes that assume a standard PKI with explicit certificates. The primitive of [16] is different; it employs implicit certificates. Therefore, a new security definition and a proof will be necessary to validate this suggestion. On the other hand, our scheme provably satisfies a very strong security definition discussed above, where the CA is only trusted not to register new keys for users without their permission. Our results also show that the Fujisaki-Okamoto transform is not needed as our scheme is very simple and yet IND-CCA secure.

Our efficient certified signature scheme resembles the proxy signature scheme of Kim, Park and Won [28] and the self-certified signature scheme of Lee and Kim [29]. Unlike our scheme, the proxy signature scheme assumes a PKI where each user already holds a public key and a digital certificate. Neither of these papers provides formal security definitions and analyses. A modification of the proxy signature scheme of [28] has been proven secure in [11], but their proof is for a primitive that differs from ours in that it assumes a PKI, explicit certificates, and involves a different security notion.

Acknowledgments

Part of the work was done while the authors were at UCSD. We thank Martin Abadi, Mihir Bellare and Burt Kaliski for useful discussions, and the anonymous reviewers for their comments. Alexandra Boldyreva is supported in part by NSF CAREER award 0545659. Marc Fischlin is supported by the Emmy Noether Program Fi 940/2-1 of the German Research Foundation (DFG). Bogdan Warinschi is supported in part by the ACI Jeunes Chercheurs JC 9005.

References

1. C. Adams and S. Farrell. Internet x.509 public key infrastructure: Certificate management protocols. Work in progress, 2004.
2. S. Al-Riyami and K. G. Paterson. Certificateless public key cryptography. In *ASIACRYPT*, volume 2894 of *LNCS*, pages 452–473. Springer-Verlag, 2003.
3. J. Baek, R. Safavi-Naini, and W. Susilo. Certificateless public key encryption without pairing. In *Information Security (ISC)*, volume 3650 of *LNCS*, pages 134–148. Springer-Verlag, 2005.
4. M. Bellare, A. Boldyreva, and J. Staddon. Multi-recipient encryption schemes: Security notions and randomness re-use. In *Public-Key Cryptography (PKC)*, volume 2567. Springer-Verlag, 2003.
5. M. Bellare, A. Desai, E. Jokipii, and P. Rogaway. A concrete security treatment of symmetric encryption. In *FOCS '97: Proceedings of the 38th Annual Symposium on Foundations of Computer Science (FOCS '97)*. IEEE Computer Society, 1997.
6. M. Bellare and P. Rogaway. Random oracles are practical: a paradigm for designing efficient protocols. In *Conference on Computer and Communications Security (CCS)*. ACM, 1993.

7. K. Bentahar, P. Farshim, J. Malone-Lee, and N.P. Smart. Generic constructions of identity-based and certificateless kems. *Cryptology ePrint Archive, Report 2005/058.*, 2005.

8. T. Beth, M. Borcherding, and B. Klein. Valuation of trust in open networks. In *Computer Security—ESORICS 94*, pages 3–18. Springer-Verlag, 1994.

9. A. Boldyreva. Threshold signatures, multisignatures and blind signatures based on the Gap-Diffie-Hellman-group signature scheme. In *Public Key Cryptography (PKC) '03*, pages 31–46, 2003.

10. A. Boldyreva, M. Fischlin, A. Palacio, and B. Warinschi. A closer look at PKI: Security and efficiency. *A full version of this paper. Available at http://www-static.cc.gatech.edu/~aboldyre/publications.html*, 2007.

11. A. Boldyreva, A. Palacio, and B. Warinschi. Secure proxy signaure schemes for delegation of signing rights. *Cryptology ePrint Archive, Report 2003/096.*, 2003.

12. D. Boneh and M. Franklin. Identity-based encryption from the Weil pairing. In *CRYPTO*, volume 2139 of *LNCS*. Springer-Verlag, 2001.

13. D.R. L. Brown, R. P. Gallant, and S. A. Vanstone. Provably secure implicit certificate schemes. In *Conference on Financial Cryptography '01*, pages 156–165. Springer-Verlag, 2002.

14. M. Burmester, Y. Desmedt, and G. Kabatianskii. Trust and security: A new look at the Byzantine generals problem. In R. N. Wright and P. G. Neumann, editors, *Network Threats, DIMACS, Series in Discrete Mathematics and Theoretical Computer Science, 1996, vol. 38*. AMS, 1998.

15. R. Canetti. Universally composable signature, certification, and authentication. In *CSFW*. IEEE Computer Society, 2004.

16. C. Castelluccia, S. Jarecki, and G. Tsudik. Secret handshakes from CA-oblivious encryption. In *ASIACRYPT*, volume 3329 of *LNCS*, pages 293–307. Springer-Verlag, 2004.

17. Z. Cheng and R. Comley. Efficient certificateless public key encryption. *Cryptology ePrint Archive, Report 2005/012.*, 2005.

18. A. W. Dent and C. Kudla. On proofs of security for certificateless cryptosystems. *Cryptology ePrint Archive, Report 2005/348.*, 2005.

19. T. ElGamal. A public key cryptosystem and signature scheme based on discrete logarithms. *IEEE Transactions on Information Theory*, Vol. 31, 1985.

20. E. Fujisaki and T. Okamoto. Secure integration of asymmetric and symmetric encryption schemes. In *CRYPTO*, volume 1666 of *LNCS*, pages 537–554, 1999.

21. C. Gentry. Certificate-based encryption and the certificate revocation problem. In *EUROCRYPT*, volume 2656 of *LNCS*, pages 272–293. Springer-Verlag, 2003.

22. S. Goldwasser and S. Micali. Probabilistic encryption. *Journal of Computer and System Science*, 1984.

23. S. Goldwasser, S. Micali, and R. L. Rivest. A digital signature scheme secure against adaptive chosen-message attacks. *SIAM Journal of Computing*, 17(2):281–308, April 1988.

24. J. Herzog, M. Liskov, and S. Micali. Plaintext awareness via key registration. In *CRYPTO*, volume 2729. Springer-Verlag, 2003.

25. B. Hu, D. Wong, Z. Zhang, and X. Deng. Key replacement attack against a generic construction of certificateless signature. In *ACISP*, volume 4058 of *LNCS*, pages 235–246. Springer-Verlag, 2006.

26. A. Josang. Trust-based decision making for electronic transactions. In *Fourth Nordic Workshop on Secure IT Systems (NORDSEC'99)*, pages 99–105, 1999.

27. B. Kaliski. An unknown key-share attack on the mqv key agreement protocol. *ACM Transactions on Information and System Security (TISSEC)*, 4(3):275–288, 2001.

28. S. Kim, S. Park, and D. Won. Proxy signatures, revisited. In *ICICS*. Springer-Verlag, 1997.

29. B. Lee and K. Kim. Self-certified signatures. In *Indocrypt*, volume 2551 of *LNCS*. Springer-Verlag, 2002.

30. Y.-R. Lee and H.-S. Lee. An authenticated certificateless public key encryption scheme. *Cryptology ePrint Archive, Report 2004/150.*, 2004.

31. B. Libert and J.-J. Quisquater. On Constructing Certificateless Cryptosystems from Identity Based Encryption. In *Public Key Cryptography (PKC)*, LNCS. Springer-Verlag, 2006.

32. A. Lysyanskaya, R. L. Rivest, A. Sahai, and S. Wolf. Pseudonym systems. In *Selected Areas in Cryptography (SAC)*, pages 184–199. Springer-Verlag, 1999.

33. U. Maurer. Modeling public-key infrastructure. In *Computer Security—ESORICS 96*, pages 325–350. Springer-Verlag, 1996.

34. A. Menezes, M. Qu, and S. A. Vanstone. Some new key agreement protocols providing mutual implicit authentication. In *Selected Areas in Cryptography (SAC)*, 1995.

35. A. Menezes and N. Smart. Security of signature schemes in a multi-user setting. *Designs, Codes and Cryptography*, 33:261–274, 2004.

36. S. Micali, K. Ohta, and L. Reyzin. Accountable-subgroup multisignatures. In *Conference on Computer and Communications Security (CCS)*, pages 245–254. ACM, 2001.

37. M. K. Reiter and S. G. Stubblebine. Path independence for authentication in large scale systems. In *Proceedings of the 4th ACM Conference on Computer and Communications Security*, pages 57–66, 1997.

38. C. P. Schnorr. Efficient signature generation by smart cards. *Journal of Cryptology*, 4(3):161–174, 1991.

39. A. Shamir. Identity-based cryptosystems and signature schemes. In *CRYPTO*. Springer-Verlag, 1984.

40. Y. Shi and J. Li. Provable efficient certificateless public key encryption. *Cryptology ePrint Archive, Report 2005/287.*, 2005.

41. V. Shoup. On formal models for secure key exchange. *IBM Research Report RZ 3120*, 1999.

42. D. H. Yum and P. J. Lee. Generic construction of certificateless encryption. In *EuroPKI*, volume 3043 of *LNCS*, pages 802–811. Springer-Verlag, 2004.

43. D. H. Yum and P. J. Lee. Generic construction of certificateless signature. In *ACISP*, volume 3108 of *LNCS*, pages 200–211. Springer-Verlag, 2004.

44. P. R. Zimmermann. *The Official PGP User's Guide*. MIT Press, Cambridge, Massachussets, 1995.

Self-Generated-Certificate Public Key Encryption Without Pairing

Junzuo Lai[1] and Weidong Kou[2]

[1] Department of Computer Science and Engineering
Shanghai Jiao Tong University, Shanghai 200030, China
laijunzuo@sjtu.edu.cn
[2] School of Computer Science and Technology
Xi Dian University, Xi'an 710071, China
kou_weidong@yahoo.com.cn

Abstract. Certificateless Public Key Cryptography (CL-PKC) has very appealing features, namely it does not require any public key certification (cf. traditional Public Key Cryptography) nor having key escrow problem (cf. Identity-Based Cryptography). However, it does suffer to the Denial-of-Decryption (DoD) Attack called by Liu and Au [1], as its nature is similar to the well known Denial-of-Service (DoS) Attack. Based on CL-PKC, they introduced a new paradigm called Self-Generated-Certificate Public Key Cryptography (SGC-PKC) that captured the DoD Attack and proposed a first scheme derived from a novel application of Water's Identity-Based Encryption scheme. In this paper, we propose a new SGC-PKE scheme that does not depend on the bilinear pairings, which make it be more efficient and more short public keys than Liu and Au's scheme. More importantly, our scheme reaches Girault's trusted level 3 (cf. Girault's trusted level 2 of Liu and Au's scheme), the same level as is enjoyed in a traditional PKI.

Keywords: Certificateless Public Key Cryptography, Self-Generated-Certificate Public Key Cryptography, Self-Certified-Key.

1 Introduction

In traditional Public Key Cryptography (PKC), each user selects his own private key and computes the corresponding public key, which is published. If a user wants to send an encrypted message to other user, he needs to know the user's public key. However, it is easy to suffer from the man-in-the-middle attack. To address this threat, there is a need to provide an assurance to the user about the relationship between a public key and the identity (or authority) of the holder of the corresponding private key. In a traditional Public Key Infrastructure (PKI), this assurance is delivered in the form of certificate, essentially a signature by a Certification Authority (CA) on a public key. However, a PKI faces with many challenges in the practice, such as revocation, storage and distribution of certificates.

T. Okamoto and X. Wang (Eds.): PKC 2007, LNCS 4450, pp. 476–489, 2007.

Identity-Based Public Key Cryptography (ID-PKC), first proposed by Shamir [13], tackles the problem of authenticity of keys in a different way to traditional PKI. In ID-PKC, a user's public key is derived directly from certain aspects of its identity, for example, an IP address belonging to a network host, or an e-mail address associated with a user. Private keys are generated for entities by a trusted third party called a Private Key Generator (PKG). In this way, the certificate is provided implicitly due to the fact that the user will not have the ability of performing any cryptographic operations, if he hasn't obtained a correct private key associated with the published identity. The only disadvantage of ID-PKC is an unconditional trust to the PKG, which results that PKG can impersonate any user, or decrypt any ciphertext.

In order to solve for the above problem, Certificateless Public Key Cryptography (CL-PKC) was introduced by Al-Riyami and Paterson [2,3]. It is a new paradigm which lies between Identity-Based Cryptography and traditional Public Key Cryptography. The concept is to eliminate the inherent key-escrow problem of Identity-Based Cryptography (IBC). At the same time, it preserves the attractive advantage of IBC which is the absence of digital certificates (issued by Certificate Authority) and their important management overhead. Different from IBC, the user's public key is no longer an arbitrary string. Rather, it is similar to the public key used in the traditional PKC generated by the user. A crucial difference between them is that the public key in CL-PKC does not need to be explicitly certified as it has been generated using some partial private key obtained from the trusted authority called Key Generation Center (KGC). Note here that the KGC does not know the user's private keys since they contain secret information generated by the users themselves, thereby removing the escrow problem in IBC.

It seems that CL-PKC can solve the problem of explicit certification. Nevertheless it suffers Denial-of-Decryption (DoD) Attack called by Liu and Au [1]. Suppose Alice wants to send an encrypted message to Bob. She takes Bob's public key and his identity (or personal information) as input to the encryption function. However, Carol, the adversary, has replaced Bob's public key by someone's public key. Although Carol cannot decrypt the ciphertext, Bob also cannot decrypt the message while Alice is unaware of this. This is similar to Denial of Service (DoS) Attack in the way that the attacker cannot gain any secret information but precluding others from getting the normal service.

Liu and Au [1] propose a new paradigm called Self-Generated-Certificate Public Key Cryptography (SGC-PKC) to defend the above attack while preserving all advantages of Certificateless Public Key Cryptography. Similar to CL-PKC, every user is given a partial secret key by the KGC and generates his own secret key and corresponding public key. In addition, he also needs to generate a certificate using his own secret key. The purpose of this self-generated certificate is similar to the one in traditional PKC. That is, to bind the identity (or personal information) and the public key together. The main difference is that, it can be verified by using the user's identity and public key only and does not require any trusted party. It is implicitly included in the user's public key. If Carol uses her public key to replace Alice's public key (or certificate), Bob can be aware of this and he may ask Alice to send him again her public key for the encryption.

Related Work. Al-Riyami and Paterson [2,3] introduced Certificateless Public Key Cryptography and proposed a CL-encryption scheme and a CL-signature scheme. Some concrete efficient implementations were proposed in [8,9]. In addition, some generic construction were proposed in [7,5,6].

In [4], Baek et al. proposed a CL-encryption scheme without pairing, which was related to the early works on the self-certified keys [10,11]. However, their scheme can't be converted to SGC-PKE directly and only reaches Girault's trusted level 2. We modify their scheme to get a new CL-encryption scheme without pairing. Our scheme can be converted to SGC-PKE directly and reaches Girault's trusted level 3, which makes our scheme more appealing. Our works are related to the works on Self-Certificate-PKI [12].

Liu and Au proposed the first SGC-PKE scheme in [1], which defends the DoD attack that exists in CL-PKE. However, their scheme is based on a CL-encryption scheme and a CL-signature scheme that are using the same set of public parameters and user key generation algorithm. In addition, their scheme has long public keys due to their CL-PKC derived from a novel application of Water's Identity-Based Encryption scheme and only reaches Girault's trusted level 2. All there make their scheme impractical.

Contribution. In this paper, we propose a SGC-PKE scheme without pairing and prove that it is secure in a fully adaptive adversarial model, provided that the standard Computational Diffie-Hellman (CDH) problem is hard. Compared with the first scheme, our scheme is more efficient, has short public keys and reaches Girault's trusted level 3, which makes our scheme more practical.

Organization. The rest of the paper is organized as follow. We give some definitions in Section 2. We propose a CL-encryption scheme in Section 3. The proposed SGC-PKE scheme is presented in Section 4. We compare our SGC-PKE scheme to Liu and Au's scheme in Section 5. Finally a concluding remark is given in Section 6.

2   Definition

In this section we first introduce our model of CL-PKE and its security definition. Next, we recall the security definition of SGC-PKE defined by Liu and Au [1].

2.1   Certificateless Public Key Encryption

Our model of CL-PKE is similar to that of Baek et al. [4]. Only slight difference lies in our model. However, it is the crucial point that makes our scheme reach Girault's trusted level 3 and is easy to be converted to SGC-PKE. Below, we formally describe our model of CL-PKE.

Definition 1 (Certificateless Public Key Encryption). *A generic Certificateless Public Key Encryption scheme, denoted by Π, consists of the following algorithms:*

- **Setup:** is a probabilistic polynomial time (PPT) algorithms run by a Key Generation Center (KGC), given a security parameter k as input, outputs a randomly chosen master secret **mk** and a list of public parameter **param**. We write (**mk, param**) = **Setup** (k).
- **UserKeyGeneration:** is PPT algorithm, run by the user, given a list of public parameters **param** as inputs, outputs a secret key **sk** and a public key **pk**. We write (**sk, pk**) = **UserKeyGeneration** (**param**).
- **PartialKeyExtract:** Taking **param**, **mk**, a user's identity ID and **pk** received from the user, the KGC runs this PPT algorithm to generate a partial private key D_{ID} and a partial public key P_{ID}. We write (P_{ID}, D_{ID}) = **PartialKeyExtract** (**param, mk**, ID, **pk**).
- **SetPrivateKey:** Taking **param**, D_{ID} and **sk** as input, the user runs this PPT algorithm to generate a private key SK_{ID}. We write SK_{ID} = **SetPrivateKey** (**param**, D_{ID}, **sk**).
- **SetPublicKey:** Taking **param**, P_{ID} and **pk** as input, the user runs this PPT algorithm to generate a public key PK_{ID}. We write PK_{ID} = **SetPublicKey** (**param**, P_{ID}, **pk**).
- **Encrypt:** Taking a plaintext M, list of parameters **param**, a receiver's identity ID and PK_{ID} as inputs, a sender runs this PPT algorithm to create a ciphertext C. We write C = **Encrypt** (**param**, ID, PK_{ID}, M).
- **Decrypt:** Taking **param**, SK_{ID}, the ciphertext C as inputs, the user as a recipient runs this deterministic algorithm to get a decryption δ, which is either a plaintext message or a "Reject" message. We write δ = **Decrypt** (**param**, SK_{ID}, C).

For correctness, as usual we require that **Decrypt** (**param**, SK_{ID}, C) = M whenever C = **Encrypt** (**param**, ID, PK_{ID}, M).

The function of **UserKeyGeneration** algorithm is the same as the **SetSecretValue** algorithm in Baek's definition. However, note that the **UserKeyGeneration** algorithm in our definition must run precede the **PartialKeyExtract** algorithm, compared with the **PartialKeyExtract** algorithm can run precede **SetSecretValue** algorithm in Baek's definition. We emphasize that this is the crucial point to make our scheme desirable.

Security Model. According to the original scheme in [2], there are two types of adversaries. Type I adversary does not have the KGC's mater secret key but it can replace public keys of arbitrary identities with other public keys of its own choices. It can also obtain partial and full secret keys of arbitrary identities.

Type II adversary knows the master secret key (hence it can compute partial secret key by itself). It is still allowed to obtain full secret key for arbitrary identities but is not allowed to replace public keys at any time.

Definition 2 (IND-CCA Security). *A Certificateless Public Key Encryption scheme Π is IND-CCA secure if no PPT adversary $\mathcal{A}$ of Type I or Type II has a non-negligible advantage in the following game played against the challenger:*

1. The challenger takes a security parameter k and runs the **Setup** algorithm. It gives $\mathcal{A}$ the resulting system parameters **param**. If $\mathcal{A}$ is of Type I, the challenger keeps the master secret key **mk** to itself, otherwise, it gives **mk** to $\mathcal{A}$.

2. $\mathcal{A}$ is given access to the following oracles:
   - **Public-Key-Request-Oracle:** on input a user's identity ID, it computes $(\mathbf{sk}, \mathbf{pk}) = \mathbf{UserKeyGeneration}$ **(param)** and $(P_{\mathrm{ID}}, D_{\mathrm{ID}}) = \mathbf{PartialKeyExtract}$ **(param, mk, ID, pk)**. It then computes $PK_{\mathrm{ID}} = \mathbf{SetPublicKey}$ **(param, P_{ID}, pk)** and returns it to $\mathcal{A}$.
   - **Partial-Key-Extract-Oracle:** on input a user's identity ID and **pk**, it computes $(P_{\mathrm{ID}}, D_{\mathrm{ID}}) = \mathbf{PartialKeyExtract}$ **(param, mk, ID, pk)** and returns it to $\mathcal{A}$. (Note that it is only useful to Type I adversary.)
   - **Private-Key-Request-Oracle:** on input a user's identity ID, it computes $(\mathbf{sk}, \mathbf{pk}) = \mathbf{UserKeyGeneration}$ **(param)** and $(P_{\mathrm{ID}}, D_{\mathrm{ID}}) = \mathbf{PartialKeyExtract}$ **(param, mk, ID, pk)**. It then computes $SK_{\mathrm{ID}} = \mathbf{SetPrivateKey}$ **(param, D_{ID}, sk)** and returns it to $\mathcal{A}$. it outputs $\perp$ if the uesr's public key has been replaced (in the case of Type I adversary.)
   - **Public-Key-Replace-Oracle:** (For Type I adversary only) on input identity and a valid public key, it replaces the associated user's public key with the new one.
   - **Decryption-Oracle:** on input a ciphertext and an identity, returns the decrypted plaintext using the private key corresponding to the current value of the public key associated with the identity of the user.

3. After making oracle queries a polynomial times, $\mathcal{A}$ outputs and submits two message (M_0, M_1), together with an identity ID* of uncorrupted secret key to the challenger. The challenger picks a random bit $\beta \in \{0,1\}$ and computers C^*, the encryption of M_β under the current public key PK_{ID^*} for ID*. If the output of the encryption is $\perp$, then $\mathcal{A}$ immediately loses the game. Otherwise C^* is delivered to $\mathcal{A}$.

4. $\mathcal{A}$ makes a new sequence of queries.

5. $\mathcal{A}$ outputs a bit β'. It wins if $\beta' = \beta$ and fulfills the following conditions:
   - At any time, ID* has not been submitted to **Private-Key-Request-Oracle**.
   - In Step (4), C^* has not been submitted to **Decryption-Oracle** for the combination (ID*, PK_{ID^*}) under which M_β was encrypted.
   - If it is Type I, ID* has not been submitted to both **Public-Key-Replace-Oracle** before Step (3) and **Partial-Key-Extract-Oracle** at some step.

Define the guessing advantage of $\mathcal{A}$ as $Adv_{\mathrm{CLE}}^{\mathrm{IND-CCA}}(\mathcal{A}) = |\Pr[\beta' = \beta] - \frac{1}{2}|$. A Type I adversary $\mathcal{A}_I$ breaks a IND-CCA secure CL-PKE scheme Π with

$(t, q_{par}, q_{pub}, q_{prv}, q_D, \epsilon)$ if and only if the guessing advantage of $\mathcal{A}_I$ that accesses q_{par} times **Partial-Key-Extract-Oracle**, q_{pub} times **Public-Key-Request-Oracle**, q_{prv} times **Private-Key-Request-Oracle** and q_D times **Decryption-Oracle** is greater than ϵ within running time t. The scheme Π is said to be $(t, q_{par}, q_{pub}, q_{prv}, q_D, \epsilon)$-IND-CCA secure against Type I adversary if there is no attacker $\mathcal{A}_I$ that breaks IND-CCA secure scheme Π with $(t, q_{par}, q_{pub}, q_{prv}, q_D, \epsilon)$. There is the similar definition about Type II adversary.

2.2   Self-Generated-Certificate Public Key Encryption

The definition of SGC Encryption is the same as the definition of CL-encryption given in Definition 1, except for **SetPublicKey** in which the user generates a certificate using his own secret key.

For security, in addition to IND-CCA, we require the scheme to be DoD-Free, which is formally defined as follow as a game played between the challenger and a PPT adversary (DoD Adversary), which has the same power of a Type I adversary defined in CL-encryption.

Definition 3 (DoD-Free Security). *A SGC Encryption scheme is DoD-Free secure if no PPT adversary $\mathcal{A}$ has a non-negligible advantage in the following game played against the challenger:*

1. The challenger takes a security parameter k and runs the **Setup** algorithm. It gives $\mathcal{A}$ the resulting systems parameters **param**. The challenger keeps the master secret key **mk** to itself.
2. $\mathcal{A}$ is given access to **Public-Key-Request-Oracle, Partial-Key-Extract-Oracle, Private-Key-Request-Oracle** and **Public-Key-Replace-Oracle**.
3. After making oracle queries a polynomial times, $\mathcal{A}$ outputs a message M^*, together with an identity ID^* to the challenger. The challenger computes C^*, the encryption of M^* under the current public key PK_{ID^*} for ID^*. If the output of the encryption is $\perp$, then $\mathcal{A}$ immediately losses the game. Otherwise it outputs C^*.
4. $\mathcal{A}$ wins if the following conditions are fulfilled:
   - The output of the encryption in Step (3) is not $\perp$.
   - **Decrypt** (**param**, SK_{ID^*}, C^*) $= M^*$.
   - At any time, ID^* has not been submitted to **Partial-Key-Extract-Oracle**.

Define the advantage of $\mathcal{A}$ as $Adv_{\text{SGCE}}^{\text{DoD-Free}}(\mathcal{A}) = \Pr[\mathcal{A}\ wins]$

3   Our CL-PKE Scheme Without Pairing

Our scheme modifies from the first CL-PKE Scheme without pairing [4].

3.1   Construction

Setup(k): Generate two large primes p and q such that $q|p-1$. Pick a generator g of $\mathbb{Z}_p^*$. Pick $x \in \mathbb{Z}_q^*$ uniformly at random and compute $y = g^x$. Choose hash functions $H_1 : \{0,1\}^* \times \mathbb{Z}_p^* \times \mathbb{Z}_p^* \to \mathbb{Z}_q^*$, $H_2 : \{0,1\}^{l_0} \times \{0,1\}^{l_1} \to \mathbb{Z}_q^*$ and $H_3 : \mathbb{Z}_p^* \to \{0,1\}^l$, where $l = l_0 + l_1 \in N$. Return **param** $=(p,q,g,y,H_1,H_2,H_3)$ and **mk** $=(p,q,g,x,H_1,H_2,H_3)$.

UserKeyGeneration(**param**): Pick $z \in \mathbb{Z}_q^*$ at random and compute $\mu = g^x$. Return (**sk**, **pk**) $=(z,\mu)$.

PartialKeyExtract (**param**, **mk**, ID, **pk**): Pick $s \in \mathbb{Z}_q^*$ at random and compute $w = g^s$ and $t = s + xH_1(\text{ID}, w, \textbf{pk}) = s + xH_1(\text{ID}, w, \mu)$, Return $(P_{\text{ID}}, D_{\text{ID}})$ $=(w,t)$.

SetPrivateKey (**param**, D_{ID}, **sk**): Set $SK_{\text{ID}} = (\textbf{sk}, D_{\text{ID}}) = (z,t)$. Return SK_{ID}.

SetPublicKey (**param**, P_{ID}, **pk**): Set $PK_{\text{ID}} = (\textbf{pk}, P_{\text{ID}}) = (\mu, w)$. Return PK_{ID}.

Encrypt (**param**, ID, PK_{ID}, M) where the bit-length of M is l_0: Parse PK_{ID} as (μ, w), Pick $\sigma \in \{0,1\}^{l_1}$ at random, and compute $r = H_2(M, \sigma)$. Compute $C = (c_1, c_2)$ such that $c_1 = g^r$; $c_2 = H_3((\mu w y^{H_1(\text{ID}, w, \mu)})^r) \oplus (M \| \sigma)$.

Decrypt (**param**, SK_{ID}, C): Parse C as (c_1, c_2) and SK_{ID} as (z,t). Compute $M \| \sigma = H_3((c_1)^{z+t}) \oplus c_2$. If $g^{H_1(M, \sigma)} = c_1$, return M. Else return "Reject".

Due to $g^{z+t} = g^z \cdot g^t = \mu g^{s+xH_1(\text{ID}, w, \mu)} = \mu w y^{H_1(\text{ID}, w, \mu)}$, it can be easily seen that the above decryption algorithm is consistent.

Note that in **PartialKeyExtract** algorithm, it includes **pk** generated by the user as input. It is the same binding technique used by the original certificateless encryption scheme [2,3] which raises our scheme to trust level 3 in the trust hierarchy of [10]. Now, with the binding technique in place, a KGC who replaces an entity's public key will be implicated in the event of a dispute: the existence of two working public keys for an identity can only result from the existence of two partial private keys binding that identity to two different public keys; only the KGC could have created these two partial private keys. Thus this binding technique makes the KGC's replacement of a public key apparent and equivalent to a CA forging a certificate in a traditional PKI.

3.2   Security Analysis

The security proofs of our scheme is similar to the first CL-PKE Scheme without Pairing [4]. Basically, the main idea of the security proofs given in this section is to have the CDH attacker $\mathcal{B}$ simulate the "environment" of the Type I and Type II attackers $\mathcal{A}_I$ and $\mathcal{A}_{II}$ respectively until it can compute a Diffie-Hellman key g^{ab} of g^a and g^b using the ability of $\mathcal{A}_I$ and $\mathcal{A}_{II}$.

For the attacker $\mathcal{A}_I$, $\mathcal{B}$ sets g^a as a part of the challenge ciphertext and g^b as a KGC's public key. On the other hand, for the attacker $\mathcal{A}_{II}$, $\mathcal{B}$ set g^a as a part of the challenge ciphertext but uses g^b to generate a public key associated with the challenge identity.

The following two theorems show that our scheme is IND-CCA secure in the random oracle, assuming that the CDH problem is intractable. We will give the proofs of Theorem 2 and omit the certification process of Theorem 1 due to the similarity of Theorem 2.

Theorem 1. *The CL-PKE scheme is* $(t, q_{H_1}, q_{H_2}, q_{H_3}, q_{par}, q_{pub}, q_{prv}, q_D, \epsilon)$-IND-CCA *secure against the Type I attacker* $\mathcal{A}_I$ *in the random oracle assuming the CDH problem is* (t', ε')-*intractable, where* $\epsilon' > \frac{1}{q_{H_2}}(\frac{2\epsilon}{e(q_{prv}+1)} - \frac{q_{H_2}}{2^{l_1}} - \frac{q_D q_{H_2}}{2^{l_1}} - \frac{q_D}{q})$ *and* $t' > t + 2(q_{par} + q_{pub} + q_{prv})t_{ex} + 2q_D q_{H_2} q_{H_3} t_{ex} + 3t_{ex}$ *where* t_{ex} *denotes the time for computing exponentiation in* $\mathbb{Z}_p^*$.

Theorem 2. *The CL-PKE scheme is* $(t, q_{H_1}, q_{H_2}, q_{H_3}, q_{pub}, q_{prv}, q_D, \epsilon)$-IND-CCA *secure against the Type II attacker* $\mathcal{A}_{II}$ *in the random oracle assuming the CDH problem is* (t', ε')-*intractable, where* $\epsilon' > \frac{1}{q_{H_2}}(\frac{2\epsilon}{e(q_{prv}+1)} - \frac{q_{H_2}}{2^{l_1}} - \frac{q_D q_{H_2}}{2^{l_1}} - \frac{q_D}{q})$ *and* $t' > t + 2(q_{pub} + q_{prv})t_{ex} + 2q_D q_{H_2} q_{H_3} t_{ex} + 3t_{ex}$ *where* t_{ex} *denotes the time for computing exponentiation in* $\mathbb{Z}_p^*$.

Proof. Assume there is a Type II adversary $\mathcal{A}_{II}$ exists. We are going to construct another PPT $\mathcal{B}$ that make uses of $\mathcal{A}_{II}$ to solve the CDH problem with probability at least ϵ' and in the time at most t'.

$\mathcal{B}$ is given (p, q, g, g^a, g^b) as an instance of the CDH problem. In order to use $\mathcal{A}_{II}$ to solve for the problem, $\mathcal{B}$ needs to simulates a challenger and all oracles for $\mathcal{A}_{II}$. $\mathcal{B}$ does it in the following way.

<u>Setup.</u> $\mathcal{B}$ picks $x \in \mathbb{Z}_q^*$ uniformly at random and computes $y = g^x$, then sets **param** $=(p, q, g, y, H_1, H_2, H_3)$ and **mk** $=(p, q, g, x, H_1, H_2, H_3)$. Finally gives $\mathcal{A}_{II}$ **param** and **mk**.

We suppose that H_1, H_2, H_3 are random oracles [14]. Adversary $\mathcal{A}_{II}$ may make queries of all random oracles at any time during its attack. $\mathcal{B}$ handles as follows:

H_1 **queries:** On receiving a query $(\mathtt{ID}, w, \mu)$ to H_1:

1. If $\langle(\mathtt{ID}, w, \mu), e\rangle$ exists in $\mathbf{H_1 List}$, return e as answer.
2. Otherwise, pick $e \in \mathbb{Z}_q^*$ at random, add $\langle(\mathtt{ID}, w, \mu), e\rangle$ to $\mathbf{H_1 List}$ and return e as answer.

H_2 **queries:** On receiving a query (M, σ) to H_2:

1. If $\langle(M, \sigma), r\rangle$ exists in $\mathbf{H_2 List}$, return r as answer.
2. Otherwise, pick $r \in \mathbb{Z}_q^*$ at random, add $\langle(M, \sigma), r\rangle$ to $\mathbf{H_2 List}$ and return r as answer.

H_3 **queries:** On receiving a query k to H_3:

1. If $\langle k, R\rangle$ exists in $\mathbf{H_3 List}$, return R as answer.
2. Otherwise, pick $R \in \{0, 1\}^l$ at random, add $\langle k, R\rangle$ to $\mathbf{H_3 List}$ and return R as answer.

<u>Phase 1.</u> $\mathcal{A}_{II}$ can issue the following oracle queries.

Public-Key-Request: On receiving a query ID:

1. If $\langle \text{ID}, (\mu, w), coin \rangle$ exists in **PublicKeyList**, return $PK_{\text{ID}} = (\mu, w)$ as answer.
2. Otherwise, pick $coin \in \{0, 1\}$ at random, so that $\Pr[coin = 0] = \delta$. (δ will be determined later.)
3. If $coin = 0$, pick $z, s \in \mathbb{Z}_q^*$ at random and compute $\mu = g^z, w = g^s$, and $t = s + xH_1(\text{ID}, w, \mu)$; add $\langle \text{ID}, (z, t) \rangle$ to **PrivateKeyList** and $\langle \text{ID}, (\mu, w), coin \rangle$ to **PublicKeyList**; return $PK_{\text{ID}} = (\mu, w)$ as a answer.
4. Otherwise (if $coin = 1$), pick $z, s \in \mathbb{Z}_q^*$ at random and compute $\mu = g^z, w = (g^b)^s$; add $\langle \text{ID}, (z, ?) \rangle$ to **PrivateKeyList** and $\langle \text{ID}, (\mu, w), coin \rangle$ to **PublicKeyList**; return $PK_{\text{ID}} = (\mu, w)$ as a answer.

Private-Key-Request: On receiving a query ID:

1. Run **Public-Key-Request** on ID to get a tuple $\langle \text{ID}, (\mu, w), coin \rangle \in$ **PublicKeyList**.
2. If $coin = 0$, search **PrivateKeyList** for a tuple $\langle \text{ID}, (z, t) \rangle$ and return $SK_{\text{ID}} = (z, t)$ as answer.
3. Otherwise, return "Abort" and terminate.

Decryption queries: On receiving a query $(\text{ID}, PK_{\text{ID}}, C)$, where $C = (c_1, c_2)$ and $PK_{\text{ID}} = (\mu, w)$:

1. Search **PublicKeyList** for tuple $\langle \text{ID}, (\mu, w), coin \rangle$. If $coin = 0$, search **PrivateKeyList** for a tuple $\langle \text{ID}, (z, t) \rangle$. (Note that $\langle \text{ID}, (\mu, w), coin \rangle$ must exist in **PublicKeyList** and when $coin=0$, $\langle \text{ID}, (z, t) \rangle$ exist in **PrivateKeyList**.) Then set $SK_{\text{ID}} = (z, t)$ and run **Decrypt** (**param**, SK_{ID}, C). Finally, return the result of **Decrypt** algorithm.
2. Otherwise (if $coin = 1$), run H_1 **query** to get a tuple $\langle (\text{ID}, w, \mu), e \rangle$. If there exist $\langle (M, \sigma), r \rangle \in$ **H_2List** and $\langle k, R \rangle \in$ **H_3List** such that $c_1 = g^r, c_2 = R \oplus (M \| \sigma)$ and $k = (\mu w y^e)^r$, return M and "Reject" otherwise.

Challenge. $\mathcal{A}_{II}$ then output two message (M_0, M_1) and a challenge identity ID*. $\mathcal{B}$ run **Public-Key-Request** taking ID* as input to get a tuple $\langle \text{ID}^*, (\mu^*, w^*), coin \rangle \in$ **PublicKeyList**.

1. If $coin = 0$ return "Abort" and terminate.
2. Otherwise, do the following:
   (a) Search **PrivateKeyList** for a tuple $\langle \text{ID}^*, (z^*, ?), s^* \rangle$.
   (b) Pick $\sigma^* \in \{0, 1\}^{l_1}, c_2^* \in \{0, 1\}^l$ and $\beta \in \{0, 1\}$ at random.
   (c) Set $c_1^* = g^a$ and $e^* = H_1(\text{ID}^*, w^*, \mu^*)$.
   (d) Define $a = H_2(M_\beta, \sigma^*)$ and $H_3((\mu^* w^* y^{e^*})^a)$. (Note that $\mathcal{B}$ does not know "a", $(\mu^* w^* y^{e^*})^a = (g^a)^{z^*} \cdot (g^{ab})^{s^*} \cdot (g^a)^{xe^*}$.
3. Return $C^* = (c_1^*, c_2^*)$ as a target ciphertext.

Phase 2. $\mathcal{B}$ repeats the same method it used in Phase 1.

Guess. Finally, $\mathcal{A}_{II}$ output a guess β'. Now $\mathcal{B}$ choose a tuple $\langle k, R \rangle$ form the **H₃List** and outputs $(\frac{k}{(g^a)^{z^*} \cdot (g^a)^{xe^*}})^{1/s^*}$ as the solution the the CDH problem.

Analysis : From the construction of H_1, it is clear that the simulation of H_1 is perfect. As long as $\mathcal{A}_{II}$ does not query (M_β, σ^*) to H_2 nor $(\mu^* w^* y^{e^*})^a$ to H_3, the simulations of H_2 and H_3 are perfect. By **AskH₃*** we denote the event that $(\mu^* w^* y^{e^*})^a$ has not been queried to H_3. Also, by **AskH₂*** we denote the event that (M_β, σ^*) has been queried to H_2. If happens then $\mathcal{B}$ will be able to solve the CDH problem by choosing a tuple $\langle k, R \rangle$ form the **H₃List** and computing $(\frac{k}{(g^a)^{z^*} \cdot (g^a)^{xe^*}})^{1/s^*}$ with the probability at least $\frac{1}{q_{H_3}}$. Hence we have $\epsilon' \geq \frac{1}{q_{H_3}} \Pr[\mathbf{AskH_3^*}]$.

It is easy to notice that if $\mathcal{B}$ does not abort, the simulations of **Public-Key-Request**, **Private-Key-Request** and the simulated target ciphertext is identically distributed as the real one from the construction.

Now, we evaluate the simulation of the decryption oracle. If a public key PK_{ID} has been produced under $coin = 0$, the simulation is perfect as B knows the private key SK_{ID} corresponding to PK_{ID}. Otherwise, simulation errors may occur while $\mathcal{B}$ running the decryption oracle simulator specified above. Let **DecErr** be this event. We compute the probability of this event: Suppose that (ID, PK_{ID}, C), where $C = (c_1, c_2)$ and $PK_{ID} = (\mu, w)$, has been issued as a *valid* decryption query. Even if C is valid, there is a possibility that C can be produced without querying $(\mu w y^e)^r$ to H_3, where $e = H_1(ID, w, \mu)$ and $r = H_2(M, \sigma)$. Let **Valid** be an event that C is valid. Let **AskH₃** and **AskH₂** respectively be events that $(\mu w y^e)^r$ has been queried to H_3 and (M, σ) has been queried to H_2 with respect to $C = (c_1, c_2) = (g^r, H_3((\mu w y^{H_1(ID, w, \mu)})^r) \oplus (M \| \sigma))$ and $PK_{ID} = (\mu, w)$, where $r = H_2(M, \sigma)$ and $e = H_1(ID, w, \mu)$. We then have $\Pr[\mathbf{DecErr}] = q_D \Pr[\mathbf{Valid}| \neg \mathbf{AskH_3}]$. But

$$\begin{aligned} \Pr[\mathbf{Valid}| \neg \mathbf{AskH_3}] &\leq \Pr[\mathbf{Valid} \wedge \mathbf{AskH_2}| \neg \mathbf{AskH_3}] \\ &\quad + \Pr[\mathbf{Valid} \wedge \neg \mathbf{AskH_2}| \neg \mathbf{AskH_3}] \\ &\leq \Pr[\mathbf{AskH_2}| \neg \mathbf{AskH_3}] \\ &\quad + \Pr[\mathbf{Valid}| \neg \mathbf{AskH_2} \wedge \neg \mathbf{AskH_3}] \\ &\leq \frac{q_{H_2}}{2^{l_1}} + \frac{1}{q} \end{aligned}$$

So, $\Pr[\mathbf{DecErr}] \leq \frac{q_D q_{H_2}}{2^{l_1}} + \frac{q_D}{q}$.

Now, the event $(\mathbf{AskH_3^*} \vee (\mathbf{AskH_2^*}| \neg \mathbf{AskH_3^*}) \vee \mathbf{DecErr})| \neg \mathbf{Abort}$ denoted by **Good**, where **Abort** denotes an event that $\mathcal{B}$ aborts during the simulation. The probability $\neg \mathbf{Abort}$ that happens is given by $\delta^{q_{prv}}(1 - \delta)$ which is maximized at $\delta = 1 - 1/(q_{prv} - 1)$. Hence we have $\Pr[\neg \mathbf{Abort}] \leq \frac{1}{e(q_{prv}+1)}$, where e denotes the base of the natural logarithm.

If **Good** does not happen, it is clear that $\mathcal{A}_{II}$ does not gain any advantage greater than $1/2$ to guess β due to the randomness of the output of the random oracle H_3. Namely, we have $\Pr[\beta' = \beta | \neg \textbf{Good}] \leq \frac{1}{2}$.

By definition of ϵ, we then have

$$\epsilon < |\Pr[\beta' = \beta] - \frac{1}{2}|$$

$$= |\Pr[\beta' = \beta | \neg \textbf{Good}]\Pr[\neg \textbf{Good}] + \Pr[\beta' = \beta | \textbf{Good}]\Pr[\textbf{Good}] - \frac{1}{2}|$$

$$\leq |\frac{1}{2}\Pr[\neg \textbf{Good}] + \Pr[\textbf{Good}] - \frac{1}{2}|$$

$$\leq \frac{1}{2}\Pr[\textbf{Good}]$$

$$\leq \frac{1}{2\Pr[\neg \textbf{Abort}]}(\Pr[\textbf{AskH}_3^*] + \Pr[\textbf{AskH}_2^*|\neg \textbf{AskH}_3^*] + \Pr[\textbf{DecErr}])$$

$$\leq \frac{e(q_{prv}+1)}{2}(q_{H_3}\epsilon' + \frac{q_{H_2}}{2^{l_1}} + \frac{q_D q_{H_2}}{2^{l_1}} + \frac{q_D}{q})$$

Consequently, we obtain $\epsilon' > \frac{1}{q_{H_2}}(\frac{2\epsilon}{e(q_{prv}+1)} - \frac{q_{H_2}}{2^{l_1}} - \frac{q_D q_{H_2}}{2^{l_1}} - \frac{q_D}{q})$. The running time of the CDH attacker $\mathcal{B}$ is $t' > t + 2(q_{pub} + q_{prv})t_{ex} + 2q_D q_{H_2} q_{H_3} t_{ex} + 3t_{ex}$ where t_{ex} denotes the time for computing exponentiation in $\mathbb{Z}_p^*$.

4   Our SGC-PKE Scheme Without Pairing

We give our Self-Generated-Certificate (SGC) encryption scheme without pairing based on the above Certificateless encryption scheme. The most algorithms are the same as the algorithms of Certificateless encryption scheme, except for **SetPublicKey** and **Encrypt**.

In order to distinguish the algorithm of CL-encryption, we will add the prefix "**CL.**" to the corresponding algorithms. For example, we use "**CL.Setup**" to denote the encryption algorithm of the CL-encryption scheme. The proposed SGC-encryption scheme is described as follow:

Setup: Same as **CL.Setup**, outputs parameters **param** $= (p, q, g, y = g^x, H_1, H_2, H_3)$ and master secret key **mk** $= (p, q, g, x, H_1, H_2, H_3)$.

UserKeyGeneration: Same as **CL.UserKeyGeneration**, outputs (sk, pk) $= (z, g^z)$.

PartialKeyExtract: We modify **CL.PartialKeyExtract** slightly. Taking **param**, **mk**, ID and **pk** as input, it outputs $(P_{\text{ID}}, D_{\text{ID}}) = (w = g^s, t = s + xH_1(\text{ID}, w * \textbf{pk})) = s + xH_1(\text{ID}, w\mu))$. In order to make this changes, it must modify the domain of hash function $H_1 : \{0,1\}^* \times \mathbb{Z}_p^* \to \mathbb{Z}_q^*$.

SetPrivateKey: Same as **CL.SetPrivateKey**, outputs $SK_{\text{ID}} = \text{sk} + D_{\text{ID}} = z + t$.

SetPublicKey: Except for taking **param**, P_{ID} and **pk** as input, it includes ID and SK_{ID} as inputs. Chooses a new hash function $H_0 : \{0,1\}^* \times \mathbb{Z}_p^* \times \mathbb{Z}_p^* \times \mathbb{Z}_p^* \to$

$\mathbb{Z}_q^*$, then computes $PK_{\text{ID}}^1 = \mathbf{pk} * P_{\text{ID}} = \mu w$ and $PK_{\text{ID}}^2 = \mathbf{pk} * P_{\text{ID}} * y^{H_1(\text{ID},\mathbf{pk},P_{\text{ID}})} = \mu w y^{H_1(\text{ID},\mu,w)} = g^{z+t} = g^{SK_{\text{ID}}}$. Next, it does the following performances to sign the user's identity ID and $PK_{\text{ID}}^1, PK_{\text{ID}}^2$ using the user's private key SK_{ID} and Schnorr's signature scheme [15]. (1) choose a random $r \in \mathbb{Z}_q^*$, (2) compute $R = g^r \bmod p$, and (3) set the signature to be (R, σ), where $\sigma = r + SK_{\text{ID}} * H_0(\text{ID}, PK_{\text{ID}}^1, PK_{\text{ID}}^2, R)$. Finally, returns $PK_{\text{ID}} = (PK_{\text{ID}}^1, PK_{\text{ID}}^2, (R, \sigma))$.

Encrypt: Parses PK_{ID} as $(PK_{\text{ID}}^1, PK_{\text{ID}}^2, (R, \sigma))$. If $PK_{\text{ID}}^2 \neq PK_{\text{ID}}^1 * y^{H_1(\text{ID},PK_{\text{ID}}^1)}$ or $g^\sigma \neq R * (PK_{\text{ID}}^2)^{H_0(\text{ID},PK_{\text{ID}}^1,PK_{\text{ID}}^2,R)}$, it returns $\perp$, else outputs **CL.Encrypt(** param, ID, PK_{ID}, M**)**.

Decrypt: Same as **CL.Decrypt**, outputs a plaintext M for a valid ciphertext C, or "Reject" otherwise.

Security Analysis

The IND-CCA security depends on our CL-encryption scheme (defined in Section 3). In addition to IND-CCA, we require the scheme to be DoD-Free. Here we analyze the DoD-Free Security.

Theorem 3. *The SGC-encryption scheme proposed in this section in secure against DoD adversary, assuming that the Schnorr's signature scheme is secure against the adaptively chosen message attack in the random oracle model [16].*

Proof. Assume there is a DoD adversary $\mathcal{A}$ exists. We are going to construct another PPT $\mathcal{B}$ that makes use of $\mathcal{A}$ to break the Schnorr signature scheme.

$\mathcal{B}$ is now the schnorr's signature adversary. Note that in fact, the **PartialKey Extract** algorithm in our SGC-encryption scheme signs the user's identity ID using the schnorr's signature scheme. So using his signing-oracle, $\mathcal{B}$ can answer all oracle queries for $\mathcal{A}$. After a polynomial number of oracle queries, $\mathcal{A}$ outputs a message M^* and an identity ID*. $\mathcal{A}$ wins if the following conditions fulfill:

1. The public key PK_{ID^*} of ID* is valid.
2. **Decrypt(param,** $SK_{\text{ID}^*}, C^*) \neq M^*$ where $C^* =$ **Encrypt (param, ID*,** PK_{ID^*}, M^*).
3. $\mathcal{A}$ does not query the **Partial-Key-Extract-Oracle** for ID*.

If the public key of ID* has not been replaced, due to correctness we always have **Decrypt(param,** $SK_{\text{ID}^*}, C^*) = M^*$. Condition (2) implies the public key of ID* has been replaced. Together with condition (1) and (3), it implies that $\sigma^* = (PK_{\text{ID}^*}^1, PK_{\text{ID}^*}^2)$ is a successful forgery for ID*. $\mathcal{B}$ outputs it.

5   Comparison to Previous Work

Our scheme is the second SGC-encryption scheme. In this section, we compare the scheme we have presented to the first scheme in [1].

1. Our scheme has more short public keys due to their scheme based on the Water's Identity-Based Encryption scheme [17].

2. Our scheme is more efficient due to our scheme without pairing computation. In spite of the recent advances in implementation technique, the pairing computation is still considered as expensive compared with "standard" operations such as modular exponentiations in finite fields.
3. Our scheme reaches Girault's trusted level 3 (same as the traditional PKI), but their scheme only reaches Girault's trusted level 2 (a cheating KGC could replace an entity's public key bye one for which it knows the secret value without fear of being identified).
4. Their scheme is IND-CCA$^-$ (the challenger is forced to decrypt ciphertexts for which the public key has been replaced) and DoD-Free secure in the standard model. Our scheme is IND-CCA and DoD-Free secure in the random oracle model.

6   Concluding Remarks

We have presented the first SGC-encryption scheme that does not depend on the pairing. We have proven in the random oracle that the scheme is IND-CCA and DoD-Free secure, relative to the hardness of the standard CDH problem and DL problem.

However, we can only achieve security in the random oracle although our scheme has many appealing properties. It is still an open problem to design a CL-PKC and SGC-PKC scheme without pairing that is secure in the standard model.

References

1. J. K. Liu and M. H. Au. Self-Generated-Certificate Public Key Cryptosystem. Cryptology ePrint Archive, Report 2006/194, 2006. http://eprint.iacr.org/2006/194
2. S. S. Al-Riyami and K. Paterson. Certificateless public key cryptography. In Proc. ASIACRYPT 2003, LNCS 2894, pp. 452-473, Springer-Verlag, 2003.
3. S. S. Al-Riyami and K. Paterson. Certificateless public key cryptography. Cryptology ePrint Archive, Report 2003/126, 2003. http://eprint.iacr.org/2003/126.
4. J. Baek, R. Safavi-Naini, and W. Susilo. Certificateless public key encryption without pairing. In ISC 05, LNCS 3650, pp. 134-148, Springer-Verlag, 2005.
5. K. Bentahar, P. Farshim, and J. Malone-Lee. Generic constructions of identity-based and certificateless KEMs. Cryptology ePrint Archive, Report 2005/058, 2005. http://eprint.iacr.org/2005/058.
6. B. Libert and J. Quisquater. On constructing certificateless cryptosystems from identity based encryption. In PKC 2006, LNCS 3958, pp. 474-490, Springer-Verlag, 2006.
7. D. H. Yum and P. J. Lee. Generic construction of certificateless encryption. In ICCSA'04, LNCS 3040, pp. 802-811, Springer-Verlag, 2004.
8. Y. Shi and J. Li. Provable efficient certificateless public key encryption. Cryptology ePrint Archive, Report 2005/287, 2005. http://eprint.iacr.org/2005/287.
9. Z. Cheng and R. Comley. Efficient certificateless public key encryption. Cryptology ePrint Archive, Report 2005/012, 2005. http://eprint.iacr.org/2005/012.

10. M. Girault. Self-certified public keys. In Proc. EUROCRYPT 91, LNCS 547, pp. 490-497, Springer-Verlag, 1992.
11. H. Petersen and P. Horster. Self-certified keys - concepts and applications. In 3rd Int. Conference on Communications and Multimedia Security, pp. 102-116, Chapnam and Hall, 1997.
12. B. Lee and K. Kim. Self-Certificate: PKI using Self-Certified Key. In Proc. of Conference on Information Security and Cryptology 2000, Vol. 10, No. 1, pp. 65-73, 2000.
13. A. Shamir. Identity-based Cryptosystems and Signature Schemes. In Crypto '84, LNCS 196, pp. 47-53, Springer-Verlag, 1984.
14. M. Bellare and P. Rogaway. Random Oracles are Practical: A Paradigm for Designing Efficient Protocols. In ACM CCCS '93, pp. 62-73, 1993.
15. C. P. Schnorr. Efficient signature generation by smart cards. Journal of Cryptology, Vol. 4, No. 3, pp. 161-174, 1991.
16. D. Pointcheval and J. Stern. Security proofs for signature schemes. In Proc. Eurocrypt 96, LNCS 1070, pp. 387-398, Springer-Verlag, 1996.
17. B. Waters. Efficient identity-based encryption without random oracles. In Proc. EUROCRYPT 2005, LNCS 3494, pp. 114-127, Springer-Verlag, 2005.

Author Index

Lecture Notes in Computer Science

For information about Vols. 1–4345

please contact your bookseller or Springer